PRINCIPLES OF DATA PROCESSING
Concepts, Applications, and Cases

THE IRWIN SERIES IN INFORMATION AND DECISION SCIENCES

Consulting Editors Robert B. Fetter   Claude McMillan
Yale University   University of Colorado

PRINCIPLES OF DATA PROCESSING
Concepts, Applications, and Cases

RALPH M. STAIR, JR.
The Florida State University

1981

RICHARD D. IRWIN, INC. HOMEWOOD, ILLINOIS 60430

Cover and part opening photos courtesy of:
- Part I: Synertek Inc., Copyright 1979. Reproduced by permission.
- Part II: Honeywell.
- Part III: International Business Machines Corporation.
- Part IV: Hewlett-Packard.

© RICHARD D. IRWIN, INC., 1981

All rights reserved. No part of this publication may be reproduced, stored in a retrieval system, or transmitted, in any form or by any means, electronic, mechanical, photocopying, recording, or otherwise, without the prior written permission of the publisher.

ISBN 0-256-02484-7
Library of Congress Catalog Card No. 80–82447
Printed in the United States of America

4 5 6 7 8 9 0 H 8 7 6 5 4 3

TO LILA AND LESLIE

Preface

The overall purpose of this book is to provide students with an up-to-date and comprehensive introduction to the principles of computers and data processing. This book and accompanying student learning aids and language supplements are intended for the first course in computers and data processing. Previous course work and computer-related experience are not required.

Every effort has been made to make this data processing "package" one of the most effective on the market today. In order to accomplish this objective, a number of features have been built into the book, the study guide, and the language supplements.

Features of the text

To facilitate learning, the text uses an integrative approach. There is a logical flow from one topic to the next and from one chapter to the next. Whenever possible, the material in one section is related to, and integrated with, material in other sections. Furthermore, students are asked to take an active role in the learning process.

The text has been designed to be extremely flexible. The first part is Fundamentals of Data Processing and Computers. After Part I is covered, any other part may be read in any order. Furthermore, there is a direct relationship between some of the chapters in Part I and the other parts of the book. Chapter 2 (hardware) leads into Part II; Chapter 3 (software) leads into Part III; and Chapter 4 (systems) leads into Part IV, the last part in the text. Each part starts with an outline of the topics to be covered and a statement of purpose.

There is a set of integrative cases at the end of the book that tie together the chapters for each part and integrate the parts into a unified whole. One of the cases is continued for every part. Students will be able to trace a growing company and experience some of the data processing problems that can occur. Some of the cases are also continued in the instructor's manual. With all of the cases, the overall approach is to make students apply what they learn in real situations.

Each chapter is designed to be a complete learning package. Every chapter starts with a chapter outline. This is followed by several learning objectives. Each chapter contains ample illustrations and pictures, and the writing style is simple and concise. A detailed summary is at the end of every chapter. This is followed by a list of key terms and concepts and a list of short-answer questions. Following the questions, there is a miniquiz, which is self-correcting. The miniquiz tests students on the knowledge they have acquired and the extent to which they have satisfied the learning objectives. There is at least one item of interest at the end of every chapter. This item of interest is either an article from a newspaper or journal, a quotation from a key executive in the data processing industry, or an actual success story of how a profit or nonprofit organization was able to successfully use a computer system. These items of interest have been selected to strengthen a point made in the chapter and to increase student interest in data processing in general.

This book also contains several supplements to various chapters. These supplements explore careers in data processing, discuss important social issues, cover the use of inexpensive microcomputers for home, school, and business use, and investigate computer numbering systems and data representation. Depending on the purpose of the course and the desires of the instructor, these supplements can be covered or omitted without loss of continuity.

A note to students on how to use the text and supplements

How you use this text depends in part on your instructor. Your instructor has great flexibility in designing the course and in using the materials in this package. Your instructor will decide whether or not you will need the student learning aid and one or more of the language supplements. Once your instructor has determined what supplements and materials are to be used, it will be your responsibility to get the most from the assigned work. Here are some hints.

After a chapter or supplement has been assigned in the text, you should first look at the chapter outline. This will give you an overview of the major topics that will be discussed in the chapter or supplement. Next, you should read and make a note of the learning objectives. At the end of the chapter or supplement, you will be expected to have accomplished these objectives. While you are reading the chapter or supplement, you may wish to place your own notes in the margin. After reading the chapter, review the key terms and concepts and do all of the end-of-chapter questions and exercises. If you believe that you understand the material, try the miniquiz. Once you have completed the end-of-chapter questions and the miniquiz, you might want a final review before reading new material. The best way to do this is to review the chapter outline, the learning objectives, the questions, and the key terms and concepts. The review process will help you retain the material for future use.

Your learning should not be limited to this text or the courses that you are taking. Take an active part in your education. Read newspaper and magazine articles that describe how the computer has been used in your field. Computer manufacturers are willing to supply students with information on a number of subjects related to data processing and computers. If the local branch does not have the information, ask for the address and phone number of the national office. These companies realize that you may be future customers, and they are usually willing to help you in learning more about computers. You may also want to talk to several local companies about how they use computers in their business. This could give you some excellent contacts for future employment.

ACKNOWLEDGMENTS

I am indebted to a number of organizations that freely gave me information, pictures, brochures, and their encouragement. Bill Anthony, the Department of Management, and the College of Business at Florida State University gave the support I needed to complete this project. I am also indebted to Ralph Janaro, John Malley, and Roger McGrath for taking major responsibility in developing the language supplements and in making suggestions for the improvement of the text and accompanying materials. Diane Dyer helped by coordinating much of the typing and clerical work associated with this book. Thanks to David Kirkland, Henrietta Holmes, Cathy Seery, Betty K. Smith, and Elaine Martin for their help.

I would also like to thank my wife, Lila, for taking a very active role in this project.

I am grateful to a number of individuals for reviewing the text and accompanying materials and for providing useful suggestions. Claude McMillan and Robert Fetter made many useful suggestions. Some of the other reviewers that I am indebted to include: Robert Cerveny, Texas Tech University; Dwight Graham, Prairie State College; Robert T. Keim, Arizona State University; Van N. Oliphant, Memphis State University; Robert Pew, Valencia Community College; Donald Price, Sierra College; and Henry Weiman, Bronx Community College.

Contents

PART I FUNDAMENTALS

1 Information and data processing......................... 5

Information and data processing. Data processing and organizations. Data organization and movement: *Data organization. Data base concepts. Data movement.* An analogy: *The components of a manual data processing system. Placing a manual data processing system into action. The analogy and computer systems.*

The international industry: Transborder data flow, *John Eger,* **17**

2 Hardware.. 21

The analogy revisited. The central processor and temporary storage: *The central processor. Temporary storage.* Permanent storage: *Computer cards. Magnetic tape. Disk devices.* Input: *Key-to-card, tape, and disk. Terminal devices.* Output: The printer. Computer configurations.

The Diplomat Resort installs online electronic system and cuts payroll costs by $125,000, 37

3 Software.. 41

The analogy revisited. Overview of software: *Types of software. The acquisition of software.* Application software: *Machine language. Assembler language. Macroinstructions. High-level programming language.* System software: *Assemblers and compilers. Operating systems. Utility programs. Data base management systems.*

What is software? Attorneys and others disagree, depending upon their concerns. *Edith Myers,* **53**

4 Systems 57

Capabilities and limitations of a computer system. Common elements of a computer application: *Editing. Updating. Common outputs from a computer application.* Routine applications and documents. Management information: *Management information systems in perspective. Characteristics of a manage-*

xiii

ment information system. Types of management reports. How much information?

Installed at: Travelcraft, Inc., Sterling Heights, Michigan, 70

PART II HARDWARE

5 The evolution of data processing systems 75

Mechanical devices. The beginning of the computer age. The computer generations: *The first generation. The second generation. The third generation to the present.* The future.

Remarks of C. E. Exley, Jr., President of NCR Corporation, Columbia Business School Club of New York—March 20, 1979, 95

6 Central processing 97

The control and arithmetic/logic unit: *The control unit. The arithmetic/logic unit. Registers. The execution of an instruction.* Temporary storage: *Fundamentals of temporary storage. Core storage. Semiconductor storage. Bubble storage. Other temporary storage devices.* Interfacing with other components.

Is bubble memory finally ready to fly? 112

6 Supplement: Data representation 115

Decimal and binary systems. Binary coded decimal systems. The hexadecimal numbering system. Parity checking.

7 Permanent storage devices............................. 125

Fundamentals of permanent storage devices. The card system: *Card concepts. Card devices.* The tape system: *Tape concepts. Tape devices.* The disk system: *Disk concepts. Disk devices.* A comparison of permanent storage devices: *The card system. The tape system. The disk system.*

Need information on current research? Ask a computer at "The Exchange," 147

8 Input, output, and data communications................ 149

Data entry devices: *Key to storage. Multistation data entry systems. Validation, verification, and editing.* Printers: *Impact printers. Nonimpact printers.* Terminals: *Visual display terminals. Teleprinter terminals.* Data communications: *Carriers. Communication devices and networks.*

The sensuous computer: Gaining access to systems through touch, voice, signature and other personal methods, *Paul Meissner,* **170**

9 Special purpose hardware............................. 173

Input and output: *Input devices. Output devices. Devices for input and output.* Permanent storage and central processing: *Permanent storage devices. Central processing devices.*

Xerox converts stockroom into supply supermarket, 193

Contents

10 Computer systems **195**

Microcomputers. Minicomputers. Small computer systems. Medium and large computer systems. Centralized, decentralized, and distributed systems.

Minis help move cargo, 211

10 Supplement: Microcomputers for business, school, and personal use **213**

Microcomputer systems in action: *Individual applications. Applications for small profit and nonprofit organizations.* The components of a microcomputer system: *Input and output devices. Central processing and temporary storage. Permanent storage devices. Peripheral equipment.* Software and programming. Factors in selecting a microcomputer.

Personal computers in business: An emerging competitive edge, *Bill Langenes,* **226**

PART III SOFTWARE

11 Operating and system software **231**

Batch processing. Overlapped processing. Real time processing. Multiprocessing. Spooling. Multiprogramming. Virtual storage. Program overlays. Data base management systems.

A "software first" philosophy, 249

12 Programming languages **251**

Programming languages in perspective. The basic programming language. The FORTRAN programming language. The COBOL programming language: *The structure of a COBOL program. The identification division. The environment division. The data division. The procedure division.* The PASCAL programming language. Other programming languages: *RPG and RPG II. PL/1. APL. Additional programming languages.* Language comparison.

Untraditional software designing serves untraditional mini, micro market, *Yale A. Grayson,* **268**

13 Program and application development **271**

Developing application software: *1. Problem definition. 2. Analysis and design. 3. Language selection. 4. Program coding. 5. Testing and debugging. 6. Documentation. 7. Implementation. 8. Maintenance.* Purchasing application software.

Business computer improves wholesaler's operation, 284

14 Tools for program and application development **287**

Print charts and layout charts. Flowcharts: *System flowcharts. Program flowcharts.* Decision tables. Grid charts.

A development tool for programmer productivity, 303

15 Structured design.. **305**

The structured design approach: *Structure charts. Organization and design guidelines.* HIPO: *Visual table of contents. HIPO diagrams.* Structured programming concepts: *Structured programming. Structured flowcharting. Pseudocode.* Managing structured systems: *Chief-programmer teams. Structured walkthroughs.* Implementing a structured system: *The top-down approach. Other implementation techniques.*

Programmer productivity in a structured environment, Kenneth Hamilton and Arthur Block, **328**

Part IV SYSTEMS

16 Systems analysis and design............................ **335**

Systems investigation. Systems analysis: *Assembling the study team. Data collection. Data analysis. Report on the existing system.* Systems design: *System design considerations. Generating system design alternatives. System evaluation and selection. The contract.* Systems implementation: *Personnel: Hiring and training. Site preparation. Data preparation. Installation. Final testing. Start up.* Buying system methodology.

Users drive harder bargains, 352

17 Management information and decision support systems..... **355**

MIS and DSS in perspective. The systems framework: *The systems approach. The use of models. General model of the organization. Theory of management.* The functional approach. Design and implementation considerations.

DSS: An executive mind-support system, P. G. Keen and G. R. Wagner, **370**

18 The data processing industry........................... **375**

General computer manufacturers. Small, mini, and micro computer manufacturers. Peripheral equipment manufacturers. Computer dealers and distributors. Leasing companies. Time-sharing companies. Service companies. Software companies. Supply companies. The international data processing industry.

Gene Amdahl takes aim at IBM, Bro Uttal, **390**

18 Supplement: Social issues............................. **391**

Computer waste and mistakes. Crime and fraud. Privacy.

DP crime laws enacted in only 10 states; Congress working on "Model" Federal Bill, Marguerite Zientara, **400**

19 The data processing department........................ **403**

Location of the DP center. Organization of the DP department: *Users, systems analysts, and programmers. Data processing managers, data entry operators, and other personnel.* Operation of the DP department: *General considerations. Systems considerations. The DP audit.* Disaster recovery planning.

Remarks of Williams S. Anderson, Chairman of NCR Corporation, 417

19 Supplement: Careers in data processing **419**

Data processing careers in perspective. Career opportunities in data processing: *The data processing manager. The systems analyst. The computer programmer. The system operator. The data entry operator. Other career opportunities in data processing.* Finding the right job: *Traditional approaches to job hunting. The job finding strategy. The résumé and the interview. Factors in job selection.* Starting a career in data processing.

The changing role of the MIS executive, *Joseph Ferreira and James F. Collins, Jr.,* **433**

INTEGRATIVE CASES

About the cases, **439**

  Case for Part I: Bryan's I, **441**
  Cases for Part II: Bryan's II, **444**
  Greenville Community College, **446**
  Cases for Part III: Bryan's III (A), **448**
  Leboeuf Financial, **450**
  Cases for Part IV: Bryan's IV (A), **451**
  Resnik Distributors, **453**

Glossary **455**

Index **467**

PRINCIPLES OF DATA PROCESSING
Concepts, Applications, and Cases

about part I

The purpose of Part I is to give you a broad overview of business data processing. Chapter 1 investigates fundamental concepts of data and information processing. Chapter 2 covers the fundamentals of computer systems and hardware. This chapter serves as an introduction to Part II of the book, which covers computer hardware in detail. Next, Chapter 3 investigates the fundamentals of computer programming and software. These topics are covered in detail in Part III. Finally, Chapter 4 gives an introduction to systems in action and provides an introduction to Part IV of the book.

    Chapters 2, 3, and 4 present fundamental computer concepts that are covered in detail in Parts II, III, and IV. You will note that the titles of these chapters are the same as the titles of the corresponding parts. After you finish Part I, you will be able to cover the other chapters in any order you wish.

1	Fundamentals of information and data processing
2	Hardware
3	Software
4	Systems

PART I
FUNDAMENTALS

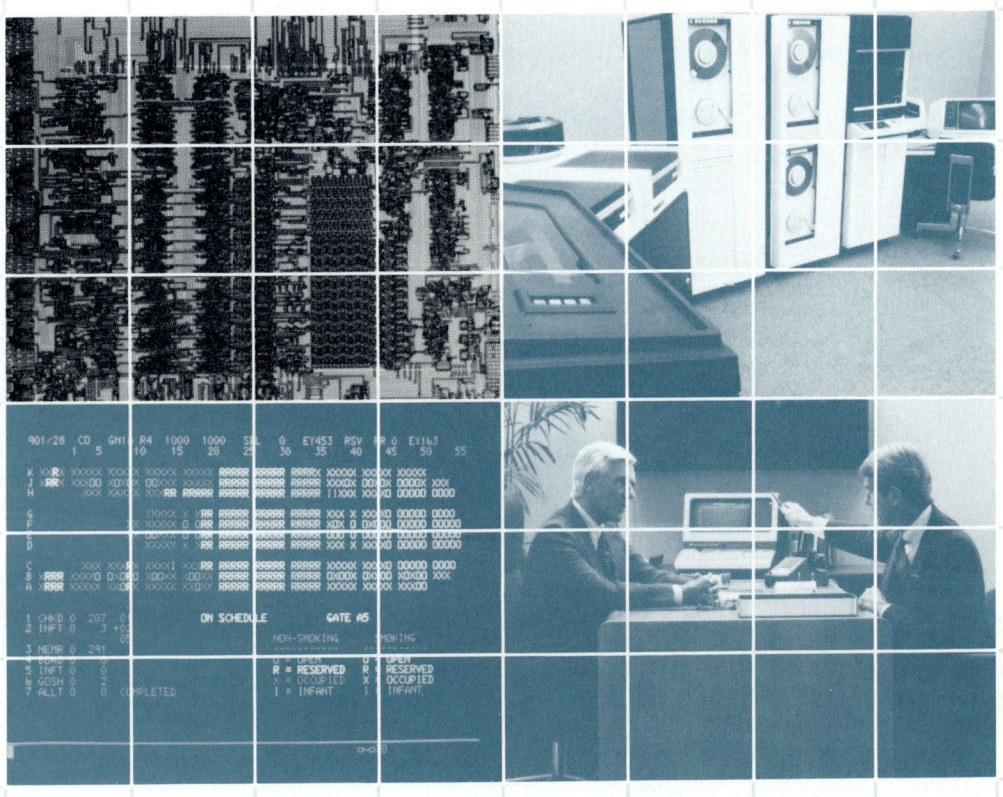

Fundamentals of information and data processing

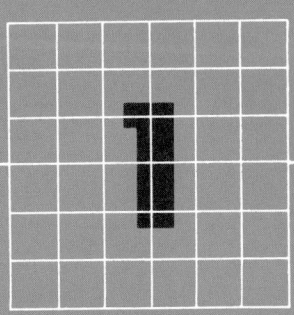

INFORMATION AND DATA PROCESSING
DATA PROCESSING AND ORGANIZATIONS
DATA ORGANIZATION AND MOVEMENT
    Data organization
    Data base concepts
    Data movement
AN ANALOGY
    The components of a manual data processing system
    Placing a manual data processing system into action
    The analogy and computer systems

After completing Chapter 1, you will be able to:

- Describe the differences between data and information.
- Discuss how data processing systems can be used in organizations.
- Explain how data moves through an organization and how it is organized into facts, records, files, and data bases.
- List the components of a manual data processing system and develop instructions that will cause this system to perform routine business applications.

The first business computer was installed at the *General Electric Appliance Park* in Kentucky in 1954. Since this time, tremendous progress has been made in business data processing. Even with this progress, ten years ago only large businesses could afford to use computers. Computers were expensive, and the applications they performed were limited to accounting and financial activities. With decreasing costs, and increasing technology, computerization is a feasible alternative for even small businesses. Furthermore, these machines are doing much more than simply performing accounting functions. Computers are helping managers reduce inventory costs, analyze new markets and the performance of salespersons, and make sophisticated financial analyses. They are being used to reduce the number of uncollected bills, more accurately determine production costs, forecast personnel and labor needs, and eliminate production bottlenecks.

Over half the world's scientific knowledge has been obtained since the construction of the first electronic computer in the 1940s. This is not a coincidence. Without computers, the body of scientific knowledge would not be as great as it is today. While business applications require the handling of a large number of documents, the scientific community requires speed and accuracy in making complex computations. For simple computations, the average individual can make from five to ten computations per minute. For complex computations that may require logarithms, trigonometry, exponents, and so forth, the average individual may require more than one minute for such a computation. The average computer can make 10,000 computations per second, and fast computers can make millions of calculations per second. Computations that would take a computer a few seconds to complete would take you a few months or a few years to complete. Furthermore, the computer would be more accurate and it would make fewer mistakes. This speed and accuracy has greatly expanded our scientific knowledge and has been an invaluable aid to engineers.

The government of the United States could not function without computers. This is true of many other governments as well. For all practical purposes, it would be impossible for the U.S. government to go back to a manual data processing system. It would take too many human beings with their desks, filing cabinets, and so forth, to make the change. Our government is dependent on the computer.

The U.S. government is the largest user of computer equipment in the world. The annual federal budget for computers and data processing is greater than $4 billion according to estimates made by the *Office of Management and Budget* (OMB). It is also estimated that the total number of persons employed in a computer or data processing related job by the federal government is over 130,000. In addition, the number of computer systems used by the federal government is placed at over 10,000.

Computers have had a profound impact on our lives. In the future, this impact will be even greater.

In this and the other chapters in Part I, the fundamentals of data processing systems will be investigated. These fundamentals will apply to a manual or clerical data processing system as well as a computer system. Furthermore, these fundamental concepts can be used to understand a microcomputer costing less than $500 or a very large computer system costing over $5 million. In addition, the approach will be to present material that will not be out of date in the near future. You will be able to place the new device or concept in the framework that will be developed in this part. Since a single clerk and a complex computer both perform the same function (they process data), let us begin by carefully examining the meaning of information and data processing.

INFORMATION AND DATA PROCESSING

When you think of information and data processing, what activities or tasks come to mind? Multiplying, dividing, adding, and subtracting are some examples. Many managers think of payroll, inventory control, customer billing and other tasks that may be associated with data processing. Students may think of registration or computerized grading. When you analyze each of these activities in detail, you will find that only a few basic functions are being performed. These functions are:

1. Input
2. Processing
    a. Classifying
    b. Sorting
    c. Summarizing
    d. Reproducing
    e. Calculating
    f. Storing
3. Output

Whether you are doing your homework with a pencil and paper or a computer is doing a sophisticated payroll application, one or more of the above functions is being performed. The first function is **input**. This involves capturing or obtaining the original data such as time cards which are used to produce paychecks. These original documents are called *source documents*. Then, depending on what is to be done, the input data can be manipulated; that is classified, sorted, summarized, calculated, then stored for future use. This is called **processing**. Finally, the results of these activities are communicated to those who will be using the information. This is called **output**. See Figure 1–1.

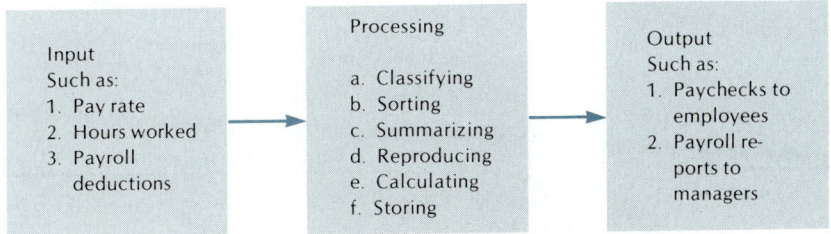

FIGURE 1–1
An overview of data processing using a payroll example

Now we are in a position to make a distinction between data and information. Like raw materials for a manufacturing plant, **data** is the raw material or input to any data processing system. A collection of sales orders, time sheets or cards, and class registration cards are a few examples of raw data. The data goes through a series of planned activities called processing to produce a desired result which is the output, such as bills and paychecks. When this output can be used to help people make decisions, it is called **information**.

Information can reduce uncertainty. It can alert a manager to low inventory levels, customers that are bad credit risks, labor costs that are getting too high, and more. This information can lead to better decision making and a savings of thousands of dollars. In general, the value of information is related to how it can reduce uncertainty, help managers make better decisions, and assist the organization in reaching its goals, such as increased profits. To be of value to managers, information should be *timely, accurate, complete, reliable,* and *concise.*

With an understanding of data and information, data processing and information processing can be defined. **Data processing** is that procedure of transforming data into desired output. The output, however, does not have to be information. **Information processing**, a special case of data processing, is the procedure of transforming data into information which can be used to make better decisions. A **data processing system** includes all people, procedures, and devices that are used to produce desirable output, and an **information processing system** includes all people, procedures, and devices that are used to produce useful information.

DATA PROCESSING AND ORGANIZATIONS

Like a thermostat controlling the temperature of a room, a data processing system has the potential of controlling the operation of an organization. In both cases, data about the system is gathered, analyzed, and then used to control the system. This is called a **feedback loop.** In an organization, data is collected and fed into the data processing system. The data processing system converts the data into information that is used by managers and decision makers in guiding the organization toward its goals. The information

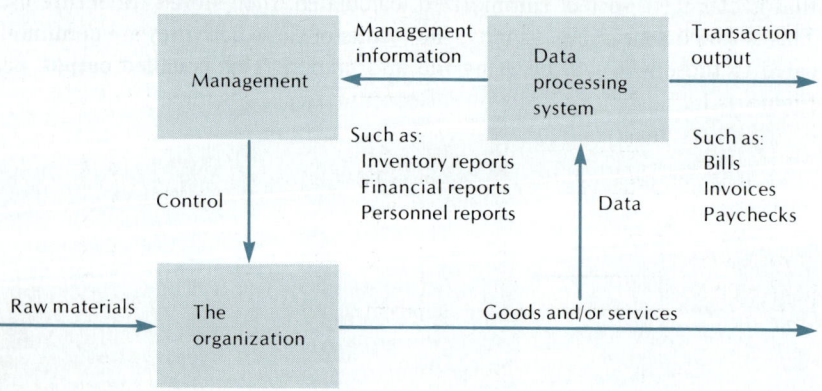

FIGURE 1–2
Data processing in the organization

1 Information and data processing

that is produced by the data processing system for managers is called **management information**. The other outputs are called **transaction outputs** or **bookkeeping reports**. See Figure 1–2.

In order to utilize a data processing system to its potential, the data must be well organized and it must move through the data processing system in an efficient manner. Regardless of whether the data processing system is a manual one or a computerized one, data organization and movement are the same.

DATA ORGANIZATION AND MOVEMENT

Data organization

Data are facts or items. A **fact** or **item** is a number, a name, or a combination of characters. A collection of related facts or items is a **record**. An employee record would be a collection of facts about one employee. These facts would include the employee's name, address, phone number, pay rate, earnings made to date, and so forth. An inventory record would be all of the facts collected about one item in inventory. For example, the part name, part number, price, and quantity for one item would be called the inventory record. A collection of related records is a **file**. For example, a collection of all employee records for one company would be an employee file. What is an inventory file? It is a collection of all inventory records for a particular company or organization. Figure 1–3 reveals the relationship between facts or items, records, and files.

The file described in Figure 1–3 is a **permanent file**. The data stored in a permanent file should be as accurate and current as possible. The permanent files for an organization are called **master files**. An *employee master file* would be a permanent file of all employees of an organization. A permanent file of all the customers that owe money to a company is called an *accounts receivable master file*. An *accounts payable master file* is a file containing all suppliers to which the organization owes money for supplies or materials.

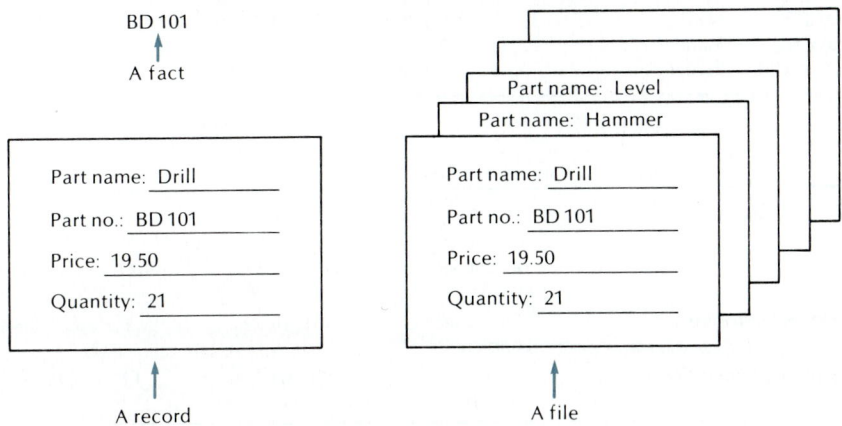

FIGURE 1–3
Facts, records, and files

Another important type of file is a transaction file. A **transaction file** (also called a **detail file**) is a temporary file that represents the transactions of the business or organization. Selling merchandise is a business transaction. Thus, a file containing the sales orders for the day would be the *sales order transaction file*. Time sheets containing the number of hours employees worked, changes that are to be made to an employee master file, new stock that has just arrived from a supplier, and bills that have been sent to the organization for collection are all examples of transactions that would be stored in transaction files. Data from these transaction files will then be used to complete a business transaction or activity.

Employees will be paid, new stock will be included with the existing inventory, and bills will be paid. Most of the above activities will also cause one or more master files to be changed or modified as well. The earnings in the employee master file will be updated, the inventory levels in the inventory master file will be changed, and the accounts payable master file will reflect the fact that a bill has been paid. Thus, the data in a transaction file normally requires the data in a master file to be changed. **Master file maintenance** is the process of making these changes in the appropriate master files.

To give you a better understanding of data organization, a simplified inventory master file and a simplified sales order transaction file will be presented. Table 1–1 contains the data that might be found in a typical inventory master file, and Table 1–2 contains the data that might be found in a sales order transaction file.

TABLE 1–1
Data stored in an inventory master file for B and H Hardware

Part number	Part name	Price per unit	Quantity on hand
ACE 1100	Bolt	$ 0.21	4,000
ACE 40	Brush	1.50	200
BD 101	Drill	19.50	21
G 110	Glue	2.75	110
BD 11	Hammer	5.65	40
ACE 41	Knife	4.60	5
ACE 101	Level	4.20	8
ACE 5	Nails	0.05	14,000
SW 61	Paint	10.61	11
ACE 10	Screw	0.12	9,610

TABLE 1–2
Data stored in a sales order transaction file for B and H Hardware

Customer name	Customer address	Part number	Quantity ordered
True Value Construction	Tallahassee, Florida	ACE 1100	400
Home Hardware	New Orleans, Louisiana	ACE 40	6
Ramsing Renovation	Eugene, Oregon	BD 101	11

1   Information and data processing

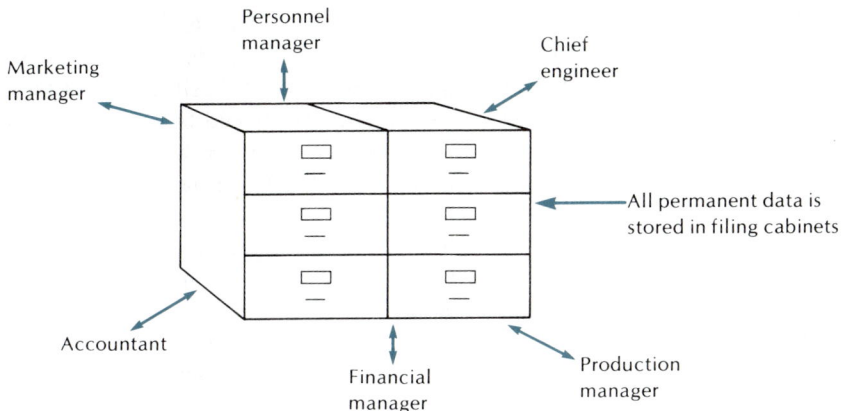

FIGURE 1–4
A manual data base system

The two tables reveal an inventory master file for B and H Hardware and three sales orders received by B and H Hardware in the sales order transaction file.

Data base concepts

The heart of a data processing system within an organization is its collection of master files. A *data base* is a collection of integrated and related master files. A data base is used as the raw material or input data for all of the applications or data processing performed by the organization. See Figures 1–4 and 1–5.

Data movement

So far, data has been discussed from a static point of view—where and how it is stored. Like unfinished goods moving through a manufacturing plant, data is constantly on the move through an organization. Data, however,

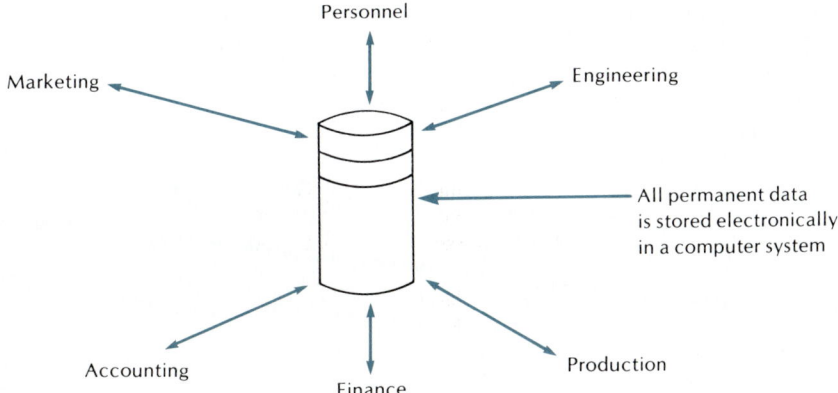

FIGURE 1–5
A computerized data base system

does not move like a physical item or part. Data moves by being *copied* or *reproduced* from the old location to the new location. This is true for both a manual and a computerized data processing system. Thus, the original source of the data does not get destroyed when the data is placed elsewhere. You could copy a sentence from a textbook into your notebook thousands of times. The sentence, of course, remains in the textbook. Likewise, data can be printed or outputted by a computer thousands of times, but the data still remains in the computer system.

As you will soon realize, the way a computer processes data is very similar to the way you would process data by hand using pencil and paper. Functionally, you and the computer are doing the same thing. This fact will be used to make it easier for you to understand computers. In the rest of this chapter, you will see a manual approach to processing data. Then this approach will be used as an analogy to ease the burden of understanding how a computer system is used to process data.

AN ANALOGY

In the following pages, you will see a manual data processing system in action. First of all, the components of a manual data processing system will be discussed; then these components will be placed into action.

The components of a manual data processing system

Although there are many devices one could use when processing data by hand, the most commonly used components would include a desk, filing cabinets, and trays to organize incoming and outgoing documents. These components are shown in Figure 1–6.

The components shown in Figure 1–6 can be named to reflect their function in the data processing system. The person is in the center of all processing,

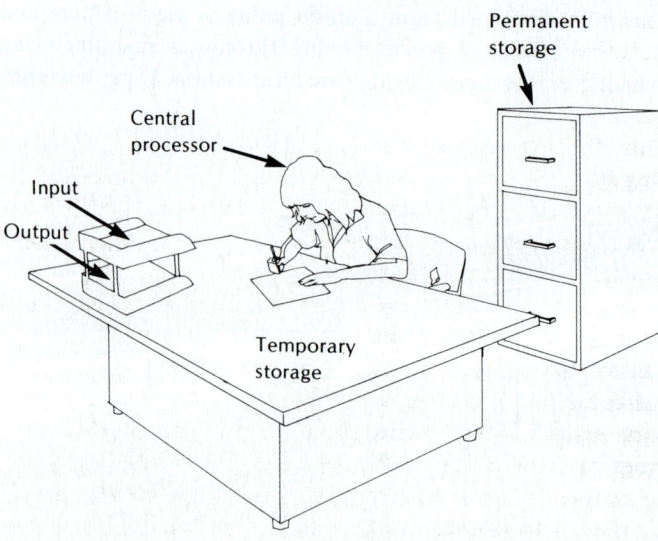

FIGURE 1–6
Components of a manual data processing system

and thus this person can be called the **central processor**. The filing cabinets provide **permanent storage** for the data. The desk is a **temporary storage** device. Finally, the trays used to organize incoming and outgoing documents can be labeled **input devices** and **output devices**.

Placing a manual data processing system into action

Assume that you have a manual data processing system like the one shown in Figure 1–6 at your command. In other words, you have the use of a clerk, the clerk's desk, filing cabinets, and trays for organizing incoming and outgoing documents. Of course, the clerk will do absolutely nothing until you supply a set of instructions for the clerk to follow. How could we instruct the clerk to find the total of a set of numbers?

Placed in one of the filing cabinets, permanent storage, is a file folder called *payroll file* containing the gross amount that was paid to all employees who worked for Honest Value Lumber last week. Since the president of Honest Value Lumber is concerned with rising payroll costs, she would like to know the total amount that was paid to employees last week. Thus, she would like the clerk to find the payroll file, add up the gross paychecks for employees who worked last week, and print the total on a *payroll report*. Here is the procedure that the president might give to the clerk to find the total. See Figure 1–7.

The analogy and computer systems

In this section, we investigated a manual data processing system. First, the components of the manual data processing system were presented. Then, these manual data processing components were placed into action by providing the clerk with a set of instructions to compute a total of a set of numbers. Both the components of the manual data processing system and the instructions that were used to place it into action perform the same functions as the components of a computer system and the instructions we give to the computer to place it into action.

The components of a computer system are called **hardware**. Like the manual data processing system, computer systems have one or more central processors, temporary storage devices, permanent storage devices, input devices and output devices. These hardware devices perform the same functions and have similar characteristics to the components in the manual data processing system. Some of the standard hardware devices will be introduced to you in Chapter 2 and explored in detail in Part II.

The series of instructions given to a computer system to make it perform a particular task, like finding the total of a set of numbers, is called a **program**, also called **software**. As with the instructions given to the manual data processing system, a program consists of a collection of statements or commands that instruct the computer to perform a particular task. This software is the key to getting the computer system to perform the applications and jobs

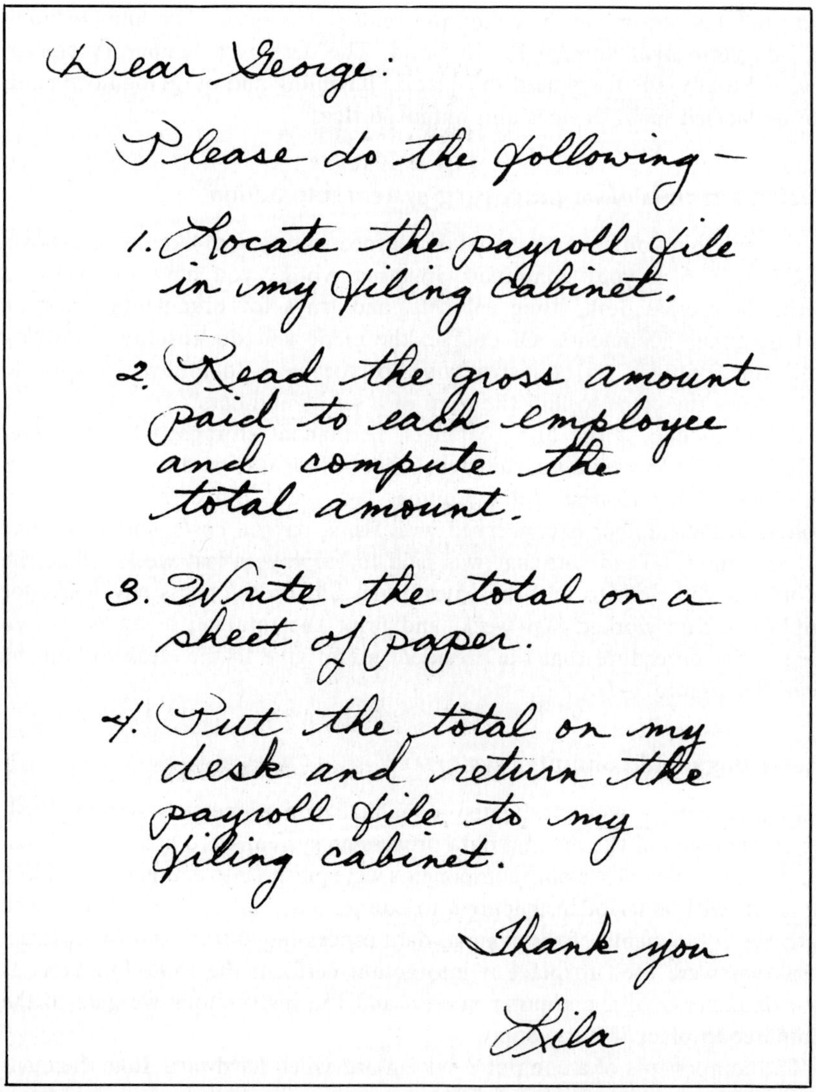

FIGURE 1–7
Calculating the total payroll

> Dear George:
>
> Please do the following—
>
> 1. Locate the payroll file in my filing cabinet.
>
> 2. Read the gross amount paid to each employee and compute the total amount.
>
> 3. Write the total on a sheet of paper.
>
> 4. Put the total on my desk and return the payroll file to my filing cabinet.
>
> Thank you
> Lila

we want. The fundamental concepts of software will be introduced to you in Chapter 3 and covered in detail in Part III of the book.

Hardware and software working together allow people to use computer systems to their benefit. Getting the most from a computer system requires cooperation between computer professionals and the people that will be using the computer system. In Chapter 4, we will investigate a number of topics related to getting more from the computer system and placing the computer system into action for the benefit of the people that it serves. The topics of Chapter 4 will be expanded and covered in detail in Part IV, the last part of the book.

1 Information and data processing

SUMMARY

Although there are hundreds of activities that can be associated with data processing, all data processing activities can be broken down into input, processing, and output. These functions allow us to take raw data and to convert it to meaningful information. The value of the information is directly related to how it can reduce uncertainty, help decision makers, and assist an organization obtain its goals, such as the maximization of profits. A data processing system can be valuable to an organization by providing management information and other outputs, called transaction outputs.

The basic building block of data is the fact, such as a word or number. A record is a collection of related facts, a file is a collection of related records, and a data base is a collection of related files. Unlike physical objects, data moves or is transferred from one location to another by being reproduced or copied. In most organizations, files can be classified into master files and transaction files. A master file is a permanent file, while a transaction file typically contains data concerning a business transaction, such as sales orders or the number of hours employees worked during a period of time.

A data processing system has one or more central processors, temporary storages, permanent storage devices, input devices, and output devices. For these devices to perform, a set of instructions, called software in a computer system, is needed. The components or devices in a computer system [...]. In the next chapter, computer hardware will be investigated, [...] computer software will be explored, and in Chapter 4, [...]tion will be discussed.

KEY TERMS AND CONCEPTS

Information	Permanent file
Information processing	Permanent storage
[In]put	Processing
[Inpu]t devices	Record
	Reproducing
[Managem]ent information	Software
[Da]ta processing	Sorting
	Storing
	Summarizing
[Maint]enance	Temporary storage
	Transaction file
	Transaction outputs

1–2. What is the difference between data and information?

1-3. Discuss the difference between transaction outputs and management information. Give examples of both.

1-4. What is the meaning of each of the following terms? Fact, Record, File, and Data Base.

1-5. What is the difference between a master file and a transaction file?

1-6. What are the functional components of a manual data processing system?

1-7. What is master file maintenance?

MINIQUIZ

ANSWERS

1. F
2. T
3. F
4. F
5. F
6. F
7. T
8. T
9. F
10. T

True or False

_____ 1. A source document means the same as a master file.
_____ 2. When output from a data processing system can be used to help people make decisions, it is called information.
_____ 3. The major purpose of a data processing system is to produce the maximum number of reports and business documents possible.
_____ 4. A record is a collection of related files.
_____ 5. A collection of related data bases is called a file.
_____ 6. An accounts receivable master file contains a list of all employees that the company owes money to.
_____ 7. Another name for a transaction file is a detail file.
_____ 8. Master file maintenance is the process of making the appropriate changes in a master file.
_____ 9. When data is transferred from one location to another, it is deleted from the original or source location.
_____ 10. Hardware in a computer system is analogous to the equipment in a clerical data processing system.

The international industry: Transborder data flow
John Eger

"The liberal vision of a pacific and mutually beneficial international order supported by growing economic interdependence is wearing very thin," Stephen D. Krasner of UCLA commented sadly in a *Wall Street Journal* review of Raymond Vernon's *Storm Over the Multinationals.* "The state will not be worn away by the ebb and flow of economic transactions; if need be, it will build dikes. That reality is going to be difficult for us to deal with."

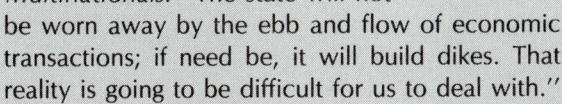

The dikes, it may be argued, are being built. Ironically, the dikes include laws ostensibly dealing with the privacy, security, and confidentiality of information flowing across national boundaries. Application, interpretation, and enforcement of these laws may actually cut off the flow of information, the central nervous system of transnational communications, which are vital not only to the United States, but also to the far-flung activities of multinational corporations.

Of equal consequence, the export of "information products," a concept not yet well defined but of increasing importance in the scheme of world trade, may suffer the same crippling effect.

Eighteen nations now have privacy or other so-called data protection laws on the books or in the making. Other nations have similar laws in force or under consideration. These laws present an imminent threat to the world economy and to all nations increasingly dependent upon the free flow of information across national borders. In the United States, where communications are most advanced, the threat looms large indeed.

Every government function from security and national defense to weather prediction and disaster relief is increasingly dependent on computer and telecommunications technology. It is clear, therefore, that taxes, tariffs, laws, regulations, and other barriers to the free flow of information adversely affect not only our multinational corporations, but all others transacting business and exchanging scientific or cultural information across national borders.

Perhaps less clear is what these barriers portend for the future of our so-called information industry and our related "information products." While no exact accounting of our information products is available from a 1976 study released by the U.S. Department of Commerce, we do know that our service sector (which depends in large part upon the production, use, storage, and transfer of information and is itself better defined by recorded statistics), accounts for two thirds of our labor force. The same study found that one fifth of our exports were "services" as opposed to "goods," from either farms or factories. According to a more recent Commerce study, approximately 46 percent of the American work force is comprised of "information workers"—men and women employed not on farms or in factories but in the information industry. Almost half the GNP is now made up of information services and technology. In the next few years, by other estimates, 70 percent of our labor income will be from such "information activity."

We are increasingly dependent on this broadly defined "information" for the growth and health of our economy, the smooth functioning of our institutions, and the quality of our individual lives. Information has become a marketable, transferable, exportable commodity. Information, therefore, means national and individual income and well-being.

Traditional restrictions The United States in recent years has seen restrictions on the more traditional forms of information flow. Television, for instance, has become a prime target of restriction. In Canada, commercial messages are sometimes

---
Source: Reprinted with permission of DATAMATION® magazine. © Copyright by Technical Publishing Company, a Dun & Bradstreet Company, 1978—all rights reserved.

deleted from U.S. programs relayed by Canadian cable tv systems, and a 15 percent tax on all non-Canadian programming has been proposed. In Brazil, the government has set up policy censors at all post offices to intercept incoming publications which might contain anything "contrary to public order or morality." The Brazilian government has also proposed that 70 percent of their radio and television programs be domestically produced.

Many of the countries resisting or blocking the export of our information are not concerned with competition in any literal sense. They have no information technology or industry of their own and therefore cannot hope presently to compete with technologically rich nations—and in that fact may lie the reason for their opposition and their fear.

What many fear is cultural inundation or annihilation. They are resisting what they call "electronic colonialization" or "electronic imperialism." They do not want their minds, banks, governments, news, literature, music, or any other aspect of their lives to be Americanized. Neither do they want to be Anglicized, Sovietized, or otherwise victimized by advanced technology and information that freely flows across their borders, thus possibly causing their own identities to become extinct.

It is lamentable but undeniable that while we see ourselves as offering the developing nations of the world information they need to survive, such as medical and other scientific data, they perceive, beyond the images and printouts of data bits, a threat of vast and unwelcome change. More specifically, they see changes in their governments and their leadership groups. Our information, particularly when it is delivered via a computer-satellite link to a battery-operated tv or radio receiver, appears as an imminent threat to national status, power, and lifestyle.

New forms Among the industrialized nations, the more recent information disputes are taking different forms, and stem from different motives. Long frustrated by our lead in the computer and communications field, Europe, according to some observers, had turned to a new form of protectionism. One need only listen to France's Magistrate of Justice, Louis Joinet, who stated the European concern most directly at a symposium in Vienna in September 1977: "Information is power, and economic information is economic power. Information has an economic value and the ability to store and process certain types of data may well give one country political and technological advantage over other countries. This in turn may lead to a loss of national sovereignty through supranational data flows."

To protect their "national sovereignty" against this perceived threat, many European nations are proposing a variety of data protection laws. Most of these laws are being passed in the name of personal privacy and individual rights. Many countries in Europe have no concern, perhaps, but to protect the privacy of personal data, a concern which neither the American public nor any member of a democratic society can fault. The problem, of course, comes when these new laws are used not to protect just privacy but domestic economic interests.

According to Rep. Barry Goldwater, Jr. (R-Calif.), coauthor of the 1974 Privacy Act and himself a champion of individual privacy, that is precisely what is starting to happen.

All these protectionist steps are leading to some other potentially serious problems. First, there is the very real possibility that in a world where the flow of information is predominantly regulated, "data havens" or "data refuges" will spring up in those countries with either few or no laws restricting the storage, transmission, and use of data. Because computer communications technology is essential not only to business and commerce but to all human activity, laws will not end the information revolution. Instead, data banks in countries where it has become impossible, too expensive or cumbersome to operate, or where privacy of the data cannot be secure, will leave and move to such a "data haven." The loss of revenue, as much as the loss of control over the information, is unthinkable to most nations.

Sweden's data act The first nation to restrict the flow of information in the name of privacy was Sweden, which passed its Data Act in 1973 as a response to the discovery that material on

Swedish citizens was stored or processed in more than 2,000 data systems outside the country. Under Sweden's law, a Data Inspection Board must now approve any export of data files or transmission of personal data outside Sweden.

The impact and interpretation of the new laws being enacted and discussed elsewhere is still uncertain. West Germany's new Federal Data Protection Act requires German data processors to stop the improper input, access, communication, transport, and manipulation of stored data. Belgium and France are making it a criminal offense even to record or transmit some data. In France, violators could pay up to $400,000 in fines and serve prison terms of up to five years for recording or transmitting data defined only as "sensitive." The Swiss, who offer what many consider to be attractive numbered bank accounts, are considering laws to regulate strictly all electronic trade and business data transmission across their borders.

Spain requires money to be deposited in an escrow account before data files can be transmitted electronically or manually out of the country. Canada has warned U.S. industry of its concern over the one-way flow of information to the United States. In addition, certain Canadian provinces have enacted their own regulations blocking data movement at the provincial level. The warnings, nevertheless, have had effect: one medical information bureau owned by U.S. insurance companies has already set up a Toronto subsidiary just for Canadian data. Some also see a potential major threat in Britain, where existing law requires that the British Post Office be able to read any transmitted message—a rule which, if applied to electronic data, would force firms to share their confidential cryptographic codes and data compression formulas with a government body.

The obstacles to building and using global networks with or without minimum restrictions, however, are not limited to national privacy or data protection laws alone.

In the United Nations and the International Telecommunications Union (ITU), the questions of information flow, orbital slots, and frequency allocations have been exploited by the Soviet Union and Third World countries. European Ministries of Posts, Telephones, and Telegraphs (PTT's), the government-controlled telephone postal monopolies, now price their facilities at rates and schedules that are prohibitive for the development of private or user-controlled data networks. In other forums, new proposals have been put forth which threaten elimination of private lines altogether, and protocols (or standards) have been suggested which likewise threaten to wrest the control of international data processing away from the user completely.

DISCUSSION QUESTIONS

1. Why is transborder data flow an important issue?
2. Why are some countries trying to block transborder data flow?
3. What are some of the techniques and laws used to regulate transborder data flow?

Hardware 2

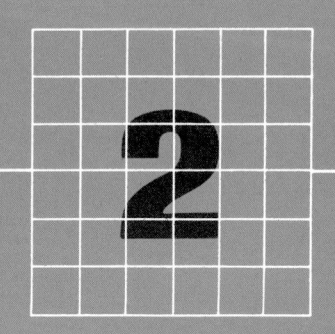

THE ANALOGY REVISITED
THE CENTRAL PROCESSOR AND TEMPORARY STORAGE
    The central processor
    Temporary storage
PERMANENT STORAGE
    Computer cards
    Magnetic tape
    Disk devices
INPUT
    Key-to-card, tape, and disk
    Terminal devices
OUTPUT: THE PRINTER
COMPUTER CONFIGURATIONS

After completing Chapter 2, you will be able to:

- List the various types of components in a computer system.
- Discuss the important factors of the Central Processing Unit and Temporary Storage.
- Describe and give advantages and disadvantages of the different permanent storage devices.
- Define data entry and data input and describe the devices that perform the input function.
- Contrast the various output devices.
- Distinguish the different ways in which computer components are put together to form a complete computer system.

Computer systems come in all different sizes, types, and price ranges. Like certain species of plants or animals, computer systems have a number of characteristics that set them apart from mechanical calculators, adding machines, and other data processing devices. To begin with, computers have the ability to **input, process,** and **output** data and information without human intervention. Computer systems have the ability to *store data* and *instructions* and to follow a set of stored instructions (a program) in producing a desired output or result. Computer systems have these common characteristics, but the types and uses of computer systems vary tremendously.

There are basically two different types of computers, **analog** and **digital.** Analog means to measure, and digital means to count. In a hospital, a patient's blood pressure can be measured and fed directly into a computer. In a chemical manufacturing plant, the temperature and pressure of a chemical can be measured and inputted directly into a computer that is controlling the process. These computers are analog computers. Although analog computers are fast, they are not extremely accurate. Most analog computers cannot process numbers to more than a few significant digits. Thus, if you were adding millions of dollars on an analog computer, the computations might be hundreds of dollars off the correct answer. A digital computer, which counts, can be more accurate. In fact, many digital computers can be exact to more than 16 significant digits. Most business and scientific computers are digital computers.

Some computer manufacturers have attempted to combine an analog and digital computer. This type of computer system is called a **hybrid** computer. These computers attempt to combine the advantages of both computers. Some hybrid computers are faster than digital computers and more accurate than analog computers. Even so, a digital computer, which can be programmed or instructed to act like an analog computer, is the most popular type of computer.

Some digital computers are **special purpose** computers. That is, they only have the ability to do one type of job, like navigation on a ship. Most digital computers, however, are **general purpose** computers. These computers can be programmed or instructed to do a variety of business and scientific applications. Regardless of type, size, purpose, or price tag, all computers use components, called *hardware,* to perform the same types of functions. When connected together, these components form a *computer system.*

THE ANALOGY REVISITED

Like a manual data processing system, all computer systems perform the same types of functions: input, output, central processing, temporary storage, and permanent storage. There are devices in a computer system that perform the same function as the clerk, the input and output trays, the desk, and the filing cabinets. Furthermore, many of these components in the manual data processing system have the same characteristics as their computer counterparts. Figure 2–1 is an overview of some commonly used components for a computer system.

2 Hardware

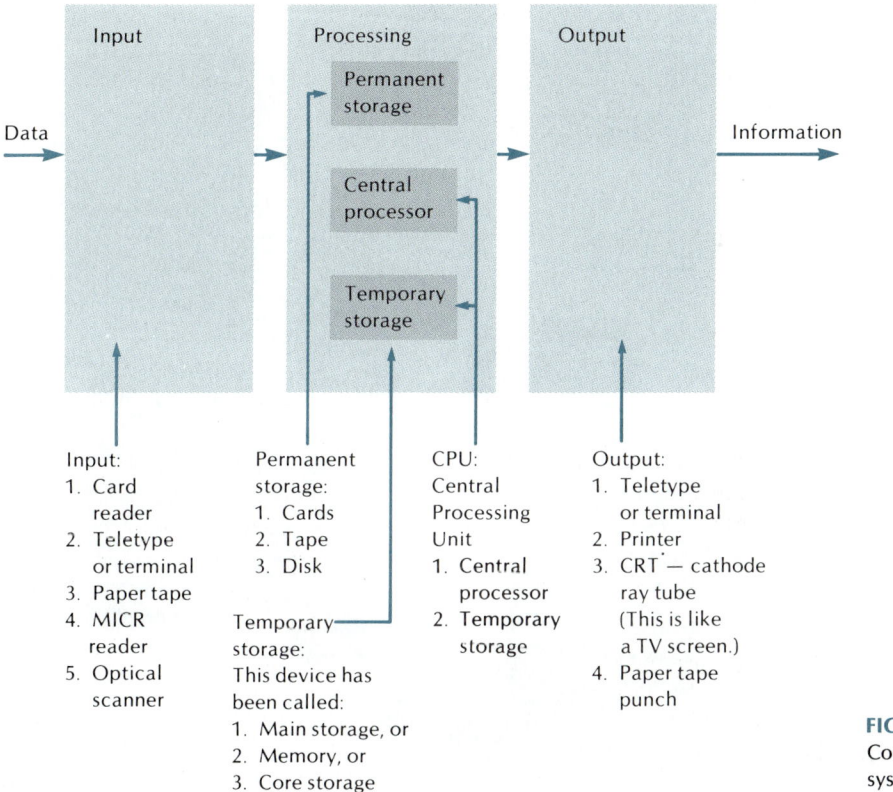

FIGURE 2–1
Components of a computer system

Input:
1. Card reader
2. Teletype or terminal
3. Paper tape
4. MICR reader
5. Optical scanner

Permanent storage:
1. Cards
2. Tape
3. Disk

Temporary storage:
This device has been called:
1. Main storage, or
2. Memory, or
3. Core storage

CPU: Central Processing Unit
1. Central processor
2. Temporary storage

Output:
1. Teletype or terminal
2. Printer
3. CRT — cathode ray tube (This is like a TV screen.)
4. Paper tape punch

THE CENTRAL PROCESSOR AND TEMPORARY STORAGE

The central processor and the temporary storage device are normally housed in the same box or cabinet. Usually this box or cabinet is called the *central processing unit* (CPU).

Often called the *main frame,* the CPU is the center or heart of the computer system. All other devices are tied directly or indirectly into the CPU. The name of the complete computer system takes on the same name as the CPU for that computer system. A Burroughs B2800 is the name of a CPU, but it is also the name of a complete computer system that has a Burroughs B2800 for its CPU. Figure 2–2 shows a typical CPU.

The central processor

In the manual data processing system, the clerk executed each instruction and performed the arithmetic operations. Working logically from one instruction to the next, the clerk controlled the system. Like the clerk, the central processor performs *control, arithmetic,* and *logic* functions. In addition, most central processors act as an internal time clock keeping track of the time actually spent on each set of instructions.

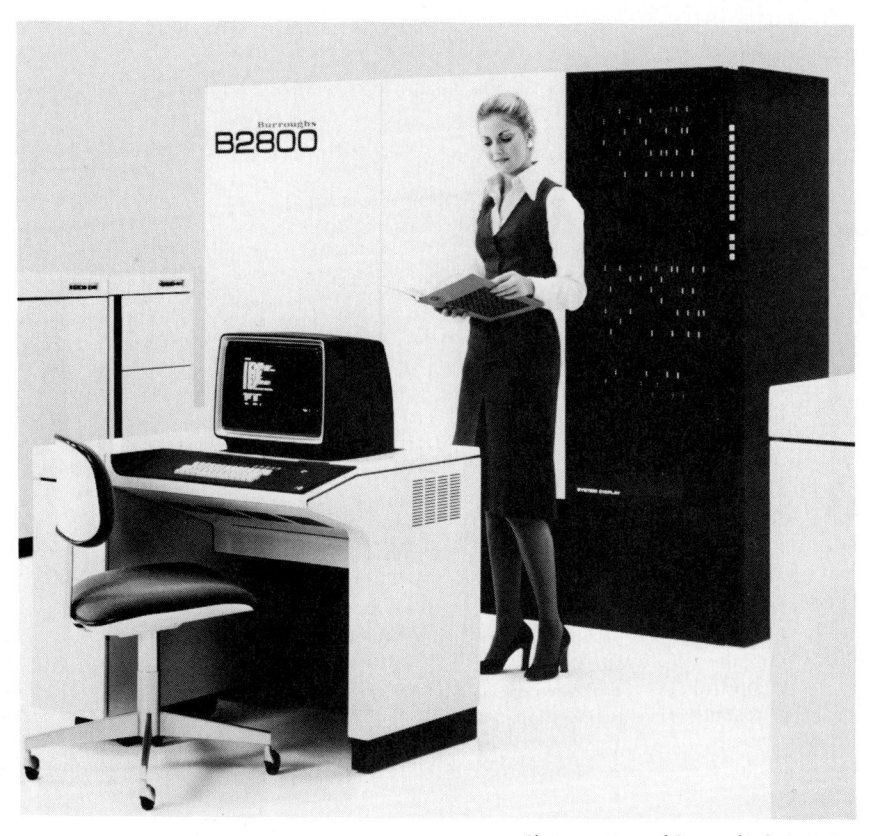

FIGURE 2–2
A CPU

Photo courtesy of Burroughs Corporation

Central processors can cost under $10 or over a $1,000. What is the main reason for the difference in price? It is *speed*. The older and less expensive processors had operating speeds measured in milliseconds and microseconds. A **millisecond** is one thousandth of one second ($\frac{1}{1000}$ second). A **microsecond** is one millionth of one second ($\frac{1}{1,000,000}$ second). The speed of modern computers is measured in *nanoseconds* and *picoseconds*. A **nanosecond** is one billionth of one second ($\frac{1}{1,000,000,000}$ second), and a **picosecond** is one trillionth of a second ($\frac{1}{1,000,000,000,000}$ second). Figure 2–3 presents some comparisons.

Temporary storage

All data processing systems require temporary storage. In the manual data processing system, a desk was used as the temporary storage device. The main purpose of the desk was to provide a working area for the clerk. The instructions and the data currently being processed were kept on the desk. The desk provides fast access to desired instructions or data. In a computer system, temporary storage performs the same function as the desk. The main purpose of temporary storage is to provide the CPU with a working storage area. Also like the desk, temporary storage devices for computer

FIGURE 2–3
The impact of technology

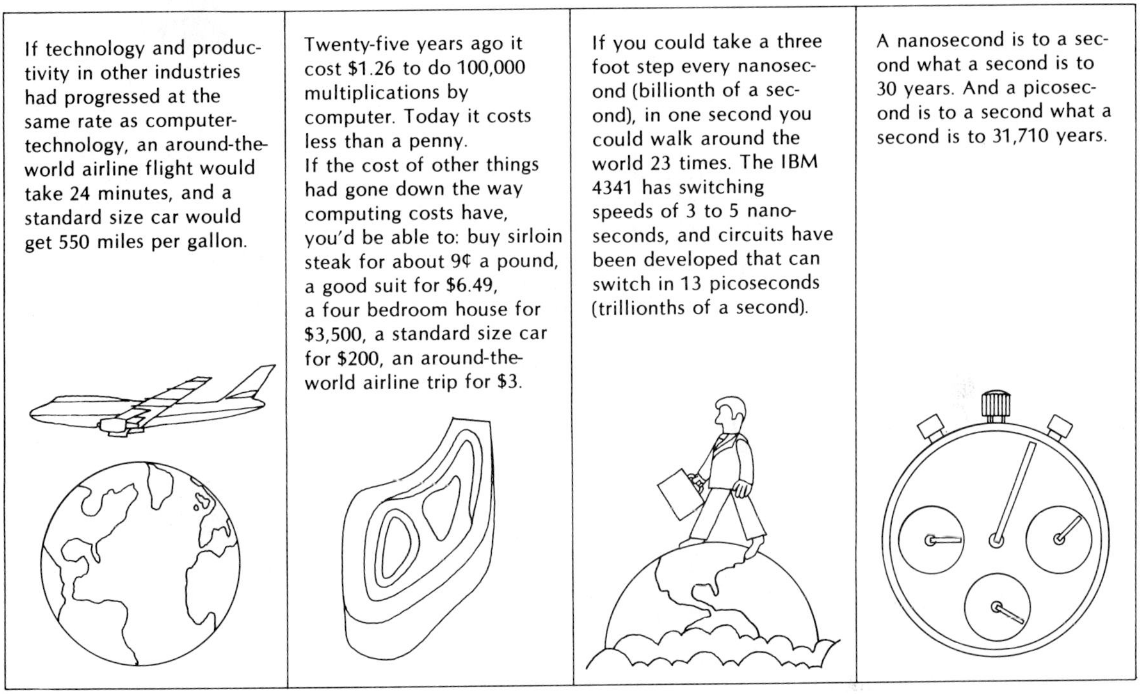

| If technology and productivity in other industries had progressed at the same rate as computer-technology, an around-the-world airline flight would take 24 minutes, and a standard size car would get 550 miles per gallon. | Twenty-five years ago it cost $1.26 to do 100,000 multiplications by computer. Today it costs less than a penny. If the cost of other things had gone down the way computing costs have, you'd be able to: buy sirloin steak for about 9¢ a pound, a good suit for $6.49, a four bedroom house for $3,500, a standard size car for $200, an around-the-world airline trip for $3. | If you could take a three foot step every nanosecond (billionth of a second), in one second you could walk around the world 23 times. The IBM 4341 has switching speeds of 3 to 5 nanoseconds, and circuits have been developed that can switch in 13 picoseconds (trillionths of a second). | A nanosecond is to a second what a second is to 30 years. And a picosecond is to a second what a second is to 31,710 years. |

Courtesy of IBM

systems usually hold one or more sets of instructions called programs and some data that is being processed currently. As seen in Figure 2–4, temporary storage literally ties together all of the functional components of a computer system.

There are many names for temporary storage. Some of the more popular ones are: *main storage, main memory, memory, primary storage,* and *core storage.* The term core storage evolved because some temporary storage devices were made of small iron rings or "cores." The major factor with temporary storage is *storage capacity* or size. In general, enough temporary storage is needed to hold one or more sets of instructions or programs and the data that is currently being processed. In most cases, the storage capacity is measured in bytes, where one *byte* is approximately equal to one character.

The letter *K* means 1,024 and the word *mega* means million. Thus, a storage device that has 16K can hold 16,384 bytes, and a storage device that holds 5 megabytes holds 5 million bytes of storage.

Some companies use different approaches to specify the size of temporary storage. Common approaches include specifying the number of words, blocks, or bits. These conventions will be fully explored along with computer numbering systems, central processors, and temporary storage devices in Chapter 6.

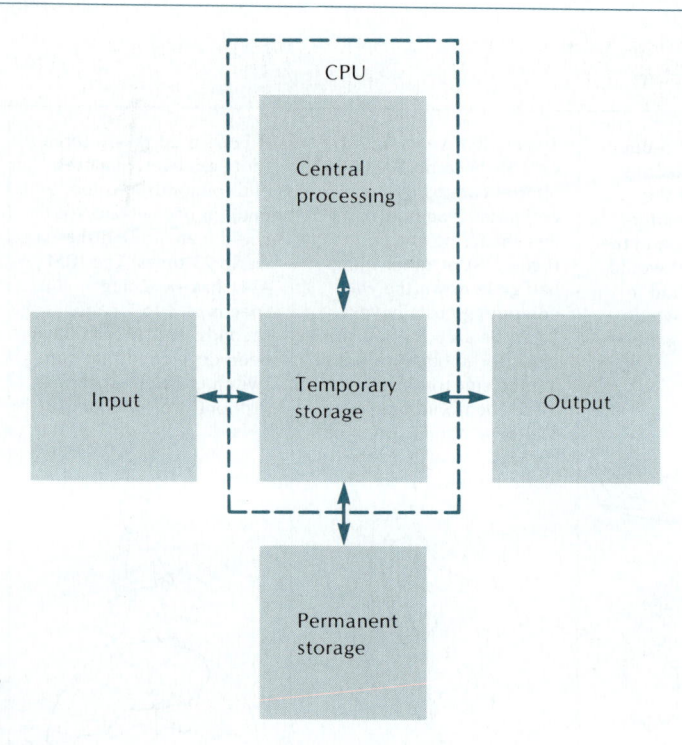

FIGURE 2–4
The components of a computer system

PERMANENT STORAGE

Data processing systems require the ability to store all of the data and instructions on a permanent basis. This type of storage is called *permanent storage, secondary storage,* or *auxiliary storage.* Although there are many ways of storing data on a permanent basis, *computer cards, magnetic tape,* and *disk devices* are the most commonly used media for permanent storage.

Computer cards

One of the oldest methods of permanently storing data is to use computer cards. The standard card has 80 columns. One character can be stored in each column. Normally one record is stored on one card, and thus they are known as *unit records,* while card devices have been called *unit record equipment.* Standard computer cards are shown in Figure 2–5.

Although there are many different devices used to manipulate data stored on cards, the *card reader* and *card punch* are essential in getting the data to and from the computer system. In some of the newer systems, one device is used for both card reading and card punching. See Figure 2–6.

Magnetic tape

Another popular way of storing data is to use magnetic tape. The average reel of tape is 2,400 feet long and ½ inch wide. One character occupies a

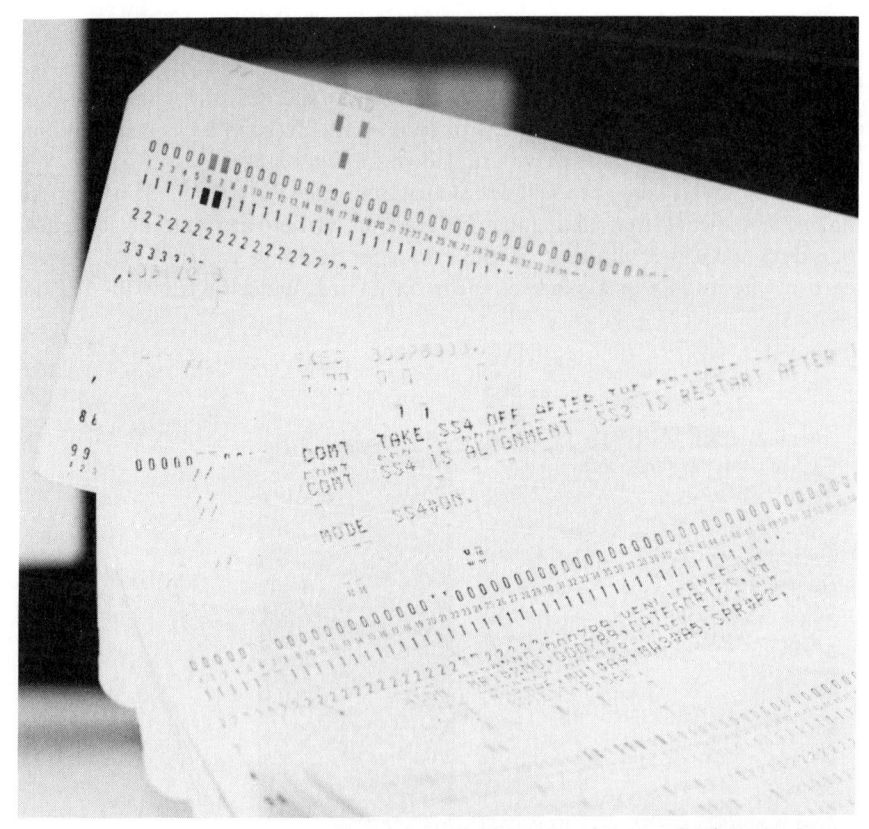

FIGURE 2–5
Computer cards

Photo courtesy of Honeywell Information Systems

FIGURE 2–6
A card reader punch

Photo courtesy of Honeywell Information Systems

narrow and invisible column that cuts across the tape. Usually, there are seven or nine areas or tracks that run through the tape. Some tape devices can store up to 1,600 characters on 1 inch of tape. Certain characters are represented by having certain areas or spots magnetized in any given column. A reel of tape and a tape drive are shown in Figure 2–7.

Both cards and tape are **sequential access storage devices** (SASD). Sequential access means that data must be read or written in order of sequence, one data item after another. If the computer is going to read data from a card in the middle of a stack of cards on a card reader or from the middle

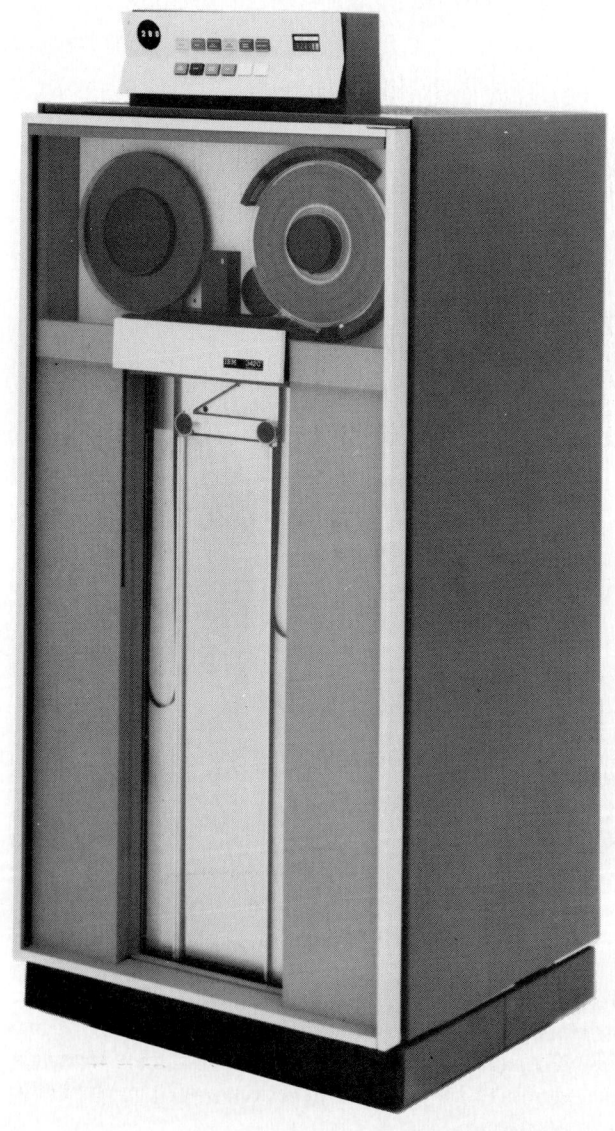

FIGURE 2–7
Standard magnetic tape and tape device

Photo courtesy of IBM

2 Hardware

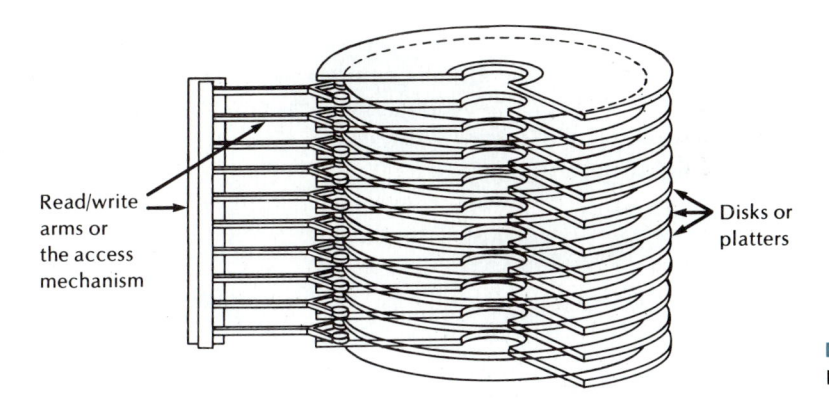

FIGURE 2–8
Disks and read/write arms

of a reel of tape, all of the cards or tape before the desired piece of data must be passed over sequentially before getting to the desired piece of data. Sequential access is one disadvantage of cards or tape. Although more expensive, the disk has the potential of eliminating this disadvantage.

Disk devices

Most disk devices have several disks or platters stacked on top of one another with enough room between each disk or platter to allow a read/write arm to access information stored on the top and bottom of the disks. Refer to Figure 2–8.

The operation of disk devices is somewhat similar to the operation of a record player. The disks, which are mounted in a disk drive, rotate at a rapid speed. Data is either read from or written to the disk surface, which is a magnetic material, using access arms. These access arms can be either fixed or they can be moved in and out over the disk area. A disk drive with disk is shown in Figure 2–9.

In reading or writing data, the access arm will position itself over the desired track. Then it will either read data from the disk or write data to the disk when the appropriate area rotates over the access arm. With a disk device, the computer can go directly to the desired piece of data when reading or writing. Thus the disk is called a **direct access storage device** (DASD). Direct access is also called random access.

Speed and storage capacity are the major factors in selecting the appropriate permanent storage device. In general, the disk, which offers direct access, is faster than magnetic tape, and magnetic tape is generally faster than card systems. As you would expect, the systems with the faster access speeds are more expensive. With any permanent storage system, the storage capacity must be large enough to accommodate all of the data and programs used by the computer system. Storage capacity for permanent storage is specified in the same manner as temporary storage. Permanent storage concepts will be explored in detail in Chapter 7.

FIGURE 2–9
A disk device

Photo courtesy of Control Data Corporation

INPUT

In the manual data processing system, input trays were used to transfer data into the system. In a computer system there are many more options. Regardless of how the data is transferred into the computer system, the same process is occurring. Input is the process of transferring data that is human readable, such as a sales order, into the computer system. In some instances this is a two-stage process. First, the human readable data is converted into a form that a computer system can interpret—machine readable. This is called **data preparation** or **data entry.** The second stage is to transfer the machine readable data into the computer system. This is **data input.**

Key-to-card, tape, and disk

A keyboard that transfers human readable data directly on to computer cards, magnetic tape, and disk devices is the most popular method of performing data preparation or entry. Some of the newer data entry devices allow

FIGURE 2–10
A data entry device

Photo courtesy of IBM

the data to be checked for errors before it is entered on to cards, tape, or disks. See Figure 2–10.

A keypunch operator reads the data and then hits the appropriate keys on a keyboard that resembles the keyboard on a typewriter. The keypunch machine punches holes in a computer card that can be sensed and interpreted by the computer system. Key-to-tape and key-to-disk work basically the same. Data is entered through a keyboard onto a magnetic tape, a cassette, a disk, or a flexible disk. In addition, some of these devices can have a buffer storage area or a microcomputer to assist in entering the data.

Terminal devices

Terminal devices are becoming very attractive for limited data input and output. These devices perform both data entry and data input at the same time. Data is keyed into the terminal which converts the data into machine readable form and transfers the data to the computer system. Normally connected directed to the computer by telephone lines, terminals can be placed in offices, warehouses, homes, and anywhere that phone lines can be placed.

Most terminals can be classified as either *teleprinter terminals* or *display terminals* depending on how the data is outputted. The teleprinter terminal has a printing device and the display terminal has a *cathode ray tube* (CRT), which is similar to a TV screen. See Figure 2–11.

FIGURE 2–11
A display terminal

Photo courtesy of IBM

There are a number of other input devices that can be used with computer systems. These devices include *point of sale* (POS) devices, *speech recognition devices, magnetic ink character recognition* (MICR) devices, *optical character recognition* (OCR) devices, and *paper tape* reading devices. These and other devices will be covered in Chapters 8 and 9.

OUTPUT: THE PRINTER

The purpose of any output device is to get data and information stored in the computer system into a form that is human readable and understandable. Unlike input, output normally occurs in one stage. Although there are many different types of output devices, the most commonly used ones are **printers** and **terminals.** Terminals are also used for input, and they were introduced to you in the previous section.

Printers are available with different speeds, features, and capabilities. Some printers print one character at a time, some print a complete line of characters at a time (line printers), and some printers can print an entire page at one time. A line printer is shown in Figure 2–12. Printers are set up to accommodate different paper forms. These forms may be blank check forms, blank invoice forms, and so forth. Forms may be in different colors with several copies that are routed to various departments.

2 Hardware

FIGURE 2–12
A printer

Photo courtesy of IBM

FIGURE 2–13
A large computer system

Photo courtesy of NCR Corporation

Other output devices include *computer output microfilm* (COM), *plotters,* and *voice response.* These devices along with various printer devices will be covered completely in Chapters 8 and 9 in Part II.

COMPUTER CONFIGURATIONS

A computer system consists of those devices or components that are directly and electronically connected together. Like a home stereo system, computer systems may be built from a large number of different components, and new components may be added at a later date. The components of one computer system may all be *centralized* in one room; they may be spread across town; or they may be located all over the country or the world. As long as the devices are connected together electronically, these devices comprise the complete computer system.

Computer systems vary in both size and configuration. Some microcomputers cost less than $500, while some large computer systems cost more than $5 million. Figure 2–13 shows a typical computer system.

All of the computer facilities can be located at one location *(centralized);* different computers can operate independently at different locations *(decentralized);* or computers can be located at different locations but be connected together to share data processing tasks *(distributed).* The prices, characteristics, sizes, and configurations of various computer systems are covered in detail in Chapter 10.

SUMMARY

Computers are electronic devices that have the ability to input, process, output, and store data and instructions. In general, computer systems can be classified into analog devices that measure, digital devices that count, and hybrid devices that attempt to do both. Today, most computers are digital systems. In addition, computer systems can be further classified as general purpose or special purpose; most computer systems are now general purpose. Like a manual data processing system, all of the components of a computer system can be classified into input devices, output devices, and processing devices that perform the functions of central processing, permanent storage and temporary storage.

The central processor and temporary storage device are normally placed in the same cabinet or device called the central processing unit (CPU). The central processor performs control, arithmetic, and logic functions. The temporary storage device provides storage for the data and instructions that currently are being processed by the computer system. The major factor for the central processor is speed while the major factor of temporary storage is storage capacity.

Permanent storage, also called secondary and auxiliary storage, is performed in most cases by computer cards, magnetic tape, and the disk. Computer cards and magnetic tape are both sequential access storage devices (SASD), while a disk is a direct access storage device (DASD). Speed and storage capacity are both important factors in selecting a permanent storage device in addition to access method (sequential or direct).

To input data into a computer system, data entry and data input are both required. Data entry devices include keypunch machines, key-to-disk, and key-to-tape devices. Data input devices include the card reader, the tape drive, and the disk drive. Terminals are also appropriate for a limited amount of input and output. Terminals can be classified into visual display and teleprinter terminals.

The major output device is the printer. Printers can print a character at a time, a line at a time, or an entire page at a time. Other output devices include computer output microfilm, plotters, and voice response devices.

A computer system includes all of the hardware devices that are electronically connected together. Depending upon the configuration of these devices, computers can be centralized, decentralized, or distributed. Furthermore, computer systems can cost under $500 (microcomputers) or more than $5 million (large computers).

KEY TERMS AND CONCEPTS

Analog
Auxiliary storage
Bytes
Cathode ray tube (CRT)
Central processing unit (CPU)
Computer
Computer cards
Computer system
Core storage
Data entry
Data preparation
Digital
Direct access storage device (DASD)
Disk devices
Display terminals

General purpose computer
Hardware
Hybrid computer
Input
K
Key-to-card
Key-to-disk
Key-to-tape
Line printer
Magnetic tape
Main frame
Main memory
Main storage
Mega
Megabytes
Memory
Microsecond

Millisecond
Nanosecond
Output
Permanent storage
Picosecond
Primary storage
Printer
Random access
Secondary storage
Sequential access storage device (SASD)
Special purpose computer
Teleprinter terminals
Temporary storage
Terminal
Unit record equipment

QUESTIONS

2–1. Describe the difference between an analog computer and a digital computer. What is a hybrid computer?

2–2. What are the functions of any computer system? Give an example of a component that performs each of these functions.

2–3. What functions does the central processing unit perform, and what is the major consideration in selecting a central processing unit?

2–4. What are some of the other names associated with temporary storage? Describe how the storage capacity for temporary storage is measured. Give several examples of storage capacity.

2–5. List the commonly used permanent storage devices.

2–6. What is the difference between sequential access and direct or random access? Which permanent storage devices are sequential and which devices are direct?

2–7. What is the difference between data entry and data input? Give some examples of data entry devices and data input devices.

2–8. Describe some of the different types of terminal devices.

2–9. List some of the different computer sizes and configurations.

ANSWERS

1. T
2. T
3. T
4. T
5. T
6. F
7. F
8. F
9. T
10. T

MINIQUIZ

True or False

___T___ 1. A digital computer counts instead of measures.
___T___ 2. Today, most business computers are digital computers.
___T___ 3. A hybrid computer is a computer that attempts to combine the advantages of an analog computer with the advantages of a digital computer.
___T___ 4. A special purpose computer is a computer that only has the ability to perform one type of job, like the navigation of a ship.
___T___ 5. The components of a computer system are called hardware.
___F___ 6. The main frame is another name for a permanent storage device.
___F___ 7. A picosecond is $1/100$ second.
___F___ 8. Temporary storage is normally performed by the disk or magnetic tape in a computer system.
___T___ 9. A storage device that can hold 5 megabytes holds 5 million bytes of storage.
___T___ 10. The process of transferring machine readable or understandable data into the computer system is called "data input."

The Diplomat Resort
installs online electronic system and cuts payroll costs by $125,000

On New Year's Eve, a sell-out crowd greeted 1977 and headliners Liza Minelli and Sammy Davis Jr., at the posh *Diplomat Resort* located on the famous Florida Gold Coast, between Ft. Lauderdale and Miami Beach.

Traditionally, such sellouts have been a mixed blessing for the resort's management and employees . . . because heavy traffic has always required hours of overtime and frenzied activity for restaurant and lounge checkers, front-desk cashiers, and auditors, as well as heightened management's concern about operating without the reassurance of a daily trial balance . . . but 1976's New Year's Eve was special.

For the first time in many years, the posting of guest charges didn't drag into the next afternoon. In fact, by 4:45 A.M., more than 10,000 food and beverage charges had been posted to guest accounts automatically and accurately with the aid of NCR "online" electronic terminals. As a result, this year employees went home on schedule, and management had the desired trial balance to begin the new year.

Roger deWardt Lane, treasurer of the resort complex, commented, "Prior to our switch to NCR online electronic terminals, it was not possible to get daily trial balances because it was often 7 A.M. on the following day before all items (especially night club charges) had been posted, and by then, it was time to start checking out guests."

"We actually went from mid-December 1975 until April 25, 1976, before we obtained a trial balance. Luckily, we were within a few hundred dollars . . . but the risks of going through another season with a $2 million trial balance that was not 'proved' was an important factor in our decision to switch to the NCR *HOST* (Hotel On-Line System) technique."

The Diplomat Resort consists of three distinct properties which offer a total of 1,200 guest rooms. It also includes two country clubs, two 18-hole golf courses, 19 tennis courts, 10 restaurants and lounges, a solarium, and a shopping arcade. Before the new system was installed, services charged at these various facilities, plus long distance phone charges, kept front desk cashiers re-posting as many as 7,000 charges on a busy day.

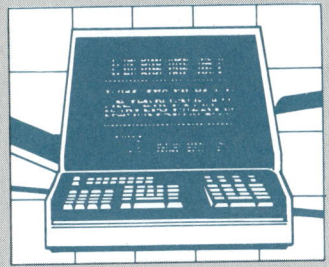

The new NCR *HOST* system has been designed to have guest charges posted into the system from 42 terminals located throughout the complex, thereby eliminating the need for re-posting at the front desk; to provide trial balances daily, as soon as all charges have been posted into the system; to process new guest reservation information so that this data is immediately available to all interested departments—reservations, housekeeping, telephone center, and so forth; to quickly produce various departmental reports that were not readily available prior to the *HOST* installation; and to permit "interface" of additional services, such as HOBIC (Hotel Billing Computer System) and *Dial-a-Maid*.

The posting of guest charges directly into the system from POS (point of sale) terminals located all around the complex has eliminated excessive overtime, reduced posting errors, established guest credit controls, and permitted the transformation of front office cashiers into service personnel, who now have more time to give hospitable service to guests requiring change or questioning resort services and accounts.

In addition, the former manual system required credit personnel to analyze all account records in trying to spot high balances of people who were known to be "overchargers," and often credit problems weren't discovered until they were excessive. "Now," says Mr. Lane, "we are able to plug maximum credit limits into our computer program. Guests are assigned limits when they check in, and when a guest exceeds his limit, his name automati-

Source: *Resort Management* (December 1977).

cally appears on a credit office report. At the same time, each charge for meals or service in excess of his limit causes a message to appear on the terminal for the operator to notify the credit office immediately. We believe this will help nip potential credit problems in the bud."

The new online system, in addition to permitting trial balances daily, also has enhanced the resort's internal controls, and provides additional data for special departmental reports; for example, information can easily be retrieved to analyze menu selection and to project inventory needs. Under the pre-check system installed for food and beverage service, the chefs and bartenders can't release food or drinks until they are presented with a guest check which has already been rung up on an offline service terminal.

Then, at settlement time, the same check is totaled and rung up on an online terminal, as a one-line item. If the guest has signed the check, the terminal operator keys in the first letters of the guest's name to verify the room number. Then the customer's name and number are printed in the validation area on the check. At the end of the day, the totals for the service terminal should balance with the totals for the settlement terminal. Without pre-checking, the resort has no way of determining if there was a discrepancy between what was served and billed.

This detailed service information can also be used in menu analysis and in maintaining inventory reports. The popularity of special items, such as perishable lobsters, can be closely monitored, and by comparing inventory with frequency-of-purchase reports, service can be improved and food waste reduced.

The introduction of new guest registration information into the system is especially important in the servicing of incoming telephone calls and messages. Formerly the 12 or 13 telephone operators had to depend on rack slip information to verify guest arrivals and room numbers, and often the information shown on these rack slips had to be hand delivered to the telephone center from the resort's three front desks, one located a mile away.

On late night arrivals, rack slip data at times was not available until the following morning . . . and even if the calling party was certain the guest had arrived, the operators had to call each front desk to try to locate the person, while the caller waited on the line. Now, the operators use the NCR data display terminals which tell them instantly whether the person has checked in, checked out, cancelled, or is still expected. Since the board handles up to 150,000 calls a day, it's important to get the messages to the right people. Spelling of last name, initials, and status can be verified while looking at the screen, making service fast and efficient.

The new software also has solved another telephone related problem at the front desk. An interface with Southern Bell's *HOBIC* makes it possible to automatically post between 1,000 and 2,000 daily long distance telephone charges to guest accounts, eliminating all front desk handling. With the automatic posting of these long distance charges, as well as those for restaurant, lounge and other services, front desk posting now rarely exceeds 200 items per day, and these are handled on one online POS terminal.

In addition, since top quality service is one of the resort's primary concerns, *The Diplomat* employs more than 300 housekeepers to keep luxurious rooms inviting, with 11 inspectresses who are responsible for checking each room before it is assigned to a guest. Formerly, the complicated and time consuming communications process involving the inspectresses, the housekeeping office and three front desks, couldn't prevent occasional dirty rooms being assigned. This was especially a problem during back-to-back convention periods, when 800 or more rooms would turn over in a few hours.

By installing the *Dial-a-Maid* system to tie in with NCR's *HOST*, as soon as an inspectress has verified that a room is clean, she uses the touch-tone phone in the room to direct dial the computer which adds the room to the available inventory. The whole process takes less than 15 seconds, while at the front desk, clerks use data display terminals to verify reservations and automatically assign guests to the inventoried rooms.

Although *The Diplomat* has only 1,200 rooms

to assign, the computer is programmed to handle a total of 4,600 "rooms," permitting the resort to carry more accounts online. For example, if during a big convention, the resort is out of rooms and guests have to be put up in other nearby hotels, some 1,000 of these "room" numbers can be assigned to them. This permits them to have the same charge privileges as other guests staying at the resort, without being charged a daily room rate. The remaining accounts are set up for area business people or residents who often entertain clients or friends at *The Diplomat,* or use the facilities for other business or social functions.

The Diplomat, which installed its first computer (an early mechanical processor) some 12 years ago, has had considerable experience to data processing. In its pre-*HOST* days, the resort developed more than 350 computer programs to perform tasks which ranged from forecasting staff requirements to maintaining a long range, advance reservation file. Yet, despite its previous sophistication. *The Diplomat* has found that *HOST* has significantly improved its ability to provide customers with quality services, as well as reduce payrolls by $125,000 during its first year of service, and, says Mr. Lane, "we saw the impact in our payroll analysis within 30 days, and believe that is only half of what we will be able to achieve."

DISCUSSION QUESTIONS

1. How is The Diplomat Resort able to use their computer to make their operation more efficient and effective?
2. What hardware devices are being used by The Diplomat Resort to help them in running their business?

Software   3

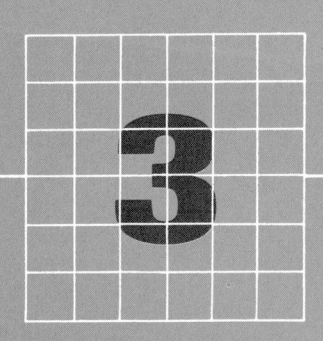

THE ANALOGY REVISITED
OVERVIEW OF SOFTWARE
    Types of software
    The acquisition of software
APPLICATION SOFTWARE
    Machine language
    Assembler language
    Macroinstructions
    High-level programming languages
SYSTEM SOFTWARE
    Assemblers and compilers
    Operating systems
    Utility programs
    Data base management systems

After completing Chapter 3, you will be able to:

- Discuss the importance of software.
- List the different types of software.
- Describe application software and what is involved in acquiring it.
- Explain the importance and functions of the different types of system software.

A paint brush and palette have never been given credit for a masterpiece painting. Nor should computer hardware be given credit for the successful or profitable operation of a computer system. Brushes, palettes, and computer hardware are tools of the trade. Of course, these devices are important but success is dependent on how these devices are used or misused. In both cases, the people using the devices make the difference. In a computer system, people control the activities of the computer by supplying it with a set of instructions.

THE ANALOGY REVISITED

In Chapter 1, a set of instructions was given to a manual data processing system to compute the total of a string of numbers. A similar set of instructions can be given to a computer to make the same calculations, as seen below.

```
PROCEDURE DIVISION.
SET-UP.
   OPEN INPUT PAYROLL-FILE.
   OPEN OUTPUT PAYROLL-REPORT.
READ-CALCULATE ROUTINE.
   READ DATA RECORD AT END GO TO PRINT-ROUTINE.
   ADD NUMBER TO TOTAL.
   GO TO READ-CALCULATE-ROUTINE.
PRINT-ROUTINE.
   WRITE TOTAL.
END-OF-JOB.
   CLOSE PAYROLL-FILE.
   CLOSE PAYROLL-REPORT.
   STOP RUN.
```

The computer would execute the above instructions in a manner very similar to how the clerk executed the instructions for the manual data processing system. In the SET-UP paragraph, the computer opens the input and output files for processing. In the READ-CALCULATE ROUTINE, the computer reads the payroll amounts and computes the total payroll. Next, the computer prints the TOTAL in the PRINT-ROUTINE. Finally, the input and output files are closed and the computer is instructed to STOP as a result of the END-OF-JOB paragraph.

OVERVIEW OF SOFTWARE

A computer program is a set of instructions given to the computer system to perform a task or activity. The instructions above are a part of a program written in a programming language called COBOL, which stands for COmmon Business Oriented Language. These instructions would actually cause a computer to compute the total payroll. A more detailed discussion of COBOL and other programming languages is given later in this chapter and in Part III.

__Software__ consists of one or more computer __programs and other documents that describe the programs and how they are to be used__. These other documents include __flowcharts__, __decision tables__, manuals that describe the programs and how they are to be used, and more. These types of documents will be discussed in more detail in Part III. While there is a difference between programs and software, most people use these terms interchangeably.

Types of software

In many instances, the phrase *software package* is used to describe or define one or more programs or sets of instructions. As you might imagine, there is an unbelievably large number of different software packages available today. In general, however, software packages can be classified into *application packages* and *system packages.*

An **application package** is one or more programs designed to solve a problem or perform a task for one or more individuals or organizations. All of the instructions and programs discussed in this book to this point are application packages. In business, there are many application packages. A payroll package produces paychecks as the major transaction document. The Accounts Receivable package keeps a record of customers owing the company money and produces monthly statements. An Accounts Payable package keeps a record of those individuals or groups to which the company owes money and writes checks to these individuals or groups to satisfy the outstanding debts. Other packages include inventory control, production scheduling, general ledger, work in process, and labor costing and distribution. There are packages for other organizations as well. In science and engineering, application packages include complex matrix manipulations, the solution of simultaneous equations, and a host of very specific applications that relate to particular fields in the engineering or science disciplines. Likewise, a significant collection of application packages exists for hospitals, governmental agencies, and so on. Application packages can be written without a knowledge of how the computer works with words like READ, DIVIDE, PRINT, and so on.

A **system package** is one or more programs that makes the operation of the computer system more effective and efficient. Good system software allows the application packages to be run on the computer system with less time and effort. Without system software, application packages could not be run on the computer system. System packages include *assemblers* and *compilers, operating systems, data base management systems,* and *utility* programs. Assemblers and compilers translate computer programs into a machine language that is understandable by the computer system. Operating systems actually operate or manage the computer system. In Chapter 1, the concept of data bases was introduced to you. Data Base Management Systems (DBMS) are system packages that facilitate the use of data bases. Finally, utility programs are a collection of miscellaneous system packages that are used to do a number of common functions, such as sorting, merging, and transferring data files from one device to another. System packages usually require a knowledge of how the computer works, and the instructions are machine related and dependent, like 11011101; MVN, FIELD 1, FIELD 2; and 00011101.

In the recent past, some instructions and programs have been placed on small chips and inserted into the computer system. These chips, some of which are ¼ inch square, can contain complete and sophisticated programs. Because these small chips are hardware devices that contain software, the difference between hardware and software is not as clear as it was earlier. As a result, these chips are called **firmware,** the programs are called **microprograms,** and the instructions that make up the programs are called **microinstructions** or **microcode.**

The acquisition of software

At one time, when you purchased a computer from a computer manufacturer, application and system software were included in the price; it was *bundled*. Today, however, this is usually not the case. Software is not included; it is *unbundled*. While most computer manufacturers supply their customers with a minimum of system software, the customer normally has the responsibility of acquiring application software.

Basically, there are two ways of obtaining software. You can either *buy* an existing package or you can make or *develop* your own package. If you decide to buy the software packages, there are many financial options. Software can be purchased; it can be leased or rented; and it can be obtained through a lease-purchase agreement. Each option has certain financial advantages which must be considered.

If an organization decides to buy its software, there are several sources. Software can be purchased from the computer manufacturer, a company that specializes in developing and selling software, called a *software company* or *software house,* or it can be purchased from a company that only sells software that another company develops, called a *software broker*. Software can also be obtained from *user groups* that are groups of people or organizations that use the same computer and share their software. If the software is to be developed in-house, there are a number of detailed steps that are needed to plan, develop, test, implement, and maintain the computer programs. These detailed steps are called **application development** or **software development,** and they will be covered completely in Part III.

APPLICATION SOFTWARE

Whether it is purchased or developed, application software is obtained by writing one or more programs in a programming language. A *computer programming language* consists of a specific set of rules that are used to develop a computer program. These rules are like the rules of grammar of the English language. If they are not followed carefully, the computer system will not be able to understand instructions, and thus, it will not be able to perform the desired activities or tasks.

Machine language

The first computer programmers had to write programs using a language that the particular computer could directly understand. This is **machine lan-**

3 Software

guage or **object code.** Each instruction was usually broken into two parts—the **operation code** (op code) and the **operand.** The operation code specified what operation was to be done, and the operand gave the location or address of the data that was to be operated upon or processed. It could take four long and complex instructions of zeros and ones to make a simple computation and to store the results. Figure 3–1 shows how the computer executes or runs a program in machine language. Note that error messages are generated if there are problems.

Machine language has a number of disadvantages. Because it is all zeros and ones, it is difficult to learn. Furthermore, the language is completely different for different computer systems. Acquiring a new computer system means learning a new language. Errors are also difficult to find; each statement has to be checked carefully. When an error is found, it and all of the statements below it have to be rewritten. In brief, machine language is a very cumbersome way to write instructions for a computer.

Assembler language

One improvement over memorizing the meaning of ones and zeros used in machine language is to use letters or abbreviations that stand for certain

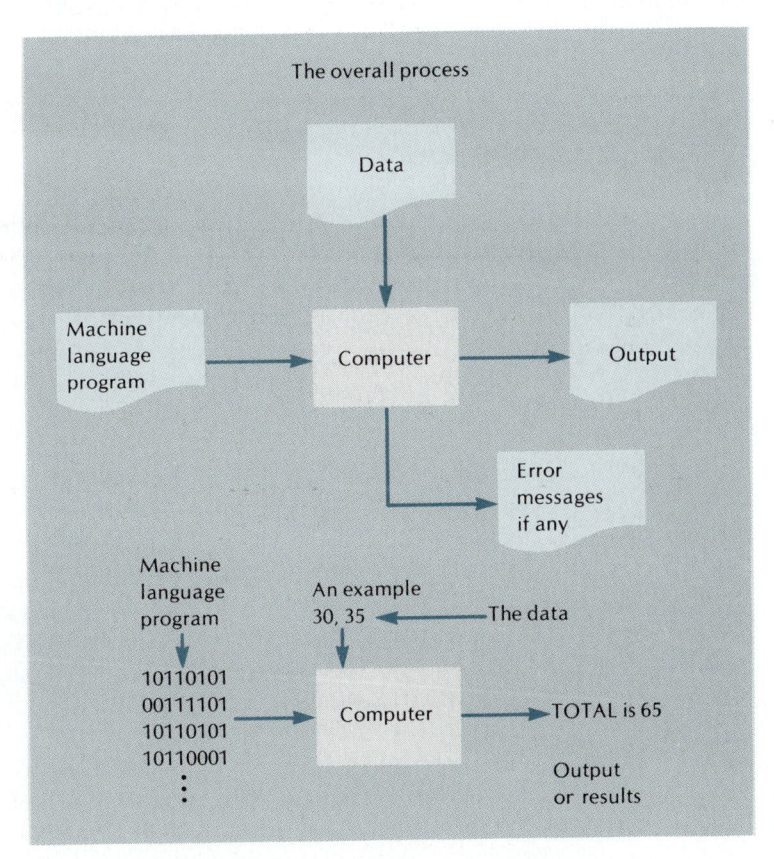

FIGURE 3–1
Using machine language

operations. This type of language is called **assembler** or **symbolic language.** For example, the letter A could mean add, the letter D could represent division, M could mean multiply, and S could mean subtract. Because it is easier to learn and read characters rather than zeros and ones, it is a vast improvement over programming in machine language. A typical instruction might be:

MVN Field 1, Field 2

MVN on some computer systems means *mo*ve *n*umerics. This instruction would direct the computer to move the number stored in the computer at a location called Field 2 to a new storage location within the computer called Field 1. The only difficulty is that the computer does not automatically understand these letters or abbreviations used in assembler or symbolic language. Thus, there must be a way to translate from assembler or symbolic language into machine language. This translation is actually done with a program that reads instructions in assembler and outputs the instructions in machine language. This program is called the *Assembler*. Then the computer can be run as shown in Figure 3–1. This translation process is shown in Figure 3–2.

The Assembler language program is also called the **source program,** and the resulting machine language program is also called the **object program.**

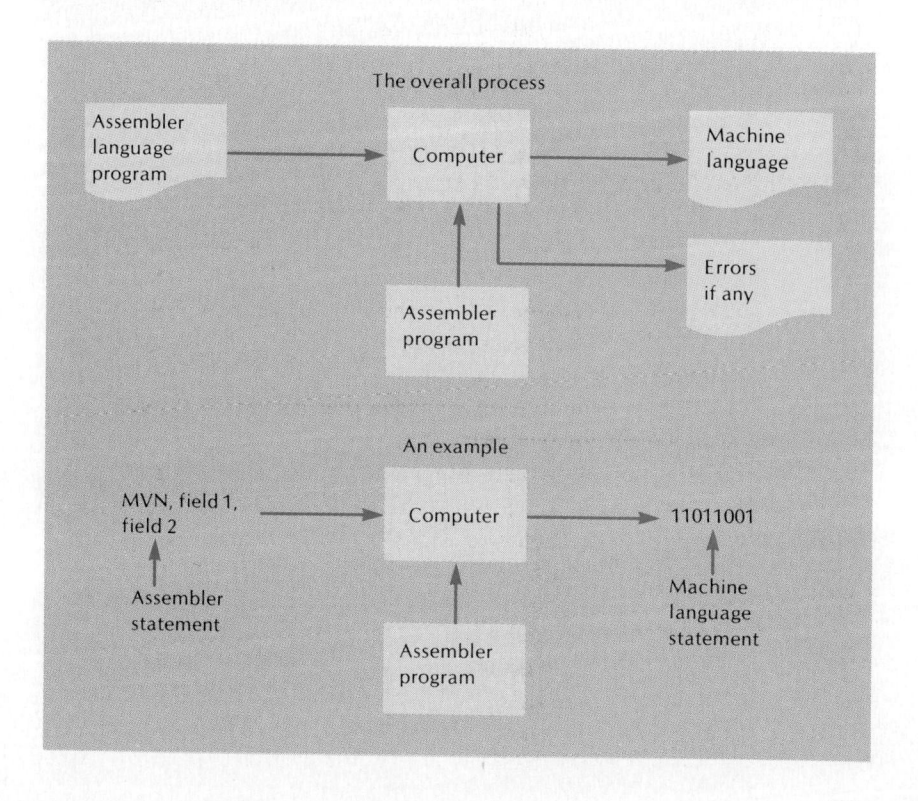

FIGURE 3–2
Translating assembler into machine language

Macroinstructions

When assembler languages were originally developed there was a one-to-one translation from assembler to machine language. That is, every instruction in assembler became one instruction in machine language. Over time, it was realized that there were several instructions that were commonly done in a certain sequence. This led to the development of *macroinstructions.* A **macroinstruction** translates into several instructions in machine language, thus making the assembler programs shorter and easier to write. These, of course, were dramatic improvements but the improvements were not enough.

High-level programming language

There were still many problems with assembler languages and macroinstructions. These languages and instructions varied from computer system to computer system. If an organization changed computers, all of its programs had to be rewritten. Furthermore, these languages were still not easy to learn. These problems, coupled with a desire to make programming easier and more efficient, caused **high-level programming languages** to be developed. These languages are the most commonly used languages in developing application software. As with assembler languages, there is a need to translate one of the high-level programming languages into machine language. This is done with a program called the **Compiler.** This process is shown in the Figure 3-3.

The high-level language program is also called the **source program,** and the resulting machine language program is called the **object program.**

There are many high-level programming languages. One of the newer languages is BASIC. BASIC stands for Beginners All-purpose Symbolic Instruction Code. This language is easy to understand, and it is an excellent language to use when the input and output are to be on a terminal device. Another language very similar to BASIC is *FORTRAN.* FORTRAN, which stands for FORmula TRANslator, is one of the older scientific languages developed in the 1950s. FORTRAN has come a long way, and it is also easy to use. To show the similarity between BASIC and FORTRAN, Figure 3-4 contains a few statements in each language that determine the value of $110 invested at 6 percent for one year.

In the late 1950s and early 1960s, one of the first business oriented languages was developed. It was called COBOL, which is an acronym for COmmon Business Oriented Language. This language was designed to handle business type problems, and the language itself was designed to be written like a manager would write a report or an author would write a book. Thus, a COBOL program may be written using *sentences.* The sentences can form *paragraphs,* which in turn form *sections.* Finally, the sections are placed into one of four major *divisions.* You saw a sample PROCEDURE DIVISION earlier at the beginning of this chapter. Below are several instructions or sentences that you might find in the PROCEDURE DIVISION.

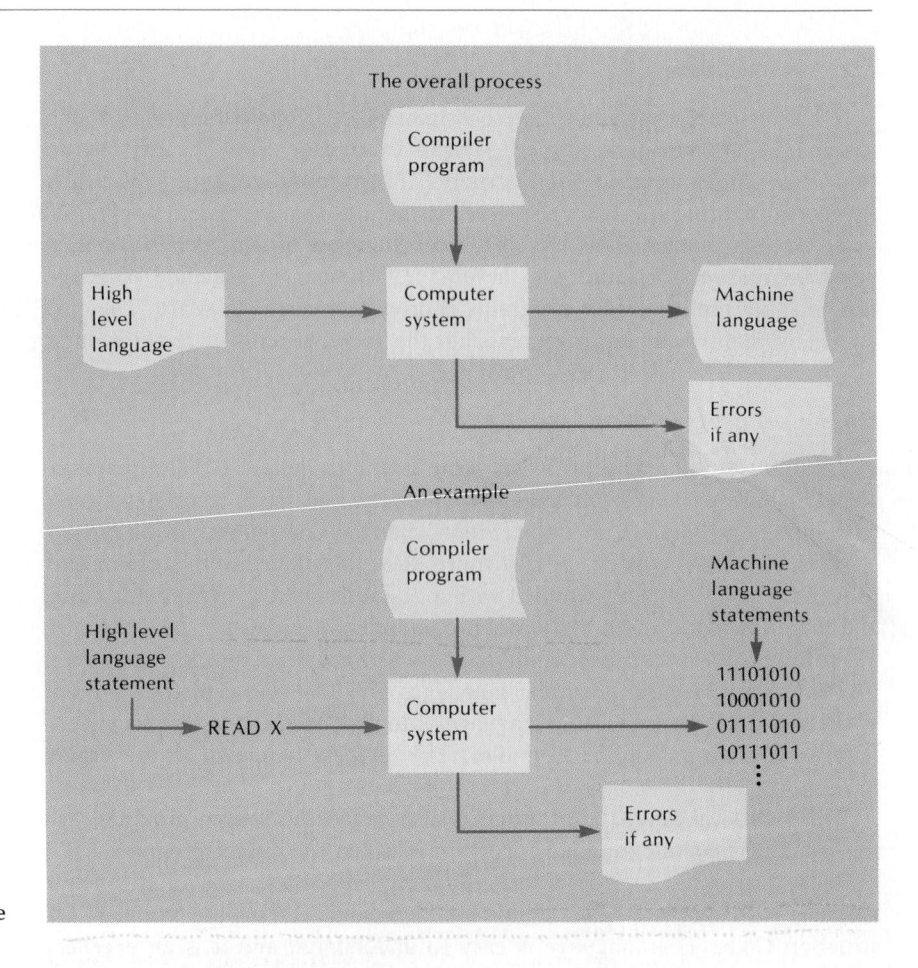

FIGURE 3–3
Translating from a high-level language to machine language

ADD QUANTITY TO TOTAL.
DIVIDE A INTO B.
SUBTRACT DEDUCTIONS FROM GROSS.

There are a number of other high-level programming languages. Report Program Generator (RPG) is a problem-oriented language that was developed originally for some of the smaller computer systems using cards for permanent storage. Today, newer versions of this language, RPG II and RPG III, have been used for a variety of applications on medium- and large-sized computers as well. Programming Language 1 (PL/1) is another general purpose high-level programming language. In addition to these programming languages, there are literally hundreds of other high-level programming languages. Some of the languages are general purpose languages like the ones described above. Other high-level programming languages are designed to perform a specific task, such as performing computer simulation or statistical computations. Programming languages will be discussed in Part III.

```
        BASIC                    FORTRAN
     statements                statements
10 LET R = .06            RATE = .06
20 LET A = 110.00         AMOUNT = 110.00
30 LET V = A * (1 + R)    VALUE = AMOUNT * (1 + RATE)
40 PRINT V                WRITE (3, 100) VALUE
                          100 FORMAT (F6.2)
50 END                    STOP
                          END
```

FIGURE 3–4
A BASIC and a FORTRAN program

SYSTEM SOFTWARE

The overall purpose of **system software** is to make the operation of the computer system more efficient and effective. Since system software is normally written in machine language, system software written for one type of computer will usually not work on another computer manufactured by a different computer company. Thus, most system software is obtained from the computer manufacturer. In the past, system software was included at no charge with the computer hardware, but today many manufacturers are selling their system software separately. In this section, assemblers and compilers, operating systems, utility programs, and data base management systems will be covered.

Assemblers and compilers

Assemblers and compilers were briefly introduced under programming languages. See Figures 3–2 and 3–3. The overall purpose of an **assembler** or **compiler** is to translate from a programming language to machine language. In addition, the programs are carefully checked for syntax errors. When an error is encountered, the computer prints an error message. Once all of the errors have been detected and removed, the program is converted into machine language and then run or executed on the computer system.

A different compiler or assembler is needed for each programming language. If your computer system uses COBOL, then your computer system must have a COBOL compiler. Furthermore, it is possible to purchase additional compilers. An organization may want to purchase a BASIC compiler, which would allow computer programs to be written in the BASIC language.

Operating systems

The purpose of an **operating system** is to provide the computer system with a set of instructions that manages or supervises the functioning or operation of the computer. A clerk could be given instructions on what jobs are to be done first or when a job should be interrupted for something more important. Likewise, a computer system needs a set of instructions that direct its activities. Also called the *monitor, supervisor,* or *executive,* the operating system is an essential part of every computer system.

In the earlier computer systems, programs or computer cards were run in a batch, one stacked on top of another. This is called *batch processing* or *stacked job processing*. While it would take minutes to get data in and out of the computer systems on input and output devices, it would take the central processing unit a fraction of a second to make the necessary computations. Thus, the CPU was idle most of the time. To avoid having one of the most expensive components idle most of the time, sophisticated operating systems were developed to make the operation of the computer more efficient.

Today, many individuals can be using the same computer at the same time. There are several techniques employed by operating systems to render the computer more efficient. These include *overlapped processing, multiprocessing, virtual storage, paging, spooling,* and more. These are fancy names for some straight-forward techniques that are very effective. These techniques will be discussed in detail in Part III.

Utility programs

There are certain day-to-day activities that all computer systems perform. These common types of activities require a set of computer programs. For a lack of a better name, these types of programs have been called **utility programs.** For example, there is always a need to sort a data file into various categories or to merge two or more data files into one. There are also programs that transfer data from one device to another. For example, it may be desirable to transfer one or more data files from the disk to magnetic tape, or from magnetic tape to computer cards. These and similar "housekeeping" programs are called utility programs, and they are normally supplied by the computer manufacturer.

Data base management systems

Data is the lifeblood of any organization. Collectively, data is one of the most valuable resources of any organization. It is essential in running a profit or nonprofit organization, and it is the foundation of good decision making. The ability of an organization to effectively use a computer depends on the organization's ability to effectively capture, manage, and maintain data.

Perhaps one of the greatest advancements in system software is the continued development and increased use of **data base management systems.** A Data Base Management System (DBMS) is a software package that manages and maintains data to facilitate the processing of multiple applications. Furthermore, most data base management systems structure the data in a predefined manner, eliminate or reduce redundant data, and retain the relationships between data elements or items in the data base.

A DBMS acts like a buffer between the data and the application programs.

In the past, when the structure of the data was changed on a device like magnetic tape or the disk, the application packages were also changed. With DBMS, programmers and other computer professionals don't have to worry about how the data is stored physically. The application packages address or access the DBMS. This is called a Logical Access Path (LAP). Then the DBMS accesses or locates the physically stored data. This is called a Physical Access Path (PAP). As a result, the application programs do not have to be modified or changed every time the physical structure of the data changes. Most DBMS offer other advantages. A DBMS can allow any application to access all or any part of the data regardless of how data is stored or organized. Updating data, locating data errors, and correcting data errors can be enhanced. A good DBMS can provide better data security and help prevent unauthorized persons from gaining access to sensitive data. Chapter 11 discusses DBMS in more detail.

SUMMARY

Software can be divided into application software and system software. Application software solves a problem, like performing inventory control, while system software makes the computer system run more efficiently and effectively. The sources of software include the computer manufacturer, a software house, a software broker, and user groups. Software can also be developed within the organization.

One of the first languages was machine language. The instructions in machine language can be understood directly by the computer system. Usually consisting of zeros and ones, machine language is difficult to learn and is different for different computer systems. Assembler language uses abbreviations, such as D for divide and M for multiply, instead of zeros and ones. Each statement in assembler translates into one statement in machine language. Macroinstructions allow one statement to be converted into several machine language instructions. High-level programming languages allow programmers to write programs using English-like words, such as READ, WRITE, and so on. In most cases, these programming languages can be used on different computer systems with only minor modifications. Examples of high-level programming languages are BASIC, FORTRAN, and COBOL.

Assemblers and compilers are examples of system software that translate programming languages into machine language. An assembler converts a program written in the assembler language into machine language. A compiler translates a high-level language into machine language. In both cases, error messages are generated if there are any problems with the translation. Operating systems, another example of system software, are responsible for controlling the entire computer system. Utility programs are a collection of miscellaneous programs that sort, merge, and perform other routine functions. A Data Base Management System (DBMS) is used to manage an organization's data. It acts like a buffer between application programs and the actual data.

KEY TERMS AND CONCEPTS

Application packages
Application software
Assemblers
Assembler language
BASIC — *high level language*
Batch processing
Bundled — *hardware/software*
Canned programs
COBOL — *computer language*
Compiler
Data Base Management System (DBMS)
Executive
FORTRAN — *high level language*

High-level programming language
Logical access path
Machine language
Macroinstructions
Monitor
Object code
Object deck
Operand
Operation code (OP Code)
Operating systems
Physical access path
PL/1
Program
RPG

Software — *programs, instructions*
Software brokers
Software company
Software house
Software package
Source deck
Stacked job processing
Supervisor
Symbolic language
System packages
System software
Unbundled — *software sold separately*
Utility programs

QUESTIONS

3–1. What are the different types of software? Give examples of each type.

3–2. What is meant by an application package?

3–3. Why is system software important? Give several examples of system software.

3–4. What are some of the ways of acquiring software? How is system software normally obtained?

3–5. What is a macroinstruction?

3–6. List some of the commonly used programming languages.

3–7. What is the difference between an assembler and a compiler?

3–8. Give some examples of utility programs.

3–9. What is the overall purpose of an operating system?

3–10. Describe the advantages of using a data base management system.

MINIQUIZ

ANSWERS
1. F
2. T
3. F
4. T
5. T
6. F
7. F
8. F
9. F
10. T

True or False

___F___ 1. COBOL is an example of a hardware device.

___T___ 2. Most software can be divided into application software and system software.

___F___ 3. A data base management system is an example of application software.

___T___ 4. The purpose of an assembler or compiler is to translate a computer program into a form that the computer can understand and use.

___T___ 5. Today, there is a trend to unbundle software.

___F___ 6. Today, most computer programs that are used for business applications are written in machine language.

___F___ 7. The operand specifies what operation is to be performed.

___F___ 8. FORTRAN, which stands for Formula Translator, is an example of a symbolic programming language.

___F___ 9. One disadvantage of COBOL is that the instructions are not at all similar to English words or abbreviations.

___T___ 10. An example of a utility program is a program that sorts or merges data files.

What is software?
Attorneys and others disagree, depending upon their concerns.
Edith Myers

"A rose by any other name would smell as sweet . . ."

So says Shakespeare. Lawyers involved with computing should only have such a simplistic attitude toward software. To them there's much in a name, a name they'd like to have clearly defined and in differing ways depending upon their concerns.

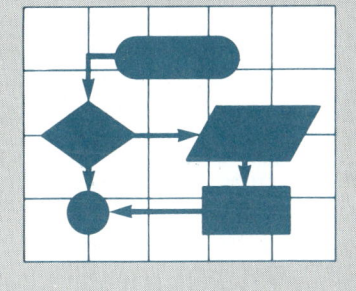

Stephen N. Hollman, general counsel for Optimum Systems Inc., Santa Clara, Calif., and a member of California's Sales Tax Action Group (STAG), is concerned with the imposition of sales taxes on sales of software. He blamed some of the software tax problems on a group of computer lawyers meeting in Los Angeles in January for their "loose use of software as a term."

"They (the taxing bodies) think they are taxing software. No, they are taxing computer programs. Computer programs are a subset of software."

Reed Lawlor, a Pasadena, Calif., attorney, in a paper prepared for the same meeting, the 1979 West Coast Conference of the Computer Law Assn., took a slightly different view. "We use the term software to refer to computer programs. We further distinguish between computer programs *per se*, that is listings of instructions on an eye-readable document and computer programs that are embodied in a physical device that can form part of a machine. This distinction must not be overlooked."

Lawlor's concern is the patentability of computer programs. He believes software is patentable.

Webster's definition is more broad than Hollman's or Lawlor's. "Software: the entire set of programs, procedures and related documentation associated with a system and especially a computer system, specifically computer programs."

Martin A. Goetz, senior vice president, Applied Data Research Inc., Princeton, N.J., in a presentation at the last National Computer Conference titled "The What Is Software Legal Snafu," listed the kinds of people asking the question, what is software?

Financial people, when analyzing a corporation's assets and liabilities.

State and federal tax authorities, when viewing new revenue sources.

The IRS, when considering the investment tax credits question.

The Copyright Office, when deciding whether software comes under their jurisdiction.

The Patent Office, when deciding whether the inventive concepts in a program constitute patentable subject matter.

Lawyers, when drawing up contracts.

Judges, when deciding cases involving ownership of software.

The State Department, when licensing and exporting high technology products to Eastern Bloc countries.

The Justice Department, in current IBM antitrust cases.

Goetz has his definition. "Software is a machine component of a computer system, similar to a computer circuit component or a terminal component, or a disk component. This software machine component can be in two forms—in source form (the source program) or in machine form (the object program)."

All laws, says Goetz, that apply to machines or to machine components should apply to software.

He takes the position that software is tangible and that software products should be subject to sales tax, as hardware products are.

And all while opponents of the imposition of sales tax on software sales are trying to establish the intangibility of software.

A puzzled attendee at the January Computer Law Association meeting wondered, after listening to those who would have software considered in-

---
Source: Reprinted with permission from DATAMATION® Magazine. © Copyright by Technical Publishing Company, a Dun & Bradstreet Company, 1979—all rights reserved.

tangible for tax purposes and others who were arguing for its tangibility for patent reasons, if the Association shouldn't come up with a uniform definition.

"We may not want uniformity," said Lawlor. "Everything may be uniformly bad."

An often cited case when the question of software's tangibility or intangibility comes up is that of Texas Instruments (TI) versus the U.S. government, now before the Fifth Circuit Court of Appeals. A TI subsidiary, Geophysical Service Inc., claimed an investment tax credit for seismic data tapes and films it produced for use in its speculative oil and gas exploration business.

The government took TI to court contending the credit shouldn't apply because "the costs represent investments in the speculative seismic data, not in the pieces of tape and film on which it is recorded, and that this information is indisputably intangible property, ineligible for the investment credit."

In its appeals brief, TI claims that the seismic data tapes and films "have intrinsic value because the seismic information contained thereon does not exist as property separate from the physical manifestation."

In a reply brief in the same action, the company contends that "if the seismic data tapes and films were destroyed (the company) would retain nothing. In order to reproduce the seismic data tapes and films the entire productive process must be repeated." The appellate court has yet to decide.

Those fighting the battle against imposition of sales tax on software probably would be best served by a government win, which would set a precedent for the intangibility of software.

California's STAG is optimistic, although conditionally so. It hopes the state's rule 1502, covering taxation of Automatic Data Processing Services and Equipment, soon will be rewritten to its liking. A STAG committee has had five meetings with staff members from the state's Board of Equalization on "trying to do to 1502 what needs to be done."

The next step was to be presentation to the state board of suggested rewording of 1502. Then the board would have to give 30 days notice of a public hearing on the rewording.

A STAG spokesman said his group intends "to pack the room again" (as it did for a public hearing held last May which led to the committee meetings with the board staff). In the meantime, he said, assessments, many retroactive, have continued but "a lot are being sent back (from the board) to local offices for review."

"We can't legislate, we can't litigate, so we're chipping away," said Hollman at the Computer Law Association meeting. He said litigation was difficult because "nobody wants to be a test case." Legislative relief in California, he said, is difficult since the passage of Proposition 13, the property tax relief initiative which "has made the legislature unsympathetic to any special interest group seeking tax relief."

And as for the "chipping away," Hollman said the meetings between STAG and the Board of Equalization have at least resulted "in an informed consensus that inclusion of custom programs is probably ill-advised and that all of the services related to custom software consequently also would fall by the way."

He also said the meetings had modified the board's thinking that packaged programs had to be 100 percent modified before being put in the "custom" category is unrealistic and that 20 percent is a more realistic breakpoint.

Hollman took issue with the language used by the Commission on New Technological Uses of Copyrighted Works (CONTU) in its recommendation to Congress that copyright be expressly provided to computer programs. He called it (the language) "abominable." He didn't point to anything specific and neither the word tangible nor the word intangible appear in the CONTU recommendation. But the implications of the committee's report are that software has value and substance and he could have been referring to such sentences as: "In considering the 'quality of life' in this country, to fail to consider the positive contributions of computers and the programs with which they are used would indeed be a mistake."

Others who quarrel with the CONTU report, including Lawlor, worry about its preemption of trade secret protection. Miles Gilbourne, Irell & Manella, Los Angeles, said at the Computer Law

Association meeting that the CONTU report states that, "The availability of copyright for computer programs does not, of course, affect the availability of trade secrecy protection." But, he noted, the report of CONTU's Software Subcommittee "appeared to be mildly in favor of construing the 1976 Copyright Act as preempting trade secret protection."

Roger S. Borovoy of Intel Corp., Santa Clara, Calif., wants copyright protection in any case and he wants it for chip topography. Intel sued the Copyright Office to force it to grant a registered copyright for its 8755 erasable programmable read-only memory. The office "finally agreed to accept the chip with a pile of disclaimers."

But not all the definition concerns at the Computer Law Association meeting were with software. Susan H. Nycum, Chickering & Gregory, San Francisco, talked about security and was concerned with the nature of value. "What do we protect? What are we concerned about? I once asked an IBM lawyer what he most wanted to protect and he said, customer lists."

Nycum also talked about intentional violations of computer systems noting, in dealing with these, "you have to think like a criminal and out-think the perpetrator." And she had a definition of nice people: "Nice people are not quite as inventive as not so nice people."

DISCUSSION QUESTIONS

1. Why is the definition of software important?
2. What are some of the legal ways of protecting software?

Systems 4

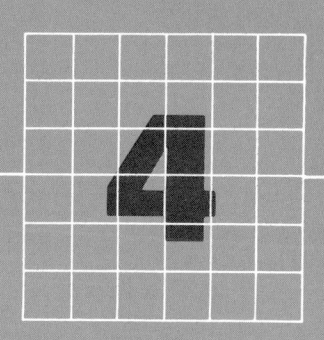

CAPABILITIES AND LIMITATIONS OF A COMPUTER SYSTEM
COMMON ELEMENTS OF A COMPUTER APPLICATION
    Editing
    Updating
    Common outputs from a computer application
ROUTINE APPLICATIONS AND DOCUMENTS
MANAGEMENT INFORMATION
    Management information in perspective
    Characteristics of a management information system
    Types of management reports
    How much information

After completing Chapter 4, you will be able to:

- Describe the capabilities and limitations of a computer system.
- Recognize the differences between routine documents and management information.

In this chapter we will investigate computer systems in action. First of all, the capabilities and limitations of computer systems will be explored. Then, some of the common features or elements of computer applications will be covered. Computerized business applications have the ability to produce both routine documents and management information, and these types of outputs will be discussed and compared.

CAPABILITIES AND LIMITATIONS OF A COMPUTER SYSTEM

Listing all of the capabilities, limitations, and applications of a computer would be like listing the capabilities, limitations, and applications of electricity. The list would be long indeed. Yet knowing the capabilities and limitations of a computer system helps a manager know what to expect or demand from the computer. A manager should know at least two things about the capabilities and limitations of computer systems. What computer systems can do in general and what his or her computer system can do in particular. We will begin the discussion with what computer systems can do in general.

Because manual data processing systems perform the same functions as a computer system, we can use the manual data processing system to help us learn the general capabilities and limitations of a computer system. In fact, the following analogy can be made: If you can give instructions to a clerical data processing system to accomplish a certain task, it is very likely that a computer program could be written to accomplish the same task on a computer system. The opposite is also true. If you cannot develop instructions for a clerical data processing system to accomplish a given task, then it is unlikely that a computer program can be written to accomplish the same task on a computer system.

Here are some examples. You know that you can instruct a clerk to write checks, to prepare invoices and bills, and to update master files. The computer can do the same. A clerk can be instructed to give you a list of all employees earning over $600 this week. A computer can do the same. Could a clerk be instructed to compute *exactly* what sales will be next month? No. Thus, a computer could not be programmed to compute *exactly* what sales will be next month either. Could a clerk be instructed to determine the exact weather conditions next month or how the stock market will do next year? Again, the answer is no. Therefore, you could not expect a computer to have the ability to perform these activities. Of course, you could instruct the clerk to guess or predict the weather or the stock market, and a computer could be programmed to guess or predict these values as well. Using the clerical analogy to determine the general capabilities of a computer system is helpful, but it doesn't tell you how well your specific computer system will perform these functions or activities.

The ability of a specific computer system to perform certain functions efficiently and effectively depends on the hardware and software of the computer system. Hardware can limit the activities of the computer system. The existing number of keypunch devices and the speed of the card reader might limit the amount of input data that can be entered during the day. A line printer with only 80 print positions or columns may prevent the computer system from printing large and complex reports and tables. The size of main storage or memory can prevent some long and complex programs from being used on the computer system, and a lack of a plotter might prevent the computer system from preparing accurate graphs and pictures. Software can also limit the operation of the entire computer system. The computer's operating system may not allow additional computers to be connected to the main computer system. If the only compiler is a BASIC programming compiler, you will not be able to run programs written in other languages such as FORTRAN or COBOL.

In this section, we have investigated *what* a computer system can do. The next question is *how* are these various activities and functions performed. As you might have concluded, there is almost an infinite number of possible computer applications. How are these applications performed on a computer system? If you study a large number of these applications, you will see that there are some common elements or activities in virtually all applications. If you know these common elements and activities, it will be far easier for you to understand the many applications performed by a computer system.

Every application has certain common elements. They include **editing, updating, transaction documents, management reports,** and **transaction listings** or **registers.** Though applications differ significantly, these common elements can be found in almost every application.

COMMON ELEMENTS OF A COMPUTER APPLICATION

Editing

All applications use one or more input files. But before these input files are used in an application, they should be checked carefully for errors. This is editing (see Figure 4–1).

The input data for an application is stored in transaction files (1). The transaction files are converted into a machine understandable form by a data entry device. The information from the original documents is normally placed on computer cards, magnetic tape, or the disk. This data is the input to the edit program (2), which checks this incoming data for errors. Perhaps an employee put 400 hours instead of 40 hours on a weekly time sheet. This error would be detected in the edit program. Or perhaps a new sales person wrote the wrong part number on a sales order. This type of error would also be detected. These errors are printed on the error report by the edit program (3). This information is then used to correct the transaction file. Once corrected, the edit program generates the edited transaction file which could be stored on the disk, magnetic tape, or computer cards (4).

Updating

Almost all applications require the use of master files. The inventory control application uses an inventory master file. The accounts receivable application uses a customer master file. The payroll application requires an employee

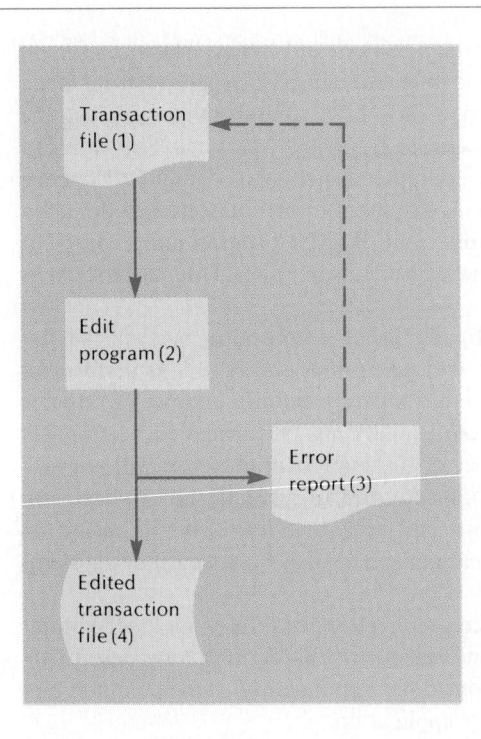

FIGURE 4–1
The editing program

master file, and so on. Master files change; they get old and out of date. **Updating** is the process of keeping the master files current and accurate. This is also called **master file maintenance.** The process of updating or master file maintenance is displayed in Figure 4–2.

Inputs to this program are the old master file (1) and a list of changes (2). A new inventory item added to the product line, a female employee getting married and using her husband's last name, and a customer changing his or her address and phone number are all examples of changes that must be reflected in the master file. If these changes are not incorporated into the master files, then the application either will not run at all or the output from the application will be wrong. These changes are placed in a machine understandable form and are input to the update program (3). The update program either makes the appropriate changes in the existing master file or it makes a completely new master file (4). If a new master file is made, the old master file should be kept for several months as a back up in case something happens to the updated master file. It is also important to have the update program print a change report (5). This report contains a list of all changes that have been made to the master file. Thus, if there is any question as to whether a change has been made, the change report can be reviewed.

Common outputs from a computer application

The edited transaction files and updated master files are the major inputs to the application program. The primary outputs of the application program

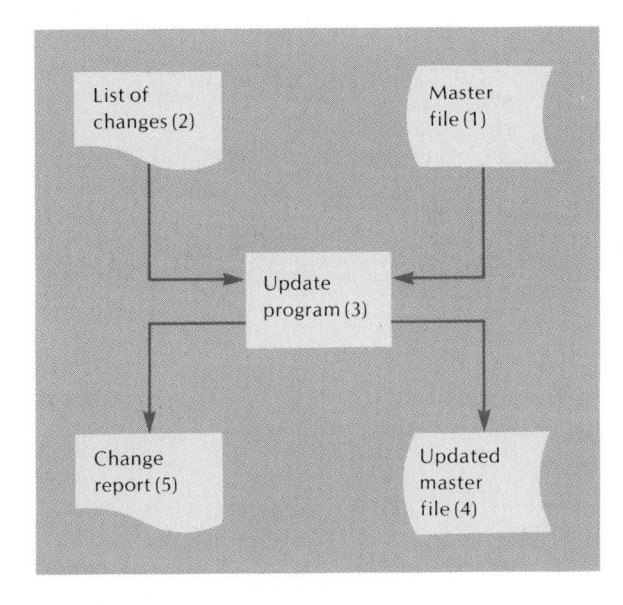

FIGURE 4–2
The update program

are *transaction documents, management reports,* and the *transaction listing* or *register*. The **transaction documents** are the required bookkeeping documents that are generated by the application. Notices to customers that sales orders have been received, shipping documents, invoices, bills, paychecks, and checks to other companies for purchases are examples of transaction documents. Another type of output from the application program, **management reports,** provides information to managers.

Finally, good application programs should produce a **transaction listing** or **register** each time the application is run or executed. This is a detailed listing of every action that was taken by the application program. If there is ever any question as to what an application program did on a particular date, the transaction listing or register can be consulted. Furthermore, this listing may be used by auditors who must, in part, validate the accuracy of the computerized application.

All of these common elements can be put together to form a standard application. These common elements are shown in Figure 4–3.

Some applications employ several master files and several transaction files. In this case, each master file is updated and each transaction file is edited before the application program is run. In addition, most applications have built-in control procedures or functions. For example, *control totals* are used to make sure that all documents have been processed. If there are 451 sales orders to be processed by a sales ordering application, then there should be 451 sales orders in the edited transaction file, and 451 notices printed to customers telling them that their order has been received and is being processed. If one of these totals does not match the original total, there is a problem. There are also other control procedures that have been designed to detect errors or problems with the execution of applications. Many of

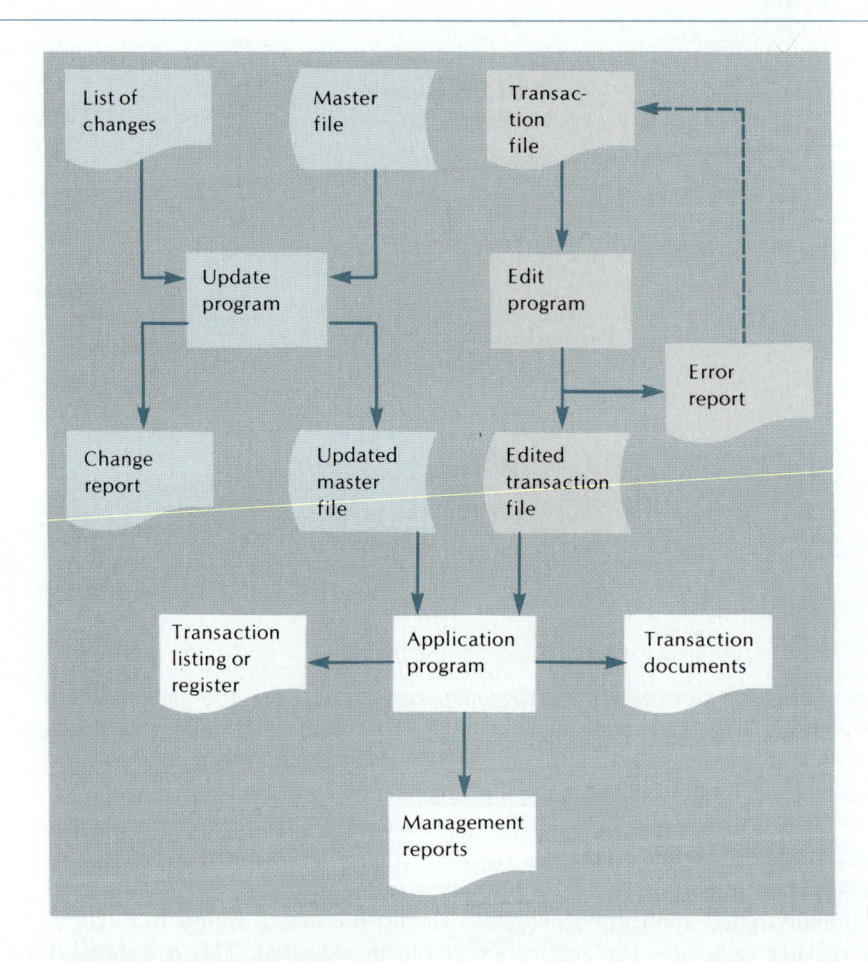

FIGURE 4–3
Common elements of a standard application

these procedures depend on the computer devices used for data input and permanent storage, and thus these control procedures will be explored when these devices are investigated in more detail in Part II.

Like bricks for a building, the common elements of a computerized application are joined together to form a complete and unique application. In the next two sections, we will explore some of the application programs that produce routine business documents and management information. As you study these applications, remember that they all incorporate the common elements of a computerized application discussed in this section.

ROUTINE APPLICATIONS AND DOCUMENTS

Several major documents are produced as a direct result of a sales order placed by a customer. The applications that produce these major documents are: the *sales ordering application,* the *inventory control application,* the *invoicing application,* and the *accounts receivable application.* These applications along with their primary documents are shown in Figure 4–4.

Typically, sales orders are generated by salespersons in consultation with

4 Systems

customers. Once received, the sales orders are converted into a machine understandable form and entered into a **sales ordering application** or program. The major document is a notice to customers that the order has been received and is being processed. The sales ordering application also activates the **inventory control** application. This is done, in some cases, by having the sales ordering application output sales ordering information on magnetic tape or the disk. This information is the input to activate the inventory control application. New stock and adjustments to inventory are other inputs to the inventory control application. The adjustments could be due to returned

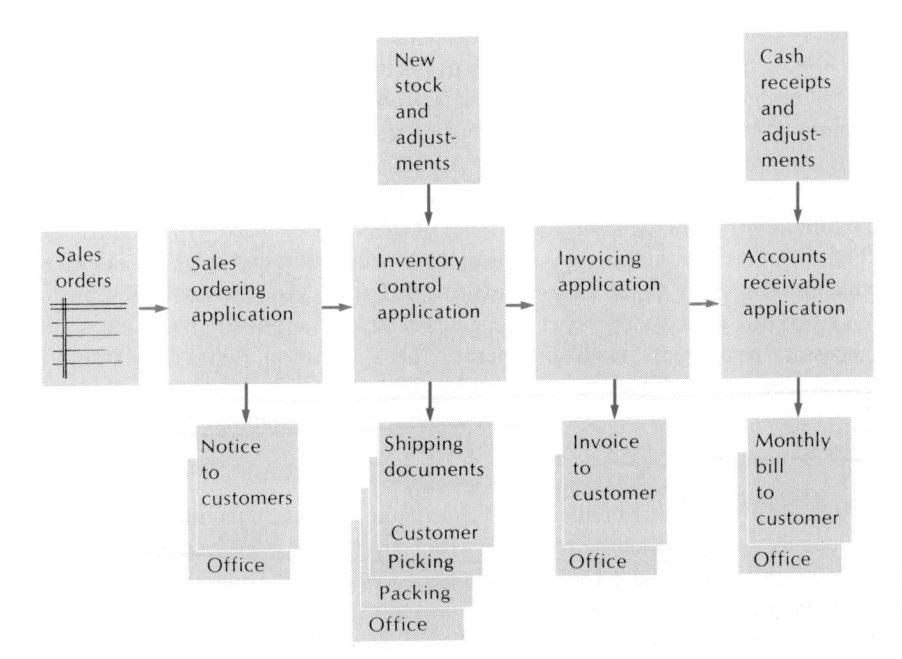

FIGURE 4-4
Overview of major documents produced as a result of a sales order

merchandise, damaged merchandise, or lost or misplaced inventory. The major documents from the inventory control application are the shipping documents. One copy is sent to the customer. Another is used by the individual that actually locates or picks the inventory from the shelves. This *picking copy* is used to physically locate the order, and it can even contain the exact location of the merchandise. The *packing copy* is enclosed with the merchandise when it is shipped, and the office copy is kept in case there are questions or difficulties with the shipment. The inventory control application then activates or triggers the **invoicing application.** The major document of this application is the invoice which is sent to the customer for payment. The invoicing application next activates the **accounts receivable application.** Other inputs to this application are cash receipts from customers and adjustments. The major document from this application is the monthly bill or statement that is sent to the customers.

In addition to the above applications, there are other routine business applications that must be performed as well. Some of the more important applications are:

1. Payroll.
2. Accounts payable.
3. Sales analysis.
4. General ledger.

The **payroll application** inputs employee number and hours worked from time sheets or cards. In some instances, this information can be collected directly by using data collection devices, and automatically stored on magnetic tape, cassette, or disk. The major output document is paychecks to employees. Most organizations purchase materials from other organizations. The **accounts payable** application takes invoices from other vendors or companies and pays these vendors the correct amount by producing checks that are sent to the vendors for payment. The **sales analysis** application inputs items sold or shipped and generates a number of sales reports used by management. These reports include **sales-by-item, sales-by-customer,** and **sales-by-salesperson.** Other reports might include slow-moving-items reports, stockout reports, and inventory usage reports. The **general ledger** application produces the necessary periodic financial statements. This application inputs daily transactions. The outputs from this application include *income statements, balance sheet statements, sources and uses of funds,* and other similar financial statements.

MANAGEMENT INFORMATION

One of the greatest challenges to computer professionals and mainstream managers alike is to get better information from computer systems. Whereas computers have been used successfully to produce routine business documents, they have not been used to any great extent to provide information for decision makers. The success of any organization depends on good decision making, and good decision making depends on good information. What is good information and how can it be obtained? In this section, we will take a closer look at management information.

Management information systems in perspective

To begin with, the importance of the information can be linked directly to its impact on decisions, and the value of information can be linked directly to how it helps decision makers reach the goals and objectives of the organization. For businesses, the value of the information can be measured in how the information is able to increase the profits of the company. What is the value of the market forecast information? If this information allows us to make an additional profit of $10,000, then the value of this information is $10,000.

What is important is not the *source* of the information but the *use* of the information. Information obtained through a game of golf may be more valuable than the information obtained from a million dollar computer. The sources of management information can be both *informal* (a golf game) and *formal* (a computer). Systems that provide management information, both formal and informal, possess some common characteristics.

Characteristics of a management information system

Management information systems that have successfully provided managers with valuable information have a number of common characteristics. In developing or designing a management information system, these characteristics should be considered and incorporated into the system whenever possible. Management information should be:

1. Timely.
2. Accurate.
3. Flexible.
4. Economical.
5. Reliable.
6. Simple.

If management information is not timely and accurate, it is worthless. Information that arrives too late or that is wrong has no value to a decision maker. Furthermore, if the information is wrong, it actually may do more harm than good. In addition, the management information system should be *flexible* in what it can do and *economical* to use. It should also be *reliable* and *simple*. A management information system with these characteristics has a much greater chance of successfully providing valuable information to decision makers. These are the characteristics of a good management information system, but how is this information produced? What are the different types of reports that contain management information?

Types of management reports

When management information is informal, the types and sources of the information are varied and numerous. The source may be a friend, a secretary, a partner in a tennis game, your boss, a competitor, an employee of the firm, and so on. The type of information can also vary tremendously. While most informal information is delivered verbally, the information may be contained in a letter, a newspaper, an internal office memo, a magazine, and so on. Some experts believe that information is conveyed in gestures and body posture. This is called *body language*. A wink or nod may be packed full of information. In the rest of this section we will concentrate on the computer system as a source of information.

Printers and terminals are the primary sources of management information from a computer system, although other output devices are also used. Today, the trend is toward using terminal devices to produce management information.

There are three types of reports that are normally used in producing management information. These are: (1) _scheduled reports_, (2) _demand reports_, and (3) _exception reports_. A **scheduled report** will be generated every time a particular computer program is run or executed. A sales ordering program could be modified to produce a report that contains the total sales over a period of time. This is an example of a scheduled report. Every time the sales order program is run to prepare invoices, a report is also generated that contains the total sales for the period. There are many other examples of scheduled reports. Every time the accounts receivable application is run, you may wish to get a copy of the aged trial balance. This is a report containing every customer that owes the company money. The report also contains the amount and how long the debt is outstanding.

The second type of report is the _demand report._ While the scheduled report is produced automatically every time the application program is run, the **demand report** is produced _only_ when requested by a manager. A manager might want to know the hourly rate for an employee, the amount owed to the company by a customer, the number of sales orders received today, the performance of a salesperson in total sales for last week, and so on. A computer can be programmed to produce these types of reports when requested by a manager. These reports are all examples of demand reports.

The third type of report is the **exception report.** This type of report is neither produced every time a program is run like the scheduled report, nor is it produced only when requested by a manager. Instead, this report is produced when an _exceptional situation_ occurs. It is produced only _if_ certain conditions exist while a program is being run. How would you control inventory levels if you had 10,000 inventory items? If you used a scheduled report, you would get a list of all 10,000 items every time an inventory program is run. Reading this report would be a waste of your time. If you use demand reports, you would have to demand that all 10,000 inventory items be printed. Demanding all of these reports would be a waste of your time. Using an exception report, you could have a report printed _only_ when some inventory items need reordering. Furthermore, the report would contain only those items that need to be ordered. This can be done using the following type of statement in an inventory control program:

IF INVENTORY LEVEL IS LOW FOR AN ITEM,
PRINT A REORDER REPORT

While the above statement is not a real programming statement, it is very similar to statements that you would find in many of the popular programming languages. Indeed, an exception report can be obtained by only adding a handful of program statements to an existing program. While it could cost a few dollars to include these types of statements in a program, they could save thousands of dollars every month in preventing stockouts. Almost every programming language has IF statements, and these types of statements are the key to getting exception reports. Of course, there are many other examples of exception reports. A report of customers owing a company more than a given amount of money, a report of all employees who worked more than 55 hours last week, and a report of all salespersons who did not meet their sales quota last month are examples of exception reports. Based on the principle of *management by exception,* most managers only take action when there is an exceptional or unusual situation. The overall purpose of the exception report is to alert a manager to an exceptional situation so the appropriate action can be taken.

How much information?

When computers were first used in business, managers received very little or no information from the computer system. Today, the pendulum has swung in the other direction and some managers have been buried in a blizzard of paper from the computer system. A time management expert, after seeing all of the useless paper generated from the computer system concluded that EDP really means "Electronic Data Pollution" instead of Electronic Data Processing. Too much information is just as bad as not enough information.

The amount of information produced by a computer system should be carefully balanced against the *value* of the information in obtaining the goals and objectives for the organization. A list of the gross earnings of 5,000 employees may be of no value to a manager. In fact, it may have a negative value. If the manager's time is worth $100 per hour, and four hours are wasted in reading this report, the value of this information is $-$ $400. On the other hand, if a manager gets a report of all inventory items that should be reordered, this report could save thousands of dollars in preventing stockouts and lost sales.

Sometimes, however, it is very difficult to measure the value of the information. Since information helps decision makers take appropriate actions, another approach is to relate information to the actions it causes a decision maker to take. If information will never cause a decision maker to take any action, it is of no value. Thus, a practical approach to determining if the information is needed, is to ask the following questions:

1. Does this report cause a decision maker to take a specific action?
2. Does every page in the report cause a decision maker to take a specific action?
3. Does every line in the report cause a decision maker to take a specific action?

If a report never causes a decision maker to take a specific action, it should never be produced.

In a similar fashion, every page of the report and every line of the report should be given the same test. If a page in a report never causes a decision maker to take an action, it is of little value, and it should be eliminated from the report. The same is true of every line in a report. This is a tough rule for reports to meet, but it can substantially reduce the amount of useless reports that are generated by the computer system. If the information is never used, it should not be produced.

SUMMARY

Computer systems perform the same functions as a manual data processing system. In general, if a manual data processing system is capable of performing a certain activity, a computer system is also able to perform the same activity. Computers, however, are limited by the capabilities of their hardware and software.

Most computerized applications contain common elements that include editing, updating, transaction documents, management reports, and the transaction register. Editing is the process of checking transaction files for errors and potential problems, and updating is the process of keeping master files current and up to date. Transaction documents are the major documents produced from an application. Examples are paychecks, invoices, bills, sales orders, and so on. The transaction register is a listing of the actions taken by the computer application, and it is a tool used to audit the accuracy and integrity of a computer system. Management reports provide managers with helpful information.

Most businesses have a number of routine applications that are started as a result of a customer placing an order. These applications are started in the following order: sales ordering, inventory control, invoicing, and accounts receivable. Other important routine applications include payroll, accounts payable, sales analysis, and general ledger.

Information that can be used by managers in the decision making process is called management information. The source of management information can be informal (a golf game) or formal (a computer system). Management information systems should be (1) timely, (2) accurate, (3) flexible, (4) economical, (5) reliable, and (6) simple. The types of management reports are usually either scheduled reports, demand reports, or exception reports. In general, the amount of information produced for managers should be a function of the value of the information. If information from a report is never used, it is of little value, and it should not be included in the report in the future.

KEY TERMS AND CONCEPTS

Accounts payable	General ledger	Sales analysis
Accounts receivable	Inventory control	Sales ordering
Change report	Invoicing	Scheduled reports
Demand reports	Management by exception	Transaction documents
Edit program	Management information	Transaction listings
Edited transaction file	Management reports	Update program
Editing	Payroll	Updated master file
Error report	Registers	Updating
Exception report	Routine applications	

QUESTIONS

4–1. Is a computer capable of determining oil imports for next year? Explain your answer.

4–2. What common elements would you expect to find in a payroll application? What types of files would be used in this application?

4–3. Discuss the documents produced by routine applications.

4–4. What is the difference between management information and transaction documents?

4–5. What are the types of management reports? Give several examples.

4–6. Describe the characteristics of a successful management information system.

4–7. How do you determine the amount of information to generate from the computer?

ANSWERS

1. F
2. T
3. T
4. F
5. F
6. F
7. T
8. F
9. T
10. T

MINIQUIZ

True or False

___ 1. In general, the size of main storage or memory does not limit the computer system to the size and complexity of computer programs that are being run.

___ 2. The common elements of an application are editing, updating, producing transaction documents, producing management reports, and producing transaction listings.

___ 3. Updating is the process of keeping master files current and accurate.

___ 4. Notices to customers that sales orders have been received, shipping documents, invoices, and bills are all examples of management reports.

___ 5. The major document from the inventory application is a notice to customers that the order has been received and is being processed.

___ 6. When the invoicing application is completed, it triggers or activates the inventory control application.

___ 7. The major document from the accounts receivable application is the monthly bill or statement that is sent to customers.

___ 8. The computerized general ledger application is used by primarily medium and large size businesses.

___ 9. The major types of reports that are normally used in producing management information include scheduled reports, demand reports, and exception reports.

___ 10. A demand report is produced only when a manager requests certain information or data.

**Installed at: Travelcraft, Inc.
Sterling Heights, Michigan**

Travelcraft, Inc. is one of two worldwide travel agency offices owned and operated by Gerald I. Choma. The agency has been in existence since 1971 and is appointed by the Air Traffic Conference (ATC) and the International Air Transport Association (IATA) and is a member of the American Society of Travel Agents.

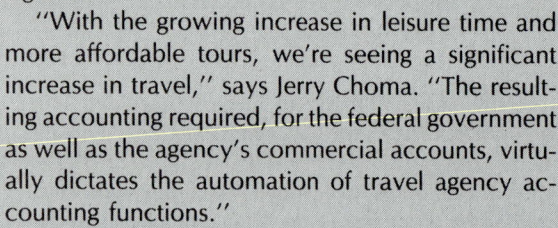

"With the growing increase in leisure time and more affordable tours, we're seeing a significant increase in travel," says Jerry Choma. "The resulting accounting required, for the federal government as well as the agency's commercial accounts, virtually dictates the automation of travel agency accounting functions."

"Knowing the agency's current financial position is critical," he says, "because the ATC's seven day reporting system allows the agency's bank to automatically draw funds due the airlines from the agency's account every Wednesday. The available account balance must cover the withdrawal. We're in a business where we're responsible for a lot of money that isn't ours. With the 5100, we've been better able to manage our business and our all important cash flow."

Commercial accounts generate a substantial portion of the agency's cash flow. Prior to installing their IBM 5100 Portable Computer, Travelcraft billed their commercial accounts on a monthly basis with mailing taking place ten days to two weeks after month end. Today, utilizing the Travel Agency Accounting System and their new 5100, commercial accounts are billed twice monthly. "In just a few months," says Jerry Choma, "our savings in cash flow have more than justified the addition of our IBM 5100 computer."

Major functions

1. Sales and refunds.
2. Profit and loss statement.
3. Balance sheet accounting.
4. Journal entries.
5. Bank balance records.
6. Disbursement journal accounting.
7. Commercial account invoicing.
8. Weekly ATC reporting.
9. Employee productivity.
10. Employee payroll.
11. Airline ticket and itinerary writing.

Highlights

1. Knowing the exact financial position of the agency at all times is an aid to management in reducing credit losses and improving savings.
2. Timely billing helps generate an improved cash flow.
3. Enables the travel agent to automate the basic accounting functions of travel agency operation.
4. Designed with the assistance of a Certified Public Accountant who applied years of experience to help insure that the accounting practices, statements, and reports are in compliance with established professional standards.
5. Allows personnel to be relieved of repetitive accounting functions and be available for productive sales activity.
6. Minimizes the manual input required; transactions are recorded only once but used many times by the system to provide information for management reports.
7. Provides security check procedures to help guard against unauthorized access to payroll, bank account, and other confidential information.
8. Through prompting on the display screen, the system guides the operator to key in data from daily transaction forms. The system edits the input for operator and mathematical errors. If

---

Source: IBM Corporation.

errors occur, the system prompts the operator to take corrective action.
9. System input is done at the operator's convenience and speed.
10. System produced reports and statements:
    a. Accounts receivable journal
    b. Airline ticket itinerary
    c. Cash receipts report
    d. Disbursement account income details
    e. Disbursement journal
    f. Employee sales recap
    g. Invoice
    h. Open transactions journal
    i. Payroll check
    j. Payroll journal
    k. Profit and loss statement
    l. Refund journal
    m. Sales journal
    n. Weekly ATC report "tapes"
    o. Weekly ATC report detail

System description

The overall objective of the Travel Agency Accounting System is to automate the basic accounting requirements common to most travel agencies. The system is designed to perform the following:

1. Incorporate into the accounting system, on a daily basis, information from receipts, checks, credit memos, bank deposit forms, and on a weekly basis travel agents' sales summary.
2. Print credit and cash sales listing required for weekly ATC Reporting.
3. Print commercial account invoices carrying balances forward, crediting payments, and noting past due balances.
4. Provide management with the following monthly reports:
    a. Sales Journal of receipts/invoices, by cash, commercial account charge, and credit card sale.
    b. Refund Journal of all refunds issued by cash or commercial account charge.
    c. Disbursement Journal of all checks issued by customer transaction or expense category.
    d. Open Transactions Journal detailing out-of-balance customer records.
    e. Cash Receipts Report of all cash received from commissions, customer payments, and other receipts.
    f. Accounts Receivable Journal for agency's commercial accounts.
5. Prints employee payroll checks and register.
6. Provides Profit & Loss Statement and Balance Sheet.
7. Prepares airline ticket and itinerary.
8. Generates four flight tickets with up to three conjunctive tickets.
9. Maintains Employee Productivity and Product Line Sales Report.
10. Provides management with access to and control over confidential date on agency sales, bank account status, and payroll information.

DISCUSSION QUESTIONS

1. What are some of the routine business applications that are being performed by computer for Travelcraft, Inc.?
2. What are some of the reports being produced to help Travelcraft manage its business?

about part II

The purpose of Part II is to cover computer hardware in detail. These topics were introduced to you in Chapter 2. If you have not read this chapter, you should go back and read it carefully before you read any chapter in this part. After you have completed Chapter 2, you can read the chapters in this part in any order, although it is recommended that you cover the chapters sequentially.

Part II starts with a discussion of the evolution of data processing systems. Then, the central processing unit and temporary storage devices are covered in Chapter 6. Card, tape, and disk systems are discussed in Chapter 7, and Chapter 8 investigates input, output, and data communications devices. Chapter 9 covers various special purpose hardware devices, and Chapter 10 reveals how hardware components can be combined into complete computer systems. Chapter 10 also investigates various computer system configurations.

There are two supplements in this part. The Supplement to Chapter 6 discusses how data is stored and represented in a computer system. The Supplement to Chapter 10 investigates one of the fastest growing segments of the data processing industry, inexpensive microcomputers.

5	The evolution of data processing systems
6	Central processing
6 SUPPLEMENT	Data representation
7	Permanent storage
8	Input, output, and data communications
9	Special purpose hardware
10	Computer systems
10 SUPPLEMENT	Microcomputers for business, school, and personal use

PART II
HARDWARE

The evolution of data processing systems

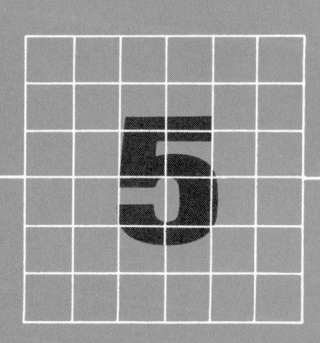

5

MECHANICAL DEVICES
THE BEGINNING OF THE COMPUTER AGE
THE COMPUTER GENERATIONS
    The first generation
    The second generation
    The third generation to the present
THE FUTURE

After completing Chapter 5 you will be able to:

- Discuss the development of mechanical calculating devices.
- Trace the beginning of the computer age.
- Describe the various computer generations.

Humans have been eating, sleeping, and processing data since the beginning of time. Five thousand years ago, devices were used to help humans process data, and over the centuries, there have been many improvements in these tools. As we live our day-to-day lives, it is difficult to realize how rapidly our world is changing. People were fumbling with mechanical devices for thousands of years. With the advent of electronic computers, it has only taken us a few short decades to make giant strides. Did you know that about half of the research done in the United States has been done in the last ten years? It is estimated that the amount of scientific information is doubling every ten years. An enlightening way to perceive the tremendous change that will take place in the next few years is to see how we have progressed in the past. As you read about mechanical devices, the beginning of the computer age, the computer generations, and today's computer systems, think about how our technology is increasing and how our lives are changing at an increasing rate. Think about what is in store for us tomorrow.

MECHANICAL DEVICES

One of the first recognized calculating devices was the **abacus.** Although the exact development date for the abacus is unknown, it has been estimated that the abacus may have been in use as early as 5,000 B.C. Refer to Figure 5–1. The abacus pictured here is Chinese. Similar devices were developed by the Romans and the Japanese.

In the early 1600s, *John Napier,* a Scottish mathematician and politician, invented logarithms and a device called **Napier's bones.** Constructed from strips of bone or wood, this device allowed the multiplication and division of large numbers quickly and accurately.

One of the first mechanical calculators was developed by **Blaise Pascal** in 1642 when he was 19 years of age. Without the use of books, this Frenchman developed a workable calculating machine and many useful mathematical

FIGURE 5–1
An abacus

Photo courtesy of IBM

5 The evolution of data processing systems 77

FIGURE 5–2A
Blaise Pascal

Photo courtesy of IBM

theorems. His calculator is displayed in Figure 5–2B. Pascal's calculating machine was developed because he was tired of adding long columns of numbers by hand at his father's tax collection office. The construction of the device was straightforward. A series of gears was used. Each gear had ten teeth, and the device had the ability to "carry" digits to the next gear. The same type of construction was used for hundreds of years. Some of the manual calculators today use the same principle. The dedication of the first model was to the Chancellor of France.

Pascal was always trying to find a better way. After waiting for transportation, he developed ideas for the first taxi service for Paris, France, and it is also said that he invented the wrist watch after growing tired of searching for his pocket watch.

About 30 years after Pascal developed his calculating device, Gottfried Wilhelm Leibnitz developed the **Leibnitz Calculating Machine.** Developed in 1671, this was the first machine to perform direct division and multiplication. This calculating device had a number of advantages over Pascal's calculating machine. One of Leibnitz's calculating machines is on display in the Library of Hanover, West Germany. Refer to Figure 5–3B.

Joseph Marie Jacquard, a French weaver, developed a weaving device called **Jacquard's Loom** that used punched cards in 1801. With this device,

FIGURE 5-2B
Pascal's calculating device

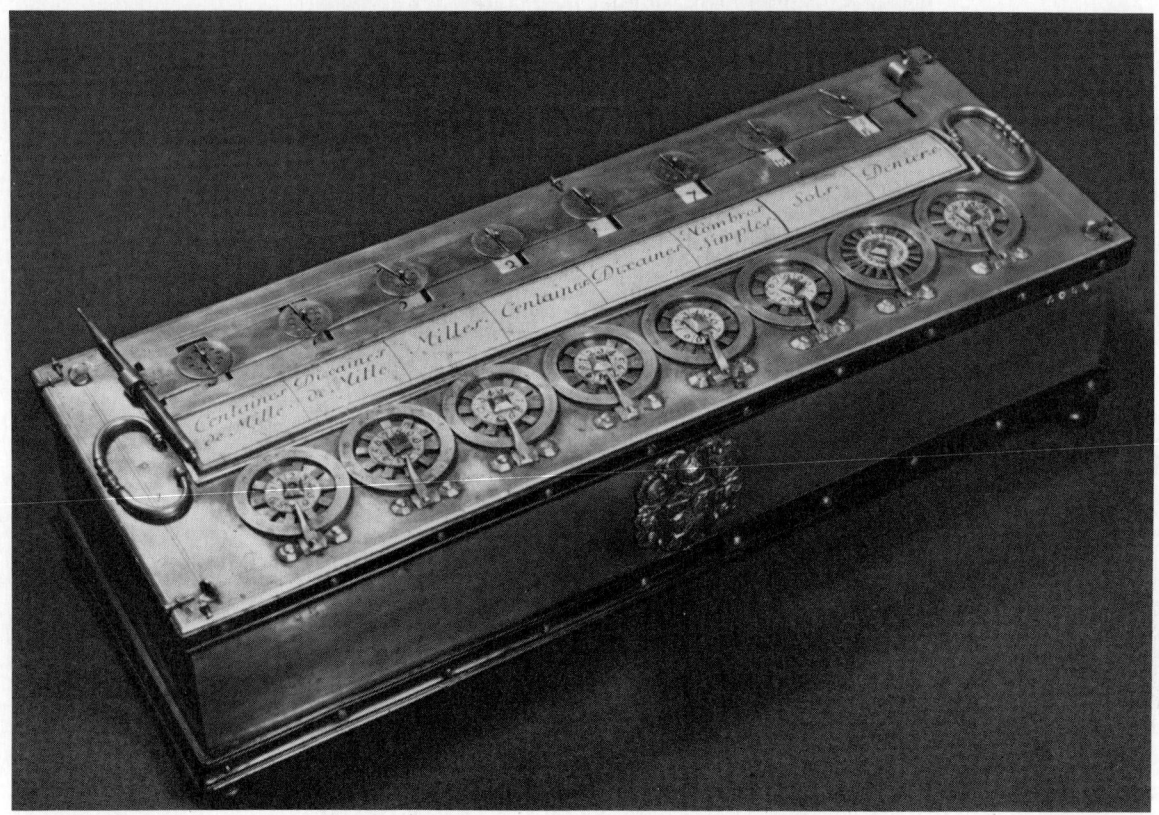

Photo courtesy of IBM

intricate patterns and designs could be produced. Requiring about 20,000 punched cards, a portrait of Jacquard was woven. This woven portrait found its way into the home of another important pioneer, **Charles Babbage.**

The idea started one evening when Babbage and a friend, John Herschel, were carefully checking astronomical calculations by hand. It was in the early 1800s, Napoleon was in power, and steam power was being used in industrial settings. After hours of grueling work, Babbage said, "I wish to God these calculations had been executed by steam." John Herschel responded, "It is quite possible." It is believed that this was the start of Babbage's idea to develop a steam powered calculator, which would evolve to become the **Difference Engine.** Babbage started the design in 1822, and he received a government grant in 1823. This device, however, was never fully constructed by Babbage. See Figure 5–4B.

One of the reasons that Babbage stopped his work on the Difference Engine was his desire to develop an unbelievable calculating machine with many unheard of capabilities. This new machine was the **Analytical Engine.** The

5 *The evolution of data processing systems*

FIGURE 5–3A
Gottfried Wilhelm Leibnitz

Photo courtesy of IBM

FIGURE 5–3B
The Leibnitz calculator

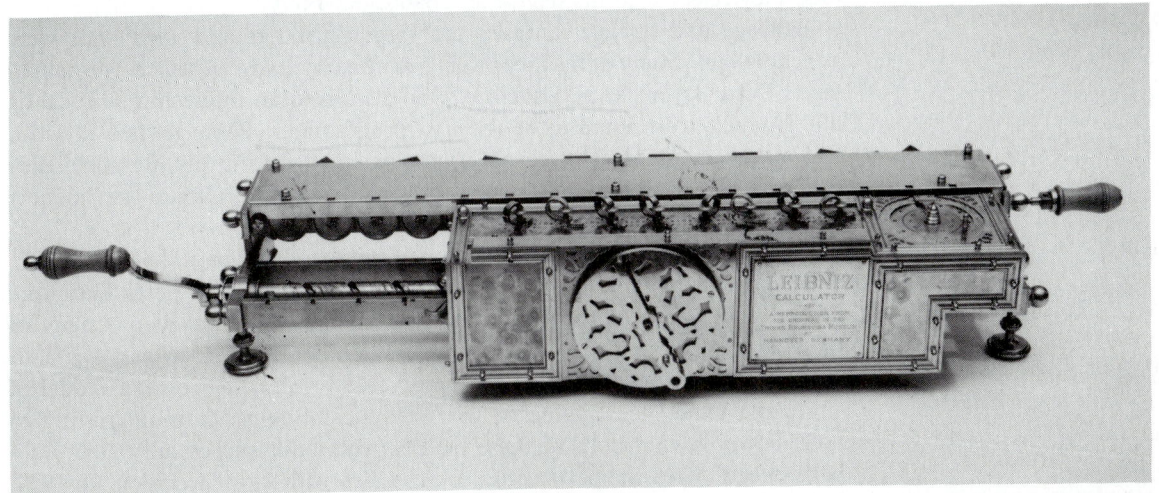

Photo courtesy of IBM

FIGURE 5–4A
Charles Babbage

Photo courtesy of IBM

device was to contain a memory unit that could actually store numbers and computations. Furthermore, the device was to have an automatic printing device, data input using punched cards, and the ability to follow a set of instructions. Babbage's Analytical Engine was to have many of the functions of today's modern computers. Many of his colleagues called him an old fool; they referred to his device as "Babbage's Folly."

Babbage had strange fantasies that organ grinders and vagabonds were attacking him. Many of his ideas were recorded by Lady Lovelace, the daughter of Lord Bryon. Lady Lovelace, who also lived an interesting and exotic life, is credited by some to be the first programmer. Babbage died in 1871, and although his ideas were never implemented during his life time, they can be seen in modern computers. Today, many experts call him the "pioneer of modern computers."

Early developers, including Pascal, Leibnitz, and Babbage, had great difficulty in actually building their calculating machines. The parts that were needed could not be manufactured with enough precision. Thus, many of these first calculating devices did not function correctly or were never built at all. For example, Babbage was never able to make a working model of either the Difference Engine or the Analytical Engine. It is interesting to note, however, that both of these devices were built successfully after Babbage's death when the parts could be produced with more precision. In 1854,

5 The evolution of data processing systems

FIGURE 5–4B
The Difference Engine

Photo courtesy of IBM

George Scheutz, a Swedish printer, successfully constructed the Difference Engine.

At this stage in history, the United States was a young and growing country. One of the great difficulties was keeping track of all the new citizens. The Census Bureau could not keep up with the great population increase. In the last years of the 19th century, a better way of processing all of the census data was needed. In 1887, *Herman Hollerith* came to the rescue by developing a punched card tabulating machine. Refer to Figure 5–5B. As a result of the **tabulating machine,** the 1890 census took about one third of the time of the 1880 census. This device could sort over 200 cards per minute. The Tabulating Machine Company was formed by Dr. Hollerith in 1896. This company merged with over ten other companies to become International Business Machines (IBM).

In the 1880s, other devices were being designed and developed by other

FIGURE 5–5A
Herman Hollerith

Photo courtesy of IBM

FIGURE 5–5B
The tabulating machine

Photo courtesy of IBM

5 The evolution of data processing systems

FIGURE 5-5C
The Scientific American, August 30, 1890

Photo courtesy of IBM

companies. An example is the **W. S. Burroughs Calculating Machine,** which was patented August 21, 1888. The overall design is seen in Figure 5-6.

The late 1800s and early 1900s also marked the beginning of several computer manufacturers. *James Ritty* developed the first cash register in 1878.

FIGURE 5–6
The W. S. Burroughs calculating machine

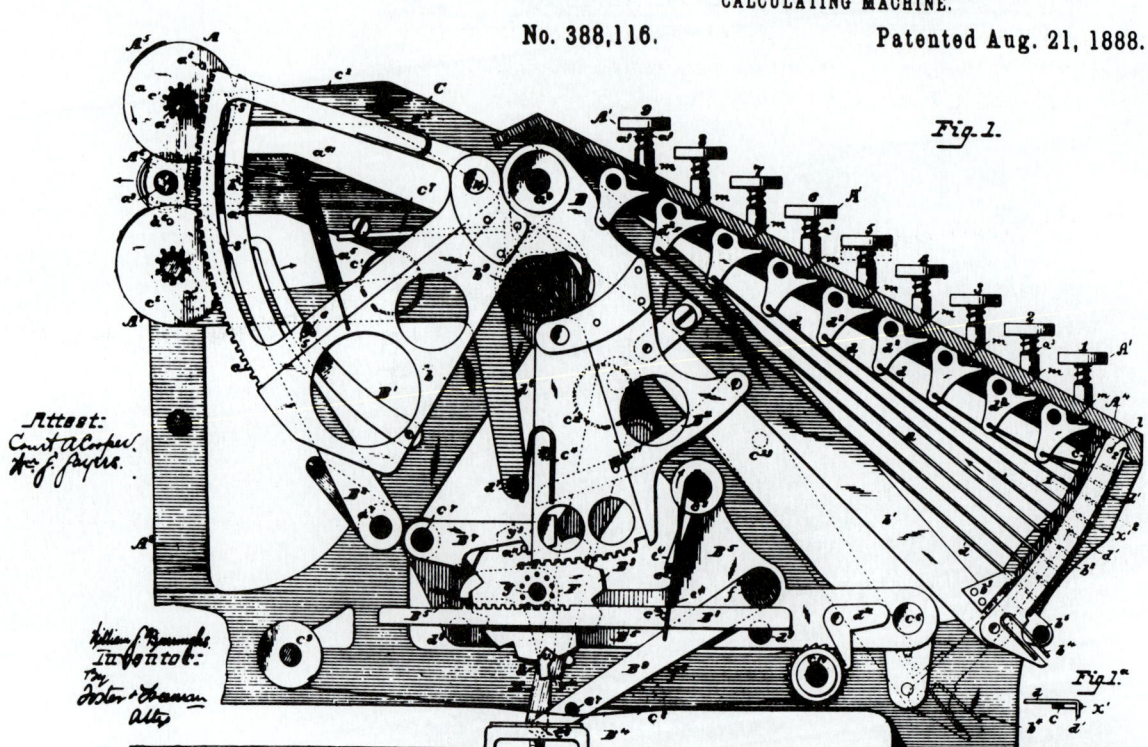

Courtesy of Burroughs Corporation

The small company was sold to *Jacob Eckert,* who formed the **National Cash Register Company.** *William S. Burroughs* formed the **American Arithmometer Company** in 1886, which became the **Burroughs Corporation** in 1953. In 1911, *James Powers* formed the **Powers Accounting Machine Company** to manufacture tabulating equipment for the U.S. Census Bureau. This company then became the **Tabulating Machine Division of Remington Rand Corporation** in 1927, and in 1955, the company merged with Sperry Gyroscope to become the **Sperry Rand Corporation.**

THE BEGINNING OF THE COMPUTER AGE

The next stage in the data processing evolution was the development of electromechanical devices. Some of the earlier devices were built at the Bell Telephone Laboratories. Most of these devices used relatively large relays or electric switches that could be either on or off. This was also the beginning of binary components.

5 The evolution of data processing systems

One of the most significant developments since the work of Babbage was the **Automatic Sequence Controlled Calculator**. More commonly called the **MARK I**, this electromechanical device was developed by *Howard H. Aiken* in 1937 and a few engineers from a new and growing company, IBM. This device could multiply ten digit numbers in less than ten seconds. It contained about 760,000 parts (switches, tubes, and so on) and about 500 miles of wire. The MARK I, which was completed in 1944, can be seen in Figure 5–7.

FIGURE 5–7
The MARK I

Photo courtesy of IBM

In 1942, *John V. Atanasoff* and his assistant, *Clifford Berry,* developed the ABC (Atanasoff-Berry Computer). Later, Atanasoff formed a research company, which was eventually sold to Aerojet General Corporation.

These early electromechanical devices were large and clumsy. The relays or switches had a tendency to stick. This pointed the way to the first all electronic digital computer. This computer was the **ENIAC** which was developed by *Dr. John W. Mauchly* and *J. Presper Eckert.* The ENIAC was developed around 1946; it is shown in Figure 5–8. The ENIAC, which stands for Electronic Numerical Integrator And Calculator, offered many advantages over devices like the MARK I. While electromechanical devices could make a few multiplications per second, the ENIAC could make hundreds of multiplications per second. Vacuum tubes were used instead of relays and electromagnetic switches. The ENIAC occupied more than 1,500 square feet, contained about 18,000 vacuum tubes, and weighed more than 30 tons. It could perform approximately 300 calculations per second.

In the early days as today, the emphasis was to make computing devices smaller, faster, and more capable. In 1952, the **EDVAC** was completed. Although design on this device started before the ENIAC, the EDVAC was smaller and had greater capabilities than the ENIAC. The EDVAC could

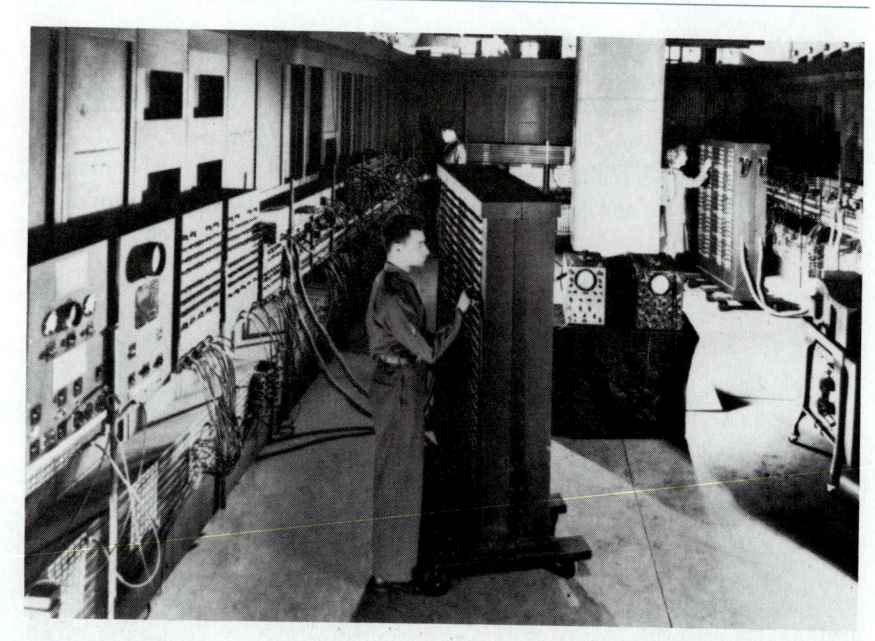

FIGURE 5-8
The ENIAC

Photo courtesy of Sperry-Univac

store programs and perform arithmetic/logic activities without assistance from a human operator. These electromechanical and electrical machines generated new ideas which led to newer and faster computers. Since the 1950s, new technologies have been developed which have resulted in several generations of computers.

THE COMPUTER GENERATIONS

In the last three decades, tremendous strides have been made in the construction and use of computer systems. Each major breakthrough caused the previous models to become technologically obsolete. The ENIAC and EDVAC used tubes instead of electromagnetic relays. This was the benchmark for the first generation of computers.

The first generation

The first generation of computers started in 1951 with the development of the UNIVersal Automatic Computer I (UNIVAC I). This computer, like all other computers of the first generation, used tubes. Refer to Figure 5–9. *Eckert* and *Mauchly* began development of the UNIVAC I at the University of Pennsylvania in 1946. It was completed and presented to the Census Bureau on June 14, 1951. Here it was used 24 hours a day for about 12 years. The company founded by Eckert and Mauchly to build the UNIVAC I eventually became the Sperry-Univac division of Sperry Rand Corporation. Up to this time, the computer was used primarily for scientific calculations. The UNIVAC I changed this in 1954 when it was used by *General Electric* in Louisville, Kentucky for business applications.

Other computer manufacturers started to produce computing devices that employed vacuum tubes. IBM developed the IBM 701 and the IBM 650 in the mid 1950s. These computers were used for business data processing. They were very popular, and some experts believe that this was the start of IBM's dominance of the computer market.

Competition between computer manufacturers was stiff even during the first generation. After lengthy litigation, UNIVAC was able to get a basic patent on electronic computers as a result of the extensive work of Eckert and Mauchly. Honeywell was then sued by UNIVAC for royalties. After a long and difficult court battle, the court ruled that Atanasoff was the primary developer of the electronic digital computer. Mauchly was knowledgeable of Atanasoff's work. He had conversations with Atanasoff at Atanasoff's home in 1940, and it is likely that this was a factor in the court ruling.

FIGURE 5–9
The UNIVAC I

Photo courtesy of Sperry-Univac

The first generation of computers also marked the start of programs and programming languages. Many of the first generation computers had to be programmed in machine language, consisting of a series of 0's and 1's. Machine language was difficult to learn and use (refer to Chapter 3 for a discussion of machine language). As a result, symbolic and assembler languages were developed. These newer languages used symbols like D for divide, and M for multiply, but there had to be a program to translate symbolic or assembler language into machine language. In 1952, *Dr. Grace Hooper* developed one of the first program translators at the University of Pennsylvania. This was the start of the development of programming languages. Other translating programs developed in the 1950s are *Soap* for the IBM 650 and *Sap* for the IBM 704.

During the first generation, computer systems were used to produce financial and bookkeeping reports for businesses. Such applications as payroll, accounts receivable, and accounts payable were common computerized applications. The people running the computer in the data processing department normally had a technical background. In most cases, these individuals had to understand the internal workings of the computer system to write programs and to operate the computer system. Hardware was the most important factor in running these first generation computer systems, and most of the data processing budget was expended for hardware.

The first generation also marked the beginning of data processing organizations. Several tabulating machine supervisors in the Chicago area formed the Machine Accountants Association over lunch in March of 1949. In the next year, the membership was over 100, and in 1951, the *National Machine Accountants Association* (NMAA) was formed.

While the first generation computers were an improvement over earlier computers, their use of vacuum tubes left much to be desired. The tubes produced a great amount of heat and furthermore, they were always burning out. These problems and a desire to produce a better computer system encouraged the development of transistors. This was the beginning of the second generation of computers.

The second generation

The **second generation** of computers used transistors instead of tubes. Transistors had many advantages: They were smaller, faster, more reliable, and produced far less heat during operation. The second generation of computers goes from about 1959 to about 1965.

There are several different computer systems that typify the second generation. IBM had several models that were in this category. Some of them were the IBM 1401, the IBM 1620, and the IBM 7090. Other manufacturers also contributed computers to the second generation. Honeywell developed the Model 800. Burroughs produced the Burroughs 5000. National Cash Register (NCR), Radio Corporation of America (RCA), and Philco developed second generation computers. The UNIVAC III, and Control Data Corporation's CDC 1604 were also products of the second generation.

A number of hardware improvements accompanied the second generation. Permanent storage on computer cards diminished, and the use of magnetic tape and disk devices was introduced. For the first time, the computer system could directly access permanently stored data using the disk. Input and output devices also were improved. Better printers, terminals, card readers, and so on were developed. In addition, cores were being used to a greater extent for memory (temporary storage). Hardware devices were also modular, an improvement that made the location of hardware problems and maintenance easier.

5 The evolution of data processing systems

The second generation of computers marked the common use of high-level languages. FORTRAN, developed in 1957, was being used for scientific purposes, and COBOL, developed in 1961, was being used for business applications. These languages were discussed in Chapter 3.

There were also improvements in system software. Operating systems were replacing many of the functions that were performed by the person operating the computer system. Compilers were developed to translate high-level languages into machine language, and utility programs were developed to merge, sort, and transfer data files from one storage location to another.

The second generation witnessed a shift of emphasis from hardware to software. In many computer installations, the cost of the software approached the cost of the hardware. Furthermore, some companies started to use the computer to supply its managers with information that could help them increase profits and run the company. This was the start of *computerized management information systems.*

Additional data processing organizations started to spring up. A few of these organizations specialized in the various functions within the data processing industry such as software and data processing service organizations. In the early 1960s, the National Machine Accountants Association (**NMAA**) evolved into the *Data Processing Management Association* (**DPMA**) with about 16,000 members. During this time, many of the early data processing organizations became concerned about the quality of data processing personnel. In 1962, the first **Certificate in Data Processing** (**CDP**) exam was given.

Although the use of transistors greatly increased the capabilities of the second generation computers, scientists and engineers were striving for new and improved technology. This led to miniaturized circuits and the third generation of computers.

The third generation to the present

The *third generation* of computers started with the introduction of the IBM 360, which occurred about 1965. Transistors gave way to integrated and miniaturized circuits. Since 1965, computer development has been very rapid, and there have been many improvements in all aspects of computer systems. These improvements include:

1. Increased processing speeds.
2. Increased accuracy.
3. Integration of hardware and software.
4. The ability to perform several operations simultaneously.
5. Data communications advances.
6. Improved performance to price ratio.

Hardware devices continue to be improved during the third generation. *Integrated Circuits* (**IC**) and *Large-Scale Integration* (**LSI**) technology are making third generation computers faster and smaller. New memory devices, including *bubble memory* and *Charge-Coupled Devices* (**CCD**) have improved storage capabilities. Magnetic tape and disk devices are now faster and less expensive. Input and output devices are also being improved, and many of these devices contain microprocessors. Some terminals, for example, have microprocessors to improve their data handling capabilities. In addition, a number of special purpose hardware devices have been developed. *Point of Sale* (POS) devices are used at grocery stores, *Magnetic Ink Character Recognition* (MICR) is being used by banks to process checks, *Computer Output Microfilm* (COM) is being used to store data, and more. There are devices that allow us to talk to the computer (speech recognition devices), and there are devices that allow the computer to talk to us (voice response units). These advancements and more will be covered fully in this part.

Software has also significantly improved, and today the major cost of a computer system is software. In the near future, software could be as much as 75 percent of the total cost of the computer system. High-level languages are used almost exclusively to develop application programs, and there have been a number of new high-level languages. The trend is to make these languages easier to use. There are also improved ways to design and develop application software. One example is *structured design*. There have also been dramatic improvements in system software. Operating systems, compilers and assemblers, and utility programs are all improving. Newer system software techniques like *virtual storage, multiprogramming,* and *multiprocessing* are making today's computers do more. All of these techniques will be covered fully in Part III. One of the biggest advances in system software is the development of *Data Base Management Systems* (DBMS). These systems have allowed organizations to gain better control over one of their most valuable resources, data and information. Part III describes DBMS and other software advances in more detail.

Computer systems and their operation have seen change. *Data communications* is allowing computer systems to be connected together in almost any configuration or network. Computer terminals and devices are now being placed where the action is—at the checkout stand, at the warehouse, on the shop floor, and in the offices of managers and executives. Furthermore, more emphasis is being given to providing information *(management information systems)* and supporting decisions *(decision support systems)*. Data processing personnel now need managerial and human relations skills to interface with the people that will be using the computer system.

Data processing organizations have continued to increase. These organizations are now publishing a number of specialized journals on computers and data processing. As new organizations are formed, older accomplishments are recognized. In 1969, Dr. Grace Hooper was named the first *Computer Sciences Man-of-the Year* for her work in developing language translators.

From the 1965 models to today's computers, there have been so many developments that it has been impossible to neatly classify further generations of computers. As computer technology has progressed from tubes to the chip, improvements have been made in software and vendor support. See Figure 5–10.

Today, computer manufacturers have changed from selling only hardware

Photo courtesy of IBM

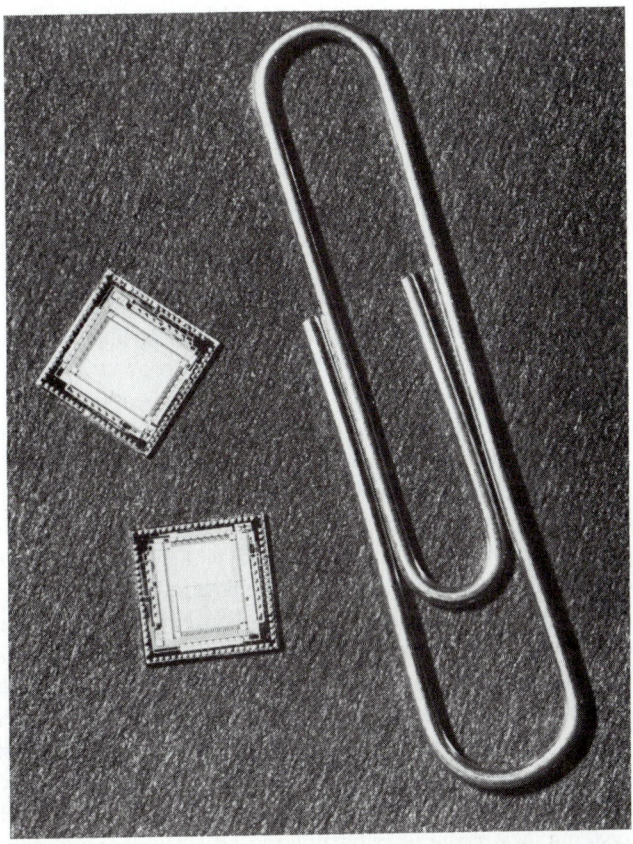

FIGURE 5–10
Chips

to offering complete and ready to use computer systems with training, maintenance, management, consulting, and other services.

While specific technological breakthroughs are nearly impossible to predict, the overall trend is clear. In the past, technology has increased at an increasing rate, and this rate of explosion in technology is expected to continue in the future.

Solid state hardware devices will continue to be improved. *Bipolar Large Scale Integration* (LSI), *fiber optics, bubble memories,* and *charge-coupled devices* will be used to a greater extent. Although some of these devices have not been put into production as soon as originally expected, these devices will have a significant effect on computer storage and operation. Some experts predict that as these technologies are improved, they may eventually replace magnetic tape and disk devices for permanent storage. Mechanical hardware devices, such as printers and card readers, will not be improved dramatically, however. Many hardware devices will contain *microprocessors,* like today's *intelligent terminals,* to help them perform their function and to expand their capabilities. Hardware devices and systems will also be more fault toler-

THE FUTURE

ant, and hardware malfunctions will be taken care of automatically by the computer system using duplicate circuitry or by automatically transferring the work to other processors.

Some of the most significant improvements are expected with software. Programs and applications, such as payroll and inventory control, will be placed on chips, called *firmware*. Techniques to develop programs, such as structured design, will be used to a greater extent, and a number of new programming languages will be developed. These languages will be problem oriented, making it easier to get valuable information from the computer system. Future software will provide a reduction in data redundancy, improved data integrity and security, and faster and cheaper access. Continued improvements in system software will also occur. In general, future system and application software will allow more people to use computer systems. These improvements will also reduce the cost of software, which has been increasing in the recent past.

There will be an increased use of data communication equipment to connect computer systems together. Increasingly computer devices will be placed where the action is, and connected to a network of processors using data communications equipment. In the future, it is expected that events will be directly connected to the computer system. The computer will monitor and control air conditioning systems, lighting, inventory levels, patient's blood pressure and temperature, and so on. This will allow factories, hospitals, universities, offices, and other facilities to become more fully automated.

Microcomputers will continue to change radically how people and small businesses process data. These inexpensive and small devices are also being used by large companies and organizations to supplement their large computer systems. *Microcomputer* hardware and software will evolve to be as sophisticated and powerful as those for today's medium and large computers.

Today, about 30 percent of the work force depends on the computer. In the near future, it is expected that from 50 to 80 percent of the work force will depend on the computer. While future computers will be easier to use, massive training and new educational programs will be required to allow people to fully realize the potential of future computer systems.

SUMMARY

One of the first mechanical devices was the abacus, developed by the Chinese as early as 5,000 B.C. In 1642, Blaise Pascal developed Pascal's calculating machine when he was 19 years old; and in 1671, Gottfried Wilhelm Leibnitz developed a calculating device that could automatically divide and multiply. Two of the most significant developments in mechanical devices were made by Charles Babbage. In 1822, he designed the Difference Engine, and in the 1830s he was working on the Analytical Engine. Although these devices were not built during his lifetime, the principles he developed can be seen in today's computer systems. In 1887, Herman Hollerith developed a tabulating machine that was used to tabulate the 1890 census. Later the company formed by Hollerith merged with several other companies to form International Business Machines (IBM).

5 The evolution of data processing systems

The MARK I was the beginning of the computer age. This electromechanical device was developed by Howard Aiken in 1937 along with engineers from IBM. Other early computing devices include the ENIAC and the EDVAC.

The first generation of computers was started in 1951 with the introduction of the UNIVAC I. Other first generation computers include the IBM 650, the Burroughs E101, and the Honeywell Datamatic 1000. These and other first generation computers used vacuum tubes. They were programmed in machine langauge in most cases.

Second generation computers dominated the period from 1959 to 1965. They used transistors instead of tubes. Examples of second generation computers are the IBM 1620, the Honeywell Model 800, and the Burroughs 5000. The second generation is also the start of the use of high-level programming languages, the use and development of management information systems, and the development of data processing organizations, such as the Data Processing Management Association (DPMA).

Third generation computers started in 1965 with the introduction of the IBM 360. Third generation computers use integrated circuits (IC's) instead of transistors. High-level languages are used to write application programs, and significant improvements were made with system software. An example is the development of Data Base Management Systems (DBMS). In the future, we should see the same rate of technological growth. While hardware devices will be faster and cheaper, we will see the greatest improvement in software. Software will harden into firmware by being placed on chips. New programming languages will be introduced and program development will be improved. These advances should reduce the spiral of increasing software costs. Although these hardware and software improvements will make computers easier to use, training programs and educational institutions will have to be improved to help people use future computer systems to their potential.

KEY TERMS AND CONCEPTS

Abacus	Honeywell Model 800	MARK I
Analytical Engine	Howard H. Aiken	Pascal's Calculating
Automatic sequence controlled calculator	IBM 360	Machine
	IBM 650	Relays
Blaise Pascal	IBM 701	Second generation
Burroughs 5000	IBM 1401	Sperry-Univac
CDC 1604	IBM 1620	Tabulating machine
Charles Babbage	IBM 7090	Tabulating Machine
Difference Engine	International Business	Company
EDVAC	Machines (IBM)	Third generation
ENIAC	Jacquard's Loom	Transistors
First generation	J. Presper Eckert	UNIVAC I
Herman Hollerith	John W. Mauchly	Vacuum tubes

QUESTIONS

5–1. Discuss some of the earlier mechanical calculating devices.

5–2. What was the major technological difference between the MARK I and the ENIAC?

5–3. What is a first generation computer? Give several examples.

5–4. What is the primary difference between first and second generation computers? What were some of the advantages of the second generation computers over the first generation computers?

5–5. When did the third generation of computers start? What technological advances were used in third generation computers?

ANSWERS

1. F
2. F
3. F
4. T
5. F
6. T
7. F
8. F
9. T
10. T

MINIQUIZ

True or False

___F___ 1. The abacus was first developed in Japan in the early 1500s.
___F___ 2. Pascal developed one of the first mechanical calculators in the 1800s when he was 19 years of age.
___F___ 3. Leibnitz developed one of the first electronic calculating devices that employed cylinders.
___T___ 4. One of Babbage's first devices was the Difference Engine, designed in 1822.
___F___ 5. Herman Hollerith, in 1887, developed the Analytical Engine.
___T___ 6. The automatic sequence controlled calculator is another name for the Mark I.
___F___ 7. The ENIAC was the first electromechanical digital computer.
___F___ 8. The IBM 701 and the IBM 650 are examples of second generation computers.
___T___ 9. Second generation computers use transistors instead of tubes.
___T___ 10. Third generation computers started with the introduction of the IBM 360 in about 1965.

**Remarks of C. E. Exley, Jr., President of NCR Corporation
Columbia Business School Club of New York—March 20, 1979**

Technological advances in electronics are one of our major weapons for offsetting the impact of inflation, but product innovation is not the exclusive province of our electronics engineers. Better design and new materials are also making possible dramatic improvements in the mechanical components of our products.

Source: Reprinted courtesy of NCR Corporation.

As we look to the future there is no sign of slackening in the rate of technological change. In fact, the period between 1980 and 1985 will probably be the most dramatic in the industry's history in terms of changing technology. As the Arthur D. Little organization has predicted for the computer industry, the 1980s will make the 1970s seem like a "stagnant decade" by comparison.

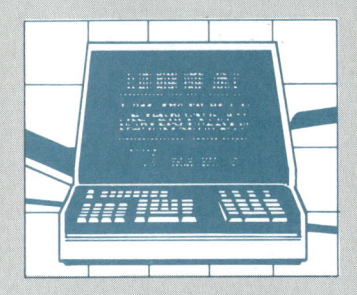

Photo courtesy of NCR

DISCUSSION QUESTIONS

1. Do you think the computer industry will experience the same growth in the next ten to twenty years as it has in the past?
2. Do you think the greatest growth will be in mechanical devices like printers and card readers or in solid state devices like the central processing unit?

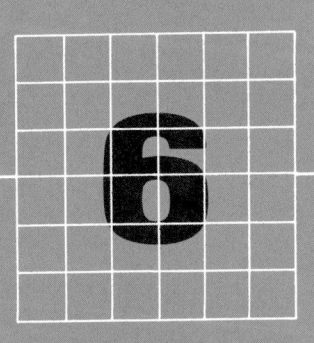

Central processing   6

THE CONTROL AND ARITHMETIC/LOGIC UNIT
    The control unit
    The arithmetic/logic unit
    Registers
    The execution of an instruction
TEMPORARY STORAGE
    Fundamentals of temporary storage
    Core storage
    Semiconductor storage
    Bubble storage
    Other temporary storage devices
INTERFACING WITH OTHER COMPONENTS

After completing Chapter 6, you will be able to:

- Describe the use of the control and arithmetic/logic unit.
- Discuss the fundamentals of temporary storage devices.
- List and explain the devices that are used to interface the central processing unit with other devices.

THE CONTROL AND ARITHMETIC/LOGIC UNIT

The center or heart of a computer system is the **central processing unit.** It controls the entire computer system and executes the instructions we give it. A typical Central Processing Unit (CPU) can be seen in Figure 6–1.

The CPU contains the *central processor* and the *temporary storage* device. The central processor is divided into the *control unit* and the *arithmetic/logic unit.* The temporary storage unit is divided into four areas. These areas include *input storage, output storage, instruction storage* and *working storage.* See Figure 6–2.

The central processor includes the control unit and the arithmetic/logic unit. Furthermore, this unit contains small storage units called registers and accumulators. In this section we will investigate these devices and how they are used to execute a set of instructions.

The control unit

As the name implies, the **control unit** directs and controls all of the devices in the computer system. The control unit tells the card reader when to read a computer card and the printer when to print a line of output. Any operation that is performed by the computer system is performed as a direct result of the control unit.

The control unit receives its instructions from computer programs. For example, we may develop a set of computer programs that performs the

FIGURE 6–1
A central processing unit

Courtesy of IBM

6 Central processing

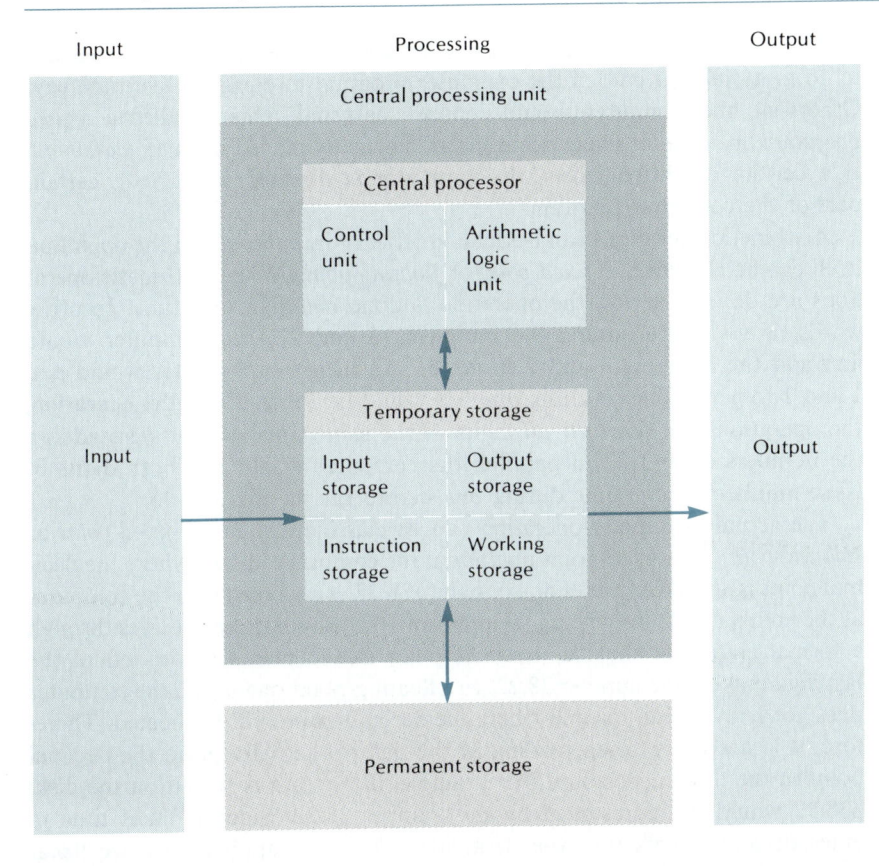

FIGURE 6–2
Components of the central processing unit

payroll application. The central processing unit executes the instructions in the programs and directs the other devices in the computer system to take the appropriate action. In some cases an arithmetic computation is required or a logical decision has to be made. In these cases, the control unit transfers the instruction to the arithmetic/logic unit.

The arithmetic/logic unit

One of the purposes of the arithmetic/logic unit is to perform all of the mathematical computations. In preparing paychecks, for example, it is necessary to compute gross wages, deductions, and so forth. All of these calculations are called arithmetic operations, and they are performed in the arithmetic/logic unit. Once these computations are performed, the control unit again takes over in directing the entire computer system.

The other function of the arithmetic/logic unit is to allow the computer system to make *decisions* during the execution of a program. The control unit is a sequential instruction executor. This means that the control unit will execute one instruction after another. In some cases, a decision has to be made that changes the sequence of the instructions. For example, if an employee worked more than 40 hours for a given week, it may be necessary to go to a different part of the computer program to compute overtime pay. Otherwise, the computer should continue as usual. This is called a *logical operation* or *decision*. These decisions are normally placed in an *IF statement*. If a certain condition exists, the computer is directed to go to a certain part of the computer program.

Arithmetic operations can be done in *series* or in *parallel* and the operation itself can be classified as *fixed-point* or *floating-point*. When arithmetic operations are done in **series,** the operation is done *one* digit at a time. In other words, if you were adding the numbers 13 and 22, the computer would first add the numbers 3 and 2 to get 5, and then the computer would add 1 and 2 to get 3. The resulting number would be 35. In a **parallel operation,** the operations are done on *all* digits at the same time. If you were adding the numbers 13 and 22 in parallel, the computer would add both digits of these numbers at *one* time during *one* step to get the number 35.

The actual arithmetic operation can be classified as either *fixed-point* or *floating-point*. In a fixed-point operation, the computer knows where the decimal point is ahead of time. For example, $38.22 can be read into the computer as the number 3822. In writing the program, the programmer specifies through a format statement that the decimal point is two places to the left of the last digit making the number 38.22. In a floating-point operation, the computer does not know ahead of time where the decimal point will be located. Therefore, it is necessary when reading in the data to actually place the decimal point in the desired position. For example, if the data is stored on the disk, $38.22 would be represented by the number 38.22. Since it takes time to enter decimal points into the data, many business applications use fixed-point arithmetic operations.

Both the control unit and the arithmetic/logic unit require a small amount of storage to hold the instruction and data currently being processed. These small storage units are called registers.

Registers

A *register* is a small storage area that is used to hold instructions and data currently being processed by the control unit or the arithmetic/logic unit. In most cases, registers can only hold one number or one instruction. Some registers are *general-purpose registers* that can be used in a number of different ways. In addition, there are a number of special purpose registers that are used to perform specific activities. An *accumulator register* is used to hold the results of an arithmetic operation. An *instruction register* is used to hold an instruction until it can be executed. A *storage register* is used to hold data until it can be processed, and an *address register* is used to store the location or address of an instruction that is to be executed. Some registers are used exclusively by the computer system. These are called *privileged registers,* and the computer programmer has no control over their use. Other registers can be controlled by the programmer.

The execution of an instruction

So far, we have investigated the components of the central processing unit. Now we will investigate how it executes an instruction. A computer statement, in a programming language such as BASIC, FORTRAN, or COBOL, is translated into one or more machine level instructions. This is done by a compiler, as discussed in Part I. Each machine level instruction contains *one operation code,* also called *OP code,* and two or more *Operands.* The operation code tells the central processor what has to be done, and the operands tell the central processor the location of the data that is to be manipulated.

The execution of any machine level instruction involves two phases. During the first phase, the instruction to be executed is brought into the central processor from temporary storage. This instruction is decoded so the central processor can understand what is to be done and the location of the next instruction is identified. This is called the *instruction cycle,* and the time it takes to perform this cycle is called the **instruction time** (I-time). The second phase, which begins after the instruction cycle, is the *execution cycle.* During this cycle the computer does what it is instructed to do. This could involve making an arithmetic computation, reading data, printing a bill, and more. The time it takes to complete the execution cycle is called the **execution time** (E-time). After both of these cycles have been completed for one instruction, the instruction cycle and the execution cycle are performed for the second instruction, and so on. After the instruction has been executed, the results are transferred to the temporary storage device.

TEMPORARY STORAGE

As shown in Figure 6-2, temporary storage is divided into four areas. These areas include *input storage, output storage, instruction storage* and *working storage.* In this section, we will investigate the fundamental concepts of temporary storage. Then we will discuss several different types of temporary storage units including core storage, semiconductor storage, and bubble storage.

Fundamentals of temporary storage

All temporary storage devices are made up of *locations* in which data and instructions can be placed. Each location is specified by its *address.* This is a reference name for that particular location. Furthermore, each location will have data or an instruction stored in it. This is called the *contents* of the storage location.

As seen in Figure 6-3, a mail box has an address and contents. The address indicates where letters or packages are to be stored, and the contents are the actual letters or packages. Storage locations in temporary storage are arranged exactly the same. Each location has a unique address, which identifies that particular location. The data or instructions at a particular location are the contents.

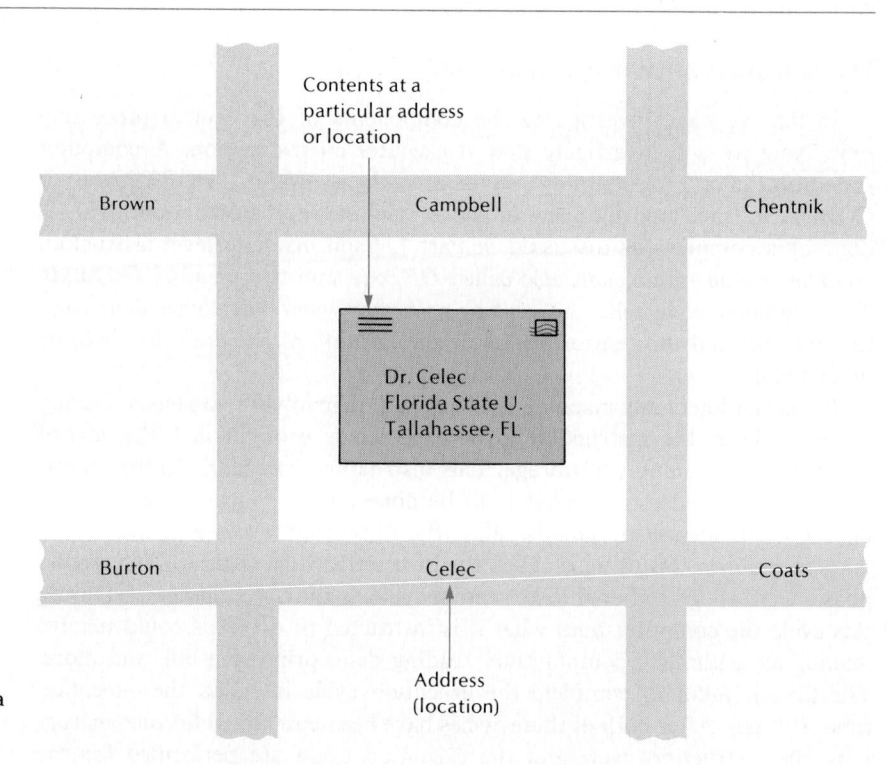

FIGURE 6–3
The address and contents of a mailbox

Depending on how much data is to be stored at a single address, the temporary storage device can be classified as either *character addressable* or *word addressable*. A character addressable temporary storage device is also called a **variable-word length device**, and a word addressable storage device is also called a **fixed-word length device**. In a character addressable storage device, each character has one unique location with its own address. This concept is shown in Figure 6–4.

As you can see, the number − 362 requires four different storage locations.

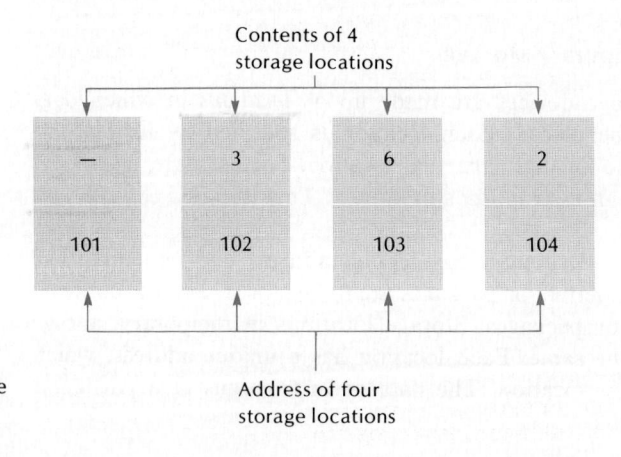

FIGURE 6–4
Storing the number − 362 in a character addressable storage device

6 Central processing

The negative sign is stored at address 101, the number 3 is stored at address 102, the number 6 is stored at address 103, and the number 2 is stored at address 104. In retrieving this number from storage, the computer will have to access each of these four locations in order to obtain the number − 362. In a word addressable storage device, one location with its own address is used to store an entire number or word. This is shown in Figure 6–5.

Contents of 1 storage location

− 362

101

Address of one storage location

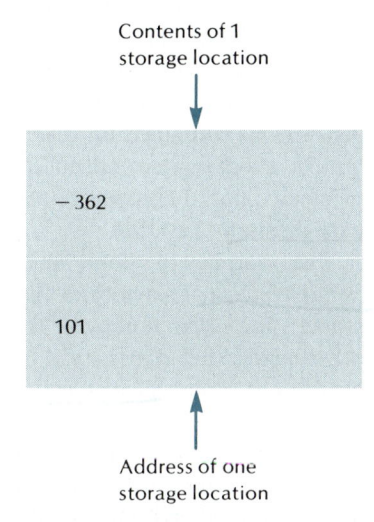

FIGURE 6–5
Storing the number − 362 in a word addressable storage device

As you can see, the entire number is stored at one location. This location has the address of 101. The major advantage of a character addressable device is that it is very efficient in terms of storage capacity. In a word addressable device, there can be wasted space. The instruction or data held at the one location normally does not use the entire space that is available. For example, a word addressable device may have the capacity of storing eight characters. However, if you have only one character to store, it still takes the same amount of space (eight characters or a word). This excess space cannot be used to store any other information. The major disadvantage of a character addressable storage device is slower access speed. To obtain a number, each character must be accessed one at a time. In a word addressable storage device, the entire word can be accessed at one time. Thus the major trade-off is between storage efficiency and access speed. Character addressable devices are more efficient in terms of storage, but their access speed is slower. Word addressable devices are inefficient in terms of storage, but they have faster access speeds. Because most business applications require a large amount of data, character addressable storage devices are normally preferred. In many new computer systems, both character addressable and word addressable storage can be used.

In any temporary storage device, the computer programmer has the ability to store data and then to *randomly* or *directly* access the data at a later time. This type of access is called **random access memory** (RAM). In addition to RAM, some computer manufacturers have installed special memory chips containing instructions that may be used to make the processing of data more efficient. To prevent accidental destruction of the data, the computer manufacturers have designed these chips in such a way that data can only be read. This type of storage is called **read only memory (ROM)**. The instructions that are contained in ROM have been called **microinstructions** or **microcode**. These instructions are not like the software discussed previously. They are contained on chips and supplied by the computer manufacturers. Because these microinstructions are somewhere between hardware and software, they are commonly called *firmware*. In some cases, it is possible to reprogram instructions contained on read only memory. But special procedures are required. Programmers normally do not have the ability to reprogram these memory chips. This type of temporary storage is called **programmable read only memory** (PROM).

The output of data and instructions from temporary storage is *nondestructive.* This means that when data is the output from temporary storage, the original copy of the data in temporary storage remains. On the other hand, when data is read into temporary storage, the old data is replaced by the new data. This is called *destructive* reading. With some temporary storage devices, a loss of power or current to the devices will result in the loss of all data and information. A temporary storage device that has this property is called a *volatile* device. A *nonvolatile* storage device does not lose its contents with a loss of power.

In general, any component or device within the computer system can be

FIGURE 6–6
A picture of core storage

Courtesy of IBM

6 Central processing

classified as being in one of two possible states or conditions. When we let the number 1 represent one state or condition and the number 0 represent another state or condition, it is possible to use the *binary numbering system* to represent the state of any component or circuit in the computer system. For example, a device that is *magnetized* or a circuit that is *on* can be represented by the number *1*. A device that is *not magnetized* or a circuit that is *off* can be represented by the number 0. A device or circuit of this nature can contain a *binary piece of information* (1 or 0). A *bit,* which stands for *bi*nary digi*t,* is one binary piece of information. One binary device or circuit can store one bit. Normally, it requires several bits to represent one character or symbol. Many computers require six, seven, or eight bits (or computer circuits or devices) that can be in one of two possible conditions to represent a particular character or symbol. Eight bits is called one *byte.* It is interesting to note that four bits is exactly between one bit and one byte and has been called a *nibble.*

Data is represented in a temporary storage device by using a number of devices or circuits that can be in one of two possible states. But how are these components and circuits constructed and how are they used? The following sections will answer these questions.

Core storage

One of the older and still very popular devices used primarily with larger computer systems to store data on a temporary basis is **core storage.** Core storage is a storage device composed of small doughnut shaped magnetic rings that can be magnetized in one of two directions. Figure 6–6 contains a picture of several cores.

Magnetic core storage consists of literally thousands of these cores that are strung on interconnecting wires.

In Figure 6–7, you can see that each core has two wires passing through it. These two wires are used to magnetize the cores. The total current required to magnetize one core is divided in half. Half of the current is sent down one wire and the other half current is sent down the other wire. At the intersection of the two wires, there is enough current to magnetize that particular core while all other cores remain as they are. Thus, by sending half of the necessary current down the appropriate two wires, it is possible to magnetize any given core. This is how data is placed on the cores. When the core is magnetized, it is in the 1 state, and when it is not magnetized, it is in the 0 state. In order to retrieve data from core storage, two additional wires, which are not shown in Figure 6–7, are required. One wire is the *sensing wire,* and when it is activated, a current will flow through it if the core was previously magnetized. If the core was not previously magnetized, a current will not flow through this sense wire. A fourth wire is also required to *restore* the original state of the core if it was previously magnetized.

Magnetic core storage has a number of advantages. It is reliable and durable. Furthermore, it requires very little electrical current, and it is also

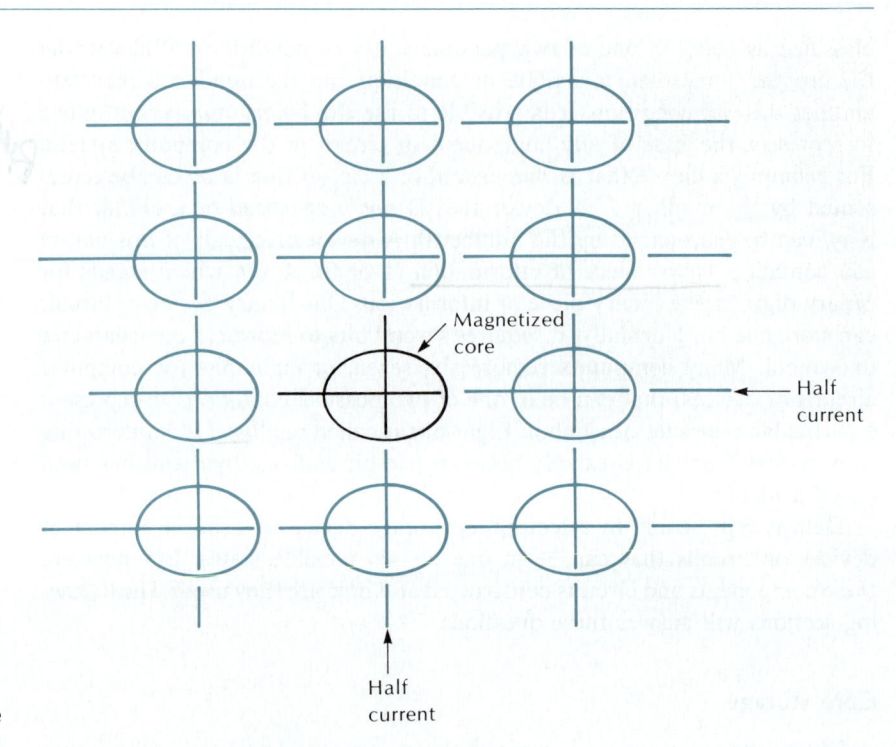

FIGURE 6–7
The operation of core storage

nonvolatile. This means that a power shortage or interruption will not change or alter its contents.

Semiconductor storage

Since the 1970s, semiconductor storage has become popular especially with minicomputers and microcomputers. **Semiconductor** storage is made up of thousands of tiny memory chips that contain complete and integrated circuits that are etched into a chip. Since the circuits are *integrated* and there are a *large* number of them, this type of technology is called **large scale integration** (LSI). Chips that are smaller than a thumbnail can contain literally thousands of words in storage. A typical semiconductor chip is shown in Figure 6–8.

The circuits contained on these small chips can be in one of two states. Like the lights in a room, the circuits can be switched either *on* or *off.* This concept is shown in Figure 6–9.

The typical circuit in a chip consists of a power source and a switching mechanism. When the switch is open, the circuit is off. This is represented by the binary number 0. When the switch is closed the circuit is on. This is represented by the binary number 1.

Semiconductor temporary storage offers many advantages over traditional core storage. Semiconductor storage is *smaller, faster,* and *cheaper* than core

6   Central processing

Photo courtesy of NCR Corporation

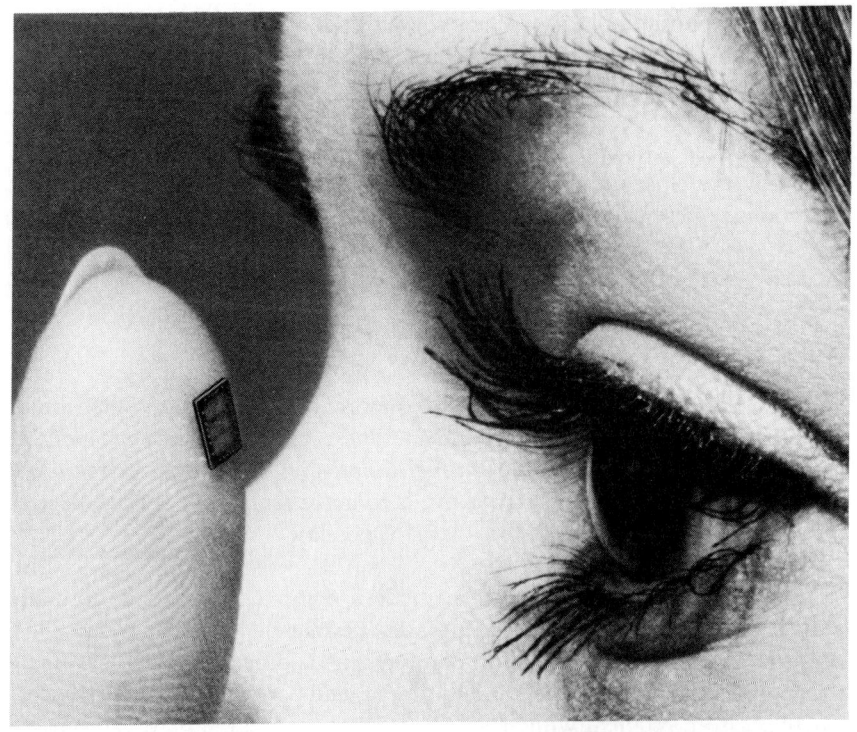

FIGURE 6–8
A chip

storage. Furthermore, it is expected that semiconductor storage will become even smaller, faster, and cheaper in the future. One of the major drawbacks of semiconductor storage is its *volatile* nature. This means that a loss or interruption of power will result in the loss of its contents.

Bubble storage

Bubble storage, also called magnetic bubble memory, is still in its infancy, but its future is bright. Constructed from small integrated circuit chips, magnetic bubble storage works on the principle of *magnetic fields*. When a magnetic field is applied to these chips, some areas of the chips strengthen and others weaken. This causes isolated areas to form that are surrounded by

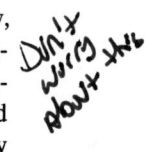

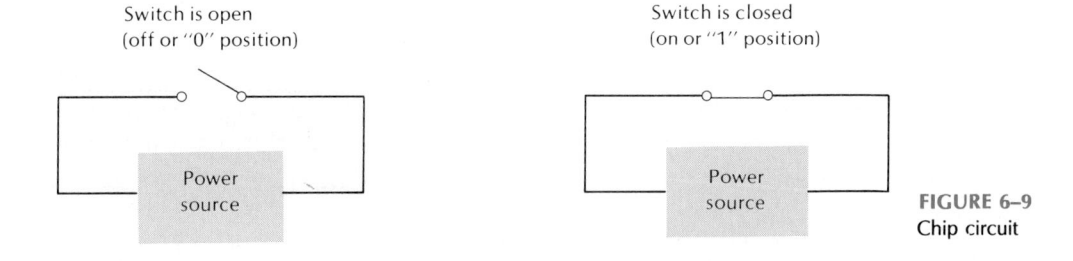

Switch is open
(off or "0" position)

Power source

Switch is closed
(on or "1" position)

Power source

FIGURE 6–9
Chip circuit

charges of opposite polarity. When viewed under a microscope, these areas take on the appearance of bubbles, and thus this type of storage has been called bubble storage.

Bubble storage works on the same binary principle as other temporary storage devices. The appearance of a bubble at a particular location is represented by the binary number 1, and the absence of a bubble at a particular location is represented by the binary number 0. Being *inexpensive* to construct and *nonvolatile* in nature, it is expected that bubble memory will compete favorably with other temporary storage devices.

Other temporary storage devices

There are a large number of other temporary storage devices that are in use or at various stages of development. These devices include *photodigital storage, laser beam storage, charge-coupled devices* (CCD), and *electron beam access memory* (EBAM). The objective is to make temporary storage devices faster, smaller, cheaper, and nonvolatile if possible.

INTERFACING WITH OTHER COMPONENTS

The central processing unit of a modern computer system is normally attached to a number of input, output, and permanent storage devices. This, however, can cause problems. How does the central processing unit coordinate the activities of all the different input, output, and permanent storage devices? There is also a problem with speed. The central processing unit can operate much faster than permanent storage devices and input and output devices. If these other devices are so much slower, how can we keep the central

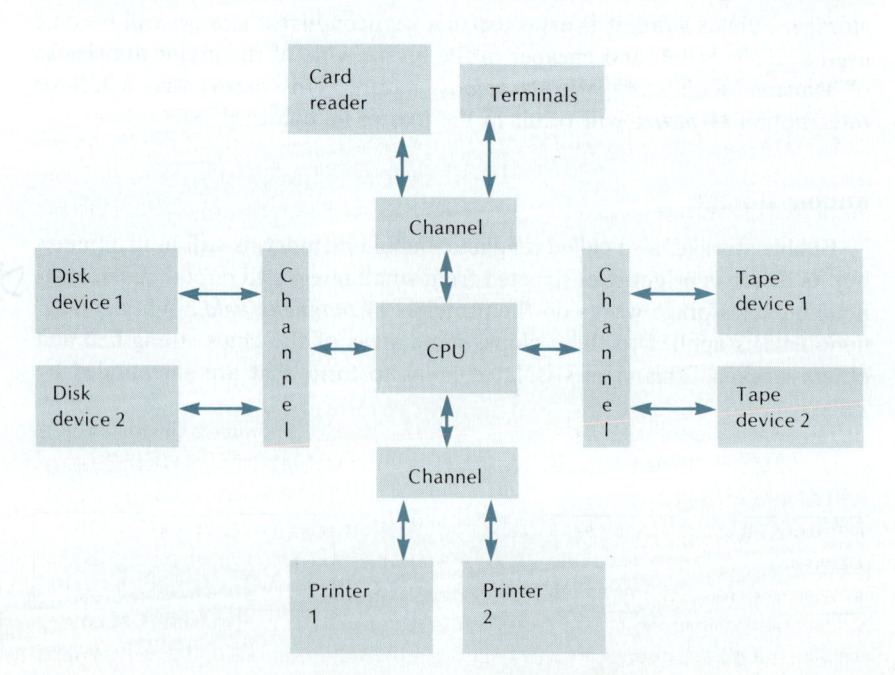

FIGURE 6–10
The use of channels

6 Central processing

processing unit from being idle most of the time? In part, these problems have been solved by using *channels* and *buffers*.

A **channel** is a device that coordinates the flow of data to and from the central processing unit. A channel may coordinate several devices and there may be several channels that interact with one central processing unit. This is shown in Figure 6–10.

In Figure 6–10, there are four channels that interact with the central processing unit. With channels, the central processing unit is able to operate more efficiently and more effectively. Furthermore, there is less idle time when the channels handle the data flow rather than the central processing unit.

To help to eliminate the problem of different operating speeds and transfer rates, small storage areas called **buffers** are used. The data from any sending device is fed into a buffer at its speed, and then when enough data is collected in the buffer, it is sent to a receiving device at its speed. In other words, this small temporary storage area literally acts as a buffer between two computer components with different operating speeds or transfer rates.

SUMMARY

The heart or center of a computer system is the central processing unit (CPU). It controls the entire computer system and executes the instructions we give it. The CPU contains the central processor and the temporary storage device.

The central processor includes the control unit and the arithmetic/logic unit. The control unit directs and controls the operation of all of the devices in the computer system. The purpose of the arithmetic/logic unit is to make mathematical computations and logical decisions during the execution of a computer program. Arithmetic operations can be done in series or parallel, and the operation itself can be classified as fixed point or floating point.

Both the control unit and the arithmetic/logic unit require small storage areas called registers. Registers can be general purpose or special purpose. Some of the special purpose registers include accumulator registers, instruction registers, storage registers, and address registers.

The execution of an instruction involves two phases. The first phase is the instruction cycle, and the time it takes to complete this phase is called instruction time or I-Time. The second phase is the execution phase, and the time that it takes to perform this phase is called execution time or E-Time.

The temporary storage device is divided into four areas, which are input storage, output storage, instruction storage, and working storage. Each storage area is divided into a number of locations that contain data or instructions, and each location has an address. Storage locations can be either character addressable or word addressable. Character addressable has also been called variable-word length, and word addressable has been called fixed-word length. Storage areas can be random access memory (RAM), read only memory (ROM), or programmable read only memory (PROM). Temporary storage can also be volatile or nonvolatile depending on whether or not the contents of memory are destroyed with a loss of power.

Storage capacity can be measured in bits and bytes. A bit is one binary digit, and a byte is normally 8 bits. Other ways of measuring storage capacity include words, blocks, and nibbles. These terms may have slightly different definitions for different computer manufacturers.

Core storage is one of the older devices used for temporary storage. Core storage is made from small iron rings through which four wires are passed. Core storage is nonvolatile in nature.

Other popular temporary storage devices include semiconductor storage and bubble storage. In addition, other temporary storage devices are being developed such as photodigital storage, laser beam storage, charge-coupled devices, and electron beam access memory.

KEY TERMS AND CONCEPTS

Accumulator register	Firmware	Privileged register
Address register	Fixed-point operation	Programmable read only
Arithmetic/logic unit	Fixed-word length	memory (PROM)
Binary	Floating-point operation	Random access memory (RAM)
Bit	General purpose registers	Read only memory (ROM)
Bubble storage	Instruction cycle	Registers
Buffer	Instruction register	Restore wire
Byte	Instruction time	Semiconductor storage
Channel	Large scale integration (LSI)	Sensing wire
Character addressable	Microcode	Series operation
Charge-coupled device (CCD)	Microinstruction	Special purpose registers
Control unit	Nibble	Storage address
Core storage	Nondestructive	Storage location
Destructive	Nonvolatile	Storage register
Electronic beam access memory (EBAM)	OP Code	Temporary storage
	Operand	Variable-word length
Execution cycle	Parallel operation	Volatile
Execution time	Photodigital storage	Word addressable

QUESTIONS

6–1. What is the basic function of the control unit and arithmetic/logic unit?

6–2. Briefly describe the purpose of registers and accumulators. How are these used in the central processor?

6–3. What is the difference between instruction time and execution time?

6–4. Describe the difference between contents and the address of a particular storage location.

6–5. What is volatile and nonvolatile storage?

6–6. Describe the difference between RAM, ROM, and PROM.

6–7. Briefly describe the construction of core storage, semiconductor storage and bubble storage.

6–8. List some of the other temporary storage devices.

6–9. Briefly describe channels and buffers. How are they used in interfacing the central processing unit with other computer components?

MINIQUIZ

ANSWERS

1. F
2. F
3. T
4. T
5. F
6. T
7. F
8. F
9. T
10. F

True or False

_____ 1. Registers and accumulators are part of the permanent storage device.
_____ 2. Mathematical computations are performed by the control rods.
_____ 3. One of the functions of the arithmetic/logic unit is to make decisions during the execution of a program.
_____ 4. The operation code tells the central processor what has to be done.
_____ 5. Temporary storage is divided into input storage, output storage, instruction storage, and disk storage.
_____ 6. In a character addressable storage device, each character has one unique location with its own address.
_____ 7. A volatile storage device does not lose its contents with a loss of power.
_____ 8. Eight bytes is called one bit.
_____ 9. A charge-coupled device is an example of a temporary storage device.
_____ 10. To help eliminate the problem of different operating speeds and transfer rates, small storage areas called channels are used.

Is bubble memory finally ready to fly?

Without a doubt, the magnetic bubble memory is one of the most important new technologies now emerging for storing computer data—so important, in fact, that such giants as International Business Machines Corp. and Texas Instruments Inc. are basing much of their future strategy in information processing on the low-cost storage devices. The trouble is that the memory is taking far longer than anyone expected to get into production. Now Bell Telephone Laboratories Inc., which invented the technique more than a decade ago, has come up with a new design that could give bubble memories a strong push forward.

Because of its powerful potential, bubble memory development has accelerated in the past year or two at more than a half dozen U.S. companies, with the investments ranging from tens of millions of dollars to an estimated $100 million-plus at IBM. But nearly everyone working on bubbles—so called because data are stored in magnetic spots that look like bubbles floating on the tiny semiconductor chip—has run into one technical problem after another. And even Bell, IBM, and TI have had to back off from earlier predictions.

Bell's new design could make the bubble memory much easier and cheaper to build. And the key to its success will be low cost. Despite the bubble's other advantages—it is far more reliable, for example, than current mass memory units such as rotating-disk memories—no other factor will influence its growth so much as low prices, which the Bell development promises. For one thing, it eliminates the magnetic coils now needed to move the bubbles around the chip. Instead, Bell uses perforated metal plates that quadruple bubble density and cut package size by two thirds.

Conventional methods. As a result, bubble memories that can store as many as 500,000 characters (4 million bits) on a single fingernail-size chip should be available at a much earlier date, researchers predict. By contrast, the most powerful semiconductor chip now available can store 8,000 characters.

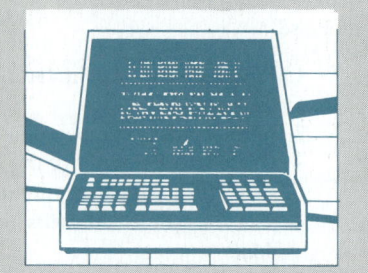

Bell disclosed its work on March 12 at a California technical conference, and researchers from other companies were impressed. "It makes the future brighter for the whole industry," says Richmond B. Clover, engineering vice president at Intel Corp.'s magnetic unit, which is expected to announce a commercial product shortly. Rockwell International Corp., which is racing to build up a major bubble business, likes the new technique because it is based on conventional semiconductor manufacturing methods. "It means we won't have to go back to the drawing boards (to develop the larger devices)," says John L. Archer, director of bubble memories at Rockwell. Observers are assuming that Bell Labs will license its new design to the rest of the industry.

IBM announced a design of its own that should speed the larger devices, but both the computer giant and Bell will build bubble memories only for their own equipment, not to sell in the outside market. That market is being chased by TI and Rockwell, the only two companies that thus far have commercial products, although they can store only 32,000 characters. It is a U.S. dominated technology for now, but the Japanese are also pouring money into bubble development and are expected to provide increasingly stiff competition.

Too optimistic. TI opened the commercial market two years ago but ran into trouble moving into production. As a result, its forecasts for how fast prices would decline and the market would grow were overly optimistic. However, TI is now building production rapidly and is shipping several thousand devices a month. Instead of hitting $100 million this year, as expected, the market is estimated by Venture Development Corp., a Wellesley (Mass.) consulting firm, to total only $11 million. But Venture and manufacturers alike see a sharp growth curve ahead; the consultant estimates 1983 sales at $231 million.

Source: Reprinted from the March 26, 1979 issue of *Business Week* by special permission, © 1979 by McGraw-Hill, Inc. All rights reserved.

Although bubble memories are much more expensive than standard disk memories, they already are finding their way into such products as cash registers, portable computer terminals, and communications equipment because of their small size and lack of moving parts.

Andrew H. Bobeck, leader of the Bell Labs team, figures that memories made with the new Bell design could be in production within a year, but other bubble developers are skeptical. Their consensus is that it will take nearer to three years and it will be the mid-1980s before the new design begins affecting sales. "Bubbles should now exceed previous market predictions" of $500 million in annual sales by the mid-1980s, predicts Rockwell's Archer.

DISCUSSION QUESTIONS

1. Why has there been a delay in the use of bubble memory devices in computer systems and equipment?
2. What advantages does bubble memory offer over other storage devices?

SUPPLEMENT 6
Data representation

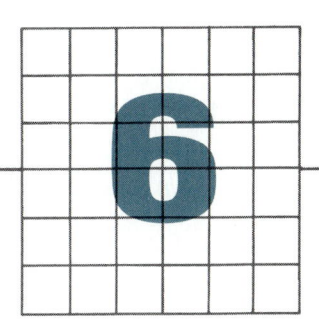

DECIMAL AND BINARY SYSTEMS
BINARY CODED DECIMAL SYSTEMS
THE HEXADECIMAL NUMBERING SYSTEM
PARITY CHECKING

After completing this supplement, you will be able to:

- Describe the decimal and binary numbering systems.
- Discuss the importance and use of binary coded decimal systems.
- List the uses of hexadecimal and parity checking.

In the last chapter, you were introduced to the concepts and construction of various temporary storage devices. In this supplement, we will investigate how these temporary storage devices store data and instructions.

DECIMAL AND BINARY SYSTEMS

The numbering system that we use every day is called the **decimal numbering system,** and it uses ten as the base. This is due to the fact that before the use of electrical and mechanical devices, human beings used ten fingers to count. The structure of our decimal numbering system is shown in Figure S6–1.

The ten allowable characters are:
0, 1, 2, 3, 4, 5, 6, 7, 8, 9

Thousand's	Hundred's	Ten's	One's	Places
10^3	10^2	10^1	10^0	Powers
1,000	100	10	1	Values
		1	3	The number 13

$(1)(10) + 3(1) = 13$

FIGURE S6–1
The decimal system

Like any other numbering system, the decimal numbering system is founded on the idea of places. Refer to the top row of Figure S6–1. As you can see, there is a place for the number of 1's, a place for the number of 10's, a place for the number of 100's, a place for the number of 1,000's, and so on. These places are determined by taking the base number ten to different powers. Ten to the zero power (10^0) is 1. This creates the first place. Ten to the first power (10^1) is 10, and this creates the place for the number of tens. Ten to the second power (10^2) is 100 and this creates a place for the number of one hundreds. Finally, ten to the third power (10^3) is 1,000 and this is how we arrive at the thousands place. The number 13, for example, means that there is one ten and three ones. This, of course, totals 13.

Computer systems do not have fingers to count, but they do have circuits, and a circuit can either be *on* or *off*. If the circuit or device is on, we can represent this with the number 1. If the circuit or device is off, we can represent this with the number 0. This is why the binary numbering system is used. The binary numbering system is generated in exactly the same way as the decimal numbering system. This is shown in Figure S6–2.

Instead of using ten as a base, the binary numbering system uses the

6 Supplement: Data representation

The two allowable characters are:
0, 1

Sixteens	Eights	Fours	Twos	Ones	Places
2^4	2^3	2^2	2^1	2^0	Powers
16	8	4	2	1	Values
	1	1	0	1	The number 13 in decimal expressed in binary

$(1)(8) \; (1)(4) + (0)(2) + (1)(1) = 13$

Converting the number 13 in the decimal system to binary

Step 1: $16 \overline{)13}$ with quotient 0 ← There are no 16's

Step 2: $8 \overline{)13}$ with quotient 1 ← There is one 8
$\quad\quad\quad \underline{8}$
$\quad\quad\quad 5$ ← 5 is the remainder

Step 3: $4 \overline{)5}$ with quotient 1 ← There is one 4
$\quad\quad\quad \underline{4}$
$\quad\quad\quad 1$ ← 1 is the remainder

Step 4: $2 \overline{)1}$ with quotient 0 ← There are no 2's

Step 5: $1 \overline{)1}$ with quotient 1 ← There is one 1

Step 6: The binary number is 1101

FIGURE S6–2
The binary system

number 2. Thus, the places are generated by taking the base 2 to different powers. Two to the zero power (2^0) is 1. This is the first place or the one's place. Two to the first power (2^1) is 2. This is the two's place. Two to the second power (2^2) is 4. This is the four's place. Two to the third power (2^3) is 8. This is the eight's place. Finally, two to the fourth power (2^4) is 16. This is the sixteen's place. Of course, this process could be continued.

In the binary numbering system, there are only two allowable characters. These characters are 0 and 1. But how do we convert the number *13* in the decimal numbering system to the equivalent number in binary? As you can see at the top of Figure S6–2, there is 1 eight, 1 four, 0 twos, and 1 one in the number 13. Therefore, the binary number 1101 is the same as the decimal number of 13. This approach can be used to convert any number in a given numbering system to another number in any other numbering system. All we have to do is to generate the places for a given numbering system and to determine how many of these places are required to make up the number we are trying to convert.

Here is another approach. See the bottom of Figure S6–2. The *first step* is to determine how many 16's there are in the number 13. Since there are no 16's, we ignore this place. See Figure S6–2. The *second step* is to determine how many 8's there are in 13. There is *one* 8 and the remainder is 5. The *third step* is to determine how many 4's there are in the remainder of 5. There is *one* 4 and the remainder is 1. The *fourth step* is to determine how many 2's there are in the remainder of 1. As you can see in Figure S6–2, there are *no* 2's. The *fifth step* is to realize that there is *one* 1 that remains. The *sixth step* is to read the binary number from top to bottom. Thus, the number 13 in the decimal system is the same as the number 1101 in the binary numbering system. Because you are using remainders this is called the *remainder system*.

The number 13 in decimal is the same as the number 1101 in binary. But how does this fact relate to temporary storage devices? If we were using core storage, we could magnetize the first core, magnetize the second core, leave the third core not magnetized, and magnetize the fourth core. If we let the number 1 represent a core being magnetized and the number 0 represent a core not being magnetized then 1101 would describe the current state or condition of the first four cores. In general, we can convert any decimal number into a binary number consisting of 0's and 1's. Then, we can turn circuits *on* or *off* to represent the 1's and 0's. One of the biggest disadvantages of using the binary numbering system is the fact that we cannot represent letters or other characters. To get around this disadvantage, **binary coded decimal** (BCD) systems were developed.

BINARY CODED DECIMAL SYSTEMS

The purpose of any binary coded decimal system is to convert every character that we use into a unique series of 1's and 0's. An example is the *4-bit binary coded decimal system* (4-bit BCD). This system is used to convert decimal numbers into a series of 0's and 1's. Refer to Figure S6–3.

As you can see, every decimal number has a unique series of 0's and 1's that are used to represent it. Each digit in a decimal number will require four digits of 0's and 1's. For example, the number 1 is represented by three 0's followed by a 1. The number 3 is represented by 0011. Therefore, the number 13 in a 4-bit BCD system would be 0001 (representing the number 1) 0011 (representing the number 3). In other words, the number 13 would be 0001 0011.

In order to include letters and special characters, the 4-bit BCD has been extended to 6-bit BCD, 7-bit BCD, and a number of different versions of 8-bit BCD. Again, the approach is the same. Every character is represented

6 *Supplement: Data representation*

Decimal numbers	4-bit BCD places			
	8	4	2	1
0	0	0	0	0
1	0	0	0	1
2	0	0	1	0
3	0	0	1	1
4	0	1	0	0
5	0	1	0	1
6	0	1	1	0
7	0	1	1	1
8	1	0	0	0
9	1	0	0	1

0001   0011 ←— The number 13
  ↑   ↑   in 4-bit BCD
  1   3

FIGURE S6–3
The 4-bit BCD system

by a unique series of 0's and 1's. Some of the more popular binary coded decimal systems appear in Figure S6–4.

Figure S6–4 shows a 6-bit system and a 7-bit system. The 7-bit system, ASCII-7, was developed by the *American National Standards Institute* (ANSI) in the 1960s to bring about greater compatibility among the various computer systems. As you can see, there is also an ASCII-8 coding system. EBCDIC, which stands for *extended binary coded decimal interchange code,* was developed by IBM. Today, the most popular coding systems are the 8-bit BCD systems. These systems allow a large number of characters to be represented. Furthermore, it is possible to pack two numbers into one 8-bit code. This is done by breaking the *8*-bit BCD code into *two 4*-bit BCD codes. When two numbers are placed in one *8*-bit BCD code, this is called *packing.* Of course, packing is only possible with an *8*-bit BCD code.

THE HEXADECIMAL NUMBERING SYSTEM

Occasionally, it is necessary to print the exact contents of temporary storage. Since temporary storage consists of thousands of on-off devices, this means printing thousands of 0's and 1's. Trying to decipher a long list of 0's and 1's is difficult indeed. As a result, the hexadecimal numbering system is commonly used in printing or *dumping* the contents of temporary storage. The *hexadecimal numbering system* is a numbering system to the base 16 (*Hexa* = 6, *decimal* = 10, thus *Hexadecimal* = 16). The hexadecimal numbering system requires 16 different characters. The first 10 characters are the numbers 0 through 9, but how do we represent the remaining 6 characters? In the hexadecimal system, they are represented by the letters A, B, C, D, E, and F. The hexadecimal numbering system is displayed in Figure S6–5.

As you can see, four binary digits can be represented by one hexadecimal number. The number 0001 in binary, for example, is the hexadecimal number

Characters (place)	4-bit BCD 8421	6-bit BCD BA8421	ASCII-7 CBA8421	EBCDIC 84218421	ASCII-8 84218421
0	0000	001010	0110000	11110000	10110000
1	0001	000001	0110001	11110001	10110001
2	0010	000010	0110010	11110010	10110010
3	0011	000011	0110011	11110011	10110011
4	0100	000100	0110100	11110100	10110100
5	0101	000101	0110101	11110101	10110101
6	0110	000110	0110110	11110110	10110110
7	0111	000111	0110111	11110111	10110111
8	1000	001000	0111000	11111000	10111000
9	1001	001001	0111001	11111001	10111001
A		110001	1000001	11000001	11000001
B		110010	1000010	11000010	11000010
C		110011	1000011	11000011	11000011
D		110100	1000100	11000100	11000100
E		110101	1000101	11000101	11000101
F		110110	1000110	11000110	11000110
G		110111	1000111	11000111	11000111
H		111000	1001000	11001000	11001000
I		111001	1001001	11001001	11001001
J		100001	1001010	11010001	11001010
K		100010	1001011	11010010	11001011
L		100011	1001100	11010011	11001100
M		100100	1001101	11010100	11001101
N		100101	1001110	11010101	11001110
O		100110	1001111	11010110	11001111
P		100111	1010000	11010111	11010000
Q		101000	1010001	11011000	11010001
R		101001	1010010	11011001	11010010
S		010010	1010011	11100010	11010011
T		010011	1010100	11100011	11010100
U		010100	1010101	11100100	11010101
V		010101	1010110	11100101	11010110
W		010110	1010111	11100110	11010111
X		010111	1011000	11100111	11011000
Y		011000	1011001	11101000	11011001
Z		011001	1011010	11101001	11011010
+		010000	0101011	01001110	10101011
−		100000	1011111	01101101	11011111
,		011011	0101100	01101011	10101100
.		111011	0101110	01001011	10101110

FIGURE S6–4
Binary coded decimal systems

1. 1111 in binary is the hexadecimal character F. Using the hexadecimal numbering system, we can reduce the total space required in dumping storage contents by a factor of 4 over binary, while making it easier for humans to read.

PARITY CHECKING

Millions of pieces of data are stored in both temporary and permanent storage devices. This data is constantly being moved, modified, and manipulated. Thus, there is a need to check the accuracy of the data that is stored within the computer system. But how is this accuracy maintained? One approach is to use *parity checking*. Under this system, an additional parity

6 Supplement: Data representation

Hexadecimal	Binary	Decimal
0	0000	0
1	0001	1
2	0010	2
3	0011	3
4	0100	4
5	0101	5
6	0110	6
7	0111	7
8	1000	8
9	1001	9
A	1010	10
B	1011	11
C	1100	12
D	1101	13
E	1110	14
F	1111	15

FIGURE S6–5
The hexadecimal numbering system

bit is added to existing binary coded decimal systems. Computer manufacturers can either use *even parity* or *odd parity*. With an even parity system, the total number of bits must be an even number. With an odd parity system, the total number of "on" or "1" bits (including the parity bit) must be an odd number. This concept is shown in Figure S6–6.

In an even parity system, if the total number of "on" or "1" bits is already even, the parity bit is zero. If, on the other hand, the total number of "on"

Even parity for the letter A

Parity bit	The letter A in EBCDIC or ASCII-8	Total of the "on" or "1" bits
1	11000001	4

Even parity

Odd parity for the letter A

Parity bit	The letter A in EBCDIC or ASCII-8	Total of the "on" or "1" bits
0	11000001	3

Odd parity

FIGURE S6–6
Parity checking

or "1" bits is odd, the parity bit is turned on to the "1" or "on" position. This makes the total number of "on" or "1" bits, including the parity bit, an even number. The same type of concept applies to odd parity. When the total number of "on" or "1" bits is already odd, the odd parity is left off. When the total number of "1" or "on" bits is even, the parity bit is turned "on" to the "1" position such that the total number of "1" or "on" bits including the parity bit will be an odd number.

SUMMARY

Because we have ten fingers, we use a numbering system to the base ten. Computers, on the other hand, are constructed from electronic components that can be either on or off. If we let the number 1 represent a situation where a circuit or component is on and the number 0 represents a situation when a circuit or component is off, the binary numbering system can be used to represent the contents or states of a computer system. One of the limitations of using binary is the inability to represent letters and other special symbols.

Binary coded decimal systems are used by most computer systems to represent data and the states of the various components of a computer system. There are 4-bit, 6-bit, 7-bit, and 8-bit binary coded decimal systems. The 4-bit system, however, can only be used to represent numbers. When using an 8-bit system, it is possible to represent two numbers in one 8-bit code. Each number is translated into a 4-bit code. This is called packing, and it allows the storage of numbers to take half of the storage space when an 8-bit code is used.

When the contents of a storage device is to be dumped or displayed, it is sometimes useful to use the hexadecimal numbering system. This system allows four binary digits to be represented with one hexadecimal digit. The hexadecimal digits are the numbers 0 through 9 and the letters A, B, C, D, E, and F.

Parity is a checking procedure that allows the computer system to automatically check the accuracy of data as it is being transferred from one device to another. This is done by adding a parity bit. With even parity, a parity bit is added to make the total number of "on" or "1" bits sum to an even number, including the parity bit. With odd parity, a parity bit is added to make the total of "on" or "1" bits equal an odd number including the parity bit.

KEY TERMS AND CONCEPTS

ASCII-7	Decimal	4-Bit BCD
ASCII-8	EBCDIC	6-Bit BCD
Binary	Hexadecimal	7-Bit BCD
Binary Coded Decimal	Parity	8-Bit BCD

6 Supplement: Data representation

QUESTIONS

S6–1. Why is a binary coded system used in representing data and instructions in a temporary storage device?

S6–2. What is the purpose and function of the hexadecimal numbering system?

S6–3. Define parity checking and discuss how it is used.

ANSWERS

1. F
2. T
3. F
4. F
5. T
6. F
7. T
8. T
9. T
10. T

MINIQUIZ

True or False

_____ 1. The binary numbering system allows for two characters, which are 1 and 2.

_____ 2. The binary numbering system can be used to represent numbers in a computer system.

_____ 3. 4-bit BCD can be used to represent numbers and letters in a computer system.

_____ 4. Packing is the process of placing two 8-bit BCD codes into one 4-bit BCD code.

_____ 5. Extended binary coded decimal interchange code is an example of an 8-bit BCD.

_____ 6. Hexadecimal is a numbering system to the base 18.

_____ 7. The number 10 in the decimal numbering system is the same as the number 1010 in the binary numbering system.

_____ 8. The symbol A in hexadecimal is the same as the number 10 in the decimal numbering system.

_____ 9. 7-bit BCD can be used to represent letters, numbers, and other special characters.

_____ 10. The hexadecimal numbering system can represent four binary digits.

Permanent storage devices 7

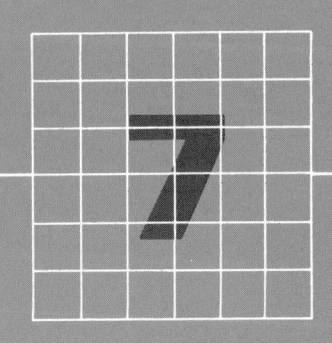

FUNDAMENTALS OF PERMANENT STORAGE DEVICES
THE CARD SYSTEM
    Card concepts
    Card devices
THE TAPE SYSTEM
    Tape concepts
    Tape devices
THE DISK SYSTEM
    Disk concepts
    Disk devices
A COMPARISON OF PERMANENT STORAGE DEVICES
    The card system
    The tape system
    The disk system

After completing Chapter 7, you will be able to:

- Discuss the card system
- Discuss the tape system
- Discuss the disk system
- Compare the advantages and disadvantages of card, tape, and disk systems.

Core storage and semiconductor storage, discussed in the last chapter, provide the CPU with extremely fast access to data. Unfortunately, these devices are too expensive to be used to store all of the data and programs that are used in a computerized system. Thus, these types of storage devices are temporary storage devices that only hold the programs and data that are currently being processed. In addition, a computer system needs one or more devices to hold all of the data and programs on a permanent basis. These types of devices are called **permanent storage devices**. They are slower than temporary storage devices, but they are much less expensive.

A common way to classify a computer system is according to the main type of permanent storage device that is used. By far, the most popular permanent storage devices are computer cards, magnetic tape, and the disk. A computer using primarily cards for permanent storage is called a *card system*, a computer using primarily magnetic tape for permanent storage is called a *tape system*, and a computer using primarily disks for permanent storage is called a *disk system*.

FUNDAMENTALS OF PERMANENT STORAGE DEVICES

Like temporary storage devices, permanent storage devices have a number of properties in common. Some of these properties are the same. For example, most permanent storage devices have *destructive reading* characteristics. This means that if data is read, the previous data that is stored at the same location is lost or destroyed. The major exception to this is the card system, where each card can only be used once. Like temporary storage, all permanent storage devices have *nondestructive writing*. This means that data can be written from a permanent storage device to any other device without disturbing or destroying the original data. Permanent storage devices use *parity checking* to assure the accuracy of the data. The concept of parity checking was discussed in the supplement to Chapter 6.

There are also a few characteristics that are unique to permanent storage devices. Since a permanent storage device holds all of the data and programs for a computer system, it is usually a good idea to have *backup* and *security* files. These files are merely copies of the original files. The backup files are used in case of accidental destruction of the data, and the security files are stored in a fireproof and secure location in case of a disaster such as a fire, tornado, and so forth. The ease of creating backup and security files are important considerations in the selection of a permanent storage device. Another important consideration is whether or not the device allows *direct access* or *sequential access*. The disk, which is a *direct access storage device* (DASD), allows the computer system to locate the needed data directly without searching through a large amount of data. Card and tape systems are *sequential access storage devices* (SASD). These concepts were discussed in Chapter 2.

Although permanent storage devices perform the same types of functions, how they perform these functions differs considerably. *Speed, capacity, ease of operation,* and *cost* are only a few of the factors that should be carefully

7 Permanent storage devices

analyzed before a permanent storage system is selected. We will begin our discussion with card systems.

THE CARD SYSTEM

In 1887, Herman Hollerith developed a punched card system to process the 1890 census. Since that time, computer cards have been an important factor in computer systems. Although tape and disk systems are gaining in popularity, a large number of organizations are still using computer cards as a permanent storage medium.

Card concepts *sequential*

For many applications, it is possible to place one *record* on each card. Records and data organization were discussed in Part I. Thus, a card is also called a *unit record,* and card devices are called *unit record devices.* The oldest type of computer card, the *standard card* or the *Hollerith card,* has 80 columns in which data can be placed. One column is used to record one character, and therefore the standard 80-column card can hold a maximum of 80 characters. A standard 80-column card is shown in Figure 7–1.

Carefully study Figure 7–1. As you can see, all characters are printed at the top of the card. Card devices read the holes that are directly below each character. Indeed, each character has a unique pattern of holes. There are 12 positions in each column where a hole may be punched. The 12 positions for all 80 columns make up 12 rows across the computer card.

Each of these rows is specified by a row number. The bottom row is the 9 row, and since it is on the bottom of the card, the bottom of the card is called the *9 edge.* The 8 row is above the 9 row, the 7 row is above the 8 row, and so on. The 0 row through the 9 row are called the *digit rows* in which a *digit punch* may be placed. The number 0 is represented by a punch in the 0 row, the number 1 is represented by a punch in the 1 row, the number 2 is represented by a punch in the 2 row, and so forth.

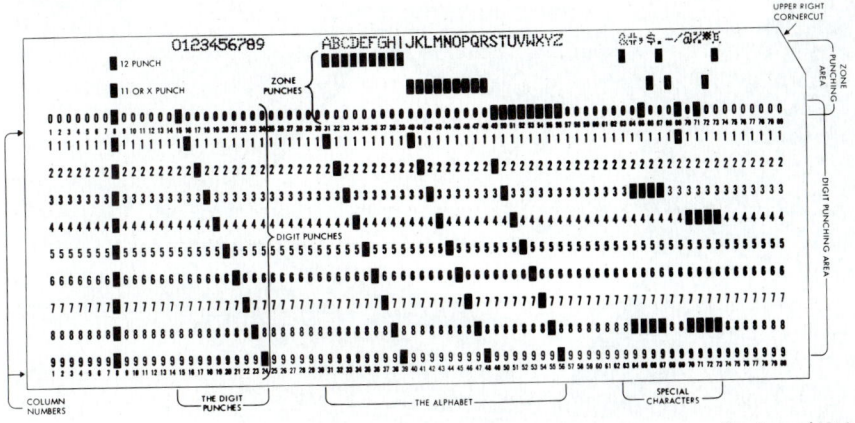

FIGURE 7–1
The 80-column card

Courtesy of IBM

To represent some letters or special characters, two punches in the same column are required. One punch is in a digit position, discussed above, and the other punch is in a *zone position*. There are 3 zone positions for any column. They make up 3 zone rows for the computer card. The top punch position is called the 12 punch, and the top row is called the 12 row. The *12 edge* means the *top edge* of the card. The 11 or x row is below the 12 row. Below the 11 row is the 0 row. These are the 3 zone rows or punch positions. The 0 row is used as both a digit row and a zone row.

In 1969, IBM introduced a new type of computer card used initially on the IBM System 3. This card is smaller in size, yet, it can hold more data than the standard 80-column card. Figure 7–2 reveals the relative size of these cards.

The new IBM card is divided into a *print area* and a *punch area*. There are 3 rows in each area with 32 possible columns for printing and punching in each. Thus, the total number of characters that can be placed on this new card is a 96 (96 = [3 rows] [32 columns/row]). Thus, this card is called the *96-column card*.

There are 3 tiers or areas in the *punching area*, where holes are punched to correspond with the data printed in the printing area. Tier 1 is the punching

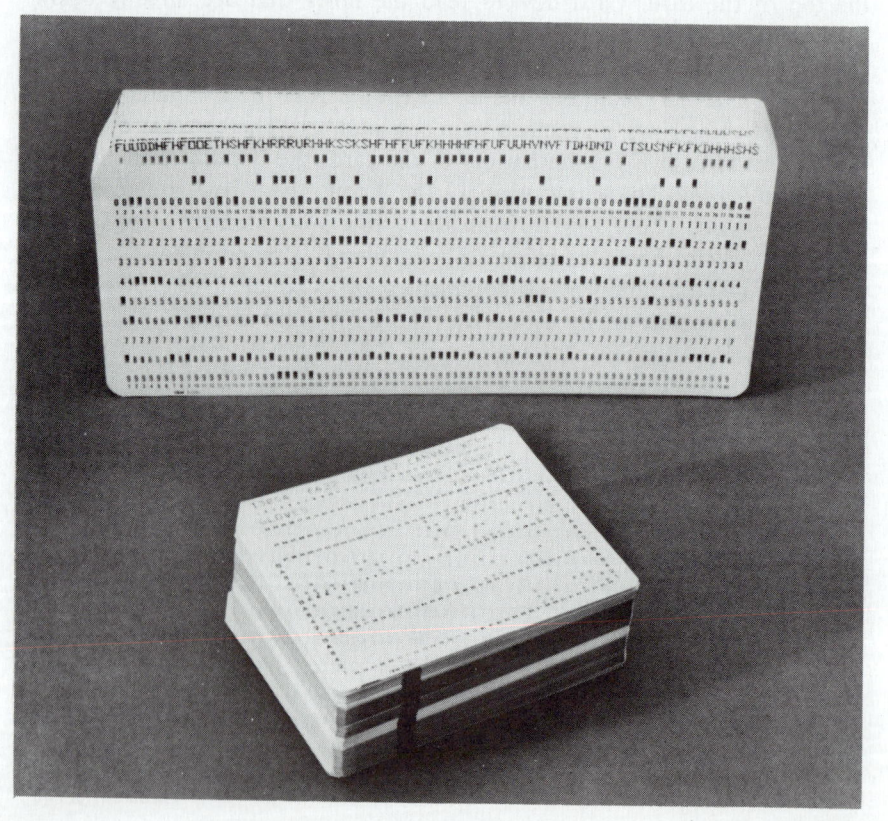

FIGURE 7–2
The 80- and 96-column card

Photo courtesy of IBM

7 Permanent storage devices

area for the top printing row, tier 2 is the punching area for the middle printing row, and tier 3 is the punching area for the bottom printing row. For any tier, holes are punched directly below the appropriate character in the printing area.

There are 6 punching positions in every column for all 3 tiers. These 6 punching areas make up the 6 punching rows for each tier. For any tier, the B row is the top row, the A row is next, and this is followed by the 8 row, the 4 row, the 2 row, and the 1 row. B and A are *zone punches,* and 8, 4, 2, 1 are the *digit punches.* These numbers correspond to the place values for the binary numbering system. Refer to Chapter 6. As with the 80-column card, every character is represented by a unique pattern of holes.

In order to use computer cards as a permanent storage media, a number of devices or components are needed. A discussion of these components is next.

Card devices

To use cards for permanent storage, a number of devices are needed to read, write, and manipulate computer cards. With earlier computer systems, one device was usually used for one specific operation. A typical **card reader** is shown in Figure 7–3.

FIGURE 7–3
A card reader

Photo courtesy of IBM

Card readers come in a number of different types with varying characteristics. A card reader can be either *serial* or *parallel.* A serial card reader starts at the side of the card and reads one character or column after another in series. A parallel card reader starts at the top or bottom edge, and reads all characters or columns at one time in parallel. A serial card reader is normally slower than a parallel card reader. Card readers can also be classified as brush type or photoelectric type. This is shown in Figure 7–4.

A. Photoelectric type

B. Brush type with compare circuitry

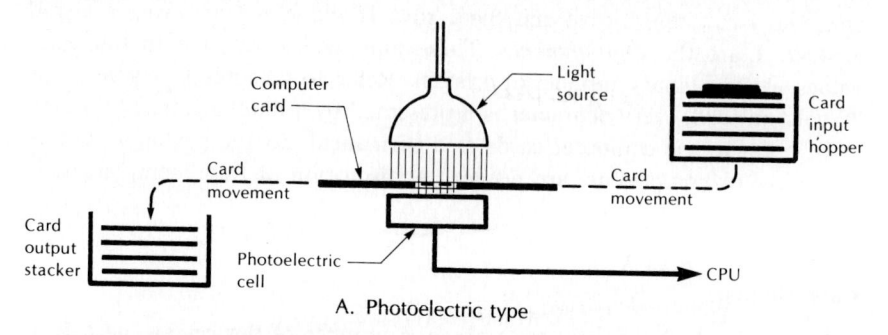

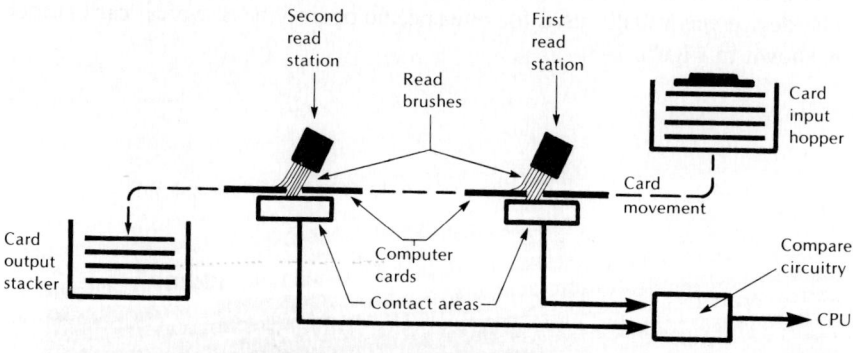

FIGURE 7–4
Photoelectric and brush type readers

In a **brush-type reader** a series of brushes will touch contact points completing an electrical circuit and sending a current to temporary storage whenever a hole is encountered in the computer card. A **photoelectric-type reader** sends a current to temporary storage whenever light passes through a hole in a computer card and shines on a photoelectric cell on the other side. Moreover, some card readers have two read situations. The second read station checks the accuracy of the first read station. See Figure 7–4B.

In order to maintain master files, permanent data and programs, a **card punch** device is needed. Some card punch devices have a read station that reads and checks each card after it has been punched for accuracy. Figure 7–5 displays a card punch device.

Another commonly used device is the **card sorter.** This device normally has one input hopper and several output bins. Card sorters are not connected

7 *Permanent storage devices*

FIGURE 7–5
A card punch device

Photo courtesy of IBM

electronically to the computer system, and thus they are not a part of the computer system.

In recent years, a card device that has the ability to perform several operations has been developed. These devices are called *multifunction card machines,* and they are available for both the 80-column and 96-column card. The major advantage of multifunction card machines is that they can significantly reduce the amount of card handling and manipulating that is required to perform a given data processing task. A multifunction card machine is shown in Figure 7–6.

Most multifunction card machines have two input hoppers and four or five output stackers. Master-file cards can be placed in one input hopper, and transaction-file cards can be placed in the other input hopper. The output stackers can be used for a number of purposes. For example, transaction-file cards can be placed in one output stacker, outdated master-file cards can be placed in a second output stacker, and the updated master-file cards can be placed in a third output stacker. Without a multifunction card machine, updating a master file on cards would have required many more steps and much more card handling.

As with cards, there are a number of different types of magnetic tapes and tape devices. In this section, we will delve into tape concepts and devices.

THE TAPE SYSTEM

FIGURE 7–6
A multifunction card machine

Photo courtesy of IBM

Tape concepts

The standard reel of magnetic tape is ½ inch wide and about 2,400 feet long. Most magnetic tapes are constructed by using a flexible plastic base upon which a red-brown magnetic material is placed. The layout of a typical magnetic tape is shown in Figure 7–7.

A *leader*, which contains no data, is at both ends of the tape. The **beginning-of-tape (BOT) marker** is a reflective marker that indicates the beginning of the usable tape, and the **end-of-tape** (EOT) marker is a reflective marker that indicates the end of the usable tape. Before the data, you will usually find a *volume* and a *header label*. The volume label identifies the tape. In most cases, each tape will have its own identification number or code. The header label describes the data that is stored on the tape. Typically it includes the name of the data file, the date when the data was placed on the tape, and the date when the data can be erased from the tape or destroyed. The *trailer label* contains the number of records in the tape along with the same information as the header label. Because it takes time for the tape device to stop and start when reading or writing information on the tape, it is necessary to have gaps between each record or each block of records. This is shown in Figure 7–8.

When each record is separated with a gap, the records may be written and read individually, and the gaps are called **interrecord gaps** (IRG). When there are several records in one block, and each block of records is written

FIGURE 7–7
A typical tape layout

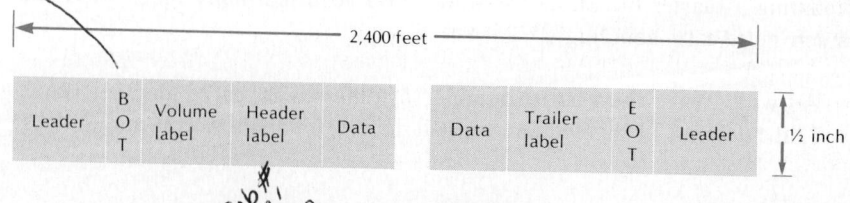

Leader	B O T	Volume label	Header label	Data		Data	Trailer label	E O T	Leader	½ inch

← 2,400 feet →

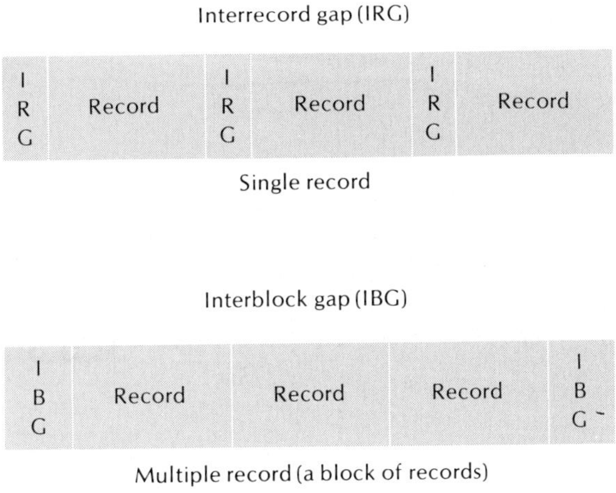

7 Permanent storage devices

Interrecord gap (IRG)

| IRG | Record | IRG | Record | IRG | Record |

Single record

Interblock gap (IBG)

| IBG | Record | Record | Record | IBG |

Multiple record (a block of records)

FIGURE 7–8
Interrecord and interblock gaps

or read at one time, the gaps are called **interblock gaps** (IBG). In general, the gaps are usually between a half inch and one inch in length. The number of records that are contained in one block is called the *blocking factor*. The tape at the bottom of Figure 7–8, for example, has a blocking factor of three. Since an entire block is read at one time, the number of records in a block depends on the storage capacity of temporary storage. Without blocking it is likely that a large portion of the tape will be empty gaps. The amount of data that can be placed over a given length of tape is called the *tape density*. Of course, a high tape density is desirable. This density is usually expressed in bytes (or characters) per inch. Tape densities can range from under 500 bytes per inch to 6,250 bytes per inch. Each letter, number, and special character is represented by a series of magnetized spots in a narrow column. This is similar to how data is represented on a computer card. Instead of holes in the card, magnetic tape uses magnetized spots on the tape. The rows in a tape that can contain magnetized spots are called *tracks*. In most tapes, there is one track for *parity checking*. Thus, if a 6 bit BCD code is used and one bit is used for parity, 7 tracks are required. This is shown in Figure 7–9.

The tape configuration shown in Figure 7–9 contains 7 invisible tracks, which are represented by dotted lines. The top track is used for parity checking. Since this system uses even parity, the magnetized bits in any column must total to an even number. Since this checks the parity of each column, this is called *vertical parity*. Vertical parity allows the computer to check the accuracy of each character. In addition to vertical parity, most tape systems use *longitudinal* or *horizontal parity*. The number of magnetized bits in any track or row must total to an even number. This is accomplished by adding a parity column. When the total number of magnetized bits in any row or track do not total to an even number, a parity bit in the parity column is magnetized. Figure 7–9 reveals a 7-track tape system that uses even parity. If an 8 bit BCD code is used, the tape will have 9 tracks, where

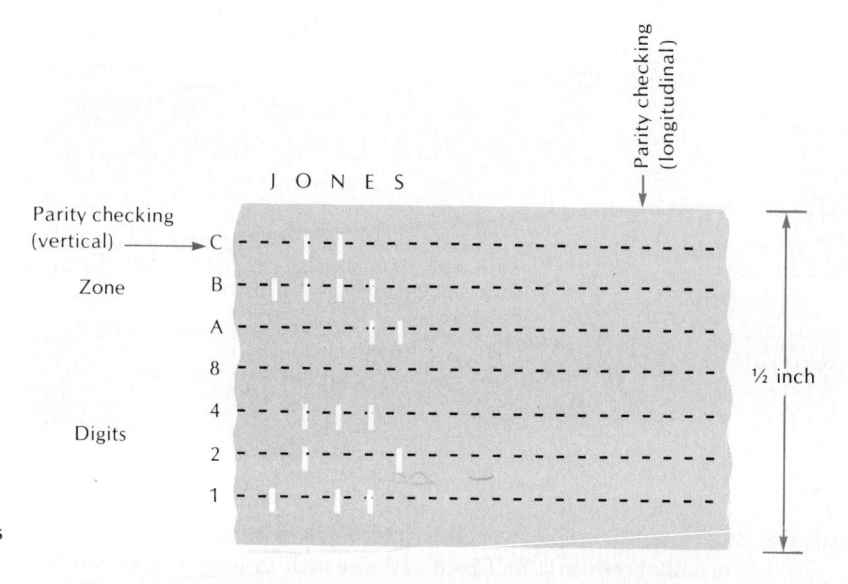

FIGURE 7–9
7-track tape with even parity where dotted lines reveal the position of the 7 invisible tracks

one track is used for parity checking. Of course, odd parity systems can be used for both 7-track and 9-track tapes. The concepts of BCD codes and parity checking were introduced to you in the previous supplement.

There are a number of different types of tapes in addition to the standard magnetic tape. Some tapes are one inch wide, and other tapes are longer or shorter than the standard magnetic tapes. There are also *cassette tapes* that are almost identical in structure to the cassette tapes that you would find in a home or car stereo system.

Tape devices

The **tape drive** is the basic tape device. These drives come in a variety of types and capacities. A tape drive that is used with a standard magnetic tape is shown in Figure 7–10.

Tape drives are made to read or write one block of records at a time, and they usually have the ability to backspace and to skip over a faulty or defective part of a tape. Moreover, some tape devices have the ability to read and write data while moving forwards and backwards.

When the tape drive is being used to read data, the operator pushes a start button, and the tape drive locates the beginning-of-tape (BOT) marker. Then, the tape drive is under the control of the program. The program reads the data contained on the volume and header label. The program checks to make sure that the tape that has been mounted is the correct tape. If the correct tape has been mounted, the program proceeds to read the appropriate data from the tape, otherwise the operator is alerted. At the end of the tape, the program encounters the trailer label. If all of the records on the

7   *Permanent storage devices*

FIGURE 7–10
A tape drive

Photo courtesy of IBM

tape have been read, the program checks to make sure that the total number of records read are the same as the total number of records that are on the tape.

When the tape drive is being used to write data on a tape, the operator must place a *file protection ring* on the reel of magnetic tape. If the file protection ring is not in place, the tape drive will not write data on the tape. After the tape is mounted with the file protection ring in place, the operator pushes the start button, and the tape drive locates the beginning of tape marker. After this, the tape is under the control of the computer program. The program reads the data on the volume and header label. If the wrong tape is mounted, or if the date for tape eradication or destruction is not passed, the operator is alerted. These procedures help prevent the accidental destruction of data. After this, the program proceeds to write data on the tape. The total number of records are written on the trailer label.

One of the most important characteristics of a tape drive is the speed at which it can read or write data. This speed is normally measured in bytes or characters per second. For example, some tape drives can read and write 50,000 bytes per second. This transfer rate, however, can be misleading. In addition to the actual time that is required to read one or more records, time is required to start and stop the tape. It might take the typical tape drive ten milliseconds to start or stop. This starting and stopping normally occurs between each block of records, and the starting and stopping time can be greater than the time it takes to actually read or write the data.

THE DISK SYSTEM

Many applications require immediate and direct access to data. An airline or hotel reservation system would not work very well if you had to wait several minutes or hours to determine how many seats or rooms were still available. These types of applications must be able to read data from and write data to a permanent storage device in a few seconds instead of a few minutes or hours. In addition, many managers and decision makers want immediate access to permanent data. It is no wonder that disk devices, which have the ability to satisfy these needs, have become common place.

Disk concepts

Although disk devices vary in size and capacity, they function in basically the same way. A disk system consists of one or more circular platters or disks. When mounted on a disk drive, these disks or platters rotate at a high speed. As the disks rotate, read/write heads access data on the surface of the disk. Disk surfaces are covered with a magnetic material. A typical disk surface is shown in Figure 7–11.

Each disk surface is divided into a number of concentric circles called

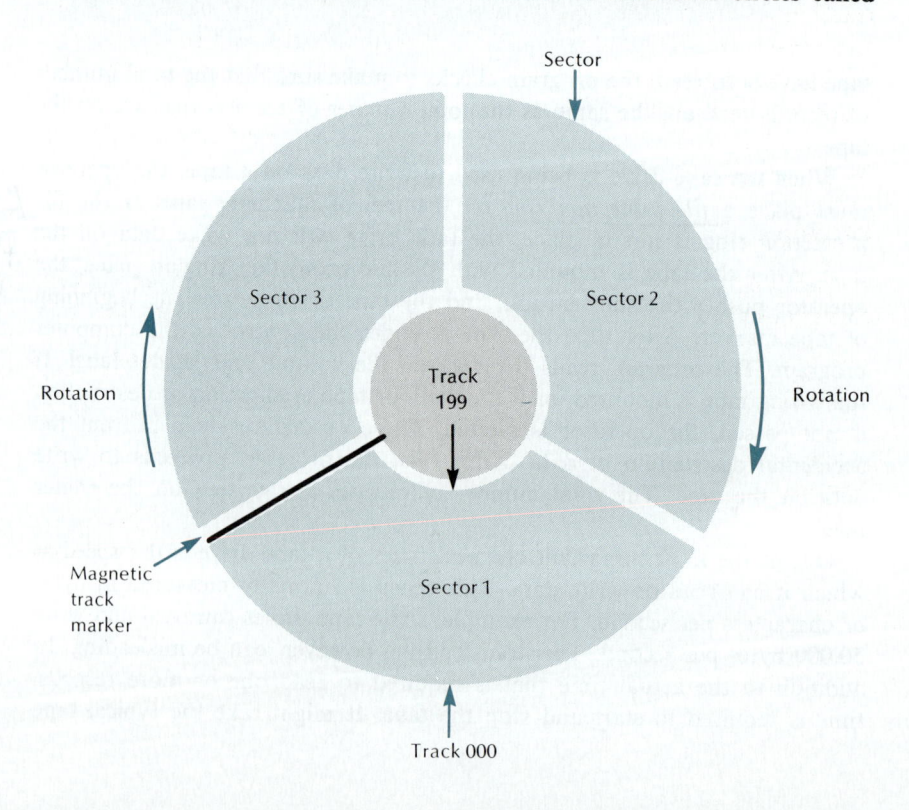

FIGURE 7–11
A disk surface

tracks. The tracks are numbered consecutively from 000, which is the outside track, to the inside track. In the disk surface shown in Figure 7–11, there are 200 tracks. The innermost track is numbered 199. Although the size of the tracks decrease as you move to the center of the disk, each track can hold the same number of characters or bytes. Each character is represented by a series of magnetized spots along the track. Depending on the number of bytes or characters per record, the typical track can hold one or more records. The portion or part of any track that holds one record is called a *sector*. As seen in Figure 7–11, there are 3 sectors or 3 records per track. Thus, this particular disk surface can hold 600 records (600 = [200 tracks] [3 records/track]).

Some disks use a *magnetic track marker,* which is a magnetic line running from the center of the disk to the outside edge. The magnetic track marker indicates where the data begins on any track. The computer is then able to locate data on a track by knowing how far the data is from the magnetic track marker.

The normal disk contains six or more disk platters with enough space between them to allow for one or more read/write heads. Because the top surface of the top disk and the bottom surface of the bottom disk can be scratched or damaged when being handled, these surfaces normally do not contain any data. When data is placed on the disk, one track is filled with records. This track might be track 100. After this track is filled, the same track (track 100) on the next disk surface is filled with data. Then, the same track on another disk surface is filled with data, and so on. In other words, the same track on all disk surfaces is filled before moving to another track. If you draw dotted lines on the same track for all of the disk surfaces, the drawing looks like a cylinder and is called a *cylinder of data*. See Figure 7–12.

Disk devices

The actual disks described in the above section are placed on devices, called **disk drives.** All of the electronic circuitry and other components that

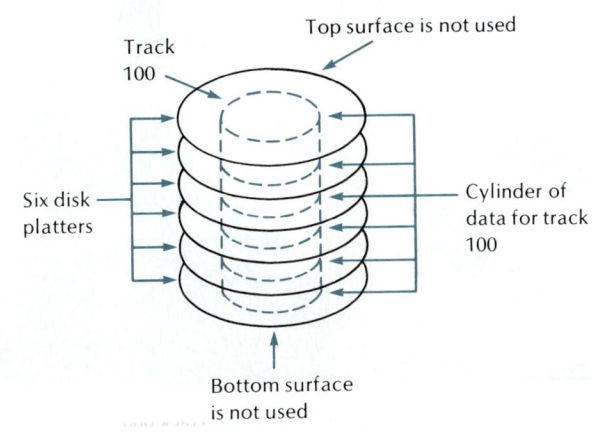

FIGURE 7–12
Cylinders of data

are needed to rotate and read and write data from the disk are part of the disk drive. The disks can either be *removable* or *nonremovable,* and they can store from 7 to over 300 million characters. A removable disk being mounted on a disk drive is shown in Figure 7–13. A plastic cover is over the disk surface. The read/write heads on a disk can be either *movable* or *fixed.* If the read/write heads are fixed, one read/write head is needed for each track. When the read/write heads are movable, all of the heads move together on one arm. This is why data is stored in cylinders of data as shown in Figure 7–12. To access data, all of the read/write heads move together to the appropriate track. One read/write head is turned on for the track containing the first record, to be read. The disk device waits for the first record contained on one of the sectors to rotate under the read/write head. This waiting time is called *rotational delay.* When the record is below the head, it is read and transferred to temporary storage in most cases. This is how the first record is read. When all of the records on the track have been read, the read/write head for the disk surface is turned off, and the next read/write head is turned on for the next disk surface on the same track. This reading process continues until all of the data is read on all disk surfaces for the same track.

Writing data on the disk takes place using the same procedures as in the read process. To check for accuracy, some disk devices automatically read each piece of data after it is written on the disk. To allow for additional data at a future date, most disks contain *overflow areas.* One or more disk surfaces are not used when the original data is placed on the disks. These

FIGURE 7–13
A disk device

Photo courtesy of Honeywell Information Systems

surfaces are the overflow areas. When additional data needs to be recorded at a future date, these overflow areas or surfaces are then used.

One of the advantages of the disk over tape and card systems is the ability to directly access data. <u>On a disk, direct access is normally accomplished by recording a reference point called a *key* in front of each record.</u> The key is normally a part of the record. An employee number would be a good key for an employee record, and an inventory part number would be a good key for an inventory part record. Then, when you want a particular record, you give the computer the appropriate key, and the computer directly retrieves the entire record. Since a record is stored on a sector of a particular track located on one of the disk surfaces, the computer must be able to convert the key, such as an inventory part number, to the exact sector, track, and disk surface at which the record is located. This is accomplished using a *transformation algorithm*. The algorithm or procedure takes the key and converts it to the location where the appropriate record is located.

While the disk has the ability to directly access data, it also can be used to store data *sequentially*. With this type of data organization, the data is stored in sequential order. When processing a large amount of data in sequence, it is faster to use sequential data organization than direct access organization with keys and transformation algorithms. The disadvantage of sequential access is that it is very time consuming to search the entire disk sequentially looking for only one piece of data.

A compromise between direct and sequential access is the *indexed sequential access method* (ISAM). With ISAM, the data is stored sequentially to handle applications where all of the data is to be processed sequentially. Then to access an individual piece of data, one or more indices are used. This is like using an index in a book. You look up the topic in the index of a book, turn to the appropriate page, and start reading the page until you encounter the topic you want, which you read in detail. With an indexed sequential system, indices are kept for the data. When one record or piece of data is to be retrieved, the index is used. The index reveals the approximate location of the record or piece of data on the disk. Then, the computer searches the area indicated by the index until it locates the desired record or piece of data. Although this process is slower than direct access, it is considerably faster than sequentially searching the entire data file until the desired record is found. With most indexed sequential access systems, two or more indices are used. The first index normally gives a general area or location of the data. This is the *coarse index*. Then another index is used to locate the data within the general area. This second index is a *fine index*.

There is one disk device that deserves special attention because of its use with small computers and its increasing popularity. This disk device is the *flexible* or *floppy* disk consisting of a plastic disk with a coating of magnetic material. Its major advantage is its low price. Many floppy disk drives can be purchased from $500 to $1,000. This low purchase price makes the floppy disk a very attractive storage device for small home computers as well as auxiliary storage for large computer systems.

The basic disk concepts discussed in this section also apply to the floppy disk. The floppy disk, however, is slower, and has a smaller storage capacity than the more traditional disk devices. It has the size and appearance of a 45 rpm record that you would play on your stereo system. A floppy disk and disk drive are shown in Figure 7–14A and B.

Photo courtesy of IBM

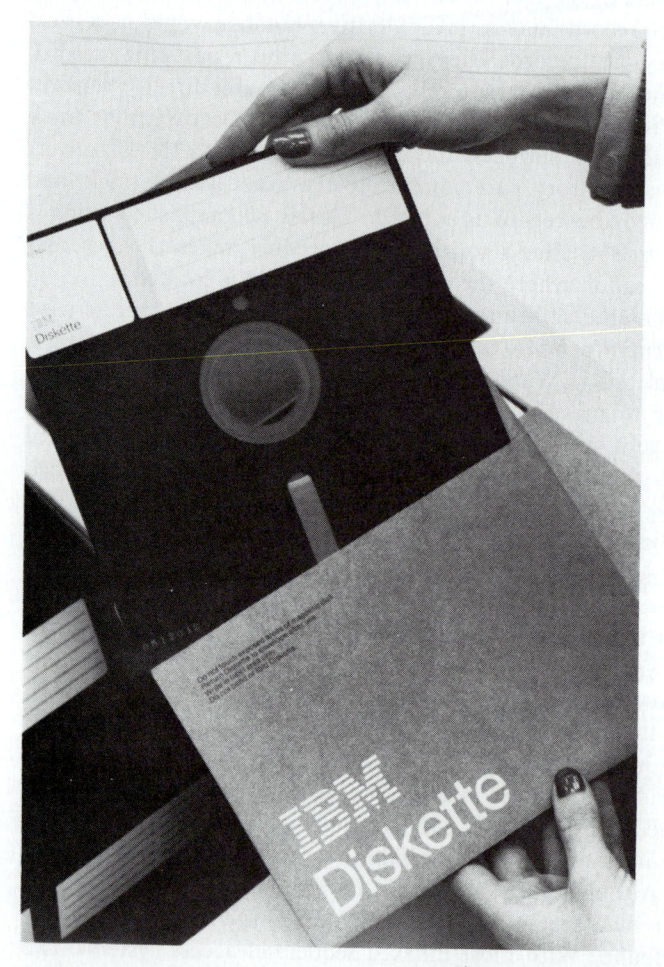

FIGURE 7–14 A
A flexible (floppy) disk

A COMPARISON OF PERMANENT STORAGE DEVICES

The primary function of any permanent storage device is to hold and maintain data and instructions on a permanent basis. Keeping the master files current and up to date is called *master file maintenance*. This concept was discussed in Part I. Master files can be updated during the running of an application such as payroll, or by using special programs that are specifically designed to update master files. In this section, we will contrast the efficiency and effectiveness of card, tape, and disk systems to maintain master files. Furthermore, we will investigate and contrast other important permanent

7 *Permanent storage devices*

FIGURE 7–14 B
A floppy (flexible) disk device

Photo courtesy of NCR Corporation

storage considerations, including storage capacity, access speed, access methods, costs, and more. We will begin with card systems.

The card system

A card system is both *inexpensive* and *flexible* compared to other permanent storage devices. The actual cards can be color coded for different applications and uses, and they can have a corner cut to help insure that they are all facing in the same direction. Furthermore, cards can be used for more than just permanent storage. Bills can be punched onto cards and sent to customers. A card containing a bill or any other document is called a *document card*. In some cases, a customer is asked to return the card with payment. This is called a *turnaround document,* and the card is called a *turnaround card*. In other cases, the customer is asked to tear off part of the card (called a stub) and to return it with payment. This type of card is called a *stub card*.

As a permanent storage device, the card system can offer a great amount of flexibility. The card media is the only media that allows an individual to directly read the data that is printed in the print position of the cards. You can also replace one or more outdated cards by hand without the need to run all of the cards through the computer.

The card system has a number of disadvantages. Cards are especially inefficient when a large amount of data is to be processed. Cards can be dropped, misplaced, lost, and mutilated, and in general they can be processed only about 50 times before they wear out. Compared to tape and disk, the card system is rather slow, and it is a sequential access storage device. Furthermore, the operator must push more buttons and spend more time in moving large quantities of cards from one card device to another.

In master file maintenance, both the cards in the master file and the cards in the transaction file must be in the same sequence. If a change is not needed in a card, the entire card is duplicated on a new card. One new card is punched for every card in the master file. For example, if there are 1,000 cards that need to be changed in a master file that contains 10,000 cards, then the 1,000 cards are changed, and the remaining 9,000 cards are punched onto 9,000 new cards. Since cards cannot be reused, this is a very inefficient and wasteful process. If a multifunction card machine is used, however, it is possible to avoid duplicating cards that do not have to be changed.

The tape system

While card devices are slightly less expensive than tape devices, the tape system offers several advantages over cards. Tape systems have faster data access and data transfer speeds, and tape systems require less operator intervention. In addition, magnetic tape can be reused a large number of times before it stretches and becomes unusable. Of course, records cannot be lost or misplaced on a magnetic tape like they can be on computer cards. In addition, tapes are an excellent way of transferring data and programs from one computer system to another. Although cards can be used for the same purpose, it is more convenient to use tapes, especially if the amount of data is large.

Tape can also be useful for purposes other than permanent storage. When output from one program is being used as input to another program, a magnetic tape can be used to hold the data. This type of file is called a *working file,* and in general, working files are used to hold intermediate results. Magnetic tape can be used to store logging files. A *logging file* is a record of all transactions or activities made at a terminal, such as a CRT. Logging files can be used to recreate files in case of a system failure to discourage crime, fraud, and the unauthorized use of the computer system.

Because tape devices are sequential access devices, the tape system has a number of disadvantages. To obtain one record or piece of data, the tape device must pass by all data that is stored before the desired piece of data. Furthermore, it is not possible for a person to read data directly from a tape. To get access to information on tape, the tape must be placed on a tape drive, and computer programs must be written to gain access to the data.

Updating a master file with a tape system is similar to updating a master file with a card system. All records must be in sequence. Any record that is not changed is copied on to the new tape containing the updated master

7 Permanent storage devices

file. Even if a few changes are required, every record on the old tape is rewritten on the new tape. This process can be time consuming if only a few changes are to be made.

With both card and tape systems, a completely new master file is created during master file maintenance. This leaves the old master file in its original state, which automatically produces a *backup file*. Since the original tape or deck of cards is not changed, it can be used along with the old transaction file to produce another updated master file at any time. Some companies keep three generations of master files. This is called the *grandfather-father-son* procedure. The grandfather (master file) can be used to create the father (master file) which can be used to create the son (master file). Thus, you have a dual backup system. Since master files and permanent data are the life blood of any organization, keeping adequate backup files is absolutely essential.

The disk system

Although more expensive, the disk system offers a number of advantages over card and tape systems. Without question, the disk is becoming the most popular permanent storage device, and its use is increasing faster than card and tape systems. The major reason for this is the ability of the disk to directly and immediately access data. This is essential for many companies and organizations. The disk system is not only faster than the card system or the tape system but it is also easier to use in master file maintenance. The master file records and transaction records do not have to be sorted into the same sequential order. With direct access, the computer can go directly to those records that need changing and make the necessary changes. Those records that do not have to be changed are not duplicated or even accessed. This process is more efficient and it takes less time.

There are, however, a number of limitations of the disk. When a disk file is updated, new data is written over the old or outdated records. Thus, the old records are destroyed. Because of this, the disk system does not automatically produce backup files when master files are updated. Thus, it is important to make a copy of the files stored on disk to generate the necessary backup files. Normally, backup files on a disk system are stored on magnetic tape.

It is also difficult to transfer data from one computer system to another with a disk device. Indeed, this would be impossible if the disks were not removable. Even with these disadvantages, the future for disk systems is bright. Many of the disadvantages of disk systems can be overcome by using magnetic tape in conjunction with, and as a back up to, a disk system.

SUMMARY

Organizations need a method of storing all data and programs on a permanent basis, and the devices that perform this function are called permanent storage devices. In general, permanent storage devices have destructive reading characteristics and nondestructive writing characteristics. Permanent storage devices use parity checking, and they require procedures for backup and security. Depending on the device, the access can either be direct or sequential.

Use of computer cards is one of the older methods of performing permanent storage. The computer card is also called a unit record, and computer card equipment has also been called unit record devices. Today, both 80-column and 96-column cards are in use.

The card reader is an important device for computers that use cards for permanent storage. Card readers can be serial or parallel readers, and the reading mechanism can be brush type or photoelectric type. Other popular card devices include the card sorter, the card punch, the reader/punch, and the multifunction card machine. The multifunction card machine performs reading, punching, and sorting, and this device significantly reduces the amount of card handling.

Magnetic tape is another popular permanent storage device. Like computer cards, magnetic tape is a sequential access storage system. The standard reel of magnetic tape is ½ inch wide and about 2,400 feet long. The actual tape normally contains a leader, beginning-of-tape marker, a volume label, a header label, the data or instructions, a trailer label, ending-of-tape marker, and a leader at the end of the tape. Interrecord gaps separate records on magnetic tape, and interblock gaps separate blocks of records.

The major device for tape handling is the tape drive, which both reads and writes data. In order to write data onto a magnetic tape, a file protection ring is needed. Most tape drives have the ability to reread data if there are problems in the reading process. Some computer systems also use cassette tapes and cassette tape devices.

The disk is one of the most popular permanent storage devices. This system allows direct access to the data. There are usually a number of disks or platters for a given disk device. Each disk platter is divided into a number of concentric circles called tracks, and each track is divided into sectors. One sector normally holds one record. The data contained on the same track for all of the disk platters is called a cylinder of data.

The disk drive is the basic device for disk systems. This device rotates the disk platters and accesses data with read/write arms. The disks can be either removable or nonremovable, and the access arms can be either fixed or movable. The time it takes for data to rotate under a read/write mechanism is called rotational delay. In order to directly access data, a reference point, called a key, is normally used. The actual access method can be direct, sequential, or indexed sequential. In addition, overflow areas are normally used with the disk to provide space for additional data that may be stored at a later date. A smaller disk, called the flexible or floppy disk, is becoming popular with both small computer systems and very large computer systems for storage of permanent data.

There are a number of factors to be considered in selecting a permanent storage device. The need for sequential or direct access is very important.

7 Permanent storage devices

Only the disk device is a direct access storage device. Other important considerations include speed, capacity, ease of operation, and cost.

KEY TERMS AND CONCEPTS

Backup file
Beginning-of-tape (BOT)
Blocking factor
Brush-type card reader
Card reader
Card system
Cassette tape
Course index
Cylinder of data
Digit punch
Digit rows
Direct access storage device (DASD)
Disk system
End-of-tape (EOT)
File protection ring
Fine index
Fixed head
Flexible disk

Floppy disk
Grandfather-father-son
Horizontal parity
Indexed sequential access method (ISAM)
Interblock gap (IBG)
Interrecord gap (IRG)
Key
Longitudinal parity
Movable head
Multifunction card machine
Nonremovable disk
Parallel reading
Parity checking
Permanent storage
Photoelectric-type card reader
Removable disk
Security backup file

Serial reading
Sequential access storage device (SASD)
Stub card
Tape drive
Tape system
Tracks
Transformation algorithm
Turnaround card
Turnaround document
Unit record
Unit record equipment
Vertical parity
Zone position
9 edge
12 edge
80-column card
96-column card

QUESTIONS

7-1. What is the difference between sequential and direct access?

7-2. What is a backup file, and why is it important?

7-3. Briefly describe the two most popular computer cards.

7-4. What are some of the devices that are used with a card system?

7-5. Describe what is contained on the typical magnetic tape. How long and wide is the standard magnetic tape?

7-6. Define IRG, IBG, blocking factor, tape density, vertical parity, and longitudinal parity.

7-7. In a disk system, what is a track, sector, and cylinder of data?

7-8. Briefly describe the difference between direct, sequential, and indexed sequential access. What are the advantages and disadvantages of each?

7-9. Contrast the advantages and disadvantages of the tape system with the disk system.

ANSWERS

1. F
2. F
3. T
4. F
5. F
6. T
7. F
8. T
9. T
10. F

MINIQUIZ

True or False

_____ 1. DASD stands for Data Access Storage Device.
_____ 2. Another name for a tape device is a unit record device.
_____ 3. A serial card reader starts at the side of the card and reads one character or column after another.
_____ 4. The interblock gap is a space that is placed between the header label and the volume label.
_____ 5. The weight of the tape per square inch is called the tape density.
_____ 6. For most tapes, there is a one track for parity checking.
_____ 7. When the file protection ring is placed on the magnetic tape, the tape drive will not be able to write data on the tape.
_____ 8. The data that can be read with one positioning of the read/write heads on a disk, is called a cylinder of data.
_____ 9. On a disk system, direct access is normally accomplished by recording a reference point called a key in front of each record.
_____ 10. When a master file is updated using a disk system, a backup file is automatically generated.

**Need information on current research?
Ask a computer at "The Exchange"**

WASHINGTON, D.C., ... If you're a trial lawyer in search of an expert witness, an inventor in the market for new ideas, a researcher in pursuit of a possible source of funding, or just a science buff who wants to keep up with ongoing research in your area of interest, where do you go?

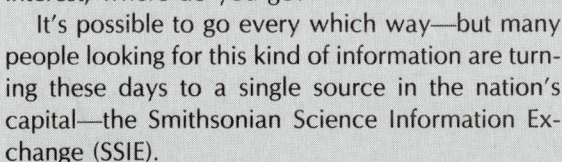

It's possible to go every which way—but many people looking for this kind of information are turning these days to a single source in the nation's capital—the Smithsonian Science Information Exchange (SSIE).

A non-profit corporation affiliated with the Smithsonian Institution, the Exchange maintains computerized files of pertinent, up-to-date information on 300,000 research projects in progress in just about every field of science and technology.

From terminals linked to an IBM computer, SSIE's staff of 50 scientists can "browse" through the computerized files and instantly retrieve or update information—from the most general to the most detailed.

And depending on the nature of a request, they can provide one page printouts of research projects the same day, or complete *custom* searches for information tailored to individual needs within about three days.

The Exchange supplies information to about 25,000 users in federal, state and local governments, at research centers and universities, in private industry, and at foreign research organizations.

In addition to locating experts to testify at trials, lawyers have used SSIE's computer files as a source of unbiased evidence for trials or comparative evidence for regulatory proceedings.

"Some lawyers who use our service feel that unlike the information they get from an agency that may have an inherently biased orientation, SSIE's collection of information is valuable because it comes from various sources and is indexed independently by trained scientists," said Dr. Donald Elliott, vice president of the division of scientific affairs.

Elliott said lawyers have also used information on research for developing regulatory standards, and patent attorneys have tapped the files to find out if a certain product is in the public domain.

The information is used in a variety of other ways, from revealing gaps in overall research efforts and identifying new research techniques, to learning about the work of a specific investigator and stimulating new research and innovation in the private sector.

"Immediate access to accurate and complete information on ongoing research projects helps bridge the critical gap—which can be years—between the time a research project begins and the time its results are published," Dr. Elliott noted.

At the center of all the activity at the Exchange is an IBM System/370 Model 138, which stores extensively indexed information on government and nongovernment research projects active during the past two to three years. The details are gathered from more than a thousand organizations that support research.

"The Exchange is the only national source of information on research in progress in all fields of basic and applied research in the life, physical, social and engineering sciences," Dr. Elliott said.

Every day an average of 400 new and updated project descriptions are entered into the computer and cross indexed by scientists who are trained in each of the major disciplines.

"Each project record is indexed to an average of 50 subject and administrative codes, so projects in broad subject areas as well as highly specific research topics are easily accessible from the file," Dr. Elliott noted.

One page printouts produced by the computer usually include the project title; supporting and performing organizations, names and addresses, inves-

Source: IBM Corporation.

tigator's name and specialty, level of funding, and a 200 to 300 word technical description of the project. Fees vary according to the nature of the request.

Searches for information can be ordered from SSIE by telephone (202-381-4211), cable (Telex 89495) or by writing to SSIE, Room 300, 1730 M Street, N.W., Washington, D.C. 20036

DISCUSSION QUESTIONS

1. What types of research projects are on file at SSIE? How many research projects are maintained at SSIE?
2. What types of permanent storage devices would be required for direct and immediate access of this type of data?
3. How would you provide backup and data security in this type of system?

Input, output, and data communications

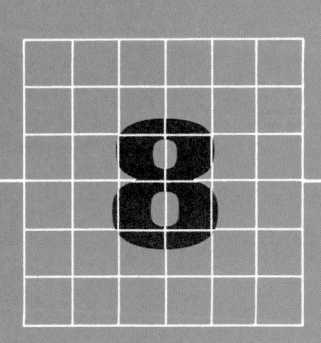

8

DATA ENTRY DEVICES
    Key to storage
    Multistation data entry systems
    Validation, verification, and editing
PRINTERS
    Impact printers
    Nonimpact printers
TERMINALS
    Visual display terminals
    Teleprinter terminals
DATA COMMUNICATIONS
    Carriers
    Communication devices and networks

After completing Chapter 8, you will be able to:

- Describe data entry devices and procedures.
- Contrast impact and nonimpact printers.
- Discuss the need and use of terminals.
- Describe the use of carriers, communication devices, and networks.

The link between any computer system and the people that use it is made with input, output, and data communication devices. Due to the fast speeds of the central processor, the bottleneck in getting more from the computer system has been the slower input and output devices. Thus, the selection and use of these devices is an important factor in realizing the potential of the computer system.

DATA ENTRY DEVICES

Some computer installations spend half of their total data processing budget on getting data into a form that the computer system can understand and use. This process is called **data entry**. Since the major forms of permanent storage are cards, tape, and disk, there are data entry devices for each type.

Key to storage

One of the oldest data entry devices is the keypunch or key-to-card device. This device allows an operator to convert data recorded on paper or other source documents to data placed on punched cards. Over the years, these devices have been easier and faster to use. Keypunch machines exist for both the standard 80-column card and the newer 96-column card. A typical keypunch machine is shown in Figure 8–1.

The newer keypunch machines contain electronic circuits and *buffers* that allow them to temporarily store data, which allows the keypunch operator to edit and correct errors before the data is punched on cards.

FIGURE 8–1
A keypunch machine

Photo courtesy of IBM

8 Input, output, and data communications

Key-to-tape devices allow data entry operators to place data directly on magnetic tape. This type of operation is especially useful when the computer system uses magnetic tapes for permanent storage. Key-to-tape devices are available for the standard tape, the cassette tape, and other tape systems. A typical key-to-tape device is shown in Figure 8–2.

Photo courtesy of IBM

FIGURE 8–2
A key-to-tape device

In recent years, the key-to-disk system has become an important means of performing data entry. As more companies and organizations start using disks and floppy disks for permanent storage, there will be a greater demand for key-to-disk devices. Like key-to-card and key-to-tape, the key-to-disk device takes data entered through a keyboard and places it directly on a disk. Some key-to-disk devices come with buffer storage and a small central processor that can be used to allow the data entry operator to edit and verify the data.

Multistation data entry systems

A **multistation data entry system** is a system that allows one or more data entry devices. In most cases, a multistation data entry system is a small computer system with a central processor and one or more permanent storage devices, such as disk drives and tape drives. A typical multistation data entry system is shown in Figure 8–3.

The multistation data entry system in Figure 8–3 contains six data entry stations that consist of a keyboard and a CRT or display unit. These stations

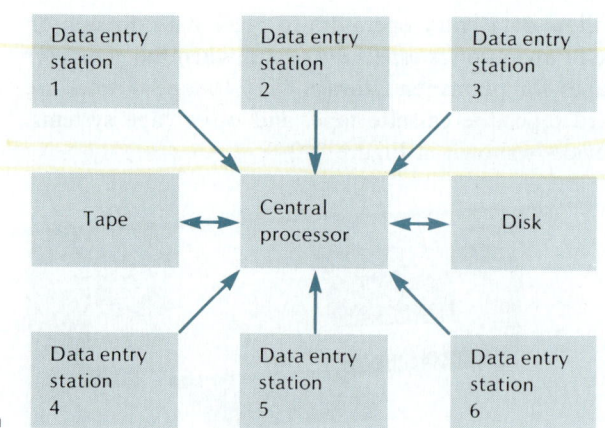

FIGURE 8–3A
A multistation data entry system

are connected to a central processor and a temporary storage unit, which are connected to a tape drive and a disk drive. Multistation data entry systems have the potential to be faster and more efficient than other data entry systems. Furthermore, with the central processing unit, multistation data entry systems have the ability to effectively check the accuracy of the data before it is used in a computerized application.

FIGURE 8–3B
Six data entry stations

Photo courtesy of IBM

8 Input, output, and data communications

The two most important characteristics of any data entry system are speed and accuracy. *Speed* is measured in terms of how fast operators can convert data that is human understandable into a form that the computer can understand and use. *Accuracy* is measured in terms of how many data items or facts stored by a computer device are correct and reflect actual conditions. In data entry, accuracy is controlled through validation, verification, and editing procedures.

Validation, verification, and editing

The data entry process begins with the recording of data onto forms or other documents. An employee works 40 hours this week, and the number of hours is recorded on a time sheet. A customer orders a product, and this order is recorded on a sales order. In most cases, a clerk will check to make sure that the forms and documents from a particular transaction are correct. This process is called *validation*.

After the data has been placed on a source document, such as a time sheet, then the next phase is to convert this data into a form that can be understood and used by the computer system. The data contained on cards, tape, or disk is checked against the original document to make sure that there are no errors in the conversion process. This is called *verification*. With a card system, there is a specific piece of equipment, the *verifier*, that is used to check the accuracy of the cards. The operator of the verifier places the newly punched computer cards in the input hopper and then types the data from the source documents on the keyboard. The data from the keyboard is compared to the data on the computer cards, and if there are any errors, a small notch is punched on the computer card. These notched cards are checked and repunched to eliminate the errors. For the other key-to-storage devices, the overall approach to verification is the same. In some cases, verification can be accomplished by using a CRT or a display screen. The newly entered data can be displayed and checked against the source documents.

The third phase in the data entry process is *editing*, which was discussed in Chapter 4. This takes place before the data is entered into the computer system for processing. In the editing phase, the data is checked to make sure that it is in a form that can be processed by the application programs. Editing can also serve as a backup checking procedure. If there are any errors or problems, an error report is generated and is used to correct or edit the data. The edit program can be used to convert from one storage media to another. For example, if the data were originally on cards, the editing program can output the data onto magnetic tape or the disk.

Paper is generated as a result of almost everything we do. We buy a car, get married, work a month, take out a loan, have a meal at a restaurant, and as a result of all of these transactions, some type of paper or document is produced. When a computer is used, the paper is normally generated by a printer. See Figure 8–4A and B.

PRINTERS

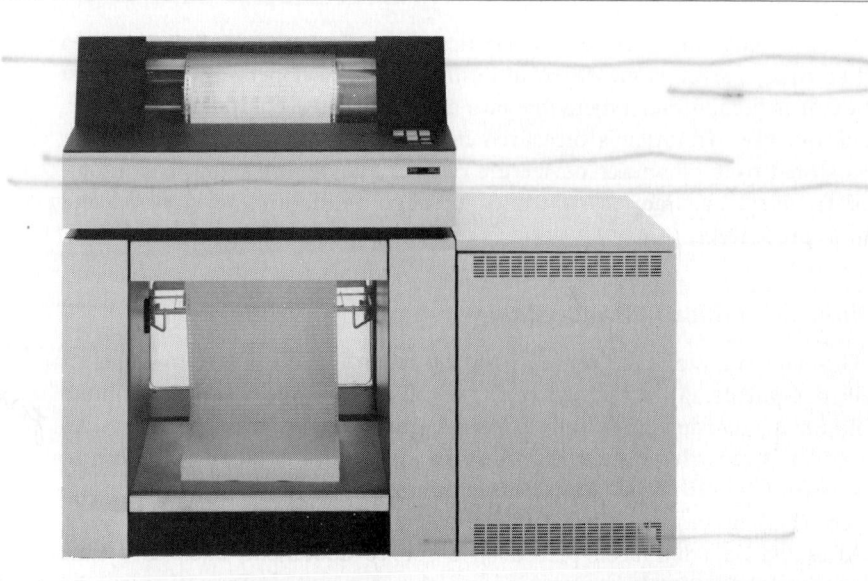

FIGURE 8–4A
A printer

Photo courtesy of IBM

A printer is simply a device that converts data that is stored in the computer system into human understandable data that is placed on paper (called *hard copy*). For most applications, the paper is continuous form or cut form paper. **Continuous form** paper, as the name implies, is paper that comes prefolded with perforated sections or in rolls. Sprocket holes may be along the side of the paper that fits into the sprockets of the printer. **Cut form** paper can be cards or any paper document that comes in precut or standard sizes. Printers also vary depending on the number of print positions or columns. The most common range is from about 100 print positions or columns to 150. In addition, printers can vary in the number of characters that can be printed. Printers can print a character at a time *(serial printers),* a line at a time *(line printers),* and a page at a time. The most common type of printer is the line printer. Printer speeds, measured in *l*ines *per m*inute (lpm), range from under 100 lpm to over 10,000 lpm. Finally, printers can vary in the type of printing mechanism that is used. An *impact* printer strikes or impacts the paper in placing a character on the paper. A *nonimpact* printer does not use a striker, hammer or other impacting mechanism.

Impact printers

There are a large number of impact printers, but the overall functioning is the same—part of the device strikes the paper. The different types of impact printers include *chain, drum, train, belt, ball, wheel,* and *matrix printers.*

A **chain printer** consists of a circular chain of characters (normally five complete character sets) that rotates at a high speed on one side of the

8 Input, output, and data communications

FIGURE 8–4B
New paper is being placed on the printer

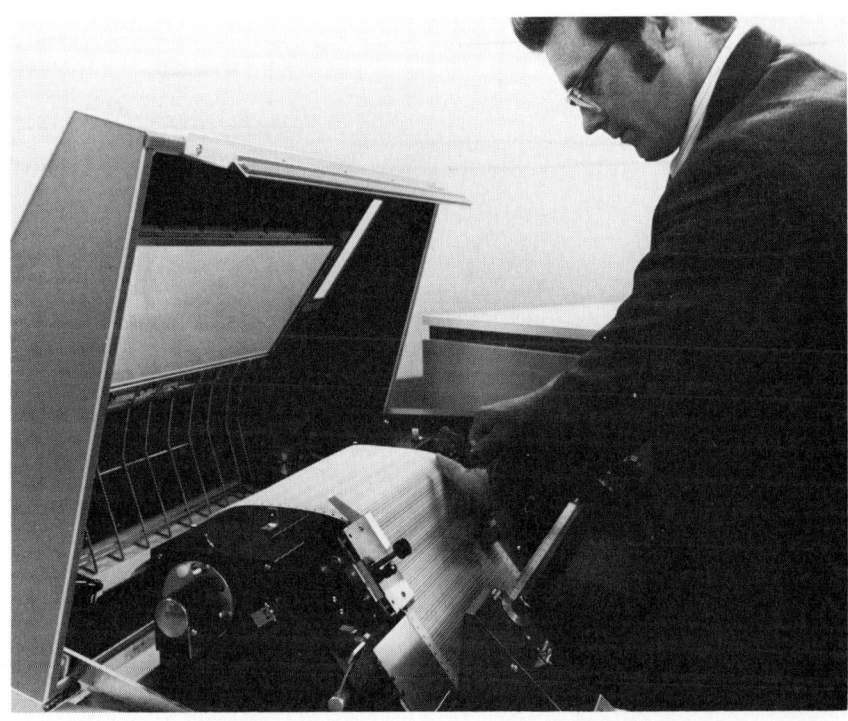

Photo courtesy of General Automation

paper. There is a hammer or a striker for each print position which is on the other side of the paper that strikes the appropriate character as it rotates to the desired position. With one striker or hammer for each position on a line, this type of printer can print thousands of lines per minute. Furthermore, the printer chains can be changed to give different character sets and print styles. After one revolution or less, an entire line is printed. A print chain is shown in Figure 8–5.

A **drum printer** consists of raised character sets placed in circles around the drum. There is one circle of characters for every print position or column, and there is a complete set of letters, numbers, and other characters for each circle of characters. Like the chain, the drum rotates, and after one complete revolution of the printer, a complete line is printed. See Figure 8–6.

There are also *train* and *belt* printers, which are similar to the chain printer. There are *wheel* printers, where the characters are placed on the outside of a spinning wheel, and there are printers that use *balls,* like the IBM Selectric typewriter. Another impact printing device, which is slightly different from the ones described above, is the *matrix* (also called *dot matrix* or *wire matrix*) printer. The principle is similar to the scoreboards that you would find in many high school and college gymnasiums that have a matrix of positions or lights that can be turned on or off to make any number. In

FIGURE 8–5
A print chain

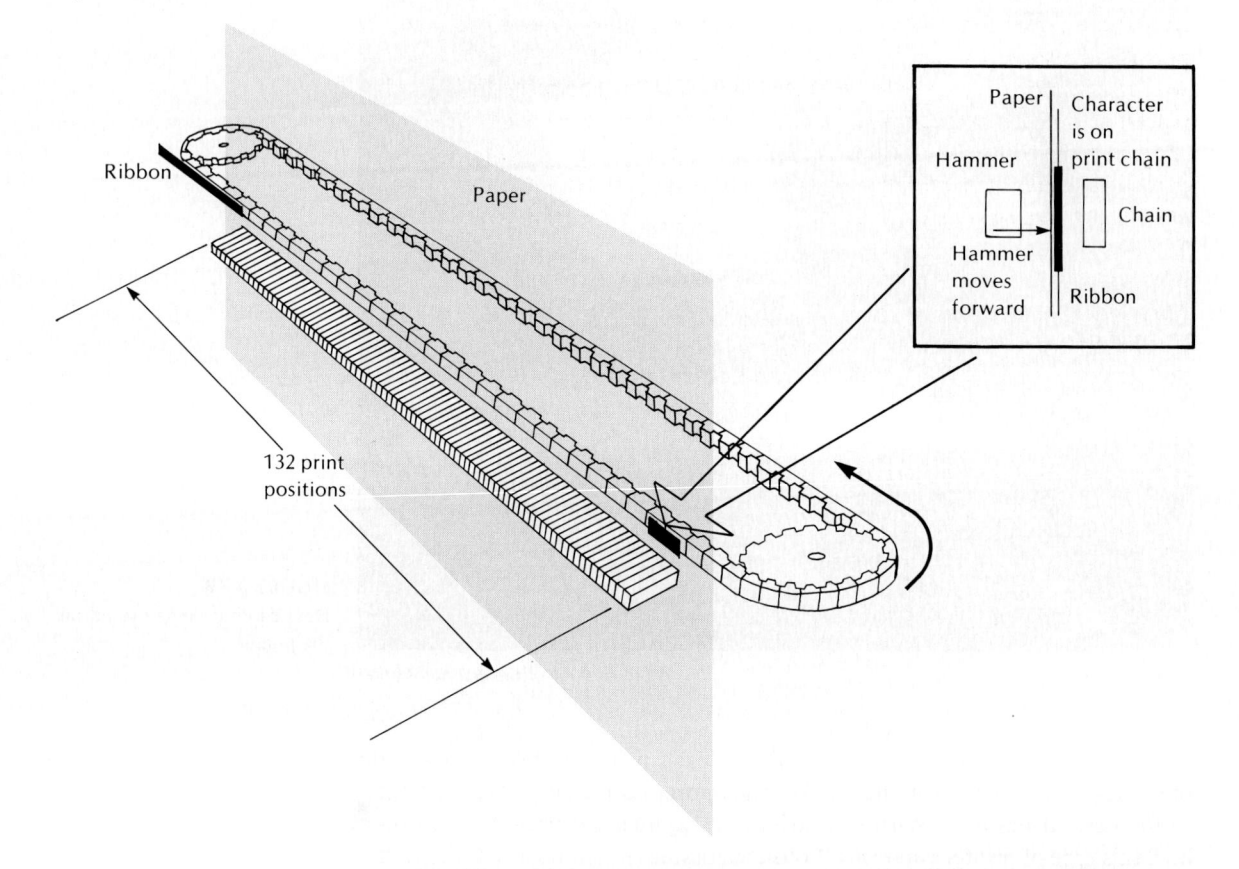

a similar fashion, a matrix printer will print a character using a matrix wires. Selected wires are pushed out to hit the paper in the appropriate place to make the character. This type of printer is a serial or character-at-a-time printer. Figure 8–7 shows how five strikes can produce the number 7.

Nonimpact printers

While impact printers physically strike the paper, nonimpact printers perform some type of operation to the paper. To print characters with nonimpact printers, the paper can be sprayed with ink, magnetized, electrically charged, heated, placed under pressure, or struck by laser beams. In most cases, the paper needs to be sensitized to the particular process or operation.

The **ink jet printer** uses a nozzle and sprays ink onto the paper to form the appropriate characters. In order to get the correct character, the ink is directed with a valve and one or more electronic deflectors that control the vertical and horizontal position of the jet stream of ink. With this process,

8 Input, output, and data communications 157

it is possible to print a number of different characters with different type styles. An ink jet printer is shown in Figure 8–8. With most other nonimpact printers, a sensitized paper is normally required. In a **thermal** printer, the paper is sensitive to heat. The print head consists of wires, similar to the wire matrix printer, that may be heated individually. The heated wires, when placed near the heat sensitized paper, cause the character to be burned into the paper. With the **electrostatic printer,** the matrix of wires or pins in the print head are electronically charged. The paper, which is sensitive to an electrical charge, picks up the charge. The sensitized paper passes through a toner solution, and the electrically charged parts of the paper pick up ink particles that form the characters. A **magnetic printer** is slightly different. Magnetic fields are placed on a belt instead of being placed directly on paper. The belt passes through a solution picking up the ink. Then the belt is heated and pressed against paper, bonding the characters to the paper. A **laser**

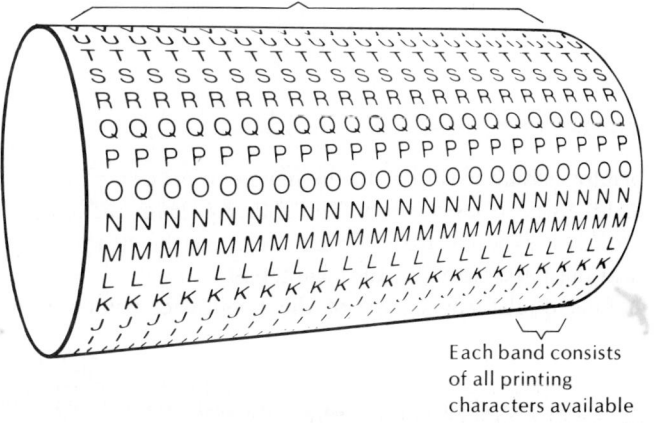

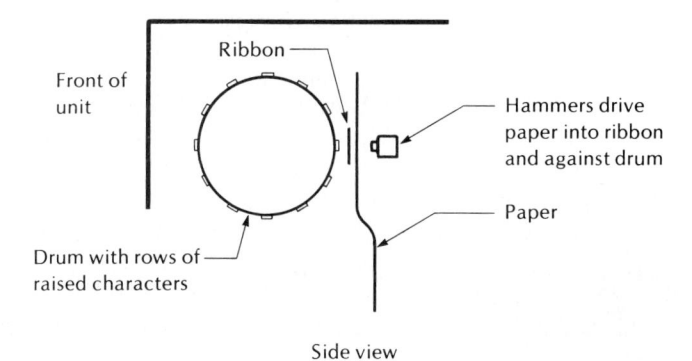

FIGURE 8–6
A drum printer

FIGURE 8–7
A matrix printer

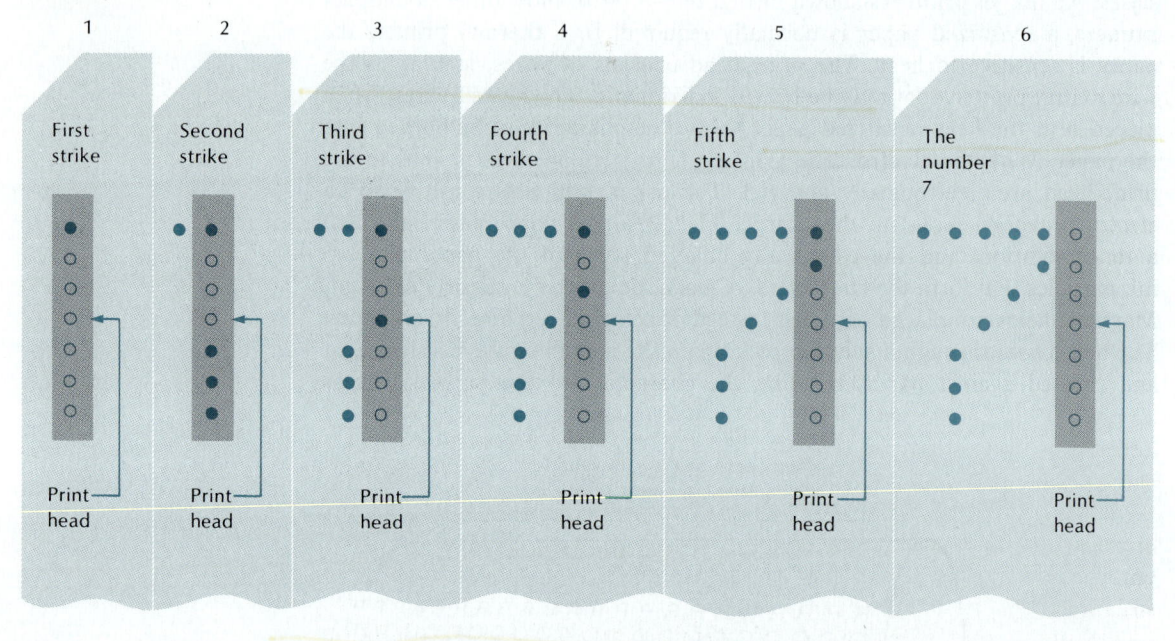

1	2	3	4	5	6
First strike	Second strike	Third strike	Fourth strike	Fifth strike	The number 7
Print head	Print head	Print head	Print head	Print head	Print head

printer, which is similar to the magnetic printer, places images on a rotating drum using a laser beam. The rotating drum picks up a toner powder on the laser exposed areas. These areas on the drums are pressed and fused into the paper forming the characters.

One of the advantages of the nonimpact printer is its silent operation.

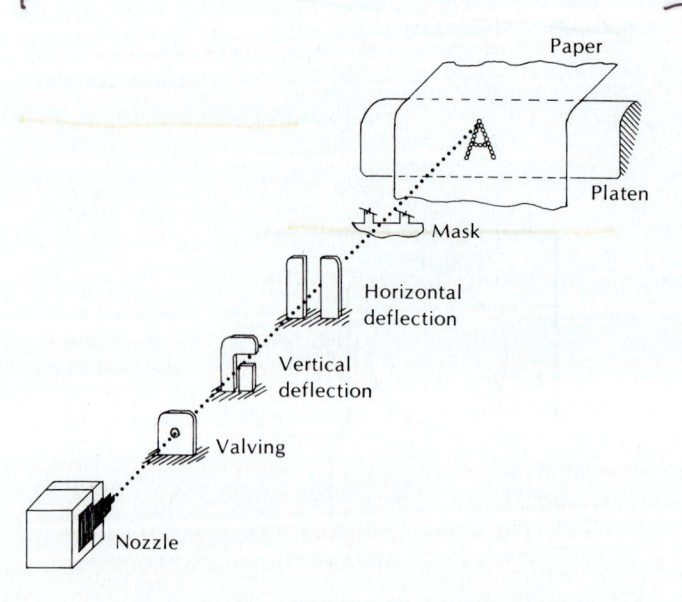

FIGURE 8–8
An ink jet printer

There are no noisy hammers, strikers, balls, or wheels that are pounding the paper. Some nonimpact printers can actually print the forms, including the company logo, on the paper in addition to data and information. This reduces the problems and expenses of having a printing company prepare paper forms. One of the biggest disadvantages, however, has been getting multiple copies from nonimpact printers. While the impact printers are noisy, they are effective when the forms are multiple copies with carbon between the forms or with the no-carbon-necessary forms. But with increasing speeds, some nonimpact printers can actually print several separate copies faster than an impact printer can print the same information on a multiple copy form.

TERMINALS

Data entry devices and printers are excellent for large amounts of data. But there are many applications that require a limited amount of input and output. An executive may want to have access to the computer in his or her office, a nurse might want immediate access to medical records, a stockbroker may wish to know the price of a stock, and a warehouse foreman might have to know the inventory level and location of a particular project or part. For these applications, large and noisy printers and keypunch machines, verifiers, and card readers are inefficient and ineffective. For these situations, a terminal is preferred.

The feature that distinguishes the **terminal** from other devices is its ability to both input and output a limited amount of data. In general, terminals are either visual display devices or teleprinters.

Visual display terminals

A visual display device has a keyboard for input and some type of visual display unit for output. In most cases, the display unit is a cathode ray tube (CRT) that has a screen similar to a TV. Figure 8–9A shows a visual display terminal.

There are two types of visual display terminals. An *alphanumeric* terminal has the ability to display numbers, letters, and other special characters on the screen. The characters that can be displayed are similar to the characters on a typewriter. The *graphical* terminal allows the screen to display a graph or drawing as well as alphanumeric information. In addition to these two types of terminals, a number of variations exist. For example, some visual display terminals can use a *light pen*. The display might contain a list of several inventory programs. One program might be used to account for new inventory and stock. Another program might be used to place an order for a particular inventory item, and so on. If a manager or clerk wanted to run a program called "New Stock," he or she would touch the pen on the screen where "New Stock" appeared, and the computer would start executing the program. Some special pens can be used with an *input tablet*. An input tablet is a flat and usually square tablet that can be used for drawing. The person using the tablet can use the pen and trace a pattern or drawing

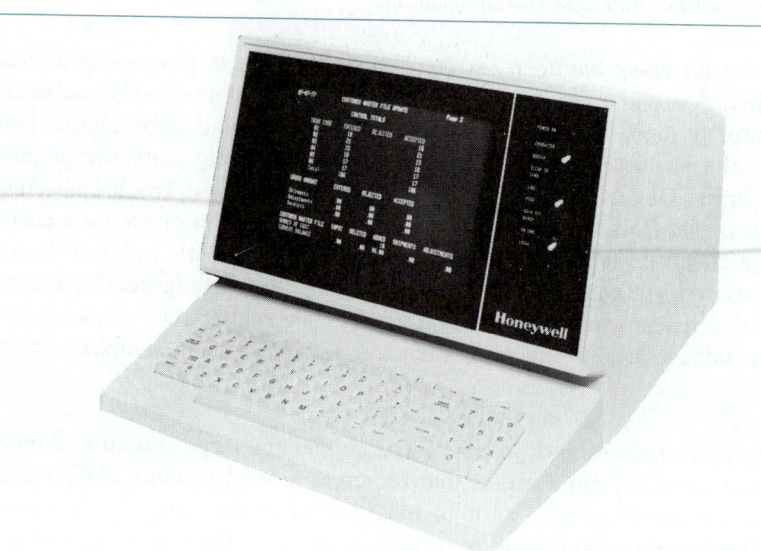

FIGURE 8–9A
A visual display terminal

Photo courtesy of Honeywell Information Systems

on the input tablet. The image that is traced is automatically transferred into the computer system. This image can then be processed. The computer can convert roughly shaped circles, squares, straight lines, into perfect circles, squares, straight lines, and so on.

A visual display terminal that deserves special mention is the *plasma* display terminal. While these terminals are more expensive than other terminals

FIGURE 8–9B
A Plato terminal

Photo courtesy of Control Data Corporation

8 Input, output, and data communications **161**

and must interface with compatible computer systems, the plasma display terminal is an excellent educational tool. Some studies claim that this terminal can teach students more effectively and in under half of the time of standard books or lectures. The *Plato* display terminal, a plasma terminal, has a number of features (Figure 8–9B). It can display any graph or drawing and it can display full color transparency slides. This terminal can flash symbols on the screen and it can buzz when it wants your attention. The screen is also sensitive to your touch. You can command it by simply touching the screen with your finger.

One of the disadvantages of the visual display terminal is its inability to produce paper output or hard copy. Some visual display terminals can produce paper output, but in most cases, this is expensive, slow, and inefficient when a moderate amount of paper output is needed. However, a teleprinter terminal can be used to overcome this problem.

Teleprinter terminals

A **teleprinter** terminal has a keyboard and a printing device. The printing device is usually a serial or character-at-a-time printer. There are also small and inexpensive printers that use the same type of printing mechanism. The main feature that distinguishes the teleprinter terminal from a printer is the keyboard. Terminals have a keyboard, while printers usually do not. Teleprinter terminals come in all different sizes and capabilities. Some can fit in a small briefcase, while others are large and would be difficult to move by one person. Like printers, the teleprinter terminal can have either an impact or nonimpact printing device. Teleprinter terminals are shown in Figure 8–10.

Terminals can also come equipped with a *microprocessor* and *temporary* or *buffer storage* areas. These additions expand the capability of the terminal. With the more advanced terminals, it is possible to program the terminal to perform different functions. Input and output data can be stored and manipulated. These types of terminals are called *intelligent* terminals. Terminals that have a microprocessor and temporary storage with limited uses are called *smart* terminals. Smart terminals cannot be programmed to do a number of activities and the data manipulation capabilities are limited. The older terminals that do not have microprocessors and temporary storage devices are called *dumb* terminals.

DATA COMMUNICATIONS

With earlier computer systems, you would have to bring all of the processing to a central room or location. All of the components of the computer system were typically located in one or two rooms. Today, computer systems are literally reaching out to us. Instead of bringing processing jobs to the computer room, we are now bringing the computer system to where the action is. But how are these remote computer devices able to communicate with each other? It is done with data communications systems.

A **data communications system** consists of *carriers,* which are used to

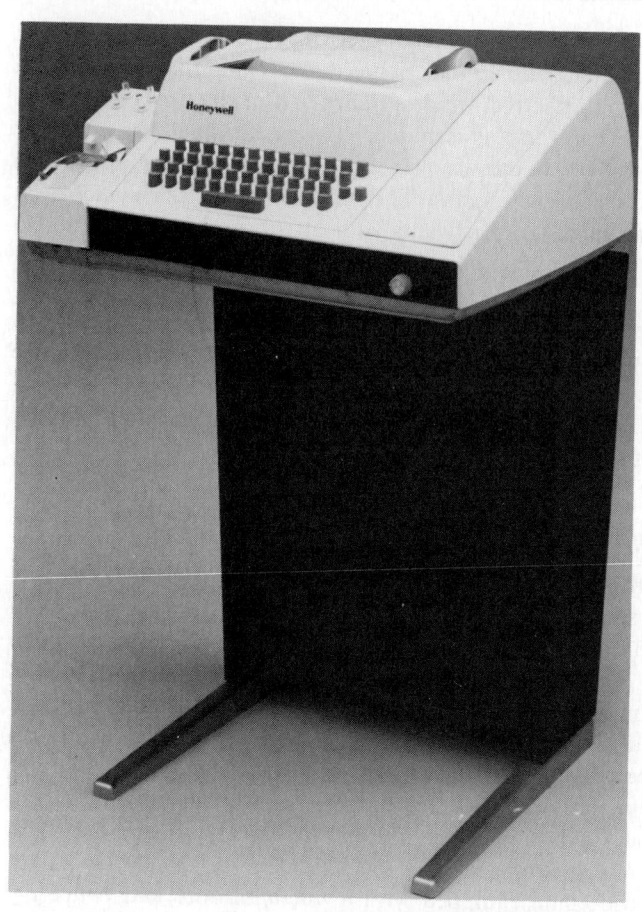

FIGURE 8–10A
A teleprinter terminal

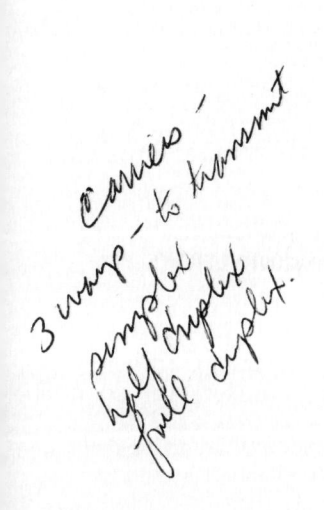

Photo courtesy of Honeywell Information Systems

transport the data from one point to another, and *devices* that connect the computer equipment to these carriers.

Carriers

A **carrier** is any system that is used to transmit data from one location to another. The capacity of a carrier is normally measured in how many bits of information can be transmitted in one second. A *baud* is one bit per second. If a carrier has a capacity of 300 baud, it can transmit 300 bits of information per second. Capacity is also measured in **characters per second** (CPS). There are three ways in which data can be transmitted. These are simplex, half duplex, and full duplex. With *simplex,* the data can only flow in one direction. You can listen to your favorite radio station, but you cannot talk back. With *half duplex,* the data can flow in both directions, but it can only flow in one direction at any point in time. This is like an amateur

8 Input, output, and data communications 163

FIGURE 8–10B
A portable teleprinter terminal

Photo courtesy of Texas Instruments, Inc.

or CB radio. You can either talk or listen, but you cannot do both at the same time. With *full duplex,* data can flow in both directions at the same time. This is like your telephone. Both parties at either end of the phone line can talk at the same time. See Figure 8–11.

But what actually carries the data from one location to another? In most cases, standard telephone lines are used, but wire lines, cables, microwave, and satellite transmission are also used.

Carriers can be classified according to their capacity or data transfer rate. *Voice grade* channels are the phone lines that we use to talk with other people. Voice grade lines have speeds ranging from about 100 to 300 characters per second (CPS). In addition to carrying a wide range of medium speed communications, voice grade lines can also carry illustrations and pictures. This type of transmission is called *facsimile transmission* (FAX). Although it may take about five minutes to transmit a drawing or other document from one location to another, this type of transmission satisfies the need for the transmission of more than just characters. A *subvoice grade channel*

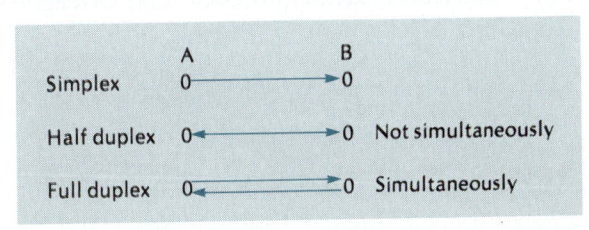

	A	B	
Simplex	0	→0	
Half duplex	0←	→0	Not simultaneously
Full duplex	0←	→0	Simultaneously

FIGURE 8–11
Simplex, half duplex, and full duplex

has a slower transfer rate. Also called *narrow-band channels,* these lines have transfer speeds that range from 10 to 100 characters per second. Although they are slower than voice grade channels, they are appropriate for slower devices such as teletypes and slow terminals. The fastest carriers are the *broadband* or *wideband* channels. Their transfer rate varies from 5,000 to 10,000 characters per second. The U.S. government, the largest user of broadband channels, often operates its own broadband equipment. It is interesting to note that several narrow-band channels can be combined to make one voice grade channel, and that several voice grade channels can be combined to make one broadband channel. When a company requires a substantial amount of data communications, they may have a line or channel *dedicated* to them. A dedicated line or channel is one that carries data for only one customer. When phone lines are used, no dialing is needed. You are always directly connected to the equipment at the other end of the line or channel. But who owns and operates these channels?

The companies and organizations that supply carriers for others to use are classified into *public carriers* and *common carriers.* Public carriers are primarily the telephone companies. These companies have been supplying data communications equipment and services for a long time. Common carriers are normally private companies that specialize in providing one type of service, and normally they only transmit data to and from large cities.

Communication devices and networks

In order to communicate data over carriers and channels, a device is needed at the sending end that can translate a digital signal from the computer system into an analog signal that can be transmitted over a carrier, such as a phone line. Then, another device is needed at the receiving end that can translate back from an analog signal to a digital signal. Translating data from digital to analog is called *modulation,* and translating data from analog to digital is called *demodulation.* Thus, these devices are *mo*dulation/*dem*odulation devices, or *modems.* Refer to Figure 8–12A and B.

Because carriers or channels are expensive, devices have been developed that concentrate several voice grade channels into one broadband channel. These devices are called *concentrators* or *multiplexers.* Figure 8–13 shows the use of multiplexers.

In addition to modems, multiplexers, and concentrators, *special communication processors* have been developed. These processors handle communications to and from a central processor. Like a receptionist at an office complex,

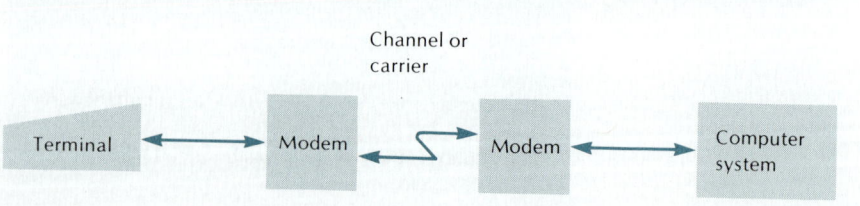

FIGURE 8–12A
Data communication with modems

8 Input, output, and data communications   **165**

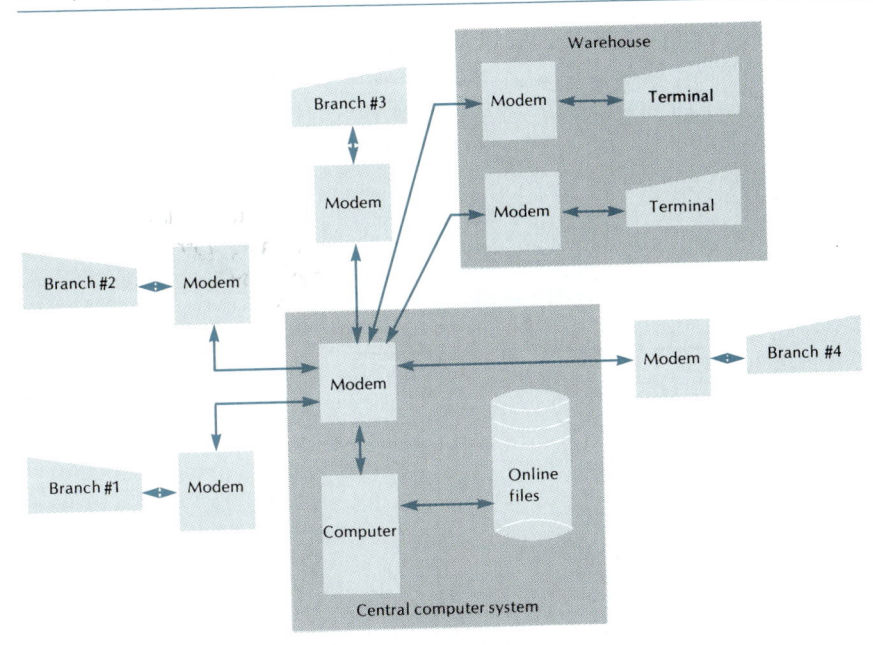

FIGURE 8–12B
The use of modems

the communications processors direct the flow of incoming and outgoing jobs. With communication processors, the main central processor is able to process more jobs without having to slow down to handle input and output activities.

With the use of communications devices and carriers, it is possible to connect several computers together. A *network* is two or more processors

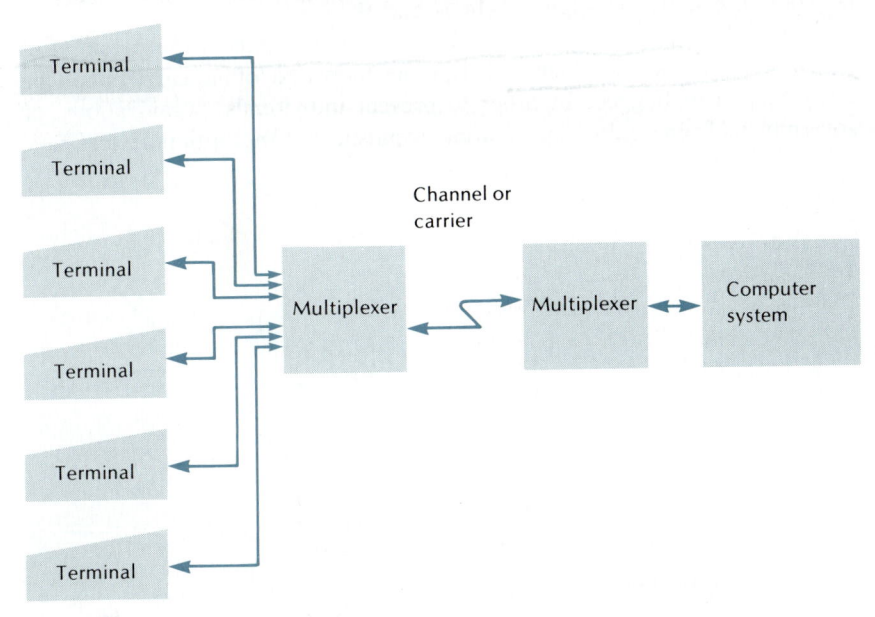

FIGURE 8–13
The use of multiplexer

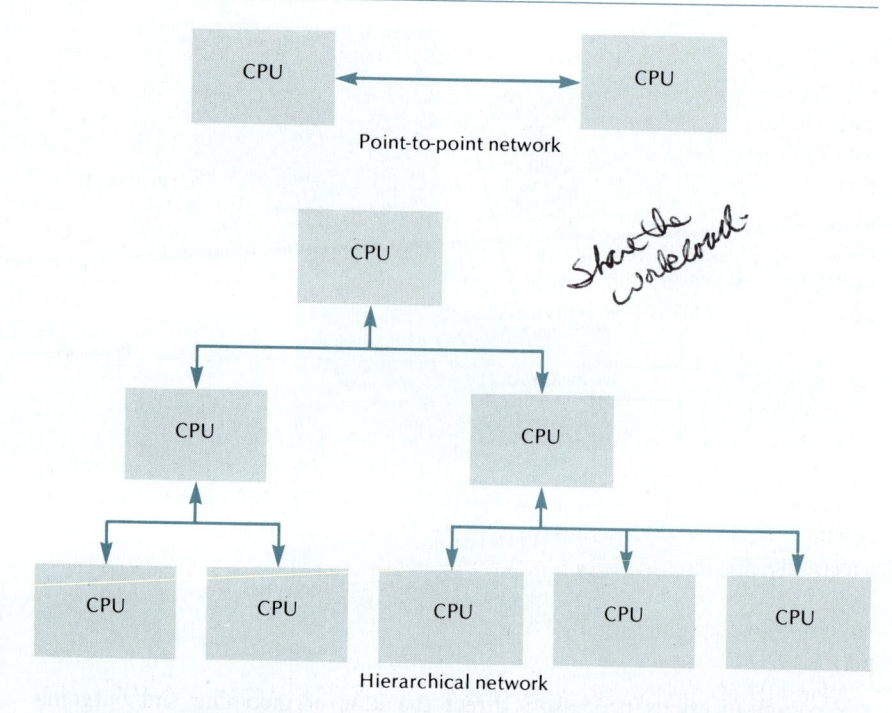

FIGURE 8–14A
Point-to-point and hierarchical networks

Point-to-point network

Hierarchical network

or computers connected with carriers and data communications devices. Although the number of possible network configurations is seemingly limitless, there are four major network configurations. They are the *point-to-point network*, the *hierarchical network*, the *star network* and the *ring network*. These networks are shown in Figure 8–14 A and B.

One of the major drawbacks of data communications is the potential of security and privacy problems. Telephone lines and other carriers can be easily tapped or bugged. In order to prevent individuals, organizations, or governments from stealing information, sophisticated encryption devices have

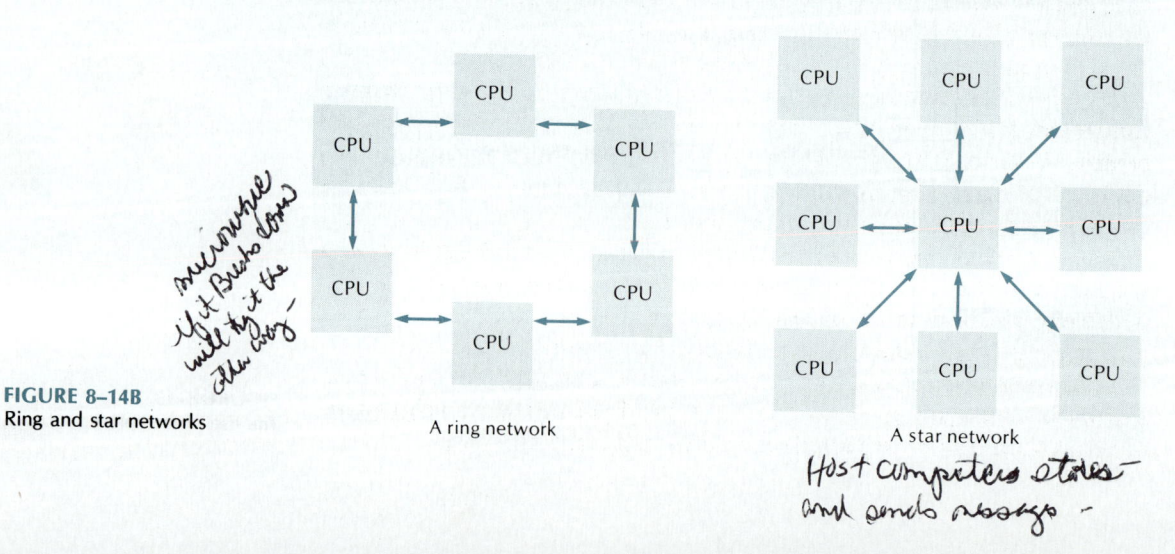

FIGURE 8–14B
Ring and star networks

A ring network

A star network

8   Input, output, and data communications

been developed. The word *encryption* comes from the Greek word *crypt* meaning to hide. These devices, which are placed at both the sending and receiving stations, use algorithms or a set of procedures to code the data being transmitted. Recently, the *National Bureau of Standards* developed the *Data Encryption Standard* (DES) to be used for national data security. Even so, most of the codes generated by encryption devices can be broken. Breaking some of the sophisticated codes, however, requires the use of powerful computers and years of processing. Examples of encryption devices include the IBM 3845 and the IBM 3846.

SUMMARY

In some cases, over half of the Data Processing budget can be spent on data entry. Today, the most popular data entry devices are the keypunch machine, the key-to-tape device, and the key-to-disk device. Some data processing installations use multistation data entry devices that usually have several key stations and one or more disk devices, tape devices, and processors. Both speed and accuracy are important factors in selecting data entry devices. In order to maintain accuracy, validation, verification, and editing can be performed.

One of the major output devices is the printer. One way to classify printers is to divide them into impact and nonimpact devices. Impact printers can use a chain, drum, train, belt, ball, wheel, or matrix device. Nonimpact printers can use ink jet, thermal, electrostatic, magnetic, or laser technology. Printers can print on continuous forms or cut forms, and they can vary in the number of print positions and the number of possible characters. Printers can print one character (serial), one line, or one page at a time.

A terminal is a popular device for a limited amount of input and output. Terminals can be divided into visual display terminals that use a cathode ray tube (CRT) and teleprinters. Visual display terminals can be further divided into alphanumeric terminals and graphical terminals. Some terminals can also use light pens and input tablets. Depending on their capabilities and the use of microprocessors, terminals can be intelligent, smart, or dumb. Some plasma terminals are even sensitive to your touch.

Data communications is a process used to transfer data and information from one location to another. Both carriers and communication devices are needed. Carriers, which can be public or common, can use simplex, half-duplex, or full-duplex transmission. Furthermore, the carriers can be subvoice (narrow-band) channels or broadband (wideband).

Modems (modulation/demodulation), concentrators, and multiplex devices are used to perform data communications. Special communication processor devices can also be used. When security and privacy are of concern, encryption products can be employed to code the data that is being transmitted.

Data communications devices can be used to connect CPU's at various locations. Almost any configuration is possible. Four standard configurations or networks are point-to-point, hierarchical, ring, and star.

KEY TERMS AND CONCEPTS

Alphanumeric terminal	Dumb terminals	Modem
Analog	Editing	Modulation
Ball printer	Electrostatic printer	Multiplexers
Band	Facsimile transmission (FAX)	Multistation data entry systems
Belt printer		
Broadband channel	Full duplex	Narrow-band channel
Carriers	Graphic terminal	Nonimpact printers
Cathode ray tube (CRT)	Half duplex	Plato terminal
Chain printer	Hard copy	Public carriers
Characters per second (CPS)	Impact printers	Simplex
	Ink jet printer	Smart terminals
Common carriers	Input tablet	Subvoice grade channel
Concentrators	Intelligent terminals	Teleprinter terminals
Continuous forms	Keypunch machine	Thermal printer
CRT	Key-to-storage	Train printer
Cut forms	Key-to-tape	Validation
Data communications	Light pen	Verification
Dedicated	Lines per minute (LPM)	Visual display terminals
Demodulation		Voice grade channel
Digital	Magnetic printer	Wheel printer
Drum printer	Matrix printer	Wideband channel

QUESTIONS

8–1. What is data entry?

8–2. Describe the popular key-to-storage data entry devices.

8–3. What is a multistation data entry system?

8–4. What is validation, verification, and editing? How are these techniques used to reduce errors?

8–5. Briefly describe some of the most popular impact printers.

8–6. What are the advantages and disadvantages of impact and nonimpact printers?

8–7. Discuss the different types of display terminals.

8–8. What is the difference between a teleprinter and a normal printer?

8–9. Describe the difference between an intelligent and a dumb terminal.

8–10. What is a carrier? Give some examples.

8–11. List the different grades of carriers. What is baud?

8–12. Briefly define a modem, a multiplexer, and a communication processor.

8–13. What is the difference between a ring and a star network?

8 Input, output, and data communications

MINIQUIZ

ANSWERS

1. F
2. F
3. T
4. T
5. T
6. T
7. F
8. F
9. T
10. T

True or False

_____ 1. A data entry device places data that is computer readable into the computer system.
_____ 2. A keypunch device is an example of a data input device.
_____ 3. A key-to-disk device is a data entry device.
_____ 4. A serial printer prints one character at a time.
_____ 5. A chain printer is an example of an impact printer.
_____ 6. A thermal printer is an example of a nonimpact printer.
_____ 7. A CRT is another name for a teleprinter.
_____ 8. A teleprinter is identical to the standard printer, but it is normally smaller.
_____ 9. A baud is one bit per second.
_____ 10. With full-duplex, data can flow in both directions at the same time.

The sensuous computer: Gaining access to systems through touch, voice, signature and other personal methods
Paul Meissner

To uphold privacy laws and ensure the security of both information and funds, sophisticated techniques are needed for verifying the identity of individuals who are authorized to use a computer system.

But no matter how sophisticated the techniques become they divide into three categories: Identity can be verified on the basis of something a person knows, something a person has or something unique about a person.

Three categories

Something a person knows should be a password, the combination to a lock or a set of facts from personal background (mother's maiden name, school teacher's name, places of residence and so forth). Passwords are presently the most common form of information used to control access to computer terminals.

Something a person has could be a key, an ID card or a credit card.

Something about a person could be a psychological attribute, such as fingerprints, handwriting, voice or the lengths of his fingers. Various other features having distinctive patterns have been considered, such as the face, ears, teeth and retina of the eye. Of course, people are most commonly recognized by their faces, but this form of identification is limited to situations in which a guard controls access to an area. There is also a serious question as to how well a guard can recognize an individual on the basis of a picture ID card if the individual is unknown to the guard.

Emphasis on physiology

Naturally, anything known to one individual could become known to another; thus if an unauthorized person learned the password to a computer system, he might gain access to the system to serve his own ends. Likewise, an object such as a key or credit card might fall into the wrong hands (or perhaps be counterfeited) and be used in an unauthorized manner. For these reasons, a great deal of emphasis is presently being placed upon the use of unique physiological attributes as a means of verifying identity.

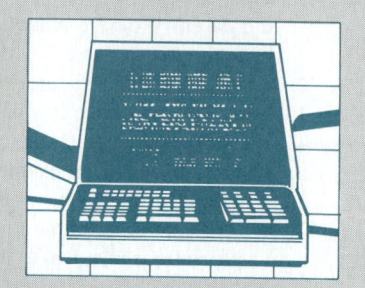

Fortunately, the computer can be of great help in such verification. With the availability of small, inexpensive computers which are nevertheless capable of rapidly executing complex programs, it is possible to extract from a single but complex attribute a representative "reference profile." This reference profile may be compared through sophisticated matching and correlation routines with measurements of that physical characteristic obtained on future occasions. And a determination can be made as to whether these measurements are within an acceptable tolerance, thereby confirming or refuting the identity of the individual.

Typically, the reference profile is obtained by "training" a recognition system through an initial set of measurements, from which a set of averages and limits are obtained. With some systems, an adaptive process is included which enables the reference profile to follow a gradually changing attribute, such as might occur with aging. A variety of systems for this type of identity verification are presently being developed in response to the growing importance and need for more reliable, inexpensive and convenient methods.

How do these work?

In general, an individual must first present a claimed identity to the recognition system. He might, for example, type his name or enter an assigned identification number. This provides the system with the information for retrieving the proper reference profile and preparing to carry out the verification process. The person then goes through

Source: *Data Management* (May 1977), pp. 23–25.

a specified "ritual," such as signing his name with an instrumented stylus, speaking into a microphone, placing his hand or finger on a scanning device or whatever is required. Signals corresponding to the measured attribute are thus produced and are analyzed by the system and compared with the reference profile.

If a match is obtained within a specified tolerance, the identity is considered to be verified. An acceptance signal can then be produced to allow the person to proceed with some authorized activity. If a match is not obtained, a rejection signal is produced. The person may then be given another opportunity to identify himself on the chance that the first attempt failed due to marginal operation. Usually not more than three attempts would be allowed in order to prevent an imposter from trying repeatedly in the hope of being accepted on the basis of chance.

Recognition systems

Recognition systems based on signatures make use of the dynamic features of the writing process (forces, velocities, accelerations) rather than the static signature image. These dynamic features are highly individualized and would be very difficult for a would-be impersonator to perceive or duplicate. It is interesting to note that the systems can be trained to perform recognitions on words other than the signature, although the signature is preferable since it is essentially a conditioned reflex action and is not under conscious control to the extent that an arbitrary word would be.

Of course, the person must be consistent in his choice of signature for this purpose. Many people have more than one signature, depending on whether they are signing formal documents, correspondence or credit receipts. Any of these signatures could be used in training the system, but thereafter the person should use that same signature for verifying his identity.

When recognition is by voice, it is necessary for the person to speak into a microphone using words that have previously been entered into the system through a process in which the computer is conditioned to recognize the characteristic features of the person's voice. But a would-be impersonator might use a recording of the person's voice in an attempt at deception. To counter this threat, the system selects phrases at random, from a set of previously stored words. The selected phrases are delivered over a loud speaker and the person must repeat them. The potential number of phrases is great enough that it would not be practical to use a recorder for reproducing the selected ones within the time available.

There are various ways for matching fingerprints automatically as a means of verifying identity. One method consists of performing an optical correlation between the live print and a file copy of the print. It is not necessary to resort to inked impressions for this process; a satisfactory image of the print can be obtained by placing the finger on a properly lighted prism. Another method is to scan the image and derive a digitized file of data representing the fingerprint "minutia." These are the distinguishing features such as the beginnings, endings and branches that occur among the ridges which constitute the fingerprint. This file of minutia data can then be compared with a reference file by using software programs that match these minutia data.

Interestingly, the lengths of people's fingers have been found to vary enough to form the basis for a recognition system (hand geometry). This was discovered by the Air Force in measuring a large number of individuals to obtain data for making gloves. This phenomenon has been incorporated in a device which measures the distance from the tips of the fingers to the web between the fingers by using a motor-driven assembly of photocells. The measurement can be made in less than one second.

Do these systems work?

There are two factors of particular interest in judging the performance of a personal recognition device: How well does it recognize the correct person, and how well does it discriminate against imposters. The rejection of correct persons is expressed by the False Alarm Rate (FAR), while the passing of imposters is expressed by the Imposter

Pass Rate (IPR). In practical systems there is generally a trade-off between these two rates and there is usually an adjustment by which one can be favored at the expense of the other. The amount of data is still quite limited, but FAR and IPR rates which are both in the range of 1 or 2 percent are being achieved and it may be possible to make one of the rates vanishingly small in some systems.

Computer security is made up of many elements, but the verification of individual identity is one of primary importance. Although the computer has opened up new possibilities for misappropriating resources and information, it has also, fortunately, provided us with a new class of techniques for verifying that a person is who he says he is. This capability can be used to establish safeguards so that we may continue to benefit from the many useful ways in which computers can serve us.

DISCUSSION QUESTIONS

1. What are some of the ways that an individual's identity can be verified before allowing the person access to a computer system?
2. What types of potential problems can be avoided with better computer security systems?

Special purpose hardware

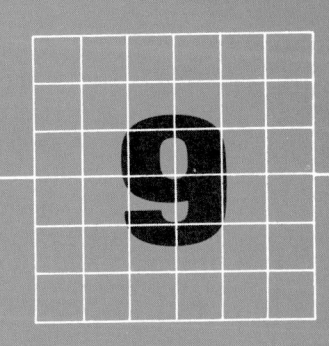

INPUT AND OUTPUT
    Input devices
    Output devices
    Devices for input and output
PERMANENT STORAGE AND CENTRAL PROCESSING
    Permanent storage devices
    Central processing devices

After completing Chapter 9, you will be able to:

- List and describe special purpose input devices.
- Discuss how special purpose output devices can be used to generate attractive and useful output.
- Compare the special purpose devices that can be used for both input and output.
- Contrast the various special purpose permanent storage devices.
- Describe the various special purpose devices that are available for central processing.

Like a home stereo system, the typical computer system can be used with a number of different devices or components. In the last several chapters, we covered some of the common devices that are used with most computer systems. These devices included card readers, line printers, magnetic tape devices, disks, and so forth. In this chapter, we will look at some *special purpose devices* or *hardware*. Although these devices are not as common as the ones previously discussed in this part, they have special and important applications.

INPUT AND OUTPUT

While there have been advances in special purpose permanent storage and central processing devices, most of the emphasis on special purpose hardware has been related to input and output. Thus, most of this chapter will be concerned with these devices.

Input devices

In the 1950s the banking industry was becoming swamped with paper in the form of checks, loan applications, bank statements, and so on. During this time, banks resembled paper factories instead of financial institutions due to the large amount of paper that had to be handled. Today, it is estimated that over 3 billion checks are processed every year alone. The *American Banking Association,* with the cooperation of representatives of the data processing industry, decided to develop a better way to process all of the paper. The objective was to use documents that both humans and the computer system could read directly. The result was **magnetic ink character recognition (MICR).** With MICR, data is placed on the bottom of the checks using a special magnetic ink that can be read by both people and the computer alike. A typical check with magnetic ink characters appears in Figure 9–1.

The magnetic ink characters, which appear at the bottom of the check in Figure 9–1, are divided into three areas. The numbers that identify the bank where the checking account is located appears on the left-hand side of the check. The account number of the checking account is placed in the middle of the check, and the amount of the check is placed on the right-hand side of the check.

The numbers that identify the bank and the checking account are placed on the checks while they are being printed. Then, when a check is cashed, the amount is placed on the check by an **MICR inscriber.** Once this is done, **MICR readers** can read the magnetic characters on the checks and make debits and credits on the appropriate accounts. Some MICR equipment is shown in Figure 9–2.

One disadvantage of MICR is its limited character set. In most cases, there are only 14 characters that are allowed, which are the 10 numeric digits and 4 other special characters. Although it is more expensive, Optical data readers can be used to increase the number of allowable characters. **Optical data readers** have the ability to read data directly from an ordinary sheet of paper. Magnetic ink or special paper is not required. Optical data

9 Special purpose hardware

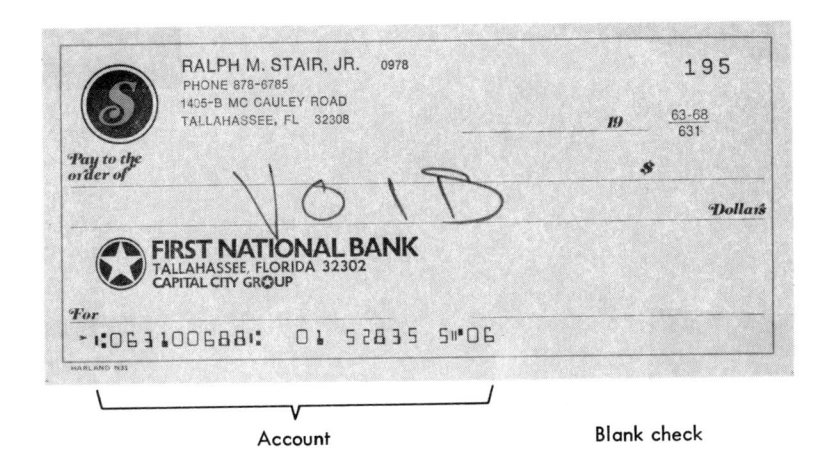

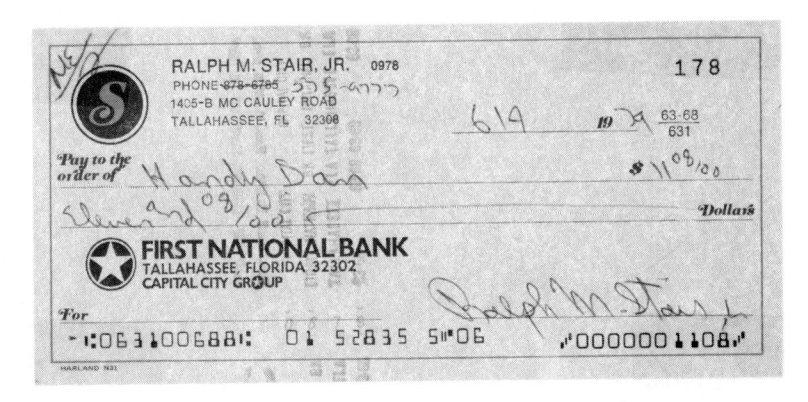

FIGURE 9–1
A check with magnetic ink characters

readers can be either **optical mark recognition** (OMR) readers or **optical character recognition** (OCR) readers.

OMR readers, in the past, were used primarily for test scoring. If you have taken a computer scored exam, it is likely that you answered the questions on OMR paper. This paper is also called a *mark sense form*. See Figures 9–3 and 9–4.

While OCR readers are more expensive than OMR readers, they are much more flexible in what they can do. These types of readers have the ability to read characters directly from an ordinary piece of paper. As you would expect, OCR readers come in a variety of different types with different capabilities. The most popular character style or font is OCR A, which was developed by the *Business Equipment Manufacturers Association* (BEMA) and adopted by the *United States American Standards Institute* (USASI). Other character fonts that can be read by some OCR readers include OCR B, *Farrington* 7B, which is used with credit cards, and E 13B, which is the same font as

FIGURE 9–2
MICR equipment—a document processing system

Photo courtesy of NCR Corporation

MICR enabling MICR documents to be read by these OCR readers. Some of the OCR fonts are shown in Figure 9–5.

Most OCR readers use reflected light to recognize various characters. Reflected light patterns from the page containing OCR characters are electronically transformed into the appropriate characters. With the use of microprocessors, it is possible for OCR readers to read hand written documents that are carefully prepared. Some OCR readers can even recognize a character when more than 80 percent of the character is missing. Other OCR readers can read an entire page at a time. While older OCR readers have a high error rate, over 15 percent in many cases, today's OCR reader can have an error or rejection rate of less than 1 percent.

In addition to MICR and optical data recognition, there are a number of other special purpose input devices. For example, there are modern **industrial data collection devices** that record the time an employee spends on a job and more. These data collection devices can be used to determine an employee's wages, a more accurate cost for jobs being done, and so on. An industrial data collection device is shown in Figure 9–6.

In addition to collecting data, industrial data collection devices can be

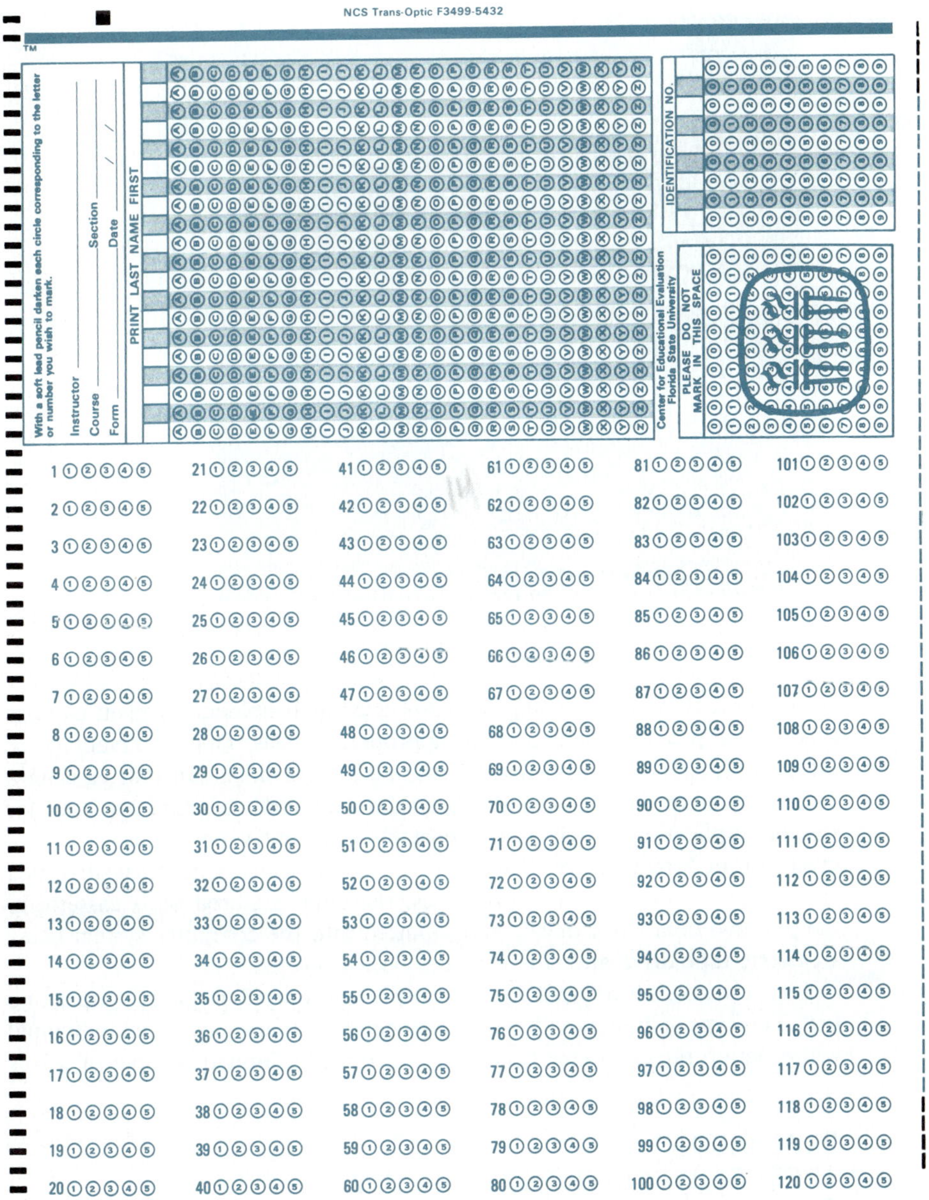

9 Special purpose hardware

FIGURE 9–3
A mark sense form

used as a security device. These security devices accept special cards or badges. If the card or badge matches the proper code, then the employee is allowed to enter into a security area.

In attempting to make data input more convenient, several companies have developed **portable data entry devices**. A **port-a-punch** allows a person to punch holes in a computer card. All of the hole positions in the card

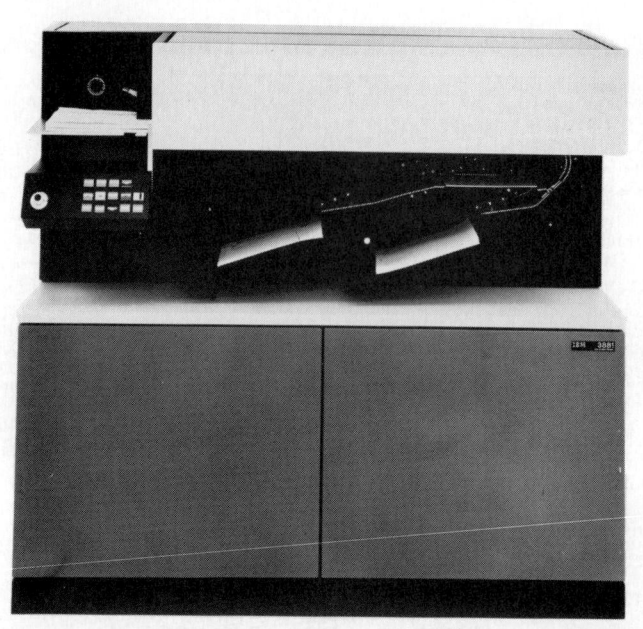

FIGURE 9–4
Optical mark reader

Photo courtesy of IBM

are perforated, and by placing the card in a small holder, a person can use a pencil or pen to punch out the appropriate holes. One disadvantage of the port-a-punch is that sometimes the perforated holes fall out, causing a data entry error. There have also been data entry devices that are used for specific applications, such as the portable data entry device used to take inventory in a retail store. Data can be entered using a light sensitive pen or through a keyboard. In most cases, the data is stored on a cassette in the portable data entry device and inputted into the computer system using a cassette tape drive after the data has been collected.

It is even possible to input data directly into a computer system by speaking to it. This type of input is called *speech recognition*. In most cases, an individual will program the computer system to understand a limited number of words

OCR A Alphanumeric
0123456789
ABCDEFGHIJKLMNOPQRSTUVWXYZ
{}%?&"*+$,.-/'=|;:

Farrington 7B
0123456789 EPH

E13B (MICR)
0123456789

FIGURE 9–5
OCR fonts

9 Special purpose hardware

FIGURE 9–6
An industrial data collection device

Photo courtesy of IBM

by speaking the words into a microphone that is connected to the computer and typing each word after it is spoken. When the individual speaks the same words to the computer at a future date, the computer will be able to recognize the word and take the appropriate action. Speech recognition has a number of applications. It can be used when an equipment operator or worker is using both hands and also needs to enter data into the computer system at the same time. It also can be used by individuals with physical disabilities. Speech recognition has also been used with security systems. A person programs the computer system to understand 16 words. Then, when the individual wants to gain access to a security area, the computer picks 4 of the 16 words at random for the individual to speak. If the spoken words match with the words previously programmed, the person is allowed access to the security area. The equipment that allows speech recognition is a *speech recognition device*. While the earlier developers of this type of equipment were hopeful that the equipment would allow people to simply talk to the computer using any words, this hope has not been realized.

The devices discussed above are only a few of the special purpose input devices. The lumber industry is now experimenting with a camera type device that can visually inspect a log as it comes into a lumber mill. The visual images of the log are fed directly into the computer system. The computer system will then determine how the log is to be cut to make the most lumber, and the saws and other lumber mill equipment will be automatically directed by the computer system to take the appropriate action. With this type of system, a human operator has the ability to override the computer's decision if necessary. In some hospitals and health care delivery centers, blood pressure, temperature, and other facts are measured and sent directly into the computer system for analysis. In these cases, the instruments are electronically connected to the computer system. This eliminates the need for a nurse to key the data into the computer, and it also makes the computer analysis of the data faster. Some computer manufacturers are now considering the possibility of wiring inventory, temperature of a building, humidity, time of the day, and so forth, directly into the computer system. Then, the computer will be able to control heating and air conditioning systems, turn lights on and off at the correct time, and automatically keep an accurate record of inventory without the need for a human to key the data into the computer system. Here the event itself is wired directly into the computer system, and thus, this type of input is called **event driven** data input.

Output devices

Starting with the first computers and continuing with today's most sophisticated computer systems, output on paper (hard copy) has been a major means of data output. In the last chapter, several popular printing devices were discussed. But in most cases, these printers are limited to printing only letters, numbers, and other characters. Many managers, however, find that tables of numbers are difficult to use. Furthermore, there have been a number of studies that reveal that it is easier for managers and decision makers to use data when it is presented graphically. For example, it is much easier to see a trend in sales when the data is presented on a graph than if the same data were placed in a large table of numbers. The device that produces drawings and graphic displays of data is the **plotter.** The output from a plotter can even be in full color. See Figures 9–7A and 9–7B for a sample of output from a plotter.

The paper used on a plotter can be up to six feet square and is placed on either a flatbed or on a drum. The graphs and drawings are placed on the paper electromechanically or electronically. With an electromechanical plotter, a pen moves over the paper. With an electronic plotter, the graphs and images are placed on microfilm using a beam, and then the microfilm is used to create the graph or drawing on paper.

Almost any graph or drawing can be produced using a plotter. These devices can be used for engineering drawings, trend lines, bar charts, pie charts, maps, organizational charts, sales forecasts, flowcharts for computer programs, population densities, and more. They have even been used to produce works of art. A plotter is shown in Figure 9–8.

9 *Special purpose hardware* 181

FIGURE 9–7A
Output from a color plotting system

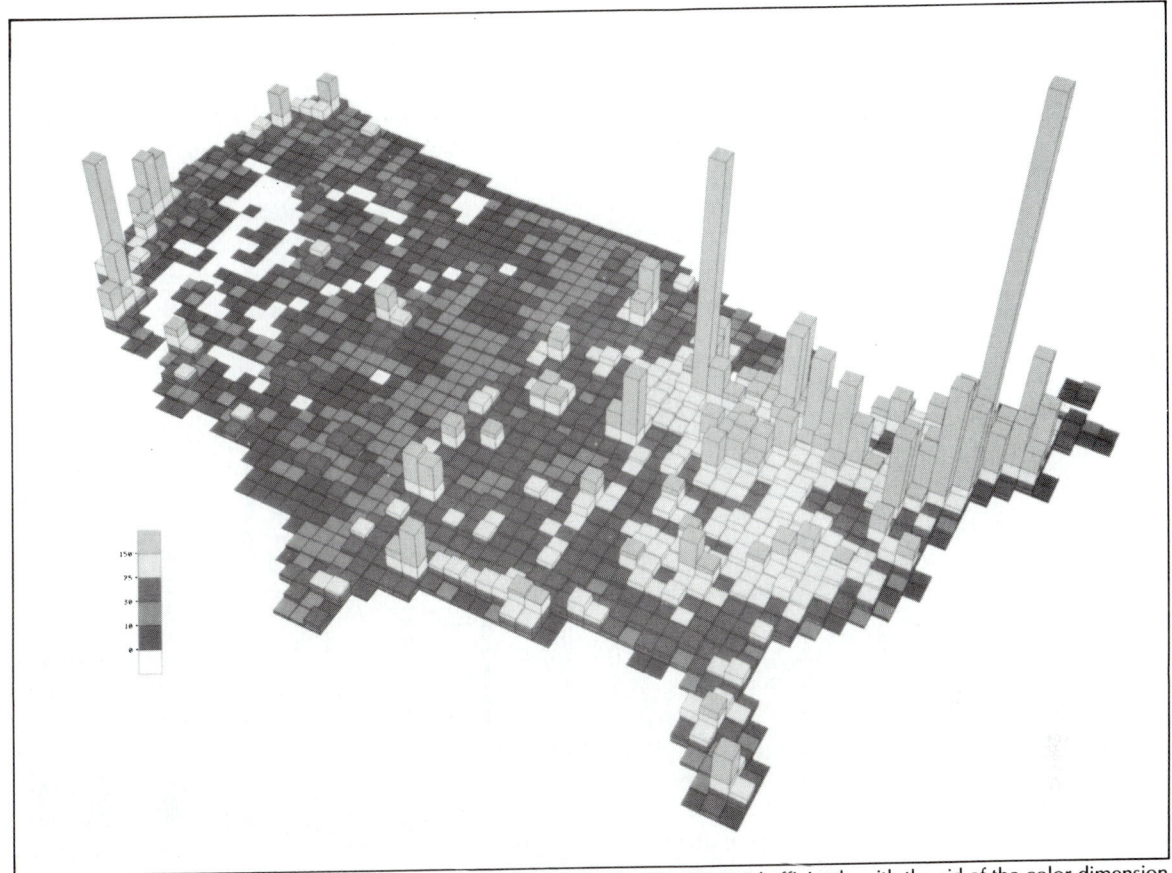

This population density map shows how a large amount of data can be presented efficiently with the aid of the color dimension. The 3D software permits the viewpoint of the observer to be changed by tilting and rotating the picture. Objects placed in the foreground automatically erase background objects that should be hidden from view.

Photo courtesy of Applicon Incorporated

Plotters are able to produce these graphs and drawings through the use of programs and software. Computer programs must be written that will accept data and convert it to a graph or drawing on the plotter. Without question, one of the major limitations of the plotter is a lack of good software to drive the plotters. With time, however, it is expected that these programs will be refined. Plotters can automatically draw labels and headings for graphs, but they must be programmed to do this. Plotters are excellent tools for providing management information, and as managers realize that their computer systems can accommodate plotters, it is expected that their use will increase.

Plotters, like normal printers, produce paper output. But too much of any form of output is undesirable. Indeed, many managers and decision mak-

FIGURE 9–7B
Output from a color plotting system

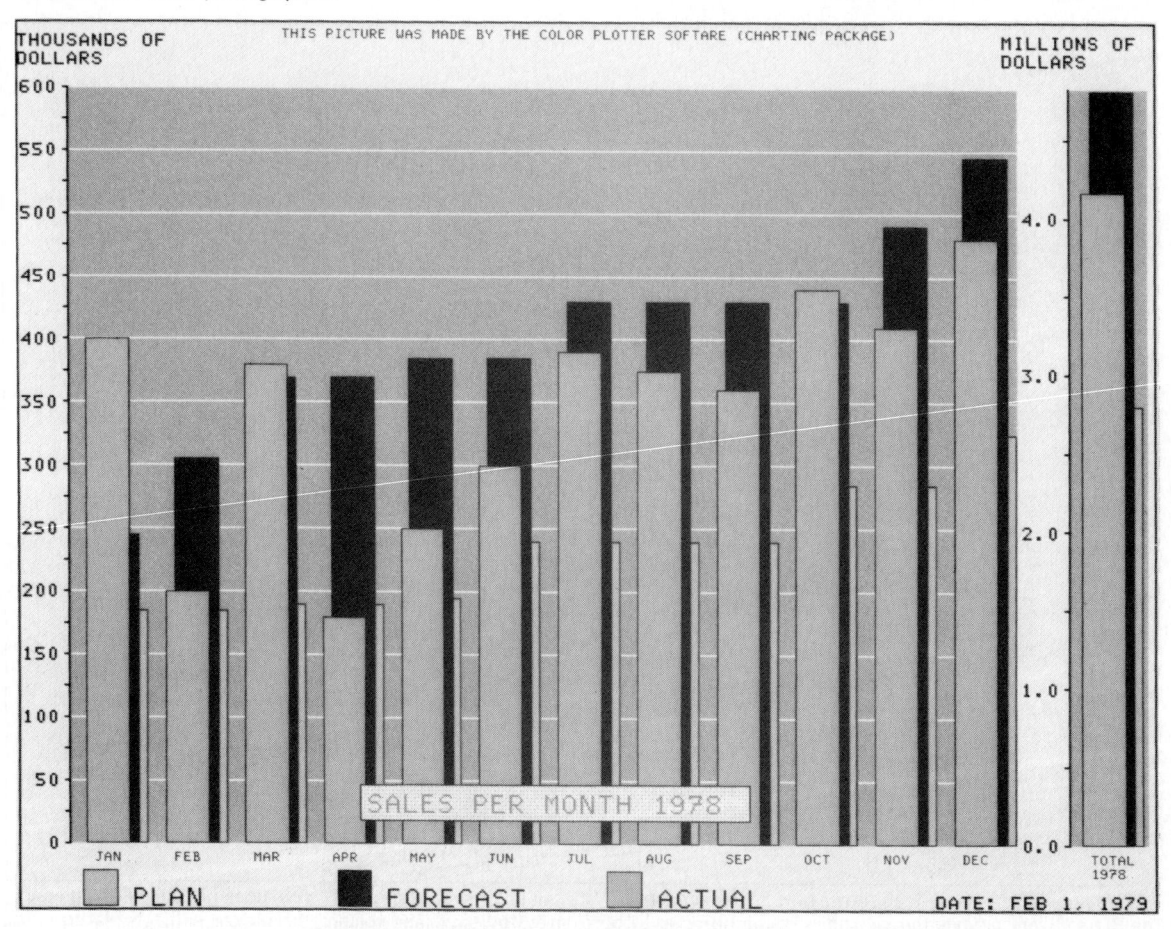

The graphics included here illustrate use of the COLOR charting software. Data scaling, axis labeling, bar segment height determination, and color legend creation are a few of the powerful features available.

Photo courtesy of Applicon Incorporated

ers are complaining about too much paper from the computer system. Dr. M. LeBouef, time management expert and author of *Working Smart,* believes that the paper blizzard from the computer system is a major time waster. To reduce the amount of paper, several alternatives have been developed, and one alternative that is attractive for companies that traditionally produce a large amount of paper is **computer output microfilm (COM)**. See Figure 9–9.

COM devices offer a number of advantages over paper output. Less storage space is required. Some companies have actually reduced storage requirements by more than 90 percent. Placing data on microfilm using a COM device is faster than using a line printer, and it is much less expensive to operate. If documents are to be sent by mail, microfilm can substantially reduce the

9 Special purpose hardware

FIGURE 9–8
The plotter

Photo courtesy of Applicon Incorporated

FIGURE 9–9
Computer output microfilm (COM)

Photo courtesy of NCR Corporation

postage costs. In addition, it can be faster to retrieve data that is on microfilm than data contained on paper documents. With these advantages, banks, universities, insurance companies, credit card companies, and telephone companies have all used COM.

The actual microfilm comes in different sizes and types but the most popular are **rolls of microfilm** and **microfiche cards,** that are usually about four inches by six inches. There are a number of devices used with microfilm. The **microfilm recorder** can input data directly from the computer system or from an auxiliary storage device such as magnetic tape. The **film developer** is like a self-contained photographic laboratory that produces the finished microfilm. Other equipment can be used to make *duplicate copies* of the microfilm, and special *printing devices* can be used to produce hard copy from the microfilm. Special readers are needed to read the microfilm. Some COM equipment is shown in Figure 9–10.

One of the biggest disadvantages of COM is the high initial expense of the COM equipment. As a result, this equipment is normally only used by companies and organizations that are large and have a great need for outputting data. Furthermore, since the data is stored offline on microfilm, it cannot be immediately accessed. In the past, there has been some difficulty in keeping the equipment in good working order. Many data processing managers did

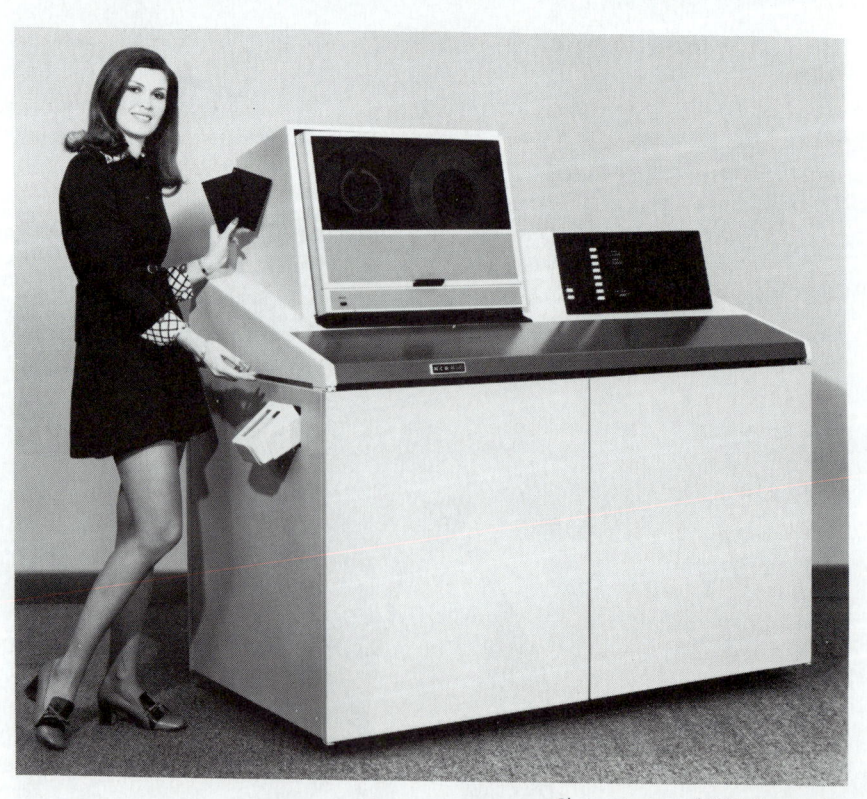

FIGURE 9–10
COM equipment

Photo courtesy of NCR Corporation

9 *Special purpose hardware*

not like the chemicals and plumbing. Some of the earlier equipment more closely resembled a photographic developing lab than a computer system. In recent years, however, many of the equipment related problems have been solved. Some COM devices use dry silver film that only requires heat.

To make the computer system easier to use, manufacturers have developed a number of other special purpose output devices. **Audio response** is an output media that produces verbal responses *from* the computer system. A computer device converts data stored in the computer system to electrical signals that can be transmitted over telephone lines.

Audio response units have a fixed number of words it can use. The list of words this device can use is called the *vocabulary* of the audio response unit. Depending on the audio response unit, the vocabulary can range from under 20 to over 200 words.

The computer can be programmed to write and play music through home stereo systems. The computer system can also assist in producing braille for the blind. Manufacturers are continuing to make output devices that generate data that we can see, hear, and feel, as long as it is convenient to use and meaningful.

Devices for input and output

An input/output device that many people already have in their home is the standard touch tone telephone. With the use of an audio response unit attached to the computer system, it is possible to convert a touch tone telephone into a computer terminal. The buttons on the phone are used for input, and the computer responds with a voice using an audio response unit. To cite an example, some banks are now using this system to allow customers to automatically obtain their balances in their accounts, to pay bills and to transfer funds from one account to another.

Retail stores are now using *special telephones* to check a customer's credit rating. There is a slot near the back of the phone, where a credit card can be placed. When a customer uses a credit card, one card is inserted in the slot which dials up the computer of the credit card company, and then the customer's credit card is inserted. If there is adequate credit, the phone shines a green light or the amount of the credit limit is given on a small screen. Otherwise a red light comes on.

Retail stores are also using a special terminal device which is helping to reduce checkout times and to keep a more accurate and more timely record of current inventory. The terminals are located at the checkout stand or the point at which the sale occurs. These devices are called **point of sale (POS) devices**. Different computer manufacturers have developed different coding systems that are placed on labels and affixed to products. At the checkout stand, these codes are read by a special wand or the product can be passed over a reading platform that is usually built into the counter.

Grocery stores have taken the lead by adopting a standardized code, called the **universal product code** (UPC). Since this code is standard for the entire

FIGURE 9–11
Universal product code (UPC)

Photo courtesy of IBM

industry, it can be placed on the product when it is manufactured. UPC was designed to satisfy a number of requirements. It can be read from any direction, and it has parity and character checking abilities. Furthermore, it was designed to have a low rejection rate, in many cases it can be less than 1 percent. In addition, UPC can be read by reading platforms, wands, and by people. See Figure 9–11.

The devices and systems that use POS in grocery stores vary. Some systems input data from the POS station directly into the computer system, while other systems place data on magnetic tape or cassettes first. Some systems use controllers, where one controller can handle over 20 POS terminals. The POS terminal inputs data to the controller, which sends the data to the computer system. Some POS equipment is shown in Figure 9–12.

POS offers a number of advantages over traditional cash registers. It is faster and requires lower operator skills. It can also be used to control credit and to reduce the number of bad debts. One of the biggest advantages of

9 *Special purpose hardware* 187

POS is its ability to be used in inventory control. POS can be used to keep an accurate record of current inventory. This will help reduce stockouts, prevent the ordering of slow moving items, and so on. Using POS can also save time and money when the products do not have to be individually marked. This, however, is one problem of POS. Many customers and consumer groups are demanding that all of the products be individually marked. An alternative to this would be to mark the price on the shelves. This problem has yet to be resolved. Even so, the future for POS systems is bright. It is estimated that in a few years, there will be more than 2 million POS terminals in operation. This could be from 50 percent to 75 percent of all retailing checkout stations.

In the near future, it is likely that a number of specialized input and output devices will be developed for the banking industry. These devices will be centered around a new system to transfer funds called **electronic funds transfer system** (EFTS). Even with the use of MICR, banks are still being plagued with paper transactions. The idea of EFTS is to transfer funds electronically instead of using paper documents. The savings to the banking industry could be enormous.

Already, we are witnessing the beginning of EFTS. Today, many banks have **automatic teller machines** (ATM) that can handle most routine banking

FIGURE 9–12
POS equipment

Photo courtesy of IBM

transactions. After inserting a card into the ATM, you can get money, pay bills, make deposits, move funds from one account to another and more. These machines can be located almost anywhere. A typical ATM is shown in Figure 9–13.

If EFTS were fully implemented, funds would be transferred electronically. This would mean that your pay check would be deposited directly into your checking or savings account. Of course, there are places where this is happening today. Furthermore, retail stores would be connected to banks and other financial institutions. Thus, if you make a purchase, your account would decrease, and the account of the retail store would increase by the amount of your purchase—instantly and automatically. With credit authorization, you could take out a short term loan at a retail store while shopping. Moreover, banks would be electronically connected. Instead of taking a few days or a week or more to transfer funds from one bank to another, the transfer could take place in seconds. This would reduce the time, called float, that it takes to complete a transaction once it is begun.

EFTS, however, has not been implemented as fast as some bankers would want. Part of the reason is due to the high cost of the equipment and a

FIGURE 9–13
An automatic teller machine (ATM)

Photo courtesy of Burroughs Corporation

9 Special purpose hardware

number of potential problems that have yet to be resolved. With any computer system, computer crime, security, privacy, and mistakes are always a potential problem. With EFTS, these potential problems become even more threatening. Until these problems have been adequately addressed and solved, it is unlikely that EFTS will be fully implemented. The Supplement to Chapter 18 discusses some recent EFTS legislation.

There are a number of other devices used for special purpose input and output. The airlines, illustrate this point. They employ special equipment that allows reservations to be made and tickets to be written automatically. As the prices of computer equipment decrease, more special purpose input and output devices will be developed.

While most of the developments in special purpose hardware has been with input and output devices, there are several special purpose permanent storage and central processing devices which will be discussed in this section.

PERMANENT STORAGE AND CENTRAL PROCESSING

Permanent storage devices

For large data users, a compromise between the disk and magnetic tape is needed. The expense of storing extremely large data files should be less than the disk, but the access speed should be much faster than magnetic tape. **Mass storage devices** have been developed to meet this compromise for large amounts of data.

One type of mass storage device is the IBM 3850, which consists of data cartridges stored in honeycomb type cells. See Figure 9–14.

Each cartridge contains a magnetic tape strip that is 3 inches by 770 inches. When data is accessed, the contents of one tape strip are automatically placed on a disk, which is then accessed by the computer system. This type of access is called *staging*. Other mass storage devices have also been developed by such companies as Control Data Corporation (CDC) and Ampex. The Ampex system uses a two inch wide strip of video tape. A single 10½ reel can hold over 5 billion bytes with access speeds of 15 seconds or less.

There are other permanent storage devices that have been developed over the years that have never become as popular as magnetic tape, the disk or the mass storage device. They include *drum storage* and *data cell storage*. The drum is coated with a magnetic material, and as it rotates, a read/write head directly accesses the data. Data cell storage consists of individual cells that contain magnetic tape strips that are about 2 inches wide by 13 inches long. When data is accessed, the computer system automatically finds the correct magnetic strip and reads or writes the appropriate data. While the data cell is an online device, it is not as fast as the disk.

Central processing devices

With the increase of computer networks and data communications, there has been more emphasis on the development of **communications processors.**

FIGURE 9–14
A mass storage device

Photo courtesy of IBM

A communications processor is a processing unit which coordinates networks and data communications. These processors are responsible for insuring that the data flows to and from different computer systems correctly and efficiently. In most cases, communication processors have temporary storage devices and circuitry that allows them to switch data and messages from an incoming computer system to its destination.

As mentioned in Part I, there are a number of special purpose central processing devices that are used by the military to control weapons and NASA to control space flights. Other central processing devices are designed to handle specific scientific and engineering applications. Some of these special purpose central processors are analog instead of digital. The difference between analog and digital computers was discussed in Part I.

With new developments in computer chips, there has been an increase in the use of **special purpose microprocessors.** These small processors are being placed in cars to monitor and in some cases control gasoline consumption and braking speeds on ice and snow. They can also be used to calculate the number of miles that can be driven without running out of gasoline given the current fuel supply and driving speed. Microprocessors are also

9 Special purpose hardware

being used in microwave ovens and watches. Microprocessors can be used to control air conditioners, heating systems, hot water heaters, lighting, and more in homes. Although some of these applications of microprocessors are relatively expensive, these small yet powerful processors will be saving energy and making our lives more enjoyable in the years to come.

SUMMARY

To accommodate the diverse needs of profit and nonprofit organizations, the companies in the data processing industry have developed a large number of special purpose hardware devices. Most of the innovations have been in input and output devices. MICR, OCR, OMR, industrial data collection devices, POS, portable data entry devices, plotters, COM, EFTS, ATM, and more are examples. Also, special purpose permanent storage devices, such as the mass storage device, the data cell, and the drum have been developed.

Communications processors and other special purpose processors for the military and NASA have also been developed to handle specific needs. One of the most exciting developments in special purpose processors has been with microprocessors. These devices are now being used in cars, watches, ovens, and homes, and it is expected that they will be used at an increasing rate in the future.

So far in this part, we have explored computer devices (hardware). When cabled together and supplied with software and people, these devices become complete computer systems. Like a stereo system or the furniture in a home, these devices can be combined in an almost limitless fashion to construct different computer systems. Since all computer systems perform the same basic functions, input, processing, and output, the major differences are their capacity and cost. In the next chapter, we will investigate computer systems that range from small computers that cost under $500 to very large computers that cost over $5,000,000.

KEY TERMS AND CONCEPTS

Audio response
Automatic teller machine (ATM)
Business Equipment Manufactures Association (BEMA)
Chips
Computer output microfilm (COM)
Data cartridge
Data cell
Drum
Electronic funds transfer system (EFTS)

Event driven
E13B
Farrington 7B
Industrial data collection
Magnetic ink character recognition (MICR)
Microfiche card
Microfilm
Microprocessors
OCR A
OCR B
Optical character recognition (OCR)

Optical mark recognition (OMR)
Plotter
Point of sale (POS)
Portable data entry
Port-a-punch
Speech recognition
United States American Standards Institute (USASI)
Universal product code (UPC)

QUESTIONS

9–1. What is MICR and how is it used?

9–2. Briefly describe the differences between OCR and OMR.

9–3. What is an industrial data collection device? Give some examples of how these devices are used.

9–4. List some of the portable data entry devices.

9–5. What is the difference between a printer and plotter? Describe some applications of the plotter.

9–6. What is COM, and under what circumstances should it be used?

9–7. Describe the meaning of POS and UPC.

9–8. How is EFTS used in the banking industry?

9–9. List and briefly describe some of the special purpose permanent storage devices.

9–10. What are some of the applications of special purpose processing devices?

MINIQUIZ

ANSWERS
1. T
2. F
3. F
4. T
5. F
6. T
7. F
8. F
9. T
10. F

True or False

_____ 1. MICR was developed by the banking industry to help ease the burden of processing checks.

_____ 2. MICR is limited to only 20 characters.

_____ 3. OMR and OCR are examples of systems that are used to process checks.

_____ 4. OCR A was developed by the Business Equipment Manufacturers Association.

_____ 5. A computer system that has the ability to understand human speech is called a voice response unit.

_____ 6. A plotter is a device that produces graphical displays of data.

_____ 7. A COM device is used by many companies to produce a higher volume of paper output than is possible with a standard printing device.

_____ 8. Microfiche is a roll of microfilm that is used by a URC device.

_____ 9. An audio response unit is an output device that produces verbal responses from the computer system.

_____ 10. A POS device is a special purpose permanent storage device.

Xerox converts stockroom into supply supermarket

Researchers, engineers and secretaries at Xerox Corp.'s research facility now pick their supplies off stockroom shelves and check them out in a matter of minutes, aided by an NCR minicomputer system which has eliminated long waiting lines and reduced paperwork. In addition, the flow of supplies has nearly doubled with only a small increase in staff, and lower overhead has been passed on directly in the form of lower markups.

The stockroom, operated by the Material Services Group (MSG), makes no profit. "We operate as a service for immediate supply needs," says Gary C. Mortensen, manager of MSG, "but we also operate under a tight budget that requires that we neither make nor lost (sic) money at the end of the year."

To meet his budget requirements, Mortensen charges back all withdrawals of stock to budget center managers, adding a markup to cover his overhead. No money changes hands, but all purchases are debited to departmental budgets. More than 5,000 people under more than 400 budget centers patronize the MSG's supermarket-style stockroom.

Until early this year, withdrawal of supplies was neither convenient nor well-controlled. People charging out goods would fill out a computer card for each item and hand it to a clerk who would pick up the item and bring it back to the counter.

Illegible signatures

The system was slow for customers and inaccurate for MSG. Customers commonly made mistakes in filling out the cards. For example, if a customer withdrew one of an item normally sold in dozens, the "1" on the card could mean either one each or one dozen. This became a problem for budget center managers who could be charged erroneously, and it also affected MSG's inventory control system. "We were asking our customers to do the input, and when you put pen to paper there's always a chance of error," Mortensen says.

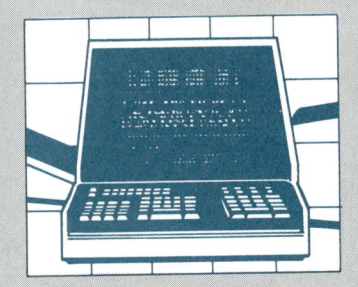

Unauthorized withdrawals also created a problem. It was impossible for the stock clerks to police everyone coming into the stockroom. Signatures often were illegible on the cards, so that neither MSG nor the budget center managers maintained any control over who purchased what items.

"I was constantly receiving calls from budget center managers, and had no way to answer their questions," Mortensen says. "We could only go by the data in the reports, so we didn't really have any more information than they did."

Mortensen began looking for an automated system that would provide accountability for every item withdrawn, control of inventory, and would take data input out of the hands of the customers. He finally installed a unique system designed for him by NCR systems analysts, one very similar to the scanning systems used in supermarkets.

Electronic terminals, similar to cash registers, use a pen-like wand to scan a tag attached to each item. A magnetic tape cassette inside the terminal records the data encoded on the tag and at the end of the day the cassettes are read into the computer.

Color-coded tags

Color-bar-coded tags issued to employees control authorization to purchase. Budget center managers designate people who may withdraw supplies, and then MSG makes up a tag identifying that person. Nobody is allowed in the stockroom without the authorization tag, so withdrawals are restricted only to authorized persons. All people entering the stockroom must pass the counter, showing their authorization tag to the clerk. Customers then are free to browse in the stockroom, picking what they need off the shelves.

As customers leave the terminal operator first passes an electronic wand over the authorization tag, recording the customer data on the terminal's

Source: *Minicomputer News*, February 1978.

tape cassette. The tags on each item then are scanned, providing an accurate, cumulative record on the tape. The clerk then puts the items in a paper bag and staples the terminal-printed receipt to the top.

"The system completely eliminates paperwork at the checkout," says Mortensen. "People have told me they now can complete transactions that used to take 45 minutes in three or four minutes. Not only does this reduce their frustration level, but it also returns a lot of researchers and engineers to their jobs sooner."

Once the data are recorded on tape, they can be processed on the NCR 8200 minicomputer. The computer uses programming developed by NCR for wholesalers, and modified to serve Mortensen's unique requirements. In all, the installation includes the 8200 with 64K words of memory, two disk units totalling 20 megabytes, a 300 line-per-minute printer, three CRTs and five cash-register-like terminals.

Inventory control

One of the system's most important functions is inventory control. The system provides daily buyers' reports and out-of-stock and below-minimum reports to MSG materials specialists so that stock levels can be maintained. The reports also aid in reducing overstocking by allowing shifting stock between stockrooms.

The system has paid for itself. Mortensen says, and he has been able to move twice the volume in the stockroom with only a slight increase in manpower. Total overhead cost, including computer and terminal rental, has decreased significantly. MSG cut its 60 percent markup to 50 percent when it switched from over-the-counter to supermarket-style sales, then to 35 percent with the new minicomputer system. An item which wholesales for $1 now costs $1.35 from MSG, rather than $1.60— a total reduction in both markup and overhead of 42 percent.

Following the supermarket analogy further, Mortensen also is studying the movement of specific items using a sales analysis prepared by the computer. A guide to what items to stock, and at what levels, the analysis also will indicate the amount of shelf space to allocate to each.

Each budget center manager receives a monthly report that lists every item withdrawn by each member of his staff, each person's name and the cost of the materials. If he wishes, he can have his staff turn in their withdrawn receipts so he can check them against the computer report. If necessary, he can call MSG any time during the month for a verbal update on his account.

"I used to get a lot of complaints from budget center managers, but because of the completeness of the reports and accuracy of the data, these calls have almost stopped," Mortensen says.

DISCUSSION QUESTIONS

1. What types of special purpose hardware devices are being used by Xerox to make their stockroom more efficient and effective?
2. What are the advantages of using this type of special purpose hardware?
3. Are there other industries or businesses that could benefit from this type of system?

Computer systems

10

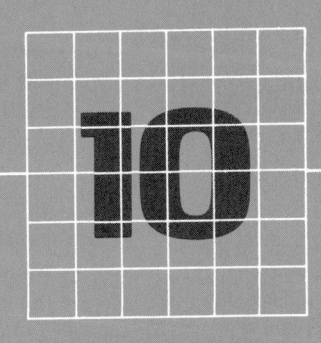

MICROCOMPUTERS
MINICOMPUTERS
SMALL COMPUTER SYSTEMS
MEDIUM AND LARGE COMPUTER SYSTEMS
CENTRALIZED, DECENTRALIZED, AND DISTRIBUTED SYSTEMS

After completing Chapter 10, you will be able to:

- Discuss the use of microcomputers and minicomputers.
- List some of the advantages and disadvantages of using small computer systems.
- Describe the applications and equipment configurations of medium and large computer systems.

A few decades ago, computer systems were large and expensive. With the development of the chip, the size and expense of computer systems have dropped, while computer capabilities have increased. Today, a complete computer system can be purchased for under $500 or for more than $5 million. This offers the user a wide selection of computer systems. Depending on the capabilities and the purchase price, computer systems can be categorized into *microcomputers, minicomputers, small computers, medium computers,* and *large computers.* With the large number of computer systems and configurations, these categories are not always clearly defined. Prices and capabilities overlap for the various categories, and thus, we will be investigating price and capability ranges.

In addition to price and equipment capabilities, there are a number of other important factors to consider in the selection and use of a computer system. These factors include the availability of application software, the personnel required to operate the computer system, the reputation and reliability of the computer manufacturer, whether or not the equipment is easy to use, methods for insuring security and privacy, and so on. The thrust of this chapter is to discuss computer systems of different sizes and capabilities. Advantages and disadvantages of these computer systems will also be explored.

MICROCOMPUTERS

With purchase prices that range from under $500 to $5,000 the **microcomputer** offers computer power to engineers, educators, students, lawyers, and other professionals. Many complete microcomputer systems can be purchased for under $500. This low price makes these computer systems attractive to the individual and small business or nonprofit organization. Also called the personal computer, microcomputers will be one of the fastest growing markets in the computer industry. Some experts even predict that the influence of the microcomputer on society will be greater than the effect of the industrial revolution.

The microcomputer contains the same types of hardware and software of larger computer systems, but because of its low purchase price, it is an attractive alternative to calculators. Today, microcomputers are being purchased for home, personal, school, and business use. A supplement at the end of this chapter covers microcomputers in detail.

MINICOMPUTERS

Costing between $2,000 and $100,000, the **minicomputer** has rapidly evolved in the last ten years. In the late 1960s, there were only about 5,000 minicomputers in use. By 1970, this figure jumped to over 10,000 and in the near future, the number of minicomputers is expected to be well over 500,000. If this trend continues, minicomputers will be the fastest growing segment of the computer industry.

Originally, the minicomputer was used for specific applications such as controlling a piece of manufacturing equipment. With advances in software and hardware coupled with price reductions, the minicomputer has become a general purpose computer system. Many minicomputers are capable of

Computer systems

10

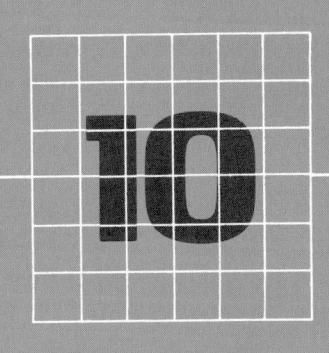

MICROCOMPUTERS
MINICOMPUTERS
SMALL COMPUTER SYSTEMS
MEDIUM AND LARGE COMPUTER SYSTEMS
CENTRALIZED, DECENTRALIZED, AND DISTRIBUTED SYSTEMS

After completing Chapter 10, you will be able to:

- Discuss the use of microcomputers and minicomputers.
- List some of the advantages and disadvantages of using small computer systems.
- Describe the applications and equipment configurations of medium and large computer systems.

A few decades ago, computer systems were large and expensive. With the development of the chip, the size and expense of computer systems have dropped, while computer capabilities have increased. Today, a complete computer system can be purchased for under $500 or for more than $5 million. This offers the user a wide selection of computer systems. Depending on the capabilities and the purchase price, computer systems can be categorized into *microcomputers, minicomputers, small computers, medium computers,* and *large computers.* With the large number of computer systems and configurations, these categories are not always clearly defined. Prices and capabilities overlap for the various categories, and thus, we will be investigating price and capability ranges.

In addition to price and equipment capabilities, there are a number of other important factors to consider in the selection and use of a computer system. These factors include the availability of application software, the personnel required to operate the computer system, the reputation and reliability of the computer manufacturer, whether or not the equipment is easy to use, methods for insuring security and privacy, and so on. The thrust of this chapter is to discuss computer systems of different sizes and capabilities. Advantages and disadvantages of these computer systems will also be explored.

MICROCOMPUTERS

With purchase prices that range from under $500 to $5,000 the **microcomputer** offers computer power to engineers, educators, students, lawyers, and other professionals. Many complete microcomputer systems can be purchased for under $500. This low price makes these computer systems attractive to the individual and small business or nonprofit organization. Also called the personal computer, microcomputers will be one of the fastest growing markets in the computer industry. Some experts even predict that the influence of the microcomputer on society will be greater than the effect of the industrial revolution.

The microcomputer contains the same types of hardware and software of larger computer systems, but because of its low purchase price, it is an attractive alternative to calculators. Today, microcomputers are being purchased for home, personal, school, and business use. A supplement at the end of this chapter covers microcomputers in detail.

MINICOMPUTERS

Costing between $2,000 and $100,000, the **minicomputer** has rapidly evolved in the last ten years. In the late 1960s, there were only about 5,000 minicomputers in use. By 1970, this figure jumped to over 10,000 and in the near future, the number of minicomputers is expected to be well over 500,000. If this trend continues, minicomputers will be the fastest growing segment of the computer industry.

Originally, the minicomputer was used for specific applications such as controlling a piece of manufacturing equipment. With advances in software and hardware coupled with price reductions, the minicomputer has become a general purpose computer system. Many minicomputers are capable of both batch and real-time processing. These topics are discussed in Chapter 11. Minicomputers are attractive to organizations of all sizes. For the small business, the minicomputer provides an attractive alternative to manually or mechanically processing data. For the larger company or nonprofit organization, the minicomputer has a number of uses. For example, a minicomputer can be used as a remote data entry device that prepares data for input into a larger computer system. Furthermore, some large companies have turned in their large computer for a number of minicomputers that operate independently at different locations. This is called a *decentralized data processing* system. In addition, minicomputers can be electronically connected to a central computer system. This is called *distributed data processing*. These concepts are discussed in the last section of this chapter.

Minicomputers are also used to control scoreboards at sports facilities, prepare mailing lists, collect laboratory data, control cash machines at banks, perform quality control, regulate temperature and pressure at chemical plants, and other specific applications. In most cases, minicomputers are word oriented, and up to ten times faster than microcomputers.

The availability of hardware and peripheral equipment for the minicomputer is greater than the less expensive microcomputer. Most minicomputers come with a main storage device that has a capacity of from 4K bytes to over 100K bytes. Input devices such as the card reader and the CRT [visual display unit] are typical with the minicomputer. As with the microcomputer, the floppy or flexible disk and cassette tape permanent storage devices are popular with the minicomputer. Standard disk, tape, and card devices are also used with minicomputers, although these devices are relatively slow. Output devices include card punch equipment, teletypewriters, video display screens, and small printers. Depending on the minicomputer, peripheral equipment and special purpose hardware devices can be purchased from the minicomputer manufacturer or a peripheral equipment manufacturer. Over the last few years, there has been a continued reduction in price, while the capabilities of the hardware have increased. Today, minicomputers are taking over the tasks that were done with small and medium computer systems. Figure 10–1 shows a typical minicomputer.

Application software packages once only available to medium and large computer users are now available to the minicomputer user. There have been complete application software packages developed for a large number of different industries and businesses. Application software for transportation companies, food companies, hospitals, paper companies, construction companies and a number of other organizations have already been developed. There have also been improvements in the system software available on minicomputers. Developments in language translators have made high-level programming languages such as FORTRAN, BASIC, RPG, COBOL, and several other languages available on minicomputers. Operating systems and utility programs are also being improved. Some minicomputer manufacturers are even boasting of data base management systems (DBMS).

One of the first manufacturers of minicomputers was Digital Equipment

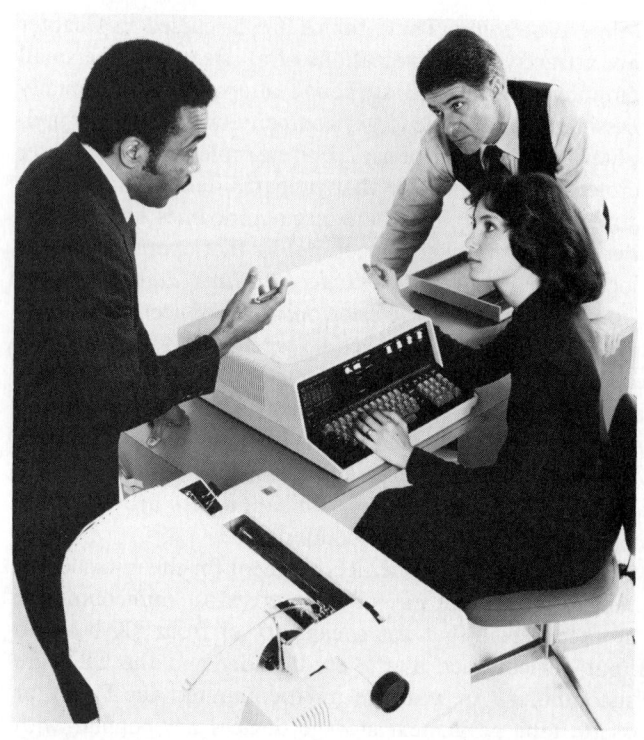

FIGURE 10-1
A minicomputer system

Photo courtesy of IBM

Corporation (DEC). Today, DEC is the leader in sales of minicomputers with over 50 percent of the market. Other manufacturers of minicomputers include Honeywell, Hewlett-Packard, Data General, Basic/Four, General Automation, Olivetti, Philips Business Systems, Tektronix, Wang Laboratories, IBM, Burroughs, and NCR. Although some of these manufacturers offer a lease/purchase option, the user is still encouraged to purchase the minicomputer. In two to five years the cost of leasing could equal the purchase price. The service and reliability of the minicomputer manufacturer varies considerably. While some minicomputer manufacturers offer excellent training, maintenance agreements, software support, and general trouble shooting and consulting, other minicomputer manufacturers provide very little service. If the user of the minicomputer is a large company with a complete staff of data processing professionals, service from the manufacturer may not be too important. On the other hand, service from the computer vendor can be critical if the user is a small, first time user of computer equipment. This is especially true if the small user is completely converting from a manual or mechanical data processing system to a minicomputer. Problems that require vendor support and service are likely to occur.

Perhaps one of the greatest advantages of using a minicomputer is the low price coupled with greater capabilities. The speeds and storage capacity of today's minicomputer are approaching the speed and capacity of older medium computer systems. Minicomputers, like microcomputers, require no special wiring and air conditioning, and they are small, portable, and easy to use. Their small size means that they can be placed in the same room with other furniture. In addition, it is not necessary to have a complete staff of data processing professionals. Depending upon the size of the minicomputer system, from one to over five people can be employed to run the minicomputer system. In many cases, existing employees are trained by the minicomputer manufacturer, and thus new employees are sometimes not required. The same types of equipment that are used with a large computer system can be used with minicomputers. This equipment can be obtained from the minicomputer manufacturer or from a number of peripheral equipment vendors that specialize in manufacturing equipment and devices for minicomputers. Software advances have also made minicomputers more attractive. As discussed previously, many application software packages have been developed for specific industries and businesses. Furthermore, there are many reputable software companies that do nothing but develop software for minicomputers. Advances in system software for minicomputers have also been made. Some of the minicomputer vendors offer **turnkey** systems. This type of system is complete with hardware, software, training, and everything that is needed to simply turn the key and operate the computer system. Some minicomputer manufacturers refer to this approach as "hand holding," where the manufacturer does virtually everything for and with the minicomputer user. For small and first time computer users, a turnkey approach is very attractive. Minicomputers are very flexible and modular. These small computers can accommodate a number of peripheral equipment devices, and they can grow with the organization. Some minicomputer manufacturers are subdividing their minicomputer systems into three categories. These three categories are the *mini-minicomputer,* the *midi-minicomputer,* and the *maxi-minicomputer.* As you go from mini-minicomputers to maxi-minicomputers, prices, capabilities, speeds, and storage capacities all increase.

There are, however, a number of disadvantages of using a minicomputer. Some jobs are simply too complex or too large for a minicomputer. While some minicomputer manufacturers are reliable and provide excellent support, a number of minicomputer manufacturers are not. Service, training, maintenance of hardware and software, and general support can be almost nonexistant with some minicomputer vendors. In addition, the peripheral equipment can be very expensive. It could cost more to purchase the needed peripheral equipment than it costs to purchase the basic computer system itself. Acquiring adequate software can also be a problem. If an application package exists that satisfies a company's needs, software costs can be moderate. Software can be 50 to 90 percent of the total cost. If the owner of the minicomputer does not have much experience with computer systems and decides to build software packages, there can be problems. This process can be very long and expensive, and the resulting software could be full of errors. Buying software from a software company can also be expensive, and if the user of the minicomputer is not experienced, the software package that is purchased could be totally inadequate. Like microcomputers, many minicomputers do not have any procedures or systems to provide security, privacy, or adequate computer crime protection. Because many minicomputer users are small and do not have previous experience with computers, a number of other problems can occur. Many minicomputer users do not plan for the possibility of fire, floods, and other disasters. One disaster could destroy the hardware and software and seriously jeopardize the functioning of the organization. Some minicomputer users forget to keep adequate back-up files. Again, if files are accidently destroyed, the small company or organization could face severe difficulties. Crime, fraud, privacy, and security can also be a problem. Even with these disadvantages, the growth of minicomputer users is expected to continue.

SMALL COMPUTER SYSTEMS

In general, the price of **small computer systems** ranges from $50,000 to $500,000, although there are small computer systems whose price falls outside of this range. Originally, small computer systems used cards for permanent storage and operated in the batch mode. Like other computer systems, increasing technology and price decreases have expanded the desirability and application of the small computer system. Today, small computer systems are both *batch oriented,* where a group or batch of transactions and jobs are processed at one time, and *transaction oriented,* where the computer system responds and takes action as the transactions occur. Now, small computer systems are also being used by large companies and organizations to supplement their larger computer systems. A small computer system is shown in Figure 10–2.

Small computer systems can accommodate a number of hardware devices. These devices are available from both the computer manufacturer and the peripheral equipment dealers. In general, more peripheral equipment is available from the small computer manufacturer. Since many small computer systems are still card oriented, some excellent card handling equipment is available. For example, many small computer systems will accommodate multifunction card machines. These machines can substantially reduce the amount of card handling that is necessary when cards are used for permanent storage. Small computer systems can also use tape and disk for permanent storage. Some small computer systems will interface with high speed disk and tape drives. Faster input and output devices are also available with small computer systems. Faster line-at-a-time printers are found on small computer systems, while slower character-at-a-time printers are common with minicomputers and microcomputers. Card readers that can read over 1,000 cards per minute are also available. The faster photoelectric sensing card readers are available with small computer systems. Most of the hardware devices discussed in this part can be interfaced with small computer systems.

Better and more complete software also can accompany the small computer system and many more application software packages are available for small computer systems compared to minicomputers. These applications can serve

FIGURE 10–2
A small computer system

Photo courtesy of Honeywell Information Systems

hospitals, banks, manufacturing companies, retail stores, transportation companies, import/export companies, scientific and engineering firms, small colleges and universities, and more. In addition to application software, there are improvements in system software. Some small computer systems are now using multiprogramming, multiprocessing, virtual storage and data base management systems. These concepts are fully discussed in Part III. Many high-level programming languages are also available. Often small computer systems can accommodate FORTRAN, COBOL, BASIC, RPG, and a number of other programming languages. There have also been improvements in language translators, operating systems, and utility programs.

There are several companies that manufacture small computer systems. These companies include IBM, NCR, Burroughs, Honeywell, DEC, and Control Data Corporation. Some of these manufacturers are large and have an excellent reputation for providing service and support to users of small computer systems. These manufacturers offer application software for a number of different industries, maintenance agreements, purchase or lease options, training programs for computer operators and other data processing personnel, and executive seminars on how to get more from the small computer system.

The small computer system has a number of advantages over microcomputers and minicomputers. More application software packages are available and the service from the computer manufacturer can be superior. Small computer systems also have an attractive price/performance ratio. Furthermore, these small computer systems are attractive for large computer users that want to use a small computer in conjunction with their large computer system. Most small computer systems are modular and flexible. This means that they can accommodate a number of devices and that they can grow with the needs of the organization. For organizations that want a batch oriented card system, a small computer system can be an excellent choice. Some of the first small computer systems were batch oriented, and these computer systems still do an excellent job with this type of processing. Small computer systems can also be used for transaction oriented processing.

Small computer systems have a number of disadvantages. A higher price has caused some small organizations to use minicomputers instead. In some cases, special wiring is required. In addition, many small computer systems require a small staff of computer personnel. A manager, a systems analyst, a programmer, and an equipment operator may be required to get the most from the computer equipment. For smaller installations, a programmer/analyst and an equipment operator may be needed. The use of specially trained computer personnel can cause special problems. If an organization relies too much on its computer personnel and a few key people leave for higher paying jobs, the company may find itself in a position of not having the needed skilled personnel to run the computer installation. With bills to send out and employees to pay, this might be a serious problem. Many small computer systems are not adequately protected against security, crime, and privacy.

MEDIUM AND LARGE COMPUTER SYSTEMS

As you move up to medium and large computer systems, it becomes even more difficult to develop categories that distinguish between medium, large, and super large computer systems. It is more a matter of degree than a matter of specific and distinguishable categories. The price of *medium computer systems* normally starts at about $150,000 and goes up to over $1,500,000. *Large computer systems* overlap this range. Prices start at about $1 million and increase beyond the $5 million amount. These computer systems are used by medium and large sized companies and nonprofit organizations. Large manufacturing companies, universities, municipal governments, national stock market and commodity exchanges, large financial institutions, stock and bond firms, airlines, hotels, large hospitals, and a number of federal agencies use medium and large computer systems. Microcomputers, minicomputers, and small computer systems can be used in conjunction with medium and large computer systems. This can be done using a number of different configurations. The smaller computer can be decentralized or distributed. These concepts are discussed later in this chapter. They can also be used

FIGURE 10–3A
Medium systems

Photo courtesy of Honeywell Information Systems

FIGURE 10–3B
Medium systems

Photo courtesy of NCR Corporation

for data entry. Both scientific and business applications are possible with these larger and faster computer systems. Medium computer systems are shown in Figures 10–3A and 10–3B.

Medium and large computer systems can support the ultimate in hardware devices and equipment. All of the devices discussed in this part can be used with medium and large computer systems. Most medium and large computer systems use several different ways of data input. Card input, visual display units, POS, MICR, OCR, voice recognition can all be used by the same computer system. Likewise, medium and large computer systems can support a number of different permanent storage devices at the same time. It is common for these computers to store data on disks with tape and card backups. There could be five or more tape and disk drives. Medium and large computer systems can also accommodate a large number of different and sophisticated output devices. It is not uncommon for a medium computer system to have two or more fast line printers. Indeed, large computer systems may have over 20 line printers connected to it that may be located thousands of miles from the main computer system. Voice response units, COM, plotters, teleprinters, and more can be connected to one large computer system. Central processing units for medium and large computer systems are large, fast and sophisticated. A large computer may have 500K bytes, and a super large computer system may have over 5,000K bytes for main storage. Processing speeds are measured in nanoseconds or picoseconds instead of microseconds or milliseconds. Processing can take place in a batch oriented environment or a transaction oriented environment. In addition, main storage can be organized using a word orientation or a character orientation. These larger computer systems are modular and flexible. It is possible to tailor make a computer system to meet specific needs. An airline reservation system, for example, might have over 200 terminals located all over the world that are connected to the same large computer system. A large bank, on the other hand, might have over 20 automatic teller machines (ATM) attached to the same computer system. A university might have a COM device to keep student records and other information on microfilm. An engineering or scientific company might have limited input and output devices, but this type of organization might have two or more large CPU's connected together to provide extremely fast processing speeds and the ability to handle complex calculations and algorithms with ease. After an organization has determined its needs, it can acquire the necessary equipment that will satisfy these needs. Large computer systems are shown in Figures 10–4A and 10–4B.

The most advanced software is available with medium and large computer systems. Most manufacturers have a complete line of application software to service banks, universities, manufacturing companies, hospitals, municipal governments, and other organizations. Furthermore, these application software packages can contain excellent *management information system* (MIS) packages. System software normally comes with virtual storage, multiprocessing, multiprogramming, and data base management systems. These concepts are explained in Part III. All of the high-level programming languages are

10 Computer systems

FIGURE 10–4A
Large systems

Photo courtesy of NCR Corporation

FIGURE 10–4B
Large systems

Photo courtesy of General Automation

available on medium and large computer systems. Excellent utility programs are also included that help in merging files, sorting data, and in transferring data from one storage device to another. Management by exception, decision support systems, and management inquiries are possible with the software available for medium and large computer systems.

Because of the complexity and cost of larger computer systems, there are a limited number of manufacturers for medium and large computer systems. Without question, IBM is the largest producer of medium and large computer systems. Other manufacturers include Burroughs, Honeywell, NCR, Control Data Corporation, Sperry Univac Division of Sperry Rand Corporation, DEC and Amdahl. These manufacturers normally offer a number of financial options. A medium or a large computer system can be purchased, leased, or rented. Lease/purchase options are also available. Generally speaking, these companies are more reputable and offer better service than computer manufacturers of smaller systems. These large computer manufacturers have offices all over the world to serve their customers. All types of training, maintenance, trouble shooting, seminars, and support are available.

There are advantages and disadvantages to consider before a medium or large computer system is acquired. Advantages include the best hardware, software, and vendor support. These computer systems are faster, more sophisticated, have larger storage capacities, and can accommodate more peripheral equipment and devices than any other computer system. For some organizations, a large computer system is the only system that will satisfy their needs. There are, however, a number of disadvantages. Large computer systems are expensive to acquire and use. Special wiring and air conditioning are usually required. In addition, a computer staff or department is required in most cases. This staff would include a data processing manager and one or more systems analysts, computer programmers, computer operators, and data entry operators. These positions are discussed in more detail in Part IV. Before a computer is installed, it may be necessary to modify one or more rooms to make space for the computer system. If the rooms were used for another purpose, there is an opportunity cost of placing the computer in these rooms. For example, if there were hospital rooms earning over $100 per day when occupied, the hospital could lose thousands of dollars each month by not having the rooms available for patients. Other rooms will be needed for the data processing staff. Acquiring a new medium or large computer system is like acquiring a new department or branch office. New personnel, equipment, procedures, office space, supplies, secretaries, and so on will be needed.

CENTRALIZED, DECENTRALIZED, AND DISTRIBUTED SYSTEMS

The first computer systems were normally placed in one or more connecting rooms, and all of the processing was conducted at this one location. This is called a *centralized data processing system*. See Figure 10–5.

In this example the company has a main office, three branch offices and two warehouses. There is one central computer system, which is located at the main office. Today, there are many organizations that still use a centralized

Computers have incalculably changed our lives. They are helping us at home, at school, and at work. With continuing technological advances, computers will have an even greater impact on society in the future.

Courtesy of IBM

Courtesy of IBM

Some special display terminals and printers can actually display computer output in full color. This is both attractive and informative. Multicolor output can be used to graphically display such things as military defense positions, parts of the body for doctors, and the airline reservation status for a particular flight.

With visual display terminals, also called cathode ray tubes (CRTs), people are able to conveniently direct and control computer systems of all sizes. Because they are small and inexpensive, display terminals can be placed in offices, on the production floor, in warehouses, at checkout stands, in the classroom, and at home.

Computer systems range from inexpensive microcomputers that cost less than $500 to large, sophisticated computer systems that cost more than $5,000,000. This great difference in price represents a vast array of equipment, software, and system configurations.

Courtesy of Honeywell

Medium computer systems can support most types of hardware and software. Multiple terminals, fast printers, and popular high-level programming languages are available with medium computer systems.

Large computer systems can support the ultimate in hardware and software. These computers are being used by large businesses, universities, and governmental agencies.

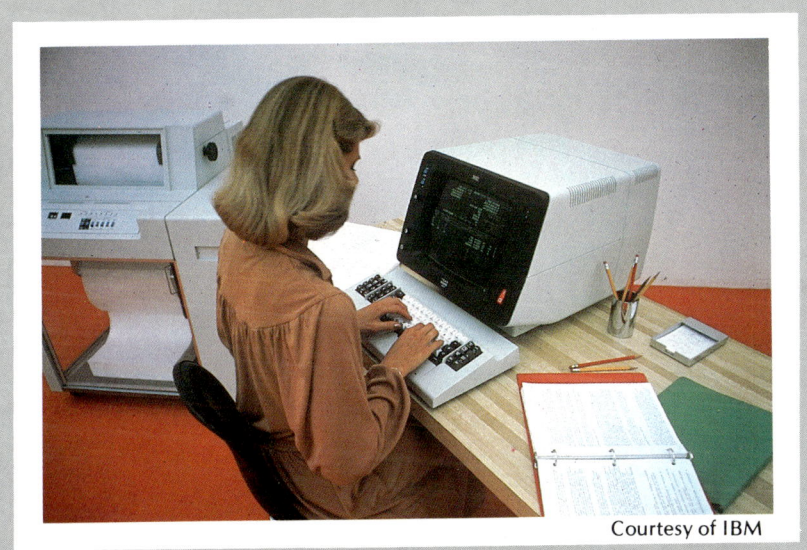

Mini- and small computer systems are the fastest growing segment in the data processing industry. These inexpensive computer systems bring the full power of computerization to small businesses and organizations.

Courtesy of IBM

Courtesy of Burroughs Corporation

In the past, processing jobs were brought to a centralized computer facility. Today, through the use of data communications and special purpose equipment, computer systems and devices are being placed where the action is.

Many large retail stores are using point of scale (POS) terminals to enter sales data. These types of terminals can be used to help control inventory, check customer credit, and more.

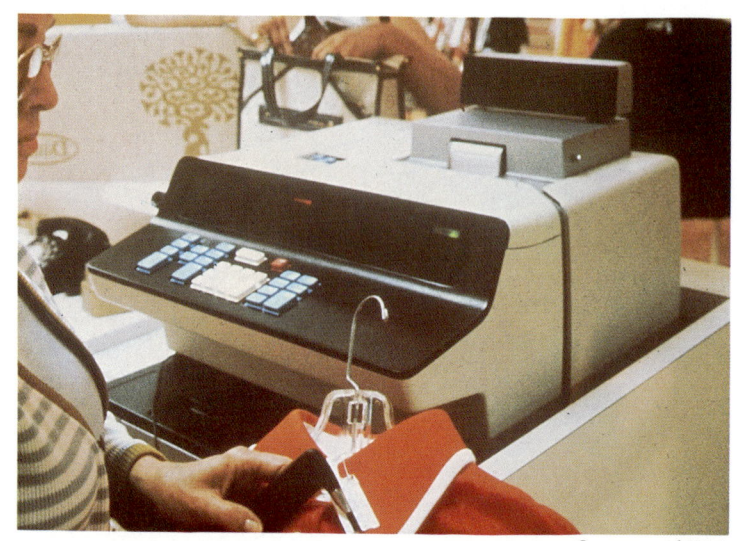

Courtesy of IBM

Timely and accurate information is a valuable commodity. On the floor of the stock options board and at investment firms all over the world, computer-displayed information is used to make split-second decisions involving millions of dollars.

Courtesy of Milt and Joan Mann/Cameramann International

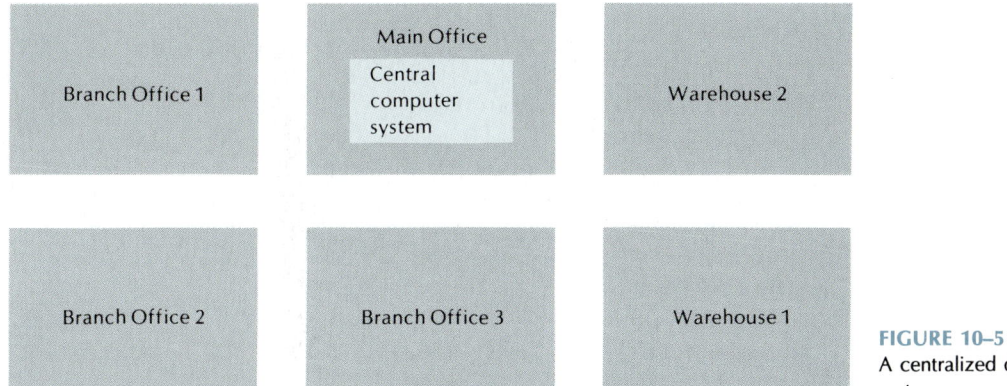

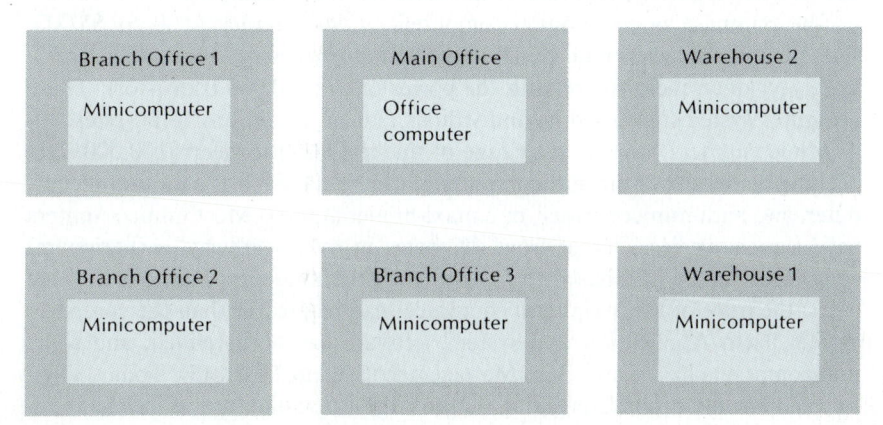

FIGURE 10–5
A centralized data processing system

data processing system. As long as the processing is done at a central location, the data processing system is called a centralized data processing system.

Another approach to locating data processing facilities is to physically place processing units at various locations within the organizations. These processing units are usually microcomputers, minicomputers, or small computer systems, which operate independently of each other. This configuration is called a *decentralized data processing system*. See Figure 10–6.

In Figure 10–6 there is a computer located at each branch office and warehouse. Furthermore, there is a computer system at the main office. With this type of placement, it is not uncommon to have a data processing manager at each computer site.

While a centralized data processing system can offer economy and efficiency, it may not allow adequate access to the computer system. A decentralized data processing system can offer immediate access to the computer system, but transferring data from one computer system to another, or coordinating data processing activities in general, can be very difficult. Another type of data processing configuration has been developed that attempts to capture the advantages of both a centralized and decentralized data processing

FIGURE 10–6
A decentralized data processing system

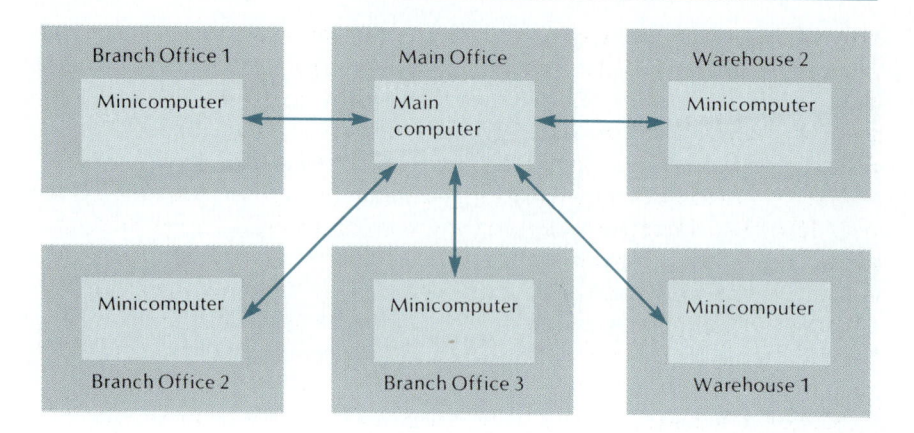

FIGURE 10–7
A distributed data processing system

[Diagram: Main computer at Main Office connected bidirectionally with Minicomputers at Branch Office 1, Branch Office 2, Branch Office 3, Warehouse 1, and Warehouse 2]

system, while eliminating some of the disadvantages of these systems. This configuration is called a *distributed data processing system*. In this type system, the CPU's are distributed throughout the organization and electrically connected together. See Figure 10–7.

Each computer can be used to process data by itself like a decentralized system. In addition, a computer at one location can transfer data and processing jobs to and from the computers at the other locations.

In this section, we have investigated purely centralized, decentralized, and distributed data processing systems. Many organizations use a combination of one or more of these systems. Processing units can be arranged in almost every conceivable way.

SUMMARY

A few years ago, only large companies and organizations could afford to use computer systems. Today, computer systems can be purchased for under $500 or for over $5,000,000. Although it is difficult to classify computer systems, price ranges and capacities can normally be used to develop approximate categories. This chapter has investigated microcomputers, minicomputers, small computers, medium computers, and large computers.

The purchase price of microcomputers is from under $500 to $5,000. These computers are made possible with microprocessors that are approximately ¼ of an inch square with the power of over 20,000 transistors. These computer systems are used by individuals and organizations of all sizes.

Minicomputers have a cost range of under $2,000 to over $100,000. Depending on the size of the minicomputer, it can be classified as a mini-minicomputer, and midi-minicomputer, or a maxi-minicomputer. Most minicomputers have a memory capacity of from 4K bytes to over 100K bytes. Peripheral equipment can be purchased to be used with the minicomputer, but in some cases, the price of the peripheral equipment can be greater than the computer system itself. Application and system software has been refined, and some minicomputers have Data Base Management Systems (DBMS). Today, Digital Equipment Corporation (DEC) is the largest manufacturer of minicomputers with over 50 percent of the market. Other manufacturers include Honeywell, NCR, IBM, Hewlett-Packard, and Wang Laboratories. The low price of minicomputers along with the increased capacities has made the minicomputer industry the fastest growing industry in data processing today. Some minicomputer systems are turnkey—completely ready to go.

The purchase price of small computers ranges from under $50,000 to over $500,000. These computer systems were originally card oriented, but today, most small computer systems can also be transaction oriented. Small computers can accommodate a large number of hardware devices, and the system and application software is more advanced than with minicomputers. On the other hand, some small computers require special wiring and air conditioning. A staff of data processing professionals may also be required.

Medium computers have purchase prices that range from about $150,000 to $1,500,000. Large computer systems have purchase prices that range from about $1,000,000 to over $5,000,000. Medium and large computer systems offer the ultimate in hardware, software, and vendor support. On the other hand, these systems require special wiring, air conditioning, rooms, and a complete data processing staff.

In the past, computer facilities were centralized in one location. Another option is to have processing devices operate independently from one another. This is called decentralized data processing. When the processing facilities are located apart but are electronically connected together, the system is called distributed.

KEY TERMS AND CONCEPTS

Centralized systems	Medium computers	Minicomputers
Decentralized systems	Microcomputers	Small computers
Distributed systems	Microprocessors	Turnkey
Large computers		

QUESTIONS

10-1. Describe the use of microprocessors in microcomputers and other devices.

10-2. What are the price range, advantages, and disadvantages of microcomputers?

10-3. What are some of the manufacturers of minicomputers?

10-4. Contrast the availability of hardware and software of minicomputers with small computer systems.

10-5. Discuss how a small computer system can be used for batch and transaction oriented processing. What equipment allows a small computer system to be used for batch processing?

10-6. What are some of the advantages and disadvantages of a small computer system?

10-7. Describe the software that is usually available with medium and large computer systems.

10-8. List the advantages and disadvantages of acquiring a medium or large computer system.

10-9. Contrast centralized and decentralized data processing systems.

10-10. What is a distributed data processing system, and what are the advantages of using it?

MINIQUIZ

ANSWERS

1. F
2. T
3. F
4. F
5. F
6. T
7. F
8. F
9. T
10. F

True or False

_____ 1. A microcomputer costs between $5,000 and $50,000.
_____ 2. A microcomputer contains the same type of hardware and software as a large computer system.
_____ 3. A CRT is the main input/output device for a large computer.
_____ 4. Originally, the minicomputer was used for business applications such as payroll and inventory control.
_____ 5. One disadvantage of the minicomputer is the fact that data base management systems are not available.
_____ 6. Many small computer systems can accommodate multifunction card machines.
_____ 7. Photoelectric sensing card readers, because of their storage requirements, are not available with small computer systems.
_____ 8. Small computer systems do not require computer personnel or special wiring or air conditioning.
_____ 9. Large computer systems have a price range of about $1,000,000 to over $5,000,000.
_____ 10. The typical large computer system has over 5 billionK bytes of main storage.

Minis help move cargo

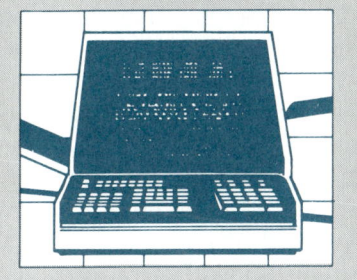

Cargo ships are not generally considered fast, but, because of technological advances that have increased the speed of ships and increased the development and acceptance of containerized shipping (putting truck bodies directly on a ship), this mode of transportation competes quite favorably on a total-time basis with other forms of transportation. For the entire cargo ship industry, however, the high speed movement of large volumes of cargo created a significant paperwork problem. In international trade, it is virtually impossible to separate the paper requirements of the various governments involved from the physical movement of the cargo.

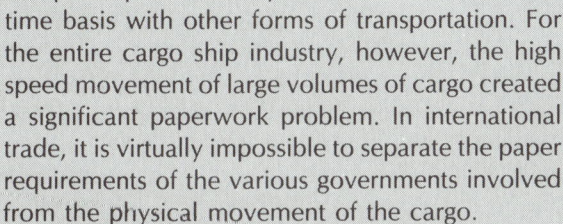

Historically, various carriers met government, operational and accounting needs physically moving paper to key locations, using any means that could get it there ahead of the ship. Airmail and courier services have been used extensively to avoid delaying ships and cargos because information was incomplete. Although many companies involved in international shipping have automated portions of their paper processing and information communications, United States Lines believes it is the first to use the full function of mimicomputers and data communications to solve its paperwork problems cost-effectively.

United States Lines has, in an attempt to expedite the mounds of paperwork associated with cargo shipments from five European ports to the United States, installed dual Wang Laboratories minicomputers in each of the five ports. The accounting and documentation capability became fully operational in July 1977, after a three-month parallel operation with prior procedures.

The benefits have been numerous and the computerized approach has been very favorably received in locations where "computers are not ingrained into the structure of living, said David L. Dawson, director, information services, United States Lines, New York. Dawson remarked that installation of the minicomputer has reduced the workload significantly, improved the working environment of each shipping office, provided employees with ready answers to customer questions and made staff personnel available to perform more needed and meaningful work. Using the minicomputers also improved the firm's cash flow and the value of data transmitted to the United States all in the most cost-effective manner possible, explained Dawson.

All programming is in BASIC and was done in Europe by United States Lines personnel, directed by a project leader. The system was two and one-half man-years in design, development and implementation. One DP person is located in Hamburg, Germany, and another in Rotterdam, The Netherlands, to maintain the system and assist operating locations, said Dawson.

A side benefit to other United States flag ocean carriers is the availability of the US Lines' programs for accounts receivable, billing and documentation at a "nominal cost" because the applications were developed as a joint project by the United States Maritime Administration and US Lines for the US ocean freight industry under a program called Shipping Operations Information Systems (SOIS).

The five Wang systems are similar and are installed in Hamburg, Rotterdam, Liverpool and Felixstowe, the United Kingdom; and LeHavre, France. Each system consists of two Wang 2200 CPUs with keyboard/CRT, 16K of memory, two 10-megabyte disk drives and communications equipment.

Dawson remarked that in today's environment, ships are faster. Time spent in each port must be limited and each ship may make an increased number of port calls, to maximize revenue. All of this affects the movement of information required for customers, cargo handling and proper accounting.

"In a highly competitive business in which the customer depends on us and in which up to 50

Source: Reprinted from *Infosystems*, March 1978, copyright Hitchcock Publishing Company.

percent of the required information for a vessel may arrive the same day the vessel sails and needs to be at the port of destination before the ship arrives, our company is under severe limitations in terms of turnaround and processing time. This time pressure mandates automation and the use of high-speed communications," Dawson said.

The Wang minicomputers are used to capture document data and other needed data in each local office, where it is used locally and also sent to Rotterdam for consolidation and transmission to the New York City headquarters.

This documentation information, Dawson explained, serves multiple functions and is a significant part of US Lines' financial and operational systems. It is the basis for the entire process of revenue accounting, accounts receivable, shipment and equipment control, as well as customer service.

Data forwarded to the US is received by and processed on dual IBM 370 computers. One of these systems also serves nine US locations with an on-line network of CRTs and printers capturing similar document information on shipments outbound from the United States. United States Lines also is getting ready to begin transmitting this information to the five Wang computers for parallel operations on ships and cargo going to European ports.

"United States Lines will use the European system as a prototype and study its possible use in other geographic locations, such as the Far East, as well as determine its suitability for implementing other applications," Dawson said.

With the present system, the Rotterdam minicomputer stores manifest data from the other locations, adds needed information and transmits the data to the US twice a week over a voice-grade line, taking no more than 45 minutes on each transmission. Transmitted at one time is all the information needed to produce arrival notices, customer manifests, due bills, accounts receivable, entries, revenue manifests and other operational documents for the 800 to 900 cargo containers associated with that specific inbound ship. Containers are 20 and 40 feet long.

The European division accounts for a substantial portion of the US Lines annual business and, therefore, was a logical candidate for initial implementation and a proving ground for the minicomputer-based system. United States Lines, as a whole, operates a fleet of 16 high-speed container ships and over 30,000 pieces of equipment between the United States, Europe and the Far East. At any given time, in excess of 80,000 active customers are on the firm's frequent shipper file.

DISCUSSION QUESTIONS

1. What types of hardware and computer systems are used to help more cargo more efficiently?
2. What are some of the benefits of computerized system for United States Lines?

SUPPLEMENT 10
Microcomputers for business, school, and personal use

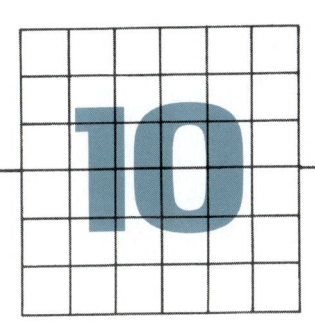

MICROCOMPUTER SYSTEMS IN ACTION
    Individual applications
    Applications for small profit and nonprofit organizations
THE COMPONENTS OF A MICROCOMPUTER SYSTEM
    Input and output devices
    Central processing and temporary storage
    Permanent storage devices
    Peripheral equipment
SOFTWARE AND PROGRAMMING
FACTORS IN SELECTING A MICROCOMPUTER

After completing this supplement, you will be able to:

- List some of the applications of a microcomputer system.
- Describe the components of a typical microcomputer.
- Discuss the importance of software and programming with a microcomputer system.
- Evaluate microcomputer systems.

Although the idea of using computers for business, school, and personal use has existed since the first generation of computers, it wasn't until 1975 that inexpensive computers first started appearing on the market. It was during this time that the Altair, costing under $400 in kit form, was first marketed. Since this time, many manufacturers of microcomputers have entered the market offering a wide range of products. These manufacturers include:

Apple computer
Atari
Basic Four Corporation
Commodore Business Machines
Digital Equipment Corporation
Imsai
Intel Corporation
Mits, Inc.
Ohio Scientific Instruments
Radio Shack
Texas Instruments
Wang Laboratories

Microcomputers, also called **personal computers,** offer many advantages over older and more expensive computer systems. Today, most microcomputers cost under $2,000. Indeed, the more popular models cost about $500 for the basic system. Special electrical wiring is not needed, and it is not necessary to have elaborate humidity control and air conditioning systems. Moreover, microcomputers are relatively small in size. They are ready to use (turnkey), and most of them can fit in the trunk or back seat of a car. Yet, these inexpensive computers can perform the same functions as computers costing thousands of dollars more.

Some experts predict that microcomputers will entirely change our lives. A few individuals have even predicted that the importance of these will be as profound as the importance of the industrial revolution, or the electric light bulb. While it is unlikely that they will change our lives to this extent, it is expected that they will help the individual as computers in general have helped businesses and government agencies.

MICROCOMPUTER SYSTEMS IN ACTION

Microcomputers are primarily used by individuals and small profit and nonprofit organizations. In both cases, the speed and storage capacity found in larger and more expensive computers are not needed. As a result, they have been used for a large number of applications.

Individual applications

There are a large number of applications that microcomputers are performing for individuals. These applications are ones that can be useful to almost everyone. The following list includes some of the applications.

1. Personal budgeting and cash management.
2. Check balancing.
3. Income tax preparation.
4. Programmed learning.
5. Games and entertainment.
6. Recipe storage and food preparation.
7. Letter writing.
8. Storing addresses.
9. Word processing.
10. Learning and memory aid.
11. Personal inventory record.

Microcomputers can be used to keep a record of all cash expenditures. This can be used to prepare a family or personal budget, after which actual cash expenditures can be compared to budgeted cash expenditures. When check numbers and other tax data are stored, the computer can be used to balance your checking account and to help prepare your income tax return.

There are many applications that are not financial. The microcomputer can be used as entertainment. Some come with a series of interesting games. You can use the computer to store the recipes of your favorite dishes. The computer also can be used to tell you the ingredients that you will need for a given recipe and a given number of servings. Furthermore, if you store your present supply of food, the computer can even tell you what additional food items have to be purchased for any given meal. The microcomputer can be used to write letters and to store addresses. This application is especially useful for small nonprofit organizations that have a newsletter or correspondence that has to be sent to its members. Some authors have used their microcomputer for word processing. They compose their original manuscript and make changes on the computer. Then, the computer can print a copy of the finished manuscript. This application, however, requires a more expensive microcomputer with additional capacity. Important dates and meetings can be stored on the computer. Printing these important dates and meetings daily or weekly will help you to remember birthdays, anniversaries, mortgage payments, meetings, and so on. A description of the items in your home or apartment can be stored in the computer system. Furthermore, you can store your driver's license number, and credit card numbers in the computer system. If anything is stolen or misplaced, you will be able to tell the insurance company and the police the items that are missing and any serial numbers, identifying numbers, or characteristics of these items.

There are other applications that are now being done by microcomputers that are more difficult to implement and require some technical expertise. For example, these computers have been used to control lighting, air conditioning, the hot water system, and so on. Your microcomputer can be used to wake you up, turn on the coffee maker, and more. These applications, however, require that your computer be interfaced or connected with one or more household appliances. As these computers become more popular, many of these interfaces may become standard equipment.

Applications for small profit and nonprofit organizations

Many small profit and nonprofit organizations are finding that for under $1,000, they can purchase a microcomputer to perform many data processing tasks that were done by hand. Furthermore, many microcomputers can perform the same types of applications as the larger and more expensive computers. These small organizations are willing to sacrifice speed and storage capacity for a smaller purchase price.

Most applications for the small organization can be divided into routine bookkeeping applications and management information applications. At the present time, most of the applications are bookkeeping or routine applications, but as organizations begin to realize the potential of their microcomputers, it is expected that more management information applications will be developed. Many management information applications can be added to existing applications that perform the routine data processing activities. See Part I for a discussion of routine applications and management information applications. Below is a list of some of the applications for small profit and nonprofit organizations.

1. Payroll.
2. Inventory control.
3. Accounts receivable.
4. Accounts payable.
5. General ledger.
6. Balance sheet and income statement.
7. Cash flow analysis.
8. Income tax.
9. Credit checking and customer file.
10. Word processing.
11. Business reminder.

Although microcomputers seldom print payroll checks, they can be used to make all of the computations that are related to payroll. These programs can compute the gross wages, all deductions, net wages, withholding information, and more. Most organizations have physical inventory, and many microcomputers are used to keep a current record of the inventory levels. Daily, weekly, or monthly inventory reports can be generated. More sophisticated inventory programs can alert the organization to items that should be ordered and to items that are slow moving. Accounts receivable and accounts payable files can be kept on the computer system. When it comes time to send out invoices or to pay bills, all of the required information can be obtained from the computer. A microcomputer can also be used to keep a general ledger and to prepare monthly or yearly balance sheets and income statements. Budgeting and cash flow analysis can also be performed by the personal computer. One of the biggest problems facing the small business is cash flow. It is essential to plan ahead and to make sure that there is enough cash to pay future bills. After you prepare a budget, you can place it on the computer and let it compare the actual cash flow with the budgeted cash flow. Information can be stored that can be used in preparing income tax returns.

Microcomputers can also be used to store a customer master file. When you need to send out invoices and bills the customer master file can be used in preparing address labels. Word processing can be done on many microcomputers. This involves such activities as letter writing, preparing memos, general correspondence, and any application that involves the output of words and sentences instead of numbers. A credit system can also be established for past customers. This will help in reducing bad debts and avoiding the mistake of not giving a good customer credit. A list of important meetings and events can be placed into storage. Once a day or once a week, you can get a list of meetings, sales calls, and other activities that need to be completed.

There are many professional applications that can be performed by microcomputers. A teacher can use one to keep and average test scores and class assignments. A doctor can use one for keeping medical records. Lawyers and accountants can also use a microcomputer. Indeed, a microcomputer can be used in almost any profession to produce routine documents and better information.

THE COMPONENTS OF A MICROCOMPUTER SYSTEM

Microcomputers contain the same type of components that you would expect to find for larger computer systems. Thus, they have *input* and *output devices*, a *central processing unit* and a *temporary storage device*, and *permanent storage devices*. While all microcomputers may not come with a permanent storage device, most of them can be expanded to include these devices. A typical microcomputer is shown in Figure S10–1.

Input and output devices

On some of the earlier microcomputers input was done through a series of *switches* located on the front panel of the computer system. The major advantage of using these switches for input is the low cost. Data input using switches, however, can be very tedious. Each piece of data is entered bit by bit.

Without question, the most commonly used input device is the *keyboard*. Keyboards for the microcomputer have the same layout as the keyboard on a typewriter. The major difference is that the keyboard for a microcomputer has a few additional keys which makes it easier to enter instructions and data.

The *video display* or *cathode ray tube* (CRT) is the most commonly used output device for a microcomputer. These devices have the appearance of a TV screen. The video display or CRT often comes as standard equipment with a microcomputer, and many times, the video display or CRT is housed in the same cabinet with the keyboard, central processor, and temporary

FIGURE S10–1
A microcomputer system

Photo courtesy of Radio Shack, a division of Tandy Corporation

storage device. Some microcomputers, however, use a standard TV screen for output.

For those applications that require a printed output, called hard copy, it may be necessary to acquire a *printer*. While most personal computers do not come with a printer, most manufacturers of microcomputers offer several printers with different capabilities and prices that are designed to be used with their computer system. See Figure S10–2.

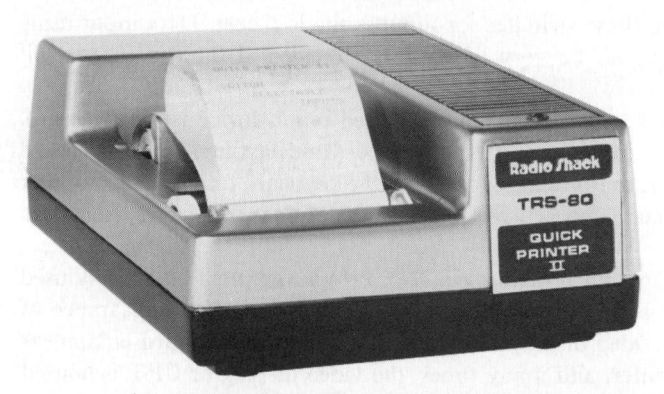

FIGURE S10–2
A small printer

Photo courtesy of Radio Shack, a division of Tandy Corporation

Central processing and temporary storage

All microcomputers have a *central processing unit* and a given amount of *temporary storage,* which has also been called main storage, core storage, or memory. The functions performed by these components are identical to that of the larger and more expensive computers. In a microcomputer, these devices are slower and have less storage capacity.

The *central processing unit* (CPU) performs two functions—arithmetic/logic and control. The arithmetic/logic unit (ALU) is responsible for making computations and logical decisions based on the instructions and data. The control unit, on the other hand, is responsible for the control and operation of the computer system.

In addition to the processing unit, a microcomputer must have a way of *temporarily storing* the data and instructions being processed. Through the use of large scale integration (LSI) circuits and new memory technology, access speeds and rates are close to medium computer systems. A microcomputer may have from 4K to over 32K bytes of storage capacity.

Temporary storage can be classified according to how it is accessed. For example, **read-only memory** (ROM) refers to temporary storage that can only be read. In other words, you cannot place data or programs into read-only memory. Special features and functions supplied by the manufacturer in both calculators and personal computers are placed in ROM.

In addition to ROM, you also need the capability of placing your own data and instructions in temporary storage and then randomly accessing the data or instructions. This type of memory is called **random-access memory** (RAM). Many calculators and most microcomputers have RAM. Another type of memory is **erasable programmable read-only memory** (EPROM or PROM). With this type of temporary storage, new programs can be placed in memory using special procedures that are normally beyond the capabilities of the typical personal computer user. Another variation of PROM is **electrically alterable read-only memory** (EAROM), which allows *you* to alter ROM through programming. Microprograms are also available to overcome the lack of certain basic instructions.

Permanent storage devices

Although permanent storage devices normally do not come as standard equipment with the microcomputer, many people using personal computers have a permanent storage device. The two most commonly used permanent storage devices for a microcomputer are the *cassette tape* and the *flexible* or *floppy disk.*

Most microcomputers allow ordinary *cassette tape* recorders to be connected to the computer system which can store up to 150,000 characters. The data to be stored on the cassette is converted into audio tones, which are then recorded on the cassette tape like you would record a piece of music or a lecture. When you want the personal computer to use the data

FIGURE S10–3
A floppy disk drive

Photo courtesy of Commodore International, Inc.

or instructions stored on the tape, the process is reversed. The biggest advantage of the cassette tape as a means of permanently storing data is the low cost compared to a flexible or floppy disk. The major disadvantage of cassette tape storage is access speed and the fact that any tape device is a *sequential access storage device* (SASD). This means that if you want to get some data or a program that is stored near the end of the tape, you must sequentially pass over all of the data and programs that are physically stored before the desired piece of data or the program.

Another permanent storage device that is popular with microcomputers is the *flexible* or *floppy disk*. Some models can store 500,000 characters. See Figure S10–3.

Although the disk is more expensive than the cassette tape, it is much

FIGURE S10–4
A microcomputer with printer and floppy disk drives

Photo courtesy of Radio Shack, a division of Tandy Corporation

faster and it allows for direct access. A microcomputer that may be used for business with a printer and floppy disk drives is shown in Figure S10–4.

Peripheral equipment

Like a component stereo system, there are many components that can be added to the basic microcomputer after it is purchased and in operation. This type of equipment is called *peripheral equipment*. With microcomputers, additional temporary storage or memory can be added at any time. One or more permanent storage devices discussed in the last section can be added to the microcomputer.

In addition to increasing the existing capabilities of the microcomputer, peripheral equipment can be added that increases the usefulness of the computer system. It is possible to add a *speech recognition* device that has the ability to understand a limited number of words. Some of these speech recognition systems come with a microphone and allow you to program the computer to understand words in your voice. With speech recognition, it is possible to program the computer or to feed it data verbally instead of using the keyboard. *Paper tape* machines and terminals can also be obtained and added to an existing microcomputer system. Printers and modified IBM Selectric *typewriters* can be added to these computer systems to allow them to produce letter-perfect typewritten documents. Other peripheral equipment can allow a microcomputer to be connected to a stereo system. Then the computer can be used to compose and play music. Another piece of peripheral equipment allows the computer to be attached to a standard color television. The computer can then be used to produce colorful and dramatic designs or to play elaborate and sophisticated games in full color.

All of the peripheral equipment mentioned is available today, but not all microcomputers have the ability to interface with this equipment. Thus, it is important to know the computers that can use the peripheral equipment you want.

SOFTWARE AND PROGRAMMING

As with any computer system, the computer equipment is of no value without a set of instructions that tell the computer what to do. All of the applications discussed previously are performed using a set of instructions called software. Also like the large computer system, the microcomputer requires both *system software* and *application software.*

Most microcomputers have at least two types of system software. An *operating system* is one type of system software that is needed to control the operation and functioning of the computer system. In addition, *compilers* are needed to translate from a computer programming language, such as BASIC, into machine language.

While systems software is needed to make the personal computer function, application software is needed to instruct the computer to perform a series of tasks or activities to complete a given application, such as payroll, inventory control, letter writing, or game playing. Most application software is written using a *high-level programming language,* and the most common high-level programming language for the microcomputer is *BASIC,* which is covered in Part III of this book.

If you want a microcomputer to perform a certain application, you can either write a program in a language such as BASIC, or you can acquire a program from an outside source. If you want to develop your own applications, you must learn a programming language, usually BASIC, that is usable on your computer system. The other choice is to acquire the programs from another source.

The price for application software normally ranges from about $20 to $200. Most software packages can be purchased from the microcomputer manufacturer for less than $100. Some examples of application software that can be purchased from microcomputer manufacturers are given below:

Business
  General ledger
  Mailing lists
  Accounts receivable
  Accounts payable
  Inventory control
  Real estate
  Word processing
  Payroll
  Fixed asset account
  Statistical analysis
  Sales analysis

Education
  Basic math
  Algebra
  BASIC programming
  FORTRAN programming
  Vocabulary
  Antonyms and synonyms
  English
  Classroom management

Personal
  Personal finance
  Memory
  Filing system
  Portfolio analysis
  Food and diet
  Income tax
  Cash management

Games
  Checkers
  Blackjack
  Casino gambling
  Music
  Military
  Space
  Tic-tac-toe
  Craps
  Slot machine
  Baccarat
  Wheel of fortune
  Artificial intelligence

You can also join a computer user's group that shares computer programs. If you don't develop the programs yourself, you should make sure that the programs that you buy or acquire will do what you expect them to do. These programs should be tested before they are used.

FACTORS IN SELECTING A MICROCOMPUTER

In determining whether or not you should own a microcomputer, it is important to carefully balance your needs against the cost of various computer systems that are on the market today. If you are seriously thinking about purchasing a microcomputer, there are several factors to consider:

1. Cost.
2. Input and output devices.
3. The central processing unit and temporary storage.
4. Permanent storage devices.
5. Software availability.
6. Programming languages.
7. Flexibility and compatibility.
8. Maintenance and repair.
9. The dealer or computer store.
10. The manufacturer of the computer system.
11. User groups and clubs.

In selecting a microcomputer, you must weigh the cost of the system against the benefits of the system. The equipment should include devices for efficient data input and output. At minimum, the central processing unit and temporary storage device should be fast enough and large enough to handle your largest program and data. Does the computer system come with a permanent storage device? What software and programming languages come with the computer system? Another important factor is flexibility and compatibility. *Flexibility* is the ability of a computer system to grow as your needs grow. Can you increase temporary storage and permanent storage at a later date. *Compatibility* is the ability of a computer system to handle or accommodate devices made by another manufacturer. Another consideration is maintenance. Will it be easy to maintain and repair your computer system? How long will a repair job take? You don't want to spend six months waiting for your computer system to be repaired. The reputation of the dealer or computer store and the manufacturer should be carefully considered. What type of service will you get from both the dealer and manufacturer? Are there any user's groups or clubs for this particular computer system? These groups and clubs can be fun to join, and the members can help you with your computer system and provide you with valuable programs and interesting applications.

Before a final selection is made, you should get a complete demonstration of the computer system. Futhermore, you might want to ask for the names of several other people that have purchased the same type of computer. You should then call these people to get their evaluation of the computer system, the dealership, and the manufacturer. You may also wish to attend a few computer shows. Microcomputing magazines, such as *Byte Magazine, Kilobaud,* or *Personal Computing,* can also be helpful to read before making any decisions concerning a personal computer.

SUMMARY

This supplement has introduced you to microcomputer systems. You were shown how microcomputers can be used for individual applications and in applications for the small profit and nonprofit organization. In addition, you were exposed to the components and software for a typical microcomputer system. Finally, this supplement investigated some of the factors in selecting a microcomputer.

KEY TERMS AND CONCEPTS

Electronically alterable read-only memory (EAROM)
Erasable programmable read-only memory (EPROM)
Microcomputers
Microprograms
Programmable read-only memory (PROM)
Peripheral equipment
Random access memory (RAM)
Read-only memory (ROM)

QUESTIONS

S10–1. Describe the beginning of microcomputer systems.

S10–2. What are some of the individual applications that can be performed on a microcomputer?

S10–3. What are some of the applications for small profit and nonprofit organizations?

S10–4. Describe the components you would expect to find in the typical microcomputer.

S10–5. What is RAM, ROM, and PROM?

S10–6. What are the most popular permanent storage devices for microcomputers? What are the advantages and disadvantages of each?

S10–7. What type of system software comes with most microcomputers?

S10–8. What is the most popular high-level programming language with microcomputers?

S10–9. Briefly describe how you would select a microcomputer system for your use.

ANSWERS

1. F
2. T
3. F
4. T
5. F
6. T
7. T
8. T
9. F
10. T

MINIQUIZ

True or False

_____ 1. Because of their small size, most microcomputers are not turnkey systems.

_____ 2. The microcomputer is basically a smaller version of the larger business or scientific computer.

_____ 3. Word processing is one application that is too complex and difficult for the typical microcomputer.

_____ 4. Microcomputers can be programmed to perform inventory control applications and other accounting applications for small businesses.

_____ 5. The major input device for a microcomputer is a card reader.

_____ 6. The flexible or floppy disk is one of the main permanent storage devices for a microcomputer.

_____ 7. The cassette tape, which is a sequential access storage device, is a typical permanent storage device for a microcomputer.

_____ 8. Peripheral equipment can be acquired that allows a microcomputer system to recognize speech patterns.

_____ 9. The most popular programming language with microcomputer systems is machine language.

_____ 10. Some application packages for microcomputers can be purchased for under $100.

Personal computers in business: An emerging competitive edge
Bill Langenes

Being competitive in business means getting important data quickly, when you need it. And this is what the personal computer does best of all.

Take, for example, a traveling insurance salesman who takes his personal computer in the car with him to keep customer and inventory information at his fingertips.

Or the senior partner in a Los Angeles law firm who calls his personal computer "my equalizer." His three-man operation uses the data and word processing capabilities of the computer to compete successfully in court with firms many times its size.

The chairman of the board of one of America's major industrial corporations has three personal computers that help him keep abreast of his company's diverse operations, while a financial analyst for a leading Wall Street investment firm uses his personal computer to keep his clients' portfolios.

These businessmen are the vanguard of a growing revolution being created by personal computers, which are bringing the power and efficiency of rapid data processing to small businesses and giving managers of larger firms "hands-on" access to business data when they need it.

Frankly, it is a revolution that is taking place faster than many of us in the personal computer industry really expected. Nearly three-quarters of a million business people are currently using small computers. They came into computer stores and made their purchases, all of which were originally identified in the "hobby" category. But, in truth, a large percentage of those hobbyists were business people learning to "do it themselves" so they could adapt the personal computer to their business needs.

As they did, they gained an advantage over their competitors who were still spending many man-hours on bookkeeping, record-keeping and report-making functions for which computers are so ideally suited.

Small computers are making new contributions to competitiveness by both increasing internal efficiency and improving customer service. A New Jersey industrial equipment distributor, Don Truesdell, discovered both benefits after installing his computer.

"For the first time in three or four years we were able to get each day's work done within a normal working day," he said. "Our computer has turned out to be an important sales tool as well. We can use the computer-generated product sales analysis reports to give our customers a comprehensive report on all the products they have purchased from us, which shows them we pay close attention to their requirements.

"The system also helps in our dealings with suppliers," Truesdell continued. "It gives us a good image, and they respect our operation. In fact, two of our leading suppliers have told us we are their most highly automated distributor."

Immediate results can often be seen from the use of a computer. An automotive parts warehouse installed a business system to handle inventory. In six months the inventory was reduced by $30,000 with no loss in effectiveness. Says the owner: "The computer more than paid for itself."

A South Carolina manufacturer's representative, Larry Kidd of CV Sales, Inc., found that his personal computer gave him more control of his managerial responsibilities, both financial and personnel.

"I feel that I know much more about the week-to-week progress of my business," Kidd says. He also wrote his own software programs—common among personal computer users—to produce semi-monthly sales summaries for his salesmen. "Now they know exactly what their customers are ordering . . . and so do I." Impressed with the possibili-

---
Source: Apple Computer, Inc.

ties of his computer, he says "I haven't yet begun to do what I can."

For the small businessman, personal computers mean that he can economically have access to the same kind of operating and accounting information previously available only to his larger competitors. Within large companies the small computer has opened up new capabilities for department heads and for managers at their individual locations.

It is within big business that computers are truly earning their "personal" distinction. There are no programmers and no operators to go through to obtain computer-stored information. Managers themselves can get the information they need when they need it.

Deere & Company is finding that line managers want their own computers. At Ford Motor Company the treasurer's office uses three small computers. The marketing manager of a multi-million dollar California corporation keeps a personal computer beside his desk to help him analyze market data and develop plans.

Sometimes it is competitive pressure that motivates business people to computerize, as was the case of a printer. When he found that a competitor was using a programmable calculator to estimate printing bids, he went out to buy his own calculator. But he discovered wisely, that he could buy a microcomputer for not much more money and have an enormously more versatile machine capable of producing bids as well as handling general accounting.

What are the special needs of the business user?

Software is certainly at the top of the list, and both manufacturers and independent software houses have reacted quickly with many new "canned" application packages.

Hardware expandability is a must. The business system should accept peripheral equipment, such as printers and disks, which are essential. The same system in other applications may require speech recognition capabilities, greater memory capacity, interfacing with a computer network, and so on.

Business system shoppers should also carefully check out the computer retailer to be certain the dealer can provide the training and after-sale service that are necessary for full utilization of the system.

Can you benefit from the use of a personal computer system? Only you can determine that for sure. Certainly current users provide a broad sample. The availability of low-cost computer power has led International Data Corporation, a leading computer industry market research firm, to predict that virtually any organization having $500,000 in annual sales will require a computer or computer services during the next few years if it is to improve its efficiency and remain competitive in the marketplace. That's why the personal computer can truly be called "An emerging competitive edge."

DISCUSSION QUESTIONS

1. What are some of the ways that a personal computer (microcomputer) can be used in a business setting?
2. What are some of the factors to consider in selecting a personal computer?

about part III

The purpose of Part III is to explore computer programming and software in more detail. These topics were introduced to you in Chapter 3. If you have not read this chapter, you should go back and read it carefully before you read any chapter in this part. After you have completed Chapter 3, you can read the chapters in this part in any order, although it is recommended that you cover the chapters sequentially.

Part III starts with a discussion of operating systems and system software. Next, various computer programming languages are covered, including BASIC, FORTRAN, COBOL, and PASCAL. Chapter 13 discusses program and application development, and Chapter 14 covers some of the traditional tools and procedures used in program and application development. Chapter 15 investigates a newer approach to application development called structured design.

11	Operating and system software
12	Programming languages
13	Program and application development
14	Tools for program and application development
15	Structured design

PART III
SOFTWARE

Operating and system software 11

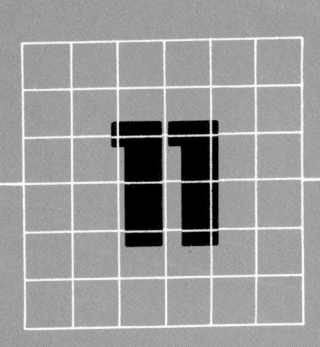

BATCH PROCESSING
OVERLAPPED PROCESSING
REAL-TIME PROCESSING
MULTIPROCESSING
SPOOLING
MULTIPROGRAMMING
VIRTUAL STORAGE
PROGRAM OVERLAYS
DATA BASE MANAGEMENT SYSTEMS

After completing Chapter 11, you will be able to:

- **Compare batch processing with overlapped and real-time processing**
- **Describe the use of multiprocessing and spooling**
- **Discuss the advantages of multiprogramming and virtual storage**
- **Describe data base concepts.**

As discussed in Chapter 3, assemblers and compilers, data base management systems, utility programs, and operating systems are all different types of system software. Since there have been some remarkable advances in operating systems and because this type of system software has the function of managing or supervising the operation of the entire computer system, most of this chapter will be devoted to operating systems.

With older computer systems, the human operator was responsible for running each of the application programs one at a time. But while the human operator was changing programs or performing other necessary tasks, the computer system was idle waiting for the operator to finish. This was very inefficient, and thus it was decided to develop a set of computer programs, called the *operating system*, to run and manage the operation of the computer system. Other terms that are used to describe this set of programs are *monitor, executive, supervisor, controller,* and *master control programs.* There have been many advances in operating systems, and as a result, modern operating systems can get more done in less time. Today most operating systems perform the following functions:

- Assign processor or processors to tasks.
- Allocate memory and other storage areas.
- Handle job-to-job transition.
- Interpret commands or instructions.
- Coordinate the use of compilers, assemblers, utility programs and other software.
- Establish a job priority system (determine the order in which jobs are to be done).
- Enforce a job priority system and maintain discipline and order in the computer system.
- Act as an internal time clock.
- Transfer control from the computer system to computer programs in the proper sequence and at the proper time.
- Schedule processing jobs and tasks.
- Coordinate and assign input and output devices while one or more programs are being executed.
- Produce dumps, traces, error messages, and other debugging and error detecting aids.
- Establish data security and integrity.
- Keep programs from interfering with each other.
- Communicate with the computer (human) operator.
- Oversee the correct execution of a program.
- Coordinate the transfer of data and files from one storage device to another.

Like the manager of a company, the operating system is responsible for the smooth and efficient operation of the entire computer system. In some cases, the operating system decides to execute a smaller program first even though it was submitted to the computer system after several larger programs. The operating system determines where data and instructions are to be stored in the computer system, when input and output devices are to be used, when data is to be transferred from one device to another, and much more. Sophisticated analysis has been conducted to make operating systems as efficient and effective as possible.

As mentioned previously, the operating system is a set of computer programs. Normally one program, called the *control program*, resides in main storage or memory. The other programs that are part of the operating system or system software, such as utility programs, compilers, assemblers, and a number of other programs that perform the tasks of the operating system described above, are stored on the disk. Then, as these programs are needed, the control program transfers these programs into memory or main storage where they are executed. Today's operating systems are very sophisticated, and they are able to substantially improve the operation of the computer system. It is refreshing to know that all of these tasks performed by the operating system and other system software are performed automatically. The functions of the operating system are *transparent* to the user. This means that you really don't see what the operating system is doing. For example, one of the first uses of an operating system was to permit a computer system to run several computer programs—one after another, without the need of a human operator to run each program individually. This is called *batch processing*.

Batch processing is one of the oldest ways of running programs on a computer system. Have you ever seen a counter or location in a computer center where people turn in a program on computer cards and come back in an hour or perhaps a day or two to pick up their cards and the output from the computer? If so, you have seen batch processing in action. A computer operator will collect these programs which have been punched on cards and stack one program or job on top of another. When a batch of these programs has been collected, they will be run on the computer system at one time. By the way, batch processing has also been called *stacked job processing*. A typical stack or batch of programs is shown in Figure 11-1. As seen in Figure 11-1, several control cards are placed before each program. For some computers, these cards are called *job control cards*, and information is placed on them using a language called *job control language* (JCL). These cards might tell the computer that your program is written in FORTRAN, and that the computer should not print more than 2,000 lines of output and take more than five seconds to execute. Next is the program itself. One statement or command is usually placed on one card. Finally, each program is followed by the data for that particular program. This procedure is typical at many colleges and universities. Students and faculty punch control cards, program cards, and data cards. These cards are turned into the computer center and run. The original cards and the output from the computer are

BATCH PROCESSING

And so on
⋮

[Data for Program 2]

[Program 2]

[Control cards for Program 2]

[Data for Program 1]

[Program 1]

[Control cards for Program 1]

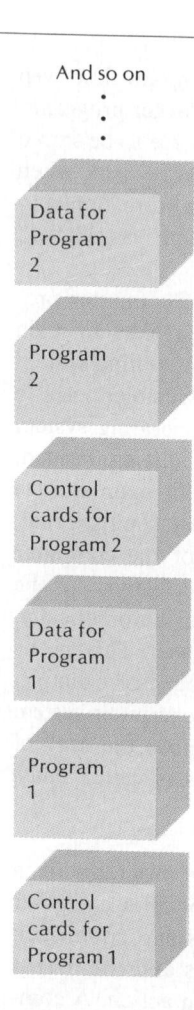

FIGURE 11–1
Batch processing

picked up in a few hours or a few days. If there are any mistakes, the bad cards are discarded, new cards are punched, and the process is repeated.

For a business, the same programs and data may be used many times. The programs and data may already be stored on disk or tape. In these situations, only control cards are needed. These control cards tell the computer which program is to be run and what data is to be used. See Figure 11–2.

As seen in Figure 11–2, the control cards for the various programs have been placed one on top of another. The human operator will place these control cards on the card reader, push a few buttons, and the computer will execute all of the programs without further assistance from the operator except for mounting tapes, etc.

Eliminating the need for an operator to run each program separately helped to eliminate some of the inefficiencies. But when one program is completely run before another program is started, there are still inefficiencies. A typical reader can read 500 cards per minute, a typical printer can print 1,000 lines

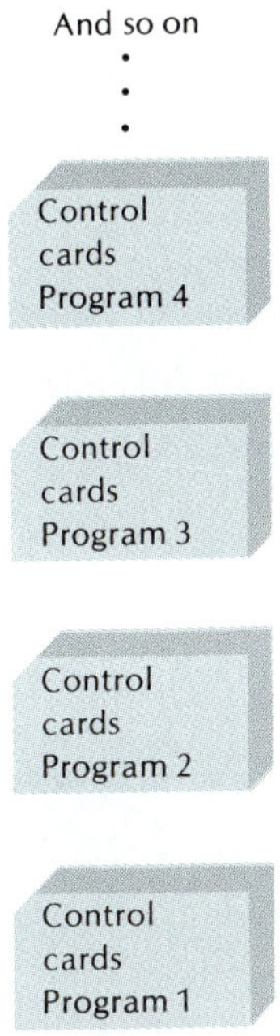

11 Operating and system software

And so on
•
•
•

Control cards Program 4

Control cards Program 3

Control cards Program 2

Control cards Program 1

FIGURE 11–2

per minute, but the typical CPU can process 10,000 instructions per second. Running one program at a time would cause the CPU to be idle most of the time. Overlapped processing helps to alleviate this problem.

In the situation described above, the input and output devices could be operating at their maximum speed, and the CPU would still be idle much of the time. This is called being *input/output bound.* The system is limited by the speed of the input and output devices. When a system is limited by the speed of the processor, the system is said to be *process bound.* In either case when there is nonoverlapped processing, a job or program is not run until the previous job or program is completely finished. When *overlapped processing* is employed, one program can undergo input, another program can be processed, and a third program can undergo output all at the same time. This simple concept can significantly reduce the time it takes to run a group of programs. Figure 11–3 reveals the possible time savings when only three programs are to be run.

As you can see in overlapped processing, the running of the programs is actually overlapped. For example, while output is occurring for job 1, processing is taking place for job 2, and input is being undertaken for job 3. The time blocks for Figure 11–3 are the same, but usually the CPU is far faster than the input and output devices. Thus in most cases even with overlapped processing, the CPU is still idle some of the time. The system is still input/output bound. A further improvement would be to have several input and output devices attached to the same CPU. While this is being done, other

OVERLAPPED PROCESSING

FIGURE 11–3
Overlapped processing versus nonoverlapped processing

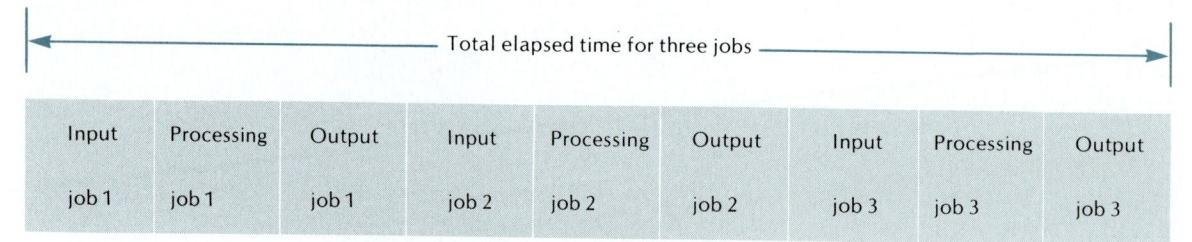

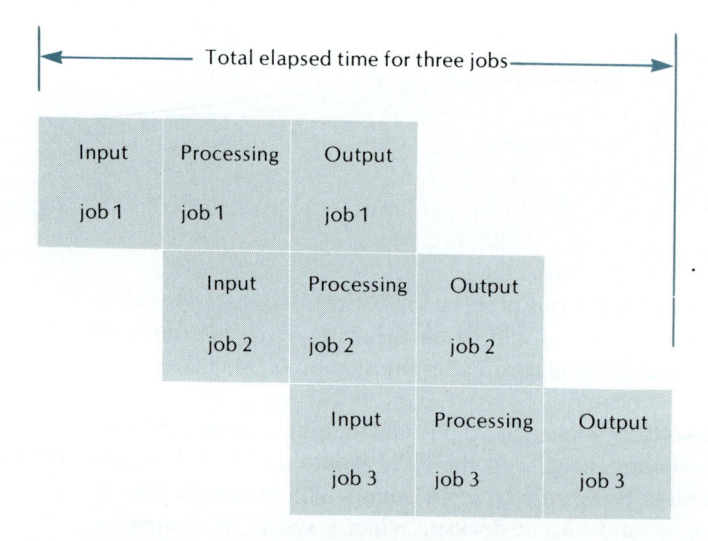

←——————— Total elapsed time for three jobs ———————→

| Input job 1 | Processing job 1 | Output job 1 | Input job 2 | Processing job 2 | Output job 2 | Input job 3 | Processing job 3 | Output job 3 |

Nonoverlapped processing

| ←——— Total elapsed time for three jobs ———→ |

Input job 1	Processing job 1	Output job 1
	Input job 2	Processing job 2	Output job 2
		Input job 3	Processing job 3	Output job 3

Overlapped processing

disadvantages of batch processing can be overcome. It can take hours or even days for the results to be obtained from a batch processing system. For an airplane or hotel reservation system, this situation is not tolerable. To avoid overbooking and other related problems, programs that actually make the reservations should be run immediately after a reservation has been made, and the data file containing the reservations that have been previously made must be kept entirely accurate. The response from the computer, when a reservation is made or from an inquiry about reservations, must be immediate and not after a few hours or a few days. This type of response is called *real time,* and a computer system that can respond immediately or within a matter of seconds is called a *real-time* processing system.

REAL-TIME PROCESSING

When immediate response is not required, batch processing is an excellent method of running programs. There are many applications, however, that

11 Operating and system software

require an immediate response from the computer, and in these cases, a real-time processing system is needed. *Real time* means immediate response from the computer. Getting a stock market quotation, finding the current level of inventory for a product, and searching a criminal data file for a possible suspect may all be actions that need to be done now without delay. As discussed in Part II, when you have a real-time system, the computer devices must be directly connected, usually by wire, cable or telephone line, to the computer system. This is called being *online,* and the computer system is referred to as an *online real-time* system. Furthermore, there may be several devices such as terminals, card readers, line printers, etc., using the computer system at the same time. This is called *time sharing.* Perhaps you have been at an airport or in a computer center where you have seen several teletypes or terminals using the same computer at the same time.

Not all computers were designed to be online, real time, and to allow time sharing. For example, you cannot take some of the older computer systems, attach several terminals to it by a cable, and expect it to work. The system software must be able to accommodate real-time processing. Even though it may appear as if several or even hundreds of terminals are using the computer system at the same time, most CPU's can only execute one instruction at a time. But as you know, the average CPU can execute thousands of instructions in a second. Thus it is possible to have a CPU execute a few instructions for literally hundreds of people in a few seconds. This is accomplished by having the CPU execute a few instructions for one user, and then a few instructions for another user a fraction of a second later, and so on. As a result, it seems that the CPU is running everyone's programs at exactly the same time when it is really executing a few instructions for each user in rapid succession. Because main storage is expensive and has a limited storage capacity, programs are normally stored on the disk and transferred into main storage when needed. This approach, called *swapping,* is useful for computer systems regardless how processing takes place.

The system software necessary for real-time processing and time sharing can be very complex. A priority system has to be set up that instructs the computer hardware when to execute the instructions for each user. Otherwise, the computer would not know what instructions are to be done first and what instructions are to be done next. The system software must also be able to handle other jobs such as data and file protection. Normally, a small portion of the disk is allocated to each individual job or user, and only that individual or user has access to that particular area on the disk.

With a real-time system, it is possible to have interactive processing. *Interactive processing* is a system that asks the user a series of questions in performing one or more applications. With interactive processing, the user does not have to know how to program a computer. The user simply answers the questions asked by the computer system. Usually this type of processing is done on a CRT, where all of the questions and the answers are displayed on the CRT screen. Interactive processing normally starts by asking the user which application is to be performed. The user might request the inven-

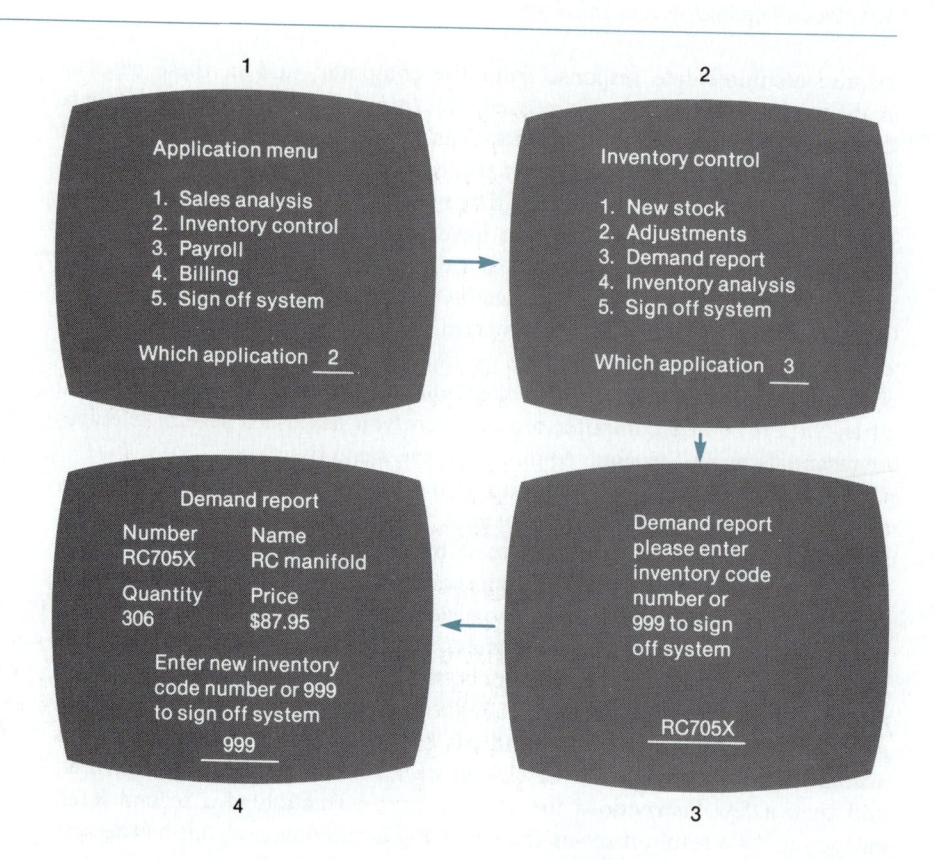

FIGURE 11-4
Interactive processing

1

Application menu

1. Sales analysis
2. Inventory control
3. Payroll
4. Billing
5. Sign off system

Which application 2

2

Inventory control

1. New stock
2. Adjustments
3. Demand report
4. Inventory analysis
5. Sign off system

Which application 3

3

Demand report please enter inventory code number or 999 to sign off system

RC705X

4

Demand report

Number   Name
RC705X   RC manifold

Quantity   Price
306        $87.95

Enter new inventory code number or 999 to sign off system
999

tory control application. The computer then asks which subapplication should be done in inventory control. The computer keeps asking questions and the user keeps responding until the desired application is performed. This process is shown in Figure 11-4.

Real-time processing and time sharing have permitted literally hundreds of users access to a computer system at the same time. Coordinating the input and output for hundreds of users has caused data communication problems. One of the solutions is to use a few smaller CPU's to do nothing more than handle input and output. This type of computer system uses *multiprocessing*.

MULTIPROCESSING

Multiprocessing means more than one processor. Whenever a computer system uses more than one CPU, the computer system uses multiprocessing. One common use of multiprocessing is to use small CPU's for input and output. A typical multiprocessing system is shown in Figure 11-5.

As seen in Figure 11-5, all of the input and output to and from the central computer at the main office goes through a small CPU at the main office. This CPU channels and coordinates all of the input and output. As a result, there is only one main stream of communication to and from the central computer, and thus the main CPU at the computer center is used

11 Operating and system software

for major processing and not for communication. In this figure, the displays at the two branch offices and the warehouse go through small computers that are at those locations. The displays in this example could be cathode ray tubes (CRT's). In some systems like this one, the small computers at the branch offices and at the warehouse can do limited processing by themselves. Thus, if there is a problem with the computer system at the main office, the branch offices and the warehouse can still do some limited processing with their small computers.

There are an almost limitless number of possible multiprocessing systems. In some systems, several small CPU's can be linked together to perform the major processing. If one of the smaller CPU's breaks down, the other CPU's will automatically take over the work. In other systems, CPU's are connected into elaborate computer networks. Distributed data processing, which was discussed in Part II, is an example. As usual, system software is needed to operate and control these different types of configurations and networks.

With multiprocessing, hundreds of people can have access to the same computer through online devices such as teletypes, CRT's and so on. These concepts, however, cause their own problems. For example, where are all of the results stored before they are dispatched to an output device? In older computer systems, input and output devices interacted directly with main storage (also called memory and core storage). Unfortunately, main storage is very expensive and it cannot hold much data. Furthermore, the CPU

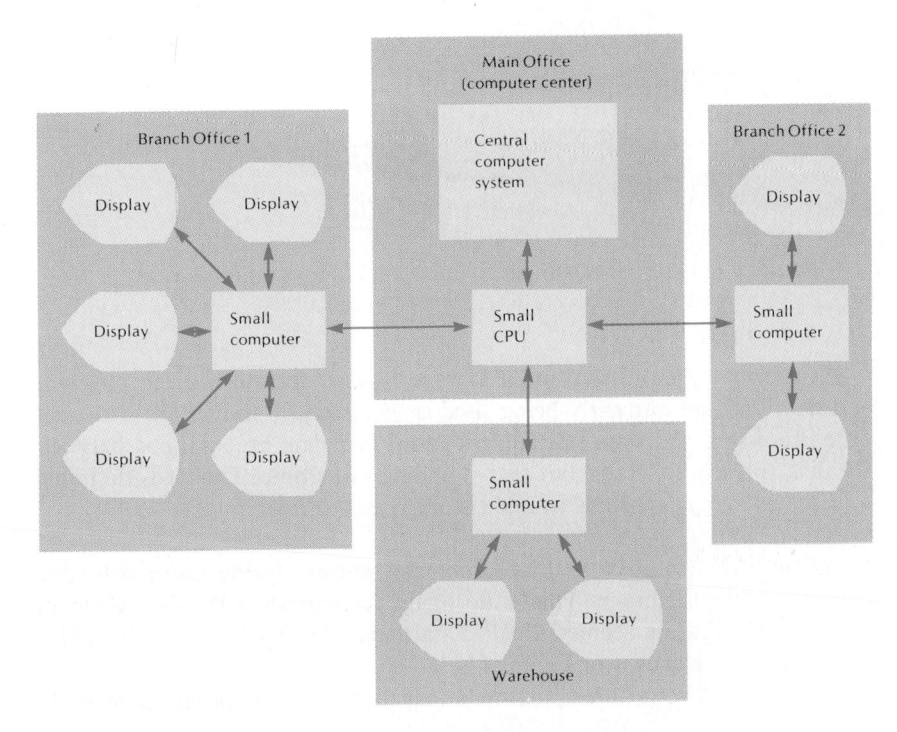

FIGURE 11-5
A multiprocessing system

interacts with main storage. If main storage is tied up with storing incoming and outgoing data, the CPU will not have enough working space to function as efficiently as it could. One solution to this problem is *spooling*.

SPOOLING

Spooling is a technique that has been successfully used on a number of computer systems. Without spooling, data from input devices and to output devices is stored in main storage. Because input devices and output devices are slow, this prevents main storage from being used for other purposes and, as a result, the CPU remains idle. Spooling is the process of placing all data that comes from an input device or goes to an output device on either the disk or magnetic tape. This is shown in Figure 11–6. Because main storage can obtain data from and place data upon a disk or a tape device much faster than typical input and output devices such as card readers and line printers, there is more space available in main storage on the average for processing. When the CPU is not too busy with other jobs, special *spooling programs* can be executed that will transfer the data from the disk or tape to main storage or an output device. In a sense, the disk or tape device acts like a buffer area between main storage which is extremely fast and input and output devices that are relatively slow. In general, spooling makes better use of main storage and the CPU.

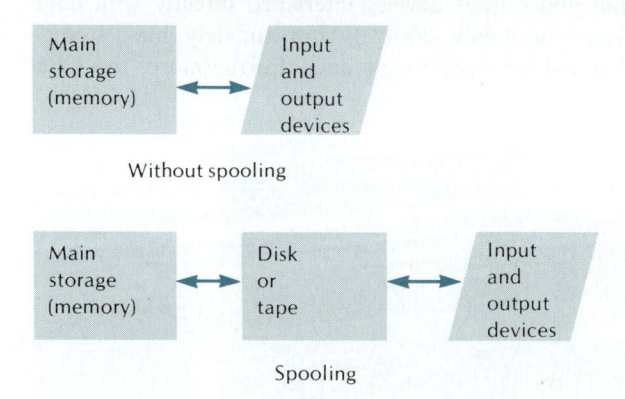

FIGURE 11–6
Spooling

As previously discussed, main storage is used for storing the program and data that are currently being used or accessed by the CPU. With real time processing and time sharing, programs and data are swapped between the disk and main storage, but this swapping takes time. Thus it is desirable to place as many programs in main storage as possible.

MULTIPROGRAMMING

As the name implies, **multiprogramming** means storing more than one program in main storage. This is normally accomplished by dividing main storage into separate segments called *partitions*. Each partition will hold a program. This is shown in Figure 11–7.

Figure 11–7 shows three partitions that may hold one program each. Of

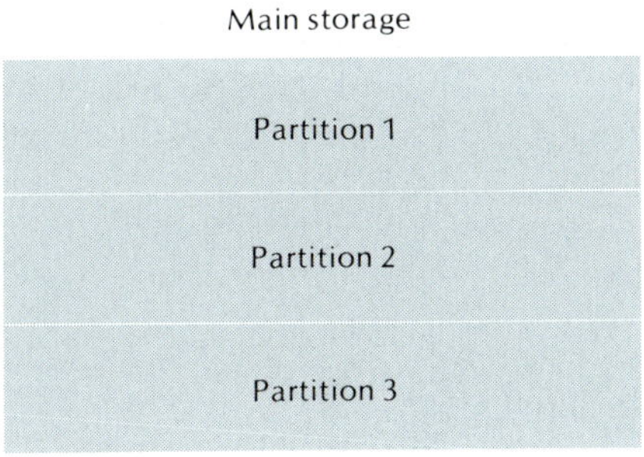

Main storage

Partition 1
Partition 2
Partition 3

FIGURE 11–7
Multiprogramming

course, in addition to programs, main storage must also store a small amount of data that is currently being processed and some system software. For some computers, the size and number of partitions is fixed, while with other systems, the size and number of partitions can be changed to increase the efficiency of processing.

With multiprogramming, the CPU can operate more efficiently. As soon as the CPU finishes with a program in one of the partitions, it can start to process another program in another partition. Then, while the CPU is processing this program, another program can be brought in from the disk to replace the program that was just executed. The swapping between the disk and main storage happens continuously, but now the CPU does not have to wait until a new program is transferred from the disk to main storage because there are several other programs already in main storage in other partitions. The CPU goes from partition to partition executing programs. When a program in a partition has been executed, it is replaced by another program from the disk while the CPU is already working with another partition. As the number of partitions increase, the size of each partition must decrease because there is only a fixed amount of total storage in main storage. If the size of the partition becomes too small, then an entire program is unable to fit in one partition. Perhaps only a small part of a program could be placed in main storage. The rest of the program would be on the disk. Depending on how large these program parts or segments are, you could have virtually any number of partial programs stored in main storage. Some computer systems actually do this, and the concept is called *virtual storage*.

VIRTUAL STORAGE

Virtual storage is nothing more than an extension of multiprogramming. Instead of storing a complete program in main storage, the computer will only be storing a small part or segment of a program in main storage. The rest of the program is stored on the disk. This concept is called virtual storage.

The number of program segments that can be placed in main storage depends on the size of the program segments. Assume that you have written a program on ten pages of computer coding forms, and that there is just enough room in main storage for this program and nothing else. Now, if

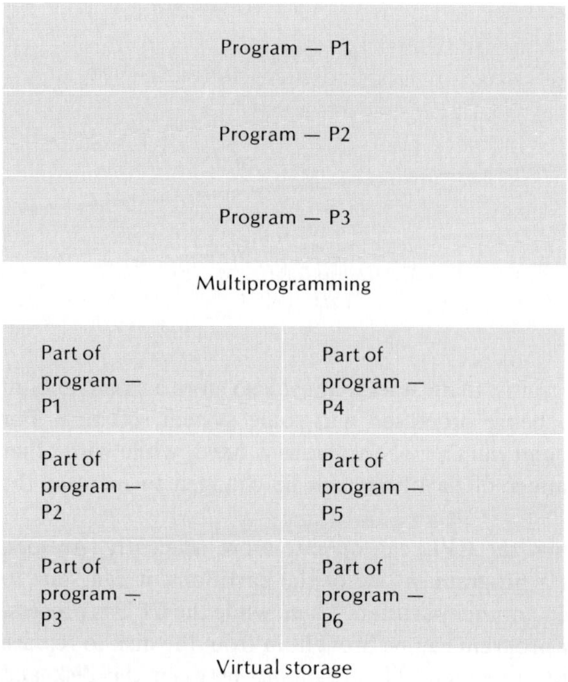

Program — P1
Program — P2
Program — P3

Multiprogramming

Part of program — P1	Part of program — P4
Part of program — P2	Part of program — P5
Part of program — P3	Part of program — P6

Virtual storage

FIGURE 11–8
A virtual storage system

you only stored a segment of this program, perhaps the first few pages, in main storage, there might be room for another program segment. In a sense, the computer would be storing only a few pages of a number of programs in main storage, and the rest of these programs would be stored on the disk. This is called *paging*. See Figure 11–8.

As can be seen in Figure 11–8, we have stored six program parts in a main storage that previously held three complete programs. What is the advantage of virtual storage?

As you may recall, when a computer system is using real-time processing and time sharing, only a few instructions are being executed for one user at a given moment in time. Then the computer executes a few instructions for another user, and so on. In a few seconds, the computer could process a few instructions for over a hundred users. Because the computer is only executing a few instructions of one user's program at one time, the complete program is not needed. With more program segments, the CPU is less likely to have to wait for programs to be transferred from the disk to main storage. This reduces CPU idle time, and increases the number of jobs or programs that can be run in a given time span. It is important to note that the physical size of main storage has remained the same. With virtual storage, the size of main storage only appears to be larger because more gets done in less time.

PROGRAM OVERLAYS

In some cases, a program will be simply too large to be stored in memory. To solve this problem, some computers use *program overlays*. A program overlay is a segment or a part of a large program. When the program is written, it is divided into a *main program* and several program overlays by the computer programmer. When the program is executed, the main program will stay in memory until the execution is completed, and the program overlays will be transferred into memory from the disk one at a time when they are needed. When a new program overlay is transferred into memory, the old program overlay will be transferred back to the disk. At any point in time, only the main program and one program overlay will be in memory. Thus, the computer programmer must be very careful when writing the program to make sure that the program is divided into a main program and program overlays in such a way that the memory of the computer can store the main program and the largest program overlay. This is shown in Figure 11–9.

When an overlay program is executed, the main program is transferred from the disk into the main program area in memory. The main program directs the computer to transfer the first program overlay into the program overlay area of memory. This overlay is executed, and then it directs the computer to transfer the second program overlay into memory while transferring the first program overlay back to the disk. This process continues until

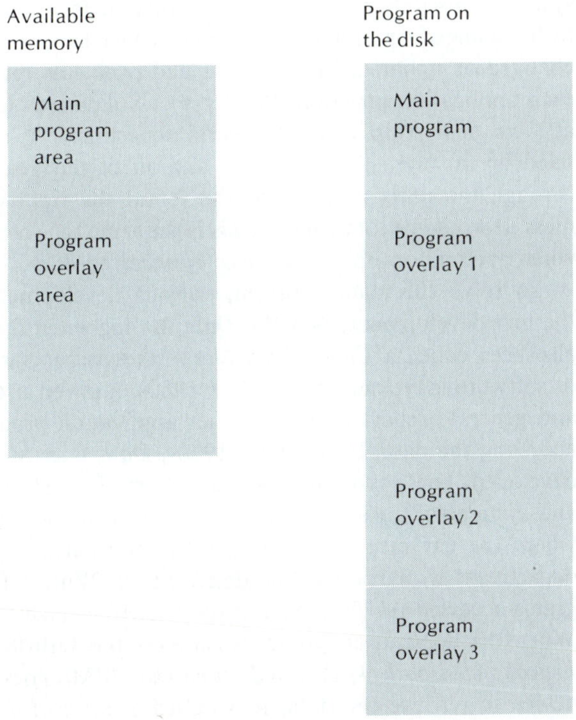

FIGURE 11–9
Program overlays

the entire program is executed. For some computer systems, this process may be slightly different, but the overall approach is the same.

DATA BASE MANAGEMENT SYSTEMS

Like other types of system software, **data base management systems** were developed to solve a problem or to find a better way. The amount of data gathered and processed by businesses and other organizations is growing at tremendous rates. Today, companies have more data and more application programs that process this data. In the past, every application program would directly access permanent storage devices to get the necessary data. See Figure 11–10.

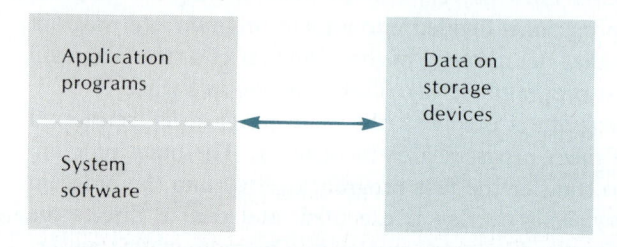

FIGURE 11–10
Software directly accessing data

In many cases, each program had its own set of data. This caused the same piece of data to be stored in several different files in the computer system. This data redundancy was very inefficient, and when the data had to be changed or updated, you were never sure if all of the data had been changed or updated. Many errors and problems resulted from this. Having each application program directly access data was like having a repair shop at a car dealership without a parts department. If all of the car parts were piled up on one side of a room and all of the mechanics would rummage through the parts until he or she found the right part, you would have a mess. It would be total chaos. This is the same type of chaos that was occurring when application programs directly accessed data.

To solve this data problem, various developments were made. One of the first developments was the *Data Management System* (DMS), which has also been called a *Generalized File Management System* (GFMS). This type of software, developed in the late 1960s, allowed users to easily access data and generate reports, but the other application programs were still directly accessing the data. In the early 1970s, *Data Base Management Systems* were developed. These systems acted like a buffer between the application programs and system software and the data. The DBMS was like a parts department, where the car mechanic would go to the parts department and the parts department would locate the desired part. With a DBMS, application programs accessed the DBMS, and the DBMS located the desired piece of data. When the application program accesses the DBMS for data, it is called a *logical access path* (LAP), and when the DBMS goes to a permanent storage device to retrieve the data, it is called a *physical access path* (PAP). In an effort to standardize and coordinate the development of DBMS, *CODASYL*

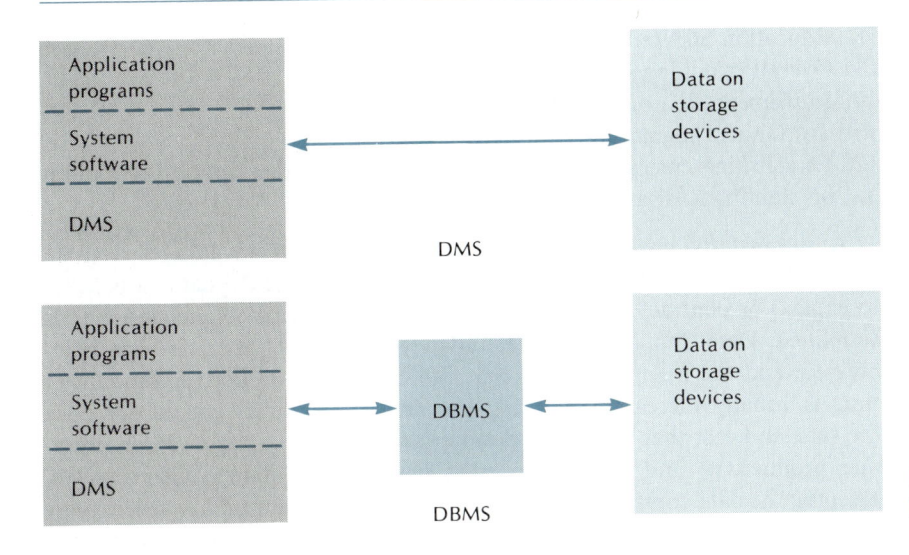

FIGURE 11–11
DMS and DBMS compared

developed a *Data Base Task Group (DBTG)*, which developed a report on data base systems and structures in 1971. Figure 11–11 shows the difference between a DMS and a DBMS.

Like any tool, the success of a data base management system depends on how it is used. In setting up a DBMS, it is necessary to clearly define the data that will be used. This is done in what is called a *data dictionary*, which is developed when the DBMS is installed. In addition, it is necessary to develop the relationships between the various data elements to be used by the DBMS. This is accomplished by developing schemas and subschemas. Using the parts department example, a *schema* is like the parts diagram for the car engine that shows the various parts that make up the engine. A *subschema* reveals the relationships between various data elements for part of the schema. It would be like having a detailed parts diagram of a carburetor, which is part of the engine. In addition to data dictionaries, schemas, and subschemas, there are other parts of a DBMS, which are beyond the scope of this book, that must be developed or considered, such as *file structure* and *organization* and *data base architecture*. In order to make sure that the DBMS will perform to its potential, most organizations hire a *Data Base Administrator (DBA)* who is responsible for managing one of the most valuable resources of any organization—its data. Most Data Base Administrators are responsible for the following areas:

1. Overall design and coordination.
2. Development of a data dictionary.
3. Development of schemas and subschemas.
4. Physical layout and organization of the data.
5. Logical layout and organization of the data.
6. System and user documentation.
7. Interface with users and managers.

8. Education and training concerning the data base.
9. Overall operation of the DBMS.
10. Implementation of the DBMS.
11. Testing and maintaining the DBMS.
12. Establishing emergency procedures in case of system failures or natural or man-made disasters.

A successfully installed DBMS offers a number of advantages over an approach where the application programs directly access the data. It is easier to expand or contract the data base, and data maintenance and updating is simplified. Data duplication or redundancy is reduced, response time is increased, and the number of jobs that can be handled in a given amount of time is usually increased. Keeping the data independent can also reduce the time and cost that it takes to develop new programs. Improved programmer productivity and greater flexibility in the use of data is also possible. Keeping the data consistent, independent, and well organized has saved many companies thousands of dollars. Since data base concepts are sophisticated and complex, most computer users do not develop their own DBMS. Today, there are thousands of companies using DBMS and there are over 20 companies that commercially produce DBMS. Like other pieces of software, the companies usually sell or lease their DBMS packages. Depending on the sophistication of the DBMS, these types of packages can cost under $15,000 to over $150,000 to purchase. Some of the more popular DBMS that are commercially available are System 2000 produced by MRI, IMS2 and GIS/2 produced by IBM, TOTAL produced by Cincom, and Mark IV which is a DMS produced by Informatics. Most of these systems require medium or large computer systems to operate, but recently there have been several DBMS designed to operate on minicomputers. These systems are being produced and developed by some of the leaders in minicomputers such as DEC and HP.

Some data base management systems also provide easy access to data. NCR TRAN-QUEST, developed by NCR Corporation, is an example. This system allows people without previous training in data processing or computers to easily access and retrieve data. A number of other data base management systems provide this type of data access as well.

SUMMARY

The efficient and effective operation of the computer system depends on good system software. One of the older types of processing was batch or stacked job processing. With this type of processing, all of the programming jobs were stacked on top of each other and run at the same time. In most cases, control cards were needed before and after each program. To help make the central processing unit more efficient, some computers use overlapped processing. Overlapped processing allows input to occur for one job, processing to occur for another job, and output to occur for a third job all at the same time. Thus, the processing of several jobs is literally overlapped. Real time means immediate access from the computer system, and it allows airlines and hotels to immediately update reservations. In order to be real time (immediate response), the computer devices must be electronically connected to the computer system. This is called being online. Another related concept is time sharing. Time sharing is the process of allowing several people, in some cases hundreds, to use the computer at the same time. In other words, these people or users are sharing the time of the computer system. Multiprocessing is a system software feature that allows more than one processor in a computer system or network, and spooling is a process that places data on a disk or magnetic tape before it is entered or retrieved from the computer system. The disk or magnetic tape device acts like a buffer, enabling the CPU to operate more efficiently. Multiprogramming is the process of allowing more than one program to reside in memory or temporary storage. Virtual storage is an extension of multiprogramming. Virtual storage permits partial programs to be stored in memory. The rest of these programs are stored on the disk. When programs are too large to fit in temporary storage, program overlays can be used. A program is broken into a main program and several program overlays. When the program is executed, each program overlay is called into memory by the main program and executed separately.

Another important type of system software is a Data Base Management System (DBMS). This type of system manages the data of an organization. A DBMS acts like a buffer between the application programs and the actual data. Logical access occurs between the application programs and the DBMS, and physical access occurs between the DBMS and the actual data.

KEY TERMS AND CONCEPTS

Batch processing
Control program
Data base administrator
 (DBA)
Data base management
 system
Data base task group
 (DBTG)
Data dictionary
Data management system
 (DMS)
Input/Output bound

Job control language
 (JCL)
Logical access path
 (LAP)
Main program
Multiprocessing
Multiprogramming
Online
Overlapped processing
Partitions
Physical access path
 (PAP)

Process bound
Program overlaps
Real time
Schema
Spooling
Spooling programs
Stacked job processing
Swapping
Time sharing
Transparent
Virtual storage

QUESTIONS

11–1. Describe what is involved in batch processing.

11–2. How can overlapped processing reduce the total time that it takes to execute several programs together?

11–3. What is real-time processing? For what applications is it useful?

11–4. What is online and time sharing? Describe situations that might require this type of processing.

11–5. What is multiprocessing? Give several examples.

11–6. Why does spooling allow the computer system to operate more efficiently?

11–7. What is meant by multiprogramming? Why is multiprogramming useful?

11–8. Briefly describe virtual storage. How does it differ from multiprogramming?

11–9. Why are programming overlays used?

11–10. What functions are performed by the data base administrator?

11–11. What is a schema, a subschema?

ANSWERS

1. T
2. F
3. T
4. T
5. F
6. F
7. F
8. T
9. T
10. F

MINIQUIZ

True or False

_____ 1. Stacked job processing is another name for batch processing.

_____ 2. A system, which is limited by the speed of the input and output devices, is called process bound.

_____ 3. A computer system that can respond immediately or within a matter of seconds to a request is called real time.

_____ 4. For a device to be real time, it must also be online.

_____ 5. A time sharing computer is one that allows two or more programs to share the time and storage facilities of the central processing unit.

_____ 6. Virtual storage is an extension of multiprocessing.

_____ 7. Spooling is a problem that occurs when there is a bottleneck in placing data on magnetic tape.

_____ 8. Multiprogramming means storing more than one program in main storage.

_____ 9. Program overlays are used when a program is too large to completely fit in main storage.

_____ 10. A data management system is a refined version of a data base management system.

A "software first" philosophy

Developing operating system software first and then building a computer that takes advantage of its features has been a predominant philosophy at Prime Computer, Inc. since the company was founded in February, 1972. This software first philosophy sets the company apart from its competitors, drives the development people to conceive and implement systems within it, and provides valuable user benefits.

In short, software first and its ramifications has been a key factor in Prime's success and rapid growth, especially over the past four years when revenues went from $10 million to $90 million, doubling almost every year. Credit for adopting and adhering to this philosophy rests with Dr. John William Poduska, a cofounder of the company. He earned bachelor's, master's and doctorate's degrees in computer science at Massachusetts Institute of Technology.

Ears wide open

While a junior faculty member at MIT between 1962–64, Poduska recalled, he contributed little but had his "ears wide open" to learn about Project MAC (multiaccess computer) and the MULTICS (multiplexed information and computing service) operating systems that used a virtual memory concept, rings of security, a utility-like approach to providing service to users, and other advanced features on a large $10 million computer.

When Poduska joined the Electronics Research Center of NASA in Tech Square, Cambridge, adjacent to the MIT campus, he and his staff implemented "a good many of the MULTICS ideas, such as virtual memory, on small minicomputers of the time—Honeywell 516 and Honeywell 832," he said.

These features and systems were part of NASA's long-term manned-space program, including the Mars mission, the lunar base station and the earth-orbiting laboratory.

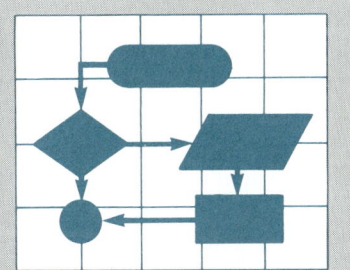

When the NASA center was closed, Poduska joined Honeywell and became director of its Information Sciences Center, also in Cambridge. By that time, Honeywell had acquired General Electric's computer operations (in 1970), and GE had provided the original large computers for the MULTICS system.

Developed at NASA

"Over that period, the ideas of how to take the MULTICS concepts and implement them on a minicomputer were forming and being implemented," Poduska said. "When Prime was founded in February, 1972," he continued, "we had available to us the software that had been developed at NASA, which was a MULTICS-like operating system running on the Honeywell 516, and a set of ideas of how to build a segmented virtual address space machine with hardware features required to support a MULTICS-like environment."

The software work done at NASA was in the public domain because of the Space Act of 1958, Poduska said, and was readily available to Prime or any other company that wanted it.

"We started with that software concept and the software development and we built the hardware to support it," Poduska said. "And so, culturally and emotionally, we are a 'software first' company."

Poduska said Prime engineers "took the instruction set of the Honeywell 516 to make it suitable for a virtual memory machine, as we had done at NASA. And we built that as the first instruction set of the Prime machine. That instruction set has since evolved so that it now supports a fully segmented, very large virtual address space memory structure. And it's been evolved from a 16-bit mode to a 32-bit mode."

The important ideas that came from this start "were numerous," Poduska said. "First of all was

---

Source: Reprinted from *Infosystems*, January 1979, copyright Hitchcock Publishing Company.

the MULTICS notion of what virtual address space should look like. The MULTICS project used both a paging structure and a segmentation structure, which has a lot of advantages. Prime has a segmentation and a paging structure, and that makes us unique in the minicomputer industry," Poduska explained. "Only Prime and the MULTICS machines have this kind of structure."

The principal user benefit: a very large virtual address space is very important to the users for creating programs that solve very large problems, he explained. "The particular MULTICS structure that was chosen maps very nicely into a user's image of his own program.

"Users like to think of programs as a main program, a number of subroutines, different data bases and communications with a supervisor," Poduska explained. "The Prime structure works very nicely into that because all those elements map into different segments on the machine and the user just references them directly." He explained that when a user makes a procedure call on the system supervisor for service, it's done the same way he would call, for example, the square root routine. "So, it's a very efficient and yet a protected mechanism for communicating; a very highly developed, very structured efficient mechanism—and up until quite recently, a very expensive one," he added. "Because of the recent availability of high-speed, bipolar, random-access memory (RAM) technology, we have been able to put that type of structure on a minicomputer-class type machine," Poduska explained.

"And now you get right to the heart of the business concept of Prime," he said. "And that is, we take that large machine functionality and we implement it using 'minicomputer' technology."

These software first observations were echoed by Joseph A. D'Angelo, Prime's director, product planning, who said that part of the MULTICS design concept was to give timesharing users a utility view of the service, similar to a public utility such as a telephone company, electric power company or gas company. That view holds that each user has the full resources of the utility available to him without hampering other users.

"In our redesigns and changes of those initial operating system characteristics, we have kept that view as fundamental," D'Angelo said. "We have a general-purpose operating system that handles many different workloads in a variety of languages. That makes Prime systems adaptable to virtually any application requirement." He also noted that Prime has maintained an isolation level in its operating system development between the hardware and software.

"This philosophy has allowed us to change the hardware implementation that supports PRIMOS (the operating system) at least three times so far without rippling those changes to our customers," he explained. "That's an important concept to us because our approach to the customer base is more like a mainframe company than a minicomputer company.

"We're interested in compatibility across a line of products and in how a customer will upgrade from old products to new products within our product lines," D'Angelo said.

D'Angelo made another key point that reflects Prime's software first philosophy: the company has developed its operating system and related software so that applications programmers and users are "insulated from the particulars of the hardware" and don't need to be concerned with tracks, sectors, pages, segments and so on.

"For virtually any user, Prime provides very sophisticated tools to solve computing problems quickly and efficiently," D'Angelo said. "And because flexibility and compatibility are built into Prime systems, the system you start with doesn't have to be the one you live with forever. Prime systems are designed to be changed—easily, efficiently and economically."

DISCUSSION QUESTIONS

1. What is Poduska's philosophy of developing operating systems and software?
2. What are some of the features of MULTICS?

Programming languages 12

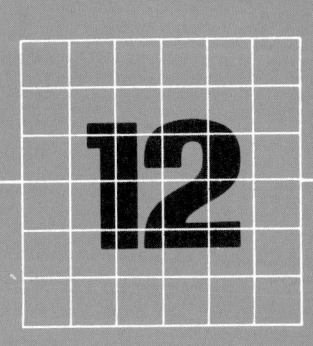

PROGRAMMING LANGUAGES IN PERSPECTIVE
THE BASIC PROGRAMMING LANGUAGE
THE FORTRAN PROGRAMMING LANGUAGE
THE COBOL PROGRAMMING LANGUAGE
    The structure of a COBOL program
    The identification division
    The environment division
    The data division
    The procedure division
THE PASCAL PROGRAMMING LANGUAGE
OTHER PROGRAMMING LANGUAGES
    RPG and RPG II
    PL/1
    APL
LANGUAGE COMPARISON

After completing Chapter 12, you will be able to:

- Discuss the various types of high level programming languages.
- List the basic characteristics of COBOL.
- Describe typical statements that are used in FORTRAN.
- Contrast the elements of BASIC with FORTRAN and COBOL.
- Describe the PASCAL programming language.
- Discuss other programming languages.

The key to making the computer system perform business applications is application software. Whether or not an organization makes its own application software or buys it, application software must be developed. If you are a computer professional, you will be directly involved in developing application software. If you are not a computer professional, you will be using application software. In either case, you should know how computer programs are written and used.

With the increased use of minicomputers and microcomputers, you may be writing short programs for your own use. Many managers who know how to program in a high-level language are finding that they are able to write programs that help them do their job. Since application software is vital to every organization, you should have an understanding of what a computer program is and how programs can be written.

As discussed in Chapter 3, programs can be written in machine language, assembler language, symbolic languages, or a high-level language. Over the years, there has been a trend towards writing application software in high-level languages. To be considered high level, a programming language should possess these characteristics.

1. The language is relatively independent of a given computer system.
2. Each statement in the language translates into several instructions in machine language.
3. The language is natural and uses abbreviations and words that are used in every day communication.
4. The language is independent of machine language instructions and other pieces of system software except for the language compiler.
5. The language is not experimental in nature and exists on more than one computer system.

Since there are over 200 high-level programming languages that meet the above qualifications, it would be impossible to investigate all programming languages in any detail. Thus, the overall approach will be to discuss the attributes of high-level languages in general and to examine a few programming languages in some detail.

PROGRAMMING LANGUAGES IN PERSPECTIVE

The purpose of a programming language is to solve a problem or to produce a desired report or output. The type of programming language that is used depends on the application. Like buying a new car, the selection of a programming language must be done carefully. Since most computers accommodate several high-level programming languages, it is important to select the right language for the particular programming problem. Thus, it is important to know the various types of programming languages and their characteristics.

Programming languages have a number of different attributes that can be used for classification purposes. See Figure 12–1.

Each of the attributes in Figure 12–1 represent two extremes, and most programming languages can be placed somewhere on the line between these extremes for each attribute. For example, some languages can only be run

Realtime ——————————————— Batch

Procedure ——————————————— Problem

Business ——————————————— Nonbusiness

General purpose ——————————————— Special purpose

FIGURE 12–1
Language attributes

in the **batch mode,** while other programs are developed to be run on a terminal in **real time.**

Programming languages can also be classified according to whether they are **procedure** oriented or **problem** oriented. Languages that are procedure oriented stress the actual procedures or manipulations that are performed, while a problem-oriented language is concerned with solving a particular type of problem. If a programming language can handle large data files and business type applications, the language is a **business** oriented language, while languages that are excellent at performing sophisticated computations but not adept at handling large data files are **nonbusiness** oriented languages. Most nonbusiness oriented languages are good at performing scientific applications. Depending on the intended purpose, a programming language can also be classified as **general purpose** or **special purpose.** A general purpose language is intended to solve a number of different types of problems, while a special purpose language is designed to handle one specific type of problem or application.

Like writing a report or a paper in English, writing a computer program requires that the programmer follow a set of *rules.* Each programming language has its own set of rules, called the **syntax** of the language. Each language also has a set of words and symbols that have a special meaning. Words like LET, FORMAT, READ, and ADD, are examples of words that are used by some programming languages. Learning a programming language requires learning the symbols, words, procedures, and rules of the language. Some new languages, such as ADAM, actually let the programmer define and use his or her own words and terms, and other new and experimental languages allow the programmer to develop programming rules or syntax. In the near future, programmers may be developing their own programming languages.

Many programming applications require the same types of activities. To avoid duplication of effort, there are *programming libraries* that contain these commonly used routines, such as sorting numbers, merging files, performing basic statistical analysis, generating random numbers, computing overtime pay for employees, performing matrix and vector manipulations, and so on. These libraries are kept by universities and by data processing departments for large organizations. There are also companies that sell or lease their libraries. For example, International Mathematics and Statistical Libraries, Inc. (IMSL) has over 200 subroutines that can be used in FORTRAN programs. Programming libraries contain complete programs, subprograms or subroutines, or both. A *subroutine* is a set of instructions that can be placed in the body of a normal program. Most programming languages have a specific set of rules that govern the development and use of subroutines for that particular language.

In the next sections, you will be introduced to the BASIC, FORTRAN, COBOL, and PASCAL programming languages in more detail. To allow you to compare these commonly used languages, the same application will be performed.

THE BASIC PROGRAMMING LANGUAGE

BASIC, which stands for Beginners All-purpose Symbolic Instruction Code, was developed at Dartmouth College in the 1960s. Because of its conversational nature, it is usually used with minicomputers and microcomputers. BASIC is becoming increasingly popular, and today, most colleges and universities teach BASIC in one or more courses.

BASIC is real time, procedure oriented, and a general purpose language. It is used for both business and non business applications. The language is made up of a series of statements. Each statement starts with a *statement number* and a *key word,* which is followed by some type of action in most cases. For example in the statement "100 LET X = 6", 100 is the statement number, LET is the key word, and X = 6 is the action. This causes the computer to set the variable X equal to 6.

In addition to statements, BASIC also has a number of *system commands* that allow the programmer to run, print, and manipulate the program. RUN, LIST, and SAVE are examples of system commands for BASIC.

Unfortunately, BASIC programming languages vary significantly from one computer system to the next. Thus, a BASIC program written on one computer may not work on another computer unless modified. At the present time the *American National Standards Institute* (ANSI) is in the process of developing a standardized BASIC programming language. This effort is a continuation of the work of the X3J2 committee of ANSI, which was formed in 1974.

The computer can be programmed to perform almost any task that can be done by hand using paper and pencil. In Figure 12–2, a BASIC program computes the total of 15 numbers.

In line 5, the computer sets T, which represents the total, equal to 0. In line 10, the computer enters a loop that consists of lines 10 through 40. In line 10, the variable I is set equal to 1, representing the first cycle or loop. In line 20, the computer reads the first number in the first DATA statement in line 60, and assigns this number to X. Thus, X becomes 16. Then the computer goes to the next line, which is line 30. In this line, T is set equal

```
5      LET T = 0
10     FOR I = 1 TO 15
20     READ   X
30     LET T = T + X
40     NEXT I
50     PRINT "THE TOTAL IS";  T
60     DATA 16, 18, 4, 8, 9
70     DATA 4, 1, 3, 7, 41
80     DATA 6, 21, 36, 44, 15
999    END


RUN
THE TOTAL IS 233
TIME   .4 sec
READY
```

FIGURE 12–2
A BASIC program to compute the total of 15 numbers

to T + X. Since T is 0 (see line 5), and X is 16, T becomes 16 (16 = 0 + 16) at this point. Line 40 sends the computer back to the beginning of the loop at line 10. In line 10, I becomes 2 for the second loop, X becomes 18, which is the second number, and T becomes 34 (34 = 16 + 18). In line 40, the computer is directed to go to line 10 to start the third loop. In the third loop, I is set equal to 3, X is set equal to 4, and T becomes 38. Then the computer loops a fourth time, and so on. After the computer has looped or cycled 15 times, reading X and computing the total, the computer is finished with the loop. Then, it drops down to line 50, where the total is printed. In this case the total is 233. Then, the program ends at line 999. How would you modify this program to compute the total of 25 numbers? You would change line 10 to: 10 FOR I = TO 25. Then, you could add 10 more numbers in additional DATA statements.

THE FORTRAN PROGRAMMING LANGUAGE

FORTRAN, which is an acronym for FORmula TRANslator, was first developed by IBM with some computer users in 1957. Since then it has gone through several revisions and changes. While FORTRAN was one of the first scientific programming languages, it is still very popular and available on a large number of computer systems.

FORTRAN is a procedure oriented, general purpose language. Originally, it was developed to be used in the batch mode, but today, most FORTRAN languages can also be processed using the real-time mode on terminals. While the original purpose of FORTRAN was to solve scientific type problems, it is also used to perform business applications.

In order to allow a program that was written on one computer system to be run on another computer system, ANSI developed a standardized FORTRAN language in the 1960s called ANSI FORTRAN. Those computer systems that have the ANSI compiler or translator can execute other ANSI FORTRAN programs written on other computers.

Like BASIC, the fundamental building block of FORTRAN is the FORTRAN statement. While spacing of the line numbers, key words, and actions in BASIC are not critical, a FORTRAN program requires that certain parts of the program be placed in certain columns. Statement numbers, which are optional in FORTRAN, are placed in columns 1 through 5. If there is a comment that a programmer would like other programmers to read but the computer to ignore, a C (Comment) is usually placed in the first column. The actual FORTRAN statement is placed in columns 7 through 72. A character in column 6 means a continuation of the above statement. Columns 73 through 80 are ignored by the computer system, and the programmer may use these columns for any purpose, like numbering each statement or for writing in a program code name. To help a programmer remember and use these columns for their proper purpose, special FORTRAN program coding forms can be used. A typical coding form is shown in Figure 12–3.

In the last section, a program in BASIC was written to compute the total of 15 numbers. A FORTRAN program can be written to make the same calculations. A program written in FORTRAN IV, one of the versions of FORTRAN, is displayed in Figure 12–4.

The FORTRAN program in Figure 12–4 functions almost identically to the BASIC program that computes the total of 15 numbers. The first statement sets the TOTAL equal to 0. The DO statement functions just like the FOR statement in BASIC. It tells the computer to *do* a loop, that

FIGURE 12–3
A FORTRAN coding form

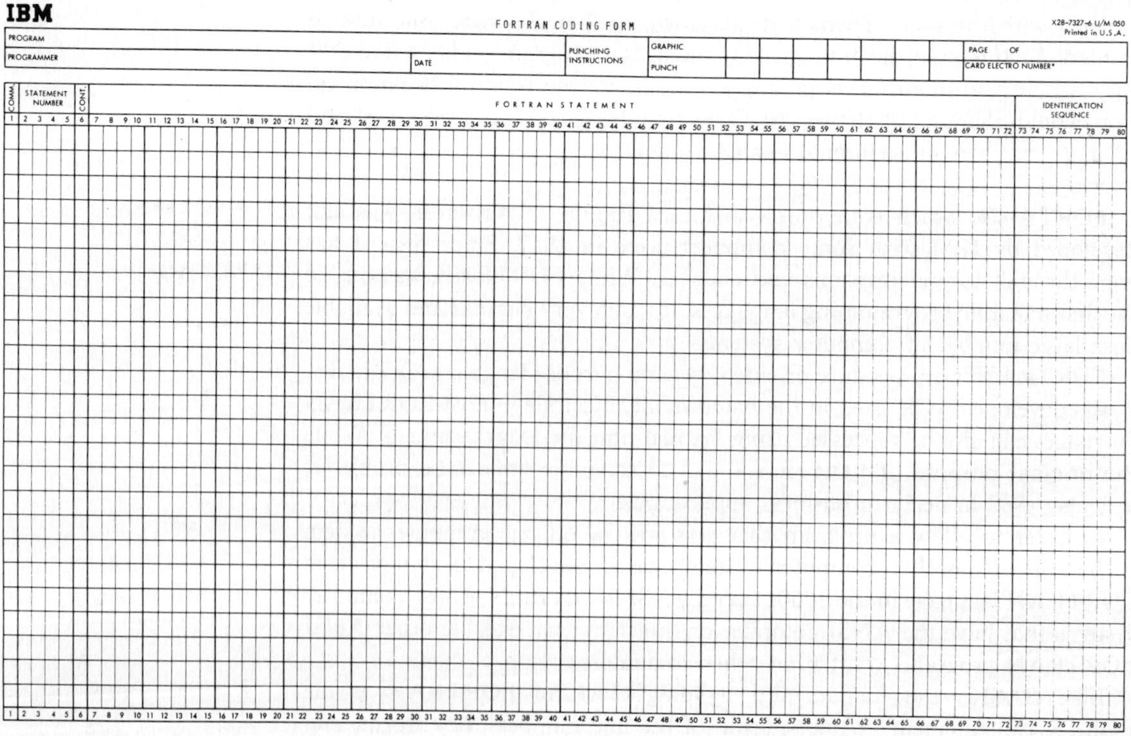

```
              TOTAL = 0
              DO 60  I = 1, 15
              READ (5, 10) X
       10     FORMAT (F8.2)
              TOTAL = TOTAL+X
       60     CONTINUE
              WRITE (6, 20) TOTAL
       20     FORMAT ( 13HTHE TOTAL IS , F15.2)
              STOP
              END
```

FIGURE 12–4
A FORTRAN program to compute the TOTAL of 15 numbers

starts at the DO statement and ends in line 60, which is a continue statement. Inside the loop, values for X are read and added to TOTAL. After the computer loops 15 times reading and accumulating the total of 15 numbers, the computer goes out of the loop and drops down to the next statement. This is the WRITE statement. The total is printed, and the computer stops. The STOP statement tells the computer to stop the execution of the program, and the END statement tells the computer that there are no more instructions or statements in the program. The data is a separate file and not contained in the program.

THE COBOL PROGRAMMING LANGUAGE

COBOL, which stands for COmmon Business Oriented Language, was developed by the CODASYL (COnference on DAta SYstems Languages) Committee in 1959 and printed by the government printing office in 1960. In the same year, the Department of Defense announced that contracts for computer systems and services must include a provision for the use of COBOL. As a result, computer manufacturers started developing compilers for COBOL. In the early 1960s, COBOL went through several updates, and in 1968, the American National Standards Institute along with several computer manufacturers developed the American National Standard COBOL or (ANS) COBOL, which was to become the industry standard for developing COBOL. In 1974, another version of (ANS) COBOL was developed. As long as these standards are followed, a COBOL program can be run on any computer system with an (ANS) COBOL compiler. The ability to write programs that are machine independent is one of the biggest advantages of using COBOL.

The structure of a COBOL program

The developers of COBOL designed COBOL to have the appearance and structure of a business report written in English. Thus, a COBOL program is constructed from *sentences, paragraphs, sections,* and *divisions.* In any COBOL program, there must be four divisions: (1) *The Identification Division,* (2) *The Environment Division,* (3) *The Data Division* and (4) *The Procedure Division.*

Most COBOL programs are written using a standard COBOL Coding Form. See Figure 12–5.

Like FORTRAN, each statement or line is broken into 80 columns. Col-

FIGURE 12-5
COBOL coding form

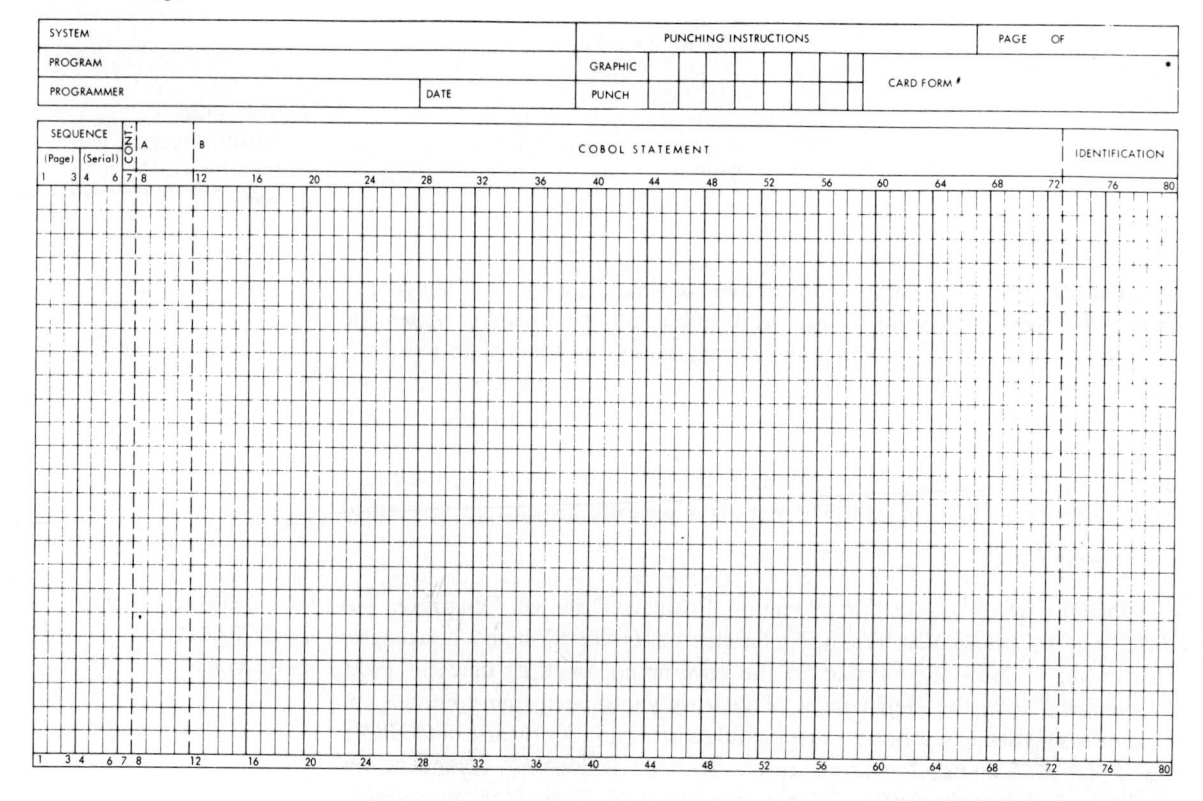

umns 1-3 are used for the page number of the coding form. Columns 4-6 identify each line number. An * in column 7 is used for remarks or program documentation.

The actual COBOL statements are placed in columns 8-72. You will notice that there are two margins: the A Margin and the B Margin. The A Margin is used to start a new *division, section,* or *paragraph*. The B Margin is used to start any *sentence*. Finally columns 73-80 can be used to identify the program name. The computer ignores these columns.

In the rest of this section, the four divisions of a COBOL program will be investigated in more detail. While doing this, we will see how a COBOL program can be written to compute the total of 15 numbers. This program will produce the same output as the FORTRAN and BASIC programs presented in the previous sections.

The identification division

The Identification Division is the first division in any COBOL program. There must be at least two sentences in this division. A typical identification division is shown in Figure 12-6.

```
                IDENTIFICATION DIVISION.
                PROGRAM ID.  TOTAL-OF-15-NUMBERS.
```

FIGURE 12-6
The identification division

IDENTIFICATION DIVISION is the first sentence in a COBOL program. This should be followed by the PROGRAM ID, which identifies the name of the program. The name of this program is TOTAL-OF-15-NUMBERS. The identification division may also specify the person who wrote the program, the date the program was written, and other remarks and identifying statements.

The environment division

The purpose of the ENVIRONMENT DIVISION is to describe the computer hardware that is to be used. Because there are different types of hardware and different hardware manufacturers, this is the only division that would have to be changed if you used an (ANS) COBOL program on another computer system. A typical environment division appears in Figure 12-7.

```
        ENVIRONMENT DIVISION.
        CONFIGURATION SECTION.
        SOURCE COMPUTER.  CYBER-74.
        OBJECT COMPUTER.  CYBER-74.
        INPUT-OUTPUT SECTION.
        FILE CONTROL.
            SELECT DATA-FILE ASSIGN TO CARD-READER-FZ.
            SELECT TOTAL-FILE ASSIGN TO PRINTER-FZ.
```

FIGURE 12-7
The environment division

The first two sentences in the environment division are ENVIRONMENT DIVISION, and CONFIGURATION SECTION. The configuration section reveals the source computer and the object computer. Normally this computer is the same. As you can see, the source computer is the CYBER-74, and the object computer is the CYBER-74. If your program was being run on a different computer system, you would replace CYBER-74 with the appropriate name of the computer. The second section in the environment division is the INPUT-OUTPUT SECTION. This section defines the files that are to be used to *input* the data and *output* the results. Furthermore, these files are assigned to specific hardware devices. These assignments are made in the two SELECT sentences. The first select sentence in the FILE CONTROL paragraph tells the computer to assign DATA-FILE to the card reader. The second select statement in the FILE CONTROL paragraph tells the computer to assign TOTAL-FILE to the printer.

The data division

In the ENVIRONMENT DIVISION, the computer system, input device, and output device were specified. In addition, the input file and output file were assigned to the appropriate input and output devices. In the DATA

DIVISION, *all* files are specified in detail. The input and output files are described in the FILE SECTION, and all intermediate or working files and results are described in the WORKING STORAGE SECTION.

In this program, there will be 15 computer cards containing the input data. There will be one card for each number. Each number is called an input fact or item, and each card is called an input record. All 15 cards or records make up the input file, which is called DATA-FILE. This file was assigned to a card reader in the Environment Division. Furthermore, the output from this program should be one line, which is THE TOTAL IS 233. This output line is called an output record, and it will be called TOTAL-LINE in this program. This line or record is made up of two items. The first item is THE TOTAL IS, and it will be called the TITLE. The second item is the number 233, and it will be called TOTAL-VALUE. The complete Data Division for the program that computes the total of 15 numbers appears in Figure 12–8.

```
DATA DIVISION.
FILE SECTION.
FD   DATA-FILE.
     LABEL RECORDS ARE OMITTED.
     DATA RECORD IS DATA-CARD.
01   DATA-CARD.
     02   DATA VALUE      PICTURE IS 9(6)V99.
     02   FILLER          PICTURE IS X(72).
FD   TOTAL-FILE.
     LABEL RECORDS ARE OMITTED.
     DATA RECORD IS TOTAL-LINE.
01   TOTAL-LINE.
     02   TITLE           PICTURE IS X(12)
                          VALUE IS "THE TOTAL IS".
     02   FILLER          PICTURE IS X(2).
     02   TOTAL-VALUE     PICTURE IS 9(13)V99.
     02   FILLER          PICTURE IS X(102).
WORKING STORAGE SECTION.
77   RUNNING-TOTAL        PICTURE IS 9(13)V99
                          VALUE IS 0.
```

FIGURE 12–8
The data division

The input and output files are completely described in the File Section. The FD DATA-FILE paragraph describes the input file, and the FD TOTAL-FILE paragraph describes the output file. FD stands for File Description. The WORKING STORAGE SECTION describes any data that is used in arriving at the final results. In calculating the total of 15 numbers, it is necessary to keep a running total. This running total is described in the Working Storage Section.

The procedure division

In the PROCEDURE DIVISION, the computer is told how the input data is to be manipulated to generate the desired output. This is done by using a series of commands or sentences. The Procedure Division for the program that computes the total of 15 numbers appears in Figure 12–9.

The PROCEDURE DIVISION consists of the BEGIN-JOB paragraph, the MAIN-LOOP paragraph, the PRINT-ROUTINE paragraph, and the END-OF-JOB paragraph. All of the files are opened in the BEGIN-JOB paragraph. This type of paragraph is fairly standard in most COBOL programs. The MAIN-LOOP paragraph reads the numbers one at a time and adds them to the RUNNING-TOTAL. This process is continued, and when there is no more data (AT END), the computer is directed to go to the PRINT-ROUTINE paragraph. In this paragraph, SPACES are moved to the TOTAL-LINE, which clears the line. Then, the RUNNING-TOTAL is moved to TOTAL-VALUE, which is a part of TOTAL-LINE. In the WRITE sentence, the TOTAL-LINE is printed. This causes the computer to print: THE TOTAL IS 233. The last paragraph is the END-OF-JOB paragraph. Here all of the files are closed, and the program is run.

```
PROCEDURE DIVISION.
BEGIN-JOB.
    OPEN INPUT DATA-FILE.
    OPEN OUTPUT TOTAL-FILE.
MAIN-LOOP.
    READ DATA-FILE AT END GO TO PRINT-ROUTINE.
    ADD DATA-VALUE TO RUNNING-TOTAL.
    GO TO MAIN-LOOP.
PRINT-ROUTINE.
    MOVE SPACES TO TOTAL-LINE.
    MOVE RUNNING-TOTAL TO TOTAL-VALUE.
    WRITE TOTAL-LINE.
END-OF-JOB.
    CLOSE DATA-FILE.
    CLOSE TOTAL-FILE.
    STOP RUN.
```

FIGURE 12–9
The procedure division

THE PASCAL PROGRAMMING LANGUAGE

PASCAL is a relatively new language with a very bright future. It is real time, general purpose, and procedural; and it can be used for business and scientific applications. It was developed by Niklaus Wirth of the Federal Institute of Technology in Zurich, Switzerland in 1968. The language is relatively easy to learn, and it allows the programmer to structure the programming problem. This language is especially well suited for microcomputers and minicomputers, and many manufacturers of these systems are investing millions of dollars into developing PASCAL compilers. PASCAL is also on many larger computer systems, and it is being taught at numerous colleges and universities.

Writing a program to find the total of a string of numbers is relatively easy and straight forward in PASCAL. See Figure 12–10.

The PASCAL program in Figure 12–10 is similar to the BASIC and FORTRAN programs that computed the total of 15 numbers. The first line contains the name of the program, SUM 15. Then, all of the variables are

```
PROGRAM SUM15 (INPUT,OUTPUT):
(* *)
(* DECLARE VARIABLES *)
    VAR  X : REAL;
         TOTAL : REAL;
         I = INTEGER;
    BEGIN
(* *)
(* INITIALIZE ACCUMULATOR *)
         TOTAL := 0;
         FOR I :=1 TO 15 DO
         BEGIN
             READ(X);
             TOTAL := TOTAL + X
         END;
         WRITELN;
         WRITELN("THE TOTAL IS ",TOTAL)
    END.
```

FIGURE 12–10
A PASCAL program to compute the total of 15 numbers

declared. The variables X and TOTAL are declared to be *real variables.* They can be assigned any real number. The variable I is declared to be an *integer variable.* The heart of the program starts with the word BEGIN and ends with the word END. First, the variable TOTAL is initialized to be equal to 0. The next line, FOR I: = 1 TO 15 DO, starts a loop that reads and computes the total of the 15 numbers. This loop is very similar to the loops that were used in the FORTRAN and BASIC programs. The various values of X are read and added to the variable TOTAL. WRITELN writes a blank line, and WRITELN ("THE TOTAL IS ", TOTAL) prints the results of the program. In this case, the results are: THE TOTAL IS 233. This is the same output as the BASIC and FORTRAN programs. The 15 numbers are the same numbers used in the BASIC program. The data, however, is not contained within the PASCAL program. It is stored separately.

OTHER PROGRAMMING LANGUAGES

The programming languages discussed above, BASIC, FORTRAN, COBOL, and PASCAL are not necessarily the most important or most popular language with every college, university, or company. These languages were presented in more detail to give you a better understanding of computer programming in general. There are many other programming languages that are just as important and popular. Some of these languages will be briefly discussed in this section.

RPG and RPG II

Report Program Generator (RPG) is a business oriented, general purpose programming language. It is problem oriented and is usually implemented in the batch mode on such computers as the IBM System/3 and System/32. Instead of writing instructions or statements, the programmer completes five *specification sheets.* These sheets specify exactly what is to be done, and then the computer uses these specification sheets to generate the necessary instructions to perform the application. Originally, RPG and the newer version **RPG II** were developed for small computer systems, but today they are being implemented on medium and large systems as well.

PL/1

Programming Language 1 (PL/1) was developed by IBM in the 1960s to combine the advantages and structures of FORTRAN and COBOL. This language has *default options,* which allow the programmer to make minor omissions or errors, and it has a division structure similar to COBOL. The language is general purpose and procedural, and it can be used for either business or scientific applications. PL/1 does require substantial memory requirements; it is not standardized like FORTRAN and COBOL, and it is not as widely used or accepted.

APL

A Programming Language (APL) was developed by Kenneth Iverson in 1962. It is general purpose and procedural in nature. This language is a real-time language that was developed for primarily *scientific applications.* APL has a free form structure, and it uses *special operators,* which look somewhat like greek letters, to perform sophisticated manipulations. Due to these special operators, a special key board is necessary. APL can be used by large and small computers. The small desk top IBM 5110, for example, can be programmed in BASIC or APL by placing a switch into the BASIC mode or the APL mode.

Additional programming languages

In addition to business and scientific languages, there are *special purpose* languages that perform simulation, network analysis, mathematical programming, computer assisted instruction, line drawing, string processing, formula processing, list processing, artificial intelligence applications, and editing functions. To show you the diversity of these languages, some of these special purpose languages have been listed in Figure 12-11.

LANGUAGE COMPARISON

Since most computer systems can be programmed in a number of different high-level programming languages, it is important to select the best language for a particular application. A comparison of some of the characteristics of a few high-level programming languages is given below.

BASIC is easy to learn, interactive in nature, and it is available on a number of different computer systems. This language has good math and character string manipulation characteristics, and it does not require a special terminal or keyboard. Because large amounts of storage are not required, this language is available on microcomputers and minicomputers, as well

FIGURE 12–11
Additional programming languages

Scientific
   ALGOL
   JOSS
   SPEAKEASY

Business
   DataBASIC
   IDS
   PL/DB

Statistics
   SPSS
   CROSSTABS
   BMD

Simulation
   GPSS
   SIMSCRIPT
   DYNAMO
   MIMIC

Networks
   GIRL
   FGRAAL

Computer-assisted instruction
   TUTOR
   PILOT
   MENTOR
   Coursewriter III

Line drawing
   B-LINE
   BUGSYS

Mathematical programming
   AMBUSH
   MPSX
   GAMMA 3

String processing
   SNOBOL
   COMIT
   VULCAN

Artificial intelligence
   Planner
   QLISP

Formula processing
   ALTRAN
   FORMAC
   FORMAL
   SCRATCHPAD
   SYMBAL

List processing
   TREET
   LPL
   MLISP 2

Multipurpose
   AED
   HAL
   JOVIAL
   OSCAR

Editing
   PAGE
   SNAP

as small, medium, and large computers. BASIC, however, is not completely standardized, and programs written on one computer system normally have to be modified before they will work on another computer system. This language is not highly efficient, English-like, or self-documenting.

FORTRAN has excellent mathematical capabilities, it is available on a large number of computer systems, and it is concise. This standardized language does not require a large amount of storage. On the other hand, FORTRAN does not manipulate character strings efficiently or easily. It is not English-like, self-documenting, and the rules of the language must be strictly followed to avoid errors.

COBOL is English-like, self-documenting, standardized, and it is easy to learn and understand. It is a very popular language for business applications. Because of its English-like nature, COBOL is easier to test and debug than many other languages. This language is available on a large number of different computers and because it is standardized, it is easy to modify COBOL programs to run on different computer systems. Only the ENVIRONMENT DIVISION has to be changed. COBOL, however, is verbose. In some cases, it can take two or three times as many statements to write the same program compared to other languages. The computational capabilities are poor, the language is not highly efficient, and large amounts of storage are required. Thus, COBOL is not normally found on microcomputers or minicomputers.

PASCAL is easy to learn, interactive in nature, and highly structured. This language has a number of default options that allow the programmer to write simple or sophisticated programs. PASCAL does not require a large amount of storage like COBOL, and it is becoming very popular on computers of all sizes. This language, however, is not self-documenting, English-like, or completely standardized.

RPG is a problem oriented language that is available on many small and medium sized computer systems. It does not require a large amount of storage, and it is relatively easy to learn. It is especially good for generating business reports and documents. This language, however, is not good for mathematical computations, and therefore, the language is not a good scientific language. RPG is not standardized nor is it English-like.

PL/1 has good mathematical capabilities, and it has a number of built in functions that make programming easier. There are a number of default options that simplify the programming process. This language can also handle character strings efficiently, and it is English-like. This language, however, requires a large amount of storage, and it is still primarily used with IBM computers.

APL is an interactive language that has good mathematical capabilities and the ability to efficiently handle character strings. APL has a free-form structure, and there are a number of special operators that allow sophisticated manipulations to be done without too much effort. APL, however, requires a large amount of storage and a special keyboard. It is not standardized or English-like.

SUMMARY

The key to making the computer system perform business applications is application software, and the purpose of this chapter was to introduce you to the various high-level programming languages that can be used in developing application software. High-level languages are relatively independent from a particular computer system; each statement is normally translated into several machine language statements, and the language is natural and easy to use. High-level languages have attributes that can range from real time to batch, procedural to problematic, business oriented to nonbusiness oriented, and general purpose to special purpose.

BASIC, a language that is popular with microcomputers and minicomputers, was developed at Dartmouth College in the 1960s. This is a real time, procedure oriented, and a general purpose language. The basis structure of this language is the statement, which consists of a line number, a key word, and in most cases an action.

FORTRAN was one of the earliest scientific programming languages, although it is also used in business applications. It was developed in 1957 by IBM. Today a standardized FORTRAN is being used. The basic structure of FORTRAN is the statement which starts in column 7. Columns 1–5 are reserved for optional statement numbers, and column 6 is used for continuing a statement.

COBOL is one of the most popular business oriented programming languages. Like FORTRAN, there is a standardized COBOL developed by the American National Standards Institute (ANSI). COBOL, which has the structure of a written report, is constructed with sentences, paragraphs, sections, and major divisions. Every COBOL program must have an IDENTIFICATION DIVISION, an ENVIRONMENT DIVISION, a DATA DIVISION, and a PROCEDURE DIVISION.

There are a number of other popular and important languages that are in use around the world and are taught at numerous colleges and universities. These languages include PASCAL, RPG and RPG II, PL/1, and APL. In addition, there are hundreds of other programs that are used in statistics, simulation, network analysis, computer-aided instruction, line drawing, mathematical programming, string processing, artificial intelligence, formula processing, list processing, and editing.

KEY TERMS AND CONCEPTS

BASIC
COBOL
FORTRAN
High-level programming languages
Real time
Batch
Procedure oriented
Problem oriented
Business oriented
Scientific oriented
General purpose
Special purpose
American National Standards Institute (ANSI)
PASCAL
RPG
RPG II
PL/1
APL
Identification division
Environment division
Data division
Procedure division

QUESTIONS

12–1. What is the purpose of a high-level programming language?

12–2. Briefly describe the development and use of the BASIC programming language?

12–3. How are BASIC programs normally executed? Describe how you would run a BASIC program on a computer system.

12–4. What was FORTRAN originally developed to do?

12–5. Briefly describe the development of the COBOL language. What is ANS COBOL?

12–6. What are the four major divisions of any COBOL program? What is a section, paragraph, sentence, and a clause?

12–7. Briefly describe the purpose of the four divisions of a COBOL program.

12–8. Contrast PASCAL, RPG, PL/1, and APL. Briefly describe the development and use of these programming languages.

MINIQUIZ

ANSWERS

1. F
2. T
3. T
4. F
5. T
6. T
7. T
8. T
9. F
10. T

True or False

_____ 1. The errors that can be generated using a particular programming language are called the syntax of the language.
_____ 2. BASIC was developed at Dartmouth College in the 1960s.
_____ 3. BASIC is a real time, procedure oriented, and a general purpose language.
_____ 4. FORTRAN was developed by NCR in 1945.
_____ 5. FORTRAN is a procedure oriented and a general purpose language.
_____ 6. In 1974, another version of (ANS) COBOL was developed.
_____ 7. A COBOL program is made up of sentences, paragraphs, sections, and divisions.
_____ 8. The divisions of a COBOL program include the identification division, the environment division, the data division, and the procedure division.
_____ 9. RPG is a scientific oriented general programming language.
_____ 10. PL/1 was developed by IBM in the 1960s to combine the advantages and structures of FORTRAN and COBOL.

Untraditional software designing serves untraditional mini, micro market

Yale A. Grayson

An unconventional software design firm, hidden in the Vermont countryside, is relying on some old-fashioned concepts when designing systems for end users of mini and microcomputers. Incentives, based in part on meeting deadlines with a quality product, help encourage computer professionals to take genuine pride in their products.

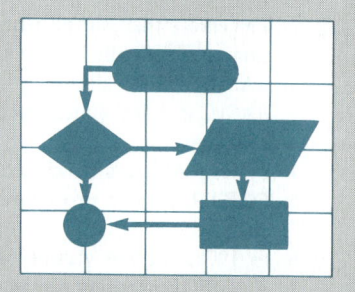

Minis and micros are returning processing to the grass-roots point of the transaction. And the information manager has a new vista of previously unknown computer operating systems and languages.

For so many in mainframes the choice of vendors is generally limited to three or four prime choices. In the mini-micro area there are currently over 50 different suppliers with complete system pricing running from $3,000 to mainframe prices. Surprisingly, many of the machine capabilities overlap at widely varying costs.

This proliferation of mini-micro products has produced an opportunity for software firms specializing in mini/micros. And, by complementing nontraditional uses of small computers, some new software firms are conducting business in equally untraditional ways. Programmers, for example, believe that programmers and systems people can function more efficiently in a relaxed rural environment (Fairlee, VT). At the same time, such a location's environment does not require the higher standard of living found in the large, urban areas.

From recent observations, it seems that many projects can be done at a savings of up to 50 percent as compared to other companies. The reason for such potential savings is two-fold. The first involves motivation of the technical staff, and the second involves an advanced "system building" technique that has been developed over several years.

Motivation

This first concept is based upon the idea that, in most operating computer systems environments, system people are compensated in straight salary, and not in relation to their individual productivity. The Country Programmers concept is to provide fair and competitive base salaries which are enchanced by incentive bonuses.

Incentives are triggered by:

- Completion on schedule.
- Clarity of documentation (as related to the number of customer calls asking for further explanation).
- Number of program bugs found after delivery of the software product (First 120 days after delivery).

System building

The systems building technique consists of two phases: The first is getting a clear definition of the problem; the second consists of an extensive set of techniques that the technical staff must follow in order to build either a mini/micro computer system or a simple time-sharing program module.

Book phase

In the first phase, a systems design book is produced with the following contents:

- *Glossary.* This contains all special terms used by the buyer with connection terms easily understood by the software development technical staff.
- *Source documents.* Complete set of all the source documents that will be used for the system. For each document there is a complete explanation for each field.
- *File formats.* This is the complete data base design, defined down to the field size, data type,

Source: *Data Management,* March 1979, pp. 24–25.

format and location in the data base for every data quantum.
- *Screen formats.* Complete layout of every format on a field/character basis with indication of entry field sizes and content.
- *Systems processes.* Complete narrative and systems flow-chart for every function to be performed by the computer system. The section is usually detailed to the subsystem level and is so constructed that it contains all the manual and automatic data flow through the system. All information is constructed so that it can readily be understood by a "non-computer oriented" executive.
- *Output formats.* This is the normal character layout for every printed report.
- *PERT chart.* This is a section containing a narrative description of the PERT chart along with a week by week description of the work to be performed.

Construction phase

The second phase is the construction phase, which is too lengthy to describe in detail here. However, several basic tenets include:

- A systems software analyst will completely analyze special conditions of the target machine software and produce a mini-micro computer software primer checklist. This will contain the special advantages of the target machine software to be used, along with any known bugs in the software, things to watch out for, or take advantage of.
- The programmers who will do the actual construction must create or work on the following in the indicated order: Program flowcharts; individual GANTT charts with at least one or more reporting points for every week of the project; and completion of the software primer checklist.
- All programs built in the system are highly structured, using top down techniques and specially created forms to produce small, highly efficient program modules.
- Weekly reporting information is entered into the computer by each programmer at the end of every week against earlier produced GANTT chart information. The computer lists any tardy entries as well as any missed target dates on an exception basis. All data is reviewed weekly by project manager.
- All programmers, analysts and project managers have automated methods for sending to and receiving from each other information concerning daily operations and reporting. This allows each individual to define his or her work day while avoiding the usual endless round of meetings.

The result is greater productivity.

This is a unique approach of a single rural mini/micro computer company assisting the information manager in selecting and building systems for a distributed data processing network.

DISCUSSION QUESTIONS

1. What types of documentation and implementation techniques do you think are being used by Country Programmers, Inc.?
2. How are programmers and systems analysts motivated? Is this a good approach to motivation, and will it result in better application programs?

Program and application development

13

DEVELOPING APPLICATION SOFTWARE
    Problem definition
    Analysis and design
    Language selection
    Program coding
    Testing and debugging
    Documentation
    Implementation
    Maintenance
PURCHASING APPLICATION SOFTWARE

After completing Chapter 13, you will be able to:

- Discuss what is involved in problem definition.
- Describe the difference between analysis and design.
- List what is involved with testing and debugging.
- Contrast the different documentation manuals.
- Discuss implementation and maintenance.

The least expensive or most expensive computer hardware can be plugged into an electrical outlet and absolutely nothing will happen. A computer will not function unless you provide it with a set of instructions (software) telling it what to do.

Over the years, the importance of software has increased. In the 1950s, software costs represented approximately *15 percent* of the total cost of computerizing. Today, approximately *50 percent* of the cost of a computer system is software costs, and by 1985, it is expected that software costs could be as much as *75 percent* or more of the total cost of computerizing. The increased importance of software is due in part to lower computer hardware costs and increasing program development costs, such as higher salaries for computer programmers and systems analysts.

Software is the key to unlocking the potential of any computer system. All of the computer applications described in this book are a direct result of application software. Software makes the difference between an effective data processing department and an ineffective data processing department, between profit and loss.

It is the purpose of this chapter to reveal to you the minimum requirements for developing good application software. In addition, the option of buying already developed application software will be explored. The steps and procedures presented in this chapter will not prevent all mistakes or problems. The chance for human error is too great to make this guarantee. But the procedures presented below will greatly help in eliminating mistakes and problems from occurring, and they will help in getting more from a computer system.

DEVELOPING APPLICATION SOFTWARE

Some books lead you to believe that very little or nothing has to be done before entering a program into a computer system; you just write the program on the back of an envelope or on a scrap piece of paper, punch it on computer cards, and then run it on the computer. Doing this for a program of any size would be like sketching plans for a house on a soiled place mat or napkin at a restaurant, and then constructing the house without any blueprints or detailed plans. In both cases, the chances of success are small.

Developing computer programs and application software that are useful to the persons using it requires a substantial amount of *detailed planning*. Through years of experience, a series of steps and planned activities have been developed to maximize the likelihood of developing profitable and useful software. Many companies and computer manufacturers have developed books, seminars, cassettes, and other materials on the application development process, with titles such as *Managing Application Development* and *Computer Problem Solving*. While the particular procedures have different names, the overall approach is basically the same. These fundamental steps are:

1. Problem definition.
2. Analysis and design.
3. Language selection.

4. Program coding.
5. Testing and debugging.
6. Documentation.
7. Implementation.
8. Maintenance.

The fundamental steps outlined above offer a number of advantages over an approach where no formal procedure is used to develop application software. These advantages include:

1. Better management control over the project.
2. The use of proven techniques and procedures.
3. Good use of data processing personnel.
4. Better estimates of project completion time.
5. Better estimates of total project costs.
6. Improved quality control over entire project.
7. Better program design which leads to fewer problems with debugging and maintenance.
8. Greater likelihood of satisfying user needs and desires.

It should be noted that one step does not have to be completely finished before the next step is started. For example, during program analysis, materials are developed that are used in documentation. Furthermore, many programmers develop test data during the initial steps that are used during the testing and debugging phase. In other cases, programmers perform all of these steps for one part of one program, and then this process is repeated until the entire program is written. A newer programming technique, called *structured design* which will be discussed in Chapter 15, uses this approach. It should also be noted that after a step has been completed, it may be modified several times before the program is completed. While a program is being written or coded, the user or a manager might want to get additional reports from the computer program. This would require the problem definition and analysis steps to be modified to include the additional reports. It is also not uncommon for a programmer to discover, while writing the necessary programs, that some of the desired outputs are either not possible or extremely difficult to obtain. These discoveries would also cause the program definition and analysis steps to be modified to reflect the reports or outputs that will not be produced.

Like links in a chain, the eight steps of developing application software provide the connection between the potential of the computer hardware and the desires of the individuals using the computer system. When one step is not adequately completed, there is a *weak link,* and the computer system will most likely not be able to perform to its potential in satisfying the needs and desires of those individuals using the computer system. These eight steps can also be used to follow the progress of the application development project by monitoring the extent to which each step has been completed over time. Perhaps the most important step is the first step, **problem definition.**

1. Problem definition

Computer programs are written because there is a problem to be solved or a need to be satisfied. Perhaps a medical clinic needs tighter controls on unpaid bills, or a police department has a problem in obtaining a fast and complete list of possible suspects for a crime. In a business, the problem could be too many stockouts or perhaps a total labor cost that is entirely too high. The problem might be that it takes too long for a company to send out bills after it receives purchase orders for its products.

In some cases, the problem is so evident that it is not necessary to conduct a long investigation. In other circumstances, the problem might be difficult to determine or define. In defining the problem, it is important to go beyond the *symptoms* and find the *true cause* of the problem. This might require extensive *interviews* with employees, customers, and managers. *Surveys* and *questionnaires* can be developed and administered, and company *documents* and *procedures* can be studied. While these efforts may appear to be a waste of time and bothersome, they may be necessary to clearly and precisely define the problem; otherwise a great deal of time and effort may be invested in a problem that is trivial or irrelevant.

After the problem has been defined, the next step is to determine what **output** should be produced from the computer system to help in solving the problem. Perhaps the problem is too many stockouts for a particular item. How could the computer be used to help in solving this problem? If the computer could print a report every time the quantity on hand for the item was 50 units or less, an order could be placed for more of these items before the quantity dropped to zero. Thus, the desired output from the computer is a report that contains all items in inventory with 50 units or less on hand. Deciding what type of report or output is needed, however, is not enough. The desired report or output from the computer system must be described in detail. The *exact form* or *layout* of the report or output must be determined. Questions about *when* the output is to be generated, *how* many copies are required, *who* gets the output, *where* the output is to be sent, *how* the output is to be produced, and *who* is responsible for producing the output need to be answered. The person or persons who will be using the output (the user) should be involved in specifying the output requirements for the outputs that they will be using.

After the output requirements have been specified, the next logical step is to determine what data is required to obtain the necessary reports or outputs from the computer system. This is called determining the **input requirements.** If a manager wants the computer to print a report consisting of the employee number and gross pay for all employees who earned over $400 in any given week, what input data is required? In order to compute gross pay, the hourly pay rate and the number of hours worked for any given week for all employees is needed. In addition, the employee number for each employee would be required. With larger and more complex programs, the process of determining the needed input data is not any more difficult. It involves starting with the desired output and working backwards determining what input data is needed to generate the desired output.

The *source* of the input data also needs to be determined. Some input data may already be stored on the computer system, while other input data has to be captured and entered into the computer system. The *accuracy* of the input data is also important. Inaccurate input data will result in inaccurate output reports. This is called **"garbage in garbage out"** (Gigo). Several documentation techniques are available to assist in problem definition. These techniques include *grid charts, layout charts,* and *print charts,* and they will be covered in the next chapter.

2. Analysis and design

The analysis and design step takes the problem definition and produces all necessary documents and performs all necessary activities that are required before the computer programs can be written. The major emphasis of **analysis** is an investigation into the *existing* problem and situation, while the major emphasis of **design** is to develop the *new* procedures that are necessary to solve the problem.

At the center of analysis is the **feasibility study.** This study determines whether the proposed solution has *technical feasibility, operational feasibility,* and *economic feasibility.* In some cases, the problem either cannot be solved or it would be too expensive to justify its solution. Included in the analysis phase is an investigation into the expected resources to be used, the structure of the organization, corporate policies and practices, marketing procedures, the existing data processing system and data processing personnel, the products and services produced by the organization, potential legal problems, customers, and so on. All of these factors can have an impact on the extent to which the problem can be solved. Usually, a feasibility study team is charged with the responsibility of conducting the feasibility study.

While analysis investigates the way things *are,* design investigates the way things *should be.* Design is concerned with developing a *new* system to solve the problem defined in the first step. In addition to the development of additional application software, this might require additional hardware and personnel.

Design is a critical phase of developing application software. Designing application software is like designing a house. The finished product will be no better than the design, and in some cases, the finished product can be worse. Data security, privacy protection, program and data backup, error detection and recovery, and audit trails to prevent fraud, should **all** be designed into the system at this stage. It is much easier and less expensive to design these features into the system than to modify the system at a later date. Likewise, it is easier and less expensive to design a four bedroom house than to design a three bedroom house and add a fourth room after the house has been completely built. Issues of data security and integrity, audit trails and fraud protection, and data backup and disaster recovery will be discussed in detail in Part IV.

There are many tools and techniques that can be used for analysis and design. Some of the traditional tools include *flowcharts* and *decision tables,* which will be covered in the next chapter. A newer approach to application software development, *structured programming and design,* will be covered in Chapter 15.

3. Language selection

In some cases, the programmer does not have a choice. Some computer systems only have one usable computer language. For example, many minicomputers and microcomputers use the BASIC language only. When there is a language choice, the type of application should be matched to the programming language.

In the last chapter, you were introduced to the characteristics of a number of different programming languages. In selecting a programming language, these characteristics must be carefully balanced against the characteristics of the particular problem to be solved. These characteristics include:

1. The difficulty of the problem.
2. The technical skill required of the computer programmers.
3. Whether or not the program is to be run using batch processing or real time processing.
4. The availability of subroutines that may be used in the program.
5. The existing hardware and software configuration.
6. The type of problem such as business or scientific.

4. Program coding

Program coding is the process of writing the necessary instructions in the language selected in Step 3 to solve the problem defined in Step 1 and analyzed and designed in Step 2. Like a contractor building a house, the computer programmer follows the plans and documents developed in the previous steps. This insures that the computer program or programs actually accomplished the desired result or solves the problem outlined in the first step.

There are several aids that a programmer can use in developing the necessary programs. Some data processing departments have a *library of programs* and *subroutines* that have already been written and tested. These programs and subroutines can be used in writing the new programs. Many programmers write the programs on *program coding forms* before the programs are entered into the computer system. There are coding forms for most languages that have the appropriate columns and positions marked. FORTRAN and COBOL coding forms were shown in Chapter 12.

The way the programs are actually written is very important. The same

13 Program and application development 277

building materials can be used to construct a sound house or a house that is ready to fall apart. The difference is how the house is constructed or built. Likewise, how a computer program is constructed or built makes the difference between a program that is sound and effective and one that is full of errors and problems. In general, programs should be as *simple* as possible *without* a large number of *loops* and *branches*.

5. Testing and debugging

Testing and debugging are vital steps in developing computer programs. A computer program may work for several months without any problems. Then, during one run, the program may start printing meaningless jibberish or it may fail to run altogether. Under such circumstances, the computer operator may state, "The program developed a bug last night" or "The program just crashed or blew up." This implies that a bug or a mistake magically appeared in the program. In reality, the mistake or problem was always there. Most computer related mistakes are caused by inadequate testing and debugging. Billions of dollars have been lost by government agencies and private companies because they did not spend the time or effort to test and debug their computer programs. In general, **testing** is the process of making sure the program performs as it was intended, and **debugging** is the process of locating errors and eliminating them.

The first step in testing is to carefully check the coding forms and the program itself for possible errors. This is called **desk checking,** and it is done before the program is tested on the computer system. The programmer checks each instruction to make sure that all of the rules of the programming language have been followed and that there are no clerical errors or misspellings.

Once the program has been desk checked, the program is checked on the computer system with test data that is consistent with the problem definition. In the first phase, the program is tested with **normal data.** This is data that is expected to be used by the program. In the next phase, the program is tested with data that is **slightly abnormal.** This data might be encountered occasionally in running the program. The third phase is to run the program with data that is completely outside the range of what is expected. This is done to see how the program reacts in **abnormal** and **unusual circumstances.** Good programs should be able to handle **abnormal data** without blowing up or generating meaningless output. If the program interacts with other programs, *system testing* is also required.

System testing is testing several programs together. If the output from one program is used as the input to another program, system testing is essential. In system testing, all of the programs that interact with each other are tested together. As with program testing, normal and abnormal data are used to locate and correct program errors.

During the testing procedure, errors that are encountered are corrected. In general, there are only two types of errors that can occur in a computer program. One type of error is a **grammatical error.** This type of error results when you don't follow the rules or syntax of the programming language. When this happens, the computer prints a list of *error messages*. The second type of error is a **logical error.** The computer actually does not know that you have made an error. It follows the program instructions and outputs the results. But the output is not correct. When a logical error occurs, all you know is that the computer is not printing the correct output. The computer does not tell you what is wrong.

There are several ways to locate and correct logical errors. One approach is to analyze the wrong output and try to determine what the problem is. Another approach is to put several print or write statements in the program that indicate the values of intermediate computations. These statements can also be used to tell you what is happening during the execution of the program. Once the errors have been found and corrected, these print and write statements are removed from the program. Other approaches include the use of a *storage dump* or a *tracing routine*. **A storage dump** is a printout of the contents stored in main storage or memory during the execution of the program, normally in hexadecimal notation. **A tracing routine** is a computer routine that is available with some computer systems that traces the operation and execution of the program.

6. Documentation

The next step is to document the program. For most applications, two different types of documentation are required, *technical documentation* and *user documentation*.

The need for program documentation is similar to the need for documentation in other areas. For example, two types of documentation or manuals are produced by most automobile manufacturers for each type of car. One manual is used by the service centers at the local dealerships. The manual is a technical description of the automobile. It includes the procedures required to repair the car. The other type of manual or documentation is the owners manual. This manual tells the car owner how to operate the vehicle. For the same reasons, most programs require both *technical documentation* and *user documentation*. The **technical documentation** is used by computer operators to execute the program and analysts and programmers in case there are problems with the program or if the program is to be modified. The **user documentation** is used by the individuals who will be using the program. This type of documentation shows the users in easy-to-understand terms how the program can and should be used.

After the first five steps, most of the technical documentation has been completed. This documentation should include the statement of the problem, the determination of the solution requirements, and all flowcharts, coding forms and all the other material developed during problem definition, analysis and design. In addition, technical documentation can include a list of potential problems and a description of how they can be solved.

13 Program and application development

User documentation is intended to tell the user how to use the program. This documentation must be clear and easy for the non-computer professional to understand. Technical terminology should not be used. Although there is no standard way to develop user documentation, at least the following material should be included:

1. A discussion of the problem that the program will solve.
2. A non-technical discussion of how the problem is solved by the computer.
3. A description of the output from the program.
4. A discussion of the data that is required to run the program.
5. A detailed explanation of how the data is to be prepared and entered into the computer.
6. A list of potential problems that may be encountered by the user.
7. A detailed explanation of how these problems can be solved when they occur.

7. Implementation

The last step in developing a new computer program is implementation. Implementation is the process of taking the program and placing it into operation.

One of the best ways to implement a new program is called **running in parallel**. Under this system, the new program is run together with the existing system. If there are any problems with the new programs, they can be corrected while the existing system is still being used. Thus, there is no interruption of service if there are problems with the new computer programs. Then after the bugs are out of the new programs, the new programs are slowly phased in while the old system is slowly phased out. If there are several new programs to be implemented, this **phase in** and **phase out** method is used for each program one at a time. When a company is converting most of its applications from a manual system to a computerized system, the payroll programs are usually the first ones to be implemented. This is usually followed by other accounting related application. Finally, all other programs are implemented one at a time.

When the computer is to be used for the first time, it is also necessary to *convert* all of the data files from manual files to computer files. This is called **data conversion** or **conversion.** To avoid an unnecessary delay, it may be necessary to hire some temporary employees to actually make this conversion.

8. Maintenance

It is hard to believe that after a computer program is written it will usually require maintenance. Yet several studies have shown that on the average, over half of the hours spent by application programmers and systems analysis personnel is on program maintenance. Furthermore, most programs have a finite or a limited useful life. Some programs are discarded before five years of use, while other programs may be useful for over ten years. The useful life of a program depends on the initial design and construction of the program and the extent to which the hardware changes over time. During the useful life of a program, program maintenance can make up over half of the cost of the total cost of the program.

The major cause of program maintenance is due to user requests, normally *changing* program enhancements. As a manager uses a computer program, there is a tendency to demand additional reports and outputs from the program. Changes in data storage and organization and program bugs and emergency program repairs are other important causes for maintenance. The remaining program maintenance is spent on hardware changes, system software changes, enhancing program documentation, and scheduled and routine debugging.

When programs are modified or changed, it is important to make sure that program documentation be changed. Not changing documentation to be consistent with the programs invites problems and mistakes in the future. You would not want to use a repair manual for a Model T Ford when you are trying to fix a Maverick. Yet, many companies don't maintain their program documentation when they change their programs. When they try to correct problems with outdated documentation, they can actually make the problems worse.

PURCHASING APPLICATION SOFTWARE

At one time, application software was provided free with the computer hardware. After IBM stopped this practice, however, many other computer manufacturers did the same. Now, most computer systems do not come with application software. This is called **unbundling,** which means that the application software is priced separately. Today, the computer user has the option of developing application software or buying it. In this section, we will consider the option of buying application software.

As discussed in Part I, there are many ways to buy application software. It can be purchased from the *computer manufacturer, software houses* that specialize in developing and selling software, or from a *software broker*. A software broker acts like a stock broker. The broker doesn't own the software but sells the software for a commission or a fee. Over the last several years, the software industry has grown rapidly. In 1975, sales of software products was approximately $500,000 and it is expected that by 1985, software sales could be in excess of $3.5 billion annually. Since the financial investment required to start a software company is far less than what is required to start a computer manufacturing company, the number of software companies has grown to over 1,000 companies, and the number of different software products is over 5,000. In addition, there are professional organizations that are only concerned with the software industry. The **Software Industry Association** (SIA), which is part of the **Association of Data Processing Service Organizations** (ADPSO) is an example.

Buying application software can offer a number of advantages over developing application software. One of the biggest differences is price. Purchased software can be obtained for less than one third of the price of developed software in some cases. Even when the purchased software has to be modified, the savings could still be substantial. For most applications, 75 to 90 percent of the code remains the same regardless of the company or organization using it. Certain computations and processing must be done for payroll, inventory control or any other application. Thus, it can be cheaper to buy the basic code or program from a software company and to modify it to the specific needs of the company or organization. Lead time can be substantially reduced. While it could take two to three months to install purchased software, it could take a year or more to develop and install software that is produced. Another potential advantage of buying application software is better program design and structure. Many companies cannot afford to hire a staff of programmers and systems analysts that have experience, a knowledge of good program design, and the ability to work with managers and users in developing application software. Better design can mean less trouble with program testing, debugging, and maintenance. Each year, good design could save a company thousands of dollars in maintenance and debugging.

A number of companies offer software service for the customers that purchase application or system software. NCR, for example, has established central software facilities that allow customers to contact specialists when software related problems occur. These centers are located in Los Angeles, Dallas, Dayton, New York, and Atlanta. Initial tests have revealed that approximately 95 percent of all problems have been solved with a single phone call.

While buying application software can save an organization money and time, and provide a better designed package of programs, these potentials are not guaranteed. Another danger is not getting what is really needed or desired from the purchased application package. Selecting the best software product and software company is important.

When application software is purchased instead of developed, a logical and systematic procedure should be followed. It is possible to buy an expensive software package that is totally worthless unless necessary time and effort are spent to make a good choice. The first step is to determine exactly what you want the package to do. Next, you should analyze the available software packages. There are several professional organizations that list and evaluate software packages.

In analyzing the existing packages, a company should talk to other users of the packages, and insist upon a demonstration of the package on their computer system. The company should also evaluate the package in terms of how it meets its needs. The *reliability* and *reputation* of the software company should also be considered. The amount of *support* and *service* from the software company after the package has been installed is important as well.

The next step is to negotiate the contract. Although software companies are likely to have a standard contract, it may be necessary to modify the contract or to develop one that more closely satisfies company needs. Once the final decision has been made and the contract has been signed, the company should follow through by *monitoring* the installation and checking the performance of software in action after it has been installed.

SUMMARY

This chapter has investigated the development of computer programs and applications. Computer programs and applications are the key to unlocking the potential of any computer system. Without good application software, the computer equipment is of little value. It would be like owning a very expensive stereo system with no records, tapes or radio stations to listen to. Application software is what makes the computer work for us. A knowledge of how to develop or obtain application software is a knowledge of how to use the computer system to your benefit.

In this chapter, only some of the more important aspects of developing computer programs and applications have been outlined for you. There are many other techniques that are useful in developing good application software. Some of the more commonly used techniques are discussed in Chapters 14 and 15.

KEY TERMS AND CONCEPTS

Analysis	Interviews	Software house
Conversion	Language	Storage dump
Debugging	Logical error	Structured programming
Desk checking	Maintenance	Subroutines
Design	Operational documentation	Surveys and questionnaires
Documentation	Operational feasibility	System testing
Economic feasibility	Phase in-phase out	Technical documentation
Feasibility study	Problem definition	Technical feasibility
Feasibility study team	Program coding	Testing
Grammatical error	Program library	Tracing routine
Implementation	Running in parallel	Unbundle

QUESTIONS

13–1. Briefly discuss what is required in defining the problem and in determining solution requirements.

13–2. Why is problem analysis important and how can it be accomplished?

13–3. Briefly discuss program coding.

13–4. What is desk checking?

13–5. What types of errors can occur in a computer program?

13–6. Discuss the different types of documentation.

13–7. What is involved in implementation and maintenance?

13–8. Discuss the differences between buying and developing application software.

MINIQUIZ

True or False

ANSWERS

1. F
2. T
3. F
4. T
5. T
6. T
7. F
8. F
9. T
10. T

_____ 1. The second step in application development is problem definition.
_____ 2. During problem definition, the exact form or layout of all reports and outputs must be determined.
_____ 3. After the input requirements have been specified, the next step is to develop the output requirements during the problem definition stage.
_____ 4. The emphasis of analysis is an investigation into the existing system, while the emphasis of design is to develop new procedures and systems.
_____ 5. After analysis and design, the next step is language selection.
_____ 6. Checking the coding forms and the program itself by hand is called desk checking.
_____ 7. System testing is testing one program at a time to make sure that the input data is compatible with the desired outputs.
_____ 8. A logical error results in an error message.
_____ 9. Programs require both technical and user documentation.
_____ 10. The major cause of program maintenance is due to user requests, normally program enhancements.

Business computer improves wholesaler's operation

Park City Food Products, Inc., Stratford, Conn., a wholesale supplier of food, paper, and cleaning products to hospitals, schools, restaurants, and other institutions, is an example of a small operation that has successfully maintained its efficiency with the aid of computer technology. Park Food recently installed a minicomputer-based business data processing system to relieve its growing paperwork problems. Park Foods' customer base consists of more than 1,000 institutions which account for an annual volume in excess of $4 million.

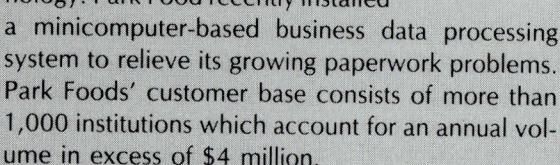

According to Edward Greene, president, the business is one of small but frequent changes in prices, quantity packed per carton, new products replacing old, and so on. A hundred changes sometimes occur in a week. Any given change is routine unless it is not made or it is made incorrectly.

Edward Greene and his brother Joseph, vice president, tried many methods to speed data handling. Beginning with hand-posting, progress of the business forced a search for a supplementary means of handling inventory figures. Park Foods implemented an accounting machine and quickly outgrew its capacity. A card system was brought in next, but cards eventually proved too cumbersome. By using the card system combined with the services of a data processing center, things proceeded smoothly until business volume required all the service bureau time to handle inventory alone. The next logical step was to implement their own computer system.

Since Messrs. Greene had become well versed in computers and the problems of business data handling by this time, their appraisal of several available computer systems was a well informed process. According to Robert J. Steinus, vice president, Compudata Systems Inc., Westport, Conn., ultimate supplier of the system: "Park Foods had a good idea of what it wanted and, because of its involvement in changing from system to system over the years, was able to help us a great deal with the design of its system." While Compudata Systems, Inc. was the company's service bureau prior to selection of the system, the Greenes stressed that this was not a consideration.

The system itself is based on a Digital Equipment Corp. DATASYSTEM 340 with ongoing maintenance under a service contract. Application programming was done largely by John Fiedler of Compudata. The system was ordered last September and almost completely operational in less than 90 days. The firm knew exactly what it wanted. Instant access to the entire data base to make changes and receive information was a primary need. Since changes funneled through the president, he needed a terminal in his office. Another terminal, preferably one that required minimum operator retraining, was to be used for input. A printer was needed for invoices, purchase orders and reports. The entire system, organized on a file basis, called for numerous long list file matching to update inventory, create price lists, etc.

The system installed is built around a PDP-8/E processor with 32K of core, two DECpack disk drives, two VT05 input and inquiry terminals, and a 165-character-per-line printer. Expansion can continue up to 64K of core, up to six CRT terminals and six disk drives, or equipment can be added for cards, paper tape, magnetic tape, or data link communications between computers. All input now is through two CRT terminals providing immediate visual confirmation.

The heart of the system, according to Edward Greene, is the programming. Within the environment of Digital Equipment's COS-300 COMMERCIAL OPERATING SYSTEM, application programming by Compudata brings it together in a usable system tailored to Park Foods' needs, both immediate and future. DIBOL (Digital's Business Oriented Language) is a kind of uncomplicated hy-

Source: *Office Magazine*, vol. 79, June 19, 1974. Reprinted with permission from The Office and Digital Equipment Corp.

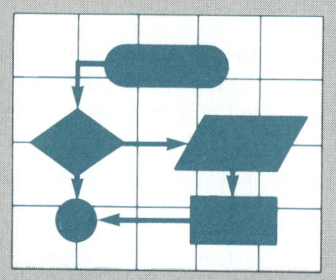

brid of COBOL and FORTRAN IV; it takes relatively little time to learn and is quite powerful. Mr. Greene spent two weeks in the training school at Digital Equipment's offices in Maynard, Mass., and now does all special report programming himself in minutes. Since the computer allows foreground-background processing, an operator can print invoices on the line printer at the same time Edward Greene is entering a price change from his desk. When Joseph Greene writes a new program, that, too, is entered through the CRT.

The disk-resident data base comprises a complete file of customers including names, addresses and other pertinent information; a continually updated inventory file; a vendor file with names, addresses and telephone numbers; a file of all purchases by vendor and product, including last-ordered quantities and prices; a file of open purchases (goods not yet received); a file of orders broken down by salesmen; and records of all transactions.

From these inputs and records maintained with the system come essentially all documents needed to run the business. Orders give rise to invoices, warehouse picking lists, shipping documents and customer order-price lists. Shipping documents include number of cases, cubic footage and weights of all orders assigned to one truck to be sure its capacity will not be exceeded. There are monthly statements, cash received reports, aging account lists, sales reports by customer and by salesman, salesmen's price books and a daily invoice register. Also purchase orders, receiving reports and inventory status report (including goods in transit), a buy guide (inventory level history by product) and a quarterly report of product usage by each customer.

A salesman typically makes a survey of each new customer's needs based on his menu. From this, an order form is created just for that customer. The multipart form, printed by the computer, contains the product's name, brand, size, company's identification number, price per carton, price per unit, price per portion, number of servings per carton and per unit. This helps the customer food manager's planning. Other pages of the form contain product names, brands, sizes and identification numbers but, instead of price information, vertical columns that the customer fills in to do his weekly ordering. For customers who do not order weekly, a printed form listing the 400 most commonly used products offers similar convenience. Edward Greene said, "Order entry on the CRT is fantastic. Fast response, visual indication and an erasure function combine to reduce the order entry process from four hours to 35 minutes."

All orders received are gathered at the end of each day, sorted in delivery route sequence, copies of each separated for routing purposes and sent to the computer room. An operator at the CRT terminal keys in the customer number of the first order.

A credit check confirms acceptable status or, if a balance is overdue or the customer is on credit hold, prints out on the CRT the recent accounts receivable history for a decision. If credit is approved, the order is entered. Order entry includes validity checks of product numbers and automatic substitution where appropriate. If an order item will drop a product's inventory level below a predetermined figure, the customer's record is examined to see if a substitute product has been authorized. If so, substitution is made and automatically noted for invoicing. Taxes on each order are computed for the state where the institution is located. Then a picking list and shipping document are generated and, once shipping has confirmed the actual items pulled from inventory, a mirror image of the invoice is created in storage. At the same time, the inventory file is updated.

When a food broker visits the firm, all vendors represented by that broker are listed sequentially in a computer file. Edward Greene can instantly bring to his screen a list of all items bought from that vendor, the quantity of each in inventory, the last cost for each and the average weekly movement. If there is to be a price change Mr. Greene enters the change and the effective date. On that date, all prices for that product in the system will change automatically. When an order is entered for an item, he merely types in the quantity and, if there was a change since the last order, the price.

A purchase order will be created when the purchase order file is run.

Many suppliers extend small discounts to nonprofit organizations, particularly schools, when presented with valid documentary evidence of quantities sold to eligible institutions. The tedious and time-consuming rebate bookkeeping made it impossible to recover these discounts for any but a few products going to the largest customers. Now, a simple program runs once a month gathering and printing the specific information on every eligible product sold to any customer, regardless of how small the quantity. According to Edward Greene, these rebates alone nearly cover the cost of the system each month.

In addition to the functions outlined, Joseph Greene soon expects to put accounts payable on the computer and even financial statements. The system costs the company $1,500 a month, including programming and a service contract. Edward Greene said his previous service bureau time and internal card handling cost as much but provided fewer useful functions and were relatively inflexible. Decision making, especially in a fast moving business like wholesale food distribution, depends on getting current, accurate data on prices, orders, inventories, etc. Here the system has thoroughly established itself as an integral tool by providing a surer basis for decisions.

Any product that is not ordered by a customer during three quarters is dropped from his printed price-order sheet. The system provides daily, week-to-date, and month-to-date order figures by product category (fruit, vegetable, cleaning supplies) broken down by individual salesmen. This enables Mr. Greene to monitor and work selectively with each salesman whose abilities may differ in selling different products. The whole business still begins in the salesman's price book. "Now," he says, "a salesman can come in and ask for a new price book. He has it in ten minutes."

DISCUSSION QUESTIONS

1. What are the characteristics of the DIBOL programming language?
2. What are some of the applications that are being performed by the computer system at Park City Food Products, Inc.?

Tools for program and application development

14

PRINT CHARTS AND LAYOUT CHARTS
FLOWCHARTS
    System flowcharts
    Program flowcharts
DECISION TABLES
GRID CHARTS

After completing Chapter 14, you will be able to:

- Discuss the use of print charts and layout charts in defining input and output requirements.
- Describe the difference between system and program flowcharts.
- Contrast decision tables and flowcharts.
- Discuss the use of grid charts.

A number of tools and techniques are available to computer programmers and systems analysts to assist them in developing computer programs and applications. In this chapter, some of the more traditional tools and techniques will be covered. They include print charts and layout charts, flowcharts, decision tables, and grid charts. In the next chapter, a newer approach to application design and development will be explored—structured design and programming.

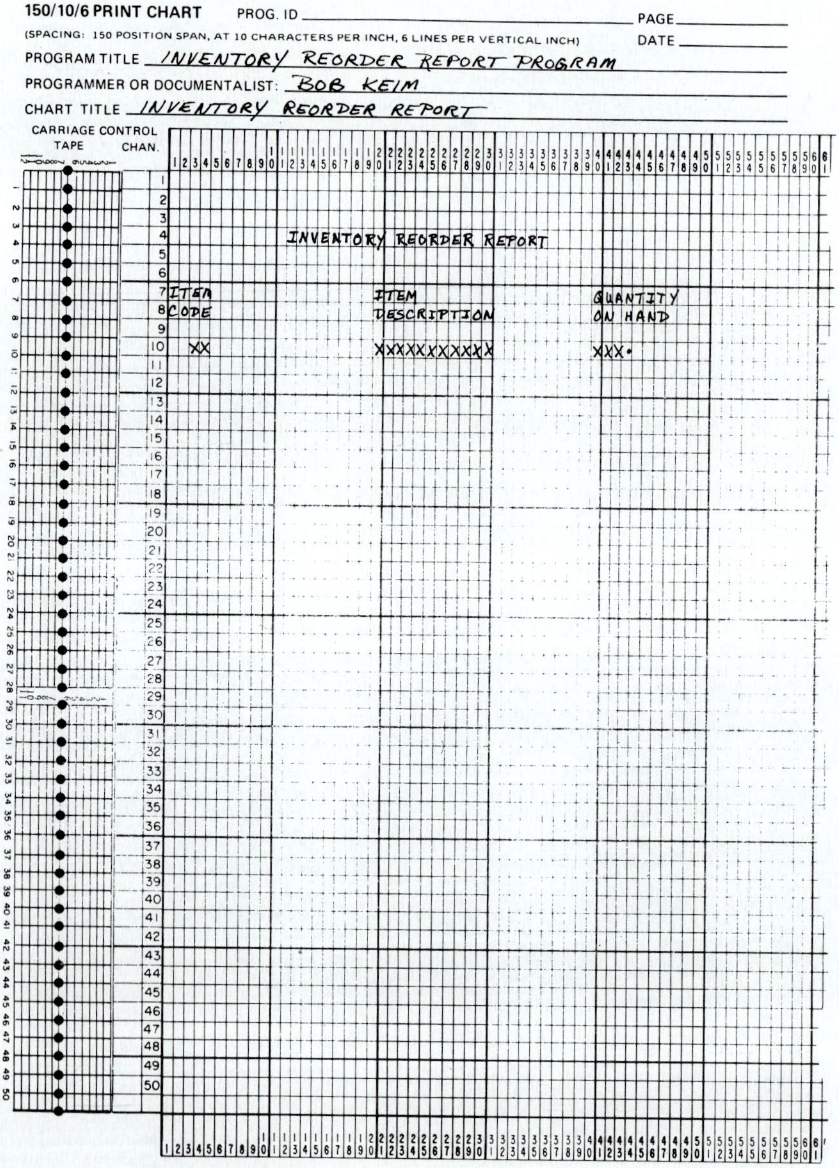

FIGURE 14–1A
A print chart

Form courtesy of IBM

14 Tools for program and application development 289

PRINT CHARTS AND LAYOUT CHARTS

A number of forms have been developed to make it easier to specify in detail the input and output from a computer application. A **print chart** is used to describe the format of an output report from a printer, and a **card layout chart** is used to describe how input data is placed on one or more computer cards. The charts shown in Figures 14–1A and B are examples of the charts that may be used. Different companies and data processing departments might use slightly different forms. In addition, there are other charts and forms that describe the exact layout or positioning of data on magnetic tape, the disk, and the display terminal or CRT.

FLOWCHARTS

Like a road map, **flowcharts** are used to reveal how to go from a starting point to the final destination, and they can be used to display any amount of detail. If you are moving from San Francisco to New Orleans, you will need a general road map of the United States to get you to the City of New Orleans, and then you will need a road map of the City of New Orleans to help you get to the desired street in New Orleans. Likewise, in developing application software, you will need a general flowchart to reveal the overall purpose and structure of the application. This general type of flowchart is usually called the **system flowchart** or **application flowchart.** Then you will need one or more detailed flowcharts that reveal how each program is to be developed. This type of flowchart is called a **program flowchart.**

Both system and program flowcharts are drawn using a special **flowcharting template.** This template contains a set of symbols you will need in developing flowcharts. Figure 14–2 is an example of such a flowcharting template.

System flowcharts

Some of the symbols are used for both system and program flowcharts while other symbols are fairly specialized. Some of the more commonly used system flowcharting symbols are presented in Figure 14–3.

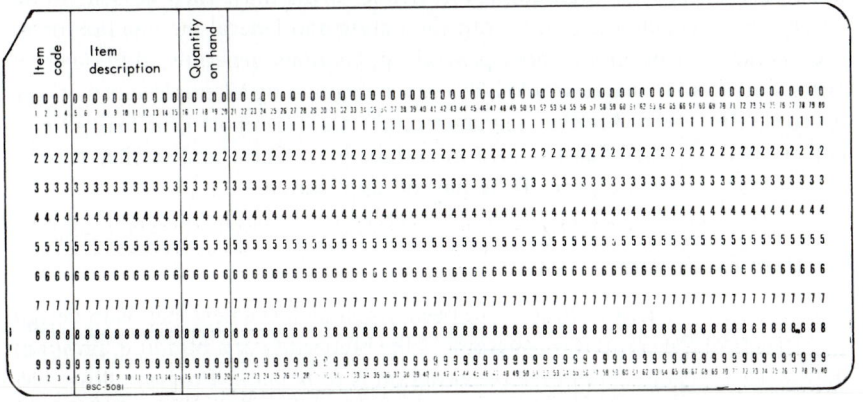

FIGURE 14–1B
Card layout chart

Form courtesy of IBM

FIGURE 14–2
A flowcharting template

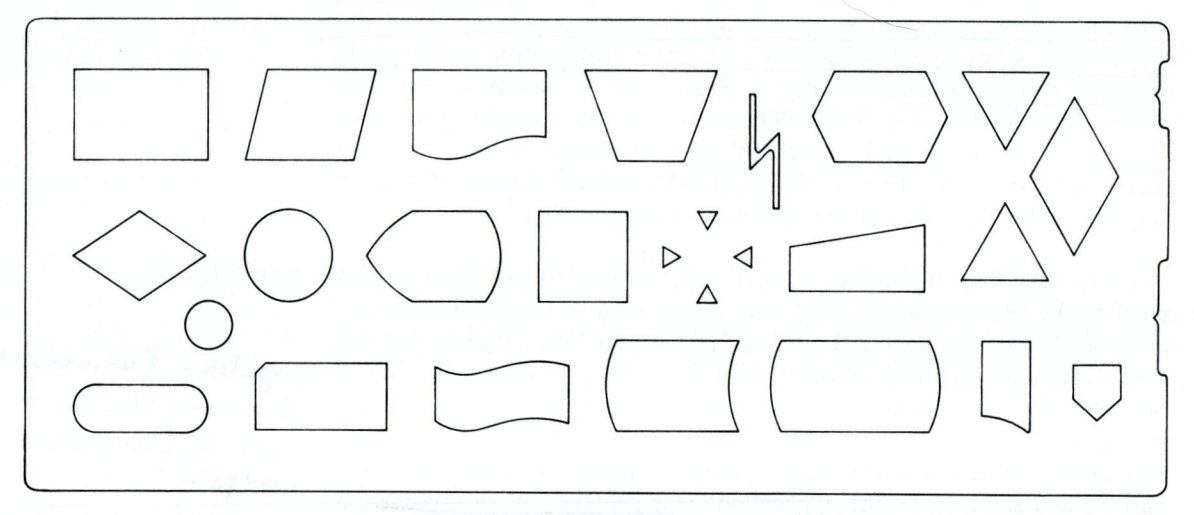

symbols that describe operations

These system flowchart symbols are used to reveal in a general fashion the relationship between the input data, the programs, and the desired output. For example, most realistic payroll applications require multiple computer programs interacting with multiple data files. A simplified system flowchart for a payroll application is displayed in Figure 14–4.

The payroll application shown in Figure 14–4 includes an update routine (symbols 1 through 6), an edit routine (symbols 7 through 11), a summary routine (symbols 15 through 17), the posted master file (symbol 14), and the checks (symbol 13). Most payroll applications are more complex and involved. For example, federal and state income tax withholding statements must be prepared for each employee. These forms must then be sent to all employees to enable them to fill out their state and federal income tax forms every year. Furthermore, most payroll applications generate additional reports. Perhaps a manager would like a report containing all employees working overtime this week. Another manager might want a report that lists all employees who are qualified to perform certain jobs. These and similar reports and outputs become a part of the payroll application.

Program flowcharts

Once the system flowcharts have been developed, the next step is to design and structure the computer programs. Like blueprints of a building, program flowcharts reveal in detail how the program is to be built. Program flowchart symbols are used to show what activities are to be performed, and the same flowcharting template, shown in Figure 14–2 is used. Some commonly used symbols for program flowcharting are shown in Figure 14–5.

A flowchart for a payroll program shown in Figure 14–4 (refer to symbol

14 Tools for program and application development

Process	Input/output	Comment, annotation	
Connector	Offpage connector	Punched card	Card file
Card deck	Document	Magnetic tape	Punched tape
Online storage	Keying	Core	Merge	Offline storage
Collate	Sort	Magnetic disk	Extract	Display
			Manual input	
Auxiliary operation	Manual operation	Magnetic drum	Tape transmittal	Communication link

FIGURE 14–3
Symbols for system flowcharts

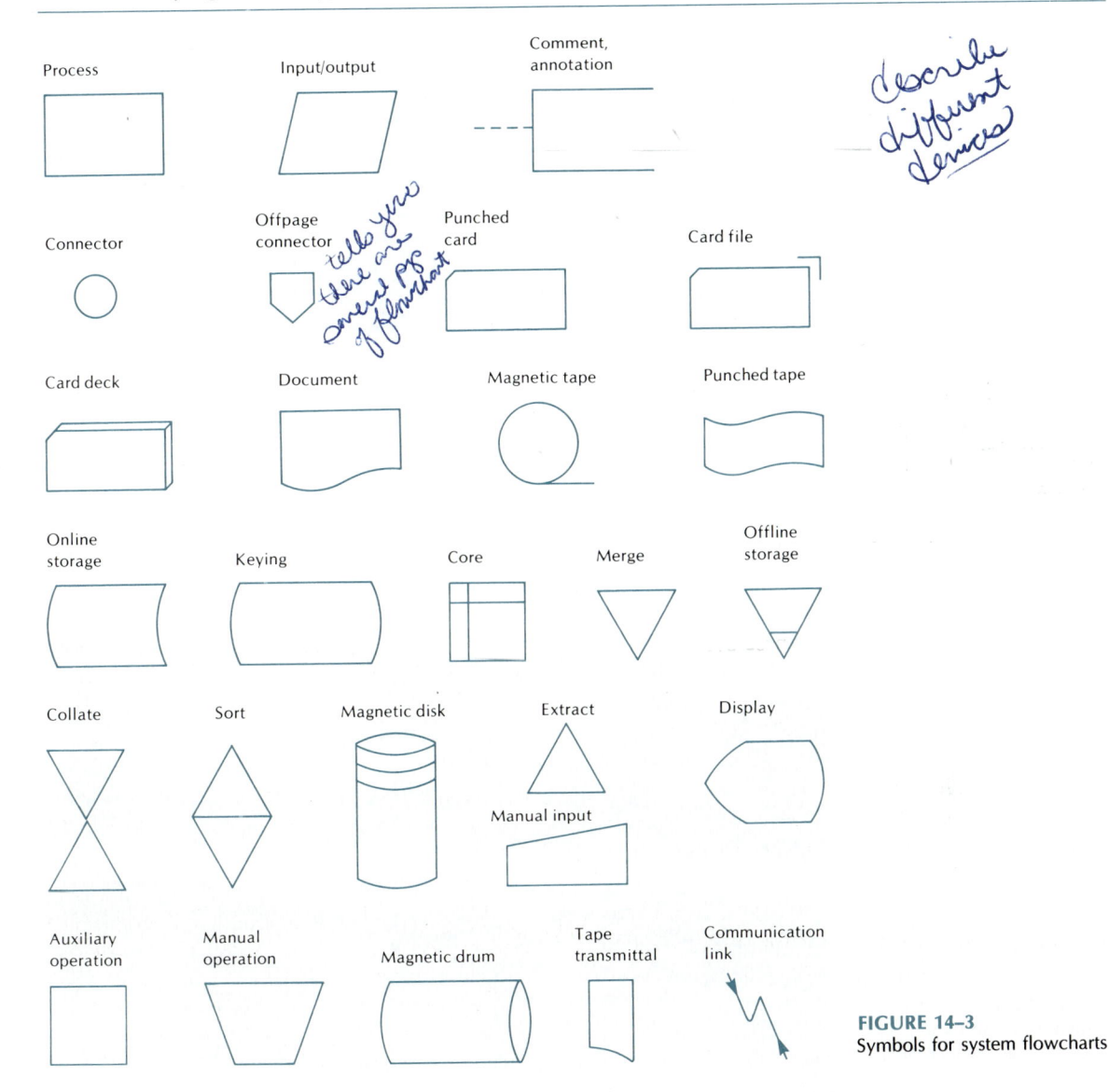

12 in Figure 14–4) can be developed. This program should read from the updated master file and the edited transaction file. It should write checks, update the master files, and prepare a summary report. The flowchart for this program is in Figure 14–6.

As you can see, a flowcharting worksheet has been used. Notice that one symbol is placed in one box and that each box has been labeled starting with A1 in the upper left-hand corner and ending with K5 in the lower right-hand corner. There are ten rows (they are labeled A through K), and there are five columns (they are labeled 1 through 5).

In both program and system flowcharts, there can be various levels of

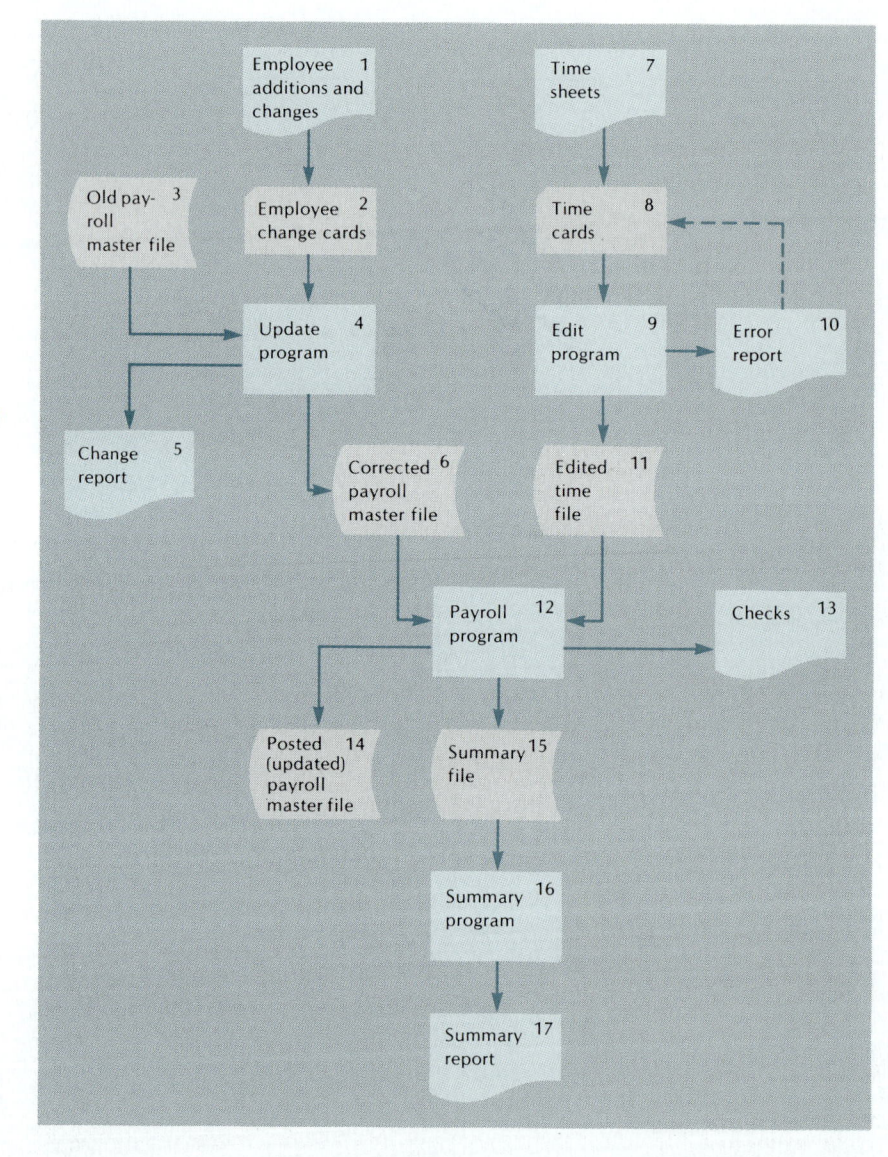

FIGURE 14–4
System flowchart for a simplified payroll application

Flowchart elements:
1. Employee additions and changes
2. Employee change cards
3. Old payroll master file
4. Update program
5. Change report
6. Corrected payroll master file
7. Time sheets
8. Time cards
9. Edit program
10. Error report
11. Edited time file
12. Payroll program
13. Checks
14. Posted (updated) payroll master file
15. Summary file
16. Summary program
17. Summary report

detail. A flowchart that shows less detail is called a *macro flowchart*, while a flowchart with more detail is called a *micro* or *detailed flowchart*. In the flowchart for the payroll program displayed in Figure 14–6, there is a "Calculate Gross Pay With Overtime" box. See symbol D3 in Figure 14–6. In order to display how overtime is computed, a detailed program flowchart can be used. This is shown in Figure 14–7.

While programmers and systems analysts have a good deal of freedom in creating system and program flowcharts, there are a number of general rules and guidelines used to help standardize the flowcharting process. These

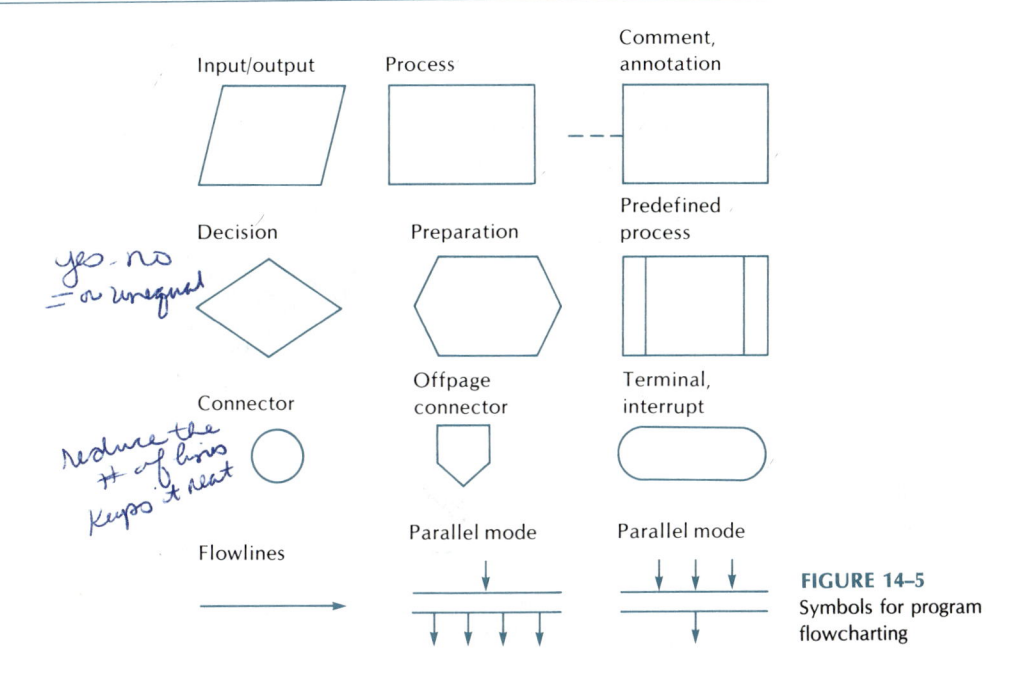

14 Tools for program and application development

FIGURE 14–5
Symbols for program flowcharting

standards are recommended by the **American National Standards Institute** (ANSI), and the various computer manufacturers and data processing departments usually have their own set of similar flowcharting standards. Some of these rules and guidelines are as follows: go from left to right and top to bottom in constructing flowcharts; when a reference for a symbol is needed, it should be placed above the symbol; if a new flowcharting page is needed, it is recommended that the flowchart be broken at an input or output file; use an annotation symbol when a more detailed explanation is needed, and so forth. Books and manuals have been developed by various companies and organizations on flowcharting, and while these specific rules are beyond the scope of this book, good flowcharting procedures require that these rules and guidelines be followed.

DECISION TABLES

A decision table can be used as an alternative to flowcharts or as an addition to flowcharts. The objective of both decision tables and flowcharts is the same. They reveal how the input data is to be manipulated to obtain the desired output. As the name implies, **decision tables** reveal what decisions or actions the computer is to take as a result of the input data. When the computer has to make a large number of decisions or if there are a large number of different branches within a program, decision tables are particularly useful. In these cases, decision tables are preferred to flowcharts.

In general, a decision table displays the different *conditions* that could exist and the different *actions* that the computer should take as a result of these conditions. Most decision tables have six parts. First, these six parts

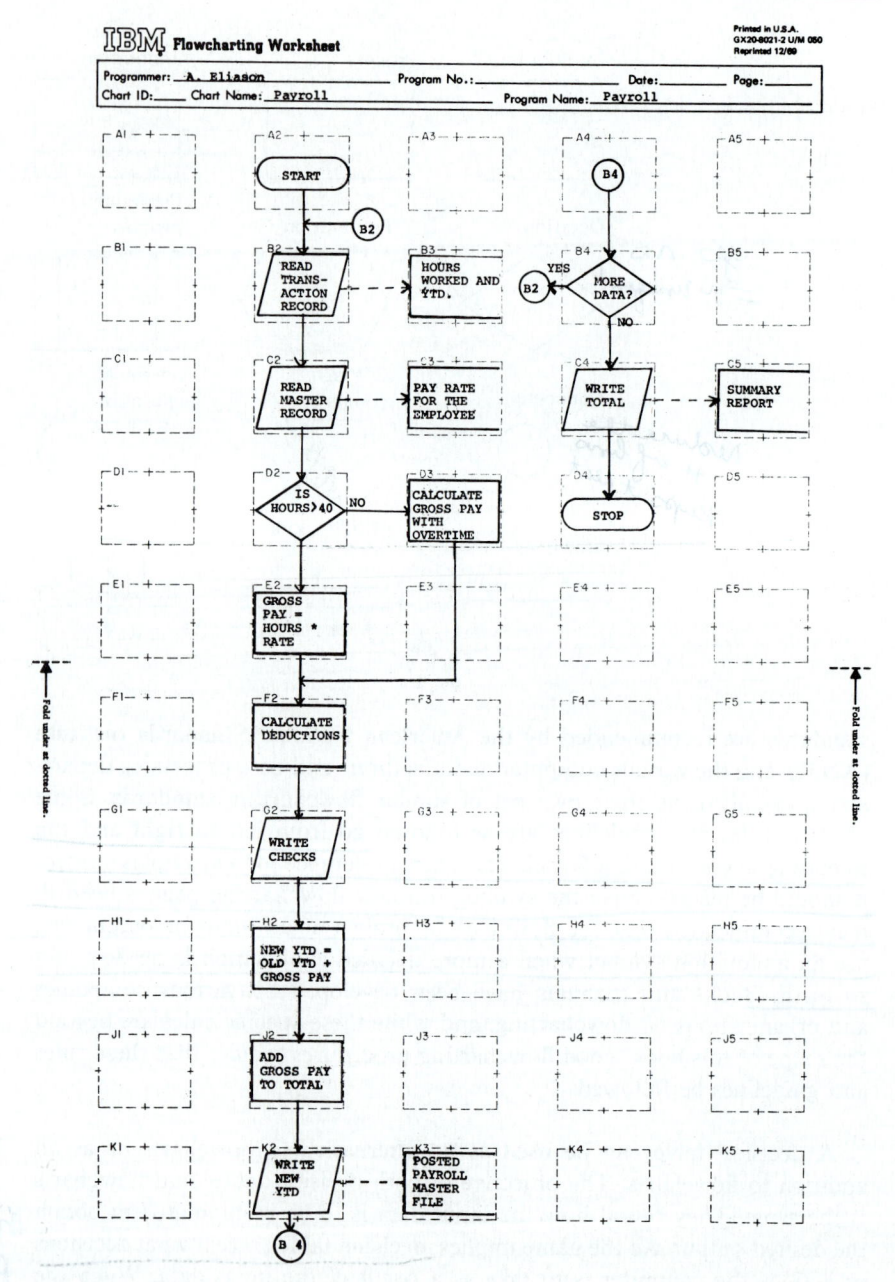

FIGURE 14-6
A flowchart for the payroll program

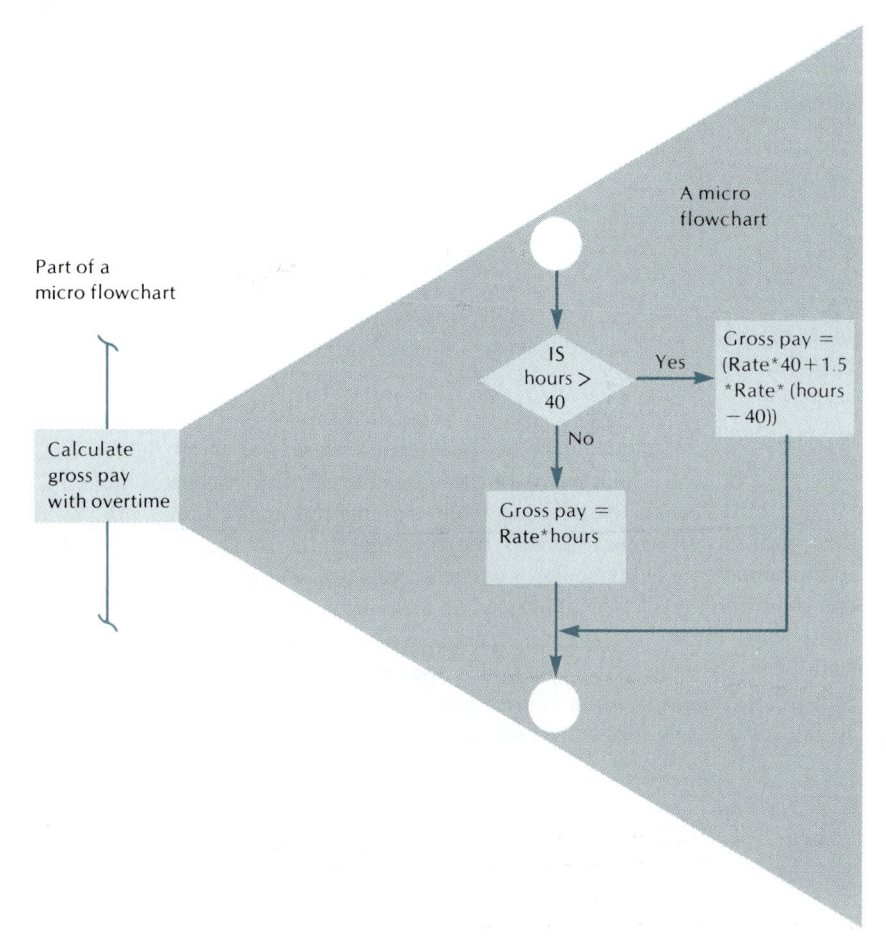

14 Tools for program and application development

FIGURE 14–7
Detailed flowchart of gross pay with overtime

will be discussed in general. Then two examples will be given to show you how decision tables can be used as an aid to the analysis and design of computer programs. The six parts of a typical decision table are given in Figure 14–8.

The first area of the decision table contains the *name and/or number of the table*. For some of the larger applications, two or more decision tables are used in the analysis part of program development. If a computer program were to be developed that made airline reservations, the decision table might be called the Airline Reservation Application. This would appear at the upper left of the decision table.

The second area of the table contains the *condition statements*. These statements describe the conditions that could exist with the input data. If the computer program is to make tourist and first class reservations, there may be four possible states or conditions. These would be: (1) a first class reservation is requested, (2) a tourist class reservation is requested, (3) a

1 (Name of decision table)	4 (Rule numbers)
2 (Condition statements)	5 (Actual conditions)
3 (Action statements)	6 (Actions taken)

FIGURE 14–8
Parts of a decision table

first class seat is available, and (4) a tourist class seat is available. These four conditions are then listed in the second area of the decision table.

The third area of the decision table contains the *action statements.* While the condition statements reveal the possible states of the input data, the action statements describe the possible actions of the computer system. Given the conditions discussed above, what types of actions might the computer take? Most airline reservation systems will either issue a first class ticket, wait-list a passenger for a first class ticket, issue a tourist class ticket, or wait-list a passenger for a tourist class ticket. The first three areas for the airline reservation application are shown in Figure 14–9.

Name of decision table: 1	*Airline reservation application*					Rule numbers: 4
	Condition statements					
	First class requested					
Condition statements: 2	First class available					Actual conditions: 5
	Tourist class requested					
	Tourist class available					
	Actions Taken					
	First class ticket issued					
Action statement: 3	Tourist class ticket issued					Action taken: 6
	First class wait listed					
	Tourist class wait listed					

providing rules for the programmer.

has as many applications in a non data processing environment as in a data processing area.

FIGURE 14–9
Name of the decision table, condition statements, and action statements

14 Tools for program and application development 297

Look at the left-hand side of the decision table in Figure 14–9. The name of the application is in the upper left hand corner. Next appears the four conditional statements. The action statements appear in the lower left-hand side of the decision table.

The right-hand side of the decision table contains the *rule numbers,* the *actual conditions,* and the *actions* taken by the computer. After this side of the decision table has been completed, each column indicates what the computer should do as a result of certain conditions. As seen in Figure 14–9, four columns have been included. These four columns correspond to four rule numbers. Under each rule number will be a given condition in *area 5* of the decision table followed by a specific action to be taken by the computer in *area 6* of the decision table. The four rule numbers, the four actual conditions, and the associated actions taken by the computer system are discussed below.

Rule 1. A first class ticket is requested, and a first class seat is available. The action by the computer should be to issue a first class ticket.
Rule 2. A first class ticket is requested, but a first class seat is not available. The computer should wait list the passenger.
Rule 3. A tourist class ticket is requested, and a tourist class seat is available. The action by the computer should be to issue a tourist class ticket.
Rule 4. A tourist class ticket is requested, but a tourist class seat is not available. The computer should wait list the passenger.

After each rule number, a given condition is stated and the actions that should be taken by the computer are described. The decision table contains exactly the same information but in a tabular form. Each column contains one rule number. Under each rule number is one condition which is followed by a specific action. A complete decision table for the airline reservation application is given in Figure 14–10.

Any column of the decision table reveals what the computer should do as a result of a given condition. Look at the column under Rule 3. A tourist class ticket is requested (Y) and a tourist class seat is available (Y). Thus, the computer should issue a tourist class ticket (X). Y means "yes" and N means "no" under the actual conditions area of the decision table. An X in the actions taken area of the decision table indicates that the computer should take this particular action. To find out what the computer should be doing for any given condition, simply read down the appropriate column and see what actions have been marked with an X.

In another example, a company is concerned with collecting overdue bills or debts that are either a large number of days overdue or for large amounts. Depending upon these two factors, number of days overdue and amount due, the company would like to take several actions. One of three letters is to be written. One letter is a gentle reminder to pay the bill, another letter is a standard credit letter, and the third letter is to be a harsh reminder that a large amount is due or the bill is long overdue. Under some circumstances, credit is to be limited to $1,000 until the past bills have been paid, and under severe conditions, all credit is to be stopped until all past bills

Name of decision table: 1	Airline reservation application	Rule number				Rule numbers: 4
		1	2	3	4	
	Condition statements					
Condition statements: 2	First class requested	Y	Y	N	N	
	First class available	Y	N	N	N	Actual conditions: 5
	Tourist class requested	N	N	Y	Y	
	Tourist class available	N	N	Y	N	
	Actions taken					
	First class ticket issued	X				
Action statement: 3	Tourist class ticket issued			X		Actions taken: 6
	First class wait listed		X			
	Tourist class wait listed				X	

FIGURE 14–10
Decision table for the airline reservation application

have been paid in full. The credit manager has decided what actions should be taken for certain conditions. These actions and conditions are shown in the decision table displayed in Figure 14–11. Try to determine exactly what actions are to be taken under the various conditions.

Read down the column for Rule 1. This corresponds to a situation where the bill is 30 days or less and the amount is $1,000 or less. See the Y (meaning Yes) by 30 days or less and $1,000 or less. What should the computer application do in this case? Read down the column and look for X marks. It can be seen that a mild letter should be sent to the customer. Then, the computer is directed to Go To Rule 1, If More Data. This tells the computer to check the next customer for one of the nine conditions or rules. What is the condition under Rule 6, and what actions should be taken? As seen in the decision table, Rule 6 is the condition where the bill is overdue by more than 60 days and the amount is $5,000 or less. The action is to send a harsh letter, send the customer's file to the collection agency, and stop all credit for purchases over $1,000. Then, another customer should be checked (Go To Rule 1, If More Data). You should notice that there is an X mark in every column for the *Go To Rule 1* action. This causes a loop that checks the outstanding bills for every customer. When there is no more data, the application is completed.

14 Tools for program and application development

Bill Collection Application	Rule number								
	1	2	3	4	5	6	7	8	9
Condition Statements									
(How old is the bill?)									
30 days or less	Y	N	N	Y	N	N	Y	N	N
31–60 days	N	Y	N	N	Y	N	N	Y	N
Over 60 days	N	N	Y	N	N	Y	N	N	Y
(What is the amount?)									
$1,000 or less	Y	Y	Y	N	N	N	N	N	N
$5,000 or less	N	N	N	Y	Y	Y	N	N	N
Over $5,000	N	N	N	N	N	N	Y	Y	Y
Actions Taken									
Send Mild Letter	X	X		X					
Send Standard Letter			X		X		X		
Send Harsh Letter						X		X	X
Collection Agency			X			X			X
Stop Credit Over $1,000						X			
Stop All Credit									X
Go To Rule 1, If More Data	X	X	X	X	X	X	X	X	X

FIGURE 14–11
Decision table for the bill collection application

In the above discussion, you have been introduced to the fundamentals of decision tables. These types of tables are called **Limited-Entry Decision Tables.** The only permissible entries are Y's, N's and X's. In an **Extended-Entry Decision Table,** other entries can be made in the right-hand side of the decision table. This may be done for convenience and to make the decision table easier to understand. For complex applications, several decision tables may be required. Thus, one of the actions in a table is to go to another decision table. Linking several decision tables together is similar to linking several programs together in a system flowchart.

GRID CHARTS

In business, the application programs are usually complex and interrelated. The same data may be used for several application programs, and the output from one program may be the input to another program. **A grid chart** is an excellent method to reveal the relationships between application programs. What data is used for several application programs? What data is used to produce different reports and documents? For which applications is the output from one application used as input data for another application? These and similar questions can be answered using grid charts. For example, the same inventory data may be used in several application programs. See the grid chart in Figure 14–12.

Inventory data \ Program	Invoice	Inventory reorder	Shipping	Sales analysis	Stock adjustment	Master file update
Item name	X	X	X	X	X	X
Item code number	X	X	X	X	X	X
Item price	X			X		X
Item amount		X		X	X	X
Reorder point		X				X
Warehouse location			X			X
Sales-to-date				X	X	X

FIGURE 14–12
The use of grid charts

The X's in the table reveal what data is used for each application program. Look at the first column. The invoice application uses the following inventory data: the item name, the item code number, and the item price. Likewise, the data that is used in any of the application programs listed in the grid chart can be found by reading down the appropriate column. In what applications is the Reorder Point data used? Going across the Reorder Point row, it can be seen that this data is used in the inventory reorder program and in the master file update program.

SUMMARY

This chapter has introduced you to a number of traditional tools and techniques for program and application development. Print charts and layout charts are used to reveal the exact layout and format of input data and output reports and documents. Both flowcharts and decision tables are used to display how the input data is to be manipulated to obtain the desired output. System flowcharts give the overall structure of the application, while program flowcharts reveal how each individual program is to be written or

14 Tools for program and application development

constructed. In addition, micro or detailed flowcharts can be used to reveal in detail how a computation or process is to be performed. This chapter also contrasted flowcharts and decision tables. In general, where there are a number of interrelated decisions or branches, a decision table is preferred over a flowchart. Of course, flowcharts and decision tables can be used together. Finally, this chapter concluded with the use of grid charts, which can relate one or more applications.

KEY TERMS AND CONCEPTS

Action statement
Actions taken
Actual conditions
Condition statement
Decision tables
Detailed flowchart
Extended-entry decision tables

Flowcharting template
Flowcharts
Grid charts
Layout charts
Limited entry decision tables

Macro flowchart
Micro flowchart
Print charts
Program flowcharts
Rule number
System flowcharts

(handwritten note: know these for test)

QUESTIONS

14–1. What is the purpose of a print chart? What is the purpose of a layout chart? Give examples of both.

14–2. Describe the difference between a system flowchart and a program flowchart. Why are both types of flowcharts useful when developing application software?

14–3. What is a macro flowchart? What is a micro or detailed flowchart?

14–4. What are the basic parts of any decision table?

14–5. Under what circumstances is a decision table preferred to a flowchart? When would a decision table not be appropriate to use?

14–6. What are some of the uses of a grid chart?

(handwritten notes:)
action chart — denotes action — a flowchart

static chart — organization chart — describes a situation.

MINIQUIZ

True or False

ANSWERS	1. A program flowchart is used to reveal in a general fashion the relationship between the input data, the programs, and the desired output.
1. F	2. Once the system flowcharts have been developed, the next step is to design and structure the computer programs using program flowcharts.
2. T	3. A flowchart that shows more detail is called a micro flowchart.
3. T	4. In general, a decision table displays the different conditions that could exist and the different actions that a computer should take as a result of these conditions.
4. T	5. Most decision tables have ten separate parts.
5. F	6. When a large number of decisions are to be made, a flowchart is the preferred method of documentation.
6. F	7. In a limited entry decision table, the only permissible entries are Y's, N's, and X's.
7. T	8. The action in one decision table may lead to another decision table.
8. T	9. A grid chart is a method that allows the relationships between application programs to be revealed.
9. T	10. Grid charts can be used in place of decision tables and flowcharts.
10. F	

A development tool for programmer productivity

"Industry's chief problem over the next decade will be programmer productivity, rather than equipment performance and costs."—AFIPS Special Report.

Not only is programmer productivity a problem, but the elapsed time and the effectiveness of the entire systems development process is an important issue in the industry.

According to Dan H. Holtz, manager of the data maintenance group at Deere & Company, a major part of the problem is the lack of the right tools and technology for the speedy implementation of application software.

Deere, the Moline, Illinois, manufacturer of tractors and other heavy equipment, is implementing data bases using the Information Management System (IMS). And it is easing the familiar programming bottleneck with an IBM program product called the Application Development Facility.

The facility helps programmers develop applications quickly and efficiently by relieving them of the need to code in detail many of the most frequently used IMS functions.

To prepare straightforward programs, the parameters are entered into the facility's tables. Then, its built-in logic retrieves, formats, screens, audits, and returns data base fields. It also can be used to implement more complex programs when its functions are augmented by conventionally coded routines.

Although he is now a confirmed proponent of the facility, Mr. Holtz says he approached the program with "guarded optimism" after it was introduced.

"The Application Development Facility did appear to offer some opportunity for addressing important problems which we were facing, but we were concerned about the performance and impact on the IMS system," he says. "We also were unsure how well our people could use the facility's method of 'rules specifications.'"

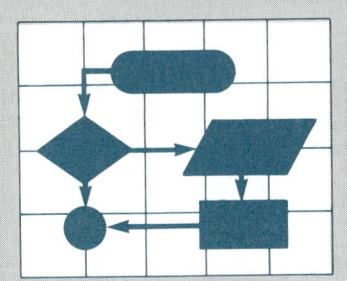

Deere installed the program on its test IMS system for a six-month trial. Three existing COBOL programs were selected as benchmarks. These applications were rewritten under the Application Development Facility while attempting to keep the screen displays and processing as close to the COBOL originals as possible. The call patterns did not end up 100 percent identical, but the facility's programs provided functionally equivalent displays to the user.

"We were extremely pleased with the results," Mr. Holtz says. "They showed that the Application Development Facility can provide significant productivity gains—in one case, ranging up to 40 times less manpower."

In addition, there was little loss of performance—user response times remained virtually the same.

The benchmarking group had expected that conversational programs developed under the facility would require more resources than nonconversational COBOL ones because of the facility's additional functions. Nonconversational programs, however, should be reasonably close to COBOL. This turned out to be the case.

"In general, performance does not appear to be a restrictive factor," Mr. Holtz says. "Some additional computer resources should be expected to be sacrificed when a higher level development tool is used. The point is that the use of computer resources is not prohibitive. It's what should reasonably be expected, given the functions the facility provides."

The programmer assigned to write the applications had only three months experience with the Deere company.

After the successful trial evaluation, the Application Development Facility was installed on production IMS systems at two Deere computer centers. The program since has been used for several production applications, with results similar to the early study.

Source: *Data Processor*, vol. 21 (September 1978), pp. 8–9.

"These production systems were done using only standard facility functions," Mr. Holtz says. "But we also used the facility for a system prototype—an order entry function that required the entry of both an order and line items on the same screen. The line items represented twin occurrences of a dependent segment, and some auxiliary COBOL processing was required to perform all the data base updates from the one input screen.

"The total time spent on the development, including the extra COBOL processing, was only twelve man days compared to an estimated 60 man days without the facility. In addition to the update function, five other inquiries were provided for the data base."

Mr. Holtz notes that evolutionary growth and expansion are inherent in implementing data bases.

"It's impossible to expect that all current and future data requirements can be effectively and efficiently modeled in a data base structure," he says.

"So, we have to be able to change data bases and the application systems without any, or with very minimal, impact on existing users. To capitalize on and to realize the benefits of common data bases, we need the ability to change and adapt.

"Although modifications and enhancements are a way of life, they can't restrict or prohibit our ability to service the user's information needs. Systems and data bases must be flexible, and that is why we believe that the Application Development Facility concept of a high level specification language provides a future direction that will become the accepted practice."

DISCUSSION QUESTIONS

1. Describe how this development tool is able to increase programmer productivity. What are some of the benefits for Deere?
2. What impact do you think the Application Development Facility will have on traditional programming tools, such as flowcharts and decision tables.

Structured design 15

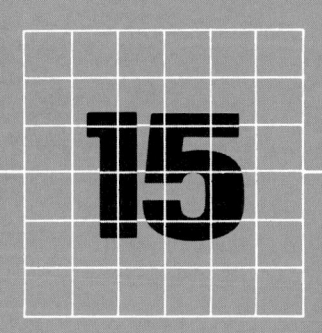

THE STRUCTURED DESIGN APPROACH
    Structure charts
    Organization and design guidelines
HIPO
    Visual table of contents
    HIPO diagrams
STRUCTURED PROGRAMMING CONCEPTS
    Structured programming
    Structured flowcharting
    Pseudocode
MANAGING STRUCTURED SYSTEMS
    Chief-programmer teams
    Structured walkthroughs
IMPLEMENTING A STRUCTURED SYSTEM
    The top down approach
    Other implementation techniques

After completing Chapter 15, you will be able to:

- Describe the advantages of a structured design approach.
- Discuss the use of HIPO in documenting a structured system.
- List the procedures in structured programming, structured flowcharting, and pseudocode.
- Contrast the top down approach of implementing a structured system with traditional approaches to implementing application software.
- Describe how structured systems can be managed with structured walkthroughs and chief-programmer teams.

In the early days of computer programming, the application programs were fairly short and simple. As computer hardware became more complex and sophisticated, application software became more complex and sophisticated. While some of the traditional approaches and techniques for application development were satisfactory for simpler and shorter programs, these same approaches and techniques became inadequate for today's longer and more complex programs.

Today, many application programs range from 20,000 to over 100,000 statements or instructions. This additional length has resulted in problems with program testing, debugging, and maintenance. And this relationship is not a constant. If the length of a program is doubled, the number of problems related to testing, debugging, and maintenance can increase by a factor of four or more. Larger and more complex programs make it more difficult to satisfy the needs of those using or benefiting from the program. Furthermore, it was very difficult to keep these larger programs on time and within original cost estimates. These problems led to a new way of thinking about application design and development. The result is structured design.

THE STRUCTURED DESIGN APPROACH

Structured design is more of a philosophy of designing and developing application software than it is a new documentation technique. The overall objective of structured design is to find the *best* possible way to develop software, although the same procedures and approaches can be used to solve other programs as well. The overall approach of structured design is to break a large and difficult problem into smaller problems that are simple enough to manage and handle but independent enough to solve separately.

Structured design has a number of potential advantages over the more traditional approaches to application development. These advantages include:

1. Better able to meet user or customer needs.
2. More reliable total project cost estimates.
3. More reliable total project completion date.
4. Improved project scheduling and planning.
5. Easier to monitor and control entire project.
6. Better designed application software.
7. More resistant to errors and problems during operation.
8. Less expensive to test and implement.
9. Less expensive to maintain or change.
10. More reliable and flexible.
11. Egoless programming teams and programs.
12. More productive use of data processing personnel.
13. More productive use of data processing resources.
14. More accurate and better developed documentation of the application packages.
15. A standardized approach to program design and coding.
16. More portable application software that is easier to adapt to different computer systems and hardware devices.

15 Structured design   **307**

17. Application software that is more efficient and effective and easier to use.

Although a structured approach can offer a number of attractive benefits, the benefits are not guaranteed because a structured approach is used. The extent to which the benefits of structured design are realized depends on *how* the large problem is broken into smaller problems. A valuable aid in visualizing the smaller problems or modules is a structure chart.

Structure charts

Structure charts show the modules or smaller problems and how they are related to each other. In a sense, a structure chart shows a *vertical slice* through the entire problem or system. A simple structure chart is shown in Figure 15–1.

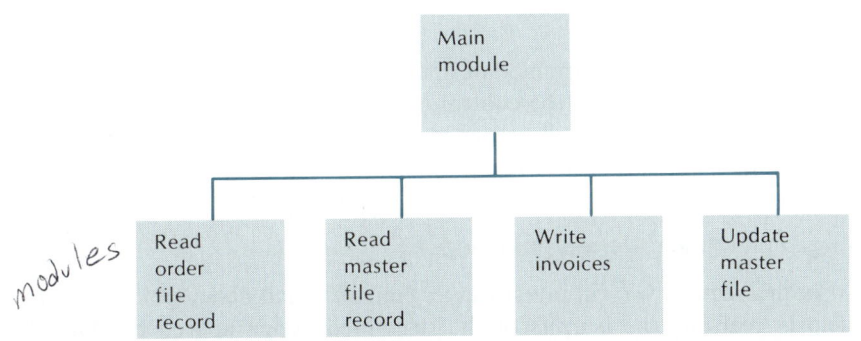

FIGURE 15–1
A simplified structure chart for processing sales orders

As with most structure charts, there is one *main module.* The first executable statement in the main module sends the computer to the first module which is the *Read Order File Module.* The Order File record is read, and the computer goes back to the main module. Next, the main module sends the computer to the next module. This is the *Read Master File Record Module.* Again, this module is executed, and then the computer goes back to the main module. Do you see the pattern? The main module sends the computer to the modules below it, one at a time. When the execution of one of these modules is completed, the computer goes back to the main module. Program control goes from *top* to *bottom* and never from side to side. Thus, for example, the *Read Order File Module* would never send the computer to the *Read Master File Module.* The only way the computer gets to the *Read Master File Module* is through the main module. For the structure chart in Figure 15–1, there are only two levels of modules. The first level is the main module, and the second level consists of the four modules below the main module. In most cases, there are three or more levels of modules. This is shown in Figure 15–2. The modules have been numbered. Module 1000 is the main module. This is the first level. This module sends the computer to the modules

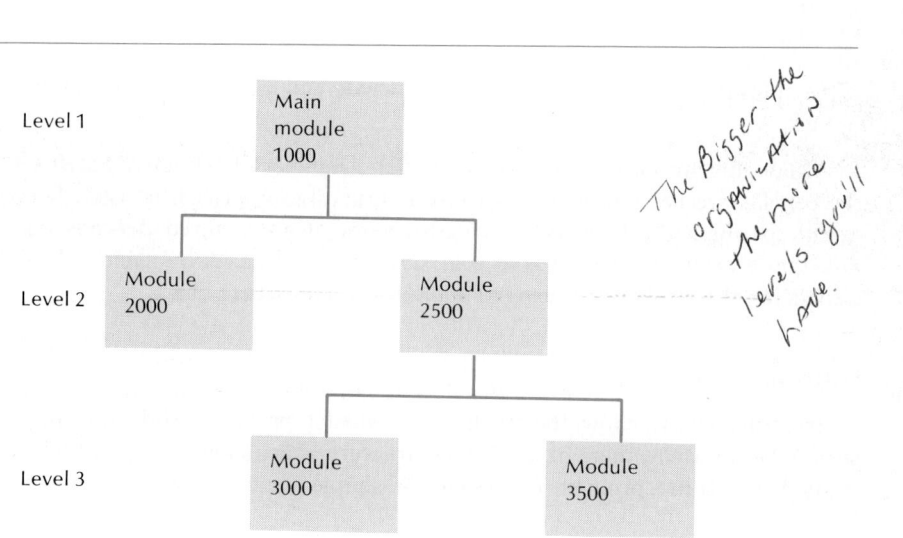

FIGURE 15–2
A structure chart for a program with three levels

Level 1: Main module 1000
Level 2: Module 2000, Module 2500
Level 3: Module 3000, Module 3500

in the second level. In turn, module 2500 sends the computer to the modules in the third level. Again, the control is always from *top to bottom*. After a module has been completely executed at any given level, it always returns to the module directly above it.

Organization and design guidelines

In this section, we will investigate organization and design guidelines that help in realizing the benefits of the structured design approach. Many of these techniques are similar to management techniques that you may have studied in a management course. For example, the structure charts in Figures 15–1 and 15–2 look like an organization chart with the president at the top, managers in the middle, and people (workers) that carry out the directives and orders of the president and managers at the bottom of the chart.

The control in a modular program should be from the top to the bottom. Each module has one entering point and one exit point. The modules at the top of the structure chart make decisions and direct and control the modules below or at the bottom of the structure chart. If a decision is made by one module, all modules that are affected by the decision should be placed below the module that makes the decision. Like the president of a company, the top or main module controls the entire program, the middle level modules act as managers in carrying out the orders of the top or main module, and the bottom level modules do the actual work—they perform the processing and input and output. When all of the input, processing, and output is performed by the modules at the lowest level of the structure chart, the program is called **completely factored**.

Each module should carry out or perform one basic function, such as reading data, making a computation, or an output of a result. The degree to which a module performs one general function is called **cohesion**. In addition, each module should represent a unique subproblem of the total problem. The activities that one module performs should be independent from the activities performed by other modules. The modules should not be related to or dependent on each other. The degree to which modules are related to or dependent on each other is called **coupling.** In general, modules should have *high cohesion* and *low coupling*.

In dividing a larger problem or program into small and managable modules, there are a number of design guidelines that can be followed to help in realizing the benefits of a structured approach. Also called **design heuristics,** these design guidelines are not hard and fast rules. They merely indicate what structured designs that over time have resulted in good design. One guideline is to make each module approximately 50 statements or instructions long. This is a managable size that allows a significant amount of processing to be accomplished without making the module too large and difficult to write, test, and debug. Another guideline is to have from three to ten modules below any given module in the structure chart. The number of modules below any given module is called **fan out** or **span of control.** The average number of modules that appear in any given module (fan out) is usually five or six in most programs. Another concern in developing modular programs is the depth of the program. The **depth** of a program is the number of levels of modules in the structure chart. The modular programs in Figure 15–1 and 15–2 have a depth of 2 and 3. This would be typical of a program up to 500 statements in length. A program with several thousand statements may have a depth of about five levels, a program with 10,000 statements or more could require about ten levels of modules, and massive programs with over 100,000 statements could have 50 or more levels of modules.

The above general guidelines are only design aids. There are exceptions to every guideline discussed above. In addition, there are several tools and techniques that are especially useful with the structured design approach. While such techniques as flowcharts and decision tables can be used with structured design, there are other techniques that use the principles and strategies of structured design. These techniques include HIPO, structured programming, structured flowcharting, pseudocode, the top down approach, chief-programmer teams, and structured walkthroughs.

HIPO, which stands for Hierarchy plus Input-Processing-Output, is both a design tool and an aid to program documentation. Like other techniques used in structured design, HIPO uses a **functional** approach. HIPO is concerned with *what* is done and not *how* a particular activity is accomplished. This is a departure from flowcharts that stress *how* something is done and not *what* is to be done. When properly used, HIPO offers the same types of advantages discussed previously in this chapter.

When using HIPO to design and document a program, a number of diagrams and visual aids are used. These diagrams and visual aids are called a *HIPO Package*. In most cases, a HIPO package consists of a visual table of contents and one or more HIPO diagrams. Like flowcharts, HIPO diagrams can be overview diagrams that reveal the overall structure of the application or detail diagrams that reveal in more detail what is happening with specific parts of the application.

Visual table of contents

The **visual table of contents** is very similar to the structure chart. In a visual table of contents, the structure chart is called a *hierarchy diagram* and each box or module is numbered. In addition, a visual table of contents may contain a *legend* and an *operational description section*. Figure 15–3 shows a visual table of contents for the sales order application first seen in the structure chart in Figure 15–1.

As you can see, each module has been numbered. The main module is 1.0, the read order file record module is 2.0, the read master file record

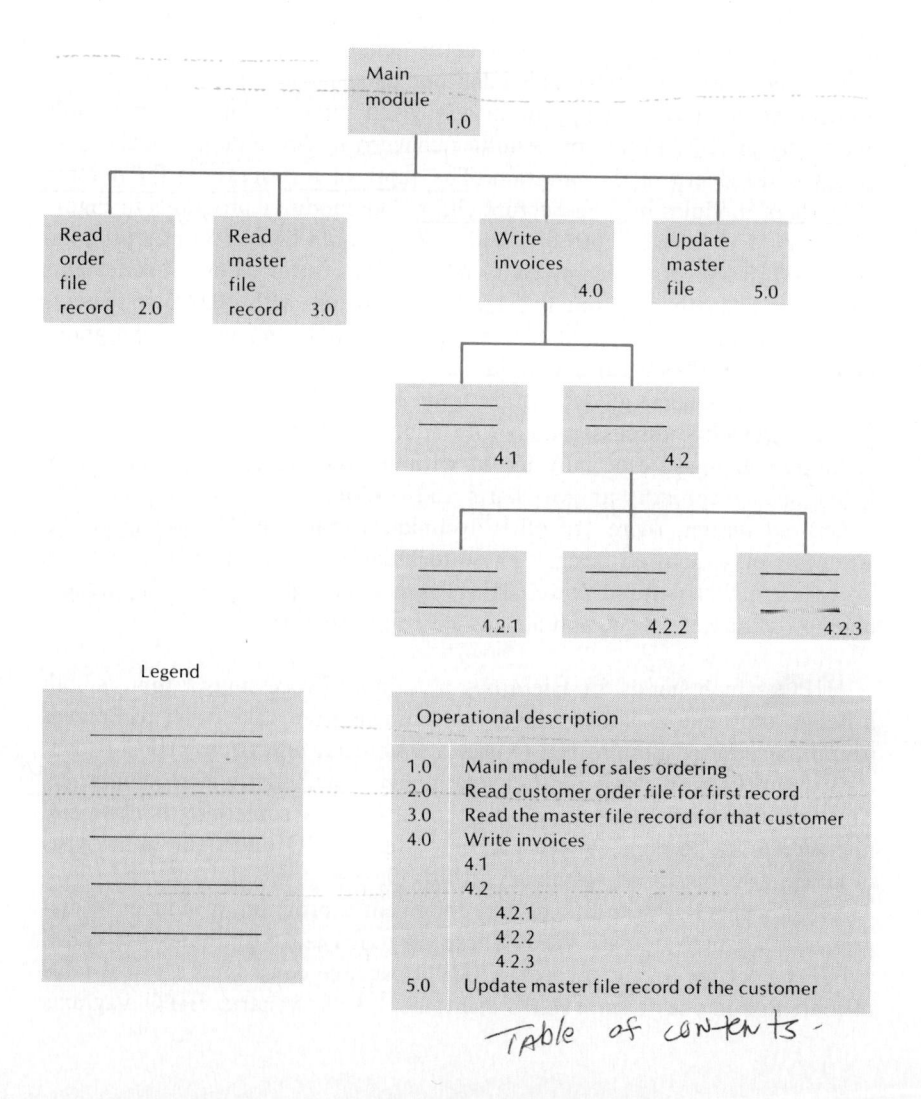

FIGURE 15–3
Visual table of contents

module is 3.0, the write invoices module is 4.0, and the update master file module is 5.0. Module 4.0, writing invoices, has been expanded into more detailed modules to show you how they would be numbered. The two modules that are directly below module 4.0 are numbered 4.1 and 4.2 respectively. Additional modules would have been numbered 4.3, 4.4, and so on. In a similar fashion, the modules below module 4.2 are also numbered to reflect their position in the visual table of contents. These modules are numbered 4.2.1, 4.2.2 and 4.2.3. The visual table of contents may also have a legend that describes any of the conventions used and an operational description that describes the modules in more detail.

Hierarchy diagrams should be read from *left to right* at any given level. In most cases, a middle module at any given level receives data from the module to its immediate left and passes the output data to the modules to its immediate right. Look at the bottom level in Figure 15-3. Module 4.2.2 gets data from module 4.2.1, and it passes the results to module 4.2.3. Hierarchy diagrams can also be read from *top to bottom*. Modules near the top describe the general function to be completed. Modules that are directly below a module give a more detailed description of what is to be done. Thus, a hierarchy diagram can be read from left to right to see what functions are being performed and from top to bottom to get a more detailed explanation of any particular function.

HIPO diagrams

HIPO diagrams are used to describe in more detail the modules that are displayed in the visual table of contents. Usually, there is one HIPO diagram for each module in the visual table of contents. Overview HIPO diagrams reveal the overall functions that are being performed in a module, and detail diagrams reveal in more detail what is happening with one specific part of one of the main functions or modules. HIPO diagrams are usually numbered to correspond to the modules in the visual table of contents, which are also numbered. For example, a HIPO diagram can be developed for the update master file module (module number 5.0) in the visual table of contents shown in Figure 15-3. This HIPO diagram is displayed in Figure 15-4.

In the HIPO diagram, the inputs are the inventory transaction record and inventory master record. If these records are sorted according to an inventory key on magnetic tape, the process box reveals the processing that takes place. A master and transaction record are read. If their keys match (they are the same inventory item), the master file is updated and another master and transaction record are read. When the transaction key is greater than the master key, the master record does not need to be changed. The old master record is copied on the update tape, and more master records are read until there is a match. When there is a match, the master record is updated. What happens if there is a mistake, and there is a transaction record that does not have a corresponding master record? For example, the

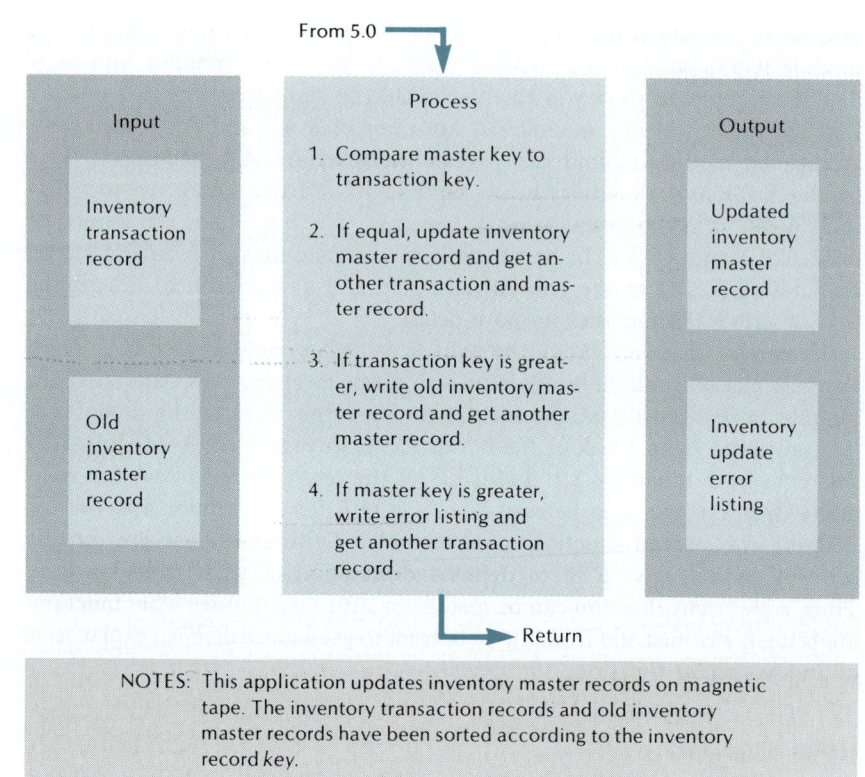

FIGURE 15–4
HIPO diagram for the inventory update application

From 5.0

Input

Inventory transaction record

Old inventory master record

Process

1. Compare master key to transaction key.

2. If equal, update inventory master record and get another transaction and master record.

3. If transaction key is greater, write old inventory master record and get another master record.

4. If master key is greater, write error listing and get another transaction record.

Return

Output

Updated inventory master record

Inventory update error listing

NOTES: This application updates inventory master records on magnetic tape. The inventory transaction records and old inventory master records have been sorted according to the inventory record key.

first master record key might be 100, and the first transaction key might be 11. In other words, the master key is *greater than* the transaction key. Because both files have already been sorted, from low to high, the lowest master record key has to be 100. Therefore, a corresponding master record does not exist for the transaction record. In general, whenever the master key is greater than the transaction key, there is no corresponding master record and an error listing should be made.

STRUCTURED PROGRAMMING CONCEPTS

There are a number of techniques that can be used to ease the burden of computer programming or coding and to standardize the programming process. These techniques include structured programming, structured flowcharting, and pseudocode.

Structured programming

Structured programming is not a new programming language; it is a way of standardizing computer programming using existing languages. The basic idea behind structured programming is that a program can be broken down into groups of statements. There is no size restriction on how many statements can be in a group, but usually these groups are formed according to what

15 Structured design

they do or their function. One group may read data, while another group does a certain processing task.

When using the structured programming approach, statements in a group must conform to a standardized pattern or structure. To begin with, there can only be *one entering point* into the block of statements and *one exiting point* from the block of statements. Therefore, you cannot branch to or from the middle of the structured group of statements. This restriction by itself eliminates many programming errors and makes debugging the program much easier. Each group can be tested separately. What structures or patterns are allowed when you use structured programming? There are only three types. There are (1) *sequence,* (2) *decision,* and (3) *loop.* Programming statements that are typically used in each of these structures are shown in Table 15–1.

TABLE 15–1
Overview of structured programming

	Example statements		
Structure	BASIC	FORTRAN	COBOL
Sequence	10 READ T	READ TOTAL	READ TOTAL.
Decision	20 If N=0, GO TO 60	If (X) 50,50,60	If G is less than 10, GO TO PRINT ROUTINE.
Loop	40 FOR I=1 to 10 ⋮ 60 NEXT I	DO 60 I=1,10 ⋮ 60 CONTINUE	PERFORM MAIN-ROUTINE, UNTIL I>10.

In the **sequence structure,** programming statements are executed one after another. There must be a definite starting and ending point. Figure 15–5 contains a typical sequence structure. After starting the sequence, the statements are executed one after another until all of the statements in the sequence have been executed. Then the program continues to another sequence. In this figure, a value for X is read. Then Y is set equal to 3 times X. Finally, the values for X and Y are printed. Of course, other actions may be in the sequence structure as long as the statements are executed one after another in sequence.

The **decision structure** allows the computer to branch depending upon certain conditions. As with all structures, there is a starting point and an ending point for the decision structure. See Figure 15–6.

Figure 15–6 shows how the commission for a salesperson should be computed. Normally the commission is 20 percent (.2) of sales. If sales are greater than $1000, then a $50 bonus should be added to the commissions. In Figure 15–6, C is the commission and S is the total sales. Note that when S is greater than 1000, C is .2(S) + 50. Otherwise, the commission is simply 20

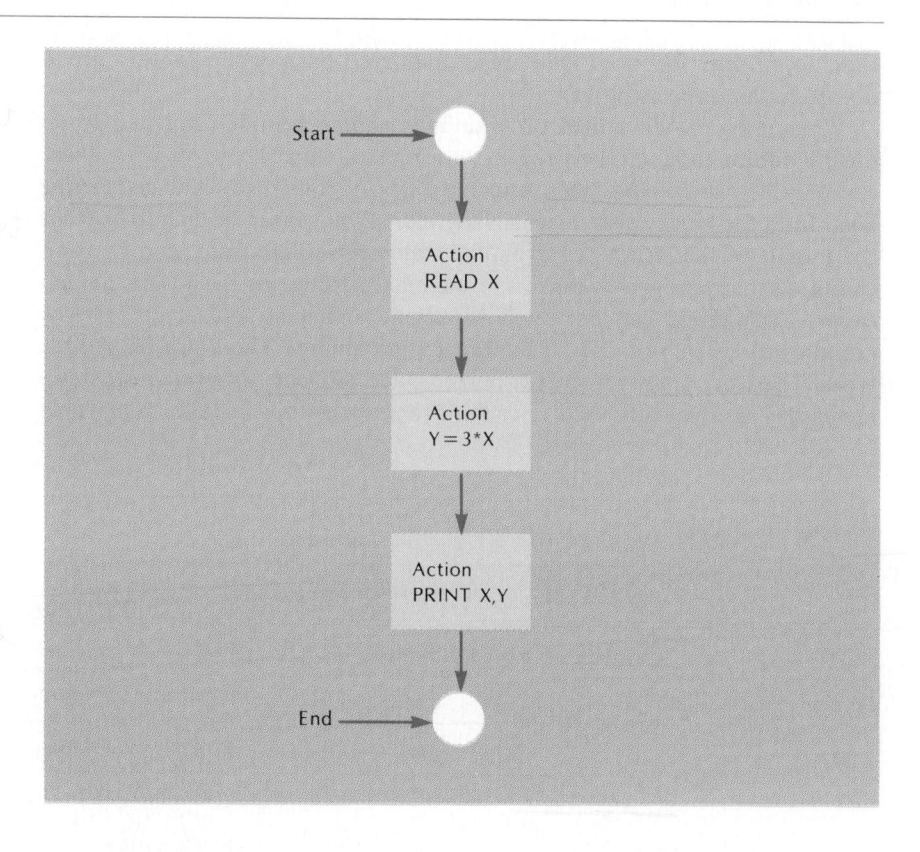

FIGURE 15–5
A sequence structure

percent of sales, C = (.2)S. It is important to note that regardless of which branch is taken in the above decision structure, the ending point is the same.

The final structure is the **loop.** Actually, there are two commonly used structures for loops. One is the **Do While** structure, and the other one is the **Do Until** structure. Both structures are shown in Figure 15–7. In both structures, the total of the ten values are obtained. This is done by the action, T = T+X(I). The action may not always total X(I) values, and there may be many statements in sequence that comprise the action inside of the loop. Both loop structures accomplish the same thing. In the *Do Until* structure, the loop is done *until* a certain condition is met. In the example used in Figure 15–7, the loop is repeated *until* I is greater than 10. For the *Do While* structure, the loop is done *while* a certain condition exists. This condition is I being less than or equal to 10.

Structured flowcharting

Along with some new ways to construct programs, there are some new ways to flowchart programs. **Structured flowcharting** is one of these techniques. It is especially appropriate for programs that are written using the structured programming approach. As with so many new approaches, there is no universally accepted method. There are many minor variations. The

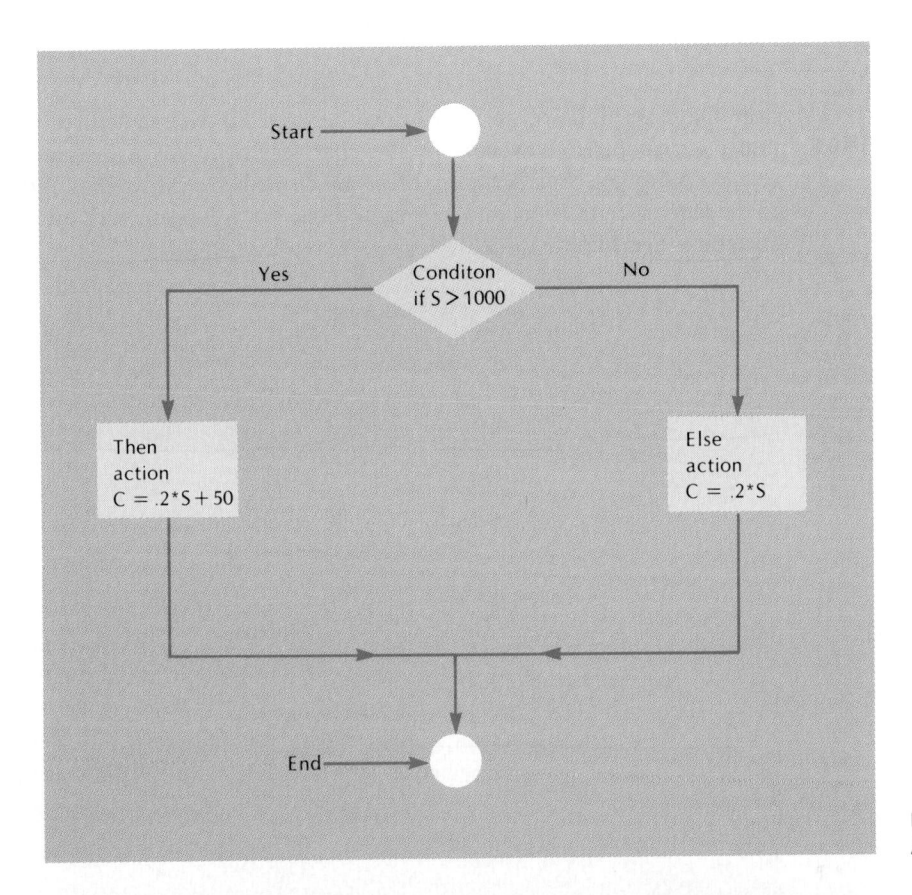

FIGURE 15–6
A decision structure

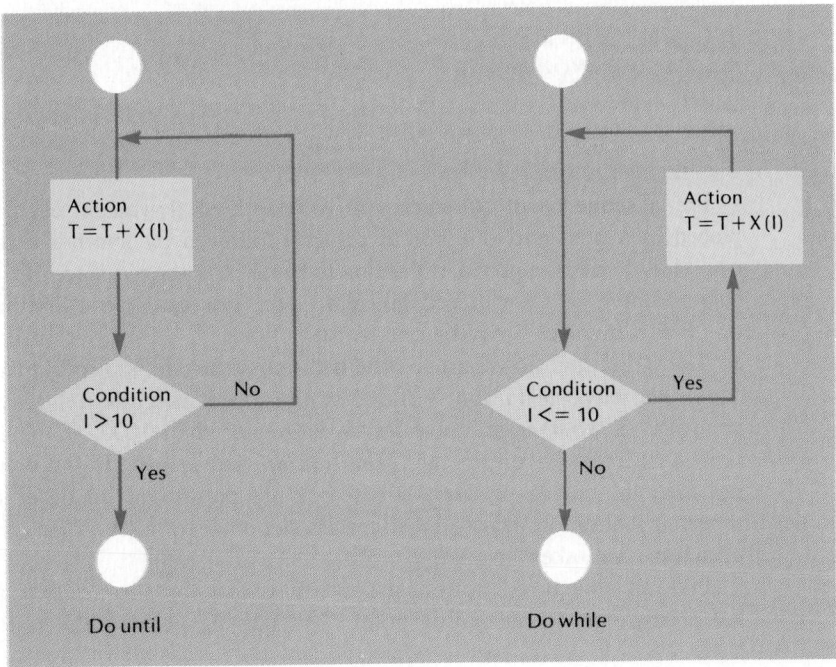

FIGURE 15–7
Two loop structures

overall approach, however, is generally the same. As with structured programming, a structured flowchart or flowchart segment has a definite starting and ending point. Furthermore, there are three basic forms that correspond to the sequence, decision, and loop structures. We will begin with the **sequence structure.** See Figure 15-8.

```
        READ X
          │
          ▼
       Y = 3*X
          │
          ▼
        PRINT
         X,Y

    Traditional
     flowchart
```

```
┌──────────────┐
│   READ X     │
├──────────────┤
│   Y = 3*X    │
├──────────────┤
│  PRINT X,Y   │
└──────────────┘

Structured flowchart
for the
sequence structure
```

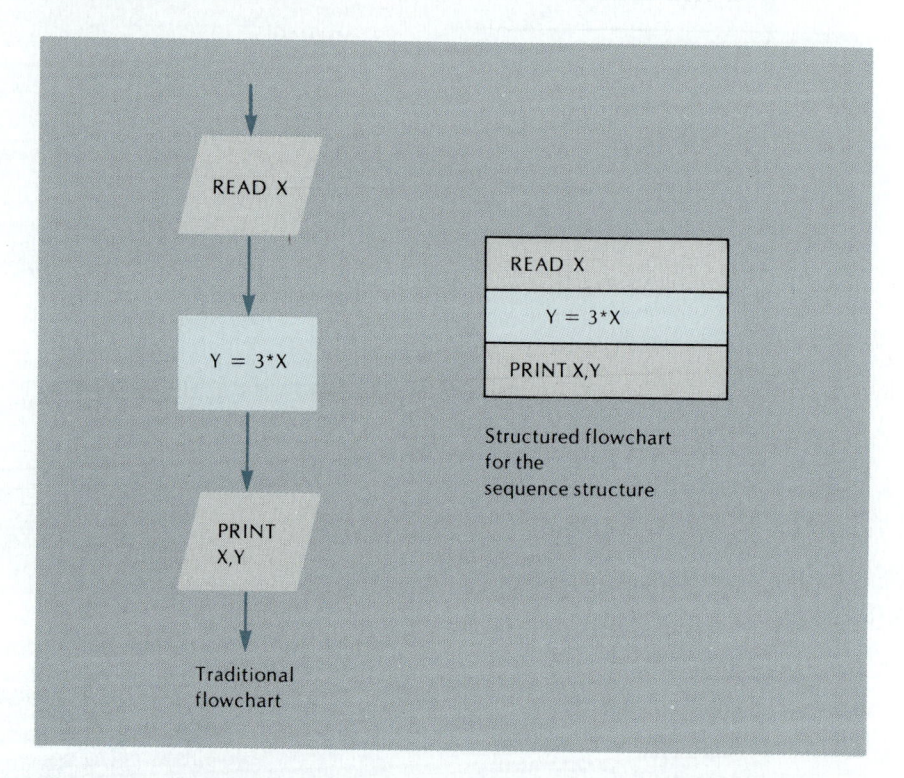

FIGURE 15-8
A structured flowchart for the sequence structure

For a sequence of statements in a structured flowchart, each action is placed in a box, and one box is directly followed by another box, and so on. If less detail is required, the action to be taken in the sequence of statements can be stated in a structured flowchart box. For example, "Compute Tax" or "Write Invoices" may be one of the actions.

The structured flowchart for the decision structure is displayed in Figure 15-9. The basic condition is stated at the top of the box. In this case, the condition is whether or not sales, S, is greater than 1000. If the condition is met, the actions under the *Then* box are performed. If the condition is not met, the actions under the *Else* box are performed. In other words, *if* a certain condition exists, *Then* certain actions are taken, *Else* another set of actions are taken.

Like all structured flowcharts, the flowchart for the decision structure has a starting and an ending point. The starting point is the statement of

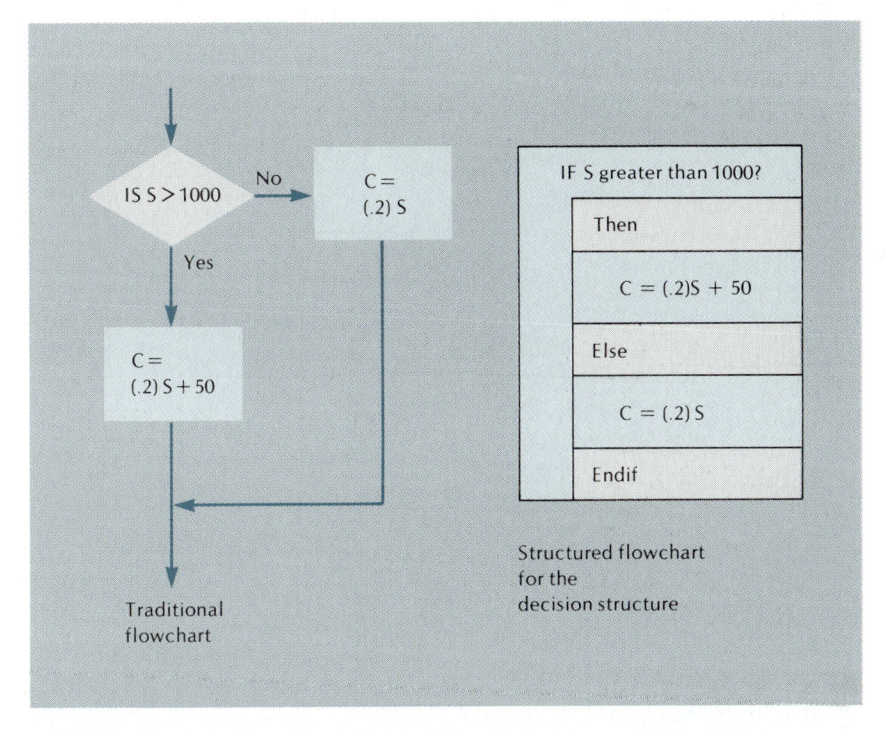

15 Structured design

FIGURE 15–9
A structured flowchart for the decision structure

the condition: If S is greater than 1000. The ending of the flowchart is the *endif* box. This literally means that this is the *end* of the *if* or decision segment of the flowchart. In a larger program, you are likely to see many of these types of flowcharts embodied in a larger structured flowchart. We will see how a larger structured flowchart can be constructed, but first, the structured flowchart for the loop structure needs to be explained.

A structured flowchart for a **loop** is shown in Figure 15–10.

The beginning of the flowchart for the loop structure is the Do While or the Do Until statement. This is followed by a series of actions. In this example, the total of the X(I) values are determined. After all of the actions have been taken in the loop, the structured flowchart ends with the *enddo* statement. See the bottom of the structured flowchart in Figure 15–10. Now, we are in a position to see how several of these structured flowchart segments can be used together in constructing a structured flowchart for a program.

For this program, assume that there are 15 salespersons who should be paid commissions this week. The normal commission is 20 percent of sales as discussed with decision structure. If the total sales are greater than $1,000, then a $50 bonus should be added to the normal commission. The total commission is to be printed, and this process is to be repeated for all 15 salespersons. This problem can be flowcharted using the traditional methods

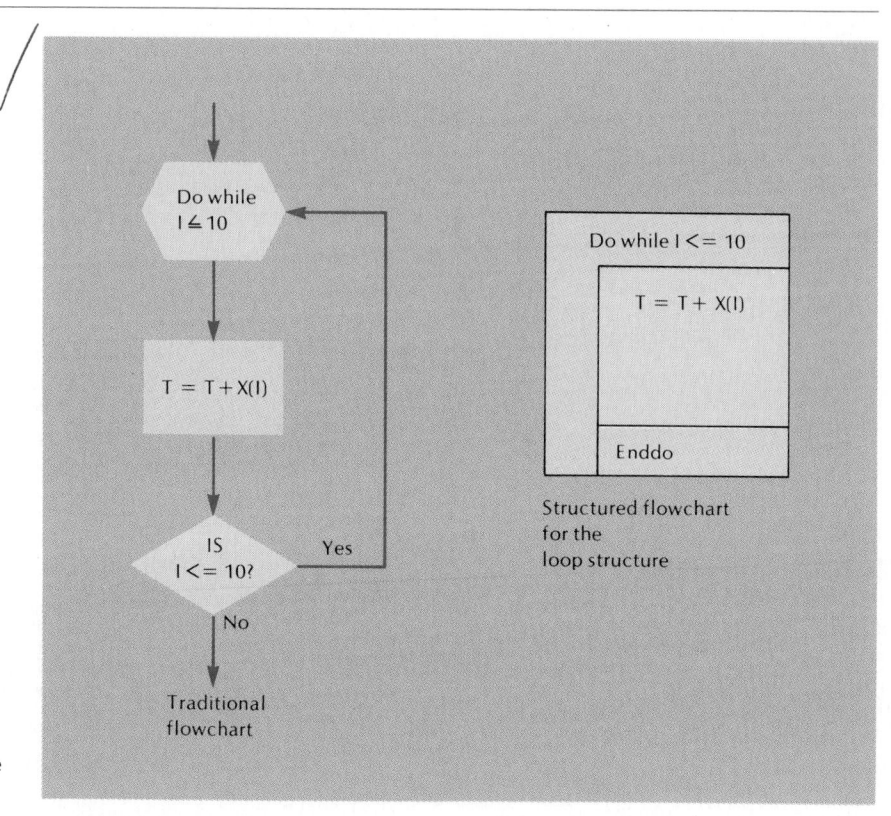

FIGURE 15-10
A structured flowchart for the loop structure

or using the structured flowcharting approach. Figure 15-11 contains both types of flowcharts.

Both the flowcharts contain the same information, but the structured flowchart is more compact in this case. Which flowchart is easier for you to understand? Perhaps the traditional flowchart is easier for you. This may be due to the fact that you have been working with traditional flowcharts for some time, while this is your first exposure to structured flowcharts. Many managers, however, find that the structured flowchart is easier to understand. It can be like reading a report or a book. There are a series of smaller boxes in larger ones that show what is to be done and in what order. These boxes are like sentences, paragraphs, and major sections within a report.

Pseudocode

In some cases, it still may be difficult to go from tools such as flowcharts, decision tables, grid charts, visual tables of contents, and HIPO diagrams to the actual programs. As an intermediate step, the programmer might decide to write, in ordinary English, the steps and procedures that the computer program must perform. These ordinary English statements will be similar to the actual program or code, and thus these statements or instructions

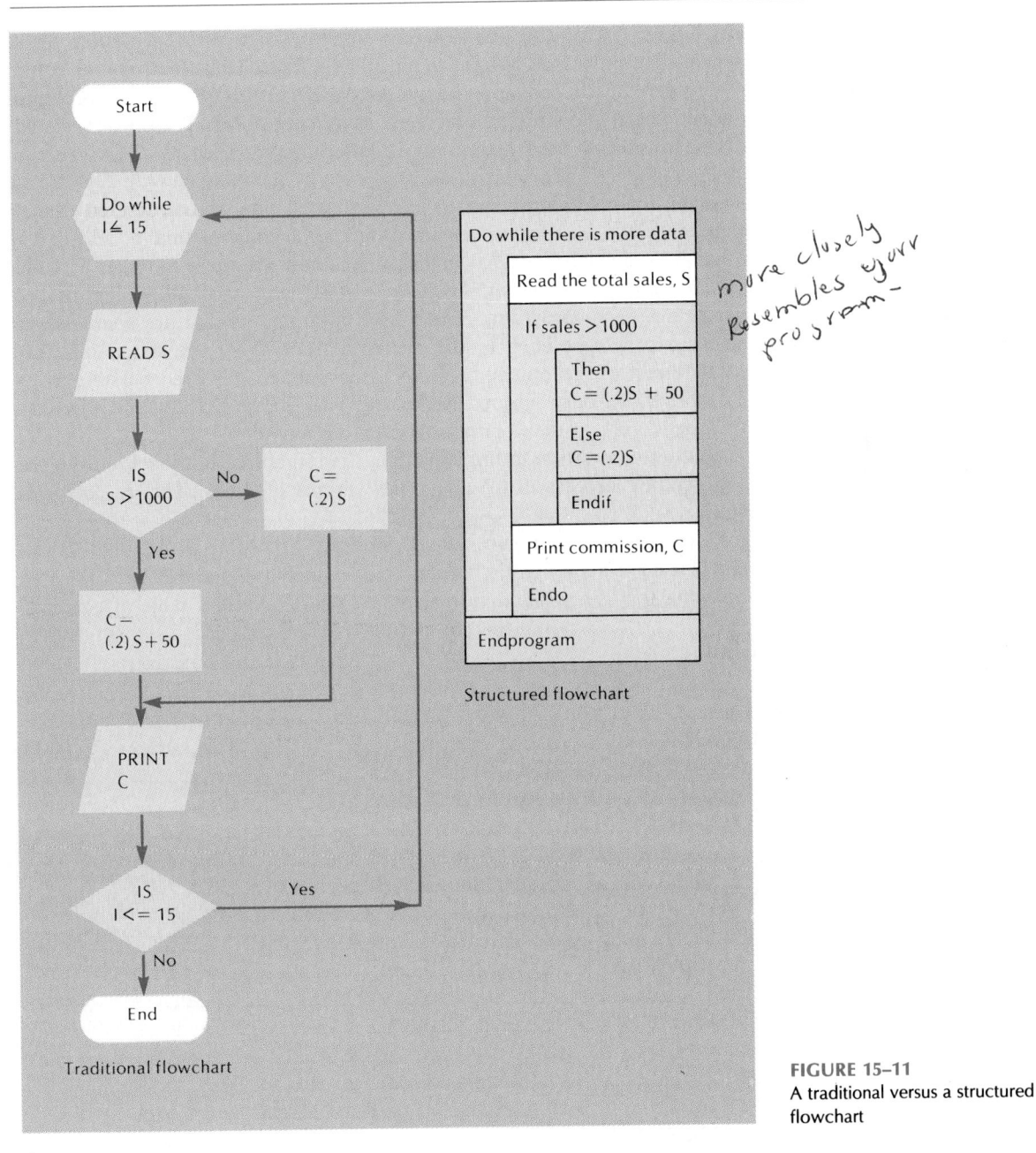

15 Structured design

Traditional flowchart:

Start → Do while I ≤ 15 → READ S → IS S > 1000?
- No → C = (.2)S
- Yes → C = (.2)S + 50

→ PRINT C → IS I <= 15?
- Yes → (loop back to Do while)
- No → End

Structured flowchart:

```
Do while there is more data
    Read the total sales, S
    If sales > 1000
        Then
        C = (.2)S + 50
        Else
        C = (.2)S
        Endif
    Print commission, C
Endo
Endprogram
```

more closely Resembles your program —

FIGURE 15–11
A traditional versus a structured flowchart

are called **pseudocode**. You may have trouble writing programs assigned to you by your instructor. One approach that many students have used successfully is to write out how they would solve the problem by hand. It will then be easier to write the actual program. If you do this, you are writing a program in pseudocode—a set of instructions which resemble a computer program. In Chapter 1, you saw how some instructions were written for a manual data processing system to calculate a total. These instructions could be considered pseudocode. Although there are no rules for writing a program in pseudocode, many programmers use **structured words.** These words would include the terms used in structured programming such as *Do While, Do Until, If Then, If Else,* and so on.

So far in this chapter, we have investigated how the structured design approach could be used to break a larger problem into smaller and easier to handle subproblems called modules. But how are these modules actually written in a programming language? Most languages allow the use of **subroutines** or **subprograms.** These are miniprograms that are contained in the main program. Then in the main program, there are statements that *call* or direct the computer to go to a subroutine. It is even possible to go to a subroutine from a subroutine. Some languages, like COBOL and ALGOL, are easier to use in developing programming modules.

Another convention in implementing the structured approach during the programming process is to indent the various modules. This is shown in Figure 15–12.

As can be seen in Figure 15–12, modules 1.0, 2.0, 3.0, 4.0, and 5.0 all start in the left-hand margin. Other modules such as 2.1 and 2.2 are indented according to their position in a structure chart or visual table of contents.

MODULE 1.0 _____

MODULE 2.0 _____

  MODULE 2.1 _____

  MODULE 2.2 _____

    MODULE 2.2.1 _____

    MODULE 2.2.2 _____

MODULE 3.0 _____

MODULE 4.0 _____

  MODULE 4.1 _____

  MODULE 4.2 _____

MODULE 5.0 _____

FIGURE 15–12
Indenting a modular program

15 Structured design

The ability to indent programming instructions is also a function of the programming language being used. With some languages, this practice is difficult to implement.

MANAGING STRUCTURED SYSTEMS

Of all the techniques and procedures outlined in this chapter, the most important element in realizing the benefits of a structured design approach is the human element. The people that manage and implement the structured approach are the key to unlocking the potential of the structured approach. Because programs that utilize the structured approach are usually large and complex, a team of people must be used to plan, design, develop, and implement the necessary computer programs in a reasonable amount of time.

In managing structured systems and programming projects, the emphasis is on *results*—the finished package of computer programs. Efforts must be made to eliminate conflict and friction among the people in the programming team. In order to get a smooth and efficient set of structured programs in operation, the programming team must operate as a unified team striving for the same overall objective. Programmer styles, personalities, and egos should be suppressed and good program design should be stressed. Programming teams that accomplish these objectives are called **egoless** and **adaptive**. In order to help programming teams work together to accomplish the objectives of the structured design approach, a number of approaches and guidelines have been developed. Some of these are discussed in this section.

Chief-programmer teams

One of the first chief-programmer teams was assembled by IBM in 1969 to undertake the New York Times Project to automate the newspaper clipping file. The software consisted of approximately 83,000 lines of source code and took about 22 months to complete. The resulting software successfully completed a solid week of testing without any errors or problems, and it ran for about 20 months before the first error occurred. This remarkable success can be directly attributable to the chief-programmer team concept.

The emphasis of the chief-programmer team is to develop a team of skilled data processing professionals to fully *design, develop,* and *implement* a structured application software package. This team has total responsibility of building the *best* application software possible.

While the actual make up of the chief-programmer team varies with the size and complexity of the computer programs to be developed, there are a number of functions or activities that must be accomplished by the members of the chief-programmer team. Each chief-programmer team should have a chief programmer or chief analyst, a backup programmer, one or more programmers, a librarian, and one or more clerks or secretaries.

The **chief programmer** or **analyst** has the overall responsibility of seeing that the entire project is successfully completed. This individual interacts with the user or end customer and managers in general. The chief programmer needs to have both managerial skills and skills in programming and structured design.

The **backup programmer** is an assistant to the chief programmer. For large and complex application packages, there may be several backup programmers. This would be like having several managers under a president of a company. The backup programmer assists the chief programmer in all aspects of the entire project. These include defining the problem, analysis of the problem, language selection, computer programming, testing and debugging, implementation, and maintenance of the software package during the life of the package. These aspects of the programming process were described in more detail in Chapter 13. Like the chief programmer, the backup programmer or programmers should have both managerial and structured design and programming skills.

The number of **programmers** in the chief-programmer team depends on the size of the programming project and the desired completion date. A larger project or a relatively short completion date requires more programmers. For simple projects, there may be as few as one or two programmers. For a large project, there could be over twenty programmers. While the programmers do not require the same managerial skills or business knowledge as the chief programmer or backup programmer, the programmers must have excellent technical skills. If possible, these individuals should have experience with large programming projects and structured design concepts.

Most data processing departments have support libraries. These libraries contain complete programs, subroutines, and program modules that have already been developed, tested, and documented, usually as a result of other programming projects. Most support libraries have a set of rules and guidelines for the use of the materials stored in the support library. As in any library you would find at a college or university, there is usually a **chief librarian** and several **librarians** under the chief librarian that maintain the library of programs, subroutines, and modules. Because of the importance of support libraries, most chief-programmer teams have a *librarian* from the data processing support library on the team. This individual alerts the chief-programmer team to the materials that are available in the support library and helps the team in using these materials.

During the entire programming process, there will be progress reports, correspondence, a final report, and other miscellaneous jobs that must be performed. While the programmers can perform most of these tasks, it is a more efficient utilization of resources if professional **clerks** and **secretaries** are used to perform these clerical and miscellaneous jobs.

Structured walkthroughs

During any programming project, there is a need to monitor the progress that is being made. Is the project on schedule? Is the project within its budget? Are there any problems with the project? These questions need to be answered periodically during the project. This monitoring process should also detect and correct errors or problems as early in the project as possible.

When structured design concepts are being used, the **structured walkthrough** is a technique used to monitor the progress of a structured project. The structured walkthrough is a *planned* and *pre-announced* review of the progress of the entire project. The overall emphasis is on the *quality* of the project at any point in time.

Like any other technique, there are a number of guidelines and suggested approaches that will improve the effectiveness of a structured walkthrough. To begin with, structured walkthroughs should be scheduled when significant progress has been made.

In most cases, the structured walkthrough is scheduled when several related modules have been completed. The structured walkthrough should be planned, and an agenda of the topics to be covered and the modules to be investigated should be sent to the people attending the meeting in advance of the meeting. The chief programmer, backup programmer, the programmers that developed the modules, and the programmers that may be affected by these modules should attend the structured walkthrough. Normally, the structured walkthroughs are conducted with five to ten people. With more than ten people, it can be difficult to make significant progress.

In reviewing existing computer code and completed modules, it is important to search for *major design flaws* and *problems*. In addition, minor problems, such as *typographical errors,* should be located and corrected. The overall objective of a structured walkthrough is to produce *error free* and *error resistant* code. Furthermore, everyone's work should be reviewed at a structured walkthrough. This includes the work of the chief programmer and backup programmer, which is reviewed by all of the other programmers attending the structured walkthrough.

The attitude that prevails in the structured walkthrough should be one of a team effort trying to reach a common goal—the best program design, development, and implementation. Emotion, whim, undue criticism, and personal conflict should be eliminated or suppressed. The chief-programmer team should strive to develop the best application packages, and the structured walkthrough should provide an environment to accomplish this objective.

IMPLEMENTING A STRUCTURED SYSTEM

Now, let's assume that a chief-programming team is faced with the task of writing a very large program. Perhaps the program is over 30,000 statements. Furthermore, the program has been broken down into modules like the ones shown in Figure 15-3. Of course, there would be many more modules and probably several additional levels. Where do you begin? How do you test each module and the entire program? How do you get all of the bugs out? In this section, we will investigate several techniques used to implement the structured approach.

The top-down approach

In general, a good approach to writing a large program is to start with the main module, and to work down to the other modules. This is the **top-down approach.** This concept is simple, but it can untangle coding and debugging problems. The structure of the modules in Figures 15–1 and 15–3 reveal a top-down design. The control of the program goes from the top down. Now, we will use the top-down approach in developing the modules. We begin by writing the main module. Next, the modules at the next level are written. This procedure continues until all of the modules have been written.

In addition to program coding, the top-down approach should be used in testing and debugging the modules. Thus, after the first or main module is written, it is tested and debugged. But the main module sends the computer to modules at the second level which have not been written yet. Thus, dummy modules at the second level are needed to send the computer back to the first or main module so it can be fully and completely tested. If errors are found in the main module, they are corrected immediately. When the main module is working, the dummy modules at the second level are discarded, and the actual modules at the second level are written. If one or more modules at the second level sends the computer to a third level, it will be necessary to develop dummy modules at the third level. Since the main module is needed to run the modules at the second level, when the second level modules are tested and debugged, the main module is again tested. Indeed, when you test a module at any level, all of the modules above it are tested again. If there are five levels, the main module will be tested at least five times. The modules at the second level will be tested at least four times. The modules at the third level will be tested at least three times, and so on. This writing, testing, and debugging sequence is summarized in Figure 15–13.

Level 1   (the main module)
  a. Write the main module
  b. Write any necessary dummy modules at the second level.
  c. Test the main module
  d. Debug the main module

Level 2   (this procedure is done for each module one at a time)
  a. Write the module
  b. Write any necessary dummy modules at the third level.
  c. Test the module (this will automatically test all of the modules that are above this one in the structure chart).
  d. Debug the module

Level n (the same procedure is repeated for all levels)

FIGURE 15–13
The top-down approach to writing, testing and debugging a modular program

Other implementation techniques

There are a number of alternative implementation techniques and modifications of the top-down approach. One implementation technique is the **bottom-up** technique. As the name implies, the bottom level modules are written first. To test these modules, dummy driver modules are written. After the lower level modules are written, tested, and debugged, the next lowest level of modules are written, tested, and debugged. This process continues until all of the modules have been completed. The process used in the bottom-up approach is exactly opposite of the approach used in the top-down approach.

One of the variations or modifications to the top-down approach is to implement some of the modules along one branch of the structure chart from the top module to a bottom-level module. Thus, instead of completing all of the modules at a given level before going to the next level, some of the modules at all levels are completed first.

When one of the modules at a lower level may be extremely difficult or complex to write, the chief-programmer team may wish to write, test, and debug this module first. Otherwise, the team may have to rewrite all of the modules above it if the complex module cannot be developed or coordinated with the modules that have already been completed. After the complex modules have been completed, the normal top down approach can be continued.

While there are a number of approaches to implementing an application package developed using structured design, the top down approach or modification of the top down approach offers a number of advantages. These advantages include:

1. The most important modules are written and tested first.
2. It is easier for users or customers to see the progress that is being made on the project.
3. It is no longer necessary to perform system and volume testing after the packages have been written.
4. Testing and debugging is easier and more efficient.
5. The use of computer resources for testing and debugging is more evenly distributed over the project.
6. The implementation is normally smoother and shorter.
7. Programmer morale and job satisfaction is increased.
8. It is easier to detect and correct time delays and cost overruns.
9. It is easier to deal with time delays and cost overruns when they occur.
10. Data processing resources are used more evenly and efficiently.

SUMMARY

This chapter has introduced you to the structured design approach. The overall philosophy of structured design is to break a large and complex problem into smaller problems that are manageable and that can be solved separately to arrive at the solution to the entire problem. In addition, this chapter introduced you to some of the techniques that are used in conjunction with the structured design approach. These techniques include structure charts, HIPO, structured programming, structured flowcharting, pseudocode, chief-programmer teams, structured walkthroughs, top-down design, and bottom-up design.

One tool that can be used for both project design and documentation is HIPO. A HIPO package consists of a visual table of contents and one or more HIPO diagrams. Like flowcharts, HIPO diagrams can show the overall purpose of the application (overview diagrams) or the detailed activities within a module (detailed diagram).

Structured programming concepts are used in simplifying and standardizing the programming process. In structured programming, only three structures are allowed. These structures are the sequence, the decision, and the loop. The GO TO type statements are discouraged in structured programming. Structured flowcharting is a documentation technique that stresses the structured programming approach. There is a flowcharting procedure for each structure-sequence, decision, and loop. Pseudocode is another aid to computer programming. Using structured words, a programmer can develop a set of English-like instructions that can aid in writing one or more computer programs.

This chapter also covered a number of techniques used to manage and implement a structured system. Chief-programmer teams are used to develop the entire package. These teams consist of a chief programmer, a backup programmer, several programmers, a librarian, and one or more clerks or secretaries. This team then uses structured walkthroughs to monitor the progress of the project. Structured walkthroughs have the objective of producing the best error free code possible. In implementing a structured system, the top-down approach is normally used. Other approaches such as the bottom-up approach and various modifications of the top-down approach can also be used. With the top-down approach a module is completely designed, written, tested and debugged, and implemented before the next module is started.

KEY TERMS AND CONCEPTS

Backup programmer	Design heuristics	Structure charts
Bottom-up approach	Fan out	Structured design
Chief programmer	HIPO	Structured flowcharting
Chief-programmer teams	Loop	Structured programming
Cohesion	Pseudocode	Structured walkthroughs
Completely factored	Sequence	Top-down approach
Coupling	Span of control	Visual table of contents
Decision		

QUESTIONS

15–1. What is the difference between a structure chart and a visual table of contents?

15–2. What is the purpose of a HIPO diagram? How does it relate to a visual table of contents?

15–3. Describe the three allowable structures used in structured programming.

15–4. What is pseudocode, and why is it used?

15–5. Describe the role of the chief programmer.

15–6. What types of individuals are used in chief-programmer teams?

15–7. What is a structured walkthrough?

15–8. Contrast the top-down approach with the bottom-up approach in implementing a structured system.

15–9. What are some of the advantages of using the top-down approach?

15 Structured design

ANSWERS

1. T
2. T
3. F
4. T
5. T
6. T
7. T
8. F
9. T
10. F

MINIQUIZ

True or False

_____ 1. A structure chart shows the modules for smaller problems that make up the larger programming problem.

_____ 2. The control in a modular program should be from the top to the bottom.

_____ 3. In general, modules should have low cohesion and high coupling.

_____ 4. The number of modules below any given module is called fan out or span of control.

_____ 5. HIPO stresses what is to be done and not how a particular activity is accomplished.

_____ 6. The three structures used in structured programming are the sequence, the decision, and the loop structure.

_____ 7. There can only be one entering point and one exit point when using structured flowcharting.

_____ 8. Pseudocode is a high-level programming language used in both business and scientific applications.

_____ 9. Backup programmers and librarians are normally used with chief programmer teams.

_____ 10. A structured walkthrough is a new programming technique that allows a computer programmer to develop more lines of computer code in machine language.

Programmer productivity in a structured environment
Kenneth Hamilton and Arthur Block

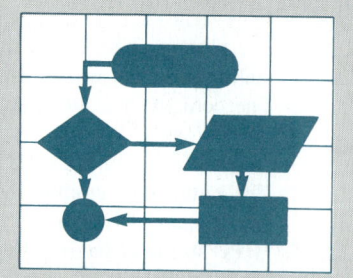

The project assignment at Manufacturers Hanover Trust Co. (MHT), New York, was to develop a wholesale demand deposit accounting system (WDDA) to replace an aging version developed during the late 60s. The term "wholesale" refers to a selection of large bank customers such as large corporations. Although the proposed system did not represent any special technological design problems, the implementation effort was considered extremely tight in light of the required delivery date—18 months from the start of design analysis.

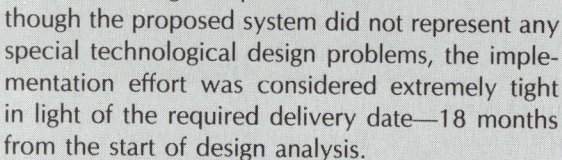

The logistics of the situation clearly required special considerations. New design and programming techniques along with our own project control approach were used in developing the new system. What follows is a synopsis of this experience and resulting findings concentrating in the area of design analysis through coding and testing. Of special interest is the use and management control over outside software firms to code and unit test the 526 separate modules that comprise the system. Also presented are statistical findings of programmer productivity in this environment.

The concepts presented are not represented as universally applicable nor limited to special situations. Rather, they provide a base on which to expand or from which to extract other ideas.

Parallel resources

The need to use parallel resources organized into multiple teams led to a requirement for a disciplined approach which would enable effective cooperation on the design task and provide explicit notations to control the communications process. The new "structured" design methodologies were considered as a key element in the solution. Such methodologies go beyond the traditional flow chart representations and provide a range of pictorial and logical notations to achieve a standardized, consistent and unambiguous means of communicating the design.

A further important benefit is derived from the new methodologies in aiding the staffing resource problem. Part of the aim of the new design methodologies is the simplification of the design and programming tasks so that they become less intuitive and inspirational and rely more on the application of well-defined procedures.

A number of design methodologies have been proposed in recent years. Each has its particular merits, philosophical basis, range of applicability, and so on. They all have a number of basic similarities such as "structured representation" of the design problem and "top down" implementation. Similarly, many have features that improve the testing, update and maintenance functions, primarily because of the clarity and traceability they provide in the dictated documentation. We chose to use the Michael Jackson methodology primarily because it appeared to be the most complete in its development. The Jackson methodology course work and supporting student material was extremely comprehensive in its "cook book" approach to design problem situations. Programmer productivity, resource and product statistics were collected so as to provide a predictive tool for future work. The analysis of these statistics will be presented.

In common with most automated systems and especially those newly developed, the question of system change quickly becomes a key element of concern. The management of change remains long after the system is delivered and throughout its use life cycle. To reduce the impact of change, the structured design methodology was augmented with a strict adherance to the "single function/single module" concept, thereby limiting functional changes to a discrete module or group of modules in the hierarchical structure. Additionally, a subset

---
Source: Reprinted from *Infosystems*, April 1979, copyright Hitchcock Publishing Company.

15 Structured design

FIGURE 1
Project life cycle

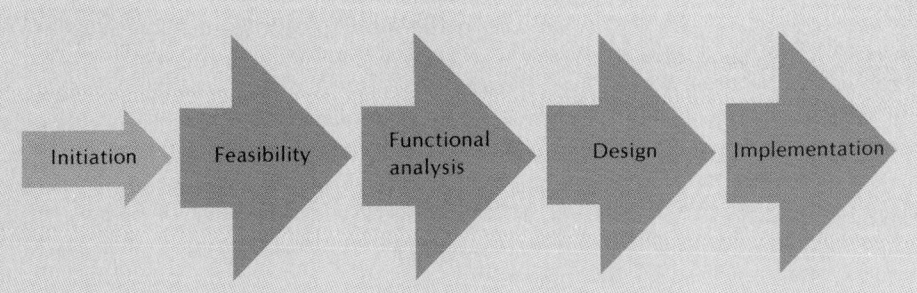

Initiation → Feasibility → Functional analysis → Design → Implementation

of the COBOL language was established as a coding standard to allow the potential for machine portability. The definition of file structures was controlled by the use of a data dictionary package which provides for the automated redefinition of file contents.

A key concept

A key concept in building a successful data processing application is the phased approach to project development (See Figure 1). By dividing the development process into a series of well-defined, easily-managed phases, MHT can present controlled cost and schedule estimates to the user.

Each phase ends in a checkpoint, where the user can decide, based on cost and system benefit information, whether to continue system development. At MHT four major phases are defined for the project life cycle as follows:

Feasibility. This phase determines whether a data processing system is feasible in terms of technical, operational and economic considerations. A feasibility study is performed, which results in a system proposal that outlines, in broad terms, the recommended approach in meeting the user's requirements.

Functional analysis. This phase determines what

FIGURE 2
Design analysis

Module, Module, Module → Component, Component → System

functions the data processing system is to perform from the user's point of view. This phase involves heavy user interaction in terms of his understanding of how the system will work and how it will be tested and installed in his area. The analysis phase produces the functional specifications which summarize system functions, input and output file considerations, and hardware and software requirements. This document is considered the "contract" between the user and systems and planning.

Design. As the analysis phase is concerned with what the system will do, the design phase is concerned with how the system will do it. During this phase, there is reduced user involvement, his primary concerns being employee training and development of acceptance test cases. This phase produces the design specifications which provide detailed information on the system design, conversion plan, and more accurate time and cost estimates.

Implementations. This phase is concerned with the actual construction of the system. Systems and planning develops programs and procedures, trains operators and users, tests and installs the system, and turns it over to the user.

The design of the WDDA system is based on a structured hierarchical network composed of components which are in turn, composed of modules (or programs) (See Figure 2). A module represents an individual unit of compiled COBOL code used to perform a single elementary function. Typically, a module is 80 procedure coding lines in length. During design analysis each module is individually designed and documented and represents the lowest level of project control and statistics gathering. A component consists of several modules (averaging 35) and represents a major system function such as editing, posting, reporting, etc. From the computer viewpoint, each component is a single link-edited, individually-loaded job step in the daily production job.

DISCUSSION QUESTIONS

1. Describe the major phases of a project for MHT.
2. What structured design techniques are being used to design the WDDA system?

about part IV

The purpose of Part IV is to explore computer systems in more detail. Many of these topics were introduced to you in Chapter 4. If you have not read Chapter 4, you should go back and read it carefully before you read any chapter in this part. After you have completed Chapter 4, you can read the chapters in this part in any order, although it is recommended that you cover the chapters sequentially.

Systems investigation, analysis, design and implementation are covered in Chapter 16. The development and use of management information systems and decision support systems are covered in Chapter 17. The data processing industry and the functioning of the data processing department are covered in Chapters 18 and 19.

This part also contains two supplements. The Supplement to Chapter 18 investigates computer waste and mistakes, crime, fraud, and privacy. The Supplement to Chapter 19 covers responsibilities, required educational backgrounds, career opportunities, salary ranges, and job-finding strategies for various data processing positions.

16	Systems analysis and design
17	Management information and decision support systems
18	The data processing industry
18 SUPPLEMENT	Social issues
19	The data processing department
19 SUPPLEMENT	Careers in Data Processing

PART IV
SYSTEMS

Systems analysis and design

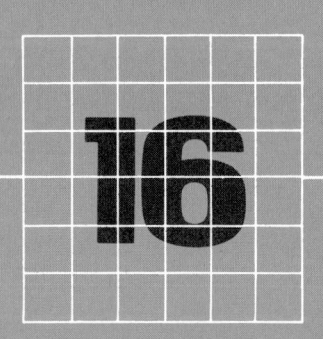

16

SYSTEMS INVESTIGATION
SYSTEMS ANALYSIS
    Assembling the study team
    Data collection
    Data analysis
    Report on the existing system
SYSTEMS DESIGN
    System design considerations
    Generating system design alternatives
    System evaluation and selection
SYSTEMS IMPLEMENTATION
    Personnel: hiring and training
    Site preparation
    Data preparation
    Installation
    Final testing
    Start up
BUYING SYSTEM METHODOLOGY

After completing Chapter 16, you will be able to:

- Describe what is involved in determining whether or not systems analysis and design should be employed for a given situation.
- List the steps of systems analysis.
- Discuss the procedures that are used in systems design.
- Describe the activities that are required for implementing the results of systems analysis and design.

During the life of any organization, there will be new problems, new needs, and a changing environment. These problems and needs call for the organization to investigate its current procedures and systems. Are the existing systems adequate? Should a new system be developed or should the old system be modified? Systems analysis and design attempts to answer these questions.

In data and information processing systems, analysis and design investigates the existing system and proposes new systems if necessary. This might require a modification of an existing computer system, the acquisition of new hardware and software, the hiring and training of data processing personnel, or in some cases, the recommended course of action may be to keep everything as it is.

The complete analysis and design cycle requires four basic steps. These are:

1. Systems investigation.
2. Systems analysis.
3. Systems design.
4. Systems implementation.

The overall purpose of *systems investigation* is to determine whether or not the entire data processing system or a part of the data processing system should be studied in detail to determine if improvements are possible and cost justified. Since systems analysis and design can be expensive and time consuming to undertake, systems investigation is one of the most important steps.

Systems analysis is a study of the existing system. The overall purpose of systems analysis is to determine if there are any problems or shortcomings concerning the existing system. If the organization or its environment is rapidly changing, systems analysis also investigates the ability of the existing system to handle future problems and situations.

Systems design is a detailed description of a new system that attempts to solve some of the problems of the existing system and to provide a superior data and information processing system. This could require major hardware and software changes or a few simple modifications of the existing system.

Systems implementation consists of all of the steps that are necessary to place the new system into operation. Depending on the complexity of the new system, implementation can be a minor task or a very difficult, time consuming, and expensive set of activities. In the rest of this chapter, we will explore the steps and procedures of systems investigation, analysis, design, and implementation.

SYSTEMS INVESTIGATION

The analysis and design cycle begins with a desire to find a better data and information processing system. The particular systems that will undergo analysis and design are determined during systems investigation. Systems investigation begins when an individual or a group suggest that a problem be investigated or that part or all of the data processing system be studied for possible improvement. The following groups or individuals have initiated this type of study:

1. Data processing manager.
2. Systems analysts.
3. Computer programmer.
4. Other data processing personnel.
5. President of the company or organization.
6. Managers.
7. Other employees of the organization.
8. Government agencies.
9. Customers.
10. Stockholders.
11. The union.
12. The competition.
13. Other outside groups.

In the past, analysis and design was initiated by someone in the data processing department, such as the data processing manager or a systems analyst. As managers and other nondata processing personnel learn more about the capabilities and limitations of computer systems, the initiation of analysis and design is being called for by people outside of the data processing department. A manager dissatisfied with the way the data processing department is filling orders may request the analysis and design of the sales ordering application. The stockholders, the union, or even the president of the company might initiate the analysis and design of a particular aspect of the data processing system. Federal agencies can indirectly cause systems analysis and design by introducing new legislation and regulations that require additional reports or modified reports and documents. The competition can also indirectly cause systems analysis and design to be conducted. If the competition is doing a better job, the data processing system may be studied to determine if it can be improved to help outdo or overcome the competition. There are a number of other ways in which systems analysis and design can be initiated. Entire companies can be bought, sold, merged, and reorganized. These types of major changes will usually result in major changes in the data processing system.

The first step in performing the systems investigation is to form an *investigation team*. This team is made up of data processing personnel and top or middle level managers. The exact make up of the team depends on the size of the company and nature of the investigation. This team is then charged with the responsibility of gathering data, analyzing the data, preparing a report on the justification of systems analysis and design, and presenting the results of their findings to top level managers, who will make the final decision concerning the proposed analysis and design. In larger organizations, several teams will be making a systems investigation at the same time. Due to limited resources, these teams usually compete with each other. After all of the presentations have been made by the teams, top level managers will select problems or needs that require the most attention or that will result in the greatest financial gain to the organization.

The actual data collection and analysis performed during systems investigation is identical to the type of data collection and analysis that is made for those projects and problem areas that are selected. Interviews, questionnaires, cost/benefit analysis, and so forth can be used at this stage. These topics will be covered in the next section.

Once the data has been collected and analyzed by the teams, a report is made on the feasibility and cost justification of performing a complete systems analysis and design study. The study teams will try to convince top management to continue the study. Therefore, this report is important, and it should be carefully drafted. Even if systems analysis and design are not undertaken for a particular system, system investigation may reveal areas that could substantially improve the system. When detailed systems analysis and design is to be undertaken for a system, the president or chairman of the board may issue a directive to all employees to support and cooperate with the analysis and design.

SYSTEMS ANALYSIS

After a project has been given approval for detailed analysis and design in the investigation stage, the next step is to perform a detailed analysis of the existing system. As discussed previously, the overall emphasis is to uncover some of the inherent problems and limitations of the existing system.

Systems analysis requires the completion of four steps that are performed in the following order:

1. Establishment of a study team.
2. Collection of appropriate data.
3. Analysis of the data and the existing system.
4. Preparation of a report on the existing system.

Assembling the study team

The first step in systems analysis is to formulate a team of individuals to study the existing system. This *study team* is not only given the responsibility of investigating the condition of the existing system, but it is usually given the responsibility of performing systems design and aiding in implementation of the new system as well.

The members of the study team usually included the members of the investigation team that completed the initial investigation report. Depending on the size of the problem or need to be investigated, a number of additional people are placed on the study team. The selection of these additional members is important. Without the support and involvement of middle and top level managers, the efforts of analysis and design may never get implemented or may never be fully utilized if it is implemented. This is due primarily to a reluctance to change on the part of managers and other employees of the organization. Today, many study teams have representatives from management, marketing, production, accounting, or finance. These individuals can help in getting acceptance of the results, in implementing the results, in negotiating for better contracts if additional hardware and software are required, and so on.

Once the study team is assembled, it develops a list of specific objectives and activities. A schedule for obtaining the objectives and completing the specific activities is also developed along with a statement of the resources that are required at each stage, such as clerical personnel, computer time, and so forth. Major milestones are normally established to help the study team monitor its progress and to determine if there are any problems or delays in performing systems analysis.

Since one objective of analysis and design is to support managerial decision making, it is important to go beyond the inadequacies of the existing system. Systems analysis should also investigate the current decision-making process and how the decision-making process could be improved if more accurate, timely, and relevent information were available. If the decision orientation is not used, it is possible to end up with a computerized system that is also inadequate and full of problems.

Data collection

In the systems investigation report, various problems or needs were outlined. It is the purpose of *data collection* to seek additional information about the problems or needs under investigation. During this process, emphasis is given to the *strengths* and *weaknesses* of the existing data and information processing system.

Data collection requires that two steps be performed in sequence. The first step is to identify and locate the various sources of data. In general, there are both *internal sources* and *external sources* of data. The second step is to actually collect or capture the data. This may require a number of tools, such as interviewing, direct observation, and the development of questionnaires.

The internal and external data sources that relate to the system under investigation are identified. Other data sources that are not relevant to the system under investigation are not identified or used. The major internal sources of data are (1) organizational charts, (2) forms and documents, (3) procedure manuals and written policies, (4) financial reports, (5) data processing documentation manuals, (6) top, middle, and low level managers, (7) other employees of the organization, (8) staff personnel such as lawyers, accountants, internal consultants, and others, (9) the data processing manager, (10) systems analysts and computer programmers, and (11) other data processing personnel. Some of the external sources of data include: (1) computer manufacturers and vendors, (2) customers, (3) suppliers, (4) stockholders, (5) government documents, (6) local, state, and federal government agencies, (7) competitors, (8) outside groups, such as environmental groups or special interest groups, (9) newspapers, (10) trade journals related to the organization,

(11) data processing journals, (12) textbooks, and (13) external consultants and other professional groups. Once the data sources have been identified, the next step is to collect data that relates to the existing system being studied.

One of the most popular and effective data collection techniques is the *interview*. In a **structured interview**, the questions are written in advance. Some structured interviews only allow for a certain type of response, such as "yes" or "no" or a response that ranges from "strongly agree" to "strongly disagree" or from "not important" to "very important." Other structured interviews are open ended responses, where the person being interviewed will respond with a few sentences for each question. In an **unstructured interview,** the questions are not written in advance, and the person doing the interview relies on his or her experience in asking the best questions to uncover some of the inherent problems and weaknesses of the existing system. Before the interview is conducted, a few sample interviews should be conducted to make sure that the right questions are being asked. This is called **pilot testing.** When the members of the study team are satisfied with the interview process, the interviews are scheduled and conducted. In conducting the interviews, it is important to select a location that is convenient, comfortable, and private. During the interview, the person conducting the interview should be straightforward and should tell the respondent that all individual responses will be kept confidential. Good interviewing is an art requiring experience and excellent personal relations skills.

Another data collection technique is **direct observation.** With this approach, one or more of the members of the study team directly observe the existing system in action. The actual operation of the data processing department and the use of the outputs of the data processing department can be directly observed. Members of the study team can see how data flows between the production department and the accounting department, how sales orders are processed, how stockouts are handled, the time it takes to transfer information from one department to another, and more. By direct observation, members of the study team can determine what forms and procedures are adequate and which ones are inadequate and need improvement. Direct observation also allows the study team to trace both *formal* and *informal* information flows. The systems and personnel that will be directly observed should be notified, but the exact data and time of the direct observation should not be disclosed. This prevents people that are being observed from changing their actual operating procedures and practices while being observed. Direct observation can reveal problems and areas of concern that otherwise would have gone undetected. Direct observation, however, does require great skill. The observer must be able to see what is *really* happening and not be influenced by his or her own attitudes or feelings. In addition, the observer needs good writing skills to record his or her observations for other study team members.

When the data sources are many and geographically spread over a wide area, *questionnaires* may be the best data collection approach. Like interviews, questionnaires can be either *structured* or *unstructured*. In most cases, a *pilot study* is conducted to fine tune the questionnaire. A *follow-up question-*

naire can also be used to capture the opinions of those who did not respond to the original questionnaire.

There are a number of other data collection techniques that can be employed. Again, the overall emphasis is to collect data on the existing system. In some cases, *phone calls* are an excellent method. In other cases, activities may be *simulated* to see how the existing system reacts. Thus, fake sales orders, stockouts, customer complaints, and data flow bottlenecks may be created to see how the existing system responds to these situations. *Statistical sampling* and *testing* techniques can also be used.

Data analysis

The data collected in its raw form from the data collection stage is usually not adequate to make a determination of the effectiveness and efficiency of the existing data processing system. This data needs to be manipulated into a form that is useable by the members of the study team. The manipulation is called *data analysis*. Some of the most commonly used techniques are:

1. Grid charts.
2. Systems flowcharts.
3. Program flowcharts.
4. Decision tables.
5. Structure charts.
6. HIPO diagrams.
7. Layout charts.

Grid charts are used to show the relationship between the various applications and systems. Data that is used by several different applications and for different purposes can be displayed in a grid chart. System and program flowcharts reveal how the various systems input and process data to produce the various reports and documents. System flowcharts reveal the overall structure of an application, while program flowcharts reveal the detailed operation of the computer programs. When a number of decisions are made, a decision table can be used to reveal what decisions are made under various conditions. If a structured approach is used, structure charts and HIPO diagrams can be used to graphically display what functions are being performed. To document inputs and outputs of the existing system, layout charts can be used. These charts reveal the exact layout and format of input and output documents. A detailed description of each of these techniques can be found in Part III.

The cost of the existing system may also be investigated. *Direct, indirect, fixed,* and *variable* costs can be identified and determined for the existing system. Direct costs are costs that are incurred as a direct result of the existing system, while indirect costs occur with or without the existing system in operation. Indirect costs include lighting, air conditioning, staff personnel, insurance costs, and so on. Fixed and variable costs can also be associated with the existing system. A fixed cost is one that is incurred whether the system is operating or not, while the variable costs are costs that are incurred when the system is in operation. Fixed costs would include the cost of equipment, hardware, software, and so on.

Report on the existing system

Systems analysis concludes with a formal report on the status of the existing system. This report contains both the strengths and weaknesses of the existing system. Particular attention is placed on those areas that could use improvement. This leads into the systems design stage. The contents of the typical report on the existing system are given in Figure 16–1.

Table of contents
Background information
Problem or need statement
Data collection
    Questionnaire results
    Interview results
    Organizational documents and forms
    Other data sources
Data analysis
    Problems of the existing system
    Cost of changing the existing system
    Benefits of changing the existing system
    Cost benefit comparison
Recommendations
Appendixes of documents, tables, and charts
Glossary of terms

FIGURE 16–1
Report on the existing system

SYSTEMS DESIGN

The emphasis of *systems design* is to develop a new system that overcomes some of the shortcomings and limitations of the existing system. If the problems are minor, only small modifications are required. On the other hand, major changes may be suggested by systems analysis. In these cases, major investments in additional hardware, software, and additional personnel may be necessary. Regardless of the complexity and scope of the new system, it is the purpose of systems design to develop the best possible new system. This involves several steps.

1. System design considerations.
2. Generating systems design alternatives.
3. Evaluating and selecting the best system.

System design considerations

The design of the new system begins with a complete description of the outputs and reports that will achieve the objectives established above. For

16 Systems analysis and design

example, one of the objectives might be to reduce the number of stockouts. This could be accomplished by keeping a current inventory master file. Then an exception report can be generated every time an inventory level drops below a specified reorder point.

Once the outputs of the new data processing system have been described, then the data that is required to produce this output is listed. In most cases, this data will already exist. All data that does not currently exist in a useable form is described and procedures necessary to capture this data are developed. In addition to determining the input requirements of the new system, detailed data base and file designs are required. While it is beyond the scope of this book to investigate file and data base design and structure, it should be pointed out that these activities need to be completed during systems design.

The resources of the organization must also be considered in systems design. Normally this means that systems design is constrained or restricted by the limited resources of the organization. One of the most important restrictions is the *cost* of the new system. Usually, a ceiling or upper cost level is set on the new system. Another important constraint is *time*. How long can the organization wait for the new system to be developed and implemented? Most organizations also place time restrictions and deadlines on new projects. Depending on the organization, there may be other constraints as well. Personnel, hardware, software, and the physical site for the new system can limit the scope and size of the new system.

The final design consideration is documentation. The documentation of the new system is very similar to the documentation of the existing system. Tools such as flowcharts, decision tables, grid charts, and so on can be employed.

Generating system design alternatives

In the past, system design ended with the documentation of the proposed new system. The new system was simply implemented and any additional hardware or software was acquired from the existing computer vendor. Today, system study teams are becoming more aggressive in obtaining cost effective systems. Fierce bargaining and competitive bidding have resulted in superior systems at the best possible price. This new approach requires generating alternative designs, evaluating these designs, and selecting the best designs for the price.

When additional hardware and software are not required, alternative designs are generated by the members of the study team. The study team may also wish to get other personnel involved in generating alternative designs if the new system is more complex and involved than the existing system. If new hardware and software is to be acquired from an outside vendor, a formal *request for proposals* (RFP) should be made. The contents of the RFP should include some background information, the procedures that are to be followed during the selection process, a description of the existing company and data processing system, a description of the proposed data processing system and its requirements, and a list of exactly what will be expected from the data processing vendor or manufacturer. The major part of the RFP is the description of the existing data processing system and the proposed data processing system.

The request for proposals should be carefully written. The procedures to be followed are especially important. The computer vendors should be told which person is to be contacted on the study team, how their proposals will be evaluated, and the deadlines for proposals. In addition, the necessary support from the data processing vendor, such as training, maintenance, installation restrictions, and so on should be stated clearly.

System evaluation and selection

The final step in systems design is to evaluate the various systems design alternatives and to select that design which meets the needs of the new system at the least cost. Normally a preliminary evaluation and a final evaluation are conducted before one of the designs is selected from the alternatives. When outside equipment, software, support, maintenance, and so on is required, a contract between the organization and outside vendor is required.

Preliminary evaluation begins after the deadline for the submission of proposals from data processing vendors. The purpose of this preliminary evaluation is to eliminate some of the proposals. Several vendors can usually be eliminated by investigating their proposals in detail. The remaining vendors are asked to make a formal presentation to the study team. Small demonstrations may also be conducted. Furthermore, the data processing vendors should be asked to supply a list of organizations that are using their equipment for a similar purpose. These organizations are then contacted and asked to evaluate their hardware, software, and the vendor. It is also a good idea to ask these companies for further references that can be contacted. After evaluating the presentations, demonstrations, and the evaluations from other companies using similar equipment, the list of data processing vendors is usually reduced to a few vendors.

The final evaluation begins with a detailed investigation of the hardware, software, and support offered by each of the remaining vendors. The data processing vendors should be asked to make a final presentation and to arrange for an extensive demonstration. The demonstration should be as close to real operating conditions as possible. Such applications as payroll, inventory control, and billing should be conducted with a large amount of test data. The same data and applications should be used by each vendor. These types of tests are called *benchmark* tests. Sometimes, it takes a day or longer for each demonstration, but this is one of the best ways to learn more about the capabilities and limitations of a proposed data processing system.

After the final presentations and demonstrations, it is necessary to make the final evaluation and selection. During this stage, a detailed analysis of the hardware, software and vendor is made. Cost comparisons, hardware performance, delivery dates, price, modularity, backup facilities, available software training, and maintenance factors are considered. Although it is good to compare computer speeds, storage capacities, and other similar characteristics, this is not enough. It is necessary to carefully analyze how the characteristics of the proposed data processing systems will help the organization or company solve its problems and obtain its goals and objectives.

Although the exact procedure that is used to make the final evaluation and selection varies from one organization to the next, there are three commonly used approaches. These are (1) *group consensus,* (2) *cost/benefit analysis,* and (3) *point evaluation.* In group consensus, a decision-making group is appointed and given the responsibility of making the final evaluation and selection. Usually, this group includes the members of the study team.

Cost/benefit analysis is an approach that lists all of the costs and benefits of each proposed data processing system. All of the costs of a proposed data processing system are listed on one side, and all of the benefits expressed in monetary values are listed on the other side.

One of the disadvantages of cost/benefit analysis is the difficulty of determining monetary values for all of the benefits. Another approach that does not use monetary value is to use a *point evaluation system.* Each factor is given an importance weight. This weight is in percent. Then, each proposed data processing system is evaluated in terms of this factor and given a score that might range from 0 to 100. The scores are multiplied by the weights, and the weighted scores are added together. The computer system with the greatest total score is selected. Figure 16–2 shows a simplified version of this process.

	System A		System B*	
Factor's importance	Evaluation	Weighted evaluation	Evaluation	Weighted evaluation
Hardware 35% Software 40% Vendor 25% support		95 × 35% = 33.25 70 × 40% = 28 85 × 25% = 21.25		75 × 35% = 26.25 95 × 40% = 38.00 90 × 25% = 22.5
Totals 100%		82.5		86.75

Note: System B is selected.

FIGURE 16–2
The point evaluation system

In actual practice, most organizations use one or more of these evaluation techniques. In some cases, the best decision is to do nothing.

The contract

One of the most important steps in the selection process is to develop a good contract if new computer facilities are to be acquired. Most computer vendors have standard contracts, but these contracts were designed to protect the computer vendor and not necessarily the organization buying the computer facilities. More and more organizations are developing their own contracts. These contracts stipulate exactly what is expected from the computer vendor and the interaction between the computer vendor and the organization. All equipment specifications, software, training, installation, maintenance, and so on are clearly stated. Furthermore, all dates for the various stages of installation and implementation are stipulated. In addition, actions to be taken by the computer vendor in case of a delay or a problem needs to be specified. Some organizations include *penalty clauses* in the contract in case the computer vendor is unable to meet its obligation at the specified date.

SYSTEMS IMPLEMENTATION

After a data processing system has been selected, a number of tasks must be completed before the system is installed and ready to operate. This preparation includes the hiring and training of personnel, site preparation, data preparation, installation, final testing and start up.

In order to have a smooth and effective implementation, a schedule is made that describes when each step of implementation is to be completed. Since a delay in one of the steps can delay the entire process, it is important to carefully monitor the progress of implementation. This can be done by establishing *milestones,* which indicate the date of completion for major activities of implementation. To help establish these milestones and deadlines, management science techniques such as **program evaluation and review technique** (PERT) or **critical path method** (CPM) can be employed. These techniques establish the earliest time that an activity can be started, the latest time that an activity can be finished without delaying the entire process, and the slack time for each activity. In addition, these techniques can be used to determine the least cost way to reducing the total implementation completion time *(crashing),* the budget that is required to complete the project *(project budgeting),* and the resources that will be required during implementation *(resource leveling).* Since these sophisticated techniques are normally covered in a management science or operations research course, they will not be covered in this book.

Personnel: Hiring and training

Depending on the size of the new data processing system, a number of data processing personnel will have to be hired and in some cases trained. A data processing manager, systems analysts, computer programmers, keypunch or data entry operators, and similar data processing personnel may be needed for the new system. Normally, the data processing manager can be hired and given the responsibility of hiring the remaining data processing personnel.

Since the eventual success of any data processing system depends on how the system is used by other people and managers within the organization, a training program should be conducted for the employees who will be using or dealing with the computer system. Fears and apprehensions about the new computer system need to be eliminated through these training programs. Employees should be acquainted with the capabilities and limitations of the computer system, and they should know how to use the new system to help them perform their jobs.

Site preparation

The actual location of the new data processing system needs to be prepared. For a small computer system, this may simply mean rearranging the furniture in an office to make room for the computer. With a larger computer system, this process is not so easy. Larger computer systems may require special wiring and air conditioning. One or two rooms may have to be completely renovated to accommodate the new computer system. Additional furniture may have to be purchased. A special flooring may have to be built under which the cables connecting the various computer components are placed, and a new security system may have to be installed to protect the computer equipment.

In addition to the actual location of the computer, other rooms and offices may have to be added or changed. The data processing manager, systems analysts, and computer programmers will need offices and space to work. Room for such devices as keypunch machines or key-to-tape devices will have to be provided. Some companies prefer to have a special room or a fireproof safe for backup tape files. A supply room will be needed to store computer cards, paper for the line printer, and so on. In general, any space, furniture, equipment or other item that is needed for the new computer system to be operational has to be arranged in advance of the computer installation.

Data preparation

If an organization has been processing its data manually, all of the master files are stored manually. These files could be stored in filing cabinets, on 3 × 5 or 5 × 7 cards, in journals, or similar devices. Employee master files, inventory master files, accounts receivable master files, accounts payable master files, and customer master files are a few examples of the files that might be stored manually. If this organization is about to computerize, all of these files must be converted into computer files. This is called *data preparation* or *conversion*. All of the permanent data must be placed on a permanent storage device such as computer cards, magnetic tape, or disk.

Usually the organization hires some part-time data entry operators or a service company to place the manual data onto computer cards, magnetic tape, or disk. Once the data has been converted from manual files into computer files, the part-time data entry operators or the service company is no longer needed. The computer programs will maintain and update these computer files.

Installation

Installation is the process of physically placing the computer equipment on the site and making it operational. Although it is normally the responsibility of the computer manufacturer to install the computer equipment, someone from the organization should oversee this process. The data processing manager is usually the person designated to oversee the installation. The data processing manager usually makes sure that all of the equipment specified in the contract is installed in the proper location. After the data processing system is installed, several tests are performed by the computer manufacturer to insure that the equipment is operating as it should.

At this point in time, the organization should have all of the hardware, software, and personnel it needs to make the data processing system fully operational. Before the data processing system is used for any processing, final testing should be conducted, and the entire system should go through a systematic start up procedure.

Final testing

Final testing involves completely testing the entire data processing system. This requires the testing of each of the individual programs, testing the entire system of programs, and volume testing. Testing each program is accomplished by developing test data that will force the computer to execute every statement in the program. In addition, each program is tested with abnormal data to determine how each program will handle problems with bad or erroneous data. System testing requires the testing of all of the programs together. It is not uncommon to have the output from one program become the input for another program. In these cases, system testing insures that the output data from one program can be used as input for another program. Finally, volume testing is performed to insure that the entire data processing system can handle a large amount of data under normal operating conditions.

Start up

Start up is the last stage of implementation. It begins with the finally tested data processing system, and when start up is finished, the data processing system will be fully operational. Although there are several approaches, one of the preferred methods is to slowly *phase in* the use of the data processing system while slowly *phasing out* the old manual system. This is accomplished by starting one application at a time, such as payroll. This application is run on the new data processing system, while it is also being run manually. When everyone is confident that the new data processing system is performing this application as expected, then the old manual system is phased out. This process is repeated for each application until the new data processing system is running every application.

After start up, final checks are performed to make sure that the entire system is operating according to specification. These controls include *hardware controls, software controls, operating controls,* and *general controls.* Some of these procedures will be covered in Chapter 19.

BUYING SYSTEM METHODOLOGY

In this chapter, we have discussed the procedures that are necessary in performing systems analysis and design. These steps include systems investigation, systems analysis, systems design, and systems implementation. These procedures can be expensive and time-consuming to perform. Furthermore, a qualified and skilled study team is needed. Some organizations simply do not have the time or the resources to undertake this type of study, and therefore, many organizations purchase system methodology.

Like application software, systems analysis and design can be performed by an outside company for a fee. This is called *buying system methodology.* Most of the large accounting firms and major computer manufacturers provide this type of service. In addition, there are companies that specialize in performing systems analysis and design.

There are a number of advantages of hiring an outside firm to perform systems analysis and design. These firms are normally experienced in this type of work, and they have the potential of doing a better job for less. In most cases, they can do the job in less time. They can also be more objective in locating the *real* problems and in suggesting the best solutions. Furthermore, the company purchasing the system methodology does not have to expend its time and manpower to perform the study. As mentioned previously, some companies don't have a choice. They simply do not have the time or resources to perform this type of study.

There are, however, a number of disadvantages of purchasing system methodology. To begin with, it can be very expensive. Accounting firms and computer manufacturers may have hidden motives for performing systems analysis and design for a company. They may put pressure on the company to purchase expensive accounting services or computer equipment. While there is nothing wrong with this, the buyer should be aware of these hidden motives. If a computer manufacturer is hired, it may be difficult or awkward to purchase computer equipment and systems from another computer manufacturer. There is no guarantee that an outside company will do a better job.

The same steps and precautions used in selecting a computer vendor should be used when buying system methodology. The company purchasing the system methodology should perform preliminary studies, send out RFP's and get references from similar clients. Presentations should be made, and a favorable contract should be negotiated. Like any other investment, the company purchasing the system methodology should carefully and completely evaluate several alternatives before any decision is made.

SUMMARY

The concepts and tools of systems analysis and design were covered in this chapter. The four basic steps are systems investigation, systems analysis, systems design, and systems implementation.

The purpose of systems investigation is to determine which systems should be studied in more detail. The actual investigation may be initiated by people inside of the organization, people outside of the organization, or governmental agencies and documents. After an individual or group has initiated the investigation, an investigation team is formed to look into the problem or need. This team does some preliminary data collection and analysis and prepares a report to managers. The report is a recommendation concerning whether or not the system should be studied in more detail.

If a complete study is to be performed, systems analysis is the first step after systems investigation. The overall purpose of systems analysis is to make a detailed investigation of the existing system. The emphasis is on problems and areas of possible improvement. Systems analysis involves establishing a study team, collection of appropriate data, analysis of the data and of the existing system, and the preparing of a report concerning the existing system.

While the systems analysis investigates the existing system, systems design is concerned with developing a new system that will solve some of the problems and needs of the existing system. Systems design includes some general systems design considerations, generating alternative designs, evaluating alternative designs, and selecting the best design.

Systems implementation begins with the final design and ends up with the final system in full operation. The overall purpose of implementation is to smoothly and efficiently place the new system into operation as soon as possible and at the least cost. The steps of systems implementation are the hiring and training of personnel, site preparation, data preparation, installation, final testing, and start up.

KEY TERMS AND CONCEPTS

Systems investigation	Unstructured interviews	HIPO diagrams
Systems design	Pilot testing	Layout charts
Systems analysis	Direct observation	Direct costs
Systems implementation	Follow up questionnaire	Indirect costs
Investigation team	Grid charts	Fixed costs
Interviews	System flowcharts	Variable costs
Questionnaires	Program flowcharts	Request for proposals (RFPs)
Cost/benefit analysis	Decision tables	Cost/benefit analysis
Structured interviews	Structure charts	Benchmark tests

QUESTIONS

16–1. Describe what is involved in the systems investigation.

16–2. What is involved in determining the system objectives?

16–3. What is an RFP? What does it contain, and how is it used in the selection phase?

16–4. Describe what is done during systems design.

16-5. What activities are performed during final evaluation and selection?

16-6. Briefly discuss the hiring and training of personnel.

16-7. What is site preparation?

16-8. Why is data preparation necessary?

16-9. Describe installation and final testing.

16-10. What is the start up process?

ANSWERS

1. T
2. T
3. F
4. T
5. T
6. F
7. F
8. T
9. T
10. F

MINIQUIZ

True or False

_____ 1. The first step in performing the systems investigation is to form an investigation team.

_____ 2. Once data has been collected and analyzed during the investigation stage, a report is made on the feasibility and cost justification of performing a complete systems analysis and design study.

_____ 3. The first step of systems analysis is to collect the appropriate data.

_____ 4. One of the most popular and effective data collection techniques is the interview.

_____ 5. Structured and unstructured questionnaires can be used during systems analysis.

_____ 6. The emphasis of systems design is to locate the shortcomings and limitations of the existing system.

_____ 7. The first step of systems design is to generate systems design alternatives.

_____ 8. A benchmark test can be used in evaluating and selecting the best data processing system.

_____ 9. To help establish milestones and deadlines for systems implementation, such techniques as program evaluation and review technique can be used.

_____ 10. Start Up is the process of selecting a date when the new system is to be implemented and the old system is to be completed removed from operation.

Users drive harder bargains

"The honeymoon is over," notes Joseph Auer, president of International Computer Negotiations in Winter Park, Florida. "Users have heard too many horror stories or experienced too many malfunctions not to want to protect themselves."

Adds Joseph Ferreira, vice president of The Diebold Group, Inc.: "In the past when you dealt with major vendors, they said: 'Here's our contract'—and that was it. You signed. But then users began dealing with some of the new people on the scene and discovered they could get concessions and set their own terms. They then turned around and began flexing their muscles against the big mainframe manufacturers."

Even with this tougher negotiating stance, however, users are still often at a disadvantage in bargaining with vendors, notes Auer, a former professional football running back for the Buffalo Bills, Miami Dolphins and Atlanta Falcons who learned about negotiating the hard way in salary battles with tough National Football League club owners. "At most, the user comes into the negotiating arena every three to five years, so he isn't really experienced," Auer explains. "And he's under the pressure of running an ongoing business, which makes his position even more difficult." The vendor, on the other hand, brings in a negotiating team that has probably put together hundreds of deals and knows every loophole and bargaining ploy in the book, observes Auer, who worked for a major software vendor after hanging up his football cleats.

Using professionals

That's where Auer's firm, and others like it, come in. They represent banks, utilities and other concerns in their transactions with computer manufacturers—and the approach Auer and his negotiating team take is instructive to any company planning to buy or lease a computer.

More often than not, ICN—which charges $1,250 a day for its negotiating services, including access to its data base of contract provisions—is brought in by a firm's top management or a financial executive rather than a data-processing professional. "The DP executive who is the least bit paranoid and insecure about his job, or who thinks he's an expert because he has negotiated three computer deals, figures he doesn't need us," says ICN vice president Ken Brindle. Interestingly, when ICN does get a call from the computer room, the DP manager is usually someone who is sure of himself and who has been able to negotiate better-than-average contracts in the past. "He recognizes that if he can do well negotiating on his own, he probably can get an even better deal for his company working with people who negotiate hundreds of conracts a year," Brindle says.

Once ICN is on the job, Auer and his associates begin preparing the client for the upcoming bargaining session. The company's DP manager, its corporate counsel and representatives from the purchasing and financial departments are each given a checklist of 110 topics that could come up in the negotiations—for example, whether the user will receive financial credits if the system malfunctions during its life span; whether the user can withhold partial payments for the computer until it has passed all tests and is fully operational; and the need for a "favored nation" provision insuring that the user is getting the vendor's maximum discount. The recipients are then asked to put a priority rating on each item, using a 1-to-10 scale.

"The idea," Auer explains, "is to come up with a compendium of items that accurately reflects the objectives of the company as a whole. That way, we've established a common ground before we enter into discussions."

Training Drill

Next, Auer puts the client's negotiating team through a training drill that would do Vince Lom-

---

Source: Reprinted with the special permission of *Dun's Review*, July 1978, Copyright 1978, Dun & Bradstreet Publications Corporation.

bardi proud. An overall bargaining strategy as well as the various tactics to be employed are mapped out, and each member of the client's negotiating team is given a specific assignment. Finally, Auer plays the devil's advocate, assuming the role of vendor as the team simulates a negotiating session.

Later, reviewing the rehearsal, which frequently is recorded on videotape, Auer and the client further refine their game plan. Auer even cues the various team members on when to be emotional and when to be calm and conciliatory. He may even suggest that one team member assume the role of "bad guy" and another play "good guy" á la the old police interrogation ploy.

DISCUSSION QUESTIONS

1. Why is the user at a disadvantage in negotiating for a computer?
2. What can be done to strengthen the position of the user or computer customer?

Management information and decision support systems

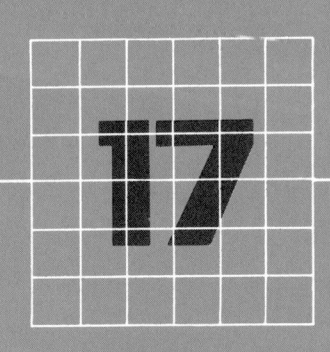

17

MIS AND DSS IN PERSPECTIVE
THE SYSTEMS FRAMEWORK
    The systems approach
    The use of models
    General model of the organization
    Theory of management
THE FUNCTIONAL APPROACH
DESIGN AND IMPLEMENTATION CONSIDERATIONS

After completing Chapter 17, you will be able to:

- Contrast data processing, management information, and decision support systems.
- Discuss the systems framework.
- Describe various functional systems.
- Discuss what is involved in designing and implementing a management information system or a decision support system.

Computers have done an excellent job of preparing pay checks, sending out invoices and bills, and reporting accounts receivable. In general, the computer has excelled at performing routine bookkeeping activities. Computers, however, have not always been helpful to managers and decision makers. Some of the problems were introduced to you as early as Chapter 1. Without a question, one of the greatest challenges of the next decade is to unlock the potential of the computer to help managers and decision makers.

The failure of computer systems to help managers and decision makers is not due to a lack of trying. Since the 1960s, data processing personnel have been attempting to develop applications and programs for this purpose with mixed results. With different types of organizations and varying management styles, it is very difficult to harness the power of the computer to help managers and decision makers perform their jobs.

During the last decade, we have seen a literal explosion in the generation of data and information. This proliferation of data and information has been so great that libraries do not have the time or resources to catalogue or cross reference the information. The data and information is just there, and it is almost impossible to retrieve it. The *President's Domestic Council Committee on the Right to Privacy* recently reported that from one-third to one-half of the *gross national product* (GNP) of the United States is attributable to the production and distribution of information and knowledge. With this explosion of knowledge and information, some computers have actually had a decline in the percent of information they store to the total information available in the company or organization. In order to fully realize the potential of any computer system, the system should be able to manipulate and use this vast information resource.

The overall purpose of this chapter is to explore how computers can be used to provide valuable information and to support managerial decision making. A system that provides management information is called a **management information system** (MIS), and a system that supports managerial decision making is called a **decision support system** (DSS). Today, the *American Association of Collegiate Schools of Business* (AACSB) member schools require coverage of MIS, and this chapter along with material throughout this book, has been developed to satisfy this requirement.

MIS AND DSS IN PERSPECTIVE

In addition to producing routine bookkeeping documents, a data processing system has the potential to help managers perform their jobs. This is accomplished by having the data processing system produce information that is used to help managers make good decisions. This process is shown in Figure 17–1. As you can see from Figure 17–1, data processing leads to information, information leads to a decision, and the decision leads to some type of perfor-

FIGURE 17–1
From data processing to performance

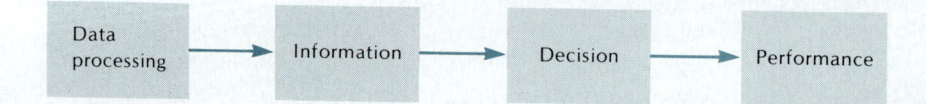

Data processing → Information → Decision → Performance

17 Management information and decision support systems

mance or result. Over the years, data processing systems have evolved into management information systems, and management information systems have evolved into decision support systems. These systems will be discussed below in more detail.

As discussed in Chapter 1, a **data processing system** is an organized collection of people, procedures, and devices used to produce useful outputs. The functions performed by a data processing system include input, classifying, sorting, summarizing, reproducing, calculating, storing, and output. The first commercial data system was installed at the General Electric Appliance Park in Kentucky in 1954. Since all computers attempt to produce useful outputs and documents, almost all computer systems are data processing systems. These outputs could be pay checks, bills, invoices, a list of accounts receivables, reports and information supplied to managers, and so forth.

A **management information system** is an organized collection of people, procedures, and devices used to provide past, present, and projection information. This information can relate to internal and external intelligence, and it can assist with planning, staffing, controlling, directing, and organizing. The overall purpose of a management information system is to provide the right information to the right manager or decision maker at the right time. As we have defined it, a management information is a specialized case of a data processing system. All management information systems are also data processing systems, but only those data processing systems that provide useful past, present, and projection information can be considered a management information system.

While the concept of using a data processing system to produce meaningful information existed since the first data processing systems, it wasn't until the mid 1950s and early 1960s that H. Luhn and S. Furth of IBM started using computers and punched card machines to produce meaningful information using a formal system. This system is called *information retrieval*. Today, most computer and data processing systems have the potential of being management information systems. As discussed in Chapter 4, most management information systems produce *scheduled reports, exception reports,* and *demand reports*. Furthermore, these systems strive to be *accurate, timely, concise,* and *relevant*.

A **decision support system** (DSS) is an organized collection of people, procedures, and devices used to support decision making. While decision support systems and management information systems appear to be the same, there are important differences. The major impact of a management information system is on structured tasks, and the major payoff has been to improve efficiency. In many cases, managers play a passive role in the development of the system. A decision support system has an impact on both *structured tasks* and *unstructured tasks* that require managerial judgment, and the major payoff has been to improve *effectiveness*. In addition, managers play an active role in the development and implementation of the system. The decision process is part of the system. A decision support system works from a managerial perspective, and it recognizes that different managerial styles and decision types require different systems. A decision support system can have a significant impact on the decision making process, while a management information system usually does not. The overall emphasis is to **support** rather than **replace** managerial decision making.[1]

It should be noted that we are in a period of dynamic change, and that there is some disagreement on the exact definition and development of data processing systems, management information systems, and decision support systems. In general, however, there is a significant amount of agreement on the fundamental concepts of these systems. A data processing system provides useful outputs, a management information produces information, and a decision support system supports the decision making process.

THE SYSTEMS FRAMEWORK

The development and use of a DPS, and MIS, or DSS is based on a systems framework or foundation. The systems approach, the use of models, the model of the organization, and the theory of management will be discussed in this section and related to DPS, MIS, and DSS.

The systems approach

The overall objective of a DPS, an MIS, and a DSS is to solve a problem or to realize a goal. Regardless of what type of system is being developed, the overall approach is basically the same. This approach is called the **systems approach,** which includes the following steps:

1. Define the problem.
2. Collect data related to the problem.
3. Analyze the data.
4. Generate alternative solutions.
5. Evaluate the alternative solutions.
6. Select the best solution.
7. Implement the solution.
8. Follow up and maintain the solution.

These steps are almost identical to the steps and procedures of *systems analysis and design* discussed in the last chapter. Defining the problem, collecting data, and analyzing the data is basically the same as systems analysis. Generating alternative solutions, evaluating alternative solutions, and selecting the best solution are basically the same as systems design. And implementing the solution and follow up and solution maintenance are basically the same as systems implementation. Designing and implementing a DPS, an MIS, or a DSS all require the use of the systems approach.

---

[1] For more information on DSS, refer to Keen and Morton, *Decision Support Systems: An Organizational Perspective* (Reading, Mass.: Addison-Wesley Publishing Co., Inc., 1978), and Alter, *Decision Support Systems: Current Practices and Continuing Challenges,* (Reading, Mass.: Addison-Wesley Publishing Co., Inc., 1978).

The use of models

The real world is complex and dynamic. Due to this fact, the systems approach normally uses models of the system under investigation instead of the system itself. A **model** is an abstraction or an approximation of reality. There are a number of different types of models, and some of these types are listed below:

1. Verbal.
2. Physical.
3. Schematic.
4. Mathematical.

A **verbal model,** as the name implies, is based on words. It is a verbal or a narrative description of reality. Both spoken and written descriptions are considered verbal models, and reports, documents, conversations concerning a system are all examples of verbal models. A salesperson describing the competition to the sales manager, a report describing the functioning of a new piece of manufacturing equipment, and a statement about the economy or future sales are all examples of verbal models.

A **physical model** is a physical representation of reality. An engineer may develop a physical model of a chemical reactor, a builder may develop a scale model or a mock up of a new shopping center, the marketing research department may develop a prototype of a new product, and a doctor may build a plastic model of a human skeleton. These are all examples of physical models—physical representations of reality. Of course, childhood toys, such as dolls and model cars, are also examples of physical models.

A **schematic model** is a graphical representation of reality. Graphs, charts, figures, diagrams, illustrations, and pictures are all examples of schematic models. Actually, you have already been studying and using schematic models throughout this book. Flowcharts, HIPO diagrams, Grid charts, decision tables, structure charts, and organizational charts are all examples of schematic models. Most data processing related models are schematic models.

A **mathematical model** is a mathematical representation of reality. While mathematical models are used in data processing, they are more prevalent in areas such as accounting, finance, management science, and production management. For example, the following mathematical model might be developed to determine the total cost of a project:

$$TC = (V)(X) + FC$$

where:

TC = Total cost
V = Variable cost per unit
X = Number of units produced
FC = Fixed cost

The above mathematical model assumes that the total cost of a project can be divided into fixed costs and variable costs. In other words, this model assumes that there are no semivariable costs. In developing any model, it is important to make it as accurate as possible. An inaccurate model will usually lead to an inaccurate solution to the problem.

Since a data processing system, a management information system, and a decision support system all attempt to benefit a particular organization or company, it is useful to develop a model of the organization. The most appropriate type of model to use in this setting is a schematic model.

General model of the organization

An organization is a *dynamic* and *complex* system. *Money, manpower, materials, machines* and *equipment, data, information* and *decisions* are constantly flowing through the organization. Furthermore, the organization is operating in a dynamic and complex environment. The *environment* can be defined to be everything not included as part of the organization. In other words, the organization and its environment make up the entire universe.

With all of the various flows through the organization and the complexity of the organization and its environment, it would seem to be impossible to develop a general model of the organization. Since we are interested primarily in data, information, and decision flows through the organization, we can de-emphasize or eliminate the other flows, such as material, manpower, and money flows. In addition, since we are interested in developing a general model of the organization, we can also de-emphasize or eliminate detail from the model. We should stop here to make an important point. A model is developed for a purpose. In this case, we want to develop a general model of the organization to study data, information, and decision flows. Thus, we will include in the model only those factors or problems that we wish to study, and we will include only as much detail as necessary in analyzing the problem or situation. With this in mind, a generalized model of the organization can be developed. See Figure 17–2.

As seen in Figure 17–2, materials, manpower, money, and so forth are inputted from the environment, go through a transformation process, and are outputted to the environment. The outputs are usually goods and services. Data flows from the inputs, from the transformation process, and from the outputs to the data and information processor. If a computer is used, the information and data processor is another name for the computer system. This data is then manipulated by the information and data processor to produce meaningful information. This information is used by managers to make decisions. These decisions can impact inputs, the transformation process, and outputs. These decisions, for example, could be to use different raw materials (inputs), to acquire a new piece of manufacturing equipment (transformation process), or to open new channels of distribution for products produced by the organization (outputs).

You will also note that the data and information processor produces data that goes back to the environment. This data is usually business documents and transactions. Examples of this data output would be pay checks, invoices,

17 Management information and decision support systems 361

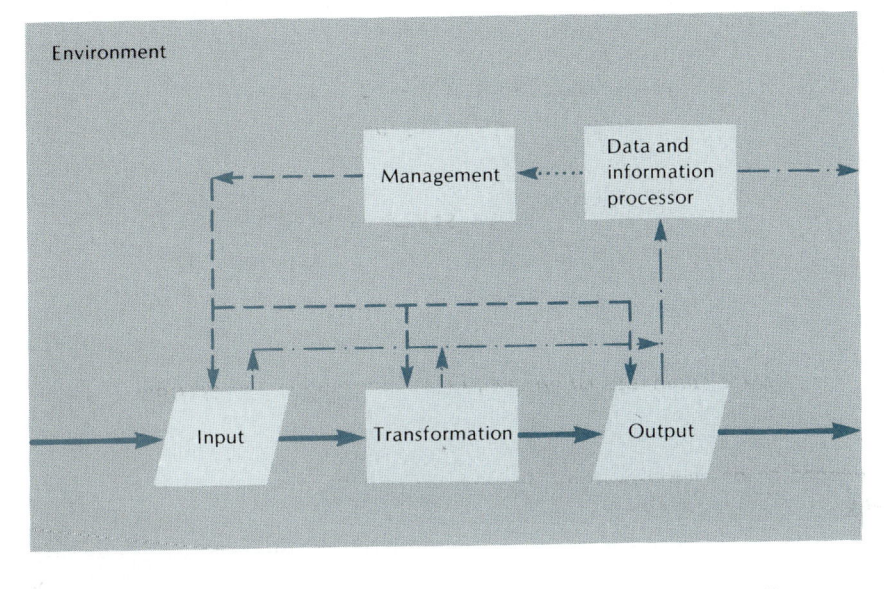

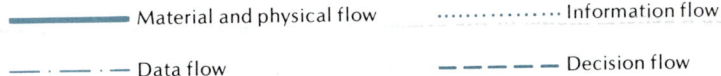

FIGURE 17-2
General model of the organization

— Material and physical flow ⋯⋯ Information flow
—·—· Data flow — — — Decision flow

bills, check to suppliers, information to stockholders, tax returns, and so on.

Theory of management

Management is the key to the success of the system shown in Figure 17-2. Thus, it is useful to understand the management process. To accomplish this, we will develop a theory of management that has been tested and validated in a number of case studies. This theory will be helpful in designing and implementing management information and decision support systems.

To begin with, the management of an organization can normally be divided into three levels. These levels are strategic, tactical, and operational. See Figure 17-3.

The **strategic** level of management consists of top level managers such as the president and vice presidents. The **tactical** level of management consists of middle level managers and decision makers, and the **operational** level consists of lower level managers and decision makers. The source of data and information, the presentation of information, and the use of information varies to some extent from one management level to the next. This is shown in Figure 17-4.

As seen in Figure 17-4, strategic or top level managers should have primarily *external sources* of data, the information should be *summarized,* and the use of the information is primarily *external*. On the other hand, operational

FIGURE 17–3
Levels of management

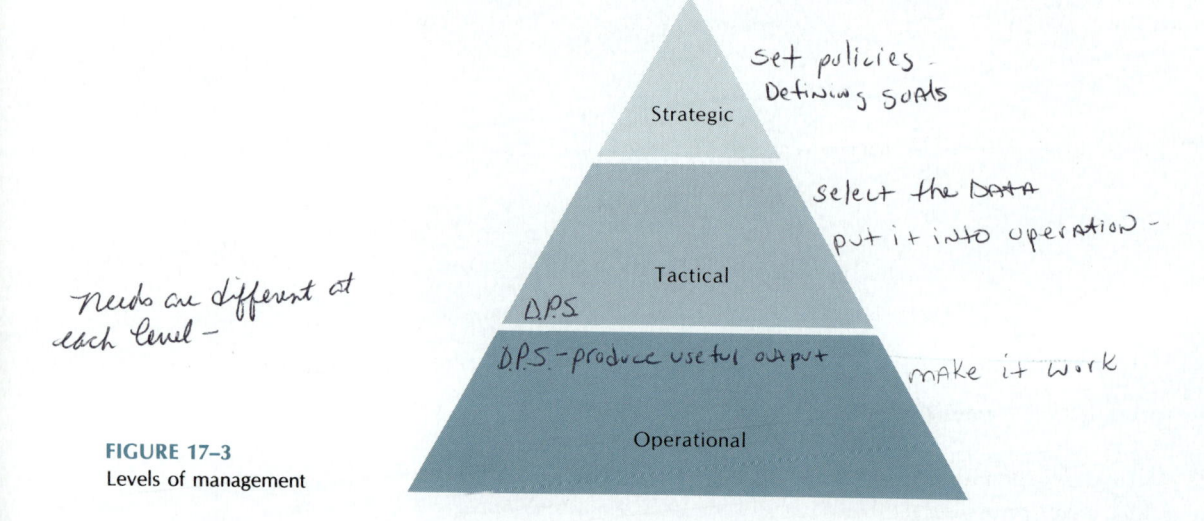

or low level managers should have primarily *internal sources* of data, the presentation should be *detailed* and the use of the information is normally *internal*. Tactical or middle level managers are somewhere between strategic and operational managers concerning the source, presentation, and use of information.

Since a management information system or a decision support system helps the managers in performing the various managerial functions, it is important to understand how the various levels of management perform these functions. In general, managers are responsible for **planning, organizing, staffing, directing,** and **controlling.** How managers and decision makers perform

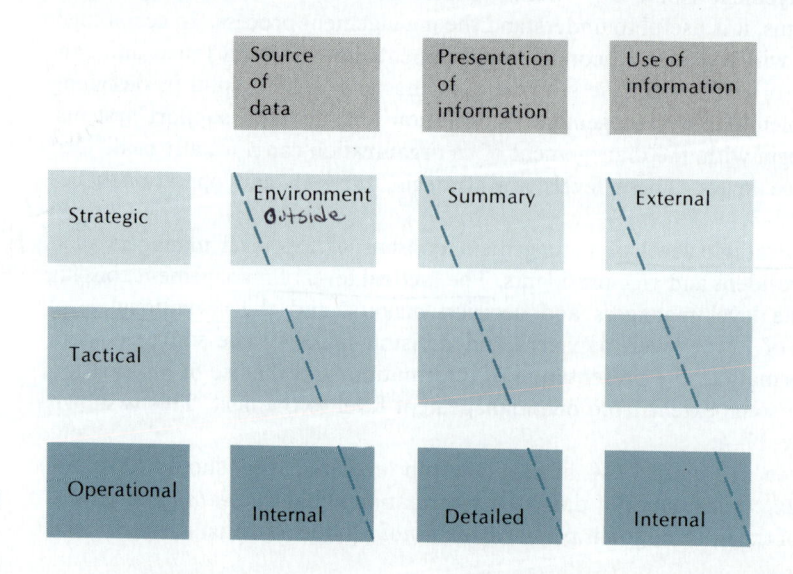

FIGURE 17–4
The source, presentation and use of information

17 Management information and decision support systems

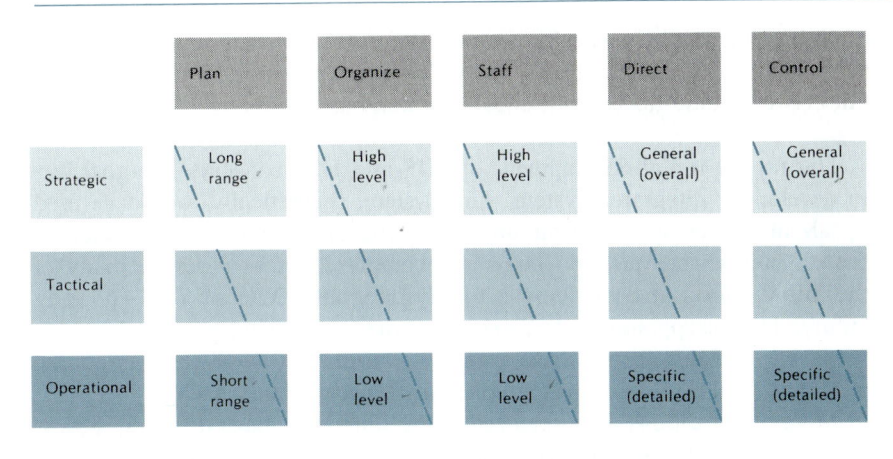

	Plan	Organize	Staff	Direct	Control
Strategic	Long range	High level	High level	General (overall)	General (overall)
Tactical					
Operational	Short range	Low level	Low level	Specific (detailed)	Specific (detailed)

FIGURE 17–5
Managerial functions

these functions depends on the managerial level (strategic, tactical, and operational). This is shown in Figure 17–5.

As seen in Figure 17–5, the three managerial levels have slightly different orientations for the five managerial functions. Strategic level managers are involved with *long range planning, high level organizing, high level staffing, overall directing,* and *overall control.* Operational level managers perform *short range planning, low level organizing, low level staffing, detailed directing,* and *detailed controlling.* As before, tactical level managers fall between strategic and operational level managers.

The decision making process also varies depending on the level (strategic, tactical, or operational) of the particular manager. See Figure 17–6.

For strategic or top level managers, the degree of problem structure is *low,* the time horizon is *long,* the amount of judgment is *high,* and each problem is usually *unique.* For operational or lower level managers, the degree

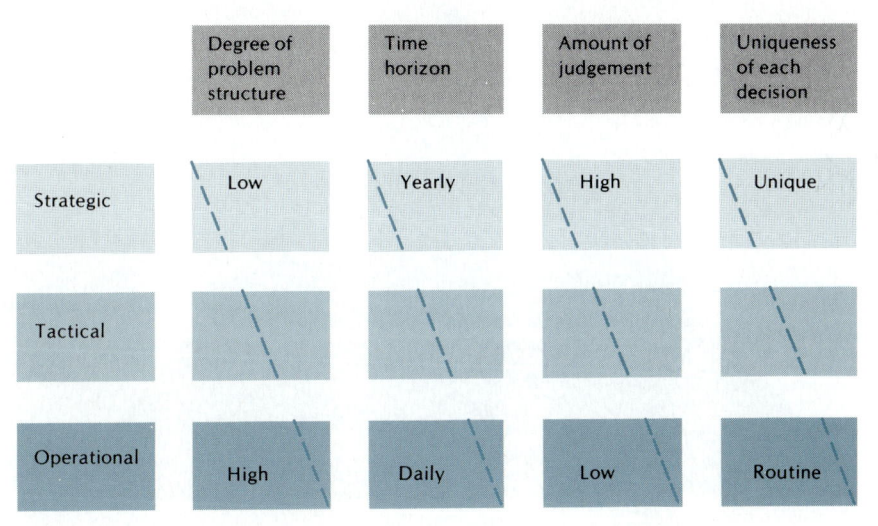

	Degree of problem structure	Time horizon	Amount of judgement	Uniqueness of each decision
Strategic	Low	Yearly	High	Unique
Tactical				
Operational	High	Daily	Low	Routine

FIGURE 17–6
Managerial levels and decision making

of problem structure is *high,* the time horizon is *short,* the amount of judgment is *low,* and the decisions are usually *routine.* Tactical or middle level managers fall between these ranges in the decision making process.

THE FUNCTIONAL APPROACH

During the initial development of MIS and DSS concepts, the goal was to develop an integrated system. This system, theoretically, would be used by all managers and decision makers in the organization. Unfortunately, these systems were just too large and complex, and as a result, many of the initial efforts at developing a totally integrated MIS or DSS ended in failure. This disappointing start prompted data processing personnel to seek better ways of developing these types of systems. Although there is no one best way, many organizations adopted the **functional approach.**

Most organizations are organized along functional lines or areas. This is usually apparent from the organization chart, which shows functional vice presidents under the president. Some of the traditional, functional areas are: (1) accounting, (2) finance, (3) marketing, (4) personnel, (5) research and development, (6) legal services, (7) operations/production management, and (8) information services. Furthermore, each of these functional areas require different information and support for decision making. In addition, each of these functional areas within the organization contain the various levels of management described previously in this chapter. Thus, in addition to horizontally slicing management into three levels (strategic, tactical, and operational), there is also a need to vertically slice management into the various functional areas. This is done in Figure 17–7.

Using a functional approach, a different information or decision support system is developed for the various functional areas and the different levels of management within each functional area. Thus, there would be a system for top level managers in accounting, middle level managers in accounting, lower level managers in accounting, top level managers in finance, middle

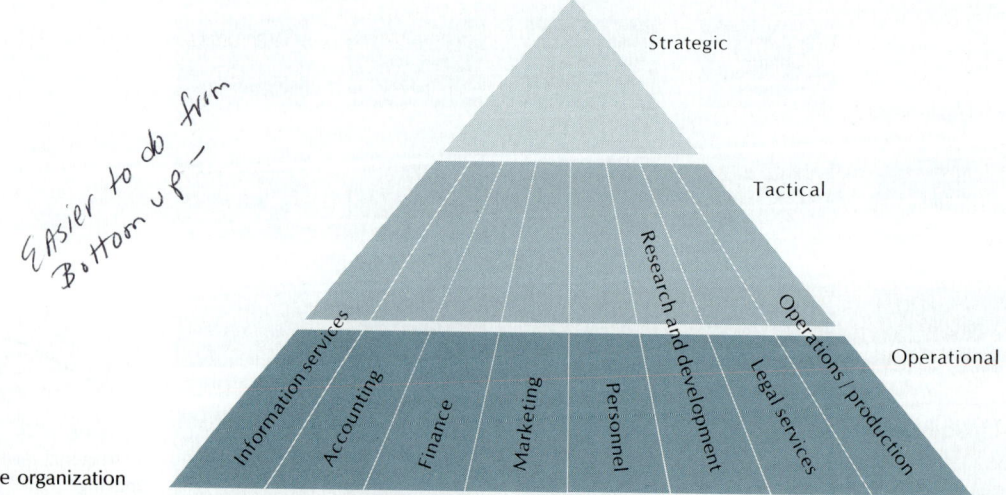

FIGURE 17–7
Functions of the organization

17 Management information and decision support systems

FIGURE 17–8
Functional data bases

Columns: Accounting, Finance, Information services, Marketing, Personnel, R and D, Legal services, Operations/production

Rows: Strategic, Tactical, Operational

Data base management system

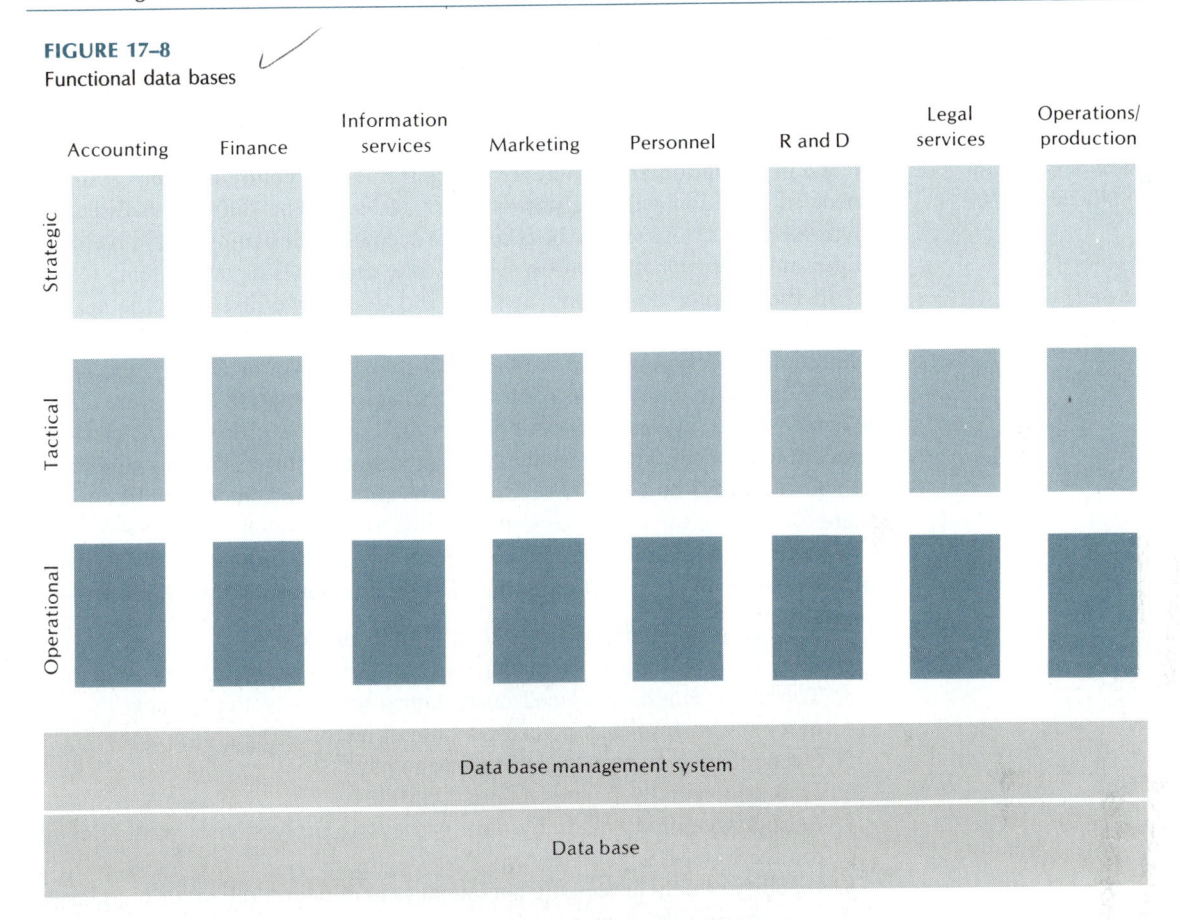

Data base

level managers in finance, lower level managers in finance, and so on. Each system will be designed to meet the particular needs of each group of managers.

When a functional approach is taken, it is necessary to try to relate or tie the various management information and decision support systems together. Otherwise, the organization might end up with a collection of disjointed and ineffective systems. With the increased use of data bases and data base management systems (DBMS), one way to unify and integrate the various systems together is through a common data base. Data bases and data base management systems were discussed in Part III. Working with a common data base and a data base management system, it is possible to develop separate data bases and application programs for each managerial level of each organizational function. This is shown in Figure 17–8.

In Figure 17–8, there are eight functional areas in the organization and three managerial levels within each functional area. A separate data base and a set of application programs can be developed for each. This would result in 24 different data bases and sets of application programs that are

DESIGN AND IMPLEMENTATION CONSIDERATIONS

all tied to the same common data base. Of course, other organizations would have a different number of data bases and sets of application programs.

In the above section, we have emphasized that different functional areas in the organization and different managerial levels require different management information and decision support systems. The differences discussed in the above sections should be taken into account in designing and implementing a management information system or a decision support system.

In the chapter on systems analysis and design, we discussed the specific aspects of analyzing, designing and implementing *any* system. The overall approach in designing and implementing an MIS or a DSS is the same. For a complete description of design and implementation procedures, read Chapter 16 on systems analysis and design. There are, however, problems and circumstances that are particularly important in the design and implementation of an MIS or a DSS. These problems and circumstances will be covered here.

To begin with, there are a number of problems that have blocked the success of an MIS or a DSS. Some of these problems are listed below:

1. Lack of goals and objectives for the MIS or DSS.
2. Lack of involvement of managers at all levels within the organization.
3. Too much emphasis placed on technical aspects of the system.
4. Not enough emphasis placed on human factors.
5. Over reliance on data processing personnel.
6. Lack of flexibility in the MIS or DSS.
7. False assumptions made by data processing professionals in developing the DSS or MIS.
8. Inability of data processing personnel to understand the needs of management during the design stage.
9. An inadequate or misdirected implementation of the MIS or DSS.
10. Inadequate control and ineffective evaluation and maintenance of the MIS or DSS after it has been installed.

One of the major problems in designing and implementing an MIS or a DSS has been due to *human factors*. Normally, there has been a *resistance* to these new systems and to change in general. Some managers have perceived these new systems as a *threat* to their power, a *threat* to their status and position, and a *threat* to their financial and job security. Managers have also perceived these new systems as creating job and role uncertainties and ambiguities, changing the relationships between top level, middle level, and lower level managers, increasing job pressures, and increasing job complexity.

A successfully designed and implemented MIS or DSS overcomes the above problems or solves them before they become a serious threat. One solution suggested by many people is to get the managers *involved* in the new system, but their involvement by itself is not enough. The involvement should directly *tie* them to the success of the system. One of the best approaches is to have the manager or user actually conceive or develop the solution. Managers should also be involved in evaluating the alternatives, selecting the best alternative, designing the new system, and implementing the new system. The overall objective of this type of involvement is to make the new system the *manager's system.*

During implementation, the new system should be *marketed* and *sold* to managers like a new product is marketed and sold to consumers. The new system should be advertised, promoted, and sold personally to managers. Some companies have used brochures, posters, and informal seminars with great success. The actual implementation of the new system should be *slow, smooth,* and *non threatening.* The people in charge of the implementation are change agents. They need to have both good interpersonal and organizational development skills and good technical skills. The implementation process requires three phases: (1) *unfreezing,* (2) *moving,* and (3) *refreezing.* Unfreezing is the process of removing or eliminating the old procedures and systems. Moving is the phase of having managers get used to the new system, and refreezing is the process of establishing new habits and behaviors concerning the use of the new system.

For organizations that have eliminated some of the problems of design and implementation, MIS and DSS are a reality and not a potential project on the drawing boards. The Kansas City Fire Department is using a computer system to find invalids in burning buildings and structures. DuPont is using an MIS to assist managers in a number of areas, including research, marketing, sales ordering, manpower requirements, cash flow, sales and return on investment, personnel, manufacturing, and technical exchange. The Educational Testing Service of Princeton, New Jersey has developed a computer system to help students in career planning and development. Gould, Inc. is using a DSS to graphically present information and support decisions using large visual display terminals. The Norsk Pacific Steamship Co. Ltd. uses an MIS to more effectively transport wood products and to project revenues and expenses for voyages. Working with First National Bank of Chicago, IBM has developed a DSS to produce color graphs and charts on a TV screen, to analyze loan portfolios, interest rates, assets and liabilities and more. Geo-Data Analysis and Display (GADS) is another example of a DSS developed by IBM to display data and information that can be related to a geographical location. GADS can assign policemen, set school attendance guidelines, evaluate zoning requirements for cities and counties, dispatch repairmen to jobs, and more.

SUMMARY

Management information systems (MIS) and decision support sytems (DSS) were introduced to you in this chapter. We started with a discussion of the differences between a data processing system, a management information system, and a decision support system. A data processing system produces meaningful output, a mangement information system produces managerial information, and a decision support system provides support for decision making.

Next, this chapter investigated the systems framework, which is a part of an MIS or DSS. In this section, the systems approach was discussed, the use of models was explained, a general model of the organization was presented, and the theory of management was discussed. These theories and models are very useful in designing and implementing new systems.

Another consideration in the design and implementation of an MIS or DSS is the functional approach. Since previous attempts of developing comprehensive and integrated systems have not been completely successful, many organizations are using a functional approach. With this approach, different systems are developed for each of the major functions of the organization and the various levels of management. With a functional approach, however, it is important to tie the systems together. This can be done by using a common data base and a data base management system (DBMS).

The last section in this chapter discussed design and implementation considerations. Since a complete description of analysis, design, and implementation was presented in Chapter 16, this section only emphasized those concerns that are particularly important to MIS and DSS. This section addressed some of the problems of design and implementation and suggested some general solutions to these problems.

KEY TERMS AND CONCEPTS

Accounting
Controlling
Data base
Data base management system (DBMS)
Data processing systems (DPS)
Decision support systems (DSS)
Directing
Environment
Finance
Functional approach
General model of the organization
Information services
Legal services
Management information systems (MIS)
Marketing
Mathematical models
Models
Moving
Operational
Operations/production management
Organizing
Personnel
Physical models
Planning
Presentation of information
Refreezing
Research and development (R&D)
Schematic models
Source of Information
Staffing
Strategic
Tactical
Unfreezing
Use of information
Verbal models

QUESTIONS

17-1. Describe the difference between DPS, MIS, and DSS.

17-2. What is a schematic model? Give several models.

17-3. What types of models are most frequently used in data processing? Give several examples of these types of models.

17-4. What is the systems approach? What steps are involved?

17-5. Describe how the different levels of management differ in their use of information, in the presentation of information, and in the source of data and information.

17-6. What functions do managers perform, and how do these functions vary for the different levels of management?

17-7. What is the functional approach, and how is it used in designing and implementing MIS and DSS?

17-8. What are some of the problems of designing and implementing new MIS and DSS? What are some of the solutions to these problems?

MINIQUIZ

ANSWERS

1. F
2. T
3. F
4. F
5. T
6. F
7. F
8. T
9. F
10. F

True or False

_____ 1. In most cases, computer programmers use mathematical models to describe and document computer programs.

_____ 2. The three levels of management are the strategic level, the tactical level, and operational level.

_____ 3. The environment is the major source of data for operational level managers.

_____ 4. A low degree of problem structure is typical for operational level managers.

_____ 5. A functional approach is often used in developing information systems for the various functions within an organization.

_____ 6. Technical and hardware problems are the major difficulties in designing and implementing a management information system or a decision support system.

_____ 7. The actual implementation of the new system should be fast and decisive.

_____ 8. A decision support is a specialized case of a data processing system.

_____ 9. It is the responsibility of the programmer to determine what reports are to be generated.

_____ 10. A mangement information system is a specialized case of a decision support system.

DSS:
An executive mind-support system
P. G. Keen and G. R. Wagner

When one asks a senior manager, "What do you use computers for?" the dialog is often predictable:

"Oh, we use them for everything. Why, we have systems on-line, interactive thus-and-so's. We're putting in a distributed such-and-such."

"Yes, but what do *you* use computers for?"

"Well, I get a lot of reports. Some of them are very helpful. . ."

"Yes, but what do you *use* computers for?"

"Well, actually—very little."

The importance of data processing to the organization and the ferverish growth in demand for hardware and software hide an inescapable reality: even now, many managers feel that the computer is only of peripheral value.

But a new concept in computer use is a foot that promises to improve this situation. New approaches are being taken that represent an entirely different philosophy. As a result, in many organizations, computers are being used by managers as *personal tools*—as extensions of the executive mind. Wrapped up in this change are some monumental implications for dp professionals.

The new managerial uses of computers are being brought about by inexorable trends in hardware, software, and business needs. This is not a single, cleancut innovation that occurred overnight, but is more like a tide moving in many currents and eddies over a period of time. What is happening is manifested in a variety of new software packages for interactive use by managerial personnel. This software is centered around two broad classes of applications: data base management (information systems) and financial planning (modeling, analysis, etc.).

Several years ago, one of us (Keen, in association with others at the Sloan School of Management) began describing the emerging new philosophy and gave it a name: decision support. A decision-support system (DDS) is a computer-based system (say, a data base management system or a set of financial models) which is used personally on an ongoing basis by managers and their immediate staffs in direct *support* of managerial activities—that is, *decisions*. Another term for DDS might be "executive mind-support system."

The other one of us (Wagner, working independently) created a planning or modeling language which is an expression of the decision-support concept. Called interactive financial planning system (IFPS), this software package is a method of creating a DSS in the form of one or more models, and then using the system on a continuing basis by manipulating the models and improving them in a learning process. The models may be linked to a data base management system to form an even broader expression of the DSS philosophy.

Here, we will elaborate on the movement toward personal use of a computer by managerial personnel in terms of decision support. We will draw on IFPS as an example of DSS philosophy.

First, it is well to explore the discouraging situation reflected in the opening dialog. What does it mean when a senior manager admits computers are of little use to him? And why is this so?

For one thing, many technical specialists have little understanding of managers. They assume the products they offer are useful to executives. Data Processing views its role as improving the operations and data flows of the organization, MIS as providing the information needed by managers, and OR/MS (operations research/management science) as developing analytic methods for decision-making. Each group works forward from technology (the means) to applications (the end). For some, the end *is* the means.

Source: Reprinted with Permission of DATAMATION® Magazine, © Copyright by Technical Publishing Company, 1979—all rights reserved.

No one can deny these traditional approaches have been fruitful. Even though we have often jumped ahead only to scuttle back, computer systems and models are indeed a central component of most functions of business.

But regardless of how indispensible such computer-based systems have become, they are incomplete from the viewpoint of the manager. Benefits of the systems are often limited to matters peripheral to the center of the manager's activities, such as reporting and control systems, delegated activities that mainly involve procedures and rules, and delegated decisions that—although they involve judgment—are of minor importance.

The central managerial activities not touched by traditional computer systems are those involving personal choices—matters that cannot be performed routinely or delegated: planning for the future, "fire fighting," and providing fast responses to unanticipated situations. Even though much of the analysis is provided by staff, the final choice must be made by the manager.

Henry Mintzberg[1] aptly characterized the senior manager's job as one of brevity, fragmentation, and variety. Managers rarely spend more than an hour at a time on any one activity; they deal with a typical problem in fragments of time scattered over a period of weeks or months; and they cover many different tasks in a given day. Furthermore, they prefer obtaining concrete information and rely on face-to-face discussions; yet they often depend on intuition.

In light of a senior manager's real job and how he does it, one may discern several reasons why computer-based systems useful to the manager's organization may provide no help at all to him personally:

1. Since his decision-making is often ad hoc and addressed to unexpected problems, standardized reporting systems lack scope, flexibility, and relevance.

1. Many classical OR/MS models that are *conceptually* useful often do not adequately fit a specific situation. Decision-making involves exceptions and qualitative issues.

3. While plenty of computer power is available, the lead time is too long for writing programs and getting answers.

4. Managers cannot specify in advance what they want from programmers and model builders. Decision-making and planning are often exploratory. Information needs and methods of analysis evolve as the decision-maker and his or her staff learn more about the problem.

Support for managerial decisions. However, systems are appearing that do provide direct, personal support for managerial decision: decision-support systems. What capabilities must such a system have to be useful to a manager? A DSS should be able to reflect the way managers think, be flexible and adaptive through ease of modification, support managers in a complex process of exploration and learning, and evolve to meet changing needs, knowledge, and situations.

In many ways, such a system is defined by its uses, and not by any specific technology. The goal is to provide managers with tools they will choose to adopt and that mesh with their own decision-making and judgment processes. The means are whatever software and hardware tools are suitable and available.

This is the essence of DSS philosophy. As far as computer systems are concerned, the foregoing capabilities translate into some specific design criteria:

- A flexible development language that allows rapid creation and modification of systems for specific applications.
- A system design architecture that allows quick and easy extensions and alterations.
- An interface that buffers the users from the "computer" and allows a dialog based on the manager's concepts, vocabulary, and definition of the decision problem.
- Communicative display devices and output generators.

The key words to this system are flexibility, ease of use, and adaptivity. A manager will not use a system lacking these attributes. It is hard to see any reason why he should.

Decision-support systems are used for many purposes, but there are certain common features. Direct, personal support of managerial decisions requires either the elements of an information system (a DBMS) for storing and retrieving data, or modeling and analysis capabilities, or both. Of course, the systems are interactive—usually on a time-shared basis.

Systems with these characteristics are becoming more prevalent as interactive processing spreads and as the software tools become available. Some decision-support systems are created by means of canned models that provide many functions. Others are developed from scratch by close staff members of the managers whose decisions are to be supported—or, in some cases, by the managers themselves.

Although it is possible to use a general purpose language, such as APL, DSS can be more easily implemented by using any of several simple special-purpose languages. For example, EXPRESS is a development language used for marketing analysis applications. A language called RAMIS is suitable for data base-oriented decision support. In addition, there are several financial planning languages.

Of course, it's not in any particular software package that the DSS philosophy is realized—it's in the way the software is used.

Of all managerial tasks, strategic planning is the least amenable to the traditional computer system approach, because it is least subject to predictability, delegation, and automation. The more continuous, ongoing aspects of planning (budgeting, capital investment analyses, and forecasting) are obvious candidates for decision-support applications. But perhaps the most spectacular use of a DSS is in a quick-turnaround, ad hoc situation. Here is a case in point.[2]

Houston Oil and Minerals Corp. was interested in a proposed joint venture with a petrochemicals company, with respect to developing a chemical plant. The executive vice president responsible for the decision wanted a Monte Carlo analysis of the risks involved in the variables of supply, demand, and price. David Simpson, manager of planning and administration, and his staff built a DSS model in a few days by means of a planning language. The results strongly suggested the project should be accepted.

Up to this point, any traditional simulation model might well have been adequate for providing answers to the expressed problem. The genuine decision-support capabilities of the model were mainly latent. They were reflected principally in the speed with which the problem statement was translated into a model the executive vp could readily understand and trust.

Then came the real test. Although the executive vp accepted the validity and value of the results, he was worried about the potential downside risk of the project—the chance of a catastrophic outcome. As Simpson tells it, his words were something like this: "I would like to see this in a different light. But I realize the amount of work you have already done, and I am 99% confident with it. I know we are short on time and we have to get back to our partners with our yes or no decision."

In short, Simpson replied that the executive vp could have the risk analysis he needed in less than an hour's time. Simpson concludes, "Within 20 minutes, there in the executive boardroom, we were reviewing the results of his 'what-if?' questions. Those results led to the eventual *dismissal* of the project which we otherwise would probably have accepted."

This was decision support in action. The particular situation is one that occurs again and again in top-level decision-making. The process began with what was really a first cut, based on the decision-maker's best initial definition of what was needed. The executive vp then responded to the results—his judgment alerted him to the need for additional analysis, so that the model needed to be modified, and *quickly*. In a sense, the first model—the one he asked for—was either incomplete or incorrect. It performed well, but the executive vp's broader sense of the situation told him something was wrong—even though he did not realize that the computer tools at hand were flexible and responsive enough to allow this result of his own learning to be followed up. In the end, he was using the system as an extension of his own mind.

In this and countless other specific applications for which decision-support systems are being created, one sees the necessary capabilities we listed earlier—reflection of the way managers think, flexibility, and ease of use, exploration, and evolution. The importance of these features is apparent in studies of DSS development and use. Without them, true DSS is impossible.

DISCUSSION QUESTIONS

1. What are some of the characteristics of a DSS?
2. How was a DSS able to help Houston Oil and Minerals Corporation?

The data processing industry 18

GENERAL COMPUTER MANUFACTURERS
SMALL, MINI, AND MICRO COMPUTER MANUFACTURERS
PERIPHERAL EQUIPMENT MANUFACTURERS
COMPUTER DEALERS AND DISTRIBUTORS
LEASING COMPANIES
TIME-SHARING COMPANIES
SERVICE COMPANIES
SOFTWARE COMPANIES
SUPPLY COMPANIES
THE INTERNATIONAL DATA PROCESSING INDUSTRY

After completing Chapter 18, you will be able to:

- List the various data processing industries.
- Contrast the advantages and disadvantages of the different sources of data processing resources.
- Discuss the world market for data processing equipment and service.

In the 1950s, the number of computers installed in both profit and nonprofit organizations was small. During this period, there were only a few companies that could be considered a part of the data processing industry. Over the last quarter of a century there has been a dramatic increase in the number of computers installed for commercial use. A curve showing the approximate growth is shown in Figure 18–1.

In 1975 the total revenues for the U.S. data processing industry were over $30 billion. About $7 billion was spent on mainframes, $13 billion on terminals and peripheral equipment, $5 billion software and services, $3 billion on minicomputers and small business computers, and $2 billion on supplies. Today, about $65 billion will be spent by U.S. customers on data processing equipment and services, and by 1985, this figure is expected to be as high as $150 billion annually. Annual data processing expenditures double about every five years. Table 18–1 reveals how this amount is allocated over various types of equipment and services.

While computer expenditures are doubling about every five years, the capabilities of computers are expanding at an even faster rate. Other products are costing more and more due to inflation, but today's computer user is getting more capacity and computing power for the same amount invested than ever before, and this trend is expected to continue. U.S. computer spending per capita and as a percent of GNP is also increasing. See Figure 18–2.

This tremendous growth has been due primarily to increasing technology, which has lowered computer prices while increasing computer capabilities. It is estimated that the typical computer cost about $3 million in 1950, while the average computer today has a cost of under $300,000. And with

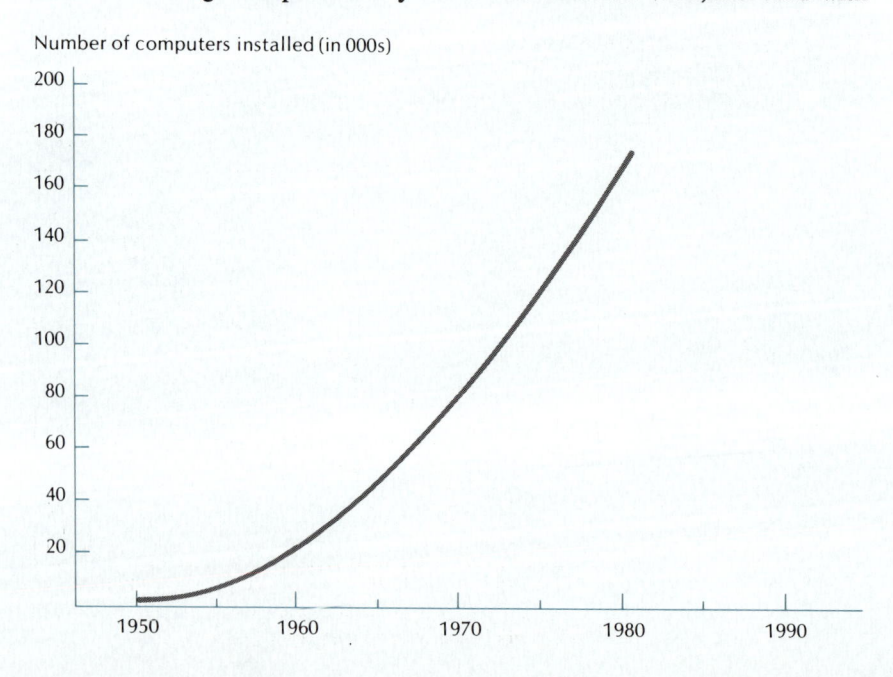

FIGURE 18–1
Number of computer installations

18 The data processing industry

TABLE 18-1
World revenues for U.S. firms

	1971 ($millions in 1971 dollars)			1976 ($ millions in 1976 dollars)			1981 ($ millions in 1976 dollars)
	U.S.	Overseas	World total	U.S.	Overseas	World total	World total
Equipment:							
General purpose computers	5,300	3,300	8,600	9,500	7,000	16,500	28,000
Mini and dedicated application computers	250	60	310	1,200	800	2,000	7,000
Peripherals:							
Data entry and terminal equip. from mainframe manufacturers	350	180	530	1,000	800	1,800	4,000
Data entry and terminal equip. from independent suppliers	165	60	225	1,600	600	2,200	5,000
Machine room peripherals from independent suppliers	180	140	320	1,000	400	1,400	2,500
Leasing	600	70	670	1,000	100	1,100	1,500
Used computer sales	40	*	40	100	*	100	300
Services:							
Batch	950	110	1,060	1,700	200	1,900	2,400
Online	500	90	590	1,400	300	1,700	5,600
Software	750	40	790	1,100	500	1,600	5,000
Education	160	*	160	60	*	60	*
Supplies	1,100	*	1,100	1,200	300	1,500	2,700
Totals	10,345	4,050	14,395	20,860	11,000	31,860	64,000

The dollar value of computer shipments should approximately double in each five year period, with the segment for minicomputers and dedicated application systems actually increasing much faster than that. (Note that some of the growth from 1971 to 1976 may be due to inflation.)

* Negligible
Source: American Federation of Information Processing Societies, Inc.

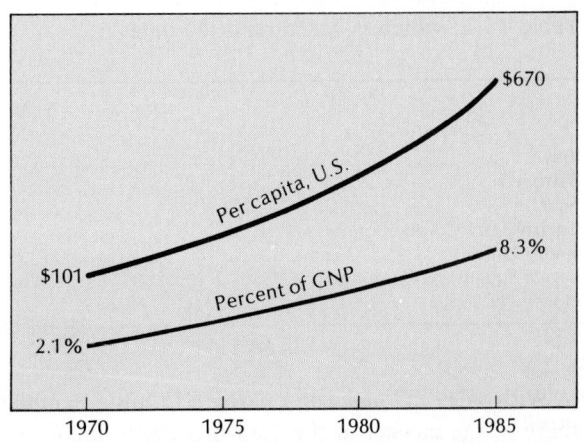

FIGURE 18–2
U.S. computer spending

Source: "Information Processing in the U.S.," report by American Federation of Information Processing Societies, Inc.

the advent of minicomputers and microcomputers, this price is expected to decrease even further.

While prices were going down, the capabilities were increasing. Computer speeds, which were measured in milliseconds (1/1,000 seconds), are now being measured in nanoseconds (1/1,000,000,000 seconds), and a computer that occupied an entire room in the 1950s can be replaced with a computer of greater capacity which is small enough to easily fit in a small closet.

While there are still under ten companies that supply a complete range of computer systems, there are literally thousands of computer related companies that specialize in satisfying a specific need in the data processing industry. Furthermore, it is expected that in the years to come, the data processing industry will further splinter into a vast number of specialty companies.

In this chapter, we will investigate:

1. General computer manufacturers.
2. Small computer manufacturers.
3. Peripheral equipment manufacturers.
4. Computer dealers and distributors.
5. Leasing companies.
6. Time-sharing companies.
7. Software companies.
8. Service companies.
9. Supply companies.
10. The International Data Processing industry.

GENERAL COMPUTER MANUFACTURERS

Although there have been a large number of companies that have entered into the data processing industry, the number of manufacturers that produce all types of computer equipment, software, and services has remained fairly small and constant. Amdahl has recently entered into the industry, while Xerox, GE, Singer and RCA have dropped out of the industry. Today, there are seven large and relatively stable general computer manufacturers. See Table 18–2, which is based on 1980 data.

TABLE 18–2
The major U.S. general computer manufactuers

Company	Approximate sales (in $ millions)
IBM	$15,000
Burroughs	1,800
NCR	1,600
Control Data Corporation	1,500
Sperry Univac	1,500
Digital Equipment Corporation	1,100
Honeywell	1,000

With sales estimated to be over $15 billion annually, IBM has the largest share of the market in the data processing industry. Amdahl, Control Data Corporation, and Itel are all directly competing with IBM. There are also several foreign computer manufacturers, such as Hitachi, who also compete with IBM.

The products that general comptuer manufacturers produce range from large computer systems costing millions of dollars to small and minicomputer systems costing thousands of dollars. These companies also offer software packages to perform all types of business and scientific applications. General computer manufacturers also offer a wide range of services including maintenance, programming assistance, facilities management, and so on.

Normally, customers either buy or lease computer equipment and software from the general computer manufacturers. In some cases, a lease-purchase arrangement is made where the ownership is transferred to the customer after a fixed number of years.

Although there are only a few general computer manufacturers, the equipment from one manufacturer is generally not compatible with the equipment from another manufacturer. Once a customer starts using a computer from one manufacturer, it is very difficult and usually expensive to switch to another. Thus, the initial selection of a general computer manufacturer is very important.

SMALL, MINI, AND MICRO COMPUTER MANUFACTURERS

While there are only seven major U.S. companies that manufacture and supply all types of computer equipment, software, and services, (See Table 18–2) there are over 100 companies that are involved with the manufacturing of small, mini, and micro computer systems. These computer systems normally cost under $100,000. It is possible, however, to expand the capabilities of these small computer systems to where the total price is well over $100,000. Table 18–3 shows approximate annual sales for some mini and micro computer manufacturers for 1980.

TABLE 18–3
Mini and micro manufacturers

Company	Approximate sales (in $ millions)	Rank in DP industry (according to sales)
Digital Equipment Corporation	$1,060	6
Hewlett-Packard	400	9
Data General	260	12
Texas Instruments	160	20
Wang Laboratories	110	28
Data Point	100	34

Small computer manufacturers offer the same types of services and software products as the general computer manufacturers. Thus, a full range of software and services is normally available. However, since many of these companies themselves are small and without the financial resources of the large general computer manufacturers, the software availability and service offerings are not usually as complete or comprehensive.

Although some small computer manufacturers offer both lease and buy options, customers are encouraged to buy the small computer systems. Moreover, as the size and price of the computer system decreases, the number of customers that buy instead of lease increases. When the purchase price is under $10,000, some small computer manufacturers do not offer a leasing option.

Many of the small computer systems do not require any special air conditioning or wiring. Some manufacturers claim that their small or minicomputers are complete and ready to use. These are called **turnkey** systems that include all hardware, software, training, and so on. The small size of these computers also means that they can be placed in existing office space along with other equipment or furniture. Larger computer systems normally require one or more rooms which must be specially wired and air conditioned.

Today, there are over 350,000 minicomputers manufactured by U.S. firms that are installed and in operation all over the world. In 1972, there were about 50,000 installed minicomputers. The annual sales growth for some of the leading minicomputer manufacturers is between 20 percent and 40 percent each year.

While the manufacturers of large computer systems sell their products to mostly end users, at least one third of the total sales of minicomputers is to **original equipment manufacturers** (OEM's). An original equipment manufacturer is a company that buys a minicomputer or microcomputer and combines it with other computer equipment and/or software and then sells the complete system to an end user.

Like minicomputer sales, microcomputer sales are also expected to soar. Sales could easily be $1 billion in the near future. These computers can be used at home, in the office, or at school, and many of these computer systems can be purchased for under $500. Some experts predict that these computers will be as popular as today's hand calculators.

In the recent past, there has been a trend to decentralize or distribute data processing facilities. This trend can sometimes be threatening to the large and centralized data processing department or center. Decentralization of data processing equipment usually means the decentralization of power and authority. As a result, there has been some reluctance on the part of some data processing departments to shed their larger centralized computers for smaller decentralized or distributed computer systems.

PERIPHERAL EQUIPMENT MANUFACTURERS

While it has been difficult for new companies to compete with the large general computer manufacturers in supplying a total line of computer equipment, software, and services, there has been an increase in the number of companies that specialize in manufacturing one or more lines of computer equipment. These companies are called **independent computer peripheral equipment manufacturers** (ICPEM's), and they have done an excellent job of producing high quality computer equipment that is completely compatible with computers produced by other manufacturers. Most of the peripheral equipment can be plugged into existing computer systems without requiring additional software or interfaces. This is called **plug-to-plug compatible.**

The success that peripheral companies have enjoyed has been the result of offering superior products at reasonable prices. Some ICPEM's offer better products at 30 percent to 50 percent off the manufacturer's cost. One disadvantage of using peripheral equipment is dealing with two or more manufacturers. If a problem occurs, the peripheral manufacturer and the general computer manufacturer might blame each other for the problem. This can place the computer user or customer in a difficult position. Furthermore, it may take longer to resolve and correct the problem when there is more than one manufacturer involved.

The list of products that are produced by peripheral equipment manufacturers is large. Some peripheral equipment manufacturers compete directly with the general computer manufacturers. These companies might specialize in manufacturing tapes, tape drives, disks, disk drives, data entry equipment, printers, and so on. Other peripheral equipment manufacturers produce computer equipment that may not be produced by one of the general computer manufacturers. For example, digital plotters and graphical display units are not produced by all of the general computer manufacturers. Other specialized devices, such as speech recognition units, voice response units, computer output on microfilm, and industrial data collection devices, are also produced by the peripheral equipment manufacturers.

COMPUTER DEALERS AND DISTRIBUTORS

A *computer dealer* or *distributor* is a company that only markets computer equipment. These companies do not manufacture any equipment. Like any other retail store, these companies stock and display a number of different computer systems from different computer manufacturers. In addition, computer equipment and software from companies specializing in the production of specific computer equipment or software can be stocked and sold at the computer dealer. This is like keeping an inventory of spare parts at a car dealership or repair shop.

At the present time, computer dealers primarily sell minicomputers and microcomputers. Since these computers are relatively inexpensive, it is possible to keep a sizable number of these computers in stock. Many manufacturers of minicomputers and microcomputers do not have the financial resources to have branch offices in every major city. Thus, the computer dealers offer a valuable service to these manufacturers.

LEASING COMPANIES

The primary financial options in acquiring computer hardware are to buy or lease. While almost all general and small computer manufacturers will lease their computer systems, there are companies that specialize in leasing computer equipment which they purchase from a computer manufacturer. These companies are *computer leasing companies*.

The financial resources required to start a computer leasing company are relatively small compared to the financial resources that are required to start a computer manufacturing company. As a result, there are a number of computer leasing companies, and the competition is fairly stiff.

The major advantage of using a computer leasing company is the lower lease price that most leasing companies offer compared to the leasing rates of the general computer manufacturers. In some cases, the rates can be 25 percent less than the rates for the computer manufacturers.

One of the major drawbacks of using a computer leasing company is service. The large computer manufacturers have national networks of competent technicians that will provide assistance in solving problems and in maintaining and repairing the computer equipment. Some leasing companies offer excellent service, but this is not always the case. Thus, it is important to know in advance what support will be available from the leasing company in maintaining, repairing, and in providing help if problems occur. For large companies that have their own staff of technical specialists, the service from a computer leasing company may not be as important.

TIME-SHARING COMPANIES

There are a number of small companies that would like the power and sophistication of a large computer system, but it may be financially impossible for these companies to lease or purchase a computer that will satisfy their needs. Furthermore, these companies do not need the capabilities of a computer system 24 hours a day. Instead, they might only require several hours of processing each day. This dilemma exists for many small business and engineering and technical companies. The ideal solution would be to allow these small companies to share the time and costs of a large computer system, and this is the idea behind a time-sharing company. A *time-sharing* company shares the time of a large computer system with many users or customers. Thousands of companies or individuals may be sharing the same computer.

In some cases, the time-sharing company has a large network of computer systems throughout the world. A customer of the time-sharing company would be able to use any computer system in the network. Thus, a company in New York could use a computer system located in Florida that was owned by the time-sharing company.

The customer of a time-sharing company usually purchases or leases one or more input/output devices. This equipment could be an inexpensive terminal or a remote job entry station with a card reader and line printer. The customer then uses these input/output devices to access the computer facilities of the time-sharing company. The customer pays for the input/output equipment and the amount of computer resources used. The customer can rent disk space, permanent storage on magnetic tape, and so on. The time-sharing company keeps a record of the number of seconds, minutes and hours the customer is connected to the computer system, the amount of CPU time used, and so forth. The customer then pays a monthly charge for the actual computer resources used, and for the input/output device if it is rented or leased from the time-sharing company.

Time-sharing companies, also called *Network Information Services (NIS)* and *Utility Companies,* have experienced a growth rate that has averaged about 25 percent over the last several years. In 1970, annual sales were over $400 million. Today, industry sales are about $2 billion, and this figure is expected to grow to $3 or $4 billion by 1985.

Time-sharing companies have provided a necessary service for companies that cannot afford their own computer facilities. Furthermore, large companies are finding that time-sharing can be useful when their large computer system is difficult to access. This is especially true if the large computer uses batch processing. The primary advantage of a time-sharing company is that the customer has the capabilities of a large and sophisticated computer system without the cost and problems associated with owning and operating a large computer system. A major disadvantage is that it becomes very expensive as the use of the time-sharing system increases. Thus, many companies that start with a time-sharing company find that their data processing needs increase to the point where their own minicomputer or small computer would be more economical.

SERVICE COMPANIES

Time-sharing companies and service companies satisfy a similar data processing need. While the purpose of a time-sharing company is to share computer facilities and resources, a service company provides some type of data processing service. In other words, the emphasis of a time-sharing company is to provide computer *facilities,* while the service company provides a *service.* Some time-sharing companies also offer data processing services, and some data processing service companies have added time-sharing to their business.

The type of services offered by service companies varies considerably from company to company. Some service companies specialize in small businesses. For a fee, which can be under $100 per month, the service company will do all of the data processing for the small business. The small business supplies the service company with its business data, and the service company performs all of the routine data processing such as payroll, accounts receivable, accounts payable, general ledger, income statements, balance sheets, and so on.

Some service companies specialize in data processing personnel. For example, a company might need some additional keypunch operators or programmers for a limited amount of time until a major project is completed. For a fee, the service company will provide these additional data processing personnel. Other service companies specialize in providing data processing service to one industry. There are service companies that have specialized programs and software to help companies in the oil industry, while other companies might specialize in import/export, retail stores, savings and loan companies, or companies in the transportation industry.

Like a time-sharing company, the service company offers the small organization the opportunity to take advantage of computerization without incurring the costs of owning and operating its own computer system. On the other hand, the company using a service company does not have complete control over the data processing equipment. A customer of a service company might have an important rush job that the service company cannot do because of commitments to other customers. Furthermore, the programs that the service company uses may not exactly satisfy the needs of the customer. While most service companies are willing to modify their software to accommodate their customers, service companies normally charge for this service and retain ownership of the new software. Even with these disadvantages, many companies begin using computer facilities through a service company. When these companies grow, they may eventually buy their own computer facilities. Service companies realize that they might lose their customers over time. As a result, some service companies are now becoming computer dealers and sell their customers complete computer systems when they no longer need a service company.

Service companies had a total sales of about $13 billion annually in 1978, and in 1980 the sales are expected to be over $15 billion annually. The industry also employs over 500,000 people. Service companies represent a substantial portion of all data processing spending. With decreasing hardware costs and increasing emphasis on service in general, service companies could capture as much as 25 percent of total industry sales in the near future.

SOFTWARE COMPANIES

As the cost of hardware decreases and the wages and salaries of programmers and systems analysts increase, the acquisition of software becomes more important. In addition, there has been a recent trend for software to be **unbundled.** This means that computer companies are no longer including software with the purchase of the computer equipment. Software must be purchased separately.

Software companies can either develop a software package for general computer users or they can develop a specific software package for a particular company.

Software packages developed for a general market are called **general software packages,** while a specific software package developed for a particular company is called a **contract software package** or **contract programming.** In some cases, there is a blend of these two approaches. The software company takes a general software package and modifies it to meet the needs of a particular company. Today, the software industry is experiencing tremendous growth in annual sales—between 25 and 30 percent.

Software companies produce and/or sell software that is compatible on a number of different computer systems. Some companies only market and sell the software that other companies produce. These companies are called *software brokers.*

Every organization using computer facilities must have both application and system software. This software can be either purchased from the manufacturer or a software company, or it can be developed. The major advantage of purchasing software is to reduce the cost of acquiring software. A software company is able to develop software for a number of different users. When this is done, the development cost of the software can be shared.

There are several disadvantages of using a software company. All software companies are not reliable, and some software companies do not produce and sell high quality software. Furthermore, it is important to know what service and assistance the software company is willing to offer after the software has been delivered and installed. Some companies offer no support after installation. Another disadvantage of using a software company is not getting what you want or getting more software than you need. In the final analysis the cost savings from a software company must be weighed against the reputation of the company and the company's ability to supply what the customer needs.

SUPPLY COMPANIES

Any company using computer facilities needs a number of supplies that are normally not produced and distributed by the computer manufacturer. These supplies include paper and ribbon for the line printer, computer cards, and so on. Companies that satisfy this need are called *supply companies*.

Although supply companies do not comprise a large share of the data processing industry, they are an essential part of any computer installation. Some supply companies specialize in supplying one type of product to its customers. For example, there are printing companies that do nothing but print the continuous forms that are used to prepare documents on the printer. These companies will assist their customers in designing forms that are attractive and useful. Most of these companies have also acquired some data processing expertise that enables them to design and produce forms that will be usable on any specific printing device. Since all companies using computer facilities need these supplies, supply companies will grow and prosper with the data processing industry.

THE INTERNATIONAL DATA PROCESSING INDUSTRY

The United States is not alone in the data processing industry. Companies in other countries are experiencing growth in data processing equipment and services as well. Aside from the United States, there are companies in Japan, France, West Germany, and Great Britain that have annual sales in data processing equipment and services that exceed $200 million dollars. While these companies do not compare to the seven largest U.S. data processing manufacturers in terms of total annual sales, they do represent a substantial portion of the world's production of computer systems. A summary of annual sales for 1980 in U.S. dollars for some of the leading foreign computer manufacturers is shown in Table 18–4.

TABLE 18–4 Foreign computer manufacturers

Country	Company	DP sales (in millions of U.S. dollars)
Japan	Fujitsu	$860
France	CII-HB	770
Japan	Hitachi	720
West Germany	Siemens	550
Japan	Nippon	400
West Germany	Nixdorf	380
Great Britian	ICL	230

Some of the foreign producers of computer systems, Japan in particular, are gearing up to compete with U.S. computer manufacturers. Japan is the second largest user of computer systems, but with the increased output of computer systems, Japan is looking for other markets. Some Japanese computer manufacturers have already established markets in the U.S., while other Japanese computer manufacturers are moving more slowly by establishing outlets in other areas of the world such as the Mideast. Although the Japanese owned computer manufacturers already have advanced hardware packages, these companies lag behind the U.S. in software and service. Some Japanese companies are now joining with U.S. firms to eliminate these deficiencies. It is not expected that we will see an all out attack on the U.S. computer market like we have seen Japan do with cars, cameras, TV's, radios, and so on, but it is expected that we will see Japan become a serious world competitor in the data processing industry.

While most of the computers produced by U.S. manufacturers are used by U.S. companies and organizations, U.S. companies exported about $3 billion of computer equipment to other countries. Other large exporters of computer equipment and systems include West Germany, Japan, the United Kingdom, and France. A list of some of the largest computer exporters in 1980 is given in Table 18–5.

TABLE 18–5
Leading computer exporting countries

Country	Exports (in millions of U.S. dollars)	Percent of total exporting market
United States	$2,950	28%
West Germany	1,640	16
Japan	1,010	10
United Kingdom	930	9
France	890	8
Italy	570	5
East Germany	440	4
Canada	390	4
Netherlands	330	3
Sweden	300	3

The United States is also one of the largest importers of computer systems from other countries. The United States alone imports over $1 billion dollars of computer equipment each year. France, West Germany, and the United Kingdom also import approximately one billion dollars of computer equipment each year. A list of the top ten computer importers for 1980 is given in Table 18–6.

The computer import/export market is dynamic. While some countries are increasing their imports of computer systems, other countries are decreasing their imports. Arab countries have had the highest growth rate of the computer importers. Perhaps as a result of their increased supply of petro dollars, the Arab countries have increased their imports of computer systems by about 25 percent annually. The United States, Canada, the Far East, and Western Europe also are increasing their imports.

While the USSR and Poland have increased their imports by about ten percent annually in recent years, many of the other Soviet Bloc countries have actually decreased their imports. Overall the Soviet Bloc countries have

TABLE 18–6
Leading computer importing countries

Country	Imports (in millions of U.S. dollars)
France	$1,200
United States	1,180
West Germany	1,170
United Kingdom	980
Canada	600
Italy	580
Japan	430
Netherlands	410
Soviet Union	320
Belgium	260

decreased their total annual imports by about five percent over the last several years. The Soviet Union and the Soviet Bloc countries in general have closed the technology gap, and this is one reason for the decline in computer imports.

One of the earlier Soviet computers was the BESM-6. Other Soviet Bloc countries were also developing their own computer systems, but in the early 1960s, the Soviet Bloc countries did not perceive a great need for computers nor did they have the resources to design and produce sophisticated computer systems that would be comparable to the U.S. computer systems. Then in 1967, the USSR and the *Council* for *Economic Mutual Assistance (CEMA)* announced that they were working on a family of upwardly compatible general purpose computer systems. The CEMA consists of Bulgaria, Czechoslovakia, German Democratic Republic (GDR), Hungary, Poland, and the USSR. The Ryad-1 and the more advanced Ryad-2 computer systems were the result. These computer systems are not only used by CEMA member countries but other countries as well, including Egypt, India, Iraq, and Finland. As the technology gap closes, it is expected that the Soviet Bloc countries will rely even less on Western countries for computer systems.

SUMMARY

This chapter has introduced you to the data processing industry. General computer manufacturers and manufacturers of small, mini, and micro computers were discussed. Computer dealers, leasing companies, and independent computer peripheral equipment manufacturers were covered. In addition, time-sharing, software, and supply companies were investigated. This chapter also introduced you to the international market for data processing equipment.

IBM, Burroughs, NCR, Control Data Corporation, Sperry Univac, Digital Equipment Corporation, and Honeywell make up the major manufacturers of computer systems. IBM has about half of the U.S. market for data processing equipment. In the area of minicomputers, Digital Equipment Corporation is the leader. Other leading companies that specialize in small or minicomputers are Hewlett-Packard, Data General, Texas Instruments, Wang Laboratories, and Data Point. In total, there are more than 100 companies that manufacture and market minicomputer systems. In addition, there is a significant market for peripheral equipment.

Aside from the computer manufacturers, there are a number of industries that are related to computer service and supply. Computer dealers and distributors buy computers from manufacturers and sell them to end customers. These companies can also offer complete software, management, and maintenance services. Time-sharing companies sell time on their computer to customers, and service companies usually provide complete data processing services to smaller companies and specialized services to larger computer users. Software companies specialize in developing and maintaining computer software, and supply companies provide computer users with computer paper, ribbons, and other supplies.

In addition to the U.S. market, there is a strong international computer market. Japan, France, West Germany, and Great Britain are all leading producers of computer equipment. The Soviet Bloc countries are making great strides in data processing equipment, and they are closing the technology gap with the Western countries.

KEY TERMS AND CONCEPTS

General computer manufacturers
Small computer manufacturers
Peripheral equipment manufacturers
Computer dealers
Computer distributors
Leasing companies
Time-sharing companies
Service companies
Software companies
Supply companies
Original equipment manufacturers (OEM)
Turnkey
Independent computer peripheral equipment manufacturers (ICPEM'S)
Plug-to-plug compatible
Unbundled
Proprietary software
Contract software
Contract programming

QUESTIONS

18–1. What products and services do general computer manufacturers provide?

18–2. What is a peripheral equipment manufacturer? Give some examples of products that may be produced by these manufacturers.

18–3. What is the difference between a computer dealer and a computer manufacturer? What type of computer systems do computer dealers offer?

18–4. Describe how a customer would use a time-sharing company.

18–5. What is the difference between a purely time-sharing company and a service company?

18–6. What are the advantages and disadvantages of using a computer leasing company?

18–7. What types of customers would you expect to find with a computer service company?

18–8. Describe the advantages and disadvantages of using a software company.

18–9. What is a supply company? What types of products do supply companies sell?

18–10. Who are the major foreign computer manufacturers?

18 The data processing industry

ANSWERS

1. T
2. F
3. F
4. T
5. T
6. F
7. F
8. T
9. T
10. T

MINIQUIZ

True or False

_____ 1. At the present time, Digital Equipment Corporation is the largest manufacturer of minicomputer systems.
_____ 2. ICPEM is an example of a software company.
_____ 3. A major disadvantage of using a computer leasing company is the higher lease price for the computer system.
_____ 4. Some time sharing companies have large networks of computer systems throughout the world.
_____ 5. One of the biggest threats to a computer service company is the increase in the sales of minicomputer systems.
_____ 6. Proprietary Software Packages are developed for a specific individual or a particular company.
_____ 7. A Canned Program is a type of operating system.
_____ 8. The United States is one of the largest importers of computer systems from other countries.
_____ 9. One of the earlier Soviet computers was the BESM-6.
_____ 10. The United States is one of the largest exporters of computer systems.

Gene Amdahl takes aim at IBM
Bro Uttal

Computer designer Gene M. Amdahl, architect of IBM's famous Series 360, is known for his original cast of mind, but when he quit IBM for the second time back in 1970 he seemed to have pushed originality to the point of eccentricity. In a bluntly worded letter of resignation, he declared his intention of competing with IBM by producing large-scale, general-purpose computers that would run on IBM software.

Such audacity doubtless caused some indulgent smiles in Armonk. With no wealthy backers, no experience in running a computer company, and a demonstrated distaste for administration, Amdahl was setting out to challenge the champion that was even then laying waste General Electric and RCA. At most, it appears from an internal document, IBM thought of Amdahl as a vague threat to a few enormous computer installations used by customers with specialized needs.

These days Mother Blue can hardly regard Gene Amdahl's ambitious undertaking as something to smile about. Amdahl Corp. has been setting the computer industry agog with a slashing attack on one of the most prestigious computers in IBM's product line—the very large Model 168 central processors that sell for upward of $2 million and will probably account for over half a billion dollars of IBM's 1977 revenues. Amdahl's weapon is an advanced machine called the 470 V/6, which offers better performance for less money and runs contentedly with IBM's software and peripheral devices.

In the little more than two years since the first 470 V/6 was installed, dozens of IBM customers—including NASA, General Motors, and the Bell System—have entered Amdahl's fold. Bell alone is using nine processors, which cost $36 million. By the end of this year, Amdahl will have shipped a total of some 90 units, about 10 percent of all the Model 168's installed worldwide.

Moreover, Amdahl Corp. seems solidly profitable. In 1976, its first full year of operations, the company reported profits of $24 million before taxes (and before tax-loss carry-forwards) on revenues of $92.8 million. This year's profits before such adjustments, FORTUNE estimates, will exceed $50 million, on revenues of $175 million to $200 million. That 25 to 29 percent pretax margin could well match IBM's. Amdahl Corp. has done so well, in fact, that it has already earned the accolade of imitation. Within the past year, both Itel and Control Data have also begun to market IBM-compatible mainframes.

Source: Reprinted by permission from *Fortune* magazine; © 1977 Time Inc.

DISCUSSION QUESTIONS

1. How is Amdahl able to compete with IBM? What product lines is Amdahl trying to capture from IBM?
2. Do you think that other companies will be attempting to produce IBM compatible systems like Amdahl?

SUPPLEMENT 18
Social issues

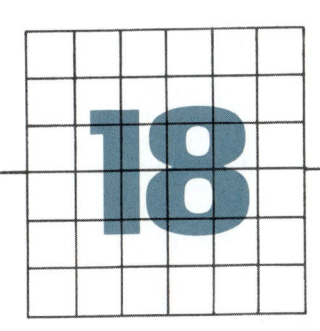

COMPUTER WASTE AND MISTAKES
CRIME AND FRAUD
PRIVACY

After completing this supplement, you will be able to:

- Discuss the problems with computer waste and mistakes.
- Describe computer crime and fraud.
- Determine your privacy rights and discuss the federal legislation that protects your privacy.

While computers have been a valuable aid to society, there are a number of real or potential problems that are a concern to both the data processing industry and society in general. Waste, mistakes, crime, fraud, and privacy are examples of these problems. These and related social issues will be explored in this chapter.

COMPUTER WASTE AND MISTAKES

The U.S. government is the largest user of computer systems, and according to some, it is also the largest misuser of computer systems.[1] The number of unused computer hours may be in the hundreds of millions of hours. Avoiding the proper computer acquisition procedures and the lack of adequate and competent data processing personnel in the federal government may also be a problem.

The same type of waste and misuse that is found in the public sector also exists in the private sector. There are expensive computer systems owned by companies that are used only a few hours a day. Too much reliance on computer salespeople and data processing professionals has resulted in the purchase of new equipment and the addition of data processing personnel when both were unnecessary.

Computers can be programmed to produce meaningful outputs, but they can also be programmed to make mistakes. Although computer related mistakes are usually covered up, many of these mistakes have been brought to the attention of the general public.

One of the classic mistakes was the "case of the missing hyphen." Apparently a hyphen (-) was left off of one computer program. As a result an $18 million Agena rocket had to be aborted. A bank in New Orleans wrote a computer program that calculated payments on a quarterly basis but actually paid its clients on a monthly basis. As a result, its customers were paid about a half of a million dollars more than they should have received. It has been reported that beneficiaries of Supplemental Security Income for the disabled, blind, and aged received about $1 billion in overpayments in part due to an untested and incomplete computer system.

There have been negative consequences from computers due to stupidity or incompetence. Most organizations keep a backup file of all permanent data. One company was having trouble with their computer; it was inadvertently destroying some of the permanent data from time to time. This company decided to duplicate all of the data files on magnetic tape for a backup. The backup data on magnetic tape was stored in the same room as the computer for easy access. One fire completely destroyed everything.

A medical clinic purchased a computer system to handle medical records and routing bookkeeping activities. The computer system was guaranteed to work by the computer manufacturer. The data processing department at the medical clinic set a date when they would fire their clerical staff and start using their new computer system. The new computer system didn't

---

[1] Victor Block, "Computer Wasteland USA: Part I," *Infosystems* (October 1977), pp. 40–46; "Computer Wasteland USA: Part II," *Infosystems* (November 1977).

18 Supplement: Social issues

work, and the clinic could not send out any bills for four months because they didn't have any clerical staff to do the job.

In less than a second, a computer can process millions of pieces of data. Computers can also be used to steal a million dollars in less than a second. Compared to robbing a bank or retail store with a gun, computer crime can be committed in the privacy of a house with a computer terminal. The crime is difficult to detect, the amount that is stolen or diverted can be substantial, and the criminal does not have to worry about a security guard who is fast with a gun.

In most cases, the computer is used as a tool to help in committing the crime. Like using dynamite to open a safe, the computer is used to give the criminal access to valuable information or the means to steal thousands or millions of dollars. There are many ways a criminal can break into a residence or commercial establishment, and there are many ways a computer criminal can break the security system of the computer for illegal purposes. Some experts estimate that the average computer fraud may be as high as $500,000. Furthermore, it has been estimated that about 100,000 individuals possess the capability and skills necessary to commit these types of crimes. Basically two capabilities are required. First of all, the criminal needs to know how to gain access to the computer system. Sometimes this requires a knowledge of an identification number and a password. Secondly, the criminal must know how to manipulate the computer system to get what is desired.

In one case, a Defense Department employee introduced fraudulent payment vouchers for items that were never delivered and walked off with $100,000. In another case, a clerk used fictitious food-stamp claims and got away with about $90,000. Some doctors are getting rich from Medicaid. This is accomplished by submitting fictitious or exaggerated bills to HEW for services that were never performed. A warehouse employee manipulated the inventory control system to cover up inventory thefts valued at more than $200,000. A bank employee altered several transactions and made several account transfers for close to $1.5 million. An employee at a brokerage house transferred about a million dollars worth of various funds into his account from other accounts. An insurance claims agent made false claims payable to friends and stole about $130,000 from the insurance company. A bank officer stole $290,000 from inactive bank accounts. An employee of a public utility company eliminated over $25,000 of customer bills for which the employee received a kickback. A group of individuals used a check-kiting scheme and data processing employees of two banks and stole about $900,000.

A computer can also be used as the object of the crime instead of the tool used to commit the crime. Millions of dollars of computer time and resources are stolen every year. Federal, state, and local government computers are sometimes left over the weekend without any security, and university computers are used for commercial purposes under the pretense of research or academic data processing. Computer equipment has also been diverted. A major computer company sold a large computer to an intermediary com-

CRIME AND FRAUD

Difficult to Detect
Take a few sec.
Becoming easier
by # amounts
over 100,000 people
have the knowledge and
skill.

pany at a $500,000 discount. This intermediary company in turn sold the same computer to a city government without the $500,000 discount. As a result of this simple paper transaction, the intermediary company made a profit of $500,000. Of course, the city would have saved the taxpayer's money if it had purchased the computer directly from the manufacturer.

While the number of potential frauds appears to be limitless, the actual methods used to commit crime and fraud are limited. A knowledge of some of these methods is helpful in preventing and detecting frauds. Some of the more common methods are given below.

1. Add, delete, or change inputs to the computer system.
2. Alter inputs that are valid.
3. Modify or develop computer programs that commit the fraud.
4. Alter or modify the data files that are used by the computer system.
5. Operate the computer system in a way to commit fraud.
6. Divert or misuse valid output from the computer system.

In the past, data processing personnel have been the major perpetrators of computer fraud and crime. Today, however, many people with limited computer background and experience are performing computer fraud and crime. As computers are becoming easier to program and use, they are also becoming vulnerable to criminals that do not have computer experience.

Because of the increased use of the computer to commit fraud and crime, there is a greater emphasis today on the prevention and detection of computer fraud and crime. All over the country, private citizens and public officials are making individual and group efforts to curb computer crime and fraud. Any company using a computer system should also be actively involved in preventing and detecting crime and fraud. One of the best ways is to design protective security systems into the computer system before it is built and placed into operation. Another strategy is to have a number of different people performing the various data processing tasks. Separating computer tasks and responsibilities helps in preventing crime and fraud because more people would have to be involved.

While existing laws may be stretched to cover computer crime and fraud, the federal government and several states are now proposing laws that specifically deal with computer fraud and crime. An example of proposed legislation aimed at computer crime and fraud is the *Federal Computer Systems Protection Act of 1977*. This act, which applies to federal agencies, fines computer criminals up to $500,000 or imprisons the computer criminal up to 15 years or both for various criminal acts performed with the assistance of a computer system. As law makers realize that the computer presents special criminal problems, it is expected that additional legislation will be proposed.

PRIVACY

Basically, the issue of privacy deals with the collection and use or misuse of computer stored data. Have you ever seen any information about you that is stored in any computer system? Do you know how many computers store information on you? Do you know where these computers are and what companies or organizations own or use these computers? Do you know if all of the information stored on you in all of the computer files is correct and error free? Most people answer "No" to these questions.

Data on you can be collected, stored, and used without your knowledge or consent. When you are born, take some high school exams, start working, enroll in a course, apply for a driver's license, purchase a car, serve in the military, buy insurance, get a library card, apply for a charge card, apply for a loan, buy a house, see a doctor or visit a hospital, get a passport, start paying taxes, or even purchase certain products, data is collected on you and stored somewhere in computer files. The federal government is perhaps one of the largest collectors of data. There are close to 4 billion records on individuals collected by about 100 federal agencies. Some of the main federal data banks are:

Veterans Administration
F.B.I.
Treasury Department
Civil Service
Department of Labor
Department of Housing and Urban Development
Social Security Administration
Bureau of Alcohol, Tobacco, and Firearms
Coast Guard
Department of Commerce
Federal Aviation Administration
Defense Department
Department of Transportation
Department of Health and Human Services
Department of Education
Small Business Administration
Federal Communications Commission
Justice Department
Securities and Exchange Commission
State Department

Other data collectors include state and local governments, and profit and nonprofit organizations of all types and sizes. Data is collected for subsequent use, and here is where an individual's rights can be abused.

Sometimes the use of information is a bother more than a real threat to individual privacy. "Junk" mail is an example. During your lifetime, you will receive your share of mail generated from data files containing your name and address. You will be asked to buy life insurance, get credit cards, purchase some seat covers for your new car, subscribe to a magazine, buy discount clothing, join the save-the-whale club, join a book or record club, buy an encyclopedia, buy a new vacuum cleaner, join a new religion, and much more, all of which are generated from computer files.

Although data files are usually used correctly and justifiably, there are potential areas for misuse. IRS tax records may have been used in the past to harass certain individuals or troublesome groups. Credit files at credit bureaus have contained errors and prevented people with excellent credit from getting a loan. Corporations have refused to hire employees due to faulty data files that contain incorrect data on individuals. Furthermore, there may be facts about you that you do not want to become common knowledge. Have you been arrested, filed bankruptcy, been divorced, expelled from school, been discharged from the military, received low scores on college entrance exams, been denied credit for any reason, had any history of medical problems, been in a mental institution, been denied a credit card, or has anyone said anything bad about you that could possibly be placed on a computerized file? If your answer is "Yes" and if you do not want this or similar information to become common knowledge, you should be concerned about privacy.

The major piece of legislation on privacy is the **Privacy Act of 1974 (PA74)**. PA74, which was enacted by President Ford, applies only to federal agencies, but it serves as a privacy guideline for private organizations as well. The act, which is about 15 pages long, is straightforward and easy to understand. The statement of purpose of the act is below.

> The purpose of this act is to provide certain safeguards for individuals against an invasion of personal privacy by requiring Federal agencies, except as otherwise provided by law to:
>
> 1. Permit an individual to determine what records pertaining to him are collected, maintained, used or disseminated by such agencies.
> 2. Permit an individual to prevent records pertaining to him obtained by such agencies for a particular purpose from being used or made available for another purpose without his consent.
> 3. Permit an individual to gain access to information pertaining to him in Federal agency records, to have a copy of all or any portion thereof, and to correct, or amend such records.
> 4. Collect, maintain, use, or disseminate any record of identifiable personal information in a manner that assures that such action is for a necessary and lawful purpose, that the information is current and accurate for its intended use, and that adequate safeguards are provided to prevent misuse of such information.
> 5. Permit exemptions from the requirements with respect to records provided by in this act only in those cases where there is an important public needed for such exemption as has been determined by specific statutory authority.
> 6. Be subject to civil suit for any damages which occur as a result of willful or intentional action which violates any individual's rights under this act.

The Privacy Act of 1974, which applies to all federal agencies except such agencies as the CIA and law enforcement agencies, established a *Privacy Study Commission* to study existing data banks and to recommend to the Congress rules and legislation which should be considered. PA74 also requires training for all federal employees who interact with a "system of records" under the act. Most of the training is being conducted by the Civil Service Commission and the Department of Defense. Another interesting aspect of PA74 concerns the use of social security numbers. Federal, state, and local governments or agencies that go into operation after January 1, 1975 cannot discriminate against any individual for *not* disclosing or reporting his or her social security number.

A number of states either have or are proposing their own privacy legislation. These states include California, Connecticut, Indiana, Maryland, Massachusetts, Mississippi, Montana, and New Jersey. Many people believe that the only way to reduce the amount of federal interference and legislation is to have the various states legislate their own privacy laws, and many states are doing just that. Some of the proposed state legislation is more comprehensive and covers more organizations than PA74. The use of social security numbers, medical records, the disclosure of unlisted telephone numbers by telephone companies, the use of credit reports by credit bureaus, the amount and type of information that can be collected and stored by state agencies, the disclosure of bank and personal financial information, or the use of criminal files, are some of the issues that are being considered by state legislators. Furthermore, many of these proposed legislative actions apply to both public agencies and private organizations and companies.

Privacy is also an international issue. For example, there is a federal French law that stipulates that data transmitted across the French border or data that is transmitted using phone lines must be registered. Spain requires that money be placed in an escrow account if data crosses its borders, and the *Swedish Data Act of 1973* stipulates that transmittal of data across its border must be approved by an inspection board. Transferring data across the borders of a country, which is called *transborder data flow,* is becoming more complex. The transborder data flow situation is further complicated with *Euronet,* which is a data processing network of the European Economic Communities.

There are a number of pieces of federal legislation that relate to privacy. The *Fair Credit Reporting Act (FCRA) of 1970* regulates the operation of credit bureaus. This law specifies how credit bureaus are to collect, store and use credit information. The *Tax Reform Act of 1976 (TRA76)* restricts the IRS in obtaining and using certain types of personal information. The *Electronic Funds Transfer (EFT) Act,* which went into effect in 1979 and 1980, stipulates the responsibilities of companies using Electronic Funds Transfer Systems and consumer rights. This act also stipulates customer liability for bank cards (debit cards).

As computers become faster and easier to use, it becomes faster and easier to violate individual privacy, and the privacy issue becomes more important. Honeywell's annual symposium on privacy which attracts people from private industry and state and federal agencies, is rapidly growing in size. In one year, the number of people attending increased by more than 50 percent.

More data and information is produced and used today than ever before. Recently, the *President's Domestic Council Committee on the Right of Privacy* stated that ". . . It is already clear that from one-third to one-half of the gross national product of the United States is currently attributable to the production and distribution of information and knowledge."

A difficult question that has yet to be answered is "Who owns the information and knowledge?" If a public or private organization expends time and resources in obtaining data, does the organization own the data, and can it use the data in any way it desires? PA74 answers these questions to some extent for federal agencies, but the questions remain unanswered for companies and other private organizations.

In 1890, Supreme Court Justice Louis Brandeis stated that the "right to be let alone" is one of the most "comprehensive of rights and the most valued by civilized man." With modern computers, the right to privacy is an especially challenging problem.

SUMMARY

This supplement has alerted you to some of the real and potential problems with computerization. Both public and private organizations waste millions of dollars every year on unnecessary computer equipment and personnel. You were also introduced to how computer related mistakes can cost millions of dollars.

Fast and easy to use computers are making computer related crime and fraud fast and easy. Some experts estimate that the average computer fraud could be over $500,000. This supplement revealed several cases of crime and fraud, how crime and fraud are typically perpetrated, and proposed legislation that is specifically aimed at preventing and discouraging computer related crime and fraud in federal agencies.

Another potential problem is personal privacy. In this supplement, how computers can be a threat to privacy was discussed, and various federal, state and international laws regulating the use of personal information were discussed. The major piece of legislation in the United States is the Privacy Act of 1974 (PA74). Other national laws that relate to privacy are the Fair Credit Reporting Act (FCRA) of 1970, the Tax Reform Act of 1976 (TRA76), and the Electronic Funds Transfer (EFT) Act implemented in 1979 and 1980.

KEY TERMS AND CONCEPTS

Computer waste
Computer mistakes
Computer crime
Computer fraud
Privacy
Federal computer systems protection act of 1977

Fair Credit Reporting Act (FCRA) of 1970
Privacy Act of 1974 (PA74)
Privacy Study Commission
Transborder data flow

Euronet
Tax Reform Act of 1976 (TRA76)
Electronic Funds Transfer (EFT) Act

18 Supplement: Social issues

QUESTIONS

S18–1. What are the major causes of computer related mistakes?

S18–2. What is being done to prevent computer related crimes?

S18–3. How is your privacy being protected? What control do you have over the use of data stored on you?

S18–4. What are some of the computer related problems that have been reported in newspapers, by magazines, or on television?

ANSWERS

1. T
2. F
3. F
4. T
5. F
6. T
7. T
8. F
9. F
10. F

MINIQUIZ

True or False

_____ 1. A missing hyphen in a computer program resulted in the loss of an expensive Agena rocket.

_____ 2. The most common way of performing computer fraud is to rewire the hardware of a computer system.

_____ 3. The average amount stolen in computer fraud is approximately the same as the average amount when the computer is not involved.

_____ 4. There are close to 4 billion records on individuals collected by about 100 federal agencies.

_____ 5. Because of the comprehensive nature of the Privacy Act of 1974, fewer than five states have their own privacy legislation.

_____ 6. The Privacy Study Commission is a federal committee to study existing data banks and to recommend to the Congress rules and legislation which should be considered.

_____ 7. The Fair Credit Reporting Act of 1970 regulates the operation of credit bureaus.

_____ 8. The Data Bank Protection Act of 1970 regulates the accuracy and integrity of federally-maintained files and data banks.

_____ 9. The Tax Reform Act of 1972 restricts the IRS in obtaining and using certain types of personal information.

_____ 10. The United States has the most comprehensive piece of privacy legislation of any other country in the free world.

DP crime laws enacted in only 10 states; Congress working on 'Model' Federal Bill

Marguerite Zientara

To date only ten states have enacted computer crime legislation. Legislative action is pending in five states and a "model" federal bill is still at the legislative grindstone.

In states without such statutes, U.S. attorneys prosecute computer-crimes under laws designed to punish such diverse crimes as mail fraud, wire fraud, theft of trade secrets and obscene telephone calls.

In 1978, Arizona and Florida became the first states to pass laws specifically against computer crime. Arizona's law defines the types of computer crime and specifies whether they are first or second degree.

With no mention of a fine imposed, the Arizona law calls for five years in prison for a first-degree felony conviction and a year and a half in prison for a second-degree felony.

Florida's bill addresses offenses against intellectual property, offenses against computer equipment or supplies and offenses against computer users. Crimes resulting in damages between $200 and $1,000 are considered third-degree felonies, while damages in excess of $1,000 belong to second-degree felony crimes.

Action in other states

States that passed computer crime bills in 1979—with varying severities of punishment—include Colorado (whose law was modeled after the Florida bill), Illinois (where types of crime range from a misdemeanor to a Class 4 felony), Michigan (where infractions are punishable by up to 10 years in prison and/or a $5,000 fine) and New Mexico (where third-degree felony is defined as a crime resulting in damages over $2,500).

North Carolina passed a bill last year that categorizes the altering, damaging or destruction of a software program, system or network as a misdemeanor. This bill also levies a felony punishment on verbal or written communications intended to extort money through a network.

Utah passed a crime bill with four classes of offense. For fraudulent acts resulting in damages greater than $25 but less than or equal to $100, the charge is a Class B misdemeanor. If the damages exceed $100 but are less than or equal to $300, the charge becomes a Class A misdemeanor.

For damages between $500 and $1,000, the charge is third-degree felony; for damages greater than $1,000, the crime becomes a second-degree felony.

Last year, too, Rhode Island and California passed similar computer crime legislation, with California even adding an amendment to include programmable pocket calculators.

The California bill, and hence the Rhode Island bill, was based on a federal computer crime bill introduced by Sen. Abraham Ribicoff (D-Conn.)

Although Ribicoff's bill was recently approved by the Senate Subcommittee on Criminal Justice, it is questionable whether it will be passed this year, according to a Ribicoff aide. It is hoped, however, that the bill will serve as a model for remaining states to initiate their own computer crime legislation.

A number of other states have introduced computer crime bills that have met various legislative fates. Hawaii, Minnesota and Missouri have carried their computer crime bills over to 1980, with action pending.

Maryland's bill, introduced last August, is currently dead but may be brought up again this year. In Massachusetts, a bill relating to computer privacy is being revamped, and Tennessee killed a computer crime bill last August.

Source: Copyright 1980 by CW Communications/Inc., Framingham, Mass. Reprinted from *Computerworld*.

DISCUSSION QUESTIONS

1. What types of laws have Arizona and Florida passed to prosecute data processing related crime?
2. What other states are now considering data processing crime legislation?

The data processing department 19

LOCATION OF THE DP DEPARTMENT
ORGANIZATION OF THE DP DEPARTMENT
    Users, systems analysts, and programmers
    Data processing managers, data entry operators, and other personnel
OPERATION OF THE DP DEPARTMENT
    General considerations
    Systems considerations
    The DP audit
DISASTER RECOVERY PLANNING

After completing Chapter 19, you will be able to:

- Discuss the placement of the data processing department.
- List the functions and roles of the members of the data processing department.
- Describe the operation of the data processing department.

The success of any computer system depends on the data processing (DP) department or center. This department contains the data processing personnel repsonsible for the efficient and effective operation of the computer equipment and facilities. In order to fully realize the potential of the computer system, the DP department should be located, organized, and operated according to proven guidelines and procedures that have been refined through years of experience. This chapter will cover these guidelines and procedures. In addition, this chapter covers disaster recovery planning—an extremely important but often ignored topic.

LOCATION OF THE DP CENTER

The first commercial computers were used primarily for *accounting* related applications. These applications included payroll, billing, accounts receivable, accounts payable, and general ledger. Therefore, the data processing center usually reported to a vice president or an executive in charge of accounting or finance. As other departments and functions such as personnel, marketing, and operations started to use the computer, the traditional placement of the data processing department became inadequate. To encourage better utilization of the computer facilities, organizations started placing the data processing department under a vice president of information services or similar position. This is shown in Figure 19–1.

This placement of the data processing center reflected a very important shift in managers' attitudes about the computer. The computer was no longer pictured as a glorified tool used to grind out bookkeeping reports. The computer was being perceived as an aid to managers and decision makers. This

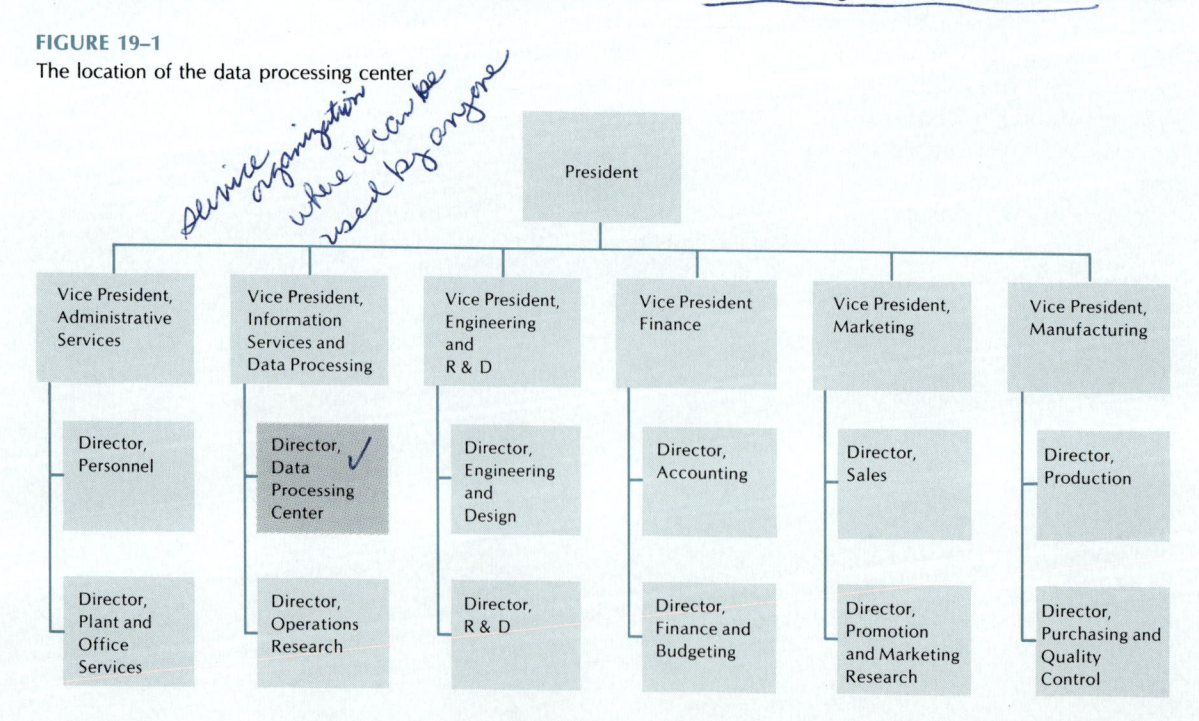

FIGURE 19–1
The location of the data processing center

trend in the location of data processing facilities allowed other functional areas, such as marketing, manufacturing, finance, administrative services, engineering and science, and management to use the computer system more frequently and effectively.

Many of the beneficial applications of the computer discussed in this book were made possible with this type of organizaton.

ORGANIZATION OF THE DP DEPARTMENT

With the earlier computer installations, the data processing department consisted of a collection of computer technicians and specialists. These individuals were primarily responsible for operating the computer equipment. Today, data processing centers employ a well rounded staff of individuals that are technically competent and able to communicate and render assistance to other people within the organization. Although the exact structure and organization of the data processing department varies, every data processing center must perform the same types of functions. These functions are shown in Figure 19–2.

As seen in Figure 19–2, a data processing center requires the functions of a *data processing manager,* a *systems analyst,* a *programmer,* a *system operator,* and a *data entry operator.* For smaller companies, these functions may be done by one or two people. For larger organizations, there may be literally hundreds of individuals that perform these activities. The organization chart for a larger data processing department is shown in Figure 19–3.

As you can see, each major function or area is divided into several layers. Under the manager of the data processing department is one or more assistant managers. Under the manager of systems analysis, there are several lead systems analysts. Under each lead systems analyst are several senior systems analysts, and under each senior systems analyst, there are several junior systems analysts. Anywhere from two to ten people at a lower level report to a person at the next higher level. In a typical data processing organizaton, you might find one manager of systems analysis, three lead systems analysts, ten senior systems analysts, and 30 junior systems analysts. Of course, the exact number of employees at any level varies from one organizaton to the other.

The same type of breakdown exists for programmers, computer or system operators, data entry operators, librarians, and data communication operators.

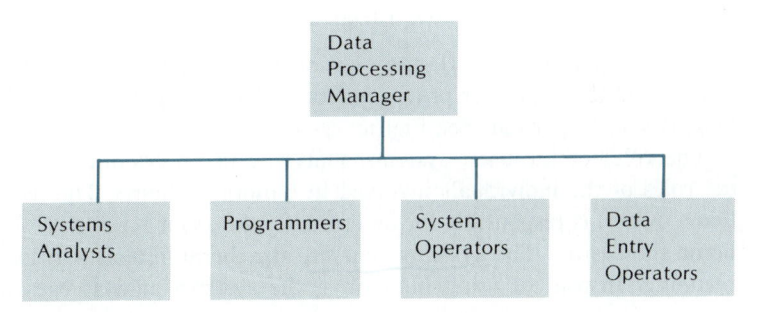

FIGURE 19–2
The data processing center

FIGURE 19-3

Organization of large DP department

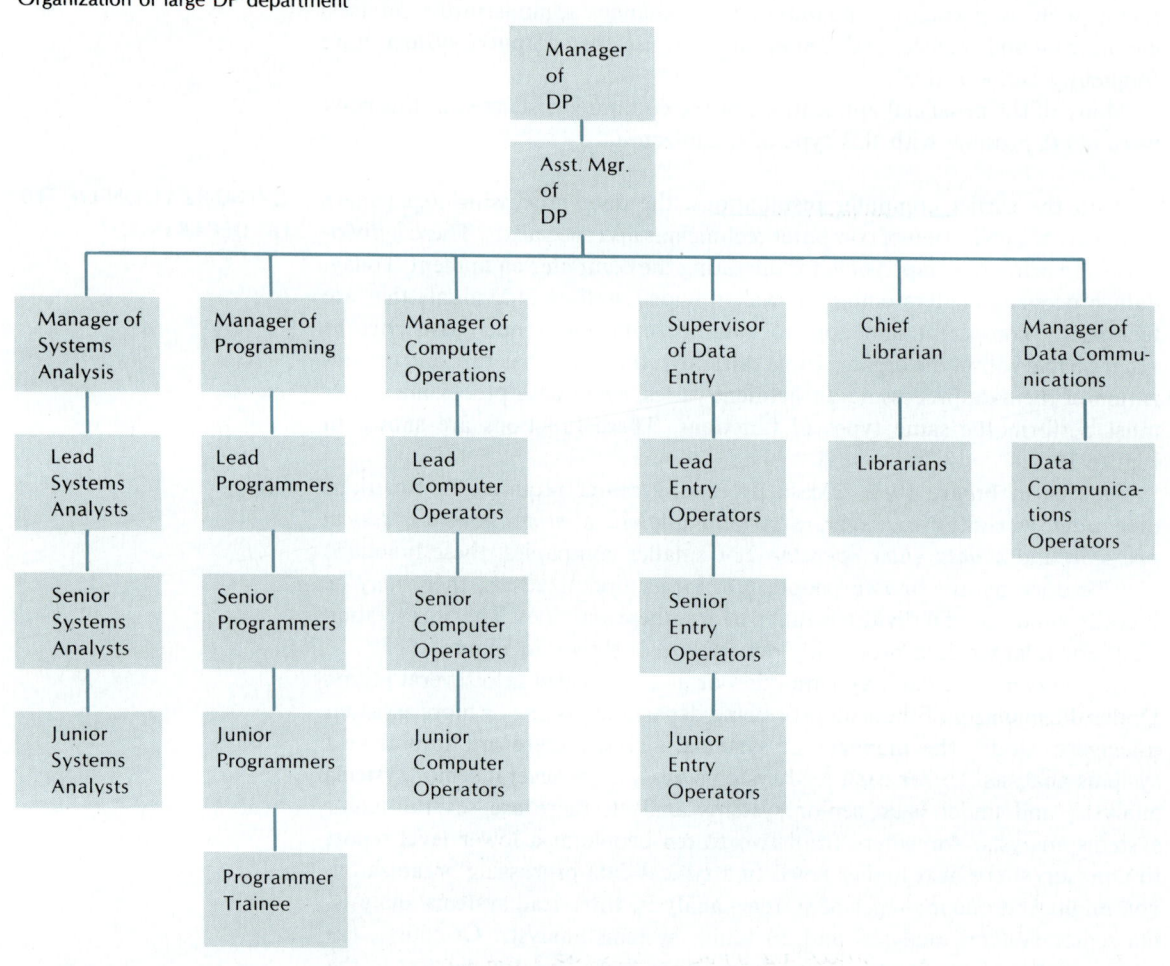

```
                          Manager
                            of
                            DP
                            |
                         Asst. Mgr.
                            of
                            DP
```

- Manager of Systems Analysis
  - Lead Systems Analysts
  - Senior Systems Analysts
  - Junior Systems Analysts
- Manager of Programming
  - Lead Programmers
  - Senior Programmers
  - Junior Programmers
  - Programmer Trainee
- Manager of Computer Operations
  - Lead Computer Operators
  - Senior Computer Operators
  - Junior Computer Operators
- Supervisor of Data Entry
  - Lead Entry Operators
  - Senior Entry Operators
  - Junior Entry Operators
- Chief Librarian
  - Librarians
- Manager of Data Communications
  - Data Communications Operators

Each of these areas performs a very important function in the data processing department.

Users, systems analysts, and programmers

As discussed in Part III, the relationship between the user, the systems analyst and the computer programmers in developing computerized applications is very important. See Figure 19–4.

The roles of the user, systems analyst, and programmer are similar to the roles of the individuals involved in building a home. The user, like the home owner, is responsible for determining the exact reports or outputs that he or she desires. The **systems analyst,** like the architect, is responsible for planning. Instead of using blueprints, the systems analyst uses tools such

19 The data processing department

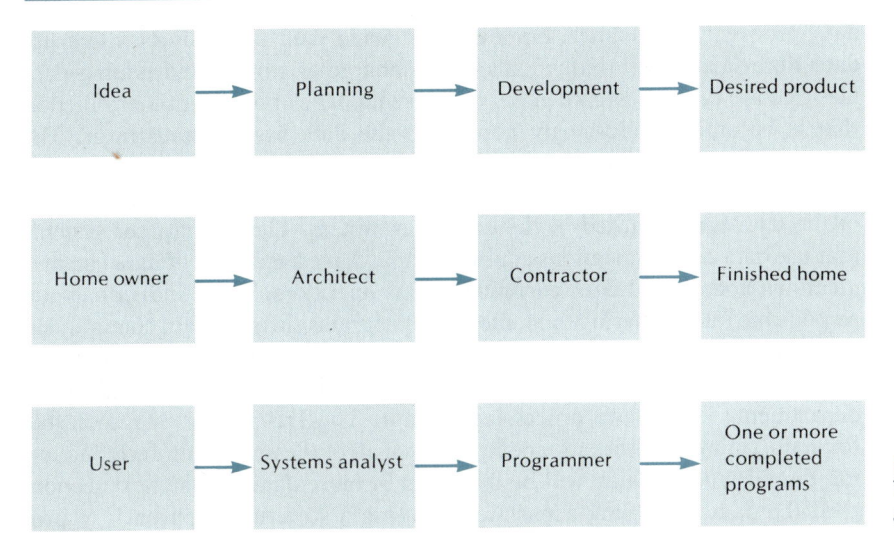

```
Idea → Planning → Development → Desired product

Home owner → Architect → Contractor → Finished home

User → Systems analyst → Programmer → One or more completed programs
```

FIGURE 19-4
The role of the user, systems analyst, and programmer

as flowcharts, decision tables, grid charts, and so on. These plans are then passed to the **computer programmer,** who like the contractor, develops or builds the necessary computer programs.

Data processing managers, data entry operators, and other personnel

As any other manager within the organization, the **data processing manager** has the responsibility of the efficient and effective operation of the data processing center. The data processing manager must possess excellent technical and managerial skills. Furthermore, as the size of the data processing center increases, the managerial skills of the data processing manager become even more important. A data processing manager must be a good organizer, a good motivator, and a good leader.

The **system** or **computer operators** are responsible for running or operating the computer equipment in the data processing center. Furthermore, these individuals should have the ability to detect minor problems that might occur with computer equipment and to take corrective action when possible.

All data processing centers must have the ability to place data in a machine understandable form. This is the purpose of the **data entry operator.** With the first computer systems, data entry operators were keypunch operators. These individuals placed data onto standard computer cards. Today, however, there are a number of alternative methods of data entry. Key-to-tape operators enter data onto magnetic tape or onto cassettes. Key-to-disk operators enter data directly onto a disk or a floppy disk. Data entry operators may also enter data using a computer terminal.

Depending on the size of the organization, there may be other types of data processing personnel. For example, some data processing centers use **data librarians.** These individuals are in charge of storing and issuing data files that are typically stored either on magnetic tape or disk. Another function that is becoming increasingly popular is the **data base administrator.** The data base administrator has the responsibility of maintaining the data base management system and in general maintaining the accuracy and the integrity of the data that is stored in the computer system. Those computer systems that use data communications equipment may have a **manager of data communications** and several **data communications operators.** These individuals are responsible for transferring data, files, and programs through data communications channels from one data processing facility to another. Data communications was discussed in Part II. Another position in large data processing departments is the **data processing auditor.** The DP auditor is responsible for maintaining the accuracy and integrity of all of the processing and conducting the DP audit, which will be discussed in more detail in the next section.

If the data processing department is using a structured approach to programming (see Part III for a discussion of structured programming), the data processing personnel discussed in this section may take on other responsibilities. As discussed in Part III, a **chief-programmer team** is assembled for every large programming project. The chief-programmer team consists of a **chief programmer,** an **assistant chief programmer,** several **programmers,** a **librarian,** one or more **clerks,** and perhaps a **data communications operator.** Assembling a chief programmer team is like taking a horizontal slice through the organization chart shown in Figure 19–3. There are usually people on the chief-programmer team from every function or area of the data processing department.

In this section, we have outlined the organization of the data processing department. You might also be interested in learning more about the specific job descriptions, salaries, required educational backgrounds, and advancement possibilities and opportunities for the various positions in the data processing department. This information and more is discussed in the supplement to this chapter.

OPERATION OF THE DP DEPARTMENT

The effective operation of the data processing department requires good hardware, good software, and good personnel. Regardless of the size or make up of the data processing department, there are several guidelines that should be followed:

1. Keep it simple.
2. Concentrate on results.
3. Suppress irrelevant data.
4. Clearly state goals and objectives.
5. Regularly appraise the status of the entire operation.
6. Get the involvement of managers.

The effective operation and management of the data processing department requires careful *planning, organization, directing, staffing* and *controlling.*

19 The data processing department

These activities are also required of any department in a company or other organization, and since these topics are usually covered in the typical management course, these general topics will not be discussed in any detail in this book. In any data processing department, however, there are some unique and very important activities that must be undertaken in the operation of a data processing department. There must be system controls and DP audits. Furthermore, there are some general considerations in the effective operation of a data processing department. We will begin by investigating some of the general considerations.

General considerations

A data processing department is a service department. The overall objective is to produce meaningful and valuable outputs from the computer system. The data processing department should strive to assist every area and department in the organization.

All projects and programs undertaken by the data processing department should be aimed at satisfying a need or solving a problem in the organization. If there is not a real need or a valid reason for the project or program, it should not be undertaken. Those programs and projects that have the greatest chance of increasing profits, improving services, or assisting the organization obtain its goals should be done first.

Every effort should be made to eliminate errors. This requires **error detection** at all stages of processing from the recording and entering of the original source documents to the production and distribution of the final reports and outputs. The primary method of reducing errors is *redundancy* or *duplication*. When any system is duplicated, it can be checked for errors. This type of redundancy should be present in the hardware, software, and in the operation of the entire computer system. Particular attention should be given to those errors that would have disasterous consequences. This can be accomplished by asking the following questions:

1. How often might the error occur?
2. What are the consequences of the error—cost and otherwise?
3. What is involved and what does it cost to detect the error?
4. What is best place and what is the best procedure for detecting and correcting the error.

There should be a *backup* for all hardware, software, and personnel. The most common backup for hardware is a similar or compatible computer owned by another company or a service bureau. Although the major computer companies are not in the business of providing hardware backup, on occasion they are willing to provide this service. The hardware backup agreement should be made in writing. Software can be backed up by making a duplicate copy of all programs, files, and data. At least two backup copies should be made for all software. One backup copy can be kept in the data processing department in case of the accidental destruction of the software. The other backup copy should be kept in a safe, secure, fireproof, and temperature and humidity controlled environment. Several companies, such as National Underground Storage (NUS), Inc. provide this type of underground security for vital records and software. There should also be a backup for data processing personnel. This can normally be accomplished by making an agreement with another data processing department or a data processing service company.

The data processing department should be protected against crime, fraud, and computer misuse and disasters. In order to protect a data processing system from data processing employees, some companies have insisted that data processing employees be *bonded,* which means that they are insured against fraud and theft, etc. Another approach is to divide the responsibility and authority within the data processing department. One employee should not be responsible for all aspects of any application or any processing. *Division of responsibility* discourages problems because the involvement of several employees is required. Additional protection procedures will be discussed later in this chapter under disaster recovery planning.

Systems considerations

There are a number of controls and procedures that are used in the actual running of the computer system by the computer operators or other authorized personnel. To begin with, most data processing departments have a set of general operating rules that help protect the computer system. Some data processing departments are *closed shops,* where only authorized computer operators can run the computers, while other data processing departments are *open shops,* where other people are also authorized to run the computer, such as programmers and systems analysts. Other rules specify expected conduct in the data processing department. Aside from these general rules, there are other considerations that include:

1. Scheduling.
2. Console and storage logs.
3. Time logs.
4. Utilization statistics.
5. Unusual occurrences report.
6. System run manuals.

All jobs and programs that enter the data processing department need to be **scheduled** to be run. There are several approaches that can be used in scheduling data processing jobs. *First in, first out* (Fifo) is a technique that processes jobs on a first come first serve basis. Another approach is *shortest operating time* (SOT). This scheduling procedure schedules jobs that take the shortest amount of computer time first. Studies have shown that SOT is an excellent method for decreasing the time it takes to run a number of jobs with different time requirements. Another scheduling procedure is to develop a *priority* system. Those jobs that are higher on the *priority* list are always done first—before jobs that are lower on priority. There are other scheduling procedures and some data processing departments use a modification of one of the methods discussed above.

Console and **storage logs** contain a detailed and complete listing of all jobs that are run on the computer system and of all data that is stored on a permanent storage device. These logs should contain the time jobs were run, any problems with the jobs, when data was stored, and where data was stored.

A **time log** is used to document how the computer system was used during the day. Run times for all jobs, necessary idle times, unnecessary idle times, program testing and debugging times, computer down or crash times, etc. are recorded. Every minute of the day should be accounted for. Time logs should also contain the program names or jobs being performed, account numbers for computer billing, description of the computer usage, the operator's signature or initials, start and stop times, downtime or problems encountered, and any messages that describe the situation of the computer during operation.

Utilization statistics are measures of the computer's performance, and they are obtained from the time log. All of the time data is accumulated for the various data processing activities, such as time spent running specific programs, time spent for testing and debugging, and down or crash time where the computer has some sort of a malfunction. Next, this data is converted into percentages of the total time. This data is then used by the computer operator and the data processing manager to determine how the computer system was used and any problem areas that require attention. Some data processing departments compute these statistics once a day, while some DP departments compute these statistics once a week or once a month.

During the operation of a computer system, unusual things are bound to happen. There will be certain problems that are difficult to explain, or the behavior of the computer may seem to be abnormal. These occurrences should be placed in the **unusual occurrences report,** which contains the date and time of the occurrence, the computer operator on duty, the nature of the problem or situation, the corrective action taken or attempted, and any other remarks that may be useful in documenting and analyzing the unusual occurrence. The unusual occurrences report is then used to solve any problems that were observed.

For every piece of software or job that is being run on the computer system, there is a **system run manual.** This manual is a complete description of how the software or job is to be run on the computer system. Also included in the manual are potential problem areas, solutions to problems if they occur, and all program documentation such as flowcharts, decision tables, structure charts, etc.

The DP audit

In addition to controlling the projects being undertaken by the data processing department, the data processing manager is also responsible for controlling the accuracy and integrity of the programs and procedures in use in the data processing department.

Audits can be used to help a data processing manager perform this type of control. An audit attempts to answer two basic questions:

1. What procedures and controls have been established?
2. Are these procedures and controls being used?

There are two types of audits. An **internal audit** is conducted by the employees of the organization, usually the DP auditor, while **external audits** are performed by accounting firms or companies and individuals not associated with the organization. In either case, a number of steps must be performed to complete the auditing function. The auditor checks and inspects all programs, documentation, control techniques, the existence of backup files, the data processing disaster plan (to be discussed next), insurance protection, fire protection, the efficiency and effectiveness of the disk or tape library, and computer access and security. This can be accomplished by interviewing data processing personnel and performing a number of tests on the data processing system.

In establishing the integrity of the computer programs and software, an *audit trail* must be established. The audit trail allows the auditor to trace any output from the computer system to the source documents, and any input or source document to the final outputs. The audit trail consists of both input and output documents that allow the auditor to trace the flow of data and information through one or more programs. The auditor may also use test data that he or she developed, a random sampling of data and output actually used, and a number of computer programs specifically designed to help the auditor in checking the various documents and control procedures of the data processing center.

In the past, auditing was normally done *around* the computer. Auditing was accomplished by investigating the printed outputs, input documents, listings of files and processing, etc. In other words, the auditor only looked at all of the inputs and outputs associated with a particular application—the computer programs were not tested. With the large number of computer programs to be checked in a data processing department and the difficulty of really knowing what the computer was doing, many auditors started auditing *through* the computer. When auditing through the computer, the auditor actually uses the computer in making the audit. This approach is more accurate, takes less time, and is more complete than auditing around the computer. Furthermore, with many of the real time and time-sharing systems today, it is extremely difficult to follow an audit trail when auditing around the computer. In many cases, there is simply no record of inputs to the computer system, and this destroys the audit trail. In auditing through the computer, the auditor investigates the actual processing in addition to the inputs and outputs of the various programs. Input data and transactions are generated to completely and thoroughly test the computer programs. Today, auditors have special computer programs that generate test data and help them in

19 The data processing department

auditing the existing computer programs, controls, and procedures through the computer system.

The last section investigated various controls and procedures to be used in the normal operation of the data processing department, but the operation of the data processing department is not always normal. Although disasters and emergency situations seldom occur, a data processing department should be prepared. The major types of disasters that have crippled the data processing department are:

1. Water damage.
2. Fire damage.
3. Electrical problems.
4. Security and personnel problems.

DISASTER RECOVERY PLANNING

Computers and water do not mix. In locating and operating a data processing department, floods, leaky roofs, steam lines, water systems, automatic water sprinkler systems, and sewer systems should be avoided. There are numerous cases of steam lines breaking, sewer systems exploding, roofs leaking, and flooding that have all caused the computer system to be completely shut down for weeks.

Fire is another serious problem. The major protection from fire is prevention. The rooms and buildings for the data processing department should be made out of fire retardant and resistant materials, and the computer room should be kept clean and free from waste paper, computer outputs, and no longer needed computer cards.

While electrical problems are not usually as severe as water or fire damage, this type of problem can cause delays and computer down time. Not only does the data processing department have to be concerned with the wiring and electrical system in the data processing department, but the utility or power company is also a concern. Computers do not function very well at half or twice their specified voltages and currents. With today's energy problems, blackouts, and brownouts, a data processing department must take corrective actions. In some cases, a *special power line* can be requested from the power companies. In other cases, the data processing department may wish to obtain their own power supply or source, called an *uninterruptible power system* (UPS). These systems can provide a computer system with power for several minutes or hours at the correct voltage and current.

Security and personnel problems can also cause data processing disasters. The problem may be as simple as a janitor smashing his floor cleaner into a disk device or as serious as a DP department employee stealing hundreds of thousands of dollars from the computer system. Alarm systems, closed circuit TV, pass keys, watchmen and guards, and security checks can be used to help prevent unauthorized persons from entering the computer room.

The overall purpose of disaster planning is to *prevent* disasters and to develop specific actions to follow in case a disaster occurs. The steps to follow in developing a disaster plan are outlined below.

1. Getting involvement and commitment of top level managers.
2. Forming the analysis team.
3. Determining the objectives of the plan.
4. Analyzing potential disasters.
5. Formulating a disaster plan.
6. Documenting the disaster plan.
7. Implementing the disaster plan.
8. Testing the disaster plan.
9. Maintaining the disaster plan.

In performing the above steps, it is a common practice to document the disaster plan. This is step 6 above. This normally requires that a *disaster plan report* or *manual* be developed. The contents of such a report is given below:

The disaster plan
    Table of contents
    Background information
    The analysis team
    The data processing center
    The staff
    The equipment
    The software (system and application software)
    Operating procedures
    The physical environment
    Analysis of potential disasters
    Disaster prevention
    The disaster plan
    Appendixes
    Index

In developing a disaster recovery plan, it is necessary to have a backup for everything—hardware, software, personnel, supplies, and so on. The transportation of the backup system to the data processing department or the transportation of the processing to the backup systems should also be worked out. Disaster planning is a complex task, and it is easy to forget an important aspect. This is why many data processing departments have *unannounced test disasters,* where a real disaster is simulated. For example, the DP manager may walk into the computer room one day and announce that this is a simulated disaster and that all of the data stored on the disk devices has been destroyed. The disaster plan can then be tested using the fake disaster. This process can be repeated to test all aspects of the disaster plan.

SUMMARY

The location, organization, and operation of the data processing department has been explored in this chapter. In addition, disaster recovery planning has been discussed.

In the past, the data processing department was often located under accounting or finance. Today, many data processing departments are located under a vice president for information services and data processing. The manager of the data processing department normally reports to this individual. In the data processing department, there are programmers, systems analysts, system operators, data entry operators, librarians, data communications operators, and one or more data base administrators. In large companies, there are usually several layers of management, such as manager, supervisor, lead, senior, junior, and trainee.

The operation of any data processing department requires general and operating considerations. Most data processing departments also use auditing procedures. In performing data processing jobs, the most important jobs that will lead to the highest profits or the obtainment of important company goals should be done first. During the actual operation of the computer facilities, scheduling, console and storage logs, time logs, utilization statistics, unusual occurrences reports, and system run manuals should be established and used.

To protect a data processing department from the potential of a disaster, a disaster recovery plan can be used. This plan is an excellent tool for protecting a data processing department from such common disasters as (1) water damage, (2) fire damage, (3) electrical problems, and (4) security and personnel problems. Careful designing, implementation, and testing are required for an effective disaster recovery plan.

KEY TERMS AND CONCEPTS

Audit around the computer
Audit through the computer
Audit trails
Bonded employees
Computer operator
Console logs
DP auditor
DP manager
Data base administrators
Data communications operator
Data entry operator

Disaster recovery planning
Division of responsibility
Duplicate circuitry
Electrical problems
External audits
Fire damage
Librarian
Internal audits
Programmer
Scheduling

Security and personnel problems
Storage logs
Systems analyst
System run manuals
Time logs
Uninterruptible Power System (UPS)
Utilization statistics
Unusual occurences report
Water damage

QUESTIONS

19-1. Briefly describe some of the alternatives in placing the data processing center within an organization.

19-2. What is the role of the systems analyst?

19-3. Describe the roles and responsibilities of the computer programmer.

19-4. What is the relationship between the user, systems analyst, and computer programmer?

19-5. Contrast internal auditing with external auditing.

19-6. What types of logs and records should be maintained in the operation of a computer system?

19-7. What is involved in developing a disaster recovery plan?

MINIQUIZ

True or False

ANSWERS

1. F
2. F
3. T
4. F
5. T
6. F
7. F
8. T
9. F
10. F

_____ 1. The first commercial computer systems were used primarily for management information related applications.

_____ 2. Today, the trend is locate the data processing department under an accounting or financial department.

_____ 3. The data processing department requires the functions of a data processing manager, a systems analyst, a programmer, a systems operator, and a data entry operator at a minimum.

_____ 4. The programmer, like the architect, is responsible for planning the necessary computer programs.

_____ 5. The data processing manager must possess excellent technical and managerial skills.

_____ 6. The data base administrator is an example of application software that is used to control and maintain accurate data files.

_____ 7. Unification of responsibility is one way to reduce crime, fraud, and computer misuse.

_____ 8. UPS can be used to avoid power related problems, such as a temporary loss of power due to a brownout.

_____ 9. Console and storage logs are maintained by the computer programmer to reveal the data to be stored and the operations to be performed in executing a computer program.

_____ 10. The audit trail allows the auditor to trace the electronic circuitry of the computer system to make sure there are no malfunctions.

Remarks of William S. Anderson, Chairman of NCR Corporation

Dr. Samuel Johnson, that very quotable 18th Century literary lion, once pointed out that "expectations improperly indulged must end in disappointment."

The very-ready James Boswell then asked Dr. Johnson what constituted an improper expectation. Johnson's reply was that an improper expectation is one that is dictated not by reason, but by desire.

And that is what often occurs in the development of management information systems. Desire overcomes reason, and an expectation gap develops.

Let's define the expectations gap a little more precisely: from the viewpoint of top management, it's the difference between what management expects from a new or improved information system, and what that system finally delivers. But from the viewpoint of the systems professional, it's the difference between the guidance and participation he expected from his top management, and what he actually got.

I'm not aware of any company, or any organization which is immune to this problem. And that's rather surprising—especially in view of the sophistication of today's information processing industry.

Consider management's dilemma: too often, the information management needs is either not available when it's needed, or its accuracy is questionable, or it conflicts with other information.

Few business managers today question the importance—indeed the necessity—of good Management Information Systems. Instead, they look upon such systems as the nerve center of the entire enterprise. The difficulty is that when management looks at this nerve center, it sometimes concludes that the organization is on the verge of a nervous breakdown.

When serious information gaps exist, management has no recourse but to muddle through. It scrapes together what information it can, largely by brute force. It adds a dash of experience and a touch of intuition, and then makes the decisions that have to be made. But usually a heavy price is paid for that kind of haphazard, seat-of-the-pants management. So what is the cure? How can the expectations gap be narrowed? The point I stress the most to our internal systems people is this: to come closer to top management's expectations, the systems professional has to become a generalist as well as a specialist. By this I mean that he has to find out what management is trying to do, what information is therefore needed, and when and how that information should be supplied.

To gain this broader perspective, the systems professional must learn how the business or organization really functions—all the way from purchasing to customer billing. That demands a working knowledge of the requirements of all divisions and departments, not just those that generate a lot of paper.

To gain this broader perspective, the systems professional should study in intimate detail how the organization is structured—to develop, produce and distribute its products or services. He also needs some degree of empathy with the chief executive. As one example, he must understand his company's competitive environment, and all the other factors that tend to keep the chief executive awake at night.

And he ought to cultivate that depth of knowledge and understanding on a continuing basis. Information requirements are constantly changing, as the organization itself changes, and as external factors change.

Source: Joint Dinner Meeting of the Association for Systems Management and Data Processing Management Association, Stouffer's Dayton Plaza, January 24, 1978. Reprinted courtesy of NCR Corporation.

Another guideline I've suggested to our own systems people is to avoid promising too much, too soon. One of the great temptations in systems development and implementation is to bite off more than we can chew. At NCR we are very much aware of that problem, because excessive promises get us as a supplier in trouble, just as they do the systems professional. We are already on the side of the systems people. We want them to succeed because that is the only way that we can succeed. So we are going to do our best to help in the implementation of a new system. However, we are not workers of miracles. Nor is any other computer supplier a worker of miracles.

DISCUSSION QUESTIONS

1. What is the expectations gap?
2. What problems are caused by the expectations gap?
3. What are some ways to prevent or to reduce the expectations gap?

SUPPLEMENT 19
Careers in data processing

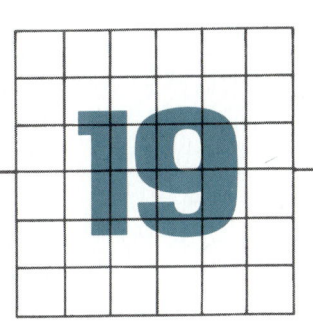

DATA PROCESSING CAREERS IN PERSPECTIVE
CAREER OPPORTUNITIES IN DATA PROCESSING
    The data processing manager
    The systems analyst
    The computer programmer
    The system operator
    The data entry operator
    Other career opportunities in data processing
FINDING THE RIGHT JOB
    Traditional approaches to job hunting
    The job finding strategy
    The résumé and the interview
    Factors in job selection
STARTING A CAREER IN DATA PROCESSING

After completing this supplement, you will be able to:
- List the educational requirements, salary ranges, job responsibilities and career opportunities in the data processing industry.
- Use a job finding strategy to help you get a good job.
- Discuss what is involved in starting and pursuing a career in data processing.

Whether or not you will be a provider of computer services (a data processing professional) or a user of computer services, you should know more about the people employed as data processing professionals. Of course, if you intend to work in the data processing industry, you will most likely be very interested in the salaries, educational requirements, and career opportunities of this profession. On the other hand, if you will be a user of data processing services, you will have to deal with data processing personnel in using the computer to help you perform your job.

The purpose of this supplement is to briefly investigate career opportunities in the data processing industry and to discuss the skills and strategies for finding the right job. Salary figures and required educational backgrounds have been obtained from the latest issues of several data processing journals immediately before the publication of this book.

DATA PROCESSING CAREERS IN PERSPECTIVE

In recent years, opportunities in the data processing industry have continued to grow. Indeed, career opportunities in the data processing industry have been better than in most other industries. The reason for this is supply and demand. The demand for data processing personnel has increased faster than the supply. Today, there are over a half a million people employed as computer operators and about 400,000 people employed as programmers and analysts. The government estimates that the growth in the number of analysts and programmers will increase 50 percent faster than the average of all occupations through 1985. According to the Department of Labor Statistics, a total of nearly 17 million new jobs will be created in the field of data processing between 1976 and 1985.

The major reason for the excellent career opportunities in the data processing industry has been due to the tremendous advances in computer technology. These advances have increased computer capabilities while reducing computer costs. This has caused a remarkable proliferation of computer systems being used by both profit and nonprofit organizations. The growth of the data processing industry was discussed in Chapter 18. With ever advancing technology, lowered prices, and the introduction of minicomputers and microcomputers, more and more people will be using computer systems in the future. Therefore, more data processing professionals will be needed to provide computer services.

CAREER OPPORTUNITIES IN DATA PROCESSING

Although some people start their own company, most data processing professionals work for a profit or nonprofit organization. If you do not work for yourself, you will have two choices. You can either work for a company or organization that provides computers systems and/or services or you can work for a company or organization that uses computer systems and/or services.

If you decide to work for a company that provides computer systems and/or services, you will have a number of different alternatives. You can work for a general computer manufacturer, a small computer manufacturer, a peripheral equipment manufacturer, a leasing company, a time sharing

19 Supplement: Careers in data processing

company, a software company, a service company or a supply company. These companies were described in Chapter 18. Like any other company or organization, these companies require managers, accountants, production foremen, and so on. These companies also require people with expertise in data processing and computers. Some of the more popular jobs that require some data processing expertise are listed below:

1. Maintenance and field service.
2. Sales and marketing.
3. Education.
4. Technical design.
5. Manufacturing research.
6. Software service.
7. Business specialists.
8. Science and engineering specialists.

While there are excellent career opportunities with companies in the data processing industry, there are even more career opportunities with companies and organizations that use computer systems and services. Some of the major positions are listed below:

1. Data processing manager.
2. Systems analyst.
3. Programmer.
4. System operator.
5. Data entry operator.

The data processing manager

The overall function of the data processing manager is to employ the hardware, software, and personnel in the data processing center in a manner that will help the company or organization obtain its goals and objectives. Depending on the size of the data processing department, there may be several people at the managerial level. Some of the job titles associated with data processing management are below:

1. Vice president of information systems.
2. Director of information systems.
3. Manager of data processing.
4. Assistant data processing manager.
5. Manager of systems analysis and design.
6. Manager of computer programming and coding.
7. Supervisor of data processing operations.
8. Supervisor of data entry and office support.

As you can see, there are many different types of management positions, and for the larger data processing centers, there may be managers in charge of the systems analysts, computer programmers, computer operators, and data entry operators. Management positions in a data processing center require both technical and managerial skills. As the data processing department increases in size, the managerial skills become more important. As a result, the trend in educational background is toward management or business. While most managers in the past were promoted from a position of a programmer or systems analyst, today many companies and organizations are seeking data processing managers with degrees in business administration and minors or support areas in data processing and computers. Of course, degrees in computer or information science with a minor or support area in business or management is also a good background for a management job in data processing. While the basic educational requirement for a management position is an undergraduate degree, many data processing managers are seeking graduate degrees such as an MBA (Masters of Business Administration) or a Masters Degree in Computer or Information Science.

The salary of the data processing managers depends on the size of the data processing department and the responsibilities of the data processing manager. The salary range for managers of data processing departments runs from $800 per month to $8,400 per month. In 1980, the average DP manager earned about $2,300 per month.

The systems analyst

The role of the systems analyst is multifaceted. Like the architect in the home building analogy, the systems analyst helps the user in determining what reports and outputs should be obtained from the computer system and the plans that are needed to develop the necessary computer programs that produce these reports and outputs.

The number and types of systems analysts is a function of the size of the data processing department. The list below contains some of the typical titles with descriptions following.

1. Assistant supervisor of systems analysis and design.
2. Senior systems analyst.
3. Systems analyst.
4. Junior systems analyst.

The educational requirements for the systems analyst are similar to those of the data processing manager. Since the systems analyst interacts with other managers and decision makers within the organization, the systems analyst should have good management and communication skills. An undergraduate degree in business with a minor in computer science or an undergraduate degree in computer science with a minor in business administration or management are common requirements for a job as a systems analyst. Furthermore, many systems analysts pursue graduate degrees in both business and computer science.

Systems analysts earn a salary that ranges from $670 to $4,200 per month. Of course, the actual salary depends on the experience and qualifications of

19 Supplement: Careers in data processing

the individual and the job duties and responsibilities. In 1980, the average monthly salary was about $1,900.

The computer programmer

The major responsibility of the computer programmer is to take the plans developed by the systems analyst and to develop one or more computer programs that will produce the desired reports and outputs. In addition, the computer programmer might be involved with flowcharting, testing, implementation, and documentation. A list of job titles for the computer programmer is given below:

1. Assistant supervisor of programming.
2. Programmer I.
3. Programmer II.
4. Senior programmer.
5. Junior programmer.
6. Coder.

Data processing departments may use different titles for different programming levels. For example, Programmer I and Programmer II reveal two different levels of programmers. The educational background for programmers also varies. While some programmers have B.S. degrees from four-year universities, many programmers have degrees from community colleges and from private training schools. The trend is toward B.S. degrees from four-year universities. Most programmers with a B.S. degree have majored in computer science, but there are a large number of programmers with backgrounds in business and other fields.

The salary for programmers ranges from $500 per month to $3,900 per month. In 1980, the average monthly salary was about $1,760. Again, the exact salary depends on the experience, educational background, and job responsibility of the programmer.

The system operator

As mentioned previously, all components that are electronically connected to the computer are part of the computer system. This equipment would include the CPU, disk drives, tape drives, card readers, printers, and similar devices. The primary function of the system operator is to operate or run all equipment that is associated with the computer system. Some of the titles that are associated with system operators are given below:

1. Supervisor of equipment and system operators.
2. Senior system operator.
3. System operator.
4. Junior system operator.
5. Console operator.
6. Unit record and card system operator.

As with all positions, there are several different levels of system operators. The educational background of operators is normally a high school degree or a certificate of completion from a technical or operator's school. In addition, system operators have degrees from community colleges, junior colleges, and from private computer schools. Some operators for the larger computer installations might have a B.S. degree from a four-year college or university.

The salary range for system operators ranges from $480 per month to $3,530 per month. In 1980, the average monthly salary was about $1,130.

The data entry operators

The major responsibility of the data entry operator is to convert data that is on a document into a form that can be used by the computer system. For example, a keypunch operator places data onto computer cards, which can be read by a card reader and entered into the computer system. Likewise, a key-to-tape operator and a key-to-disk operator place data onto magnetic tape, tape cassettes, the disk, or the floppy disk. Some of the titles associated with data entry are given below:

1. Supervisor of data entry operators.
2. Data entry operator.
3. Keypunch operator.
4. Key-to-tape operator.
5. Key-to-disk operator.
6. Verifier.
7. Data entry clerk.

The educational requirements for the data entry operator are similar to the educational requirements for the system operator. In most cases, a high school degree with a certificate of completion of training at a junior college, community college or a private school is required. The monthly earnings of the data entry operator ranges from $410 to $2,500. In 1980, the average monthly salary was $950.

Other career opportunities in data processing

Depending on the size and type of data processing department, there may be other data processing personnel. Some of the more common positions are the data base administrator, the project or team leader, the data communications operator, and the tape librarian.

The data base administrator is an important position for data processing departments that employ a data base management system (DBMS). The educational background for this position is similar to the data processing department manager. The monthly salary for a data base administrator can range from $1,250 to $4,100. In 1980, the average salary was about $2,300 per month.

In Chapter 15, the topic of structured design was introduced to you. Each major programming application has a chief programmer team that is managed by the chief programmer or project or team leader. This individual is responsible for the entire programming application. The educational background of this position is similar to the educational backgrounds of the systems analyst or the computer programmer. The monthly salary for a project or team leader can range from $900 to $14,100. The average monthly salary in 1980 was about $2,160.

Organizations that use data communications equipment may have one or more data communications operators. These individuals operate and maintain data processing equipment. This equipment was described in Part II. The educational requirements for this position are similar to computer and system operators. The monthly salary for a data communications operator can range from $650 to $2,800. In 1980, the average monthly salary was about $1,400.

For those organizations that require a large amount of data storage on magnetic tape, a tape librarian is needed. The tape librarian is responsible for the use, accuracy, and protection of data stored on magnetic tape. The educational requirements are similar to the computer operator, and some tape librarians have experience with normal libraries and the management of data and information. The monthly salary ranges from $550 to $1,840, and in 1980, the average monthly salary was about $960.

It should be noted that the salary figures and the required educational backgrounds discussed for the various positions above have been compiled from the most recent statistics prior to the publication of this book in 1980. It is expected that in the years to come the amount of formal education required for the various positions and the salary figures will increase. While the educational requirements for the various positions is not expected to increase dramatically over the next five years, the average monthly salary figures are expected to increase by 10 percent or more per year. Of course, the actual increase depends on the economy and the possible existence of wage and salary guidelines or regulations.

FINDING THE RIGHT JOB

One of the most important and difficult tasks that you will undertake is to find a good job. A person with fewer qualifications and skills could get a higher paying and more satisfying job than you by knowing how to go about getting a good job. Although it is beyond the scope of this book to deal with the subject of job finding in any detail, we will investigate the essential aspects of job hunting.

Traditional approaches to job hunting

Some of the traditional approaches to finding a job include the use of private employment agencies that usually charge for their services (head hunters), public employment agencies, college placement centers, and professional organizations. Other approaches include preparing and mailing thousands of resumes to companies and organizations throughout the country. Some people have found jobs through their friends and relatives. Some religious organizations provide career counseling and assistance.

While these traditional approaches have worked well for some individuals, they have not resulted in meaningful jobs for others. Some people have even tried all of the above approaches without success. What is needed is an approach or a strategy, which will provide you with an organized procedure for finding and obtaining a good job.

The job finding strategy

Any job finding strategy, regardless of how good it is, cannot guarantee that you will obtain a good job. Any worthwhile strategy, however, will greatly increase your chances of landing a good job. The minimum requirements for a job finding strategy are:

1. Decide what you want.
2. Gather extensive information.
3. Contact the person who has the authority to hire you.
4. Stress your strengths.

Completing the first step involves determining exactly what you want in a job. Salary and geographical location are always important factors. In addition, fringe benefits and training and development programs may be important to you. Your job description, job responsibilities and the people you will be working with will also be important to you. Of course, everyone has a different perception of a good job.

The second step is to gather extensive information. One of the major purposes of the second step is to locate those organizations that could offer you the type of job that would satisfy the desires that you listed in the first step. You will be seeking organizations that will be able to offer you a job with the salary, fringe benefits, location, and working environment that you want. But there is another purpose of the second step. This is to start the process of locating the person that has the authority and responsibility to make you an offer. You will need this information for the third step.

There are basically two sources of information—indirect and direct. The indirect sources are the ones that are most commonly used. These indirect sources include magazines, trade journals, newspapers, and other documents that describe industries, their problems, and their career opportunities. In data processing, there are many journals and data processing societies that discuss new data processing concepts, problems in the field, and career opportunities. Some of these societies and organizations will be discussed at the end of this chapter.

Gathering information directly means going to companies that employ data processing centers and talking to people, usually the data processing manager, about the data processing industry. If you are a student and you have to complete a few term papers, you will have an excellent opportunity to meet the people in data processing departments. You will be talking to these people about your term project or student assignment, and at the same time, you will get to know people who will most likely have the authority to hire you when you graduate.

The third step is to contact the person who has the authority to hire you. If you have done a good job with gathering information, you will already have a list of people that have this authority. When you talk to one person, get names of other people that may also be able to help you. You can also go to the personnel department, but in some cases, this will not lead you to the right people. Many personnel departments do little more than screen potential employees, and you do not want to be screened out of a job before you have a chance to talk to that person with the authority to hire you.

The fourth step, selling your strengths, is more of a philosophy. You always want to stress how your abilities can help the organization, in this case the data processing department.

The résumé and the interview

The résumé and the interview are common tools for any job search. The purpose of both of these tools is to communicate to a potential employer the skills, qualifications, and abilities that you will be able to use in solving problems or in helping the organization obtain its goals.

The résumé is a one to two page description of you and your qualifications and experiences. Typical contents of a résumé are below:

1. Personal information.
2. Skills and qualifications.
3. Educational background.
4. Work experience.
5. Miscellaneous information.
6. References.

Some employment agencies suggest that you print over 1,000 résumés and send out at least 500 of these résumés to companies that might be interested in your skills and qualifications. This is the shotgun approach. Unfortunately, in developing a general résumé that may appeal to a number of different companies, you might end up with a résumé that does not appeal to anyone. Instead, it is usually better to individually prepare a résumé for each company that you would like to interview. If you have done a good job in researching the data processing industry and the companies for which you would like to work, you can stress your ability to solve the problems that these companies are facing.

The interview is one of the most important aspects of getting a good job. Unfortunately, many job seekers do a completely inadequate job of preparing for an interview. Again, it is necessary to completely research the industry and the particular company that you will be interviewing. You should know how the company is organized, what the company produces, some of the problems of the company, the goals and the objectives of the company, and so on. You should also be prepared to answer some commonly-asked questions. Why do you want this job? How can you help the company? What do you expect in terms of salary, fringe benefits, working conditions, and so on?

The person interviewing you will make a judgment about you in a relatively short amount of time. Your behavior and appearance can make the difference between getting an attractive job offer and not being considered for the job. In terms of behavior, the interviewer will be carefully studying exactly what you say and how you act during the interview. In addition, your appearance will be very important. This does not mean that you need to wear a tuxedo or formal dress if you are interviewing for a programming job, but you should be neatly and appropriately dressed.

Factors in job selection

If you are fortunate enough to have several job offers, how do you make the best selection? In the first step of the job finding strategy, you listed desirable characteristics of the job you are seeking. You may give each of these characteristics or factors a weight in percent representing its importance to you. Then you can evaluate each factor for each company on a 100 point basis and calculate a weighted average that will give you a numerical score for each job. An example of this appears in Figure S19–1.

Factor	Importance rating	Evaluation of job A	Evaluation of job B
1. Salary	30%	80 × 30% = 24	70 × 30% = 21
2. Location	10	100 × 10% = 10	90 × 10% = 9
3. Work environment	5	80 × 5% = 4	100 × 5% = 5
4. Fringe benefits	15	60 × 15% = 9	80 × 15% = 12
5. Training and development	20	80 × 20% = 16	100 × 20% = 20
6. Advancement opportunities	20	70 × 20% = 14	90 × 20% = 18
Totals	100%	77	85

FIGURE S19–1

The totals for each job were obtained by multiplying the importance rating by the points given to each factor and then adding the results. Of course, the weights that you will assign to the various factors will be different, and you may have several job offers to compare. The procedure, however, remains the same.

STARTING A CAREER IN DATA PROCESSING

The career opportunities in data processing have been excellent, and it is likely that they will continue to be excellent in the future. More than other careers, data processing careers require that you have the determination to be very good at what you do. Promotion and advancement are based on performance and results, and if you are willing to put forth the time and effort, you will have the potential to advance quickly in the data processing industry.

Because the data processing industry is extremely dynamic, it will be necessary for you to keep current on the latest and newest concepts. The same increasing technology that has caused a growing data processing industry has also caused good data processing professionals to continually go through training and development programs. A career in data processing requires continuing education.

There are many data processing organizations and journals that can help you keep current. Furthermore, these organizations and journals can be a source of new career opportunities. Association for Computing Machinery (ACM), the Association of Data Processing Service Organization (ADPSO), the Data Processing Management Association (DPMA), the American Society for Information Science, and the American Federation of Information Processing Societies (AFIPS) are only a few of the data processing organizations and societies. Some of the data processing journals include *Communications of the ACM, Data Processing Digest, Infosystems, Journal of Systems Management,* and *Computer World.* In addition to these organizations and journals, there are publications produced by many of the computer manufacturers, and there are many specialized data processing organizations and publications. The address of some of these organizations is given below in case you wish to write to them directly to gather additional information about careers in data processing:

American Federation of Information Processing Societies
210 Summit Avenue
Montvale, New Jersey 07645

American Society for Information Science
1010 Sixteenth Street, N.W.
Washington, D.C. 20036

Association for Computing Machinery
1133 Avenue of the Americas
New York, New York 10036

Association for Systems Management
24587 Bagley Road
Cleveland, Ohio 44138

Data Processing Management Association
505 Busse Hwy.
Park Ridge, Ill. 60068

It is also possible to get certified in the data processing field. The Institute for Certification of Computer Professionals gives two examinations and awards two certificates, the Certificate in Computer Programming and the

Certificate in Data Processing. The first examination is intended for senior-level programmers. It is not restricted to that level but would be difficult to pass without fairly broad experience in programming. The second examination is designed for those having at least 60 months of direct experience in computer-based information systems or at least 3 years experience with college-level academic work substituted for up to 2 years experience. Certification of data processing professionals by examinations better defines the knowledge requirements of the field. For example, candidates for certification in computer programming are tested in the following areas:

1. Data and file organization.
2. Principles and techniques of programming.
3. Interaction with hardware and software.
4. Interaction with people.
4. Associated techniques including quantitative techniques and systems analysis and design.

One of the following areas of specialization is included according to the candidate's choice:

1. Specialization-business programming.
2. Specialization-scientific programming.
3. Specialization-systems programming.

Candidates for certification in data processing are tested over the following areas:

1. Data processing equipment.
2. Computer programming and software.
3. Principles of management.
4. Quantitative methods.
5. Systems analysis and design.

For more information about these examinations you can write to:

Institute for Certification of Computer Professionals 304 East 45th Street New York, New York 10017

In starting a data processing career, it is important to remember that a data processing department has the overall objective to serve the organization or company. Before you get lost in the detail of computer programming or systems analysis, it is helpful to ask yourself: "How can I help the company or organization in obtaining its goals or in solving its problems?"

SUMMARY

In this supplement, you have been introduced to careers in the data processing industry. Various career opportunities along with salaries, responsibilities, job descriptions, educational backgrounds, and career opportunities were discussed. In addition, this supplement introduced you to the fundamentals of finding the right job. A job finding strategy was presented, and techniques

19 Supplement: Careers in data processing

of developing a resume and conducting an interview were explored. This was followed by a discussion of the factors in job selection. Finally, this supplement ended with a discussion of starting a career in data processing.

KEY TERMS AND CONCEPTS

American Federation of Information Processing Societies (AFIPS)
American Society for Information Science
Association for Computer Machinery (ACM)
Association of Data Processing Service Organizations (ADPSO)
Communications of the ACM
Computer programmer
Computer World
Data base administration
Data communications operator
Data entry operator
Data Processing Digest
Data Processing Management Association (DPMA)
Data processing manager
Infosystems
Interviewing
Journal of Systems Management
Résumés
Systems analyst
System operator
Tape librarian

QUESTIONS

S19–1. What are the factors that have enhanced the opportunities of data processing careers?

S19–2. Briefly discuss the career opportunities of working for a company that is in the data processing industry, such as a computer manufacturer.

S19–3. What are the career opportunities, salary ranges, and educational requirements of a data processing manager?

S19–4. What are the differences between a career as a programmer and a career as a systems analyst?

S19–5. Describe the salary ranges, educational backgrounds, and responsibilities of the system operator and the data entry operator.

S19–6. What are some of the other career opportunities in the data processing industry?

S19–7. What are some of the traditional approaches to job hunting?

S19–8. Describe the job finding strategy.

S19–9. What are some of the factors in job selection.

S19–10. Briefly describe how to construct a resume and how to conduct a job interview.

ANSWERS

1. T
2. T
3. F
4. T
5. F
6. F
7. F
8. F
9. F
10. T

MINIQUIZ

True or False

_____ 1. According to the Department of Labor Statistics, a total of nearly 17,000,000 new jobs will be created in the field of data processing between 1976 and 1985.

_____ 2. Some of the jobs that are available for computer manufacturing companies include maintenance and field service, sales and marketing, technical design, and manufacturing research.

_____ 3. The major educational requirement for a data processing manager is a high school degree with experience with computers.

_____ 4. A typical data processing manager earned about $2,300 per month in 1980.

_____ 5. Like the contractor in a home building analogy, the systems analyst helps in actually building the necessary computer programs and systems.

_____ 6. In general, computer programmers are paid more than systems analysts.

_____ 7. The system operator and the data entry operator perform the same basic function or purpose.

_____ 8. A data base administrator is paid about the same average salary as a computer programmer.

_____ 9. The best job finding strategy is to develop thousands of resumes and to send these resumes to various companies that might employ data processing personnel.

_____ 10. It is now possible to take an exam and to acquire a certificate in computer programming.

The changing role of the MIS executive

Joseph Ferreira and *James F. Collins, Jr.*

"The future is coming. Are you ready?"

This headline in recent national advertising by a large industrial corporation could well be directed to today's MIS executive. For today, management information services (MIS), the wide-encompassing corporate function-created in a short 25 years by the spectacular achievements of data processing and communications technology, finds itself at a crucial turning point in its own further evolution. Nothing less than the professional status and organizational power base of the director of MIS operations is at stake.

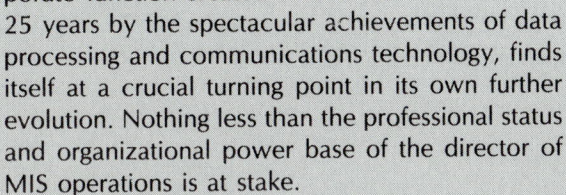

Ironically, the career predicament in which the heads of large-scale MIS operations find themselves now, or will sortly be confronted with, arises from their very success in applying the new developments in data processing and communications technologies as fast as they appeared. They provided end users in operating departments with systems and equipment that are to a large extent user transparent. This has, in effect, made it possible for operating managements to become MIS managers in their own right, pressing to extend applications to fit their particular needs. Easy-to-use minicomputers and satellite installations, and the services of computer utilities, freed them to a large extent from dependency upon the technical expertise of the central computer staff. Advances in technology made it possible for them actually to disregard technological details, and, by virtue of the flexibility of their "black boxes," to concentrate upon their business needs.

One result is that today many end users of data processing and communications technology are challenging the way the central MIS mission is carried out as well as how its goals are set. It is important to note that their dissatisfaction transcends the mere competition for available resources: it involves an important change in the way *information*—and not merely the processing of data—will be viewed in the period that lies ahead. This development will have a profound effect on MIS philosophy, on the way the MIS function fits into the corporate structure, and on how its main mission is to be conceived and implemented.

The implication for MIS managers is clear: the wheels of change are turning rapidly, and those who do not turn with them are liable either to be run over or simply left behind.

Evolution of MIS. The MIS function is no stranger to evolutionary development, and by and large it has adapted well to times of transition. The fact remains, however, that further change is now in the making, and the latest adaptive process may be traumatic for many.

Ten to 15 years ago, the principal requirements for the direction of computer operations were outstanding technical competence and the ability to provide top-grade technical management. Basically, the MIS function—indeed, not yet called by that name—was that of a service, much like accounting, to aid in the processing of transactional data and in supplying collations and summaries of data that would be useful in management decision-making. The MIS function was not, be it noted, to participate in the management decision-making process itself.

But as the function matured, the concept of "management information system" and, more broadly, "management information services" began to emerge, and the head of MIS came to be considered part of the management team. Thus it became apparent about five years ago that top MIS managers had to be good *business* managers. In addition to directing technical managers responsible for components of the MIS function, they were now expected to contribute to the business strate-

---

Source: Reprinted with permission of DATAMATION® magazine. © Copyright by Technical Publishing Company, a Dun & Bradstreet Company, 1979—all rights reserved.

gies and operational efficiencies of all corporate functions—manufacturing, finance, marketing, sales, and even research and development. MIS management had to become broad-gauged in its perception of goals and procedures, it had to come outside of the technological cocoon.

The next progression, admittedly thus far achieved in only a minority of instances, is for MIS management to be considered a logical stepping-stone to general top management positions—on an equal footing with other functions such as marketing, finance, manufacturing, and sales. But this will occur only if MIS is accepted as part of the main line of business operations. The challenge to present MIS management is to see to it that this potential is realized.

DISCUSSION QUESTIONS

1. How did the MIS executive evolve?
2. What types of skills are required for an MIS executive?
3. What are the advancement possibilities for the MIS executive?

INTEGRATIVE CASES

GLOSSARY

INDEX

ABOUT THE CASES

With any book, there is a need to integrate the material contained in the various chapters and parts. In addition, it is important to be able to apply the concepts you learn to "real-world" problems. The overall purpose of the cases is to allow you to integrate the material and to apply what you learn to real problems and situations.

The case method is a proven approach, and many colleges rely completely on this approach in the classroom. In this section of the book, you will find cases that will allow you to use the knowledge that you acquire. These cases are:

Bryan's I	Part I
Bryan's II	Part II
Greenville Community College	Part II
Bryan's III(A)	Part III
Bryan's III(B)	Instructor's Manual
LeBoeuf Financial	Part III
Bryan's IV(A)	Part IV
Bryan's IV(B)	Instructor's Manual
Resnik Distributors	Part IV

Bryan's starts out as a small clothing store (Part I), and it grows to become a large and complex national company (Parts II, III, and IV). As the company grows, its data processing needs and problems become increasingly complex. Starting with Part I, you will find a case about Bryan's that traces its growth and its problems. In these cases, you will be asked to apply what you learn to solving the data processing problems that Bryan's encounters as it emerges into a national clothing chain. You may notice that there are two cases for Bryan's, III(B) and IV(B), that are in the Instructor's Manual. These cases are a continuation of III(A) and IV(B), and your instructor may reproduce and assign these cases as well.

The other cases, Greenville Community College, LeBoeuf Financial and Resnik Distributors, also allow you to apply what you learn to "real-world" problems. Along with Bryan's, these cases will ask you to develop management information systems, design computerized applications, perform systems analysis and design, apply structured design techniques, and more.

SUGGESTIONS FOR SOLVING CASES

Another advantage of the case approach is that it allows you to develop an approach for solving problems. If your instructor does not give you any guidelines for solving the cases, you may wish to use the steps listed below:

1. Understand the overall setting.
2. Identify the problem(s).
3. List the feasible alternatives.
4. Evaluate the alternatives.
5. Select the best solution.
6. Present the solution.

The first step in solving a case is to get a feeling for the overall situation. This will help you go beyond the symptoms and concentrate on the real problems. In determining the problems, make sure to consider both equipment and technical problems as well as human relations and personnel problems. In some cases, you will find both. Make sure to list and consider all alternatives, and don't forget that doing nothing or keeping things the way they are is one alternative for all cases. The alternatives should be evaluated in terms of the overall goals and objectives of the firm. In most cases, this will be to increase overall profits or to reduce total costs. There may, however, be other goals and objectives. These might be to increase customer service, to produce a better quality product, to increase market share, and so on. If the alternatives have been correctly and completely evaluated, selecting the best solution should not be too difficult. Usually there will be several good solutions. In some cases, it may be difficult or impossible to find the *best* solution.

After you have solved the case, you will be asked to either present your findings before the class and your instructor or to prepare a report that contains your conclusions and recommendations. With either situation, the approach is basically the same. Below is an outline that can serve as major sections of a written report or as the major points of a verbal presentation:

1. Discussion of the important facts.
2. Statement of the problem(s).
3. Analysis of the alternatives.
4. Recommendations.
5. Appendix (if needed).

CASE FOR PART I

Bryan's: I

It all started on a cold Friday night. The University of Wisconsin football team had just trounced Purdue. Madison was alive, and the beer was flowing. The celebration for Steve Bryan, however, was hollow. While Steve enjoyed the game and the parties, he was deeply concerned about his future. He graduated with honors last year with a master's degree in English literature, but there were simply no jobs. For the last year and a half, Steve worked at University Fashions to make ends meet. Although the salary was more than adequate, Steve liked fine clothes and good times. His desire to always be well dressed was one of the reasons he decided to work for University Fashions, but he realized that this was a dead end job.

This Friday night was unusually cold. For Steve, going outside during the winter was like stepping into a cold shower. No matter how many clothes he had on, the cold winds seemed to always slice through him. Perhaps this is why he liked "The Library," a popular student bar. It was always warm. The walls were covered with fraternity and sorority plaques, and the atmosphere was always friendly. It was also a meeting place for Steve and his friends.

When Steve walked through the doors of "The Library," his small group of friends was already at their usual table with two half-empty pitchers of beer. Steve joined the group. It was at this time when Bob Surowsky, with a slurred voice, said to Steve, "With the clothes you buy, you should own your own clothing store." For the rest of the evening, Steve didn't say or drink very much. He just stared at his beer glass.

The four years since that Friday night at "The Library" seemed to fly by for Steve. For two years, he worked at University Fashions, learning the business and saving every penny for when he would start his own company. It took Steve two more years after he quit University Fashions to start Bryan's on State Street in Madison and to open two more locations at East City Mall and West City Mall. The road to success was not always smooth, and twice he almost went bankrupt because of cash-flow problems. Today, his cash flow is excellent, and his employees are dedicated, including Jimmy Jackson and Frank Pierson. Jimmy received his B.S. in Business from the University of Wisconsin and was now the general manager of all three stores. Frank, who was an excellent computer programmer, ran the small-batch oriented computer that used 96 column cards for permanent storage that was purchased to handle payroll and other accounting functions. Even though the cash flow was good, there were always problems to hammer out. Discussing some of these problems was the purpose of the meeting with Steve, Jimmy, and Frank.

Steve: The purpose of this meeting is to identify and to try to solve some problems that Jimmy is facing as general manager. Some of these problems may be caused by our computer, while other problems may be solved by the computer. That is why you are here, Frank. Jimmy, since you wanted to have this meeting, why don't you start?

Jimmy: I have been with this company for over a year, and I have seen it grow. Although our cash flow is good, we have a number of serious problems that need immediate attention. For example, why does it take so long to get the list of what we have in inventory? By the time I get the computer report, which was four days late last week, it was completely inaccurate. As a result we had a large number of stockouts and lost thousands of dollars in sales.

Frank: With our batch-oriented operating system and with our limited megabyte secondary storage capacity, it is difficult not to have problems. We have also had trouble with some of our main language compilers, and the inventory application just developed a bug last week.

Jimmy: I don't understand a word of that, Frank. I wish you would stop talking in your computer language and start talking in plain English. We have some real problems here.

Frank: The problem is that you know nothing about computers, Jimmy, or you would understand that we have problems, too. In plain English, there is no way we can do what you want.

Steve: This is accomplishing nothing. We are here to solve problems and not to yell at each other. Jimmy, what are some of the other problems?

Jimmy: What I was trying to say before is that we need to have accurate and up to date inventory levels. The once-a-week inventory list is inaccurate and totally useless to me. In addition, we have been having a total payroll that is entirely too high. I think that there are some people who are claiming to work over 70 hours per week. This is impossible. I need to know who these people are.

Frank: Jimmy, if you would read the weekly computer report that I send to you every week, you would know who these people are. The report contains every employee, their gross wages, deductions, overtime, and much more.

Jimmy: It takes me over three hours to read that report. It is too long. Furthermore, it is nothing more than a duplicate copy of the accounting reports. I need some reports that are designed to help me. Why don't we have a computer like University Fashions? It can determine exactly what sales will be for the next five months.

Steve: I would like both of you to get together to determine what additional reports should come from the computer and report back to me in two weeks.

Jimmy: I don't have the time for that. We are paying Frank good money to develop computer reports, and he has the responsibility to do it.

Steve: Frank, see what you can do and get back with me in a few weeks.

Cases

Questions

1. What should Jimmy know about computers?
2. What types of hardware changes would permit faster and more immediate access to data?
3. What software changes would be necessary to permit faster and more immediate access to data?
4. Frank said, "In plain English, there is no way we can do what you want." How would you respond to this statement if you were Jimmy?
5. What types of reports would you want if you were trying to control total payroll costs?
6. Do you think it is possible for the computer at University Fashions to compute exactly what sales will be for the next five months? Explain your answer.
7. Jimmy said that he would not have time to get together with Frank about possible reports for Jimmy. If you were Frank, how would you respond to this statement.

CASES FOR PART II

Bryan's: II

(This is a continuation of Bryan's: I)

The first five years for Bryan's can be characterized by rapid change. Shortly after the three stores were started in Madison, Wisconsin, Steve Bryan was talking to his lawyers about setting up another branch in Milwaukee. Steve believed that with a larger population base, Milwaukee would be an excellent location for expansion, and he was correct. The downtown branch was able to reach a break-even position in less than six months. One year after the downtown Milwaukee branch was started, Steve opened two more branches. One was also in the downtown area, and the other was in a shopping center close to Waukesha. Dick Pabst, a graduate of the business school at Indiana University with a major in marketing, headed the three new stores in the Milwaukee area.

There were also some changes at Madison. The company now operated out of an office complex in downtown Madison instead of from the first Bryan's store. Steve Bryan, chairman of the board, was now spending more of his time playing golf and drinking with the boys at the Madison Country Club. It was a sad day for Steve when "The Library" was converted into an office supply company. Jimmy Jackson was now the president of Bryan's with a new assistant, Rhonda Render.

The data processing department was also located in the new office complex for Bryan's. Steve Bryan enjoyed showing his old friends all of the new computer equipment. After a visit from the computer vendor, Steve decided that a larger computer system was needed, and a month later, a medium-size computer system was delivered. Because it was from the same manufacturer, the conversion process was not too complicated. This medium computer system had several disks to store permanent data, but it still operated in the batch mode, using computer cards as input. While Frank appreciated the larger computer system, he was upset that he was not consulted before the new system was purchased. He also did not like having the computer center constantly on public display for Steve's friends and other people that entered the main office. Frank also did not like his new assistant, Leslie Larsen, who was hired by Jimmy. She got along with managers better than he ever did, but she was not a very good programmer. For some reason, managers preferred to go through Leslie instead of Frank, and the meeting with Jimmy, Dick, and Leslie was an example.

Cases

Jimmy: Dick and I wanted to meet with you this morning because it is virtually impossible to get Frank to understand our problems. We are still having problems with accurate data files. It takes between four and five days from the time a sale is made until it is entered into the computer system. Do you have any suggestions?

Leslie: There are a number of things that could be done. They could be more expensive, but I will try to have some alternatives and the various costs associated with each for you in the near future.

Dick: At the present time, we send all of our transactions from Milwaukee to Madison by bus. Again, the problem is speed. We need to get our processing done faster. Dress Rite, Inc., one of our biggest competitors, has some type of device at each store. What are these devices, and should we get some? In addition, when the sales-ordering file was accidently destroyed last month, it took Frank over two weeks to get the file restored, and I am still not sure if the file is correct. Don't we have some type of automatic back-up system for this?

Leslie: Again, let me look into these problems, and I will get back to you in about a week.

Questions

1. Was it right to not include Frank in the decision to purchase another computer system? Who should be involved in making this type of decision, and who should have the final authority to make this type of decision?
2. Who normally has the authority to hire someone like Leslie?
3. What type of qualities should a data processing manager have?
4. What type of hardware changes would you suggest to make data entry and input faster?
5. What are the alternatives of locating computer equipment or devices in the Milwaukee store? What would you recommend to Dick?
6. Is there any type of special purpose hardware device that would help satisfy some of Dick's needs?
7. Do you think there is an automatic back up for data files at the computer center? If there are no procedures for a backup, what would you recommend?

Greenville Community College

Sandi O'Brien was very good with mathematics in high school, and as a senior, she received A's in all of her courses. It was probably her chemistry teacher who convinced her to specialize in physical chemistry in college. This teacher was very supportive and shared her books and materials with Sandi, including a small paperback on thermodynamics. Sandi found thermodynamics logical and easy to understand. She also found her college courses almost trivial, and after four years and four scholarships, Sandi received a master's degree in chemistry and taught at Greenville Community College. Two years later, she was named vice president of administrative affairs.

Sandi soon concluded that it was much easier to solve differential equations than to deal with some of the human relations problems that she faced on a daily basis. Some of the major complaints were always related to the lack of adequate computer facilities. Since Greenville Community College is a small school, the same computer system is used for administrative purposes and for teaching and research. As vice president of administrative affairs, the data processing center was one of her areas of responsibility. It seemed that teachers, students, and administrators were always complaining about the batch-oriented medium-sized computer system.

The most common complaint from teachers was that they were not able to have the computer score true-false and multiple-choice exams. While Greenville Community College was not known for faculty research, there were several members of the faculty that performed research and published articles on a regular basis. These teachers wanted better access, faster turnaround time, and the ability to perform more sophisticated data analysis.

The students, on the other hand, were always complaining about the inability to gain access to the computer system. They complained about having to walk across campus every time they had to write a computer program and then having to wait from four hours to a day and a half before they received the results. If there were a few mistakes in their programs, it could take as long as four or five days to eliminate them.

Some school administrators also complained about the inadequate computer facilities. It was extremely difficult to obtain student records. It often required a few days to get student records from the computer system. Records were stored on the disk, but for some reason, it was a lengthy process to get the desired information. Placing all of the student records on paper was also expensive and cumbersome, but most of the administrators wanted off-line storage.

QUESTIONS

1. What type of hardware improvements or additions would help solve some of the problems for the teachers, students, and other administrators?
2. Are all of the problems hardware problems?

CASES FOR PART III

Bryan's: III(A)

(This is a continuation of Bryan's: I and II)

Leslie Larsen first met Frank at a local Data Processing Management Association (DPMA) meeting. Frank was the luncheon speaker. He started his talk with a story about a new data processing manager who was given three envelopes from the previous data processing manager who was just fired. The outgoing data processing manager said to open the first envelope when the first major problem occurred, to open the second envelope with the second major problem, and to open the third envelope when the third major problem occurred. As the story goes, the message in the first envelope was to blame the first problem on the previous data processing manager, the message in the second envelope was to blame the second problem on inadequate computer facilities, and the message in the third envelope was to make three new envelopes for the next data processing manager. Leslie laughed with everyone else as the story was being told at the DPMA meeting, but now it had real meaning. Frank was recently fired as the data processing manager at Bryan's for inadequate job performance, and Leslie was named the new data processing manager.

Frank always had trouble relating to managers within Bryan's, and this was one of the reasons he was fired. Leslie, on the other hand, worked very well with managers, and she was determined to provide managers with what they wanted from the data processing department. When Dick requested three reports on sales, Leslie was eager to satisfy Dick's request. Each report is to be generated from the sales orders, which are collected and punched onto computer cards. Because there is only one line printer, the application should be designed to have one report printed on the line printer and to have the other reports listed on the disk. Then two small programs should read and print the remaining two reports one after the other. Each report is to have a title that indicates the contents of the reports. The line below the title should be "PREPARED FOR DICK PABST."

The first report is the Sales-by-Salesperson report. The major columns of this report should be the name of the salesperson, the numerical code of the salesperson, the total sales for that salesperson, the total returns and adjustments, the net sales, and the total commissions for that salesperson. The appropriate titles should be placed at the top of each column, and totals should be computed and printed under every column containing dollar amounts. The report should list the data for salesperson alphabetically.

Cases

The second report is the Sales-by-Item report. The columns for this report should be the name of the inventory item, the item number or code, the total sales for the item, the total returns and adjustments for the item, and the net sales for the item. Appropriate column headings are to be included, and the total of all dollar amounts are to be printed.

The third report is the Sales-by-Customer report. The columns for this report should be the name of the customer, the customer identification number, the total sales to that customer, the total returns and adjustments for that customer, and the net sales for the customer. Again, the appropriate column titles should be placed at the top of each column and totals for all dollar amounts should be computed and placed at the bottom of the appropriate columns.

The data that is recorded for each sales order includes the customer name, customer code number, salesperson's name and identification number, the total sales, and the returns and adjustments. The commissions are computed as 15 percent of the net sales.

QUESTIONS

1. What other information would you need if you were Leslie in defining the problem for these reports?
2. What is Leslie responsible for in developing these types of computerized applications?
3. What is Dick responsible for in developing these types of computerized applications?
4. Develop print charts for the three reports.
5. Develop card layout charts for the three reports.
6. Develop an application flowchart for the entire application.
7. Are these three reports scheduled, demand, or exception reports?

LeBoeuf Financial

With limited resources and the motto "Work Smart," Mike LeBoeuf was able to put together LeBoeuf Financial. In addition to providing investment advice, the company also made loans to qualified individuals. The loans could range from $1,000 to $6,000 in amount. Mike used current personal income and current personal debt to determine the maximum amount of the loan for every applicant. A loan up to $1,000 would be made if current debt was over $3,000 and personal income was under $10,000. A loan up to $2,000 would be made if current debt was under $3,000 and personal income was under $10,000. A loan up to $3,000 was made if current debt was over $3,000 and personal income was between $10,000 and $20,000. A loan up to $4,000 was made if current debt was under $3,000 and personal income was between $10,000 and $20,000. A loan up to $5,000 was made if current debt was over $3,000 and personal income was over $20,000. A loan up to $6,000 was made if current debt was under $3,000 and personal income was over $20,000.

For several years, Mike determined who qualified for a loan. With increasing business, this practice was becoming impossible. Furthermore, Mike wanted to computerize this process on his new microcomputer.

QUESTIONS

1. Develop a decision table for this application.
2. Develop a flowchart for this application.
3. Which analysis technique is more appropriate for this application?
4. What general guidelines would you follow in making test data for this application?
5. Develop test data for this application.

CASES FOR PART IV

Bryan's: IV(A)

(This is a continuation of Bryan's: I, II(A), and III(A))

The merger with Hamilton, a national clothing store chain, was completely unexpected. Some executives of Bryan's, including Jimmy Jackson, believed that it was because Steve Bryan was bored with Bryan's. The aging company founder was spending more and more time with his old friends at the Madison Country Club. For the past several years, Jimmy Jackson had been assuming more responsibility in making strategic and top-level decisions. In fact, Steve Bryan didn't attend the last two board meetings of Bryan's. The stated reason was illness, but Jimmy knew it was because of a lack of interest.

Hamilton has major stores in Chicago, New York, Atlanta, and Dallas. Executive offices and the data processing department for Hamilton are located in Chicago. The computer equipment is centralized, and the system is medium sized. George Lopez is the data processing manager for Hamilton. Like Bryan's, one of the complaints of the computer facilities relates to the centralized system. The branch offices at other cities complain about the lack of control over the data processing activities and the amount of time it takes to send processing jobs to Chicago.

The data processing facilities at Bryan's remain as they were organized and managed by Frank. The manager of computer programming and the manager of operations report directly to the data processing manager. The data librarian reports to the manager of computer programming, and the data entry operators report to the manager of operations. While Lesilie is not completely happy with this organization, she is satisfied with the technical qualifications of the computer programmers. There are four system programmers and one application programmer. With the new merger, all of this will change. In fact, there is a good chance that the data processing facilities will be combined, and this is the purpose of the meeting with Luke O'Neal, Leslie and George, and selected members of their respective data processing staff.

George: Before we begin, I would like to welcome Leslie and members of her data processing department to Chicago and to the data processing facilities of Hamilton. The purpose of our meeting today is to discuss with Luke O'Neal the implications of the merger for both data processing departments. Luke O'Neal is a representative of NDP (National Data Processing). Since both data processing departments have NDP equipment, I thought that this would be a good place to start. Luke, why don't you share some of your ideas with us?

Luke: As you know, we are one of the largest manufacturers of computer equipment and systems in the world. We have been able to reach this position by offering the best hardware, software, and support in the industry. Because both Bryan's and Hamilton are using our equipment, it will not be too difficult to make any conversion. What I would like to recommend is replacing the two medium-sized computer systems in Madison and Chicago with one of our large NDP 490/185 computer systems. This system could be located in Chicago, and a large remote job entry (RJE) system could be placed in Madison. You would both have access to a faster and better computer system.

Leslie: How would this change our present method of data processing, and what features does the NDP 490/185 have?

Luke: You would not notice any changes at all. This is true for both data processing centers. All of our computers are upwardly compatible. Our NDP 490/185 has virtual storage, multiprogramming, multiprocessing, spooling, and it allows time sharing, program overlays, and much more. In brief, this system represents the state of the art.

George: Thank you for your presentation, Luke. We will let you know what we decide. I would like a brief meeting after Luke leaves to discuss this matter.

Now that Luke is gone, I would like to say that I highly recommend that we obtain the NDP 490/185. None of our programs would have to be changed, and we would be able to operate as usual. We will meet again in a week to make the final decision, but I would like to go on record as being in favor of Luke's suggestions to obtain the NDP 490/185.

QUESTIONS

1. Do you think the NDP 490/185 located in Chicago will change how Leslie's department operates? What would happen if the NDP 490/185 would malfunction in Chicago?
2. Luke stated, "You would not notice any changes at all. This is true for both data processing centers." Do you think this statement is true? Explain your answer.
3. How do you feel about the approach being taken by George to merge the data processing departments?
4. What problems if any, could occur if a new NDP 490/185 were installed in Chicago with a remote data entry station in Madison?
5. Describe in detail the steps you would go through in merging the two data processing departments.
6. What are some of the other alternatives that could be considered in the merger?
7. Are there any problems with the organization of the data processing department in Madison? Explain your answer.

Resnik Distributors

Resnik construction is a family business with over 100 years of experience in delivering wood products from lumber mills to lumber stores and hardware stores. Alan Resnik, III, the current president, is as concerned about quality products and excellent service as was his grandfather, Alan Resnik, who founded the business. Over the years, the company has grown and matured into a large and stable supplier of wood products. While over 75 percent of their business is the distribution of wood products, Resnik Distributors is also in the business of manufacturing specialized wood products for their large and long-time customers.

Alan's concern for quality, service, and profitability is one reason he decided to acquire computer facilities. Five years ago, Alan almost purchased a small computer system for $235,000. A year ago, he purchased a minicomputer for $58,000 that is faster and more efficient than the small computer system he almost acquired. The minicomputer allows for distributed data processing and it has the ability to support a data base management system. With the advice of the data processing manager, Bill Lane, Alan placed terminals in executive offices, including his own office and at the main warehouse.

Although the minicomputer system has more than justified itself in terms of cost savings in producing routine documents, Alan had hoped that the computer would help managers in his company improve product quality and service. Alan was particularly concerned about credit problems. A number of customers, both new and old, have owed large amounts to the company for a long period of time. Accurately forecasting supply and demand was also very important due to the high rate of inflation and erratic supply. Paul Willis, who is in charge of shipping and warehouse operations, was having problems with inventory and product shipping. Over the last year, a large number of stockouts resulted in lost sales. While this problem was probably caused by inadequate supply, Paul could have avoided some problems if he knew in advance which products were running low in inventory. A month ago, Paul expressed a desire to be able to get information about any inventory item directly from the computer. Another related problem that Paul constantly faces is dispatching trucks that deliver wood products to some of retail stores. Paul needs a way to know what trucks are available and the most efficient way to schedule them for delivery jobs. Joan Newgren, who is a middle-level manager in charge of operations, has a few problems as well. It is her overall responsibility to control costs, and in the last six months, payroll costs and total job costs increased significantly. Joan needs a way to analyze payroll costs and to be alerted to jobs that start to have major cost overruns.

In a meeting last month with Alan and other managers of Resnik Distributors, Bill Lane was informed of these problems. After taking a management seminar, Bill realized that management is a complex and interrelated process, and thus he decided to make reports on these problems that could be used by any manager at Resnik Distributors. Furthermore, the reports would be designed to have a similar format, and they would all be generated once a day. A credit report was designed to have all creditors listed with the amount they owed and the length of time that the debt was outstanding. In a similar fashion, the inventory report was designed to contain every item in inventory with the price, code number, and the quantity on hand. All of the manufacturing jobs would be reported every day, with the percent of completion, the actual costs expended to date, and the total budgeted cost for the job. The location of all trucks and their status was produced daily, and the total payroll for the month was also generated daily. Bill was proud of these managerial reports, and because they could be of interest to other managers, he decided to have a copy of each report sent to all lower, middle level, and top level managers, including Alan Resnik. These comprehensive and detailed reports seemed to be a sure way to a promotion.

Questions

1. Has Bill developed reports to solve all of the problems mentioned by Alan and other managers at Resnik Distributors?
2. What do you think about the reports that Bill has designed to solve the problems faced by the managers of Resnik Distributors?
3. What is your opinion of the consistent format for all of the reports?
4. Is it a good idea to have all of the reports sent to other managers?
5. If you were Bill, what reports would you develop to solve the problems?

GLOSSARY

Abacus One of the first recognized mechanical devices to make computations.

Accumulator register A register used to hold the results of an arithmetic operation.

Action statements The area of a decision table which contains the statements that describe the possible actions of a computer system.

Addresses Reference names for locations.

Address register A register used to store the location or address of an instruction that is to be executed.

Alphanumeric terminal A visual display terminal which has the ability of displaying numbers, letters, and other special characters on a screen.

American National Standards Institute (ANSI) A national organization that establishes standards.

American standard code for information interchange A standard coding system that uses 7-bit codes.

Analog computer A computer based on the measuring of physical differences, such as electrical current.

Analytical A calculating machine designed by Charles Babbage which was to contain memory and to store numbers and computations.

APL programming language An acronym for *A Programming Language* which was developed by Kenneth Iverson in 1962. It is a general purpose, procedure-oriented, real-time language.

Application package One or more programs designed to solve a problem or perform a task for one or more individuals or organizations.

Arithmetic/logic unit The part of the central processor which performs all mathematical computations and logical comparisons. These logical comparisons are known as logical operations or decisions.

Assembler A system package that converts symbolic language to machine language.

Audioresponse An output medium that produces verbal responses from the computer system. A computer device converts data stored in the computer system to electrical signals that can be transmitted over telephone lines.

Auditing around An audit accomplished by investigating the printed outputs, input documents, listing of files and processing, and so on. In this case, computer programs are not tested directly.

Auditing through An audit conducted in such a way that the auditor actually uses the computer in making the audit.

Audit trail Input and output documents that allow the auditor to trace the flow of data and information through one or more programs.

Backup file The file automatically produced with both card and tape systems when a new master file is created.

Back-up programmer The individual who is an assistant to the chief programmer.

BASIC programming language An acronym that stands for *B*eginners *A*ll-purpose *S*ymbolic *I*nstruction *C*ode. This language was developed at Dartmouth College with the intention of being used with time-sharing systems. It is a general purpose, procedure-oriented language.

Batch processing The running of several computer programs one after another without the need of a human operator to run each program individually. This is also known as stacked job processing.

Baud A term of measurement that represents one bit per second. It is used in conjunction with describing the capacity of a carrier.

Beginning of tape marker (BOT) A reflective marker that indicates the beginning of usable tape.

Benchmark test A test used in the measurement of computer equipment performance under similar conditions of use.

455

Binary coded decimal system (BCD) A code system used by computers in which every character is converted into a unique series of ones and zeros. The characters include numbers, letters, and special characters.

Binary numbering system A numbering system consisting of two digits, zero and one. It is used in computers where we allow the number one to represent one state or condition and the number zero to represent another state or condition. This then represents the state of any component or circuit in a computer system.

Bit Acronym for *bi*nary digi*t* which stands for one binary piece of information. This can be either a one or a zero.

Blocking factor The number of records that are contained in one block on magnetic tape.

Bottom up technique An implementation technique wherein the bottom level modules are written, tested, and debugged after which the next lowest levels of modules are written, tested, and debugged. This process continues until all of the modules have been completed.

Broad band channel The fastest carriers which have transfer rates from 5,000 to 10,000 characters per second. These are also known as wide band channels.

Brush-type card reader A card reader in which a series of brushes will touch contact points completing an electrical curcuit and send a current to temporary storage whenever a hole is encountered in the computer card.

Bubble storage A new concept in storage making use of small integrated circuit chips and operating on the principle of magnetic fields. Another name for bubble storage is magnetic bubble storage.

Buffer A small temporary storage area which literally acts as a buffer between two computer components with different operating speeds or transfer rates. The data from any sending device is fed into a buffer at the sending device speed and when enough data is collected in the buffer it is sent to a receiving device at its speed.

Bundling The inclusion of software, service, maintenance, and so forth in the price of the CPU or computer system.

Business oriented programming language A language designed for handling large data files in business type applications.

Byte A set of bits which represents a particular character or symbol. Normally a byte consists of eight bits.

Card layout chart A form that is used to describe how input data is placed on one or more computer cards.

Card punch A data entry device that places data onto computer cards. Some card punches are also able to read and check each card after it has been punched.

Card reader A device that transfers data contained on computer cards into the computer system.

Card sorter A unit record device not connected electronically to the computer system which is used to sort cards.

Card system A computer using cards for permanent storage.

Carrier Any device that is used to transmit data from one location to another location.

Cathode ray tube (CRT) A visual display terminal that displays data on a television-like screen or tube.

Central processing unit (CPU) The center or heart of the computer system to which all other devices are directly or indirectly tied. It performs the control, arithmetic, and logic functions. (Also called the main frame.)

Central processor One of the main parts of the central processing unit which consists of the control unit and arithmetic-logic unit.

Centralized Data Processing System A computer system in which all of the processing is done at one location.

Chain printer A printer that consists of a circular chain of characters that rotates at a high speed.

Channel A device that coordinates the flow of data to and from the central processing unit.

Character addressable storage device A storage device in which each character has one unique location with its own address. Another name for character addressable storage is variable word length storage.

Charge coupled device (CCD) A temporary storage device that stores data as packets of charges in a semiconductor.

Chief programmer The individual who has the overall responsibility of seeing that an entire project is successfully completed.

Closed shop A data processing department in which only authorized computer operators can run the computers.

Glossary

COBOL programming language An acronym for *CO*mmon *B*usiness *O*riented *L*anguage which was developed in 1959 for business data processing applications.

CODASYL An acronym for *C*onference *O*n *DA*ta *SY*stems *L*anguages. This is a committee that helps to establish programming standards for various programming languages.

Coding The process of writing instructions in a programming language, such as BASIC, COBOL, FORTRAN, or PASCAL.

Cohesion The degree to which a module performs one general function.

Communcations processor A processing unit that coordinates networks and data communications. With a network, they insure that data flows to and from different computer systems correctly and efficiently. In most cases, communications processors have temporary storage devices and circuitry that allow them to switch data and messages from an incoming computer system to its destination.

Compiler A system package which converts a procedure- or problem-oriented language into machine language.

Completely factored A situation which exists when all of the input, processing, and output is performed by the modules at the lowest level of the structure chart.

Computer leasing companies Companies that specialize in leasing computer equipment which they purchase from a computer manufacturer.

Computer output microfilm (COM) An output alternative. Instead of producing output on paper, it is produced in the form of microfilm. This microfilm requires less storage space than paper, and output is faster and less expensive than using a line printer.

Computer programmer Using the information and plans handed down from the systems analyst, this individual develops or builds the necessary computer programs.

Computer system Those devices or components that are directly and electronically connected together.

Concentrators Devices that concentrate several voice grade channels into one broad band channel. These are also known as multiplexes.

Condition statements The area of a decision table that contains the statements which describe the conditions that could exist with the input data.

Continuous form Printer paper that comes prefolded with perforated sections, or in rolls.

Contract software package A specific software package developed for a particular company. It is also called contract programming.

Control unit The part of the central processor which directs and controls all the devices in the computer system. It receives its instructions from software or computer programs and executes these instructions.

Core storage A storage device for older and larger computer systems composed of small doughnut shaped magnetic cores that can be magnetized in one of two directions.

Cost benefit analysis A procedure for evaluation and selection of hardware and/or software in which lists are made of all the costs and benefits of each proposed data processing system.

Counsel For Economic Mutual Assistance (CFEMA) An organization consisting of Bulgaria, Czechoslavakia, German Democratic Republic, Hungary, Poland, and the U.S.S.R. which is working on a family of upwardly compatible general-purpose computer systems. The apparent goal is to close the technology gap between these countries and the United States so that they may rely less on Western countries for computer systems.

Counsel log A detailed and complete listing of all jobs that are run on the computer system.

Coupling The degree to which modules are related to or dependent on each other.

Course index The first index in an index sequential access system which normally gives a general area or location of the data.

Cut form Printer paper that can be in the form of cards, or any paper document that comes in precut or standard sizes.

Data The raw material or input to any data processing system.

Data base A collection of integrated and related master files.

Data base administrator The individual who has the responsibility of maintaining the data base management system, and in general maintaining the accuracy and the integrity of the data that is stored in the computer system.

Data base management system A software package that manages and maintains data to facilitate the processing of multiple applications.

Data communications operators The individual responsible for tranferring data, files, and programs through data communications from one data processing facility to another.

Data communication system A system which consists of carriers which are used to transport data from one point to another, and devices that connect the computer equipment to these carriers.

Data conversion The process of converting data files from manual files to computer files.

Data dictionary The document which contains clear definitions of the data that will be used in setting up data base management systems.

Data division One of four divisions of a COBOL program which describes the data that the object program is to accept as input, manipulate, create, or produce as output.

Data entry The conversion of human readable data into a form that a computer system can interpret. This is also called data preparation.

Data entry operator The individual who takes human understandable data and places it in machine understandable form.

Data input The transfer of machine readable data into the computer system.

Data librarian The individual responsible for storing and issuing data files that are typically stored either on magnetic tape or disk.

Data management system (DMS) Software developed in the late 1960s which allowed users to easily access data and generate reports, but with which the other application programs were still directly accessing the data. This has also been called a generalized file management system (GFMS).

Data processing The process of transforming data into desired output.

Data processing manager The individual who has the responsibility of the efficient and effective operation of the data processing center, and hence, possesses both technical and managerial skills.

Data processing system An organized collection of people, procedures, and devices used to produce useful output.

Debugging The process of locating errors in a program and eliminating them.

Decentralized data processing system A computer system in which the processing units are physically placed at various locations within the organization. These processing units are usually microcomputers, minicomputers, or small computers that operate independently of each other.

Decision table A table which displays the different conditions that could exist and the different actions that the computer should take as a result of these conditions.

Dedicated line A channel that carries data for only one customer.

Demand report A report which is produced only when requested by a manager.

Design heuristics Guidelines that can be followed when dividing a larger problem or program into smaller, more manageable modules.

Desk testing The first step in testing: to carefully check the coding forms and the program itself for possible errors.

Difference engine A device used for computing logarithms which was designed but never fully constructed by Charles Babbage.

Digital computer A computer which is based on counting.

Direct access The reading or writing of data directly. It is also known as random access.

Direct access storage device (DASD) A storage device which allows the computer system to locate specific data directly without searching through a large amount of data. Examples are disks, and drums.

Disk system A computer using primarily magnetic disk for permanent storage.

Display terminal A terminal which has a cathode ray tube similar in nature to a TV screen.

Document card A card containing a bill or other document.

Drum printer A printer which consists of raised character sets placed in circles around a drum.

Editing The process of checking the data to make sure that it is in a form that can be processed by the application program.

EDVAC An electronic computing device similar to the ENIAC although smaller, faster, and having greater capability. It was built in 1952.

Electronic funds transfer system (EFTS) A system designed to transfer funds electronically instead of using paper documents. It is expected to be fully developed and in use in the near future by the bank-

Glossary

ing industry. The forerunner of this system is the automatic teller machines which are found in many banks.

Electrostatic printer A printing device that uses a matrix of wires and pins in the printhead that are electronically charged. The paper, which is sensitive to an electronic charge, picks up to the charge. The paper then passes through a solution and the electronically charged parts of the paper pick up ink particles to form the characters.

ENIAC The first all electronic digital computer developed by Mauchly and Eckert around 1946.

Environment division One of four divisions of a COBOL program which specifies those aspects of a data processing problem that are dependent upon the physical characteristics of a particular computer.

Event driven data input Input of the type where the event itself is wired directly into the computer system. These events can be things such as temperature of a building, humidity, time of day, and more.

Exception report A report produced when an exceptional situation occurs.

Execution cycle The second phase of execution of any machine level instruction during which the computer does what it is instructed to do.

Execution time The time it takes to complete an execution cycle.

Extended binary coded decimal interchange code (EBCDIC) An eight-bit coding system developed by IBM.

Extended entry decision tables Decision tables in which entries other than Y's, N's, and X's can be made.

Fan out The number of programming modules below any given module. It is also referred to as span of control.

Feasibility study A study to determine whether the proposed solution has technical feasibility, operational feasibility, and economic feasibility.

A collection of related records.

File protection ring A protective device which is put on the reel of magnetic tape whenever the tape drive is being used to write data on that tape. Without the file protection ring in place, the tape drive will not write data on the tape.

First generation Started in 1951 with the development of UNIVAC I. The common characteristic of first generation computers is the use of vacuum tubes.

First in first out (Fifo) A technique for processing jobs on a first come, first served basis.

Floppy disk A disk device which is normally used with small computers. It is also known as a flexible disk. It is smaller than a basic disk or standard disk and has a smaller storage capacity. It is similar in size and appearance to a 45 rpm record.

Flowchart A graphical representation of the operations or procedures to be performed by a computer program.

FORTRAN programming language An acronym for *For*mula *Tran*slator. Developed by IBM in 1957, it was one of the first scientific programming languages. Fortran is considered to be a procedure-oriented, general purpose language that can be used for either batch processing or real-time processing.

Full-duplex A way in which data can be transmitted such that the data can flow in both directions at the same time.

Garbage in, garbage out A programming adage which means that inaccurate input data will result in inaccurate output.

General purpose computer A computer which can be programmed or instructed to do a variety of business and scientific applications.

General purpose programming language A programming language which is intended to solve a number of different types of problems.

Grammatical error An error which results when the rules or syntax of a programming language are not followed. It is also referred to as syntax error.

Grandfather-father-son procedure This is a procedure in which the grandfather (master file) can be used to create the father (master file) which can be used to create the son (master file). Thus, there is a dual backup system.

Graphical terminal A visual display terminal which has a screen to display a graph or drawing as well as alphanumeric information.

Grid chart A table which relates the input data with its applicable application program.

Half-duplex A way in which data can be transmitted such that the data can flow in both directions, but can only flow in any one direction at any one time.

Hardware The components of a computer system.

Header label Located before the data, it describes the data that is stored on the tape. It typically includes the name of the data file, the date when the data was placed on the tape, and the date when the data can be erased from the tape or destroyed.

Hexadecimal numbering system A numbering system to the base 16.

High-level programming language A programming language with the following characteristics:

   a. Is relatively independent of a given computer system.
   b. Each statement translates into several instructions in machine language.
   c. Is natural and uses abbreviations and words that are used in everyday communications.
   d. Is independent of machine language instructions and other pieces of system software except for the language compiler.
   e. Is not experimental in nature and exists on more than one computer system.

HIPO An acronym which stands for *H*ierarchy plus *I*nput *P*rocessing *O*utput. It is both a design tool and an aid to program documentation which is concerned with what is done rather than how a particular activity is accomplished.

Hybrid computer A combination of an analog and digital computer.

Identification division One of the four divisions of a COBOL program.

Impact printer A printer which strikes or impacts the paper.

Independent computer peripheral equipment manufacturers (ICPEM) Companies which specialize in manufacturing one or more lines of computer equipment. The computer equipment which they produce is usually of high quality and completely compatible with computers produced by other manufacturers.

Indexed sequential access method (ISAM) A method whereby data is stored sequentially to handle applications in which all of the data is to be processed sequentially. In order to access an individual piece of data, one or more indexes are used. This is similar to using an index in a book. The index reveals the approximate location of the record or piece of data on the disk, and the computer searches the area indicated by the index until it locates the desired record or piece of data.

Industrial data collection devices Input devices which can record the time an employee spends on the job, and more. These can be used to determine wages, costs for jobs being done, and so on.

Information Output which can be used to help people make decisions.

Information processing system The people, procedures, and devices that are used to produce useful information.

Ink jet printer A printing device that uses a nozzle and sprays ink onto paper to form the appropriate characters.

Input The data processing function of capturing or obtaining original data, and placing it into the data processing system.

Input/output bound A situation in which the computer system is limited by the speed of the input and output devices.

Instruction cycle The first phase of the execution of any machine level instruction during which the instruction to be executed is brought into the central processor from temporary storage and decoded.

Instruction register A register used to hold an instruction until it can be executed.

Instruction time The time it takes to perform an instruction cycle.

Inter-block gap (IBG) When several records are in one block, these gaps separate the blocks of records on tape.

Inter-record gap (IRG) The separation or gap between records on a tape.

Job control cards Control cards that are placed before each program which tell the computer such things as the language the program is written in, how many lines of output will be required, and how long the execution time might be.

Job control language (JCL) The language in which the job control instructions are written.

K A symbol used to represent 2^{10} power, which is 1,024.

Keypunch A device that is used to place data on computer cards.

Key-to-disk A device that is used to enter data onto a disk device.

Key-to-tape A device that is used to enter data onto a magnetic tape.

Large scale integration (LSI) The type of technology concerned with placing a large number of integrated circuits on semiconductors.

Glossary

Laser printer A printing device which places images on a rotating drum using a lazer beam. The drum picks up a toner powder on the lazer exposed areas. These areas on the drum are pressed and fused into the paper forming the characters.

Limited entry decision tables Those decision tables in which the only permissible entries are Y's, N's, and X's.

Line printer A printer which prints one line at a time.

Logical access path (LAP) Addressing or accessing the data base management system with application packages.

Logical error A logical error occurs when the actual logic of a program is different from the desired logic of a program.

Machine language A form that is understandable by the computer system.

Magnetic ink character recognition (MICR) An input device which prints characters with special magnetic ink that can be read by people and the computer. The major user of these devices is the banking industry.

Management information system (MIS) An organized collection of people, procedures, and devices used to provide past, present, and projected information. The overall purpose of a management information system is to provide the right information to the right manager or decision maker at the right time.

Mark I An electromechanical device developed by Howard Aiken in 1937. Another name for this device is the automatic sequence controlled calculator.

Master file A permanent file for an organization.

Master file maintenance The process of updating, changing, or modifying master files.

Matrix printer A printer that has a matrix of dots used to print characters. Small wires in the matrix printer will hit the paper in the appropriate place and make that particular character.

Microcomputer A complete small computer system consisting of hardware and software that sells for under $500 to $5,000, and whose main processing parts are made of semiconductor integrated circuits.

Microfilm recorder A device which can input data directly from the computer system or an auxiliary device, such as magnetic tape.

Microflowchart A system or program flowchart which shows a relatively large amount of detail. It is also called a detailed flowchart.

Microprocessor The central processing unit of a microcomputer. It is an integrated circuit that will perform a variety of operations in accordance with a set of instructions. Microprocessors are used widely as the control devices for business machines, game machines, household appliances, automobile electrical systems and microcomputers.

Microsecond One millionth of one second.

Millisecond One thousandth of one second.

Minicomputer A digital computer that is characterized by higher performance than microcomputers, more powerful instruction sets, a wide selection of programming languages and operating systems, and a price range between $2,000 and $100,000.

Model An abstraction or an approximation of reality.

Modems Devices which do modulations and demodulations for data communications.

Multi-function card machine A unit record device that has the ability to perform several operations.

Multiprocessing This refers to using more than one central processing unit. One common use of multiprocessing is to use small CPU's for input and output.

Multiprogramming Storing more than one program in main storage.

Multistation data entry system A system that allows one or more data entry devices or stations.

Nanosecond One billionth of one second.

Narrow band A data communications channel that handles a small amount of data and has a slow transfer rate.

Network Two or more processors or computers connected with carriers and data communications devices.

Nondestructive The output of data and instructions is not lost. This means that when data is outputted, the original copy of the data storage remains.

Nonimpact printer A printer which performs some type of operation to the paper instead of physically striking it (as in the case of an impact printer). To print characters with non-impact printers, the paper can be sprayed with ink, magnetized, electrically charged, heated, placed under pressure, and struck by laser beams.

Non-volatile storage device A storage device that will

not lose its data and information with a loss of power or current.

Object code The machine language program which has been translated either by an assembler or a compiler.

Offline A device or system that is not directly and electrically connected to the computer system.

Online A system in which the computer devices are directly connected—usually by wire, cable or telephone lines—to the computer system.

Open shops Processing departments in which people other than authorized computer operators are also authorized to run the computer, such as programmers and systems analysts.

Operand The part of a machine level instruction which tells the central processor the location of the data that is to be manipulated. Each machine level instruction contains two or more operands.

Operating system Provides the computer system with a set of instructions that manages or supervises the functioning or operation of the computer. It is sometimes called the monitor, supervisor, or executive.

Operation code (OP code) The portion of a machine level instruction which tells the central processor what has to be done. Each machine level instruction contains one operation code.

Optical character recognition reader (OCR) Input devices which have the ability to read characters directly from an ordinary piece of paper.

Optical mark recognition reader (OMR) Input devices that read marks which have been made by number two pencils on special forms called mark sense forms. A typical application of Optical Mark Recognition Readers is the scoring of computerized examinations.

Output The results of the processing activities.

Overlapped processing A technique by which one program can be inputted, another program can be processed, and a third program be outputted all at the same time.

Packing Placing two numbers in one eight-bit BCD code.

Partitions Separate segments of main storage in which individual programs are held.

Pascal programming language A relatively new real-time, general purpose, procedure-oriented language, which can be used for business and scientific applications. It was developed by Niklaus Wirth in 1968.

Permanent storage Media used to permanently store data, such as computer cards, magnetic tape, and disk devices. Other names for permanent storage are secondary storage and auxiliary storage.

PERT An acronym for *P*rogram *E*valuation and *R*eview *T*echnique, a technique used to facilitate the implementation of a computer system.

Physical access path (PAP) A procedure where the data base management system goes to a permanent storage device to retrieve data.

Picosecond One thousandth of one nanosecond.

PL/1 The acronym for *P*rogramming *L*anguage *1*. It is a general purpose, high level programming language.

Plotter An output device that produces drawings and graphical displays of data. Some plotters are capable of getting output in full color.

Plug to plug compatible Peripheral equipment which can be plugged into existing computer systems without requiring additional software or interfaces.

Point of sale (POS) A terminal device that is able to capture data from a sale at the point or place of the sale.

Print chart A form which is used to describe the format of an output report from a printer.

Printer A device that converts data that is stored in the computer system into human understandable data that is placed on paper (hard copy).

Privileged register Registers which are used exclusively by the computer system and over which the computer programmer has no control.

Problem oriented programming language A programming language which is concerned with solving a particular type of problem.

Procedure division One of the four divisions of a COBOL program which specifies the procedures to be performed by the object program by means of English-like statements.

Procedure oriented programming language A language which stresses the actual procedures or manipulations that are performed.

Process bound The situation in which the computer system is limited by the speed of the processor.

Processing The manipulation, classification, sorting, summarizing, calculating, and storage of input data to produce a desired output.

Program A set of instructions used to direct and control

Glossary

the operation of the computer in order to solve a problem or to perform a particular task.

Program coding The process of writing instructions in a programming language.

Program flowchart A diagram that uses symbols and interconnecting lines to show the logic and sequence of specific program operations.

Programmable read only memory (PROM) Similar to Read Only Memory with the exception that by using special procedures, these chips can be reprogrammed.

Program overlay A segment or part of a large program.

Pseudocode An intermediate step between tools such as flowcharts, decision tables, grid charts, and HIPO diagrams, and the actual program. These are ordinary English statements which are similar to the actual program or code.

Random access memory (RAM) A temporary storage device in which the computer programmer has the ability to store data and then randomly (directly) access that data at a later time.

Read only memory (ROM) Special memory chips containing instructions which can be read only, therefore preventing accidental destruction of the instructions.

Real-time processing system A computer system that can respond immediately or within a matter of seconds.

Record A collection of related facts or items.

Register A small storage area that is used to contain instructions and data currently being processed by the control unit or the arithmetic/logic unit.

Request for proposal (RFP) Documented request for new hardware and/or software which is to be acquired from an outside vendor.

Restore wire The second of two wires used to retrieve data from core storage. It restores the original state of a core if it were magnetized previously.

Ring network A network in which the computer system or processors are connected in a circle or a ring.

Rotational delay The time it takes for a record contained on one of the sectors of a disk to rotate under the read/write head.

RPG An acronym for *Report Program Generator*, which is a general purpose, problem-oriented language that is usually implemented in the batch mode.

RPG II programming language The newer version of RPG which was developed for small computer systems but is being implemented on large and medium systems as well.

Running in parallel The process of running a new program together with the existing system of programs.

Scheduled report A report which will be generated every time a particular computer program is run or executed.

Second generation Started about 1959 until about 1965. Second generation computers have the common characteristic of using transistors instead of tubes.

Sequence structure In structured programming, programming statements are executed one after another. After starting the sequence, the statements are executed one after another until all of the statements in the sequence have been executed.

Sequential access Data must be read or written in order of sequence, one data item after another.

Sequential access storage devices Devices such as cards and tape which require sequential access of stored data.

Service company A company which provides some type of data processing service. Some services may include the performance of all routine data processing or the provision of data processing personnel as required.

Series operations Mathematical operations which are done one digit at a time.

Shortest operating time (SOT) A scheduling procedure for scheduling jobs that take the shortest amount of computer time first.

Simplex A way in which data can be transmitted so that the data can only flow in one direction.

Software The instructions that are given to a computer system to make it perform a particular task.

Software brokers Specialists in marketing software packages.

Software companies Companies which offer both general software packages and specific software packages for sale to computer systems owners.

Software package A phrase used to describe or define one or more programs or sets of instructions.

Source document An original document, such as a time card, which is used in the input function.

Special communication processor Processors which

handle communications to and from a central processor.

Special purpose computer A digital computer which has the ability to do one type of job.

Special purpose programming language A programming language designed to handle one specific type of problem or application.

Speech recognition The ability to input data directly into a computer system by speaking to it.

Spooling The process of placing data that comes from an input device or goes to an output device on either the disk or magnetic tape. This prevents the computer from having to store the data in main storage.

Spooling programs Programs that will transfer data from the disk or tape to main storage or an output device. In this sense the data or tape device acts as a buffer area between main storage, which is extremely fast, and input and output devices that are relatively slow.

Star network A network in which there is a central computer system from which there are several carriers to other computers or processors.

Storage dump A printout of the contents stored in main storage or memory during the execution of the program.

Storage logs A detailed and complete listing of all data that is stored on a permanent storage device.

Storage register A register used to hold data until it can be processed.

Structure charts Charts which picture the modules or smaller problems and how they are related to each other.

Structured design An overall approach to break a difficult problem into smaller problems that are small enough to manage and handle, but independent enough to solve separately.

Structured flowchart A program flowchart which is designed to be used with structured programming. It consists of a series of smaller boxes and larger ones that show what is to be done and in what order. These boxes are like sentences, paragraphs, and major sections within a report.

Structured programming A technique for designing and writing computer programs that constructs the program in independent logic or data segments in a hierarchial structure. Using a limited number of basic statement types and a minimum of branching to produce programs that can be read from top to bottom, this technique is concerned with improving the programming process through better organization of programs in better programming notation to facilitate, correct, and clear descriptions of data in control structures.

Structured walkthrough A technique used to monitor the progress of a structured project when structured design concepts are being used.

Structured words Words that include the terms used in structured programming which are applied to pseudocode. Examples of such words are: *Do While, Do Until,* and *If Then.*

Stub card A card containing a document from which the customer is asked to tear off a part, called the stub, and return it with payment.

Subroutine A miniprogram that is contained in a main program. It is also referred to as a subprogram.

Sub-voice grade channel Lines which have transfer speeds that range from 10 to 100 characters per second and are appropriate for slower devices such as teletype and slow terminals. These are also called narrow-band channels.

Supply companies Companies which offer a number of supplies that may not be produced and distributed by the computer manufacturer. Such supplies include paper and ribbon for the line printer, computer cards, and so forth.

Support libraries Libraries which contain complete programs, subroutines, and program modules that have already been developed, tested, and documented, usually as a result of other programming projects.

Swapping This refers to storing programs on disk and then transferring these programs into main storage as they are needed.

Syntax The set of rules which are peculiar to a programming language. It is analogous to rules of grammar in the English language.

Systems analysis The study of an existing system, the purpose of which is to determine if there are any problems or shortcomings concerning the existing system.

Systems analyst The individual responsible for planning the information processing system. The systems analyst utilizes tools such as flowcharts, decision tables, and grid charts. These plans are then passed to the computer programmer.

Glossary

Systems design A detailed description of a new system that attempts to solve some of the problems of the existing system, and provide a superior data and information processing system.

Systems implementation All of the steps that are necessary to place a new system into operation.

Systems investigation An investigation designed to determine whether or not the entire data processing system or a part of the data processing system should be studied in detail to determine if improvements are possible and cost justified.

System (computer) operator The individual responsible for running or operating the computer equipment in the data processing system.

System package One or more programs that makes the operation of the computer system more effective and efficient.

System run manual A complete description of how the software or a job is to be run on the computer system. It also includes potential problem areas, solutions to problems if they occur, and all program documentation such as flowcharts, decision tables, structure charts, and so on.

System software Software needed to make the operation of the computer more efficient. System software is normally written in machine language and is provided by the manufacturer with the computer system.

System testing Testing together all of the programs which interact with each other.

Tabulating machine A punch card device designed by Herman Hollerith. It came about as an aid in processing census data.

Tape density The amount of data that can be placed over a given length of tape. The density is usually expressed in bytes or characters per inch. These densities can range from under 500 bytes per inch to 6,250 bytes per inch.

Tape system A computer using primarily magnetic tape for permanent storage.

Technical documentation Documentation used by computer operators to execute a program and by analysts and programmers in case there are problems with the program or if the program is to be modified. Technical documentation should include the statement of the problem, the determination of the solution requirement, and all flowcharts, coding forms, and other materials developed during problem definition, analysis and design.

Teleprinter terminal A terminal which has a keyboard and a printing device. The printing device is usually a serial or character-at-a-time printer.

Temporary storage The part of the central processing unit which provides working storage area. It can contain one or more pieces of instruction called programs, and data that is currently being processed. Other names for temporary storage are main storage, main memory, primary storage, and core storage.

Terminal devices Devices used to perform both data entry and data input at the same time, and output. These terminals can be classified as either teleprinter terminals or display terminals.

Testing The process of making sure a program performs as it was intended to perform.

Thermal printer A printing device that utilizes paper which is sensitive to heat.

Third generation Started about 1965 with the introduction of the IBM 360 computer. Third generation computers have the common characteristic of integrated and miniaturized circuits instead of transistors.

Time log Documentation of how the computer system was used during the day.

Time sharing When several devices such as terminals, card readers, line printers, or users are using the computer system all at the same time.

Time-sharing company A company which shares the time of a large computer system with many users or customers. They are also called Network Information Services (NIS).

Top down approach An approach to writing a large program in which one starts with the main module and works down to other modules. In such a program, the control of the program goes from the top down.

Tracing routine A computer routine that is available with some computer systems that traces the operation and execution of the program.

Transaction documents The required bookkeeping documents that are generated by the application.

Transaction file A temporary file that represents the transaction of the business or organization. It is also called a detail file.

Transaction listing A detailed listing of the actions that were taken by the application program. It is also called a register.

Transformation algorithm An algorithm or procedure

which takes a key and converts it to the location where an appropriate record is located on a disk device.

Turnkey systems Systems that are complete and ready to use.

Unbundling A term which means that the application software is priced separately from the computer hardware.

Unit record Another name for a card. This name came about because it is possible to place one record on one card.

Unit record device This refers to card devices.

UNIVAC I The first commercially available computer built by Eckert and Mauchly.

Universal product code (UPC) A universal or standardized code which has been adopted by grocery stores for use with point of sales devices.

Unusual occurrences report A report which contains the date and time of abnormal occurrences, the computer operator on duty, the nature of the problem or situation, the corrective action taken or attempted, and other remarks that may be useful in documenting and analyzing the unusual occurrence.

User documentation Documentation used by the individual who will be using the program. This type of documentation shows the users in easy to understand terms how the program can and should be used.

Utility program A collection of miscellaneous system packages that are used to do a number of common functions such as sorting, merging, and transferring data files from one device to another.

Utilization Statistics Measures of the computer's performance based on the time log.

Validation The process of making sure that forms and documents from a particular transaction are correct.

Verification The process by which data contained on cards, tape, or disk is checked against the original document to make sure that no errors occurred in the conversion process.

Virtual storage An extension of multiprogramming in which the computer will only be storing a small part or segment of a program in main storage. The remainder of the program is stored on disk.

Visual display terminal A device which has a keyboard for input and some type of visual display unit for output. In most cases, the display unit is a cathode ray tube (CRT).

Voice grade channels Phone lines that we use to talk to other people. They can also be used to carry illustrations and pictures. The speed of voice grade lines range from about 100 to 300 characters per second.

Voice response An output device that employs voice-like output over telephones, speakers, and so on.

Volatile storage device A temporary storage device that will lose its data and information with a loss of power or current.

Word addressable storage device A storage device in which one location with its own address is used to store an entire number or word. Another name for word addressable storage is fixed word length storage.

Word processing A processing system that has the ability to process and manipulate words, paragraphs, and so forth.

Zone position The 0, 11, and 12 rows of a standard 80 column card used to represent characters and other special symbols.

Index

A

Abacus (5,000 B.C.), 76
ABC (Atanasoff-Berry Computer), 85
Aiken, Howard H., MARK I (electromechanical device) developer, 82
Amdahl, Gene M., computer designer, 390
Amdahl Corporation, 378–79
   and medium and large computer systems, 206
American Arithmometer Company, and William S. Burroughs, 83–84
American Banking Association, and magnetic ink character recognition (MICR), 174
American Federation of Information Processing Societies (AFIPS), 429
American Society for Information Science, 429
Ampex Corp., and permanent devices, 189
Analog computer, 22
Analytical engine, 79
ANSI (American National Standards Institute), 119
   FORTRAN, 255
   and standardized BASIC programming language, 254
APL (programming language) and Kenneth Iverson, 263
Apple Computer, Inc. (minicomputers), 214
Application package, 43
Application software, 272–73
   analysis and design, 275–76
   assembler language, 45–46
   documentation, 278–79
   high-level programming language, 47–48
   implementation, 279
   language selection, 276
   machine language, 44, 47–48
   macroinstructions, 47–48
   maintenance, 279–80

Application software—*Cont.*
   problem definition, 274–75
   program coding, 276–77
   testing and debugging, 277–78
Arithmetic/logic unit (ALU), 23, 98–100
Assembler language, 45–46
Assemblers, 43, 49
Association for Computing Machinery (ACM), 429
Association for Data Processing Services Organization (ADPSO), 280, 429
Association for Systems Management, 429
Atanasoff, John V., 85
   and (Dr. John) Mauchly, 86
   primary developer of the electronic digital computer, 88
Atanasoff-Berry Computer, 85
Atari (minicomputers), 214
Automatic sequence controlled calculator, 82, 85

B

Babbage, Charles
   analytic engine, 78
   Babbage's folly, 80
   difference engine, 79
   "pioneer of modern computers," 80
Backup programmer, 322
BASIC, 255
   and ANSI, 254
   and minicomputers, 197
   real-time, procedure oriented, 265
   and small computer systems, 201
Basic Four Corporation (minicomputers), 198
Batch processing, 50, 233–35
BCD (binary coded decimal) code, 119
Bell Telephone Laboratories
   and beginnings of binary components, 82
   and electromechanical devices, 82
   and magnetic bubble memory, 112

Berry, Clifford, 85
Binary coded decimal (BCD) systems, 118–19
Bipolar large scale integration (LSI), 91
Bit (binary digit), 105
Bubble memory device, 89, 91
Bubble storage device, 107
Buffers, 109
Burroughs, William S., 82
Burroughs Calculating Machine (1888), 83
Burroughs Corporation, 82–84, 378
   Burroughs E101 computer, 88
   Burroughs 5000, 88
   and medium and large computer systems, 206
   and minicomputers, 198
   and small computer systems, 201
Business Equipment and Manufacturers Association (BEMA) and the United States Standards Institute (USASI), 175
Buying system methodology, 349
Byte (eight bits), 105

C

Card devices
   punch, 130
   reader, 124–30
   sorter, 130–31
Card system, 141–42
   card concepts, 127–29
   card devices, 129
Card reader, 129
   brush-type, 130
   photoelectric-type, 130
CCD (charge-coupled device), 108
CEMA (Counsel for Electronic Mutual Assistance) general purpose computers, Ryad-1 and Ryad-2, 387
Central processing, 23, 109–23
   control unit and arithmetic/logic unit (central processor), 98–101

467

Central processing—*Cont.*
  interfacing with other components, 108
  temporary storage, 24–25, 101–8
Central processing and temporary storage in microcomputers, 219
Central processing devices
  communications processors, 189–90
  special purpose microprocessors, 190–91
Central processor, 23–24
  arithmetic/logic unit, 99–100
  control unit, 98–99
Centralized, decentralized, and distributed systems, 206–8
Charge-coupled devices (CCD), 91, 108
  and third generation computers, 89
Chief librarian, 322
Chief programmer, 321
Chief programmer teams, 321–22
CII-HB (French computer manufacturer), 385
COBOL, 47, 189
  ANS COBOL, 257
  ANSI COBOL, 266
  COBOL programming, 257–61
  CODASYL (COnference on DAta SYstem Languages), 257
  data division, 259–60
  environment division, 258–59
  identification division, 258–59
  and minicomputers, 197
  procedures division, 260–61
  and small computer systems, 201
COM (computer output microfilm), 34, 182–84
Communication devices
  encryption devices, 166–67
  modems (modulation-demodulation) devices, 164
  multiplexer, 164–65
  networks, 165–66
  special communication processors, 164–65
Communication networks, 165
  hierarchical, 166
  point-to-point, 166
  ring, 166
  star, 166
Communications carriers
  facsimile transmission (FAX), 162–64
  full duplex, 162–63
  half duplex, 162
  simplex, 162
  voice grade, 163
Compiler program
  and high-level programming languages, 47
  and machine languages, 47
Compilers, 43, 49

Computer
  analog and digital, 22
  general purpose, 23
  hybrid, 22
  special purpose, 23
Computer applications
  editing, 59
  management reports, 61
  transaction documents, 61
  transaction registers (listings), 61
  updating, 59–60
Computer configurations
  centralized, 34
  decentralized, 34
  distributed, 34
Computer output microfilm (COM), 34, 82–84
Computer system components, 23
  hardware, 13
  software, 13–14
Computer systems, 209–12
  centralized, decentralized, and distributed systems, 206–8
  medium and large computer systems, 202–6
  microcomputers, 196
  minicomputers, 196–200
  small computer systems, 200–202
Computer use, 6
Computer waste and mistakes, 392–93
Computerized management information systems and second generation computers, 89
Control and arithmetic/logic unit, 98–101
  arithmetic/logic unit, 99–100
  control unit, 98–99
  in instruction execution, 101
  registers, 100
Control Data Corporation (CDC), 189, 378
  CDC 1604, 88
  and medium and large computer systems, 206
Council for Economic Mutual Assistance (CEMA) and the USSR, 387
CPM (critical path method), 346
CPU (central processing unit), 23, 98
  arithmetic logic, 23, 98–100
  control, 23
  input storage, 98
  instruction storage, 98
  and main storage interaction, 240
  output storage, 98
  and overlapped processing, 235–36
  and problem of input/output bound, 235
  and real-time processing, 236
  and spooling, 240
  and temporary storage devices, 22–23

Crime and fraud, 393
  and Federal Computer Systems Protection Act (1977), 394
Critical path method (CPM), 346
CRT (cathode ray tube), 37, 142

D

Dartmouth College and BASIC programming design development, 254
DASD (direct access storage device), 29
Data analysis, 341–42
Data base concepts, 11
Data base management systems (DBMS), 43, 50, 52–57
  data base task group (DBTG), 244–45
  data management system (DMS), 244
  generalized file management system (GFMS), 244
  logical access path (LAP), 51, 244
  and minicomputers, 197
  NCR TRANS-QUEST, 246
  physical access path, (PAP), 51, 244–45
Data communications, 161
  carriers, 162–64
  communication devices and networks, 164–67
  and decision support systems, 92
  and management information systems, 92
Data entry (preparation), 30
Data entry devices, 30–31
  key-to-tape device, 151
  key-to-storage, 150–51
  printers, 153
  terminals, 159
  valuation, verification, editing, 153
Data entry operator, 424
Data file
  master, 9
  master maintenance (updating), 10, 60
  permanent, 9
  random (updating), 60–61
  transaction, 10, 61
Data General Corporation, 379
  and minicomputers, 198
Data input, 30
Data movement, 11–12
Data organization
  data base, 11
  facts, 9
  master file, 9
  master file maintenance, 10
  permanent file, 9
  record, 9
  transaction file (detail file), 10

Index

Data point, 379
Data preparation (entry), 30
Data processing
 calculating, 7
 classifying, 7
 and information, 8
 reproducing, 7
 sorting, 7
 storing, 7
 summarizing, 7
Data processing career opportunities, 420, 430-31
 computer programmer, 423
 data base administrator, 424
 data entry operator, 424
 data programming manager, 421-22
 system operator, 423-24
 systems analyst, 422-23
Data processing department
 data processing center location, 404-5
 data processing department operations, 408-13
 data processing department organization, 405-8
 disaster recovery planning, 413-14
Data processing industry, 376-77, 388-90
 computer dealers and distributors, 381
 general computer manufacturers, 378-79
 international data processing industry, 386-87
 leasing companies, 381-82
 peripheral equipment manufacturers, 380-81
 service companies, 383-84
 small, mini-, and macrocomputer manufacturers, 379-80
 software companies, 384-85
 supply companies, 385-86
 time-sharing companies, 382-83
Data Processing Management Associations (DPMA), 89, 429
Data processing organizations
 and Certificate in Data Processing (CDP) exam, 89
 Data Processing Management Association (DPMA), 89
 Machine Accountants Associations, 89
 National Machine Accountants Association (NMAA), 88-89
Data processing system, 8
Data representation
 binary coded decimal systems (BCD), 118-19
 decimal and binary systems, 116-18
 hexadecimal numbering system, 119-20
 parity checking, 120-22

DBMS (data base management system)
 and CODASYL-developed data base task group (DBTG), 244-45
 and data base administrator (DBA), 245
 data base architecture, 245
 and data dictionary, 245
 file structure, 245
 and logical access path (LAP), 244
 organization, 245
 and physical access path (LAP), 244
DBMS packages
 GIS (IBM), 246
 IMS2 (IBM), 246
 MARK IV (Inoormatics), 246
 minicomputer packages (DEC and HP), 246
 System 2000 (MRI), 246
 Total (Cincom), 246
Debugging and testing, 277-78
DEC (Digital Equipment Corporation), 197-98, 201, 378-79
Decimal and binary systems, 116-18
Decision support system (DSS), 357
 and Geo-Data Analysis and Display (GADS), 367
 and human factors, 366
 managerial decision-making aid, 358
Decision tables, 42, 293-97
 extended-entry, 299
 limited-entry, 299
Design and implementation, 366-67
Design heuristics, 209
Destructive reading, 104
Difference engine, 78
 and (George) Scheutz, 81
Digital computer, 22
Digital Equipment Corporation (DEC), 378-79
 and minicomputers, 197-98, 214
 and small computer systems, 201
Direct access storage device (DASD), 29
Disk concepts
 cylinder of data, 137
 magnetic track marker, 137
 sector, 137
 tracks, 136-37
Disk devices, 137-39
Disk system
 disk concepts, 136-37
 disk devices, 137-42
 with magnetic tape backup, 143
 and master file maintenance, 143
Documentation
 technical, 278
 user, 278-79
DSS (decision support system), 356-57
 and Geo-Data Analysis and Display (GADS), 367
 and human factors, 366
 managerial decision-making aid, 358

E

E-time (execution time), 101
Eckert, Jacob, 81
Editing, 59
EDVAC, 85-86
Electromechanical data processing devices, 86-87
 ABC (Atanasoff-Berry) Computer, 85
 Automatic sequence controlled calculator (MARK I), 82-83
 and ENDVAC, 85-86
 and ENIAC (Mauchley-Eckert) Computer, 85-86
Electron beam access memory (EBAM) device, 108
Electronic Funds Transfer (EFT) Act, 397
Electronic numerical integrator and calculator (ENIAC), 85-87
Encryption devices
 and Data Encryption Standard (DES), 167
 IBM 3845 and IBM 3846, 167
Euronet, 397
Evolution of data processing systems
 beginning of the computer age, 82-86
 computer generations, 86-91
 the future, 91-92
 mechanical devices, 76-82
Execution cycle, 101
Execution time (E-time), 101
Extended binary coded decimal interchange code (EBDIC), 119

F

Facsimile transmission (FAX), 163-64
Fair Credit Reporting Act (FCRA) of 1970, 397
Federal Computer Systems Protection Act (1977), 394
Feedback loop, 8
Fiber optics, 91
Firmware, 44, 92, 104
First generation computers
 Burroughs E101, 88
 and Eckert and Mauchley, 86
 Honeywell Datamatic 1000, 87
 and (Dr. Grace) Hooper's machine language, 87
 IBM 650 and IBM 701, 87
 UNIVAC I (Universal Automatic Computer I), 87
Flowcharts, 20-21, 23-24, 42
 program flowcharts, 290-93
 system flowcharts, 289
FORTRAN programming language
 ANSI FORTRAN, 255
 and FORTRAN statement (basic building block), 255

FORTRAN programming language—*Cont.*
  and minicomputer, 197
  and second generation computers, 88–89
  and small computer systems, 201
Fujitsu (Japanese computer manufacturer), 185
Furths, S.
  and information retrieval, 357
  and (H.) Luhn, 357

G

General Automation Corporation and minicomputers, 198
General purpose computer, 22
Generalized File Management System (GFMS); *see* Data base management systems
Geo-Data Analysis and Display (GADS), 367
Grid charts, 300

H

Hardware
  central processing, 97–113
  computer configuration, 34
  computer system, 195–212
  data representation, 115–23
  evolution of data processing systems, 75–96
  input, 30–32
  input, output, and data communications, 149–72
  minicomputers for business, school, and personal use, 213–27
  permanent storage, 26–29, 125–48
  printer, 32–34
  special purpose hardware, 173–94
Hatachi (Japanese computer manufacturer), 379, 385
Hewlett-Packard, 379
  and minicomputers, 198
Hexadecimal numbering system, 119–21
High-level programming languages, 51
  BASIC, 47
  COBOL, 47, 89
  and compiler program, 47
  FORTRAN, 47, 89
  PL/1 (Programming Language 1), 48
  RPG (Report Program Generator), 48
HIPO (hierarchy plus input-processing-output), 309
  designs, 311–12
  diagrams, 141
  visual table of contents, 310–11
Hollerith, Herman, 81
  and the tabulating machine, 81

Hollerith card, 127
Honeywell
  Datamatic 1000, 88
  Honeywell 516 and Honeywell 882, 249
  and medium and large computer systems, 206
  and minicomputers, 198
  Model 800, 88
  multics, 249
Hooper, Dr. Grace, 90
  and first program translator (1952), 87
Human factors
  and DSS, 366
  and MIS, 366
Hybrid computer, 22

I

I-time (instruction time), 101
IBM (International Business Machines), 81, 85, 378–79
  IBM 360, 89
  IBM 650, 87
  IBM 701, 87
  IBM 704, 88
  IBM 1401, 88
  IBM 1620, 88
  IBM 7090, 88
  and medium and large computer systems, 206
  and minicomputers, 198
  and small computer systems, 201
ICL (British computer manufacturer), 385
ICN, 352
Impact printers
  chain, 154–55
  drum, 155
  matrix, 155
  train and belt, 155
  wheel, 155
Implementing a structured system
  bottom up technique, 224–25
  top-down approach, 223–25
Implementation of a computer system
  data conversion, 279
  phase in and phase out, 279
  running in parallel, 279
Information and data processing, 6–7, 12–19
  data organization and movement, 9–11
  data processing and organization, 8–9
  information processing system, 8
Information and data processing functions
  input, 7, 22
  output, 7, 22
  processing, 7, 22

Input, 22
  data entry, 30
  data input, 30
  key-to-card, tape, disk, 30–31
  and source documents, 7
Input, output, and data communication, 168–72
  data communications, 160–67
  data entry devices, 150–53
  printers, 153–59
  terminals, 159–61
Input devices
  event driven data input, 180
  industrial data collection devices, 176
  key-to-card, tape, and disk, 30–31
  magnetic ink character recognition (MICR), 32, 174
  MICR inscriber, 174
  MICR reader, 174
  optical character recognition (OCR), 32
  optical data reader, 177
  optical mark reproduction, 175
  paper tape reading, 32
  point of sale (POS), 32, 37
  port-a-punch, 177–78
  portable data entry, 177
  speech recognition, 32, 179
  terminal, 31
Input and output devices, 189
  automatic teller machines (ATAs), 187–88
  electronic funds transfer system (ETFS), 187–88
  point of sale (POS), 185–87
  universal product code (UPC), 185–86
Instruction cycle, 101
Instruction execution
  execution time (E-time), 101
  instruction cycle, 101
  instruction time (I-time), 101
  one operation (OP) code, 101
  operand, 101
Instruction time (I-time), 101
Integrated circuits (IC) and third generation computers, 89–90
Interactive processing on CRT, 237
Interactive programming languages
  APL, 265
  BASIC, 263
  PASCAL, 265
Interfacing central processing with other components, 108
  by buffers, 109
  by channels, 109
International Computer Negotiations, 353
International Telecommunications Union (ITU)
  and frequency allocations, 19
  and information flows, 19
  and orbital slots, 19

Index

Itel Corporation, 55, 378
  and minicomputers, 214
Iverson, Kenneth, developer of APL Computer (1962), 263

J–L

Jacquard's loom (1801), 78
Key-to-card device (key punch), 150–51
Large scale integration (LSI)
  and semiconductor storage, 106
  and third generation computers, 89–90
Layout charts, 341
Leibnitz's calculating machine (1671), 78
Levels of management
  operational, 361
  strategic, 361
  tactical, 361
Logical access path (LAP), 51, 244
Luhn, H., and Furth, S.
  and information retrieval, 357
  and management information system (MIS), 357

M

Machine language, 44
  and compiler program, 47
  object code, 46
  operand, 45
  operation code, 45
  Sap, for IBM 704, 88
  Soap, for IBM 650, 88
Macroinstructions, 47
Magnetic bubble memory device, 107
Magnetic ink character recognition (MICR), 132
  and American Banking Association, 174
  MICR inscriber, 174
  MICR reader, 174
  optical character recognition (OCR), 32, 175
  optical data reader, 174
  optical mark recognition (OMR), 174–75
Main frame (CPU), 23
Main storage (memory and core storage), 239
  and spooling, 240
Management information
  as decision support system (DSS), 356–78
  system characteristics, 65
  types of management reports, 65–67
Management information and decision support systems, 355, 368–73
  design and implementation, 366–67
  function approach, 364–66

Management information and decision support systems—*Cont.*
  MIS and DSS, 356–58
  systems frameword, 358–64
Managing structured systems
  chief-programmer teams, 321–22
  structural walkthroughs, 322–23
Manual data processing system, 22
  central processor, 23–24
  components, 12–13
  and computer systems, 13–14
  temporary storage, 24–25
MARK I (Automatic Sequence Controlled Calculator), 82, 85
Mass storage devices
  and Control Data Corporation (CDC), 189
  data cell storage, 189
  drum storage, 189
  IBM 3850, 189
  staging, 189
Master file maintenance, 10
  updating, 60
Mauchly, Dr. John
  and (John V.) Atanasoff, 87
  and (J. Presper) Eckert, 85, 86
Mechanical calculating devices
  abacus, 76
  Babbage's analytical engine, 79
  Babbage's difference engine, 79
  Burroughs' calculating machine, 83
  Hollerith's tabulating machine, 81–82
  Jacquard's loom, 78
  Leibnitz's calculating machine, 78
  Napier's bones, 76
  Pascal's calculating machine, 76–77
  Ritty's cash register, 81–82
  Scheutz's difference engine, 80–81
Medium and large computer systems
  Amdahl Corporation, 206
  Burroughs, 206
  Control Data Corporation (CDC), 206
  Digital Equipment Corporation (DEC), 206
  Honeywell, 206
  IBM, 206
  National Cash Register Corporation (NCR), 206
  Sperry Univac Division of Sperry Rand Corporation, 206
MICR inscriber, 174
MICR reader, 174
Microcomputer system, 224–27
  applications for small profit and non-profit organizations, 216–17
  factors in selecting a microcomputer, 223
  individual applications, 214–15
  software and programming, 221–23

Microcomputer system components
  central processing and temporary storage, 219
  input and output devices, 217
  peripheral equipment, 221
  permanent storage device, 219–21
Microcomputers
  components of a microcomputer system, 217–21
  microcomputer selection factors, 223
  microcomputer systems, 214–27
  software and programming, 221–23
Microinstructions (microcode), 44, 51
  and firmware, 104
  and ROM, 104
Minicomputers
  and application software packages, 197
  and BASIC, 197
  and COBOL, 197
  and DBMS, 197
  and Digital Equipment Corporation (DEC), 197–98
  and FORTRAN, 197
  and RPG, 197
  and turnkey systems, 199
MIS (management information system), 356–58
  and DuPont, 367
  and human factors, 366
  and MIS executive, 433–34
MIS and DSS
  design and implementation, 366–67
  functional approach, 364–66
  systems framework, 358–64
Mits, Inc. (minicomputers), 214
Model types
  mathematical, 359–60
  physical, 359
  schematic, 359
  verbal, 359
Modems (modulation and demodulation), 164
Multiprocessing, 239–40
  and real-time processing, 238
Multiprogramming
  and CPU operating efficiency, 241
  and main storage partitioning, 240
  and swapping, 241
  and virtual storage, 241
Multics (multiplexed information and computing service), 249
Multistation data-entry systems
  CRT, 151
  keyboard, 151

N

Napier's bones, 76
NASA
  and communications processor, 190
  and multics, 249

National Bureau of Standards, and Data Encryption Standard (DES), 167
National Cash Register Company, 88 and (Jacob) Eckert, 81–82
  NCR TRANS-QUEST, a data base management system, 246
National Machine Accountants Association (NMAA), 88–90
NCR, 378
  and medium and large computer systems, 206
  and minicomputers, 198
  and small computer systems, 201
Network Information Services (NIS), 382
Networks, 164–66
Nibble (halfway between one bit and one byte), 105
Nippon (Japanese computer manufacturer), 385
Nixdorf (West German computer manufacturer), 385
Nondestructive data output, 104
Nonimpact printer
  electrostatic, 157
  ink jet, 156–57
  laser, 157–58
  magnetic, 157
  thermal, 157

O

OCR reader, 32
  and Business Equipment Manufacturers Association (BEMA), 175
Ohio Scientific Instruments (minicomputers), 214
Olivetti (minicomputers), 198
Online devices
  CRT, 239
  teletype, 239
Operating and system software, 47–50, 232–36
  data base management systems, 244–46
  multiprocessing, 238–40
  multiprogramming, 240–41
  overlapped processing, 235
  program overlays, 243–44
  real-time processing, 236–38
  spooling, 240
  virtual storage, 241–42
Operating system functions, 323
Operating systems, 49–50
Operation of the data processing department, 408–9
  DP audit, 411–13
  system considerations, 410–11
Optical data reader
  optical character recognition (OCR), 32, 175
  optical recognition (OMR), 175

Organization of the data processing department, 415
  data processing managers, data entry operators, others, 407–8
  disaster recovery planning, 413–14
  users, systems analysts, and programmers, 406–7
Organization and design guideline functions
  cohesion, 308–9
  complete factoring, 308
  coupling, 309
  program depth, 309
  span of control, 309
Original equipment manufacturers (OEMs), 380
Output devices, 181
  audio response, 185
  computer output microfilm (COM), 34, 182–84
  microfilm reader, 184
  plotters, 180
  printers, 32
  terminals, 31
  voice response, 34
Overlapped processing
  and batch processing, 235
  and CPU, 235–36
  and real-time processing, 236
  and input/output bound, 235

P

Paging, 242
Parity checking, 120–22
Pascal, Blaise, and early mechanical calculator (1642), 76–77
PASCAL (programming language), 261–62
Peripheral equipment manufacturers
  Independent Computer Equipment Manufacturers (CPEMs), 380–81
  plug-to-plug compatible, 380
Permanent file, 9
Permanent storage, 27
  computer cards, 26
  disk devices, 29
  magnetic tape, 26, 28
Permanent storage devices, 125, 144–46, 190–91
  card system, 127–31
  data cell storage, 189
  disk system, 136–41
  drum storage, 189
  main storage, 189
  tape system, 131–36
PERT (program evaluation and review technique), 346
Philips Business Systems (minicomputers), 198
Photodigital storage device, 108

Physical access path (PAP), 51, 244
PL/1, 263
Plotters, 34, 180–83
Point of sale (POS) device, 32
President's Domestic Council Committee on the Right to Privacy, 397
PRIMOS (software system), 250
Printers
  impact, 154–56
  nonimpact, 156–59
Processing functions 7–8, 22
Privacy, 394–95
  Electronic Funds Transfer (ETF) Act, 397
  Euronet, 397
  Fair Credit Reporting Act (FCRA) of 1970, 397
  President's Domestic Counsel Committee on the Right to Privacy, 397
  Privacy Act of 1974, 396
  Privacy Study Commissions, 396
  Swedish Data Act of 1973, 397
  Tax Reform Act of 1976, 397
Program, 13
Program and application development, 283–86
  developing application software, 272–80
  purchasing application software, 280–82
Program and application development tools, 288
  decision tables, 293–99
  flowcharts, 289–93
  grid charts, 300
  print charts and layout charts, 289
Program evaluation and review technique (PERT), 346
Program flowcharts, 341
Program overlays, 243–44
Programmer, 322
Programming languages
  APL, 263, 265
  BASIC, 47, 254–55, 263
  COBOL, 47, 257, 264–65
  FORTRAN, 47, 255–57, 264
  PASCAL, 261–62, 265
  PL/1, 48, 263, 265
  RPG languages, 262–63, 265
Project MAC (multiaccess computer), 249
PROM (programmable read only memory), 104
Pseudocode, 318–21
Purchasing application software, 280–82

R

Radio Shack (minicomputers), 214
RAM (random access memory), 103

Index

Random access, 29
Real-time language, APL, 261
Real-time processing (immediate response)
　and interactive processing, 237
　and multiprocessing, 238
　and overlapped processing, 236
　and swapping, 237
　and system-software accommodation, 237
　and time sharing, 237–38
Registers
　accumulator, 100
　address, 100
　general purpose, 100
　instruction, 100
　privileged, 100
　storage, 100
Ritty, James
　and (Jacob) Eckert, 81–82
　and first cash register (1878), 81–82
RPG (report program generator), 48, 262–63
　and minicomputer, 197
　and small computer systems, 201

S

SASD (sequential access storage device), 28–29
Scheutz's difference machine (1854), 81
Second generation computers
　Burroughs 5000, 88
　CDC 1604, 88
　COBOL and FORTRAN languages, 89
　computerized management information system, 89
　Honeywell Model 800, 88
　IBM 1401, IBM 1620, and IBM 7090, 88
　UNIVAC III, 88
Semiconductor storage and large scale integration (LSI), 106
Senate Subcommittee on Criminal Justice and Data Processing Crime, 400
Sensuous computer, 170–72
Sequential access storage devices (SASD), computer cards, 28
Siemens (West German computer manufacturer), 385
Small computer systems
　and BASIC, 201
　and COBOL, 201
　and FORTRAN, 201
　and RPG, 201
Smithsonian Science Information Exchange (SSIE), 147–48
Social issues, 399–401
　computer waste and mistakes, 392–93

Social issues—Cont.
　crime and fraud, 393–94
　privacy, 394–98
Software, 42, 52–55, 224–31, 247–51, 265–71, 280–87, 300–304
　application package, 43
　application software, 44–48
　assemblers and compilers, 43, 49
　operating and system software, 332–50
　program and application development, 272–99
　programming languages, 252–61
　structural design, 305–27
　system package, 43
　system software, 48–51
　systems analysis and design, 335–63
Software acquisition, 44
Software companies, 384–85
Software Industry Association (SIA), 280
Software packages, 43
　contract programming, 384
　proprietary software packages, 384
Software types
　application package, 43
　microprograms, 44
　system package, 43
Source program, 46
　and assembler language, 47
　and compiler program, 47
　and object program, 47
Soviet Bloc computer systems, Ryad-1 and Ryad-2, 387
Special purpose computer, 22
Special purpose hardware, 792–94
　input and output, 174–89
　permanent storage and central processing, 189–91
Speech recognition device, 32
Sperry-Rand Corporation, 82
Sperry Univac, 378
Spooling
　and the CPU, 240
　and main storage, 240
　and multiprocessing, 240
SSIE computer files, 147
Storage devices, 141–43
Structure charts, 341
Structured design, 306–7, 326–28
　HIPO, 309–12
　implementing a structured system, 323–25
　managing the structured system, 321–23
　organization and design guidelines, 308–9
　structure charts, 357
　structured programming concepts, 312–21

Structured flowcharting, 314–18
Structured programming concepts
　pseudocode, 318–21
　structured flowcharting, 314–18
　structured programming, 312–14
Swedish Data Act of 1973, 18–19, 397
Symbolic language, 46
System and application, 59–61
　editing, 59
　management reports, 61
　transaction documents, 61
　transaction registers, 61
　updating, 59–60
System flowcharts, 341
System operator, 423–24
System software
　assemblers and compilers, 43, 49
　data base management systems (DBMS), 50–51, 244–46
　and interactive processing, 237
　operating systems, 49–50
　priority system for real-time processing, 237
　utility programs, 50
Systems, 69–71, 332–34
　capabilities and limitations of a computer system, 58
　common elements of a computer application, 59–62
　data processing department, 403–18
　data processing industry, 375–90
　management information, 64–68
　management information and decision support systems, 355–73
　routine applications and documents, 62–64
　social issues, 391–401
　systems analysis and design, 335–63
Systems analysis and design, 350–53
　assembling study team, 338–39
　buying system methodology, 349
　data collection, 339–41
　generating system design alternatives, 343–44
　systems analysis, 338–42
　systems design, 342–46
　systems evaluation and selection, 344–45
　systems implementation, 346–49
　systems investigations, 336–38
Systems analyst, 422–23
Systems framework
　general model of the organization, 360–61
　models, 359–60
　systems approach, 358
　theory of management, 361–64
Systems implementation
　critical path method (CPM), 346
　data preparation, 347
　final testing, 348

Systems implementation—*Cont.*
  installation, 348
  personnel: hiring and training, 346–47
  program evaluation and review technique (PERT), 346
  site preparation, 347
Systems investigations, 336–37

T

Tabulating Machine Division, Remington Rand Corporation, 82
Tape concepts, 134
  beginning-of-tape (BOT), 132
  header label, 132
  interblock gaps (BG), 132–33
  interrecord gaps (IRG), 132
  leader, 132
  parity checking, 133
  volume, 132
Tape systems, 131, 142–43
  concepts, 132–34
  devices, 134–36
Tax Reform Act of 1976, 397
Tektronix (minicomputers), 198
Temporary storage, 24–25
  bubble, 107–8
  charge-coupled device (CCD), 108
  core, 105–6
  electron beam access memory (EBAM), 108
  laser beam, 108
  photodigital, 108
  programmable read only memory (PROM), 104
  random access memory (RAM), 103–4
  read only memory (ROM), 104
  semiconductor, 106–7

Terminal devices
  cathode ray tube (CRT), 31
  magnetic ink character recognition (MICR), 32
  optical character recognition (OCR), 32
  paper tape reading, 32
  point of sale (POS), 32
  speech recognition, 32
  teleprinter, 31, 161
  visual display, 159–61
Testing and debugging
  debugging, 277
  disk checking, 277
  storage dump, 278
  system testing, 277–78
  testing, 277
  tracing routine, 278
Texas Instruments, 379
  and minicomputers, 214
Theory of management, 362–64
  design and implementation of MIS and DSS systems, 361
Third generation application software development
  assemblers and compilers, 90–91
  data base management systems (DBMS), 90–91
  operating system, 90
  structured design, 90
  utility program, 90
Third generation computer development
  bubble memory, 89
  charged-coupled devices (CCD), 89
  COM, 90
  IBM 360, 89
  integrated circuits (IC), 89
  large scale integration (LSI), 89

Third generation computer development—*Cont.*
  MICR, 90
  POS devices, 90
Time-sharing companies, 382–83
Transaction documents, 61
Transaction file, 10
Transaction register, 61
Turnkey systems, 380

U

Unbundled, 384
UNIVAC III, 88
Updating (master file maintenance), 60–61
Utility programs, 50

V

Validation, verification, and editing, 153
Virtual storage
  and multiprogramming, 241–42
  and paging, 242
Visual display terminal
  alphanumeric terminal, 159
  cathode ray tube (CRT), 159
  graphical, 159
  light pen, 159
  plasma display, 160
  Plato display, 161
Voice response, 34

W

Wang Laboratories, 379
  and microcomputers, 214
  and minicomputers, 198
Wirth, Niklaus, developer of the PASCAL programming language, 261

This book has been set Videocomp in 10 and 9 point Times Roman, leaded 2 points. The size of the type area is 27 by 48 picas.